T0189097

Lecture Notes in Computer Science 12279

More information about this series at http://www.springer.com/series/7409

Andreas Holzinger · Peter Kieseberg ·
A Min Tjoa · Edgar Weippl (Eds.)

Machine Learning and Knowledge Extraction

4th IFIP TC 5, TC 12, WG 8.4, WG 8.9, WG 12.9
International Cross-Domain Conference, CD-MAKE 2020
Dublin, Ireland, August 25–28, 2020
Proceedings

Editors
Andreas Holzinger
Human-Centered AI Lab,
Institute for Medical Informatics,
Statistics and Doumentation
Medical University Graz
Graz, Austria

xAI Lab, Alberta Machine
Intelligence Institute
University of Alberta
Edmonton, AB, Canada

A Min Tjoa
Institute of Software Technology
and Interactive Systems
Technical University of Vienna
Vienna, Austria

Peter Kieseberg
UAS St. Pölten
St. Pölten, Austria

Edgar Weippl
SBA Research
Vienna, Austria

Research Group Security and Privacy
University of Vienna
Vienna, Austria

ISSN 0302-9743 ISSN 1611-3349 (electronic)
Lecture Notes in Computer Science
ISBN 978-3-030-57320-1 ISBN 978-3-030-57321-8 (eBook)
https://doi.org/10.1007/978-3-030-57321-8

LNCS Sublibrary: SL3 – Information Systems and Applications, incl. Internet/Web, and HCI

This Springer imprint is published by the registered company Springer Nature Switzerland AG
The registered company address is: Gewerbestrasse 11, 6330 Cham, Switzerland

Preface

The International Cross Domain Conference for MAchine Learning & Knowledge Extraction (CD-MAKE) is a joint effort of IFIP TC 5, TC 12, IFIP WG 8.4, IFIP WG 8.9, and IFIP WG 12.9 and is held in conjunction with the International Conference on Availability, Reliability and Security (ARES). The 4th conference was organized at the University College Dublin, Ireland and was held as a virtual event, due to the Corona pandemic. A few words about the International Federation for Information Processing (IFIP):

IFIP is the leading multi-national, non-governmental, apolitical organization in Information and Communications Technologies and Computer Sciences, is recognized by the United Nations (UN), and was established in the year 1960 under the auspices of the UNESCO as an outcome of the first World Computer Congress held in Paris in 1959.

IFIP is incorporated in Austria by decree of the Austrian Foreign Ministry (September 20, 1996, GZ 1055.170/120-I.2/96) granting IFIP the legal status of a non-governmental international organization under the Austrian Law on the Granting of Privileges to Non-Governmental International Organizations (Federal Law Gazette 1992/174).

IFIP brings together more than 3,500 scientists without boundaries from both academia and industry, organized in more than 100 Working Groups (WGs) and 13 Technical Committees (TCs).

CD stands for "Cross-Domain" and means the integration and appraisal of different fields and application domains to provide an atmosphere to foster different perspectives and opinions. The conference fosters an integrative machine learning approach, taking into account the importance of data science and visualization for the algorithmic pipeline with a strong emphasis on privacy, data protection, safety, and security. It is dedicated to offer an international platform for novel ideas and a fresh look on methodologies to put crazy ideas into business for the benefit of humans. Serendipity is a desired effect and shall cross-fertilize methodologies and transfer of algorithmic developments.

The acronym MAKE stands for "MAchine Learning & Knowledge Extraction," a field of artificial intelligence (AI) that, while quite old in its fundamentals, has just recently begun to thrive based on both novel developments in the algorithmic area and the availability of vast computing resources at a comparatively low costs.

Machine learning (ML) studies algorithms that can learn from data to gain knowledge from experience and to generate decisions and predictions. A grand goal is in understanding intelligence for the design and development of algorithms that work autonomously (ideally without a human-in-the-loop) and can improve their learning behavior over time. The challenge is to discover relevant structural and/or temporal patterns ("knowledge") in data, which is often hidden in arbitrarily high dimensional spaces, and thus simply not accessible to humans. Knowledge extraction is one of the oldest fields in AI and sees a renaissance, particularly in the combination of statistical methods with classical ontological approaches. AI is currently undergoing a kind of Cambrian explosion and is the fastest-growing field in computer science today thanks to the usable successes in ML. There are many application domains, e.g., in medicine, etc., with many use cases from our daily lives, e.g., recommender systems, speech recognition, autonomous driving, etc. The grand challenges lie in sensemaking, in context understanding, and in decision-making under uncertainty, as well as solving the problem of explainability. Our real world is full of uncertainties and probabilistic inference enormously influenced AI generally and ML specifically. The inverse probability allows to infer unknowns, to learn from data, and to make predictions to support decision-making. Whether in social networks, recommender systems, health applications, or industrial applications, the increasingly complex data sets require a joint interdisciplinary effort bringing the human-in-control and to foster ethical, social issues, accountability, retractability, explainability, causability, and privacy, safety and security. This requires robust ML methods.

To acknowledge all those who contributed to the efforts and stimulating discussions would be impossible in a preface like this. Many people contributed to the development of this volume, either directly or indirectly, so it would be sheer impossible to list all of them. We herewith thank all local, national, and international colleagues and friends for their positive and supportive encouragement. Finally, we thank the Springer management team and the Springer production team for their professional support.

Thank you to all – Let's MAKE it!

June 2020

Andreas Holzinger
Peter Kieseberg
Edgar Weippl
A Min Tjoa

Organization

CD-MAKE Conference Organizers

Andreas Holzinger	Medical University and Graz University of Technology, Austria, and xAI Lab, Alberta Machine Intelligence Institute, University of Alberta, Canada
Peter Kieseberg	FH St.Pölten, Austria
Edgar Weippl (IFIP WG 8.4 Chair)	SBA Research, University of Vienna, Austria
A Min Tjoa (IFIP WG 8.9. Chair, Honorary Secretary IFIP)	TU Vienna, Austria

Program Committee

Amin Anjomshoaa	SENSEable City Laboratory, MIT Massachusetts Institute of Technology, USA
Jose Maria Alonso	CiTiUS, University of Santiago de Compostela, Spain
Mounir Ben Ayed	University of Sfax, Tunisia
Christian Bauckhage	ML/AI Lab, University of Bonn, Germany
Smaranda Belciug	University of Craiova, Romania
Jiang Bian	University of Florida, USA
Chris Biemann	Language Technology Group, FB Informatik, Universität Hamburg, Germany
Ivan Bratko	University of Ljubljana, Slovenia
Guido Bologna	Computer Vision and Multimedia Lab, Université de Genève, Switzerland
Francesco Buccafurri	Università degli Studi Mediterranea di Reggio Calabria, Italy
Federico Cabitza	Università degli Studi di Milano-Bicocca, DISCO, Italy
Mirko Cesarini	Università degli Studi di Milano-Bicocca, Italy
Ajay Chander	Stanford University, Fujitsu Labs of America, USA
Tim Conrad	Freie Universität Berlin, Institut für Mathematik, Medical Bioinformatics Group, Germany
Gloria Cerasela Crisan	Vasile Alecsandri University of Bacau, Romania
Andre Calero-Valdez	RWTH Aachen University, Germany
Angelo Cangelosi	Machine Learning and Robotics Lab, The University of Manchester, UK
Josep Domingo-Ferrer	UNESCO Chair in Data Privacy, Universitat Rovira i Virgili, Spain
Massimo Ferri	University of Bologna, Italy

Hugo Gamboa	PLUX Wireless Biosensors, Universidade Nova de Lisboa, Portugal
Panagiotis Germanakos	SAP SE, University of Cyprus, Cyprus
Randy Goebel	xAI Lab, University of Alberta, Canada
Pitoyo Hartono	Chukyo University, Japan
Barna Laszlo Iantovics	George Emil Palade University of Medicine, Pharmacy, Sciences and Technology of Targu Mures, Romania
Beatriz De La Iglesia	Knowledge Discovery & Data Mining Group, University of East Anglia, UK
Xiaoqian Jiang	University of California, San Diego, USA
Igor Jurisica	Krembil Research Institute, Canada
Epaminodas kapetanios	University of Westminster, UK
Andreas Kerren	ISOVIS Group, Linnaeus University, Sweden
Max Little	University of Birmingham, UK
Shujun Li	Kent Interdisciplinary Research Centre in Cyber Security (KirCCS), University of Kent, UK
Luca Longo	Technological University Dublin, Ireland
Daniele Magazzeni	Human-AI Teaming Lab, King's College London, UK
Bradley Malin	Vanderbilt University Medical Center, USA
Ljiljana Majnaric-Trtica	University of Osijek, Croatia
Yoan Miche	Nokia Bell Labs, Finland
Fabio Mercorio	Università degli Studi di Milano-Bicocca, Italy
Paolo Mignone	KDDE Lab, Università degli Studi di Bari Aldo Moro, Italy
Jan Paralic	Technical University of Kosice, Slovakia
Luca Romeo	Università Politecnica delle Marche, Istituto Italiano di Tecnologia, Italy
Pierangela Samarati	Università degli Studi di Milano-Bicocca, Italy
Andrzej Skowron	University of Warszaw, Poland
Catalin Stoean	University of Craiova, Romania
Dimitar Trajanov	Cyril and Methodius University, Macedonia
Daniel E. O'leary	University of Southern California, USA
Vasile Palade	Coventry University, UK
Camelia-M. Pintea	Technical University of Cluj-Napoca, Romania
Ivan Štajduhar	University of Rijeka, Croatia
Irena Spasic	Cardiff University, UK
Jianlong Zhou	University of Technology Sydney, Australia
Karin Verspoor	National Information and Communications Technology Australia, Australia
Jean Vanderdonckt	Université catholique de Louvain, Belgium

Contents

Explainable Artificial Intelligence: Concepts, Applications, Research Challenges and Visions

Luca Longo[1(✉)], Randy Goebel[2], Freddy Lecue[3,4], Peter Kieseberg[5], and Andreas Holzinger[2,6]

[1] School of Computer Science, Technological University Dublin, Dublin, Ireland
luca.longo@tudublin.ie
[2] xAI-Lab, Alberta Machine Intelligence Institute, University of Alberta, Edmonton, Canada
rgoebel@ualberta.ca
[3] Inria, Sophia Antipolis, Biot, France
freddy.lecue@inria.fr
[4] Thales, Montreal, Canada
[5] JRC Blockchains, University of Applied Sciences St. Pölten, Sankt Pölten, Austria
Peter.Kieseberg@fhstp.ac.at
[6] Human-Centered AI Lab, Institute for Medical Informatics, Statistics and Documentation, Medical University Graz, Graz, Austria
andreas.holzinger@medunigraz.at

Abstract. The development of theory, frameworks and tools for Explainable AI (XAI) is a very active area of research these days, and articulating any kind of coherence on a vision and challenges is itself a challenge. At least two sometimes complementary and colliding threads have emerged. The first focuses on the development of pragmatic tools for increasing the transparency of automatically learned prediction models, as for instance by deep or reinforcement learning. The second is aimed at anticipating the negative impact of opaque models with the desire to regulate or control impactful consequences of incorrect predictions, especially in sensitive areas like medicine and law. The formulation of methods to augment the construction of predictive models with domain knowledge can provide support for producing human understandable explanations for predictions. This runs in parallel with AI regulatory concerns, like the European Union General Data Protection Regulation, which sets standards for the production of explanations from automated or semi-automated decision making. Despite the fact that all this research activity is the growing acknowledgement that the topic of explainability is essential, it is important to recall that it is also among the oldest fields of computer science. In fact, early AI was re-traceable, interpretable, thus understandable by and explainable to humans. The goal of this research is to articulate the big picture ideas and their role in advancing the development of XAI systems, to acknowledge their historical roots, and to emphasise the biggest challenges to moving forward.

Published by Springer Nature Switzerland AG 2020
A. Holzinger et al. (Eds.): CD-MAKE 2020, LNCS 12279, pp. 1–16, 2020.
https://doi.org/10.1007/978-3-030-57321-8_1

Keywords: Explainable artificial intelligence · Machine learning · Explainability

1 Introduction

Machine learning is often viewed as the technology belonging to the future in many application fields [46], ranging from pure commodities like recommender systems for music, to automatic diagnosis of cancer or control models for autonomous transportation. However, one fundamental issue lies within the realm of explainability [60]. More precisely, most of the existing learning algorithms can often lead to robust and accurate models from data, but in application terms, they fail to provide end-users with descriptions on how they built them, or to produce convincing explanations for their predictions [7]. In many sensitive applications, such as in medicine, law, and other sectors where the main workers are not computer scientists or engineers, the direct application of these learning algorithms and complex models, without human oversight, is currently inappropriate. The reasons are not only technical, like the accuracy of a model, its stability to decisions and susceptibility to attacks, but often arise from sociological concerns, practically settling on the issue of trust. In fact, one of the principal reasons to produce an explanation is to gain the trust of users [13]. Trust is the main way to enhance the confidence of users with a system [66] as well as their comfort while using and governing it [41]. Trust connects to ethics and the intensity of regulatory activities, as for instance the General Data Protection Regulation in the European Union, leads to many legal and even ethical questions: responsibility for safety, liability for malfunction, and tradeoffs therein must inform decision makers at the highest level. Many methods of explainability for data-driven models have emerged in the years, at a growing rate. On the one hand, a large body of work have focused on building post-hoc methods mainly aimed at wrapping fully trained models, often referred to black-boxes, with an explainability layer [37]. A smaller body of research works, on the other hand, have concentrated on creating self-explainable and interpretable models by incorporating explainability mechanisms during their training, often referred to as the ante-hoc phase [7]. Despite the fact that all this research activity is the growing acknowledgement of the topic of explainability [68], by now referred to as Explainable Artificial Intelligence (XAI) [54], it is important to recall that it is also among the oldest fields of computer science. In fact, early AI was re-traceable, interpretable, thus understandable by and explainable to humans. For these reasons, many scholars have tried to review research works in the field [1,3,22,51,72]. These reviews reveals the needs for a variety of kinds of explanation, for the identification of methods for explainability and their evaluation as well as the need to calibrate the tradeoffs in the degree or level of explanation appropriate for a broad spectrum of applications.

The goal of this research is to articulate the big picture ideas and their role in advancing the development of XAI systems, to acknowledge their historical roots, and to emphasise the biggest challenges to moving forward. The reminder of the paper focuses on relevant notions and concepts for explainability in Sect. 2. It then continues in Sect. 3 with descriptions on the applications of methods for XAI and on domains and areas in which these can have a significant impact. A discussion on the research challenges surrounding XAI is presented in Sect. 4. Eventually, recommendations and visions follow by presenting what we believe scholars should focus on in the development of future explainable AI systems.

2 Notions and Related Concepts

A serious challenge for any attempt to articulate the current concepts for XAI is that there is a very high volume of current activity, both on the research side [22,66,72], and in aggressive industrial developments, where any XAI functions can provide a market advantage to all for profit applications of AI [23,60]. In addition, there remains a lack of consensus on terminology, for example as noted within, there are a variety of definitions for the concept of *interpretation*, but little current connection to the formal history, that means in formal theories of explanation or causation [30]. One recent paper [4] provides an organizing framework based on comparing levels of explanation with levels of autonomous driving. The goal is to identify foundational XAI concepts like relationships to historical work on explanation, especially scientific ones, or the importance of interactive explanation as well as the challenge of their evaluation. Note further that the need for a complex system to provide explanations of activities, including predictions, is not limited to those with components created by machine learning (example in [53]). Pragmatically, the abstract identification of a scientific explanation that enables an explainee to recreate an experiment or prediction can arise in very simple circumstances. For example, one can evaluate an explanation by simply noting whether it is sufficient to achieve an explainee's intended task. For example, in Fig. 1, the pragmatic value of an Ikea visual assembly "explanation" is whether the assembler explainee can achieve the assembly using the diagram.

Overall and within this broad spectrum of ideas related to explanation, there is some focus on the foundational connection between explanation and that of abductive reasoning. For example, the historical notion of *scientific explanation* has been the subject of much debate in the community of science and philosophy [70]. Some propose that a theory of explanation should include both scientific and other simpler forms of explanation. Consequently, it has been a common goal to formulate principles that can confirm an explanation as a scientific one. Aristotle is generally considered to be the first philosopher to articulate an opinion that knowledge becomes scientific when it tries to explain the causes of "why." His view urges that science should not only keep facts, but also describe them in an appropriate explanatory framework [15]. In addition to this theoretical view, empiricists also maintain a belief that the components of ideas should be acquired from perceptions with which humans become familiar through sensory experience. The development of the principles of scientific explanation from this perspective prospered with the so-called Deductive-Nomological (DN) model that was described by Hempel in [24–26], and by Hempel and Oppenheim in [27].

There is a more pragmatic AI historical research thread that connects scientific explanation to AI implementations of abductive reasoning. One such thread, among many, begins with Pople in 1973 [59], Poole et al. in 1987 [58], Muggleton in 1991 [52], to Evans et al. in 2018 [14]. Pople described an algorithm for abduction applied to medical diagnosis. Poole et al. provided an extension to first order logic which could subsume non-monotonic reasoning theories and also identify explanatory hypothesis for any application domain. Muggleton proposed a further refinement referred to as inductive logic programming where hypotheses are identified by inductive constraints within any logic, including higher-order logics. Finally, the adoption of this thread of reasoning have been generalised to explanation based on inductive logic programming by Evans et al. [14]. This most recent work connects with information theoretic ideas used to compare differences in how to learn probability distributions that are modeled by machine learning methods.

Interpreting and explaining a model trained from data by employing a machine learning technique is not an easy task. A body of literature has focused on tackling this by attempting at defining the concept of *interpretability*. This has lead to the formation of many types of explanation, with several attributes and structures. For example, it seems to human nature to assign causal attribution of events [23], and we possess an innate psychological tendency to anthropomorphism. As a consequence, an AI-based system that purports to capture *causal relations* should be capable of providing a causal explanation of its inferential process (example in [55]). Causality can been considered a fundamental attribute of explainability, especially when scientific explainability carries a responsibility to help the explainee reconstruct the inferential process leading to a prediction. Many have noted this role on how explanations should make the causal relationships between the inputs and the outputs of a model explicit [17,30,41,51].

Despite the fact that data-driven models are extremely good at discovering associations in the data, unfortunately they can not guarantee causality of these associations. The objective of significantly inferring causal relationships depends on prior knowledge, and very often some of the discovered associations might be completely unexpected, not interpretable nor explainable. As pointed by [1], the decisions taken considering the output of a model should be clearly explainable to support their *justifiability*. These explanations should allow the identification of potential flows both in a model, enhancing its *transparency*, the knowledge *discovery* process, supporting its *controllability* and *improvement* of its accuracy. Although the importance of explainability is clear, the definition of objective criteria to evaluate methods for XAI and validate their explanations is still lacking. Numerous notions underlying the effectiveness of explanations were identified from the fields of Philosophy, Psychology and Cognitive Science. These were related to the way humans define, generate, select, evaluate and present explanations [50].

3 Applications and Impact Areas

Explainable artificial intelligence has produced many methods so far and it has been applied in many domains, with different expected impacts [21]. In these applications, the production of explanations for black box predictions requires a companion method to extract or lift correlative structures from deep-learned models into vocabularies appropriate for user level explanations. Initial activities focused on deep learning image classification with explanations emerging as heat maps created on the basis of gaps in probability distributions between a learned model and an incorrect prediction [5]. However, the field has become so diverse in methods, often determined by domain specific issues and attributes, that it is scarcely possible to get in-depth knowledge on the whole of it. Additionally, one major aspect though is the problem of explainable AI, where lot of problems have been emerged and illustrated in the literature, especially from not being able to provide explanations. While all of these topics require long and in-depth discussions and are certainly of significant importance for the future of several AI methods in many application domains, we want to focus on the benefits that can be reaped from explainability. This means not focusing on the issues of incomplete and imperfect technologies as a stopping point for applications, but discussing novel solutions provided by explainable AI. A discussion of some, partly prominent and partly surprising examples follows, with arguments on why a certain amount of explainability - as a reflection - is required for more advanced AI. There are many sectors that already have fully functional applications based on machine learning, but still serious problems in applying them exist. These are often caused by failing to be capable to explain how these methods work. In other words, it is known that they work, but the concrete results cannot be explained. Many of these applications either come from safety critical or personally sensitive domains, thus a lot of attention is put on explanations of the inferences of trained models, usually predictions or classifications.

Threat Detection and Triage - The detection of threats and efficient triage have been core topics in the area of IT-Security for at least the past three decades. This started with research in the area of code analysis and signature based AntiVirus-Software, moving towards automated decompilation and code analysis, as well as supporting the automated analysis of network monitoring information for triage. Currently, fully automated threat detection and triage is not available in real life systems due to the complexity of the task and the problem with false positives, even though several different approaches exist. These also include strategies that do not try to detect actual threats, but rather filtering out all known legit network travel and thus drastically reducing the amount of information requiring manual analysis [56]. Still, a major problem without explainability lies in the opaque nature of these methods, thus not being able to fully understand their inner functioning and how an inference was reached. Explainability could greatly enhance the detection capabilities, especially since dynamic effects, such as changing user behavior, could be modelled and introduced earlier into the algorithms without generating a large set of false positives.

Explainable Object Detection - Object detection is usually performed from a large portfolio of artificial neural networks (ANN) architectures such as YOLO, trained on large amount of labelled data. In such contexts, explaining object detections is rather difficult if not impossible due to the high complexity of the hyperparameters (number of layers, filters, regularisers, optimizer, loss function) of the most accurate ANNs. Therefore, explanations of an object detection task are limited to features involved in the data and modeled in the form of saliency maps [11] or at best to examples [40], or prototypes [35]. They are the state-of-the-art approaches but explanations are limited by data frames feeding the ANNs. Industrial applications embedding object detection, such as obstacles detection for trains, do require human-like rational for ensuring the system can be guaranteed, even certified [39].

Protection Against Adversarial ML - In adversarial machine learning, attackers try to manipulate the results of learning algorithms by inserting specifically crafted data in the learning process [32], in order to lead a model to learn erroneous things. Detection of such a manipulation is not trivial, especially in contexts with big data, where no model exists before the analysis phase. While there are several proposals on how to deal with this issue [16], some of them employ neural sub-networks for differentiating between malicious and benign input data like [49]. In this specific circumstance, explainability would have a great impact as it will support the task of uncovering such a manipulation far more quickly, efficiently and without actually finding the examples that have been manipulated, thus greatly enhancing trust in machine learning inferences [31].

Open Source Intelligence (OSINT) - In Open Source Intelligence [19], information retrieval is purely reduced to openly available information, as contrary to Signals Intelligence (SIGINT). However, there are several major issues surrounding OSINT, especially referring to context, languages and the amount of information available. Similarly, another problem lies in deciding how much a source is trusted, and what level of impact news of sources shall have on the result of their aggregations. This is especially important when considering adversarial attacks against OSINT methods and systems [12]. Explainability could provide means for detecting these attacks, with an impact on mitigating their influence. Furthermore, the information that an attack against an intelligent system was launched is also a valuable input from an intelligence perspective, so explainability might lead to additional valuable information. However, not all false information exists due to malice, especially when reporting very recent events: information particles might be wrong, misleading or simply unknown at the time of reporting. OSINT becomes especially complex in case of ongoing events, where facts change every minute, either due to knew intelligence, or simply because of changes in the event itself. Explainability would allow to estimate the effects of incorrect information particles on the overall machine learning outcomes, thus allowing, for instance, to give error margins on reported numbers.

Trustworthy (autonomous) Medical Agents - Several architectures for integrating machine learning into medical decision making have been devised in the past. These are based upon a doctor-in-the-loop approach whereby doctors act as input providers to machine learning algorithms. These can lead to suggestions related to diagnosis or treatment that can be subsequently reviewed by the doctors themselves, who, in turn, can provide feedback in a loop to further enhance modeling [34]. Additionally, the mechanism can also introduces external knowledge to support decision making aimed at incorporating the latest findings in the underlying medical field.

Autonomous Vehicles - While certainly being developed within machine learning, explainability would be beneficial for the area of autonomous vehicles, especially considering autonomous cars. In cases of car accidents, explanations can help trace the reasons why an autonomous vehicle behaved in a certain why and took certain actions. Consequently this can not only lead to safer vehicles, but it also can help solve issues in court faster, greatly enhancing trust towards these novel ML-based technologies and especially the resulting artifacts [20].

4 Research Challenges

A number of research challenges surrounding the development of methods for explainability exist, including technical, legal and practical challenges.

4.1 Technical Challenges

XAI Systems Evaluation. The comprehensive study of what explanation means from a sociological viewpoint [50] begs a difficult issue that is both technical and non-technical: *how does one evaluate the quality of an explanation?* It is not a surprise that the quality or value of an explanation is at least partly determined by the receiver of an explanation, sometimes referred to as the "explainee". An easy way to frame the challenge of evaluating explanations, with respect to an explainee, arises from observing the history of the development of evaluation techniques from the field of data visualization [36]. A simple example of "visual explanation" can frame the general evaluation problem for all explanations as follows. Consider the IKEA assembly diagram, rendered in Fig. 1. A simple list of requirements to assess explanation quality emerges from considering the IKEA assembly instructions as a visual explanation of how to assemble the piece of furniture. In this case, the visual explanation is intended to guide all explainees, and not just a single individual, to the successful assembly of the furniture item. One measure of quality is simply to test whether any individual explainee can use the visual explanation to complete the assembly. Another measure is about whether the visual explanation is clear and unambiguous, so that the assembly is time efficient. In the case of Fig. 1, the sequencing of steps might be misinterpreted by an explainee, and that the simple use of circular arrows to indicate motion may also be ambiguous.

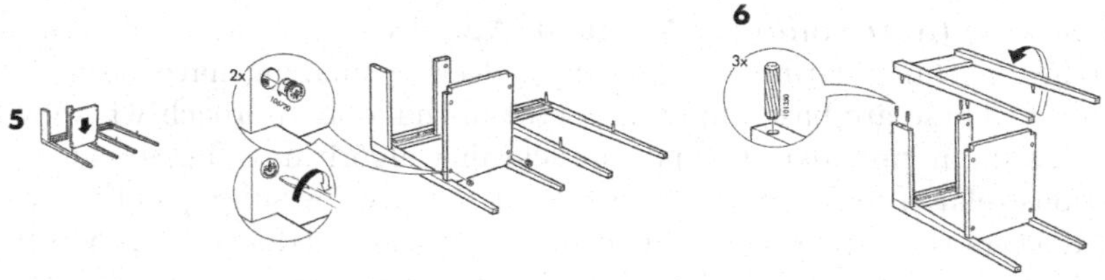

Fig. 1. An IKEA visual explanation for furniture assembly

Overall, and as anticipated in the general evaluation of explanation systems, one could design cognitive experiments to determine, over an experimental human cohort, which portions of the explanation clearly lead to correct inferences, and those which are more difficult to correctly understand. This means that XAI system requirements should include the need to produce an explicit representation of all the components in a way that supports the appropriate interpretation of the visual classification of components. One can generalize visual explanations to the full repertoire that might obtain for a general XAI system. This means a set of representations of the semantics of an underlying domain of application that can provide support to construct an explanation that is understood by a human explainee.

XAI Interpretation. Even though XAI systems are supposed to expose the functioning of a learning technique as well as a set of justification of a model's inferences, it remains rather difficult for a human to interpret them. Explanations are not the final words of an intelligent system but rather the intermediate layer that requires knowledge expertise, context and common-sense characterization for appropriate and correct human interpretation and decision-making [44,64]. Semantics, knowledge graphs [38] and their machine learning representations [6] or similar technical advancements are interesting avenues to be considered for pushing the interpretation at the next right level of knowledge expertise. These might also include the addition of argumentative capabilities, as applied in [45,61] to produce rational and justifiable explanations [62].

4.2 Legal Challenges

While the theoretical ground work in AI stays on the very theoretical side and is thus typically considered to be not problematic from a legal point of view, the actual application of XAI methods in a certain domain can have serious legal implications. This is especially important when considering working with sensitive information. Here, it has yet to be researched whether the explainability related to a model might be used to infer information about individuals, for instance, by using it with slightly different data sets. This technique has been used in many variations in IT-Security, especially considering anonymized data sets or partially released sensitive information as a basis to gather more intelligence on the people involved [9]. Similar attacks have already been proposed and carried out against machine learned models [65] and these allowed to produce a great amount of information, hidden correlations and causalities that were used to infer sensitive information.

Concepts like federated machine learning are built on the notion of executing machine learning algorithms locally on sensitive data sets and then exchanging the resulting feature sets in order to be combined centrally. These are in contrast to more traditional approaches that collect all sensitive data centrally and then run the learning algorithms. One challenge for federated machine learning is to achieve model robustness but greatly focus on protective sensitive inferences. This justifies the need for more applicable anonymisation techniques, as many of the current methods are unsuitable for many application scenarios, either due to performance or quality issues [47,48]. In addition, other legal challenges exist such as the right to be forgotten [67]. This 'reflects the claim of an individual to have certain data deleted so that third persons can no longer trace them'. This fair right is accompanied by technical difficulties ranging from the issue related to the deletion of entries in modern systems, to the problem of inferring information on individuals from aggregates and especially the removal of said individuals from the aggregation process.

Despite the aforementioned challenges, positive benefits can be brought by explainability to the area of machine learning and AI as a whole with respect to legal issues. While the issue of transparency, a key requirement in the General Data Protection Regulation (GDPR), can be a rather a hard issue to tackle, this could change with explainability providing detailed insight, where, when and to what extent personal data of a single individual was involved in a data analysis workflow [69]. While this is currently not a binding requirement to provide that level of details [69], this could be a game changer regarding acceptance of AI, as well as increasing privacy protection in a data driven society. Furthermore, a significant problem currently tackled in machine learning is bias [71], especially since simple methods for tackling the issue have shown to be ineffective [33]. Explainability could support this combat and thus provide a better legal standing for the results derived from data driven systems, especially when used for socio-economic purposes.

4.3 Practical Challenges

One of the most crucial success factors of AI generally and XAI specifically, is to ensure effective human-AI interfaces to enable a usable and useful interaction between humans and AI [2]. Such goals have been discussed in the HCI community for decades [10], but it was not really seen as important in the AI community. Now the needs and demands of XAI for 'explainable user interfaces' may finally stimulate to realise advanced human-centered concepts similar to the early visions of Vannevar Bush in 1945 [8]. Here, the goal is to explore both the explainability side, that means the artificial explanation generated by machines, as well as the human side, that means the human understanding. In an ideal world, both machine explanations and human understanding would be identical, and congruent with the ground truth, which is defined for both machines and humans equally. However, in the real world we face two significant problems:

- the ground truth cannot always be fully defined, as for instance when concerned with medical diagnoses [57] when there is high uncertainty;
- human models such as scientific, world, problem solving models, are often based on causality, in the sense of Judea Pearl [55], which is very challenging as current machine learning does not incorporate them and simply follows pure correlation.

Practically speaking, current XAI methods mainly focus on highlighting input–relevant parts, for example via heat-mapping, that significantly contributed to a certain output, or the most relevant features of a training data set that influenced the most the model accuracy. Unfortunately, they do not incorporate the notion of human model, and therefore there is a need to take also into account the concept of causability [30]. In detail, in line with the concept of usability [28], causability is defined as 'the extent to which an explanation of a statement to a human expert achieves a specified level of causal understanding with effectiveness, efficiency and satisfaction in a specified context of use and the particular contextual understanding capabilities of a human'. Following this concept, it becomes possible to measure the quality of explanations in the same terms as usability (effectiveness, efficiency and satisfaction in a specified context of use), for example with a measurement scale [29].

5 Recommendations and Visions

Machine learning, as a solid research area within artificial intelligence, has undoubtedly impacted the field by providing scholars with a robust suite of methods for modeling complex, non-linear phenomena. With the growing body of work in the last decade on deep learning, this impact has significantly expanded to many applications areas. However, despite the widely acknowledged capability of machine and deep learning to allow scholars to induce accurate models from data and extract relevant patterns, accelerating scientific discovery [18], there is the problem of their interpretability and explainability. For this reason, the last few years have seen a growing body of work on research in methods aimed at explaining the inner functioning of data-driven models and the learning techniques used to induce them. Currently and generally recognised as a core area of AI, eXplainable Artificial Intelligence (XAI) has produced a plethora of methods for model interpretability and explainability. Hundred of scientific articles are published each month in many workshops, conferences and presented at symposium around the world. Some of them focus on wrapping trained models with explanatory layers, such as knowledge graphs [39]. Other try to embed the concept of explainability during training, and some of them try to merge learning capabilities with symbolic reasoning [43]. Explainability is a concept borrowed from psychology, since it is strictly connected to humans, that is difficult to operationalise. A precise formalisation of the construct of explainability is far from being a trivial task as multiple attributes can participate in its definition [61]. Similarly, the attributes might interact with each other, adding complexity in the definition of an objective measure of explainability [42,63]. For these reasons, the last few years have seen also a growing body of research on approaches for evaluating XAI methods. In other words, approaches that are more focused on the explanations generated by XAI solutions, their structure, efficiency, efficacy and impact on humans understanding.

The first recommendation to scholars willing to perform scientific research on explainable artificial intelligence and create XAI methods is to firstly focus on the structure of explanations, the attributes of explainability and the way they can influence humans. This links computer science with psychology. The second recommendation is to define the context of explanations, taking into consideration the underlying domain of application, who they will serve and how. Ultimately, explanations are effective when they help end-users to build a complete and correct mental representation of the inferential process of a given data-driven model. Work on this direction should also focus on which type of explanation can be provided to end-users, including textual, visual, numerical, rules-based or mixed solutions. This links computer science with the behavioural and social sciences. The third recommendation is to clearly define the scope of explanations. This might involve the creation of a method that provide end-users with a suite of local explanations for each input instance or the formation of a method that focuses more on generating explanations on a global level aimed at understanding a model as a whole. This links computer science to statistics and mathematics. The final recommendation is to involve humans, as ultimate users of XAI methods, within the loop of model creation, exploitation, as well as the enhancement of its interpretability and explainability. This can include the development of interactive interfaces that allow end-users to navigate through models, understanding their inner logic at a local or global level, for existing or new input instances. This links artificial intelligence with human-computer interaction.

The visions behind explainable artificial intelligence are certainly numerous. Probably the most important is the creation of models with high accuracy as well as high explainability. The trade-off between these two sides is well known, and usually, increments in one dimension means decrements in the other dimension. Creating interpretable and explainable models that are also highly accurate is the ideal scenario, but since this has been demonstrated to be a hard problem with currents methods of learning and explainability, further research is needed. One possible solution is the creation of models that are fully transparent at all stages of model formation, exploitation and exploration and that are capable of providing local and global explanations. This leads to another vision, which is the use of methods that embed learning capabilities and symbolic reasoning. The former is aimed at generating models and representations with high accuracy for predictive and forecasting purposes, while the latter to explain these representations in highly interpretable natural language terms, aligned to the way human understand and reason.

Acknowledgements. R.Goebel would like to acknowledge the support of the Alberta Machine Intelligence Institute, which is one of the three Pan Canadian AI Centres. A.Holzinger would like to acknowledge the support of the Austrian Science Fund (FWF), Project: P-32554 "Explainable AI - A reference model of explainable Artificial Intelligence for the Medical Domain".

References

1. Adadi, A., Berrada, M.: Peeking inside the black-box: a survey on explainable artificial intelligence (XAI). IEEE Access **6**, 52138–52160 (2018)
2. Amershi, S., et al.: Guidelines for human-AI interaction. In: Proceedings of the 2019 CHI Conference on Human Factors in Computing Systems. ACM (2019)
3. Arras, L., Osman, A., Müller, K.R., Samek, W.: Evaluating recurrent neural network explanations. In: Proceedings of the 2019 ACL Workshop BlackboxNLP: Analyzing and Interpreting Neural Networks for NLP, Florence, Italy, pp. 113–126. Association for Computational Linguistics (2019)
4. Atakishiyev, S., et al.: A multi-component framework for the analysis and design of explainable artificial intelligence. (arXiv:2005.01908v1 [cs.AI]) (2020)
5. Babiker, H.K.B., Goebel, R.: An introduction to deep visual explanation. In: NIPS 2017 - Workshop Interpreting, Explaining and Visualizing Deep Learning (2017)
6. Bianchi, F., Rossiello, G., Costabello, L., Palmonari, M., Minervini, P.: Knowledge graph embeddings and explainable AI. CoRR, abs/2004.14843 (2020)
7. Biran, O., Cotton, C.: Explanation and justification in machine learning: a survey. In: IJCAI 2017 Workshop on Explainable Artificial Intelligence (XAI), Melbourne, Australia, pp. 8–13. International Joint Conferences on Artificial Intelligence Inc. (2017)
8. Bush, V.: As we may think. Atl. Mon. **176**(1), 101–108 (1945)
9. Cai, Z., He, Z., Guan, X., Li, Y.: Collective data-sanitization for preventing sensitive information inference attacks in social networks. IEEE Trans. Depend. Secure Comput. **15**(4), 577–590 (2016)
10. Card, S.K., Moran, T.P., Newell, A.: Psychol. Hum. Comput. Interact. Erlbaum, Hillsdale (NJ) (1983)
11. Chang, C.-H., Creager, E., Goldenberg, A., Duvenaud, D.: Interpreting neural network classifications with variational dropout saliency maps. Proc. NIPS **1**(2), 1–9 (2017)
12. Devine, S.M., Bastian, N.D.: Intelligent systems design for malware classification under adversarial conditions. arXiv preprint, arXiv:1907.03149 (2019)
13. Dzindolet, M.T., Peterson, S.A., Pomranky, R.A., Pierce, L.G., Beck, H.P.: The role of trust in automation reliance. Int. J. hum. Comput. Stud. **58**(6), 697–718 (2003)
14. Evans, R., Greffenstette, E.: Learning explanatory rules from noisy data. J. Artif. Intell. Res. **61**, 1–64 (2018)
15. Falcon, A.: Aristotle on causality. Stanford Encyclopedia of Philosophy (2006). (https://plato.stanford.edu
16. Feinman, R., Curtin, R.R., Shintre, S., Gardner, A.B.: Detecting adversarial samples from artifacts. arXiv preprint, arXiv:1703.00410 (2017)

17. Fox, M., Long, D., Magazzeni, D.: Explainable planning. In: IJCAI 2017 Workshop on Explainable Artificial Intelligence (XAI), Melbourne, Australia, pp. 24–30. International Joint Conferences on Artificial Intelligence Inc (2017)
18. Gil, Y., Greaves, M., Hendler, J., Hirsh, H.: Amplify scientific discovery with artificial intelligence. Science **346**(6206), 171–172 (2014)
19. Glassman, M., Kang, M.J.: Intelligence in the internet age: the emergence and evolution of open source intelligence (OSINT). Comput. Hum. Behav. **28**(2), 673–682 (2012)
20. Glomsrud, J.A., Ødegårdstuen, A., Clair, A.L.S., Smogeli, Ø.: Trustworthy versus explainable AI in autonomous vessels. In: Proceedings of the International Seminar on Safety and Security of Autonomous Vessels (ISSAV) and European STAMP Workshop and Conference (ESWC) 2019, pp. 37–47. Sciendo (2020)
21. Goebal, R., et al.: Explainable AI: the new 42? In: Holzinger, A., Kieseberg, P., Tjoa, A.M., Weippl, E. (eds.) CD-MAKE 2018. LNCS, vol. 11015, pp. 295–303. Springer, Cham (2018). https://doi.org/10.1007/978-3-319-99740-7_21
22. Guidotti, R., Monreale, A., Ruggieri, S., Turini, F., Giannotti, F., Pedreschi, D.: A survey of methods for explaining black box models. ACM Comput. Surv. (CSUR) **51**(5), 93:1–93:42 (2018)
23. Ha, T., Lee, S., Kim, S.: Designing explainability of an artificial intelligence system. In: Proceedings of the Technology, Mind, and Society, p. 1, article no. 14, Washington, District of Columbia, USA. ACM (2018)
24. Hempel, C.G.: The function of general laws in history. J. Philos. **39**(2), 35–48 (1942)
25. Hempel, C.G.: The theoretician's dilemma: a study in the logic of theory construction. Minnesota Stud. Philos. Sci. **2**, 173–226 (1958)
26. Hempel, C.G.: Aspects of Scientific Explanation. Free Press, New York (1965)
27. Hempel, C.G., Oppenheim, P.: Studies in the logic of explanation. Philos. Sci. **15**(2), 135–175 (1948)
28. Holzinger, A.: Usability engineering methods for software developers. Commun. ACM **48**(1), 71–74 (2005)
29. Holzinger, A., Carrington, A., Müller, H.: Measuring the quality of explanations: the System Causability Scale (SCS). KI - Künstliche Intelligenz **34**(2), 193–198 (2020). https://doi.org/10.1007/s13218-020-00636-z
30. Holzinger, A., Langs, G., Denk, H., Zatloukal, K., Mueller, H.: Causability and explainability of artificial intelligence in medicine. Wiley Interdiscip. Rev. Data Min. Knowl. Discov. **9**(4), e1312 (2019)
31. Holzinger, K., Mak, K., Kieseberg, P., Holzinger, A.: Can we trust machine learning results? Artificial intelligence in safety-critical decision support. ERCIM NEWS **112**, 42–43 (2018)
32. Huang, L., Joseph, A.D., Nelson, B., Rubinstein, B.I., Tygar, J.D.: Adversarial machine learning. In: Proceedings of the 4th ACM workshop on Security and artificial intelligence, pp. 43–58 (2011)
33. Kamishima, T., Akaho, S., Asoh, H., Sakuma, J.: Fairness-aware classifier with prejudice remover regularizer. In: Flach, P.A., De Bie, T., Cristianini, N. (eds.) ECML PKDD 2012. LNCS (LNAI), vol. 7524, pp. 35–50. Springer, Heidelberg (2012). https://doi.org/10.1007/978-3-642-33486-3_3
34. Kieseberg, P., Malle, B., Frühwirt, P., Weippl, E., Holzinger, A.: A tamper-proof audit and control system for the doctor in the loop. Brain Inform. **3**(4), 269–279 (2016). https://doi.org/10.1007/s40708-016-0046-2

35. Kim, B., Koyejo, O., Khanna, R.: Examples are not enough, learn to criticize! Criticism for interpretability. In: Advances in Neural Information Processing Systems 29: Annual Conference on Neural Information Processing Systems 2016, Barcelona, Spain, 5–10 December, pp. 2280–2288 (2016)
36. Lam, H., Bertini, E., Isenberg, P., Plaisant, C., Carpendale, S.: Empirical studies in information visualization: seven scenarios. IEEE Trans. Graph. Vis. Comput. **18**(9), 1520–1536 (2012)
37. Laugel, T., Lesot, M.J., Marsala, C., Renard, X., Detyniecki, M.: The dangers of post-hoc interpretability: unjustified counterfactual explanations. In: Proceedings of the Twenty-Eighth International Joint Conference on Artificial Intelligence, (IJCAI), Macao, China, pp. 2801–2807 2019. International Joint Conferences on Artificial Intelligence Organization (2019)
38. Lécué, F.: On the role of knowledge graphs in explainable AI. Semant. Web **11**(1), 41–51 (2020)
39. Lécué, F., Pommellet, T.: Feeding machine learning with knowledge graphs for explainable object detection. In: Suárez-Figueroa, M.C., Cheng, G., Gentile, A.L., Guéret, C., Keet, C.M., Bernstein, A., (eds.) Proceedings of the ISWC 2019 Satellite Tracks (Posters & Demonstrations, Industry, and Outrageous Ideas) co-located with 18th International Semantic Web Conference (ISWC 2019), 26–30 October 2019, Auckland, New Zealand, volume 2456 of CEUR Workshop Proceedings, pp. 277–280. CEUR-WS.org (2019)
40. Li, O., Liu, H., Chen, C., Rudin, C.: Deep learning for case-based reasoning through prototypes: a neural network that explains its predictions. In: Proceedings of the Thirty-Second AAAI Conference on Artificial Intelligence, (AAAI-18), 2–7 February 2018, New Orleans, Louisiana, USA, pp. 3530–3537 (2018)
41. Lipton, Z.C.: The mythos of model interpretability. Commun. ACM **61**(10), 36–43 (2018)
42. Longo, L.: Argumentation for knowledge representation, conflict resolution, defeasible inference and its integration with machine learning. In: Holzinger, A. (ed.) Machine Learning for Health Informatics. LNCS (LNAI), vol. 9605, pp. 183–208. Springer, Cham (2016). https://doi.org/10.1007/978-3-319-50478-0_9
43. Longo, L., Dondio, P.: Defeasible reasoning and argument-based systems in medical fields: an informal overview. In: 2014 IEEE 27th International Symposium on Computer-Based Medical Systems, pp. 376–381. IEEE (2014)
44. Longo, L., Hederman, L.: Argumentation theory for decision support in health-care: a comparison with machine learning. In: Imamura, K., Usui, S., Shirao, T., Kasamatsu, T., Schwabe, L., Zhong, N. (eds.) BHI 2013. LNCS (LNAI), vol. 8211, pp. 168–180. Springer, Cham (2013). https://doi.org/10.1007/978-3-319-02753-1_17
45. Longo, L., Kane, B., Hederman, L.: Argumentation theory in health care. In: 2012 25th International Symposium on Computer-Based Medical Systems (CBMS), pp. 1–6. IEEE (2012)
46. Makridakis, S.: The forthcoming artificial intelligence (AI) revolution: its impact on society and firms. Futures **90**, 46–60 (2017)
47. Malle, B., Kieseberg, P., Holzinger, A.: Do not disturb? Classifier behavior on perturbed datasets. In: Holzinger, A., Kieseberg, P., Tjoa, A.M., Weippl, E. (eds.) CD-MAKE 2017. LNCS, vol. 10410, pp. 155–173. Springer, Cham (2017). https://doi.org/10.1007/978-3-319-66808-6_11

48. Malle, B., Kieseberg, P., Weippl, E., Holzinger, A.: The right to be forgotten: towards machine learning on perturbed knowledge bases. In: Buccafurri, F., Holzinger, A., Kieseberg, P., Tjoa, A.M., Weippl, E. (eds.) CD-ARES 2016. LNCS, vol. 9817, pp. 251–266. Springer, Cham (2016). https://doi.org/10.1007/978-3-319-45507-5_17
49. Metzen, J.H., Genewein, T., Fischer, V., Bischoff, B.: On detecting adversarial perturbations. arXiv preprint, arXiv:1702.04267 (2017)
50. Miller, T.: Explanation in artificial intelligence: insights from the social sciences. Artif. Intell. **267**, 1–38 (2019)
51. Miller, T., Howe, P., Sonenberg, L.: Explainable AI: beware of inmates running the asylum or: how i learnt to stop worrying and love the social and behavioural sciences. In: IJCAI Workshop on Explainable AI (XAI), Melbourne, Australia, pp. 36–42. International Joint Conferences on Artificial Intelligence Inc. (2017)
52. Muggleton, S.: Inductive logic programming. New Generat. Comput. **8**(4), 295–318 (1991)
53. Nunes, I., Jannach, D.: A systematic review and taxonomy of explanations in decision support and recommender systems. User Model. User Adap. Interact. **27**(3), 393–444 (2017). https://doi.org/10.1007/s11257-017-9195-0
54. Páez, A.: The pragmatic turn in explainable artificial intelligence (XAI). Mind. Mach. **29**, 1–19 (2019)
55. Pearl, J.: Causality: Models, Reasoning, and Inference, 2nd edn. Cambridge University Press, Cambridge (2009)
56. Pirker, M., Kochberger, P., Schwandter, S.: Behavioural comparison of systems for anomaly detection. In: Proceedings of the 13th International Conference on Availability, Reliability and Security, pp. 1–10 (2018)
57. Pohn, B., Kargl, M., Reihs, R., Holzinger, A., Zatloukal, k., Müler, H.: Towards a deeper understanding of how a pathologist makes a diagnosis: visualization of the diagnostic process in histopathology. In: IEEE Symposium on Computers and Communications (ISCC 2019). IEEE (2019)
58. Poole, D., Goebel, R., Aleliunas, R.: Theorist: A logical reasoning system for defaults and diagnosis. The Knowledge Frontier. Symbolic Computation (Artificial Intelligence), pp. 331–352 (1987). https://doi.org/10.1007/978-1-4612-4792-0_13
59. Pople, H.: On the mechanization of abductive logic. In: IJCAI'1973: Proceedings of the 3rd International Joint Conference on Artificial Intelligence, pp. 147–152. Morgan Kaufmann Publishers (1973)
60. Preece, A.: Asking "why" in AI: explainability of intelligent systems-perspectives and challenges. Intell. Syst. Account. Financ. Manage. **25**(2), 63–72 (2018)
61. Rizzo, L., Longo, L.: Inferential models of mental workload with defeasible argumentation and non-monotonic fuzzy reasoning: a comparative study. In: Proceedings of the 2nd Workshop on Advances in Argumentation in Artificial Intelligence, co-located with XVII International Conference of the Italian Association for Artificial Intelligence, AI^3@AI*IA 2018, 20–23 November 2018, Trento, Italy, pp. 11–26 (2018)
62. Rizzo, L., Longo, L.: A qualitative investigation of the explainability of defeasible argumentation and non-monotonic fuzzy reasoning. In: Proceedings for the 26th AIAI Irish Conference on Artificial Intelligence and Cognitive Science Trinity College Dublin, 6–7 December 2018, Dublin, Ireland, pp. 138–149 (2018)
63. Rizzo, L., Longo, L.: An empirical evaluation of the inferential capacity of defeasible argumentation, non-monotonic fuzzy reasoning and expert systems. Expert Syst. Appl. **147**, 113220 (2020)

64. Rizzo, L., Majnaric, L., Longo, L.: A comparative study of defeasible argumentation and non-monotonic fuzzy reasoning for elderly survival prediction using biomarkers. In: Ghidini, C., Magnini, B., Passerini, A., Traverso, P. (eds.) AI*IA 2018. LNCS (LNAI), vol. 11298, pp. 197–209. Springer, Cham (2018). https://doi.org/10.1007/978-3-030-03840-3_15
65. Shokri, R., Stronati, M., Song, C., Shmatikov, V.: Membership inference attacks against machine learning models. In: 2017 IEEE Symposium on Security and Privacy (SP), pp. 3–18. IEEE (2017)
66. Tintarev, N., Masthoff, J.: A survey of explanations in recommender systems. In: IEEE 23rd international conference on data engineering workshop, pp. 801–810, Istanbul, Turkey. IEEE (2007)
67. Villaronga, E.F., Kieseberg, P., Li, T.: Humans forget, machines remember: artificial intelligence and the right to be forgotten. Comput. Law Secur. Rev. **34**(2), 304–313 (2018)
68. Vilone, G., Longo, L.: Explainable artificial intelligence: a systematic review. CoRR, abs/2006.00093 (2020)
69. Wachter, S., Mittelstadt, B., Floridi, L.: Transparent, explainable, and accountable AI for robotics. Sci. Robot. **2**(6) (2017)
70. Woodward, J.: Scientific explanation. Stanford Encyclopedia of Philosophy (2003). (https://plato.stanford.edu
71. Yapo, A., Weiss, J.: Ethical implications of bias in machine learning. In: HICCS 2018, Proceedings of the 51st Hawaii International Conference on System Sciences (2018)
72. Zhang, Q., Zhu, S.: Visual interpretability for deep learning: a survey. Front. Inform. Technol. Electron. Eng. **19**(1), 27–39 (2018). https://doi.org/10.1631/FITEE.1700808

The Explanation Game: Explaining Machine Learning Models Using Shapley Values

Luke Merrick([✉]) and Ankur Taly

Fiddler Labs, Palo Alto, USA
contact@lukemerrick.com, ankur.taly@gmail.com

Abstract. A number of techniques have been proposed to explain a machine learning model's prediction by attributing it to the corresponding input features. Popular among these are techniques that apply the Shapley value method from cooperative game theory. While existing papers focus on the axiomatic motivation of Shapley values, and efficient techniques for computing them, they offer little justification for the game formulations used, and do not address the uncertainty implicit in their methods' outputs. For instance, the popular SHAP algorithm's formulation may give substantial attributions to features that play no role in the model. In this work, we illustrate how subtle differences in the underlying game formulations of existing methods can cause large differences in the attributions for a prediction. We then present a general game formulation that unifies existing methods, and enables straightforward confidence intervals on their attributions. Furthermore, it allows us to interpret the attributions as *contrastive explanations* of an input relative to a distribution of reference inputs. We tie this idea to classic research in cognitive psychology on contrastive explanations, and propose a conceptual framework for generating and interpreting explanations for ML models, called *formulate, approximate, explain* (FAE). We apply this framework to explain black-box models trained on two UCI datasets and a Lending Club dataset.

1 Introduction

Complex machine learning models are rapidly spreading to high stakes tasks such as credit scoring, underwriting, medical diagnosis, and crime prediction. Consequently, it is becoming increasingly important to interpret and explain individual model predictions to decision-makers, end-users, and regulators. A common form of model explanations are based on *feature attributions*, wherein a score (*attribution*) is ascribed to each feature in proportion to the feature's contribution to the prediction. Over the last few years there has been a surge in feature attribution methods, with methods based on Shapley values from cooperative game theory being prominent among them [1,3,4,6,18,19,27].

Published by Springer Nature Switzerland AG 2020
A. Holzinger et al. (Eds.): CD-MAKE 2020, LNCS 12279, pp. 17–38, 2020.
https://doi.org/10.1007/978-3-030-57321-8_2

Shapley values [24] provide a mathematically fair and unique method to attribute the payoff of a cooperative game to the players of the game. Recently, there have been a number of Shapley-value-based methods for attributing an ML model's prediction to input features. Prominent among them are SHAP and KernelSHAP [19], TreeSHAP [18], QII [6], and IME [26]. In applying the Shapley values method to ML models, the key step is to setup a cooperative game whose players are the input features and whose payoff is the model prediction. Due to its strong axiomatic guarantees, the Shapley values method is emerging as the de facto approach to feature attribution, and some researchers even speculate that it may be the only method compliant with legal regulation such as the General Data Protection Regulation's "right to an explanation" [1].

In this work, we study several Shapley-value-based explanation techniques. Paradoxically, while all techniques lay claim to the axiomatic uniqueness of Shapley values, we discover that they yield significantly different attributions for the same input even when evaluated exactly (without approximation). In some cases, we find the attributions to be completely counter-intuitive. For instance, in Sect. 2, we show a simple model for which the popular SHAP method gives substantial attribution to a feature that is irrelevant to the model function. We trace this shortcoming and the differences across existing methods to the varying cooperative games formulated by the methods.[1] We refer to such games as *explanation games*. Unfortunately, while existing methods focus on the axiomatic motivations of Shapley values, they offer little justification for the design choices made in their explanation game formulations. The goal of this work is to shed light on these design choices, and their implications on the resulting attributions.

Our main technical result shows that various existing techniques can be unified under a common game formulation parametric on a reference distribution. The Shapley values of this unified game formulation can be decomposed into the Shapley values of *single-reference games* that model a feature's absence by replacing its value with the corresponding value from a specific *reference input*.

This decomposition is beneficial in two ways. First, it allows us to efficiently compute confidence intervals and other supplementary information about attributions, a notable advancement over existing methods (which lack confidence intervals even though they approximate metrics of random variables using finite samples). Second, it offers conceptual clarity. It unlocks the interpretation that attributions explain the prediction at an input *in contrast* to other reference inputs. The attributions vary across existing methods as each method chooses a different reference distribution to contrast with. We tie the idea to classic research in cognitive psychology, and propose a conceptual *formulate, approximate, explain* (FAE) framework to create Shapley-value-based *contrastive* feature attributions. The goal of the framework is to produce attributions that are not only axiomatically justified, but also relevant to the underlying explanation question.

[1] We note that this shortcoming, and the multiplicity of game formulations has also been noted in parallel work [14,28].

We illustrate our ideas via case studies on models trained on two UCI datasets (Bike Sharing and Adult Income) and a Lending Club dataset. We find that in these real-world situations, explanations generated using our FAE framework uncover important patterns that previous attribution methods cannot identify. In summary, we make the following key contributions:

- We highlight several shortcomings of existing Shapley-value-based feature attribution methods (Sect. 2), and analyze the root cause of these issues (Sect. 4.1).
- We present a novel game formulation that unifies existing methods (Sect. 4.2), and helps characterize their uncertainty with confidence intervals (Sect. 4.3).
- We offer a novel framework for creating and interpreting attributions (Sect. 4.4), and demonstrate its use through case studies (Sect. 5).

Table 1. Input distribution and model outputs for the mover hiring system example.

x_{male}	x_{lift}	$\Pr[\boldsymbol{X} = \boldsymbol{x}]$	$f_{male}(\boldsymbol{x})$	$f_{both}(\boldsymbol{x})$
0	0	0.1	0.0	0.0
0	1	0.0	0.0	0.0
1	0	0.4	1.0	0.0
1	1	0.5	1.0	1.0

Table 2. Attributions for the input $x_{male} = 1, x_{lift} = 1$.

Payoff formulation	f_{male}		f_{both}	
	ϕ_1 (*male*)	ϕ_2 (*lifting*)	ϕ_1 (*male*)	ϕ_2 (*lifting*)
SHAP	0.05	0.05	0.028	0.472
KernelSHAP	0.10	0.00	0.050	0.450
QII	0.10	0.00	0.075	0.475
IME	0.50	0.00	0.375	0.375

2 A Motivating Example

To probe existing Shapley-value-based model explanation methods, we evaluate them on two toy models for which it is easy to intuit correct attributions. We leverage a modified version of the example provided in [6]: a system that recommends whether a moving company should hire a mover applicant. The input vector to both models comprises two binary features "is male" and "is good lifter" (denoted by $\boldsymbol{x} = (x_{male}, x_{lift})$), and output a recommendation score between 0 ("no hire") and 1 ("hire"). We define two models—$f_{male}(\boldsymbol{x}) ::= x_{male}$ (only hire males), and $f_{both}(\boldsymbol{x}) ::= x_{male} \wedge x_{lift}$ (only hire males who are good lifters). Table 1 specifies a probability distribution over the input space, along with the predictions from the two models.

Consider the input $\boldsymbol{x} = (1, 1)$ (i.e. a male who is a good lifter), for which both models output a recommendation score of 1. Table 2 lists the attributions from several existing methods. Focusing on the relative attribution between x_{male} and x_{lift}, we make the following surprising observations. First, even though x_{lift} is irrelevant to f_{male}, the SHAP algorithm[2] results in equal attribution to both features. This contradicts our intuition around the "Dummy" axiom of Shapley values, which states that attribution to a player (feature) that never contributes to the payoff (prediction) must be zero.

Additionally, the SHAP attributions present a misleading picture from a fairness perspective: f_{male} relies solely on x_{male}, yet the attributions do not reflect this bias and instead claim that the model uses both features equally. Second, although f_{both} treats its features symmetrically, and $\boldsymbol{x}$ has identical values in both its features, many of the methods considered do not provide symmetrical attributions. This again is intuitively at odds with the "Symmetry" axiom of Shapley values, which states that players (features) that always contribute equally to the payoff (prediction) must receive equal attribution. These unintuitive behaviors surfaced by the above observations demand an in-depth study of the internal design choices of these methods. We carry out this study in Sect. 4.

3 Preliminaries

3.1 Additive Feature Attributions

Additive feature attributions [19] are attributions that sum to the difference between the explained model output $f(\boldsymbol{x})$ and a reference output value ϕ_0. In practice, ϕ_0 is typically an average model output or model output for a domain-specific "baseline" input (e.g. an empty string for text sentiment classification).

Definition 1 (Additive feature attributions). *Suppose $f : \mathcal{X} \to \mathbb{R}$ is a model mapping an M-dimensional feature space $\mathcal{X}$ to real-valued predictions. Additive feature attributions for $f(\boldsymbol{x})$ at input $\boldsymbol{x} = (x_1, \ldots, x_M) \in \mathcal{X}$ comprise of a reference (or baseline) attribution ϕ_0 and feature attributions $\boldsymbol{\phi} = (\phi_1, \phi_2, \ldots, \phi_M)$ corresponding to the M features such that $f(\boldsymbol{x}) = \phi_0 + \sum_{i=1}^{M} \phi_i$.*

There currently exist a number of competing methodologies for computing these attributions (see [2]). Given the difficulty of empirically evaluating attributions, several methods offer an axiomatic justification, often through the Shapley values method.

3.2 Shapley Values

The Shapley values method is a classic technique from game theory that fairly attributes the total payoff from a cooperative game to the game's players [24].

[2] As defined by Equation 9 in [19].

Recently, this method has found numerous applications in explaining ML models (e.g. [5,9,19]).

Formally, a cooperative game is played by a set of players $\mathcal{M} = \{1, \ldots, M\}$ termed the *grand coalition*. The game is characterized by a set function $v : 2^{\mathcal{M}} \to \mathbb{R}$ such that $v(S)$ is the payoff for any coalition of players $S \subseteq \mathcal{M}$, and $v(\emptyset) = 0$. Shapley values are built by examining the marginal contribution of a player to an existing coalition S, i.e., $v(S \cup \{i\}) - v(S)$. The Shapley value of a player i, denoted $\phi_i(v)$, is a certain weighted aggregation of its marginal contribution to all possible coalitions of players.

$$\phi_i(v) = \frac{1}{M} \sum_{S \subseteq \mathcal{M} \setminus \{i\}} \binom{M-1}{|S|}^{-1} (v(S \cup \{i\}) - v(S)) \tag{1}$$

The Shapley value method is the unique method satisfying four desirable axioms: *Dummy*, *Symmetry*, *Efficiency*, and *Linearity*. We informally describe the axioms in Appendix A, and refer the reader to [30] for formal definitions and proofs.

Approximating Shapley Values. Computing Shapley values involves evaluating the game payoff for every possible coalition of players. This makes the computation exponential in the number of players. For games with few players, it is possible to exactly compute the Shapley values, but for games with many players, the Shapley values can only be approximated. Recently there has been much progress towards the efficient approximation of Shapley values. In this work we focus on a simple sampling approximation, presenting two more popular techniques in the Appendix B. We refer the reader to [1,3,4,13,20] for a fuller picture of recent advances in Shapley value approximation.

A simple sampling approximation (used by [9], among other works) relies on the fact that the Shapley value can be expressed as the expected marginal contribution a player has when players are added to a coalition in a random order. Let $\pi(M)$ be the ordered set of permutations of M, and $\boldsymbol{O}$ be an ordering randomly sampled from $\pi(M)$. Let $\text{pre}_i(\boldsymbol{O})$ be the set of players that precede player i in $\boldsymbol{O}$. The Shapley value of player i is the expected marginal contribution of the player under all possible orderings of players.

$$\phi_i(v) = \mathop{\mathbb{E}}_{\boldsymbol{O} \sim \pi(M)} [v(\text{pre}_i(\boldsymbol{O}) \cup \{i\}) - v(\text{pre}_i(\boldsymbol{O}))] \tag{2}$$

By sampling a number of permutations and averaging the marginal contributions of each player, we can estimate this expected value for each player and approximate each player's Shapley value.

4 Explanation Games

In order to explain a model prediction with the Shapley values method, it is necessary to formulate a cooperative game with players that correspond to the features and a payoff that corresponds to the prediction. In this section, we analyze the methods examined in Sect. 2, and show that their surprising attributions are an artifact of their game formulations. We then discuss a unified game formulation and its decomposition to *single-reference games*, enabling conceptual clarity about the meanings of existing methods' attributions.

Notation. Let $\mathcal{D}^{inp}$ be the input distribution, which characterizes the process that generates model inputs. We denote the input of an explained prediction as $\boldsymbol{x} = (x_1, \ldots, x_M)$ and use $\boldsymbol{r}$ to denote another "reference" input. We use boldface to indicate when a variable or function is vector-valued, and capital letters for random variable inputs (although S continues to represent the set of contributing players/features). Thus, x_i is a scalar input, $\boldsymbol{x}$ is an input vector, and $\boldsymbol{X}$ is a *random* input vector. We use $\boldsymbol{x}_S = \{x_i : i \in S\}$ to represent a sub-vector of features indexed by S. This notation is also extended to random input vectors $\boldsymbol{X}$. Lastly, we introduce the *composite input* $\boldsymbol{z}(\boldsymbol{x}, \boldsymbol{r}, S)$, which agrees with the input $\boldsymbol{x}$ on all features in S and with $\boldsymbol{r}$ on all features not in S. Note that $\boldsymbol{z}(\boldsymbol{x}, \boldsymbol{r}, \emptyset) = \boldsymbol{r}$, and $\boldsymbol{z}(\boldsymbol{x}, \boldsymbol{r}, \mathcal{M}) = \boldsymbol{x}$.

$$\boldsymbol{z}(\boldsymbol{x}, \boldsymbol{r}, S) = (z_1, z_2, ..., z_M), \text{ where } z_i = \begin{cases} x_i & i \in S \\ r_i & i \notin S \end{cases} \tag{3}$$

4.1 Existing Game Formulations

The explanation game payoff function $v_{\boldsymbol{x}}$ must be defined for every feature subset S such that $v_{\boldsymbol{x}}(S)$ captures the contribution of $\boldsymbol{x}_S$ to the model's prediction. This allows us to compute each feature's possible marginal contributions to the prediction and derive its Shapley value (see Sect. 3.2).

By the definition of *additive feature attributions* (Definition 1) and the Shapley values' Efficiency axiom, we must define $v_{\boldsymbol{x}}(\mathcal{M}) ::= f(\boldsymbol{x}) - \phi_0$ (i.e. the payoff of the full coalition must be the difference between the explained model prediction and a baseline prediction). Although this definition is fixed, it leaves us the challenge of coming up with the payoff when some features do not contribute (that is, when they are *absent*).

We find that all existing approaches handle this feature-absent payoff by randomly sampling absent features according to a particular *reference* distribution and then computing the expected value of the prediction. The resulting game formulations differ from one another only in the reference distribution they use. Additionally, we note that in practice small samples are used to approximate the expected value present in these payoff functions. This introduces a significant source of attribution uncertainty not clearly quantified by existing work.

Conditional Distribution. The game formulation of SHAP [19], TreeSHAP [18], and [1] simulates feature absence by sampling absent features from the conditional distribution based on the values of the present (or contributing) features:

$$v_{\boldsymbol{x}}^{cond}(S) = \mathop{\mathbb{E}}_{\boldsymbol{R} \sim \mathcal{D}^{inp}} [f(\boldsymbol{z}(\boldsymbol{x}, \boldsymbol{R}, S)) \mid \boldsymbol{R}_S = \boldsymbol{x}_S] - \mathop{\mathbb{E}}_{\boldsymbol{R} \sim \mathcal{D}^{inp}} [f(\boldsymbol{R})] \tag{4}$$

Unfortunately, this is not a proper simulation of feature absence as it does not break correlations between features [14]. This could lead to unintuitive attributions. For instance, in the f_{male} example from Sect. 2, it causes the irrelevant feature x_{lift} to receive a nonzero attribution. Specifically, since the event $x_{male} = 1$ is correlated[3] with $x_{lift} = 1$, once $x_{lift} = 1$ is given, the expected prediction becomes 1. This causes the x_{lift} feature to have a non-zero marginal contribution (relative to when both features are absent), and therefore a nonzero Shapley value. More generally, whenever a feature is correlated with a model's prediction on inputs drawn from $\mathcal{D}^{inp}$, this game formulation results in non-zero attribution to the feature regardless of whether the feature directly impacts the prediction.

Input Distribution. Another option for simulating feature absence, which is used by KernelSHAP, is to sample absent features from the corresponding marginal distribution in $\mathcal{D}^{inp}$:

$$v_{\boldsymbol{x}}^{inp}(S) = \mathop{\mathbb{E}}_{\boldsymbol{R} \sim \mathcal{D}^{inp}}[f(\boldsymbol{z}(\boldsymbol{x}, \boldsymbol{R}, S))] - \mathop{\mathbb{E}}_{\boldsymbol{R} \sim \mathcal{D}^{inp}}[f(\boldsymbol{R})] \tag{5}$$

Since this formulation breaks correlation with the contributing features, it ensures irrelevant features receive no attribution (e.g. no attribution to x_{lift} when explaining $f_{male}(1, 1) = 1$). We formally describe this property via the *Insensitivity* axiom in Sect. 4.2.

We note that this formulation is still subject to artifacts of the input distribution, as evident from the asymmetrical attributions when explaining the prediction $f_{both}(1, 1) = 1$ (see Table 2). The features receive different attributions because they have different marginal distributions in $\mathcal{D}^{inp}$, not because they impact the model differently.

Joint-Marginal Distribution. QII [6] simulates feature absence by sampling absent features one at a time from their own univariate marginal distributions. In addition to breaking correlation with the contributing features, this breaks correlation between absent features as well. Formally, the QII formulation uses a distribution we term the "joint-marginal" distribution ($\mathcal{D}^{J.M.}$), where:

$$\Pr_{X \sim \mathcal{D}^{J.M.}}[X = (x_1, \ldots, x_M)] = \prod_{i=1}^{M} \Pr_{X \sim \mathcal{D}^{inp}}[X_i = x_i]$$

The joint-marginal formulation $v_{\boldsymbol{x}}^{J.M.}$ is similar to $v_{\boldsymbol{x}}^{inp}$, except that the reference distribution is $\mathcal{D}^{J.M.}$ instead of $\mathcal{D}^{inp}$:

$$v_{\boldsymbol{x}}^{J.M.}(S) = \mathop{\mathbb{E}}_{\boldsymbol{R} \sim \mathcal{D}^{J.M.}}[f(\boldsymbol{z}(\boldsymbol{x}, \boldsymbol{R}, S))] - \mathop{\mathbb{E}}_{\boldsymbol{R} \sim \mathcal{D}^{J.M.}}[f(\boldsymbol{R})] \tag{6}$$

[3] In this context, *correlation* refers to general statistical dependence, not just a nonzero Pearson correlation coefficient.

Unfortunately, like $v_{\boldsymbol{x}}^{inp}$, this game formulation is also tied to the input distribution and under-attributes features that take on common values in the background data. This is evident from the attributions for the f_{both} model shown in Table 2.

Uniform Distribution. The last formulation we study from the prior art simulates feature absence by drawing values from a uniform distribution $\mathcal{U}$ over the entire input space, as in IME [26].[4] Completely ignoring the input distribution, this payoff $v_{\boldsymbol{x}}^{unif}$ considers all possible feature values (edge-cases and common cases) with equal weighting.

$$v_{\boldsymbol{x}}^{unif}(S) = \mathop{\mathbb{E}}_{\boldsymbol{R} \sim \mathcal{U}} [f(\boldsymbol{z}(\boldsymbol{x}, \boldsymbol{R}, S))] - \mathop{\mathbb{E}}_{\boldsymbol{R} \sim \mathcal{U}} [f(\boldsymbol{R})] \tag{7}$$

In Table 2, we see that this formulation yields intuitively correct attributions for f_{male} and f_{both}. However, the uniform distribution can sample so heavily from irrelevant outlier regions of $\mathcal{X}$ that relevant patterns of model behavior become masked (we study the importance of *relevant references* both theoretically in Sect. 4.4 and empirically in Sect. 5).

4.2 A Unified Formulation

We observe that the existing game formulations $v_{\boldsymbol{x}}^{inp}$, $v_{\boldsymbol{x}}^{J.M.}$, and $v_{\boldsymbol{x}}^{unif}$ can be unified as a single game formulation $v_{\boldsymbol{x},\mathcal{D}^{ref}}$ that is parameterized by a reference distribution $\mathcal{D}^{ref}$.

$$v_{\boldsymbol{x},\mathcal{D}^{ref}}(S) = \mathop{\mathbb{E}}_{\boldsymbol{R} \sim \mathcal{D}^{ref}} [f(\boldsymbol{z}(\boldsymbol{x}, \boldsymbol{R}, S))] - \mathop{\mathbb{E}}_{\boldsymbol{R} \sim \mathcal{D}^{ref}} [f(\boldsymbol{R})] \tag{8}$$

For instance, the formulation for KernelSHAP is recovered when $\mathcal{D}^{ref} = \mathcal{D}^{inp}$, and QII is recovered when $\mathcal{D}^{ref} = \mathcal{D}^{J.M.}$. In the rest of this section, we discuss several properties of this general formulation that help us better understand its attributions. Notably, the formulation $v_{\boldsymbol{x}}^{cond}$ cannot be expressed in this framework; we discuss the reason for this later in this section.

A Decomposition in Terms of Single-Reference Games. We now introduce *single-reference games*, a conceptual building block that helps us interpret the Shapley values of the $v_{\boldsymbol{x},\mathcal{D}^{ref}}$ game. A single-reference game $v_{\boldsymbol{x},\boldsymbol{r}}$ simulates feature absence by replacing the feature value with the value from a specific reference input $\boldsymbol{r}$:

$$v_{\boldsymbol{x},\boldsymbol{r}}(S) = f(\boldsymbol{z}(\boldsymbol{x}, \boldsymbol{r}, S)) - f(\boldsymbol{r}) \tag{9}$$

The attributions from a single-reference game explain the difference between the prediction for the input and the prediction for the reference (i.e. $\sum_i \phi_i(v_{\boldsymbol{x},\boldsymbol{r}}) = v_{\boldsymbol{x},\boldsymbol{r}}(\mathcal{M}) = f(\boldsymbol{x}) - f(\boldsymbol{r})$, and $\phi_0 = f(\boldsymbol{r})$). Computing attributions relative to a single reference point (also referred to as a "baseline") is common to several others

[4] It is somewhat unclear whether IME proposes $\mathcal{U}$ or $\mathcal{D}^{inp}$, as [26] assumes $\mathcal{D}^{inp} = \mathcal{U}$, while [27] calls for values to be sampled from $\mathcal{X}$ "at random.".

methods [3,7,25,29]. However, while those works seek a neutral "informationless" reference (e.g. an all-black image for image models), we find it beneficial to consider arbitrary references and interpret the resulting attributions relative to the reference. We develop this idea further in our FAE framework (see Sect. 4.4).

We now state Proposition 1, which shows how the Shapley values of $v_{\boldsymbol{x},\mathcal{D}^{ref}}$ can be expressed as the expected Shapley values of a (randomized) single-reference game $v_{\boldsymbol{x},\boldsymbol{R}}$, where $\boldsymbol{R} \sim \mathcal{D}$. The proof (provided in Appendix C) follows from the Shapley values' Linearity axiom and the linearity of expectation.

Proposition 1. $\boldsymbol{\phi}(v_{\boldsymbol{x},\mathcal{D}^{ref}}) = \mathbb{E}_{\boldsymbol{R}\sim\mathcal{D}^{ref}}\left[\boldsymbol{\phi}(v_{\boldsymbol{x},\boldsymbol{R}})\right]$

Proposition 1 brings conceptual clarity and practical improvements (confidence intervals and supplementary metrics) to existing methods. It shows that the attributions from existing games ($v_{\boldsymbol{x}}^{inp}$, $v_{\boldsymbol{x}}^{J.M.}$, and $v_{\boldsymbol{x}}^{unif}$) are in fact differently weighted aggregations of attributions from a space of single-reference games. For instance, $v_{\boldsymbol{x}}^{unif}$ weighs attributions relative to all reference points equally, while $v_{\boldsymbol{x}}^{inp}$ weighs them using the input distribution $\mathcal{D}^{inp}$.

Insensitivity Axiom. We show that attributions from the game $v_{\boldsymbol{x},\mathcal{D}^{ref}}$ satisfy the *Insensitivity* axiom from [29], which states that a feature that is mathematically irrelevant to the model must receive zero attribution. Formally, a feature i is irrelevant to a model f if for any input, changing the feature does not change the model output. That is, $\forall \boldsymbol{x}, \boldsymbol{r} \in \mathcal{X} : \boldsymbol{x}_{\mathcal{M}\setminus\{i\}} = \boldsymbol{r}_{\mathcal{M}\setminus\{i\}} \implies f(\boldsymbol{x}) = f(\boldsymbol{r})$.

Proposition 2. *If a feature i is irrelevant to a model f then $\phi_i(v_{\boldsymbol{x},\mathcal{D}^{ref}}) = 0$ for all distributions $\mathcal{D}^{ref}$.*

Notably, the $v_{\boldsymbol{x}}^{cond}$ formulation does not obey the Insensitivity axiom (a counterexample being the f_{male} attributions from Sect. 2). Accordingly, our general formulation (Eq. 7) cannot express this formulation. In the rest of the paper, we focus on game formulations that satisfy the Insensitivity axiom. We refer to [28] for a comprehensive analysis of the axiomatic guarantees of various game formulations.

4.3 Confidence Intervals on Attributions

Existing game formulations involve computing an expected value (over a reference distribution) in every invocation of the payoff function. In practice, this expectation is approximated via sampling, which introduces uncertainty. The original formulations of these games do not lend themselves well to quantify such uncertainty. We show that by leveraging our unified game formulation, one can efficiently quantify the uncertainty using confidence intervals (CIs).

Our decomposition in Proposition 1 shows that the attributions themselves can be expressed as an expectation over (deterministic) Shapley value attributions from a distribution of single-reference games. Consequently, we can quantify attribution uncertainty by estimating the standard error of the mean (SEM) across a sample of Shapley values from single-reference games. In terms of the sample standard deviation (SSD), 95% CIs on the mean attribution ($\bar{\boldsymbol{\phi}}$) from a sample of size N are given by

$$\bar{\boldsymbol{\phi}} \pm \frac{1.96 \times \mathsf{SSD}(\{\boldsymbol{\phi}(v_{\boldsymbol{x},\boldsymbol{r}_i})\}_{i=1}^{N})}{\sqrt{N}} \tag{10}$$

We note that while one could use bootstrap [8] to obtain CIs, the SEM approach is more efficient as it requires no additional Shapley value computations.

A Unified CI. As discussed in Sect. 3.2, often the large number of features (players) in an explanation game necessitates the approximation of Shapley values. The approximation may involve random sampling, which incurs its own uncertainty. In what follows, we derive a general SEM-based CI that quantifies the combined uncertainty from sampling-based approximations of Shapley values and the sampling of references.

Let us consider a generic estimator $\hat{\phi}_i^{(\boldsymbol{G})}(v_{\boldsymbol{x},\boldsymbol{r}})$ parameterized by some random sample $\boldsymbol{G}$. An example of such an approach is the feature ordering based approximation of Eq. 2, for which $\boldsymbol{G} = (\boldsymbol{O}_j)_{j=1}^{k}$ represents a random sample of feature orderings, and:

$$\hat{\phi}_i^{(\boldsymbol{G})}(v_{\boldsymbol{x},\boldsymbol{r}}) = \frac{1}{k}\sum_{j=1}^{k} v(\mathrm{pre}_i(\boldsymbol{O}_j) \cup \{i\}) - v(\mathrm{pre}_i(\boldsymbol{O}_j))$$

As long as the generic $\hat{\phi}_i^{(\boldsymbol{G})}$ is an unbiased estimator (like the feature ordering estimator of Eq. 2), and $\boldsymbol{G}$ and $\boldsymbol{R} \sim \mathcal{D}^{ref}$ are sampled independently from one another, we can derive a unified CI using the SEM. By the estimator's unbiasedness and Proposition 1, the Shapley value attributions can be expressed as:

$$\phi_i(v_{\boldsymbol{x},\mathcal{D}^{ref}}) = \mathop{\mathbb{E}}_{\boldsymbol{R}}\mathop{\mathbb{E}}_{\boldsymbol{G}}\left[\hat{\phi}_i^{(\boldsymbol{G})}(v_{\boldsymbol{x},\boldsymbol{R}})\right] \tag{11}$$

Since $\boldsymbol{G}$ is independent of $\boldsymbol{R}$, this expectation can be Monte Carlo estimated using the sample mean of the sequence $\left(\hat{\phi}_i^{(\boldsymbol{g}_j)}(v_{\boldsymbol{x},\boldsymbol{r}_j})\right)_{j=1}^{N}$ (where $(\boldsymbol{g}_j, \boldsymbol{r}_j)_{j=1}^{N}$ is a joint sample of $(\boldsymbol{G}, \boldsymbol{R})$). As the attribution recovered by this estimation is simply the mean of a sample from a random variable, its uncertainty can be quantified by estimating the SEM. In terms of the sample standard deviation, 95% CIs on the mean attribution ($\bar{\boldsymbol{\phi}}$) from a sample of size N are given by:

$$\bar{\boldsymbol{\phi}} \pm \frac{1.96 \times \mathsf{SSD}\left(\left(\hat{\phi}_i^{(\boldsymbol{g}_j)}(v_{\boldsymbol{x},\boldsymbol{r}_j})\right)_{j=1}^{N}\right)}{\sqrt{N}} \tag{12}$$

4.4 Formulate, Approximate, Explain

So far we studied the explanation game formulations used by existing methods, and noted how the formulations impact the resulting Shapley value attributions.

We show that the attributions explain a prediction *in contrast* to a distribution of references; see Proposition 1. Existing methods differ in the attribution they produce because each of them picks a different reference distribution to contrast with. We also proposed a mechanism to quantify the approximation uncertainty incurred in computing attributions.

We now put these ideas together in a single conceptual framework *formulate, approximate, explain* (FAE). Our key insight is that rather than viewing the reference distribution as an implementation detail of the explanation method, it must by made a first-class argument to the framework. That is, the references must be consciously chosen by the explainee to obtain a specific *contrastive explanation.*

Our emphasis on treating attributions as contrastive explanations stems from cognitive psychology. Several works in cognitive psychology argue that humans frame explanations of surprising outcomes by contrasting them with to one or more normal outcomes [10–12,15,17,21,22]. In our setting, the normal outcomes are the reference predictions that the input prediction is contrasted with. The attributions essentially explain what drives the prediction at hand away from the reference predictions. The choice of references may depend on the context of the question, and may vary across explainers and explainees [15]. Moreover, it is important for the references to be *relevant* to the input at hand [11]. For instance, if we are explaining why an auto-grading software assigns a B+ to a student's submission, it would be proper to contrast with the submissions that were graded as A− (next higher grade after B+), instead of contrasting with the entire pool of submissions.

Formulate. The mandate of the Formulate step is to *generate a contrastive question that specifies one or more relevant references.* The question pins down the distribution $\mathcal{D}^{ref}$ of the chosen references. For instance, in the grading example above, the references would be all submissions obtaining an A− grade.

Approximate. Once a meaningful contrastive question and its corresponding reference distribution $\mathcal{D}^{ref}$ has been formulated, we consider the distribution of single-reference games whose references are drawn from $\mathcal{D}^{ref}$, and approximate the Shapley values of these games. Formally, we approximate the distribution of the random-valued attribution vector $\boldsymbol{\Phi}_{\boldsymbol{x},\boldsymbol{R}} = \boldsymbol{\phi}(v_{\boldsymbol{x},\boldsymbol{R}})$, where $\boldsymbol{R} \sim \mathcal{D}^{ref}$. This involves two steps: (1) sampling a sequence of references $(\boldsymbol{r}_i)_{i=1}^{N}$ from $\boldsymbol{R} \sim \mathcal{D}^{ref}$, and (2) approximating the Shapley value of the single-reference games relative each to reference in $(\boldsymbol{r}_i)_{i=1}^{N}$. This yields a sequence of approximated Shapley values. It is important to account for the uncertainty resulting from sampling in steps (1) and (2), and quantify it in the Explain step.

Explain. In the final step, we must summarize the sampled Shapley value vectors (drawn from $\boldsymbol{\Phi}_{\boldsymbol{x},\boldsymbol{R}}$) obtained from the Approximate step. One simple summarization would be the presentation of a few representative samples, in the style of the SP-LIME algorithm [23]. Another simple summarization is the sample mean, which approximates $\mathbb{E}[\boldsymbol{\Phi}_{\boldsymbol{x},\boldsymbol{R}}]$, and is equivalent to the attributions from the unified explanation game $v_{\boldsymbol{x},\mathcal{D}^{ref}}$. This is the summarization used by existing Shapley-value-based explanation methods. When using the sample mean, the framework of Sect. 4.3 can be used to quantify the uncertainty from sampling. In addition, one must be careful that the mean does not hide important information. For instance, a feature's attributions may have opposite signs relative to different references. Averaging these attributions will cause them to cancel each other out, yielding a small mean that incorrectly suggests that the feature is unimportant. We discuss a concrete example of this in Sect. 5.1. At the very least, we recommend confirming through visualization and summary statistics like variance and interquartile range that the mean is a good summarization, before relying upon it. We discuss a clustering based summarization method in Sect. 5 while leaving further research on faithful summarization methods to future work.

5 Case Studies

In this section we apply the FAE framework to LightGBM [16] Gradient Boosted Decision Trees (GBDT) models trained on real data: the UCI Bike Sharing and Adult Income datasets, and a Lending Club dataset.[5] For parsimony, we analyze models that use only five features; complete model details are provided in Appendix D. For the Bike Sharing model, we explain a randomly selected prediction of 210 rentals for a certain hour. For the Adult Income model, we explain a counter-intuitively low prediction for an individual with high *education-num*. For the Lending Club model, we explain a counter-intuitive rejection (assuming a threshold that accepts 15% of loan applications) for a high-income borrower. In the rest of this section, we present a selection of the results across all three models, while the full set of results are provided in Appendix E.

5.1 Shortcomings of Existing Methods

Recall from Sect. 4.2 that the attributions from existing methods amount to computing the mean attribution for a distribution of single-reference games $v_{\boldsymbol{x},\boldsymbol{R}}$, where the reference $\boldsymbol{R}$ is sampled from a certain distribution. The choice of distribution varies across the methods, which in turns leads to very different attribution. This is illustrated in Table 3 for the Bike sharing model.

Misleading Means. In Sect. 4.4, we discussed that the mean attribution can potentially be a misleading summarization. Here, we illustrate this using the attributions from the KernelSHAP game $v_{\boldsymbol{x}}^{inp}$ for the Bike Sharing example;

[5] In Bike Sharing we model hourly bike rentals from temporal and weather features, in Adult Income we model whether an adult earns more than $50,000 annually, and in Lending Club we model whether a borrower will default on a loan.

Table 3. Bike Sharing comparison of mean attributions. 95% CIs ranged from ±0.4 (*hum* in $\mathcal{D}^{inp}$ and $\mathcal{D}^{J.M.}$) to ±2.5 (*hr* in $\mathcal{D}^{inp}$ and $\mathcal{D}^{J.M.}$).

Game	Avg. prediction (ϕ_0)	hr	temp	work.	hum	season
$v_{\boldsymbol{x}}^{inp}$	151	3	47	1	7	2
$v_{\boldsymbol{x}}^{J.M.}$	141	6	50	1	9	3
$v_{\boldsymbol{x}}^{unif}$	128	3	60	3	12	3

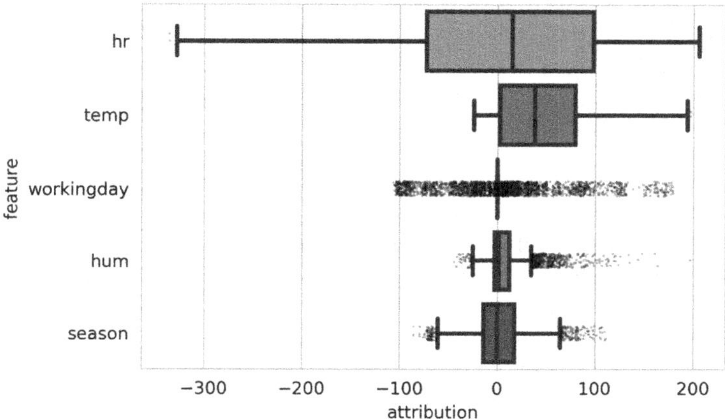

Fig. 1. Distribution of single-reference game attributions relative to the data distribution ($\mathcal{D}^{inp}$) for the Bike Sharing example.

see Table 3. The mean attribution to the feature *hr* is tiny, suggesting that the feature has little impact. However, the distribution of single-reference game attributions (Fig. 1) reveals a large spread centered close to zero. In fact, we find that by absolute value *hr* receives the largest attribution in over 60% of the single-reference games. Consequently, only examining the mean of the distribution may be misleading.

Unquantified Uncertainty. Lack of uncertainty quantification in existing techniques can result in misleading attributions. For instance, taking the mean attribution of 100 randomly-sampled Bike Sharing single-reference games[6] gives *hr* an attribution of -10 and *workingday* an attribution of 8. Without any sense of uncertainty, we do not know how accurate these (estimated) attributions are. The 95% confidence intervals (estimated using the method described in Sect. 5.2) show that they are uncertain indeed: the CIs span both positive and negative values.

[6] The official implementation of KernelSHAP [19] raises a warning if over 100 references are used.

Table 4. Adult Income comparison of mean attributions from existing game formulations (top) and from clusters obtained from k-means clustering of the single-reference game attributions relative to the input distribution (bottom). 95% CIs ranged from ±0.0004 (Cluster 2, *relationship*) to ±0.0115 (Cluster 5, *marital-status* and *age*).

Game	Size	Avg. prediction (ϕ_0)	rel.	cap.	edu.	mar.	age
$v_{\boldsymbol{x}}^{inp}$	–	0.24	−0.04	−0.03	−0.01	−0.10	−0.00
$v_{\boldsymbol{x}}^{J.M.}$	–	0.19	−0.02	−0.03	−0.01	−0.08	0.01
$v_{\boldsymbol{x}}^{unif}$	–	0.82	0.01	−0.79	0.02	−0.03	0.04
Cluster 1	10.2%	0.67	−0.15	−0.01	−0.15	−0.28	−0.02
Cluster 2	55.3%	0.04	0.01	0.00	0.00	−0.01	0.02
Cluster 3	4.4%	0.99	−0.04	−0.70	−0.06	−0.12	−0.01
Cluster 4	28.0%	0.31	−0.09	0.00	0.08	−0.21	−0.03
Cluster 5	2.1%	0.67	−0.04	0.01	−0.47	−0.14	0.03

Table 5. Lending Club comparison of mean attributions from the game $v_{\boldsymbol{x}}$ (relative to the data distribution $\mathcal{D}^{inp}$) and the game $v_{\boldsymbol{x},\mathcal{D}^{ref}}$ (relative to the distribution of accepted applications $\mathcal{D}^{accept}$). 95% CIs ranged from ±0.0004 to ±0.0007 for both games.

Game	Avg. prediction (ϕ_0)	fico.	addr.	inc.	acc.	dti
$v_{\boldsymbol{x}}^{inp}$	0.14	0.00	0.03	0.00	0.10	0.00
$v_{\boldsymbol{x},\mathcal{D}^{accept}}$	0.05	0.02	0.04	0.02	0.11	0.03

Irrelevant References. In Sect. 4.4, we noted the importance of relevant references (or norms), and how the IME game $v_{\boldsymbol{x}}^{unif}$ based on the uniform distribution $\mathcal{U}$ can focus on irrelevant references. We illustrate this on the Adult Income example; see the third row of Table 4. We find that almost all attribution from the $v_{\boldsymbol{x}}^{unif}$ game falls on the *capitalgain* feature. This is surprising as *capitalgain* is zero for the example being explained, and for over 90% of examples in the Adult Income dataset. The attributions are an artifact of uniformly sampling reference feature values, which causes nearly all references to have non-zero capital gain (as the probability of sampling an exactly zero capital gain is infinitesimal).

5.2 Applying the FAE Framework

We now consider how the FAE framework enables more faithful explanations for the three models we study.

Formulating Contrastive Questions. A key benefit of FAE is that it enables explaining predictions relative to a selected group of references. For instance, in the Lending Club model, rather than asking "Why did our rejected example receive a score of 0.28?" we ask the contrastive question "Why did our rejected example receive a score of 0.28 *relative to the examples that were accepted*?" This is a more apt question, as it explicitly discards irrelevant comparisons to other rejected applications. In terms of game formulation, the contrastive approach amounts to considering single-reference games where the reference is drawn from the distribution of accepted applications (denoted by $\mathcal{D}^{accept}$) rather than all applications. The attributions for each of these questions (shown in Table 5) turn out to be quite different. For instance, although number of recently-opened accounts (*acc*) is still the highest-attributed feature, we find that credit score (*fico*), income (*inc*), and debt-to-income ratio (*dti*) receive significantly higher attribution in the contrastive formulation. Without formulating the contrastive question, we would be misled into believing that these features are unimportant for the rejection.

Quantifying Uncertainty. When summarizing the attribution distribution with the mean, confidence intervals can be computed using the standard error of the mean (see Sect. 4.3). Returning to our Bike Sharing example, with 100 samples, the 95% confidence intervals for *hr* and *workingday* are -36 to 15, and -1 to 12, respectively. The large CIs caution us that 100 samples are perhaps too few. When using the full test set, the 95% CIs drop to 0.0 to 5.1 for *hr*, and 0.6 to 2.0 for *workingday*.

Summarizing Attribution Distributions. To obtain a more faithful summarization of the single-reference game attributions, we explore a clustering based approach. We compute attributions for single reference games relative to points sampled from the input distribution ($\mathcal{D}^{inp}$), and then apply k-means clustering to these attributions. The resulting clusters effectively group references that yield similar (contrastive) attributions for the prediction at the explained point. Consequently, the attribution distribution within each cluster has a small spread, and can be summarized via the mean.

We applied this approach to all three models and obtained promising results, wherein, clustering helps mine distinct attribution patterns. Table 4 (bottom) shows the results for the Adult Income model; results for other models are provided in Appendix E. Notice that clustering identifies a large group of irrelevant references (cluster 2) which are similar to the explained point, demonstrating low attributions and predictions. Cluster 3 discovers the same pattern that the $v_{\boldsymbol{x}}^{unif}$ formulation did: high *capitalgain* causes extremely high scores. Since over 90% of points in the dataset have zero *capitalgain*, this pattern is "washed out in the average" relative to the entire data distribution $\mathcal{D}^{inp}$ (as in KernelSHAP); see the first row of Table 4. On the other hand, the IME formulation identifies nothing but this pattern. Our clustering also helps identify other patterns. Clusters 1 and 5 show that when compared to references that obtain a high-but-not-extreme score, *marital-status*, *relationship*, and *education-num* are the primary factors accounting for the lower prediction score for the example at hand.

6 Conclusion

We perform an in-depth study of various Shapley-value-based model explanation methods. We find cases where existing methods yield counter-intuitive attributions, and we trace these misleading attributions to the cooperative games formulated by these methods. We propose a generalizing formulation that unifies attribution methods, offers clarity for interpreting each method's attributions, and admits straightforward confidence intervals for attributions.

We propose a conceptual framework for model explanations, called *formulate, approximate, explain* (FAE), which is built on principles from cognitive psychology. We advise practitioners to *formulate* contrastive explanation questions that specify the references relative to which a prediction should be explained, for example "Why did this rejected loan application receive a score of 0.28 *in contrast to the applications that were accepted?*" By *approximating* the Shapley values of games formulated relative to the chosen references, and *explaining* the distribution of approximated Shapley values, we provide a more relevant answer to the explanation question at hand.

Finally, we conclude that axiomatic guarantees do not inherently guarantee relevant explanations, and that game formulations must be constructed carefully. In summarizing attribution distributions, we caution practitioners to avoid coarse-grained summaries, and to quantify any uncertainty resulting from any approximations used.

Appendix

A Shapley Value Axioms

We briefly summarize the four Shapley value axioms.

- The *Dummy* axiom requires that if player i has no possible contribution (i.e. $v(S \cup \{i\}) = v(S)$ for all $S \subseteq \mathcal{M}$), then that player receives zero attribution.
- The *Symmetry* axiom requires that two players that always have the same contribution receive equal attribution, Formally, if $v(S \cup \{i\}) = v(S \cup \{j\})$ for all S not containing i or j then $\phi_i(v) = \phi_j(v)$.
- The *Efficiency* axiom requires that the attributions to all players sum to the total payoff of all players. Formally, $\sum_i \phi_i(v) = v(\mathcal{M})$).
- The *Linearity* axiom states that for any payoff function v that is a linear combination of two other payoff functions u and w (i.e. $v(S) = \alpha u(S) + \beta w(S)$), the Shapley values of v equal the corresponding linear combination of the Shapley values of u and w (i.e. $\phi_i(v) = \alpha\phi_i(u) + \beta\phi_i(w)$).

B Additional Shapley Value Approximations

Marginal Contribution Sampling. We can express the Shapley value of a player as the expected value of the weighted marginal contribution to a random coalition S sampled uniformly from all possible coalitions excluding that player, rather than an exhaustive weighted sum. A sampling estimator of this expectation is by nature unbiased, so this can be used as an alternative to the permutation estimator in approximating attributions with confidence intervals.

$$\phi_i(v) = \mathop{\mathbb{E}}_{S}\left[\frac{2^{M-1}}{M}\binom{M-1}{|S|}^{-1}(v(S\cup\{i\}) - v(S))\right] \tag{13}$$

Equation 13 can be approximated with a Monte Carlo estimate, i.e. by sampling from the random S and averaging the quantity within the expectation.

Weighted Least Squares. The Shapley values are the solution to a certain weighted least squares optimization problem which was popularized through its use in the KernelSHAP algorithm. For a full explanation, see https://arxiv.org/abs/1903.10464.

$$\boldsymbol{\phi} = \arg\min_{\boldsymbol{\phi}} \sum_{S\subseteq\mathcal{M}} \frac{M-1}{\binom{M}{|S|}|S|(M-|S|)}\left(v(S) - \sum_{i=1}^{M}\phi_i\right)^2 \tag{14}$$

The fraction in the left of Eq. 14 is often referred to as the Shapley kernel. In practice, an approximate objective function is minimized. The approximate objective is defined as a summation over squared error on a sample of coalitions rather than over squared error on all possible coalitions. Additionally, the "KernelSHAP trick" may be employed, wherein sampling is performed according to the Shapley kernel (rather than uniformly), and the least-squares optimization is solved with uniform weights (rather than Shapley kernel weights) to account for the adjusted sampling.

To the best of our knowledge, there exists no proof that the solution to a subsampled objective function of the form in Eq. 14 is an estimator (unbiased or otherwise) of the Shapley values. In practice, it does appear that subsampling down to even a small fraction of the total number of possible coalitions (weighted by the Shapley kernel or uniformly) does a good job of estimating the Shapley values for explanation games. Furthermore, approximation errors in such experiments do not yield signs of bias. However, we do note that using the weighted least squares approximation with our confidence interval equation does inherently imply an unproved assumption that it is an unbiased estimator.

C Proofs

In what follows, we prove the lemmas from the main paper. The proofs refer to equations and definition from the main paper.

C.1 Proof of Proposition 1

From the definitions of $v_{\boldsymbol{x},\mathcal{D}^{ref}}$ (Eq. 8) and $v_{\boldsymbol{x},\boldsymbol{r}}$ (Eq. 9), it follows that $v_{\boldsymbol{x},\mathcal{D}^{ref}}(S) = \mathbb{E}_{\boldsymbol{R}\sim\mathcal{D}^{ref}}[v_{\boldsymbol{x},\boldsymbol{R}}(S)]$. Thus, the game $v_{\boldsymbol{x},\mathcal{D}^{ref}}$ is a linear combination of games $\{v_{\boldsymbol{x},\boldsymbol{r}} \mid \boldsymbol{r} \in \mathcal{X}\}$ with weights defined by the distribution $\mathcal{D}^{ref}$.

From the Linearity axiom of Shapley values, it follows that the Shapley values of the game $v_{\boldsymbol{x},\mathcal{D}^{ref}}$ must be a corresponding linear combination of the Shapley values of the games $\{v_{\boldsymbol{x},\boldsymbol{r}} \mid \boldsymbol{r} \in \mathcal{X}\}$ (with weights defined by the distribution $\mathcal{D}^{ref}$). Thus, $\boldsymbol{\phi}(v_{\boldsymbol{x},\mathcal{D}^{ref}}) = \mathbb{E}_{\boldsymbol{R}\sim\mathcal{D}^{ref}}[\boldsymbol{\phi}(v_{\boldsymbol{x},\boldsymbol{R}})]$. □

C.2 Proof of Proposition 2

From Proposition 1, we have $\phi_i(v_{\boldsymbol{x},\mathcal{D}^{ref}}) = \mathbb{E}_{\boldsymbol{R}\sim\mathcal{D}^{ref}}[\phi_i(v_{\boldsymbol{x},\boldsymbol{R}})]$. Thus, to prove this lemma, it suffices to show that for any irrelevant feature i, the Shapley value from the game $v_{\boldsymbol{x},\boldsymbol{r}}$ is zero for all references $r \in \mathcal{X}$. That is,

$$\forall \boldsymbol{r} \in \mathcal{X} \;\; \phi_i(v_{\boldsymbol{x},\boldsymbol{r}}) = 0 \tag{15}$$

From the definition of Shapley values (Eq. 1), we have:

$$\phi_i(v_{\boldsymbol{x},\boldsymbol{r}}) = \frac{1}{M} \sum_{S \subseteq \mathcal{M}\setminus\{i\}} \binom{M-1}{|S|}^{-1} (v_{\boldsymbol{x},\boldsymbol{r}}(S \cup \{i\}) - v_{\boldsymbol{x},\boldsymbol{r}}(S)) \tag{16}$$

Thus, to prove Eq. 15 it suffices to show the marginal contribution $(v_{\boldsymbol{x},\boldsymbol{r}}(S \cup \{i\}) - v_{\boldsymbol{x},\boldsymbol{r}}(S))$ of an irrelevant feature i to any subset of features $S \subseteq \mathcal{M} \setminus \{i\}$ is always zero. From the definition of the game $v_{\boldsymbol{x},\boldsymbol{r}}$, we have:

$$v_{\boldsymbol{x},\boldsymbol{r}}(S \cup \{i\}) - v_{\boldsymbol{x},\boldsymbol{r}}(S) = f(\boldsymbol{z}(\boldsymbol{x},\boldsymbol{r},S \cup \{i\})) - f(\boldsymbol{z}(\boldsymbol{x},\boldsymbol{r},S)) \tag{17}$$

From the definition of composite inputs $\boldsymbol{z}$ (Eq. 3), it follows that the inputs $\boldsymbol{z}(\boldsymbol{x},\boldsymbol{r},S \cup \{i\})$ and $\boldsymbol{z}(\boldsymbol{x},\boldsymbol{r},S)$ agree on all features except i. Thus, if feature i is irrelevant, $f(\boldsymbol{z}(\boldsymbol{x},\boldsymbol{r},S \cup \{i\})) = f(\boldsymbol{z}(\boldsymbol{x},\boldsymbol{r},S))$, and consequently by Eq. 16, $v_{\boldsymbol{x},\boldsymbol{r}}(S \cup \{i\}) - v_{\boldsymbol{x},\boldsymbol{r}}(S) = 0$ for all subsets $S \subseteq \mathcal{M} \setminus \{i\}$. Combining this with the definition of Shapley values (Eq. 1) proves Eq. 15. □

D Reproducibility

For brevity, we omitted from the main paper many of the mundane choices in the design of our toy examples and case studies. To further transparency and reproducibility, we include them here.

D.1 Fitting Models

For both case studies, we used the LightGBM package configured with default parameters to fit a Gradient Boosted Decision Trees (GBDT) model. For the Bike Sharing dataset, we fit on all examples from 2011 while holding out the 2012 examples for testing. We omitted the *attempt* feature, as it is highly correlated to *temp* ($r = 0.98$), and the *instant* feature because the tree-based GBDT model cannot capture its time-series trend. For parsimony, we refitted the model to the top five most important features by cumulative gain (*hr*, *temp*, *workingday*, *hum*, and *season*). This lowered test-set r^2 from 0.64 to 0.63. For the Adult Income dataset, we used the pre-defined train/test split. Again, we refitted the model to the top five features by cumulative gain feature importance (*relationship*, *capitalgain*, *education-num*, *marital-status*, and *age*). This increased test-set misclassification error from 14.73% to 10.97%.

D.2 Selection of Points to Explain

For the Bike Share case study, we sampled ten points at random from the test set. We selected one whose prediction was close to the middle of the range observed over the entire test set (predictions ranged approximately from 0 to 600). Specifically, we selected instant 11729 (2012-05-08, 9 pm). We examined other points from the same sample of ten to suggest a random but meaningful comparative question. We found another point with comparable *workingday*, *hum*, and *season*: instant 11362. This point caught our eye because it differed only in *hr* (2 pm rather than 9 pm), and *temp* (0.36 rather than 0.64) but had a much lower prediction.

For the Adult Income case study, we wanted to explain why a point was scored as likely to have low income, a task roughly analogous to that of explaining why an application for credit is rejected by a creditworthiness model in a lending setting. We sampled points at random with scores between 0.01 and 0.1, and chose the 9880th point in the test set due to its strikingly high *education-num* (most of the low-scoring points sampled had lower *education-num*).

For the Lending Club data, we chose an open-source subset of the dataset that has been pre-cleaned to a predictive task on 3-year loans. For the five-feature model, we selected the top five features by cumulative gain feature importance from a model fit to the full set of features.

D.3 K-means Clustering

We choose $k = 5$ arbitrarily, having observed a general tradeoff of conciseness for precision as k increases. In the extremes, $k = 1$ maintains the overall attribution distribution, while $k = N$ examines each single-reference game separately.

E Case Study Supplemental Material

See Tables 6, 7 and 8.

References

1. Aas, K., Jullum, M., Løland, A.: Explaining individual predictions when features are dependent: more accurate approximations to shapley values. arXiv preprint arXiv:1903.10464 (2019)
2. Ancona, M., Ceolini, E., Öztireli, C., Gross, M.: Towards better understanding of gradient-based attribution methods for deep neural networks. In: International Conference on Learning Representations (2018)
3. Ancona, M., Oztireli, C., Gross, M.: Explaining deep neural networks with a polynomial time algorithm for shapley value approximation. In: Proceedings of the 36th International Conference on Machine Learning (2019)
4. Chen, J., Song, L., Wainwright, M.J., Jordan, M.I.: L-shapley and c-shapley: efficient model interpretation for structured data. arXiv preprint arXiv:1808.02610 (2018)

Table 6. Bike Sharing comparison of mean attributions. 95% CIs ranged from ±0.4 (*hum* in $\mathcal{D}^{inp}$ and $\mathcal{D}^{J.M.}$) to ±2.5 (*hr* in $\mathcal{D}^{inp}$ and $\mathcal{D}^{J.M.}$).

Game formulation	Size	Avg. prediction (ϕ_0)	hr	temp	work.	hum	season
$v_{\boldsymbol{x}}^{inp}$	100%	151	3	47	1	7	2
$v_{\boldsymbol{x}}^{J.M.}$	100%	141	6	50	1	9	3
$v_{\boldsymbol{x}}^{unif}$	100%	128	3	60	3	12	3
Cluster 1	12.9%	309	−86	14	−28	3	−1
Cluster 2	27.6%	28	140	32	0	9	0
Cluster 3	10.5%	375	−247	58	16	9	−1
Cluster 4	32.5%	131	31	38	3	4	2
Cluster 5	16.5%	128	−57	107	13	9	9

Table 7. Adult Income comparison of mean attributions. 95% CIs ranged from ±0.0004 (Cluster 2, *relationship*) to ±0.0115 (Cluster 5, *marital-status* and *age*).

Game	Size	Avg. prediction (ϕ_0)	rel.	cap.	edu.	mar.	age
$v_{\boldsymbol{x}}^{inp}$	100%	0.24	−0.04	−0.03	−0.01	−0.10	−0.00
$v_{\boldsymbol{x}}^{J.M.}$	100%	0.19	−0.02	−0.03	−0.01	−0.08	0.01
$v_{\boldsymbol{x}}^{unif}$	100%	0.82	0.01	−0.79	0.02	−0.03	0.04
Cluster 1	10.2%	0.67	−0.15	−0.01	−0.15	−0.28	−0.02
Cluster 2	55.3%	0.04	0.01	0.00	0.00	−0.01	0.02
Cluster 3	4.4%	0.99	−0.04	−0.70	−0.06	−0.12	−0.01
Cluster 4	28.0%	0.31	−0.09	0.00	0.08	−0.21	−0.03
Cluster 5	2.1%	0.67	−0.04	0.01	−0.47	−0.14	0.03

Table 8. Lending Club comparison of mean attributions. 95% CIs ranged from ±0.0004 to ±0.0007 for all games.

Game	Size	Avg. prediction (ϕ_0)	fico.	addr.	inc.	acc.	dti
$v_{\boldsymbol{x},\mathcal{D}^{ref}}$	20%	0.05	0.02	0.04	0.02	0.11	0.03
$v_{\boldsymbol{x}}^{inp}$	100%	0.14	0.00	0.03	0.00	0.10	0.00
$v_{\boldsymbol{x}}^{J.M.}$	100%	0.14	0.01	0.03	0.01	0.10	0.00
$v_{\boldsymbol{x}}^{unif}$	100%	0.11	0.05	0.07	−0.01	0.03	0.02
Cluster 1	28.5%	0.11	0.01	0.06	0.00	0.08	0.01
Cluster 2	24.4%	0.10	0.01	0.00	0.01	0.11	0.04
Cluster 3	15.4%	0.18	0.00	0.01	0.00	0.14	−0.05
Cluster 4	17.6%	0.16	−0.01	0.01	0.03	0.09	−0.01
Cluster 5	14.0%	0.22	−0.01	0.05	−0.02	0.08	−0.06

5. Cohen, S.B., Ruppin, E., Dror, G.: Feature selection based on the shapley value. IJCAI **5**, 665–670 (2005)

6. Datta, A., Sen, S., Zick, Y.: Algorithmic transparency via quantitative input influence: theory and experiments with learning systems. In: 2016 IEEE Symposium on Security and Privacy (SP), pp. 598–617. IEEE (2016)
7. Dhurandhar, A., et al.: Explanations based on the missing: towards contrastive explanations with pertinent negatives. CoRR (2018). http://arxiv.org/abs/1802.07623
8. Efron, B., Tibshirani, R.: The bootstrap method for standard errors and confidence intervals of the adjusted attributable risk. Stat. Sci. **1**(1), 54–75 (1986). https://doi.org/10.1214/ss/1177013815
9. Ghorbani, A., Zou, J.: Data shapley: equitable valuation of data for machine learning. In: Proceedings of the 36th International Conference on Machine Learning (2019)
10. Hesslow, G.: The problem of causal selection. In: Hilton, D.J. (ed.) Contemporary Science and Natural Explanation: Commonsense Conceptions of Causality. New York University Press, New York (1988)
11. Hitchcock, C., Knobecaus, J.: Cause and norm. J. Philos. **106**(11), 587–612 (2009)
12. Holzinger, A., Kickmeier-Rust, M., Müller, H.: KANDINSKY patterns as IQ-test for machine learning. In: Holzinger, A., Kieseberg, P., Tjoa, A.M., Weippl, E. (eds.) CD-MAKE 2019. LNCS, vol. 11713, pp. 1–14. Springer, Cham (2019). https://doi.org/10.1007/978-3-030-29726-8_1
13. Hunt, X.J., Abbey, R., Tharrington, R., Huiskens, J., Wesdorp, N.: An AI-augmented lesion detection framework for liver metastases with model interpretability. arXiv preprint arXiv:1907.07713 (2019)
14. Janzing, D., Minorics, L., Blöbaum, P.: Feature relevance quantification in explainable AI: a causal problem. arXiv preprint arXiv:1910.13413 (2019)
15. Kahneman, D., Miller, D.T.: Norm theory: comparing reality to its alternatives. Psychol. Rev. **93**(2), 136 (1986)
16. Ke, G., et al.: LightGBM: a highly efficient gradient boosting decision tree. In: Advances in Neural Information Processing Systems, pp. 3146–3154 (2017)
17. Lipton, P.: Contrastive explanation. R. Inst. Philos. Suppl. **27**, 247–266 (1990). https://doi.org/10.1017/S1358246100005130
18. Lundberg, S.M., Erion, G.G., Lee, S.I.: Consistent individualized feature attribution for tree ensembles. arXiv preprint arXiv:1802.03888 (2018)
19. Lundberg, S.M., Lee, S.I.: A unified approach to interpreting model predictions. In: Advances in Neural Information Processing Systems, pp. 4765–4774 (2017)
20. Maleki, S., Tran-Thanh, L., Hines, G., Rahwan, T., Rogers, A.: Bounding the estimation error of sampling-based shapley value approximation. arXiv preprint arXiv:1306.4265 (2013)
21. Miller, T.: Explanation in artificial intelligence: insights from the social sciences. arXiv preprint arXiv:1706.07269 (2017)
22. Mittelstadt, B., Russell, C., Wachter, S.: Explaining explanations in AI. In: Proceedings of the Conference on Fairness, Accountability, and Transparency, pp. 279–288. ACM (2019)
23. Ribeiro, M.T., Singh, S., Guestrin, C.: Why should I trust you?: explaining the predictions of any classifier. In: SIGKDD International Conference on Knowledge Discovery and Data Mining, pp. 1135–1144 (2016)
24. Shapley, L.S.: A value for n-person games. Contrib. Theory Games **2**(28), 307–317 (1953)
25. Shrikumar, A., Greenside, P., Kundaje, A.: Learning important features through propagating activation differences. In: 34th International Conference on Machine Learning-Volume 70, pp. 3145–3153 (2017)

26. Štrumbelj, E., Kononenko, I.: An efficient explanation of individual classifications using game theory. J. Mach. Learn. Res. **11**, 1–18 (2010)
27. Štrumbelj, E., Kononenko, I.: Explaining prediction models and individual predictions with feature contributions. Knowl. Inf. Syst. **41**(3), 647–665 (2013). https://doi.org/10.1007/s10115-013-0679-x
28. Sundararajan, M., Najmi, A.: The many shapley values for model explanation. arXiv preprint arXiv:1908.08474 (2019)
29. Sundararajan, M., Taly, A., Yan, Q.: Axiomatic attribution for deep networks. In: Proceedings of the 34th International Conference on Machine Learning-Volume 70, pp. 3319–3328 (2017). JMLR.org
30. Young, H.P.: Monotonic solutions of cooperative games. Int. J. Game Theory **14**, 65–72 (1985)

Back to the Feature: A Neural-Symbolic Perspective on Explainable AI

Andrea Campagner(✉) and Federico Cabitza

Universitá degli Studi di Milano-Bicocca, Milan, Italy
a.campagner@campus.unimib.it

Abstract. We discuss a perspective aimed at making black box models more eXplainable, within the eXplainable AI (XAI) strand of research. We argue that the traditional end-to-end learning approach used to train Deep Learning (DL) models does not fit the tenets and aims of XAI. Going back to the idea of hand-crafted feature engineering, we suggest a hybrid DL approach to XAI: instead of employing end-to-end learning, we suggest to use DL for the automatic detection of meaningful, hand-crafted high-level symbolic features, which are then to be used by a standard and more interpretable learning model. We exemplify this hybrid learning model in a proof of concept, based on the recently proposed Kandinsky Patterns benchmark, that focuses on the symbolic learning part of the pipeline by using both Logic Tensor Networks and interpretable rule ensembles. After showing that the proposed methodology is able to deliver highly accurate and explainable models, we then discuss potential implementation issues and future directions that can be explored.

Keywords: Explainable AI · Symbolic machine learning · Deep Learning · Kandinsky Patterns

1 Introduction

In the recent years, there has been a significant growth in the popularity of Machine Learning (ML) solutions, mainly driven by the increasing success of a specific type of ML, i.e., Deep Learning (DL), in a number of various applications: from game playing [41,70] and natural language processing [81], to self-driving vehicles [58] and computer-assisted medicine [21,32,33,36]. These two latter domains shed light on what has been one of the more severe limitations of the DL methodology, that is its black-box nature and lack of explainability [13], a topic that is becoming of primary importance, also in light of recent regulations like the GDPR [17,29], which stipulates that any significant or legally related decision should be explainable if reached in non-supervised automated processes.

This limitation should be considered along a twofold perspective: from a decision-support perspective, because decision makers are typically required to be accountable for their decisions in critical domains (like juridic and medical

Published by Springer Nature Switzerland AG 2020
A. Holzinger et al. (Eds.): CD-MAKE 2020, LNCS 12279, pp. 39–55, 2020.
https://doi.org/10.1007/978-3-030-57321-8_3

settings) and give indications about their interpretations and judgments; and from a system-oriented perspective, because the lack of explainability makes it difficult to reason about the robustness and actual skills of a ML system (and the socio-technical system relying on its operation), as it is shown by phenomena like adversarial examples [28], misguided usage of context information [61], or general data quality issues [11,12].

In order to address the above limitations, many approaches toward *eXplainable AI* (XAI) have been proposed and discussed [31] and different proposals to evaluate the explainability and causability [37,38] of ML models have been developed [39]. The techniques to achieve explainability can be distinguished in two broad categories: approaches that are based on the development of *instrinsically* interpretable ML models (e.g. decision rules [44,79], decision trees or linear classifiers [77]); or so-called *post-hoc* approaches, whose goal is to *make* an already existing model *understandable*, either through methods that explain the general model behaviour (e.g. using interpretable surrogate models [9] or visualization techniques, such as *saliency maps* [71]), or through local explanation techniques that only attempt to explain how the ML model arrived at its conclusion *for a specific instance* [30,61].

Drawing on recent research [3,4,26] that shows some relevant limitations in post-hoc explainability approaches, we argue that these approaches toward XAI are currently insufficient, also because they do not enable a true understanding of the causal properties of the ML models they are meant to explain [37]. More generally, we posit that the major obstacles toward building truly explainable AI systems reside in two properties of how Deep Learning is *currently used*: first, the end-to-end training process that, while allowing the development of highly accurate models, results in the discovery of *features* which are typically not guaranteed to be understandable by humans [34]; second, their essentially propositional nature, which contrasts with the fact that human knowledge is usually relational [35].

The main goal of this position paper is to put forward a perspective toward tackling the two above-mentioned issues, based on an hybrid subsymbolic-symbolic learning paradigm, a framework reconciling ML and Knowledge Representation & Reasoning (KRR) that has been attracting increasing interest and has recently been advocated as a way-forward for the field of Artificial Intelligence [18,20], also due to advancements in Statistical Relational Learning (SRL) [57] and Neuro-Symbolic (NeSy) [24,52] computation. Under this framework, we promote an integration of Deep Learning and symbolic ML techniques, in order to profit of the advantages of both methodologies. Specifically, going back to the notion of *feature engineering* [82], we propose to use the superior pattern recognition performance of Deep Learning in order to automatize the detection of *high-level, hand-crafted features*, that ideally should also be *verifiable* (e.g. object detection in image classification tasks), which are then to be employed for the training of highly interpretable symbolic models.

In the rest of this paper we discuss this proposal, specifically in Sect. 2, after providing a background of relevant DL and Explainable AI techniques, we describe the proposed methodology. We then also present a prototypical example, focusing on the symbolic learning part of the proposed framework through the usage of Logic Tensor Networks (LTN) [68] and rule ensembles, in the context of two datasets generated from the recently proposed *Kandinsky Patterns* [39] benchmark for XAI. The results of these experiments are reported in Sect. 4. Finally, in Sect. 5 we discuss the obtained results, the implications of the proposed methodologies, its current advantages and limitations and possible directions for further exploration.

2 Methods

2.1 Background

In this section we briefly recall basic notions about Deep Learning architectures and the black box problem, then we present a brief introduction to XAI techniques.

Deep Learning and Neural Networks. Deep Learning [27] is a ML paradigm, based on Artificial Neural Networks (ANN), which involves fitting an highly non-linear, differentiable, parametric model defined by the composition of non-linear functions collected in layers (see Fig. 1a for an example of such models).

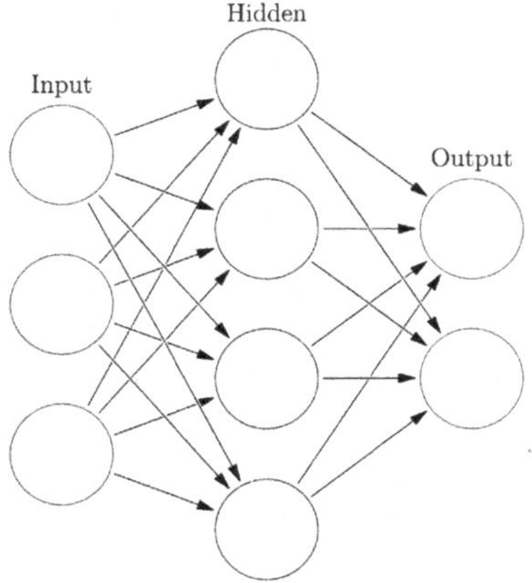

(a) An example of a deep learning model, with a single hidden layer model, visualized as a network.

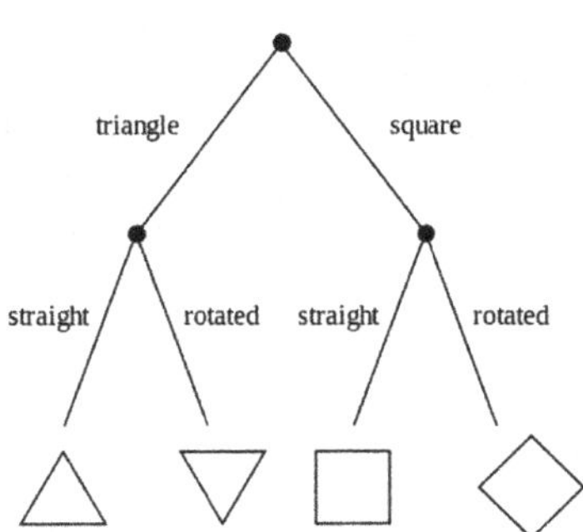

(b) An example of a Decision Tree, one of the most common transparent ML models.

Fig. 1. Examples of black box and interpretable models.

Despite being first studied as far as the late '60s [40,48] and in its modern form from the '80s [23,65], this paradigm received a boost in popularity starting from 2012 [14,43], due to advancements in hardware technology [56], optimization and regularization methods [42,76], the availability of large amount of data, and its increasing success in real-world applications, especially in regard to image recognition and natural language processing tasks.

The training of Deep Learning models involves the optimization of the parameters of the underlying network (i.e. the weights connecting the units in different layers) with respect to a loss function, typically using local search techniques such as stochastic gradient descent.

A particularly effective Deep Learning architecture for image classification tasks is represented by Convolutional Neural Networks. These architectures are composed by an alternation of convolutional layers (in which regions of the input image are processed by trainable filters which are supposed to detect and isolate low-level features) and pooling layers (which are used for dimensionality reduction).

Despite the huge success of Deep Learning architectures they have recently been criticized for their *black box* nature and lack of explainability: despite achieving high accuracy, the model learned by a DL architecture is often imperscrutable (due to the complex interactions between the high number of non-linear functions) [13] and possibly subject to a variety of attacks [28]: both problems (also in combination) could hinder the actual applicability of these systems in critical application domains, like medicine.

Explainable AI. In order to address these limitations, an increasing interest has recently been placed on the development of so-called Explainable AI techniques [55]. We can distinguish between post-hoc explainability techniques and intrinsic explainability (or transparency).

Post-hoc explainability refers to methodologies that aim to make an already existing and trained black box model explainable, or interpretable. These methodologies can be further differentiated between *global* and *local* methodologies. In the former case, the goal is to train an interpretable model that provides a good approximation of the underlying black box model. To this aim, the most common techniques are: Decision Tree induction [78,80], rule extraction methods [10,69] or architecture-specific methodologies such as Layer-wise Relevance Propagation for CNNs [54]. Although a vast number of these techniques have been proposed in the literature, sometimes with high approximation accuracy, their applicability to cases with large numbers of features or with low-level features (e.g. in image-related tasks) have recently been questioned [2].

Local explainability, on the other hand, tries to produce justifications why the black box model made a specific decision for *specific instances*. Also in this case, different methods have been proposed, such as LIME [61], or the related *anchors* [62] *Leave-One-Covariate-Out* [47], which ground on the idea of finding relevant features and associated decision rules for explaining single predictions, or approaches for local interpretability of CNN models such as saliency (or activation) maps [71]. Despite the great interest in these techniques, and some recent efforts to provide a theoretical understanding and to find mutual relationships among different local explainability approaches [51], recent research has casted some doubt on their real relevance and robustness. For instance, Mittelstadt et al. [53] criticize post-hoc explainability approaches and argue for a broader perspective on explainability; Barocas et al. and Laugel et al. [5,45,46] recently highlighted hidden assumptions required for feature-based local explainability techniques to properly work; Slack et al. [73] showed how LIME and related methods can be subject to adversarial attacks making them hide potential biases in the underlying black model; Sixt et al. [72] recently questioned the explaination capacity of attribution methods for CNNs (such as Layer-wise Relevance Propagation and saliency maps).

In light of these criticisms towards post-hoc explainability methods, calls to avoid the use of black box models augmented with explainability methods in high-stakes domains have recently been made [64], urging for the adoption of transparent (or, intrinsically interpretable) models in these contexts.

In this case, the goal is to directly train and use in the considered domain ML models which are intrinsically transparent and interpretable: such as shallow decision trees [9], Bayesian Networks [8] or rule lists [44,79] (see Fig. 1b) or relational approaches such as those based on inductive logic programming [66].

However, the same limitations that apply to global interpretability techniques also apply to transparent models [2], especially in regard to their loss of transparency when the number of relevant feature grows, and in regard to the fact that they are not currently capable to match the performance of DL approaches in tasks such as imaging-related diagnosis.

The approach that we propose, and that we describe in the next section, tries to address both this limitation and the black-box problem of Deep Learning through a combination of these two approaches.

2.2 Proposed Methodology

The approach that we propose, to tackle both the black-box problem of Deep Learning models and the limitations of symbolic transparent models, is based on an integration of the two approaches.

We argue that the main source of the black-box problem in Deep Learning models is not an intrinsic property of the model family or the technique in se, but rather a consequence of how they are typically used.

The former problem is related to the end-to-end approach that is usually employed to train these models. This learning paradigm allows the DL models to learn highly accurate parameter assignments by automatically finding high-level features that arise as complex non-linear combinations of the low-level ones originally present in input representation. The *classifier* part of the DL model is usually implemented as a (jointly trained) simple logistic regression layer on the highest-level features. The learned features, however, are usually inscrutable to a human user.

In contrast, the approach that was traditionally used to achieve high accuracy with standard classifiers (e.g. Support Vector Classifiers or Boosting models) was based on *hand-crafted* informative features [82].

Our approach is based on an integration of these two paradigms: instead of jointly training both a feature detector and a classifier, our proposal consists in directly training a DL model solely as a feature detector for high-level, informative and hand-crafted features.

In particular, we focus on models for feature detection in image recognition tasks. In this case, features represent specific *objects* or *artifacts* that should be detected in the input images: some examples are the presence of fractures (e.g. in bone MRIs), or of nodules or other anomalous objects (e.g. in mastography or similar diagnostic imaging). Compared to the traditional feature engineering (FE) pipeline, this approach has many advantages:

- The human annotators are only required to specify the set of *features* that could be detected in the given domain, and provide annotations for these features in a limited set of training examples that can then be used to train a DL model to automatically detect these features in any future image;
- Compared to the traditional FE pipeline that either employs hand-crafted algorithms or traditional ML models, this approach allows to benefit from the (usually) superior performance of DL models. In fact, specific DL architectures have been developed that could be applied to this task: for example *object detection* or *semantic segmentation* architectures such as Fully Convolutional networks [49], YOLO networks [59] or Faster R-CNN [60], which have been shown to be highly effective in real-world tasks, can be applied to implement this feature-detection task;
- Compared with the traditional end-to-end learning approach for DL models, this approach guarantees that the learned features are both interpretable (as they have previously been identified by human users) and also *testable.* By this term, we mean that their presence and nature could easily be checked in the original images by an external human user: this could be implemented by simply requiring that the DL detection model provides the identified patterns or features, as well their location in the original image (e.g. via a bounding box);
- The feature annotation task to be performed by the DL models is, naturally, a multi-target learning problem: this type of tasks have been shown to act as a regularization method for the DL models (as the shared weights are required to be optimized to several tasks simultaneously) and hence may result in improved generalization and reduce overfitting [63];

The second problem relates to the fact that the classifier used in DL models (usually a simple logic regression layer), while it uses high-level but uninterpretable features, can usually be only understood in terms of very low-level (e.g. pixel-based in imaging tasks) features.

In our approach, on the other hand, the *classifier* component of the learning architecture is separated from the feature detection component, so that more expressive and inherently interpretable learning algorithms can be applied. In this article, we will consider these two approaches, namely *Logic Tensor Networks* and *rule ensembles.*

Logic Tensor Network [68] is a neuro-symbolic computational model integrating neural network and a first-order fuzzy logic called *real logic*. It allows for the combination of the learning capabilities of Deep neural networks with the expressivity and interpretability of logic programming, and it has been shown to be effective in knowledge completion tasks [68], semantic image interpretation [67] and deductive reasoning [7]. The main advantage of this model typology is that, since it is based on a first-order fuzzy logic, it natively allows for the expression of relational concepts and that it is fully compatible with traditional DL models. This latter characteristic could be particularly meaningful in the approach that we propose as it could allow users to recover a sort of end-to-end learning. From a technical point of view, as presented in [68], a Logic Tensor Network is defined by a multi-layer neural network enscoding a collection of (prenex, conjunctive Skolemized) clauses expressed in the language of first-order real logic, i.e. logical formulas in the following form:

$$\begin{aligned}&\forall \mathbf{x} = \langle x_1, ..., x_n \rangle . \\ &P_1(f_1^1(\mathbf{x}), ..., f_h^1(\mathbf{x})) \vee ... \vee P_k(f_1^k(\mathbf{x}), ..., f_m^k(\mathbf{x})) \vee \\ &\vee \neg P_{k+1}(f_1^{k+1}(\mathbf{x}), ..., f_r^{k+1}(\mathbf{x})) \vee ... \vee \neg P_l(f_1^l(\mathbf{x}), ..., f_s^l(\mathbf{x})),\end{aligned} \tag{1}$$

where each P_i is a symbol predicate and each f_j^i is a symbol function. The clauses are represented as multi-layer neural network by associating to each symbol predicate P a neural tensor network [75] in the form:

$$\mathbf{N}(P) = \sigma(u_P^T * tanh(\mathbf{x}^T W_P \mathbf{x} + V_P \mathbf{x})), \tag{2}$$

where σ is the sigmoid function, W_P and V_P are tensors. The different networks corresponding to the predicates are then joined (according to a specified clause) by defining $\neg$ to be a fuzzy negation (e.g. $\neg(x) = 1 - x$) and $\vee$ to be a t-conorm (e.g. $\vee(x, y) = max(x, y)$). The parameters of the resulting network are then trained via standard backpropagation by maximizing the satisfiability of the clauses. For a more in-depth introduction to Logic Tensor Network we refer the reader to [67,68].

Rule ensembles [22], on the other hand, are based on training an ensemble of rules, where each rule is an expression of the form if $att_1 = val_1 \wedge ...att_n = val_n$ then $class = y$, where att_i represents one of the features and val_i a possible value for that feature, where n (i.e. the number of features involved in the rule) is small. In particular, each rule is trained in order to have high accuracy at detecting a specific class. Rule ensembles allow to obtain interpretable but very robust classifiers, which often achieve a performance that is comparable with other ensemble models (e.g. Random Forest). The main advantage of this model class is that there is a large availability of out-of-the-box computationally efficient techniques and algorithms for training such classifiers based on techniques similar to gradient boosting (e.g. SLIPPER [16] or RuleFit [22]), maximum likelihood estimation [19], Rough Sets [74] or simply by extracting rules from decision trees. Notably, these algorithms are not only computationally efficient but they also have been showed to usually provide good performance even with small sample sizes. Furthermore, while these models are based on propositional logic (as they are represent as conjunctions over ground feature values, not involving relations among them or quantifiers), simple post-processing steps can be performed to transform the rules into a relational form.

2.3 Kandinsky Patterns and Proof-of-Concept Experiments

In order to demonstrate the feasibility and effectiveness of the proposed subsymbolic-symbolic integration approach, with the two specific implementations based on LTN and rule ensembles, we provide a proof-of-concept experimental evaluation of the approach based on two datasets from the Kandinsky Patterns benchmark [39]. Kandinsky Patterns are datasets composed of patterns of geometric shapes described by either first-order logical formulas or mathematical expressions. Each pattern describes a binary classification problem in which the goal is to discriminate between images that belong to the pattern (i.e. positive examples) and images that do not belong to the pattern (i.e. negative examples).

In particular, we considered two benchmark datasets that are shown in Figs. 2 and 3. In the first benchmark, denoted as *OneRed* the positive class is composed of images containing at least one red shape. In the second benchmark, denoted as *TwoPairs*, the positive class is composed of images containing exactly four shapes in two pairs: the first pair consists of two objects with same shape and same color, while the second pair consists of two objects with same shape but different colors. We selected these two benchmarks as they do not involve overlapping figures or complex spatial patterns: for this reason, they are relatively easy tasks for a DL-based object recognition model.

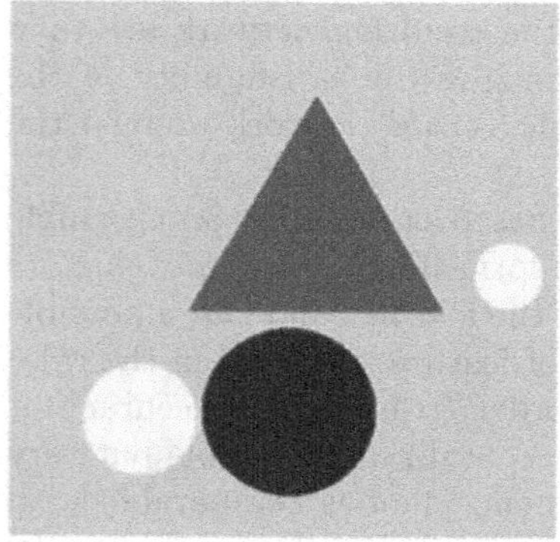

(a) Positive example: its vector-representation is $\langle t, r, c, y, c, y, c, b \rangle$

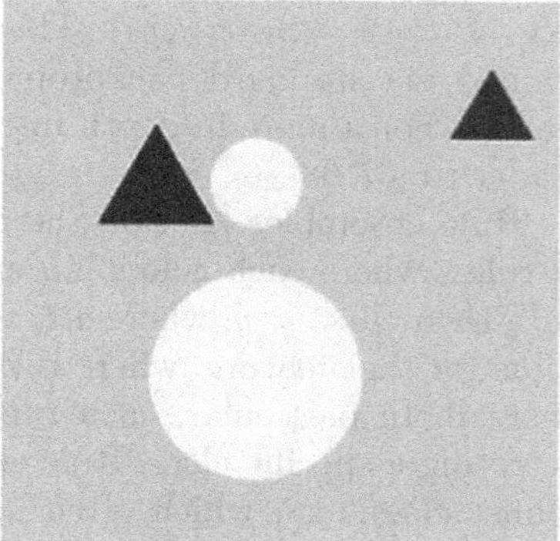

(b) Negative example: its vector-representation is $\langle t, b, t, b, c, y, c, y \rangle$

Fig. 2. The *OneRed* benchmark.

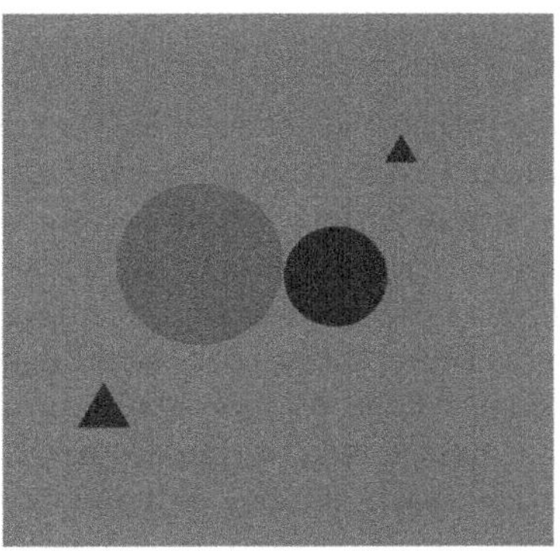

(a) Positive example: its vector-representation is $\langle 0,0,0,1,0,2 \rangle$

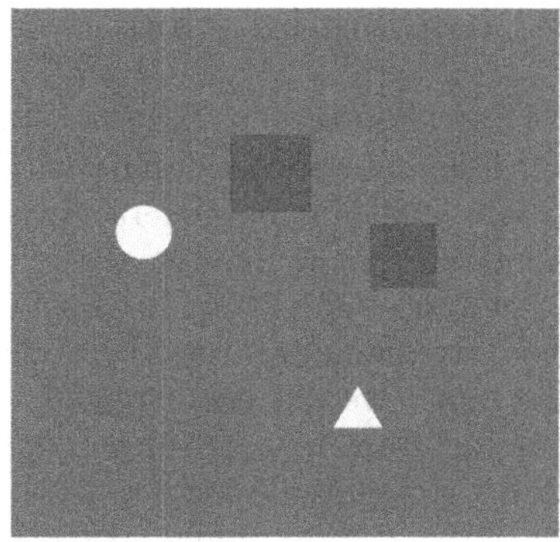

(b) Negative example: its vector-representation is $\langle 0,2,0,0,0,0 \rangle$

Fig. 3. The *TwoPairs* benchmark.

We considered, for both benchmarks, images with exactly 4 objects in order to adopt a fixed-length vector representation as input of the symbolic models. For the *OneRed* benchmark imags are represented as vectors $\langle sh_1, col_1, ..., sh_4, col_4 \rangle$, where

$$sh_i \in \{triangle(t), square(s), circle(c)\} \tag{3}$$

$$col_i \in \{red(r), blue(b), yellow(y)\} \tag{4}$$

On the other hand, for the *TwoPairs* benchmark we adopted an higher-level representation as the task is inherently more complex (as it involves comparison of pairs of objects). This is particularly relevant for the ensemble rule learning: indeed, if we were to employ a representation similar to the one for the *OneRed* benchmark, the learned classifier would be composed of a large number of rules. Thus, each image is represented as a vector $\langle eq_{1,2}, eq_{1,3}, eq_{1,4}, eq_{2,3}, eq_{2,4}, eq_{3,4} \rangle$, where $eq_{i,j} \in \{0,1,2\}$ and the semantics of these values is defined as follows:

- $eq_{i,j} = 2$ means that objects i, j have both the same shape and the same color;
- $eq_{i,j} = 1$ means that objects i, j have the same shape but different colors;
- $eq_{i,j} = 0$ means that objects i, j differ in both shape and color.

Thus, for the *OneRed* benchmark the positive examples are those for which

$$\exists i \in \{1, ..., 4\} \text{ s.t. } color_i = red \tag{5}$$

while for the *TwoPairs* benchmark the positive examples are those described by the formula

$$\exists i \neq j \neq k \neq l \text{ s.t. } eq_{i,j} = 2 \wedge eq_{k,l} = 1 \tag{6}$$

We notice that the *OneRed* benchmark consists of 6561 possible different vector encodings (in the adopted representation), while the *TwoPairs* benchmark consists of 29 possible distinct patterns.

3 Implementation

For the *OneRed* and *TwoPairs* benchmark, we generated, respectively, 1000 and 400 different random inputs with balanced classes: in order to avoid overfitting we checked via the generation script that no two images in the dataset were identical. As the main goal of the proof-of-concept experiment was to show the effectiveness of feature annotation combined with symbolic models for obtaining accurate and interpretable models, we directly generated the vector encodings and hence we did not explicitly trained a DL model for the feature annotation starting from images (although, as we previously mentioned, we expect a DL object recognition model to perform effectively in these tasks as they only involve simple, non-overlapping geometric shapes).

In order to train and evaluate the considered models we performed a 75%/25% train-test split of the two datasets.

The Logic Tensor Network models were implemented using the Tensorflow [1] framework with the logictensornetworks[1] API. The models for both benchmarks have been defined by a single predicate (representing the target to be learned) and two axioms establishing the value of predicates on the positive and negative examples of the training set respectively.

On the other hand, as regards rule ensembles, we implemented the model using the skope-rules library[2], which implements a rule ensemble algorithm based on rule extraction from Random Forests estimators.

4 Results

Logic Tensor Network models obtained 90% accuracy for the *OneRed* benchmark and 75% accuracy for the *TwoPairs* benchmarks, on the test set, while the rule ensemble models obtained 100% accuracy for both benchmarks and the learned rules were the correct description of the target class, albeit in propositional form. For the *OneRed* benchmark, the learned rules are:

- $color_1 = red \implies OneRed = 1;$
- $color_2 = red \implies OneRed = 1;$
- $color_3 = red \implies OneRed = 1;$
- $color_4 = red \implies OneRed = 1.$

where by $OneRed = 1$ we mean that the algorithm predicts that the instance is a positive one.

Similarly, for the *TwoPairs* benchmark the learned rules are:

- $eq_{1,2} = 2 \wedge eq_{3,4} = 1 \implies TwoPairs = 1;$
- $eq_{1,3} = 2 \wedge eq_{2,4} = 1 \implies TwoPairs = 1;$
- $eq_{1,4} = 2 \wedge eq_{2,3} = 1 \implies TwoPairs = 1;$
- $eq_{2,3} = 2 \wedge eq_{1,4} = 1 \implies TwoPairs = 1;$

[1] https://github.com/logictensornetworks/logictensornetworks.

[2] https://github.com/scikit-learn-contrib/skope-rules.

- $eq_{2,4} = 2 \wedge eq_{3,4} = 1 \implies TwoPairs = 1$;
- $eq_{3,4} = 2 \wedge eq_{1,2} = 1 \implies TwoPairs = 1$;

Since the learned rules correctly represent the target concepts, and there was no overlap between the train and test sets, we can claim that the perfect accuracy obtained by rule ensemble models were not due to overfitting. Furthermore, it is evident that the learned rules are fully interpretable and could be used by a human decision-maker to understand the reasons for classifying a given novel instance.

5 Discussion and Conclusion

The results reported above show that the proposed methodology could be an effective way to integrate DL models, as feature detectors, and symbolic models, in order to obtain interpretable and verifiable models which are, nonetheless, very accurate. Rule ensemble models, in particular, showed to be robust and effective models for the purpose of our proof-of-concept experimentation, as they achieved perfect accuracy while resulting in transparent and understandable models. We notice however, as a limitation, that the considered benchmarks were actually quite simple and this has a clear influence on the achieved model accuracy.

Our goal was twofold: primarily, to show the effectiveness of symbolic models also in perceptual tasks (such as image classification), when they are supplied with relevant high-level features; then, to show the effectiveness of feature engineering to obtain transparent models. For this reason, we did not explicitly trained a model to perform the required feature annotation; this allowed us to ignore the explicit interaction between the output of the DL models and the symbolic models. In the setting of a real experiment, however, this integration step is important and a careful analysis of how this is performed should be necessary, e.g. with reference to what the output format is of the DL feature detectors: would it be preferable a threshold arg-max binarization of the features (as assumed in our proof-of concept), or to directly supply the symbolic models with the un-thresholded output of the final soft-max layer of the network? The former choice would result in more interpretable binary classifiers for the symbolic component of the pipeline; the latter solution, on the otehr hand, may allow for symbolic models that employ noisy information even in cases of mis-detection of the features (whereas, in this case, the arg-max solution would supply the symbolic models with incorrect information). In this latter case, in order to properly manage this uncertain and partial form of information about the features, more expressive symbolic models could be employed, e.g. models based on fuzzy logic or other formalisms for uncertainty management. Similarly, one should consider the level of abstractness of the annotations that the DL model is trained to reproduce: indeed, our example show two different levels of abstractness, ranging from the simple object-level representation adopted for the *OneRed* benchmark, to the more complex pair-level representation adopted for the *TwoPairs* benchmark. This shows that in the proposed approach there is a measurable trade-off between interpretability, achieved by adopting a more expressive representation for the instances, and annotation easiness, as one should expect lower-level representations to be both more easily elicitable (by the human raters) and also more easy to discriminate (by the DL model).

Finally, another aspect that should be taken in consideration regards the process of feature annotation: in our proof-of-concept, this process was automatically performed via a script during the image generation step. In real-world tasks, we could expect that this process would be performed by expert human annotators in the multi-rater settings (i.e. settings in which multiple human raters annotate a given dataset): as noted in recent research [12], this annotation task could incur in annotation errors that may impact the quality of the ground truths and, hence, the performance of the DL feature detectors trained on them. Also in this case, employing symbolic formalism for uncertainty management may be useful.

Another interesting aspect that should be considered in the multi-rater settings regards how the annotations, and their influence on the related target label, are represented. Indeed, in this work, we employed a simple vector-valued representation of the features all together with the assigned target label, with no explicit relationship between the two (i.e. we employed no direct specification of which annotated feature or feature value were relevant for the target decision). However, one could also conjecture that, in complex annotation tasks, more expressive logic-based formalisms should be employed: e.g. for a given case instance, a human rater could specify that a specific target label is assigned (e.g. the instance is a positive example) because a specific subset of features is present (e.g., in a medical setting, the presence of a specific type of tissue lesion). This setting, which is based on the computational modeling of argumentation [6] and may benefit from recent research in learning from argumentation [15] and integration of DL with argumentation [25], could allow for a more explicit and informative representation of the inter-relationship among the annotated features and the target labels, expressed in the argumentative formalism which have been shown to be effective in complex decision-making settings such as the medical one [50]. For this reason, this could be a relevant further direction to explore.

References

1. Abadi, M., Barham, P., Chen, J., et al.: Tensorflow: a system for large-scale machine learning. In: 12th USENIX OSDI Symposium, pp. 265–283 (2016)
2. Adadi, A., Berrada, M.: Peeking inside the black-box: a survey on explainable artificial intelligence (xai). IEEE Access **6**, 52138–52160 (2018)
3. Adebayo, J., Gilmer, J., Goodfellow, I.J., Kim, B.: Local explanation methods for deep neural networks lack sensitivity to parameter values. CoRR abs/1810.03307 (2018)
4. Adebayo, J., Gilmer, J., Muelly, M., Goodfellow, I., Hardt, M., Kim, B.: Sanity checks for saliency maps. In: Advances in Neural Information Processing Systems, pp. 9505–9515 (2018)
5. Barocas, S., Selbst, A.D., Raghavan, M.: The hidden assumptions behind counterfactual explanations and principal reasons. In: Proceedings of the 2020 Conference on Fairness, Accountability, and Transparency, pp. 80–89 (2020)

6. Baroni, P., Gabbay, D.M., Giacomin, M., van der Torre, L.: Handbook of Formal Argumentation. College Publications, United Kingdom (2018)
7. Bianchi, F., Hitzler, P.: On the capabilities of logic tensor networks for deductive reasoning. In: AAAI Spring Symposium: Combining Machine Learning with Knowledge Engineering (2019)
8. Bielza, C., Larrañaga, P.: Discrete Bayesian network classifiers: a survey. ACM Comput. Surv. **47**, 1–43 (2014)
9. Blanco-Justicia, A., Domingo-Ferrer, J.: Machine learning explainability through comprehensible decision trees. In: Holzinger, A., Kieseberg, P., Tjoa, A.M., Weippl, E. (eds.) CD-MAKE 2019. LNCS, vol. 11713, pp. 15–26. Springer, Cham (2019). https://doi.org/10.1007/978-3-030-29726-8_2
10. Bologna, G., Hayashi, Y.: A comparison study on rule extraction from neural network ensembles, boosted shallow trees, and SVMs. Appl. Comput. Intell. Soft Comput. **2018**, 20 (2018)
11. Cabitza, F., Campagner, A., Sconfienza, L.: As if sand were stone new concepts and metrics to probe the ground on which to build trustable AI. In: BMC Medical Informatics and Decision Making (2020), submitted
12. Cabitza, F., Ciucci, D., Rasoini, R.: A giant with feet of clay: on the validity of the data that feed machine learning in medicine. In: Organizing for the Digital World, pp. 121–136. Springer (2019). https://doi.org/10.1007/978-3-319-90503-7_10
13. Castelvecchi, D.: Can we open the black box of AI? Nature News **538**(7623), 20 (2016)
14. Ciregan, D., Meier, U., Schmidhuber, J.: Multi-column deep neural networks for image classification. In: 2012 IEEE Conference on Computer Vision and Pattern Recognition, pp. 3642–3649. IEEE (2012)
15. Cocarascu, O., Toni, F.: Argumentation for machine learning: a survey. In: COMMA, pp. 219–230 (2016)
16. Cohen, W.W., Singer, Y.: A simple, fast, and effective rule learner. AAAI/IAAI **99**(335–342), 3 (1999)
17. Crockett, K., Goltz, S., Garratt, M.: GDPR impact on computational intelligence research. In: 2018 International Joint Conference on Neural Networks (IJCNN), pp. 1–7. IEEE (2018)
18. De Raedt, L., Dumančić, S., Manhaeve, R., Marra, G.: From statistical relational to neuro-symbolic artificial intelligence (2020). arXiv preprint arXiv:2003.08316
19. Dembczyński, K., Kotłowski, W., Słowiński, R.: Maximum likelihood rule ensembles. In: Proceedings of the 25th International Conference on Machine Learning, pp. 224–231 (2008)
20. Dubois, D., Prade, H.: Towards a reconciliation between reasoning and learning - a position paper. In: Ben Amor, N., Quost, B., Theobald, M. (eds.) SUM 2019. LNCS (LNAI), vol. 11940, pp. 153–168. Springer, Cham (2019). https://doi.org/10.1007/978-3-030-35514-2_12
21. Esteva, A., et al.: Dermatologist-level classification of skin cancer with deep neural networks. Nature **542**(7639), 115 (2017)
22. Friedman, J.H., Popescu, B.E., et al.: Predictive learning via rule ensembles. Ann. Appl. Stat. **2**(3), 916–954 (2008)
23. Fukushima, K.: Neocognitron: a self-organizing neural network model for a mechanism of pattern recognition unaffected by shift in position. Biol. Cybern. **36**(4), 193–202 (1980)
24. Garcez, A.D., Gori, M., Lamb, L.C., Serafini, L., Spranger, M., Tran, S.N.: Neural-symbolic computing: an effective methodology for principled integration of machine learning and reasoning (2019). arXiv preprint arXiv:1905.06088

25. Garcez, A.S.D., Gabbay, D.M., Lamb, L.C.: A neural cognitive model of argumentation with application to legal inference and decision making. J. Appl. Logic **12**(2), 109–127 (2014)
26. Gilpin, L.H., Bau, D., Yuan, B.Z., et al.: Explaining explanations: an overview of interpretability of machine learning. In: 2018 IEEE 5th DSAA International Conference, pp. 80–89. IEEE (2018)
27. Goodfellow, I., Bengio, Y., Courville, A.: Deep Learning. MIT Press, Cambridge (2016)
28. Goodfellow, I.J., Shlens, J., Szegedy, C.: Explaining and harnessing adversarial examples (2014). arXiv preprint arXiv:1412.6572
29. Goodman, B., Flaxman, S.: European union regulations on algorithmic decision-making and a "right to explanation". AI Mag. **38**(3), 50–57 (2017)
30. Guidotti, R., Monreale, A., Ruggieri, S., et al.: Local rule-based explanations of black box decision systems (2018). arXiv preprint arXiv:1805.10820
31. Guidotti, R., Monreale, A., Ruggieri, S., et al.: A survey of methods for explaining black box models. ACM Comput. Surv. (CSUR) **51**(5), 1–42 (2018)
32. Gulshan, V., Peng, L., Coram, M., et al.: Development and validation of a deep learning algorithm for detection of diabetic retinopathy in retinal fundus photographs. JAMA **316**(22), 2402–2410 (2016)
33. Haenssle, H., Fink, C., Schneiderbauer, R., et al.: Man against machine: diagnostic performance of a deep learning convolutional neural network for dermoscopic melanoma recognition in comparison to 58 dermatologists. Annals Oncol. **29**(8), 1836–1842 (2018)
34. Hagras, H.: Toward human-understandable, explainable AI. Computer **51**(9), 28–36 (2018)
35. Halford, G.S., Wilson, W.H., Phillips, S.: Relational knowledge: the foundation of higher cognition. Trends Cogn. Sci. **14**(11), 497–505 (2010)
36. Han, S.S., Park, G.H., Lim, W., et al.: Deep neural networks show an equivalent and often superior performance to dermatologists in onychomycosis diagnosis: automatic construction of onychomycosis datasets by region-based convolutional deep neural network. PloS One **13**(1), e0191493 (2018)
37. Holzinger, A., Langs, G., Denk, H., Zatloukal, K., Mueller, H.: Causability and explainability of AI in medicine. Data Min. Knowl. Discovery **10**, e1312 (2019)
38. Holzinger, A., Carrington, A., Mueller, H.: Measuring the quality of explanations:the system causability scale (SCS) comparing human and machine explanations. KI - Kunstliche Intelligenz **34**(2), 1–6 (2020). https://doi.org/10.1007/s13218-020-00636-z
39. Holzinger, A., Kickmeier-Rust, M., Müller, H.: KANDINSKY patterns as IQ-test for machine learning. In: Holzinger, A., Kieseberg, P., Tjoa, A.M., Weippl, E. (eds.) CD-MAKE 2019. LNCS, vol. 11713, pp. 1–14. Springer, Cham (2019). https://doi.org/10.1007/978-3-030-29726-8_1
40. Ivakhnenko, A.G., Lapa, V.G.: Cybernetics and forecasting techniques (1967)
41. Justesen, N., Bontrager, P., Togelius, J., Risi, S.: Deep learning for video game playing. IEEE Trans. Games **12**(1), 1–20 (2019)
42. Kingma, D.P., Ba, J.: Adam: A method for stochastic optimization (2014). arXiv preprint arXiv:1412.6980
43. Krizhevsky, A., Sutskever, I., Hinton, G.E.: Imagenet classification with deep convolutional neural networks. In: Advances in Neural Information Processing Systems, pp. 1097–1105 (2012)

44. Lakkaraju, H., Bach, S.H., Leskovec, J.: Interpretable decision sets: a joint framework for description and prediction. In: Proceedings of the 22nd ACM SIGKDD International Conference on Knowledge Discovery and Data Mining, pp. 1675–1684 (2016)
45. Laugel, T., Lesot, M.J., Marsala, C., Detyniecki, M.: Issues with post-hoc counterfactual explanations: a discussion (2019). arXiv preprint arXiv:1906.04774
46. Laugel, T., Lesot, M.J., Marsala, C., Renard, X., Detyniecki, M.: The dangers of post-hoc interpretability: Unjustified counterfactual explanations (2019). arXiv preprint arXiv:1907.09294
47. Lei, J., G'Sell, M., Rinaldo, A., Tibshirani, R.J., Wasserman, L.: Distribution-free predictive inference for regression. J. Am. Stat. Assoc. **113**(523), 1094–1111 (2018)
48. Linnainmaa, S.: The representation of the cumulative rounding error of an algorithm as a taylor expansion of the local rounding errors. Master's Thesis (in Finnish), University of Helsinki, pp. 6–7 (1970)
49. Long, J., Shelhamer, E., Darrell, T.: Fully convolutional networks for semantic segmentation. In: Proceedings of the IEEE Conference on Computer Vision and Pattern Recognition, pp. 3431–3440 (2015)
50. Longo, L., Hederman, L.: Argumentation theory for decision support in healthcare: a comparison with machine learning. In: Imamura, K., Usui, S., Shirao, T., Kasamatsu, T., Schwabe, L., Zhong, N. (eds.) BHI 2013. LNCS (LNAI), vol. 8211, pp. 168–180. Springer, Cham (2013). https://doi.org/10.1007/978-3-319-02753-1_17
51. Lundberg, S.M., Lee, S.I.: A unified approach to interpreting model predictions. In: Advances in Neural Information Processing Systems, pp. 4765–4774 (2017)
52. Mao, J., Gan, C., Kohli, P., Tenenbaum, J.B., Wu, J.: The neuro-symbolic concept learner: Interpreting scenes, words, and sentences from natural supervision (2019). arXiv preprint arXiv:1904.12584
53. Mittelstadt, B., Russell, C., Wachter, S.: Explaining explanations in AI. In: Proceedings of the Conference on Fairness, Accountability, and Transparency (2019)
54. Montavon, G., Binder, A., Lapuschkin, S., Samek, W., Müller, K.-R.: Layer-wise relevance propagation: an overview. In: Samek, W., Montavon, G., Vedaldi, A., Hansen, L.K., Müller, K.-R. (eds.) Explainable AI: Interpreting, Explaining and Visualizing Deep Learning. LNCS (LNAI), vol. 11700, pp. 193–209. Springer, Cham (2019). https://doi.org/10.1007/978-3-030-28954-6_10
55. Murdoch, W.J., Singh, C., Kumbier, K., Abbasi-Asl, R., Yu, B.: Interpretable machine learning: definitions, methods, and applications (2019). arXiv preprint arXiv:1901.04592
56. Oh, K.S., Jung, K.: GPU implementation of neural networks. Pattern Recogn. **37**(6), 1311–1314 (2004)
57. Raedt, L.D., Kersting, K., Natarajan, S., Poole, D.: Statistical relational artificial intelligence: logic, probability, and computation. Synth. Lect. Artif. Intell. Mach. Learn. **10**(2), 1–189 (2016)
58. Rao, Q., Frtunikj, J.: Deep learning for self-driving cars: chances and challenges. In: Proceedings of the 1st International Workshop on Software Engineering for AI in Autonomous Systems, pp. 35–38 (2018)
59. Redmon, J., Farhadi, A.: Yolov3: An incremental improvement arXiv (2018)
60. Ren, S., He, K., Girshick, R., Sun, J.: Faster r-cnn: towards real-time object detection with region proposal networks. In: Advances in Neural Information Processing Systems, pp. 91–99 (2015)
61. Ribeiro, M.T., Singh, S., Guestrin, C.: "Why should I trust you?": explaining the predictions of any classifier. CoRR abs/1602.04938 (2016)

62. Ribeiro, M.T., Singh, S., Guestrin, C.: Anchors: high-precision model-agnostic explanations. In: Thirty-Second AAAI Conference on Artificial Intelligence (2018)
63. Ruder, S.: An overview of multi-task learning in deep neural networks (2017). arXiv preprint arXiv:1706.05098
64. Rudin, C.: Stop explaining black box machine learning models for high stakes decisions and use interpretable models instead. Nat. Mach. Intell. **1**(5), 206–215 (2019)
65. Rumelhart, D.E., Hinton, G.E., Williams, R.J.: Learning representations by back-propagating errors. Nature **323**(6088), 533–536 (1986)
66. Schmid, U.: Inductive programming as approach to comprehensible machine learning. In: Proceedings of DKB-2018 and KIK-2018 (2018)
67. Serafini, L., Donadello, I., Garcez, A.D.: Learning and reasoning in logic tensor networks: theory and application to semantic image interpretation. In: Proceedings of the Symposium on Applied Computing, pp. 125–130 (2017)
68. Serafini, L., d Avila Garcez, A.S.: Learning and reasoning with logic tensor networks. In: Adorni, G., Cagnoni, S., Gori, M., Maratea, M. (eds.) AIIA 2016. LNCS (LNAI), vol. 10037, pp. 334–348. Springer, Cham (2016). https://doi.org/10.1007/978-3-319-49130-1_25
69. Setiono, R., Baesens, B., Mues, C.: Recursive neural network rule extraction for data with mixed attributes. IEEE Trans. Neural Networks **19**(2), 299–307 (2008)
70. Silver, D., Schrittwieser, J., Simonyan, K., et al.: Mastering the game of go without human knowledge. Nature **550**(7676), 354–359 (2017)
71. Simonyan, K., Vedaldi, A., Zisserman, A.: Deep inside convolutional networks: Visualising image classification models and saliency maps (2013). arXiv preprint arXiv:1312.6034
72. Sixt, L., Granz, M., Landgraf, T.: When explanations lie: Why many modified bp attributions fail (2019)
73. Slack, D., Hilgard, S., Jia, E., Singh, S., Lakkaraju, H.: Fooling lime and shap: adversarial attacks on post hoc explanation methods. In: Proceedings of the AAAI/ACM Conference on AI, Ethics, and Society, pp. 180–186 (2020)
74. Ślęzak, D., Widz, S.: Rough-set-inspired feature subset selection, classifier construction, and rule aggregation. In: Yao, J.T., Ramanna, S., Wang, G., Suraj, Z. (eds.) RSKT 2011. LNCS (LNAI), vol. 6954, pp. 81–88. Springer, Heidelberg (2011). https://doi.org/10.1007/978-3-642-24425-4_13
75. Socher, R., Chen, D., Manning, C.D., Ng, A.: Reasoning with neural tensor networks for knowledge base completion. In: Advances in Neural Information Processing Systems, pp. 926–934 (2013)
76. Srivastava, N., Hinton, G., Krizhevsky, A., et al.: Dropout: a simple way to prevent neural networks from overfitting. J. Mach. Learn. Res. **15**(1), 1929–1958 (2014)
77. Ustun, B., Rudin, C.: Methods and models for interpretable linear classification (2014). arXiv preprint arXiv:1405.4047
78. Van Assche, A., Blockeel, H.: Seeing the forest through the trees: learning a comprehensible model from an ensemble. In: Kok, J.N., Koronacki, J., Mantaras, R.L., Matwin, S., Mladenič, D., Skowron, A. (eds.) ECML 2007. LNCS (LNAI), vol. 4701, pp. 418–429. Springer, Heidelberg (2007). https://doi.org/10.1007/978-3-540-74958-5_39
79. Wang, T., Rudin, C., Doshi-Velez, F., Liu, Y., Klampfl, E., MacNeille, P.: A Bayesian framework for learning rule sets for interpretable classification. J. Mach. Learn. Res. **18**(1), 2357–2393 (2017)
80. Yang, C., Rangarajan, A., Ranka, S.: Global model interpretation via recursive partitioning. In: 2018 IEEE 4th DSS Conference, pp. 1563–1570. IEEE (2018)

81. Young, T., Hazarika, D., Poria, S., et al.: Recent trends in deep learning based natural language processing. IEEE Comp. Intell. Mag. **13**(3), 55–75 (2018)
82. Zheng, A., Casari, A.: Feature Engineering for Machine Learning: Principles and Techniques for Data Scientists. O'Reilly Media, Inc., Massachusetts (2018)

Explain Graph Neural Networks to Understand Weighted Graph Features in Node Classification

Xiaoxiao Li[1](✉) and João Saúde[2](✉)

[1] Yale University, New Haven, USA
xiaoxiao.li@yale.edu
[2] JP Morgan AI Research, New York, USA
jsaude@alumni.cmu.edu

Abstract. Real data collected from different applications that have additional topological structures and connection information are amenable to be represented as a weighted graph. Considering the node labeling problem, Graph Neural Networks (GNNs) is a powerful tool, which can mimic experts' decision on node labeling. GNNs combine node features, connection patterns, and graph structure by using a neural network to embed node information and pass it through edges in the graph. We want to identify the patterns in the input data used by the GNN model to make a decision and examine if the model works as we desire. However, due to the complex data representation and non-linear transformations, explaining decisions made by GNNs is challenging. In this work, we propose new graph features' explanation methods to identify the informative components and important node features. Besides, we propose a pipeline to identify the critical factors used for node classification. We use four datasets (two synthetic and two real) to validate our methods. Our results demonstrate that our explanation approach can mimic data patterns used for node classification by human interpretation and disentangle different features in the graphs. Furthermore, our explanation methods can be used for understanding data, debugging GNN models, and examine model decisions.

Keywords: Explainability · Graph Neural Networks · Classification

1 Introduction

Our contemporary society relies heavily on interpersonal/cultural relations (social networks), our economy is densely connected and structured (commercial relations, financial transfers, supply/distribution chains). Moreover, those complex network structures also appear in nature. For instance, in biology, like the brain, vascular and nervous systems, on chemical systems, atoms' connections on molecules. This data is hugely structured and depends heavily on the relations within the networks. Therefore, it makes sense to represent the data as a graph, where nodes represent entities, and the edges the connections between them, their intensity, and type (vector edge weights).

Published by Springer Nature Switzerland AG 2020
A. Holzinger et al. (Eds.): CD-MAKE 2020, LNCS 12279, pp. 57–76, 2020.
https://doi.org/10.1007/978-3-030-57321-8_4

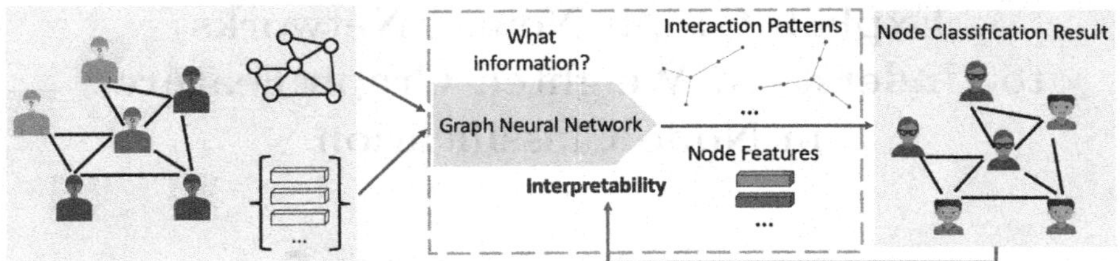

Fig. 1. Framework to explain GNN node classification.

Graph Neural Networks (GNNs) such as GCN [12], GraphSage [10], can handle graph-structured data by preserving the information structure of graphs. Our primary focus is on the node labeling problem. Examples are fraud detection, classification of users in social networks, or role assignment in biological structures. GNNs can combine node features, connection patterns, and graph structure by using a neural network to embed the node information and pass it through edges in the graph. However, due to the complex data representation and non-linear transformations performed on the data, explaining decisions made by GNNs is a challenging problem. Therefore we want to identify the patterns in the input data that are used by a given GNN model to make a decision and examine if the model works as we desire, as depicted in Fig. 1.

Related Work: Explainable artificial intelligence (AI) is an active field of research, see [3,7,9], for a general introduction, challenges, and its possible solutions. As important as having tools to explain AI results, is how to interpret those results and to compare them with human interpretations and explanations. See [14] for an overview and [11] for an evaluation tool (System Causability Scale) to measure the quality of an explanation.

Although, deep learning model visualization techniques have been developed in the convolution neural network (CNN), those methods are not directly applicable to explain weighted graphs that use node features for the classification task. A few works have tackle the explaining GNN problem [4,16,21,22].

However, to our best knowledge, no work has been done on explaining comprehensive features (namely node feature, edge feature, and connecting patterns) in a weighted graph, especially for node classification problems.

Our Contribution: Here we propose a few post-hoc graph feature explanation methods to formulate an explanation on nodes and edges. Our experiments on synthetic and real data demonstrate that our proposed methods and pipeline can generate similar explanations and evidence as human interpretation. Furthermore, that helps to understand whether the node features or graph typologies are the key factors used in the GNN node classification of a weighted graph. Our contribution is summarized as follows:

1. We propose the formula of **weight graph pattern** (learned by GNN) explanation as two perspectives: *Informative Components Detection and Node Feature Importance.*
2. We extend the current GNN explanation methods, which mainly focus on the undirected-unweighted graph to directed weighted graph. We adapt the well-know CNN visualization methods to GNN explanation.
3. We propose a pipeline, including novel evaluation methods, to find whether topological information or node features are the key factors in node classification. We also propose a way to discover group similarities from the disentangled results.

Paper Structure: In Sect. 2, we define necessary graph's notations and introduce the Graph Neural Networks (GNN). Then in Sect. 3, we describe the formula of graph explanation, and the corresponding methods are extended in Sect. 4 and 5. In Sect. 6, we propose the evaluation metrics and methods. The experiments and results are presented in Sect. 7. We conclude the paper in Sect. 8.

2 Graph Neural Networks

2.1 Data Representation – Weighted Graph

In this section, we introduce the necessary notation and definitions. We denote a graph by $G = (V, \mathcal{E})$ where V is the set of nodes, $\mathcal{E}$ the set of edges linking the nodes and X the set of nodes' features. For every pair of connected nodes, $u, v \in V$, we denote by $e_{vu} \in \mathbb{R}$ the weight of the edge $(v, u) \in \mathcal{E}$ linking them. We denote $E[v, u] = e_{vu}$, where $E \in \mathbb{R}^{|\mathcal{E}|}$. For each node, u, we associate a d-dimensional vector of features, $X_u \in \mathbb{R}^d$ and denote the set of all features as $X = \{X_u : u \in V\} \in (\mathbb{R}^d)^{|V|}$.

Edge features contain important information about graphs. For instances, the graph G may represent a banking system, where the nodes V represents different banks, and the edges E are the transaction between them; or graph G may represent a social network, where the nodes V represent different users, and the edges E is the contacting frequencies between the users.

We consider a node classification task, where each node u is assigned a label $y_u \in I_C = \{0, \ldots, C-1\}$. The two explanation perspectives correspond to the informative explanation on E and X of the weighted graph.

2.2 GNN Utilizing Edge Weight

Different from the state of art GNN architecture, *i.e.* graph convolution networks (GCN) [12] and graph attention networks (GAT) [20], some GNNs can exploit the edge information on graph [8,18,21]. Here, we consider weighted and directed graphs and develop the graph neural network that uses both nodes and edges weights, where edge weights affect message aggregation. Not only can our approach handle directed and weighted graphs, but it also preserves edge information in the propagation of GNNs. Preserving and using edges information is important in many real-world graphs such as banking payment networks, recommendation systems (that use the social network), and other systems that heavily rely on the topology of the connections. Since apart from the node (atomic) features, also the attributes of edges (bonds) are important for predicting local and global properties of graphs. Generally speaking, GNNs inductively learn a node representation by recursively aggregating and transforming the feature vectors of its neighboring nodes. Following [5,23,24], a per-layer update of the GNN in our setting involves these three computations, message passing Eq. (1), message aggregation Eq. (2), and updating node representation Eq. (3), which can be expressed as:

$$\mathbf{m}_{vu}^{(l)} = \mathrm{MSG}(\mathbf{h}_u^{(l-1)}, \mathbf{h}_v^{(l-1)}, e_{vu}) \tag{1}$$

$$\mathbf{M}_u^{(l)} = \mathrm{AGG}(\{\mathbf{m}_{vu}^{(l)}, e_{vu}\} \mid v \in \mathcal{N}(u)\}) \tag{2}$$

$$\mathbf{h}_u^{(l)} = \mathrm{UPDATE}(M_u^{(l)}, \mathbf{h}_u^{(l-1)}) \tag{3}$$

where $\mathbf{h}_u^{(l)}$ is the embedded representation of node u on the layer l; e_{vu} is the weighted edge pointing from v to u; $\mathcal{N}(u)$ is u's neighborhood from where it collects information to update its aggregated message $\mathbf{M}_u$. Specifically, $\mathbf{h}_u^{(0)} = \mathbf{x}_u$ as initial, and $\mathbf{h}_u^{(L)}$ is the final embedding for node u of an L-layer GNN node classifier.

Here, following [17], we set $h^{(l)} \in \mathbb{R}^{d^{(l)}}$ and define the propagation model for calculating the forward-pass update of node representation as:

$$\mathbf{h}_u^{(l)} = \sigma\Big(W_0^{(l-1)}\mathbf{h}_u^{(l-1)} + \sum_{v\in\mathcal{N}(u)} \phi\left(W_1^{(l-1)}\mathbf{h}_v^{(l-1)}, \mathbf{h}_u^{(l)}, e_{vu}\right)\Big), \tag{4}$$

where $\mathcal{N}(u)$ denotes the set of neighbors of node u and e_{vu} denotes the directed edge from v to u, W denotes the model's parameters to be learned, and ϕ is any linear/nonlinear function that can be applied on neighbour nodes' feature embedding. $d^{(l)}$ is the dimension of the lth layer representation.

Our method can deal with negative edges-weighted by re-normalizing them to a positive interval; for instance, $[0, 1]$, therefore in what follows, we use only positive weighted edges. Hence, in the existing literature and different experiment settings, based on the nature of the input graph and edge weights, they usually play two roles: 1) message filtering; and 2) node embedding.

Type I: Edge Weights for Message Filtering. As the graph convolution operations in [8], the edge feature matrices will be used as filters to multiply the node feature matrix. The GNN layer using edge weight for filtering can be formed as the following steps:

$$\mathbf{m}_{vu}^{(l)} = W_1^{(l-1)}\mathbf{h}_v^{(l-1)} \qquad \text{(message)} \tag{5}$$

$$\mathbf{M}_u^{(l)} = \sum_{v\in\mathcal{N}(u)} g(\mathbf{m}_{vu}^{(l)}, \mathbf{h}_u^{(l-1)}, e_{vu}) \qquad \text{(aggregate)} \tag{6}$$

$$\mathbf{h}_u^{(l)} = \sigma(W_0^{(l-1)}\mathbf{h}_u^{(l-1)} + \mathbf{M}_u^{(l)}) \qquad \text{(update)} \tag{7}$$

To avoid increasing the scale of output features by multiplication, the edge features need to be normalized, as in GAT [20] and GCN [12]. Due to the aggregation mechanism, we normalize the weights by in-degree $\bar{e}_{vu} = e_{vu} / \sum_{v \in \mathcal{N}(u)} e_{vu}$. Depending on the the problem:

- g can simply defined as: $g = \bar{e}_{vu}\mathbf{m}_{vu}^{(l)}$;
  or
- g can be a gate function, such as a RNN-type block of $\mathbf{m}_{vu}^{(l)}$, *i.e.*: $g = GRU(\bar{e}_{vu}\mathbf{m}_{vu}^{(l)}, \mathbf{h}_u^{(l-1)})$.

Type II: Edge Weights for Node Embedding. If e_{vu} contributes to node u's feature embedding, $g = f(e_{vu})\mathbf{m}_{vu}^{(l)}$, where $f(e_{vu})$ is composition of one fully-connected (FC) layer and reshape operation, mapping $\mathbb{R} \mapsto \mathbb{R}^{d^{(l)} \times d^{(l-1)}}$. In this case, we will replace Eq. (5) and (6) by:

$$\mathbf{m}_{vu}^{(l)} = f(e_{vu})\mathbf{h}_v^{(l-1)} \qquad \text{(message)} \tag{8}$$

$$\mathbf{M}_u^{(l)} = \sum_{v \in \mathcal{N}(u)} g(\mathbf{m}_{vu}^{(l)}, \mathbf{h}_u^{(l-1)}) \qquad \text{(aggregate)} \tag{9}$$

Similarly, g can be $g = \mathbf{m}_{vu}^{(l)}$ or $g = GRU(\mathbf{m}_{vu}^{(l)}, \mathbf{h}_u^{(l-1)})$.

For the final prediction, we apply an Fully Connected (FC) layer:

$$\hat{\mathbf{y}}_u = \mathit{softmax}(W_c\mathbf{h}_u^{(L)} + b_c) \tag{10}$$

Since Type II can be converted to unweighted graph explanation, which has been studied in existing literature [16,22], the following explanation will focus on Type I. For generalizations, we focus on model agnostic and post-hoc explanation, without retraining GNN and modifying pre-trained GNN architectures.

3 Formula of Graph Explanation

We consider the weighted graph feature explanation problem as a two-stage pipeline.

First, we train a node classification function, in this case, a GNN. The GNN inputs are a graph $G = (V, \mathcal{E})$, its associated node feature X and its true nodes labels Y. We represent this classifier as $\Phi : G \mapsto (u \mapsto y_u)$, where $y_u \in I_C$. The advantage of the GNN is that it keeps the flow of information across nodes and the structure of our data. Furthermore, it is invariant to permutations on the ordering. Hence it keeps the relational inductive biases of the input data (see [5]).

Second, given the node classification model and node's true label , the explanation part will provide a subgraph and a subset of features retrieved from the k-hop neighborhood of each node u, for $k \in \mathbb{N}$ and $u \in V$. Theoretically, the subgraph, along with the subset of features is the minimal set of information and information flow across neighbor nodes of u, that the GNN used to compute the node's label.

We define $G_S = (V_S, \mathcal{E}_S)$ to be a subgraph of G, where $G_S \subseteq G$, if $V_S \subseteq V$ and $\mathcal{E}_S \subseteq \mathcal{E}$. Consider the classification $y_u \in I_C$ of node u, then our Weighted Graph Explanation methods has two explanation components:

- **Informative Components Detection**. Our method computes a subgraph, G_S, containing u, that aims to explain the classification task by looking at the edge connectivity patterns $\mathcal{E}_S$ and their connecting nodes V_S. This provides insights on the characteristics of the graph that contribute to the node's label.
- **Node feature Importance**. Our method assigns to each node feature a score indicating its importance and ranking.

4 Informative Components Detection

Relational structures in graphs often contain crucial information for node classification, such as graph's topology and information flow (i.e., direction and amplitude). Therefore, knowing which edges contribute the most to the information flow towards or from a node is important to understand the node classification evidence. In this section, we discuss methods to identify the informative components on weighted graphs.

4.1 Computational Graph

Due to the properties of the GNN (2), we only need to consider the graph structure used in aggregation, *i.e.* the *computational graph* w.r.t node u is defined as $G_c(u)$ containing N' nodes, where $N' \leq |V|$. The node feature set associated with the $G_c(u)$ is $X_c(u) = \{x_v | v \in V_c(u)\}$. The prediction of GNN Φ is given by $\hat{y}_u = \Phi(G_c(u), X_c(u))$, which can be considered as a distribution $P_\Phi(Y|G_c, X_c)$ mapping by GNN. Our goal is to identity a subgraph $G_S \subseteq G_c(u)$ (and its associated features $X_S = \{\mathbf{x}_w | w \in V_S\}$, or a subset of them) which the GNN uses to predict u's label. In the following subsections, we introduce three approaches to detect explainable components within the computational graph: 1) Maximal Mutual Information (MMI) Mask; and 2) Guided Gradient Salience.

4.2 Maximal Mutual Information (MMI) Mask

We first introduce some definitions. We define the Shannon entropy of a discrete random variable, X, by $H(X) = \mathbb{E}[-\log(P(X))]$, where $P(X)$ is the probability mass function. Furthermore, the conditional entropy is defined as:

$$H[Y|X] = -\sum_{x \in \mathcal{X}, y \in \mathcal{Y}} p(x, y) \log \frac{p(x, y)}{p(x)},$$

where $\mathcal{X}$ and $\mathcal{Y}$ are the sample spaces. Finally, we define the mutual information (MI) between two random variables as $I(Y, X) = H(Y) - H(Y|X)$, this measures the mutual dependence between both variables.

Using ideas from Information theory [6] and following GNNExplainer [22], the informative explainable subgraph and nodes features subset are chosen to maximize the mutual information (MI):

$$\max_{G_S} I(Y, (G_S, X_S)) = H(Y|G, X) - H(Y|G_S, X_S) \tag{11}$$

Since the trained GNN node classifier Φ is fixed, the $H(Y)$ term of Eq. (11) is constant. As a result, it is equivalent to minimize the conditional entropy $H(Y|G_S, X_S)$.

$$-\mathbb{E}_{Y|G_S,X_S}[\log P_\Phi(Y|G_S, X_S)] \tag{12}$$

Therefore, the explanation to the graph components with prediction power w.r.t node u's prediction $\hat{y}_u$ is a subgraph G_S and its associated feature set X_S, that minimize (12). The objective of the explanation thus aims to pick the top informative edges and its connecting neighbours, which form a subgraph, for predicting u's label. Because, probably some edges in u's computational graph $G_c(u)$ form important message-passing (6) pathways, which allow useful node information to be propagated across $G_c(u)$ and aggregated at u for prediction; while some edges in $G_c(u)$ might not be informative for prediction. Instead of directly optimize G_S in Eq. (12), as it is not tractable and there are exponentially many discrete structures $G_S \subseteq G_c(u)$ containing N' nodes, GNNExplainer [22] optimizes a mask $\mathcal{M}_{sym}^{N' \times N'}[0, 1]$ on the binary adjacent matrix, which allows gradient descent to be performed on G_S.

If the edge weights are used for node embedding, the connection can be treated as binary and fit into the original GNNExplainer. However, if edge weights are used as filtering, the mask should affect filtering and normalization. We extend the original GNNExplainer method by considering edge weights and improving the method by adding extra regularization. Unlike GNNExplainer, where there are no constraints on the mask value, we add constraints to the value learned by the mask

$$\begin{cases} \sum_w \mathcal{M}_{vw} e_{vw} = 1 \\ \mathcal{M}_{vw} \geq 0, & \text{for } (v, w) \in \mathcal{E}_c(u) \end{cases} \tag{13}$$

and perform a projected gradient decent optimization. Therefore, rather than optimizing a relaxed adjacency matrix in GNNExplainer, we optimize a mask $\mathcal{M} \in [0, 1]^Q$ on weighted edges, supposing there are Q edges in $G_c(u)$. Then $E_c^{\mathcal{M}} = E_c \odot \mathcal{M}$, where $\odot$ is element-wise multiplication of two matrix. The masked edge $E_c^{\mathcal{M}}$ is subject to the constraint that $E_c^{\mathcal{M}}[v, w] \leq E_c[v, w], \forall (v, w) \in \mathcal{E}_c(u)$. Then the objective function can be written as:

$$\min_M - \sum_{c=1}^{C} \mathbb{I}[y = c] \log P_\Phi(Y|G_c = (V_c, E_c \odot \mathcal{M}), X_c) \tag{14}$$

Algorithm 1. Optimize mask for weighted graph

Input: 1. $G_c(u)$, computation graph of node u; 2. Pre-trained GNN model Φ; 3. y_u, node u's real label; 4. $\mathcal{M}$, learnable mask; 5. K, number of optimization iterations; 6. L, number of layers of GNN.

$\mathcal{M} \leftarrow$ randomize parameters ▷ initialize, $\mathcal{M} \in [0,1]^Q$

$\mathbf{h}_v^{(0)} \leftarrow \mathbf{x}_v$, for $v \in G_c(u)$

for $k = 1$ to K **do**

  $\mathcal{M}_{vw} \leftarrow \frac{exp(\mathcal{M}_{vw} e_{vw})}{\sum_v exp(\mathcal{M}_{vw} e_{vw})}$ ▷ renormalize mask

  for $l = 1$ to L **do**

    $\mathbf{m}_{vu}^{(l)} \leftarrow W_1^{(l-1)} \mathbf{h}_v^{(l-1)}$ ▷ message

    $M_u^{(l)} \leftarrow \sum_v g(\mathcal{M}_{vu} \mathbf{m}_{vu}^{(l)}, \mathbf{h}_u^{(l-1)})$ ▷ aggregate

    $\mathbf{h}_u^{(l)} \leftarrow \sigma(W_0 \mathbf{h}_u^{(l-1)} + M_u^{(l)})$ ▷ update

  end for

  $\hat{\mathbf{y}}_u \leftarrow softmax(\mathbf{h}_u^{(L)})$ ▷ predict on masked graph

  $loss \leftarrow crossentropy(\mathbf{y}_u, \hat{\mathbf{y}}_u) + regularizations$

  $\mathcal{M} \leftarrow optimizer(loss, \mathcal{M})$ ▷ update mask

end for

Return: $\mathcal{M}$

In GNNExplainer, the top k edges may not form a connected component including the node (saying u) under prediction i. Hence, we added the entropy of the $(E_c \odot \mathcal{M})_{vu}$ for all the node v pointing to node u' as a regularization term, to ensure that at least one edge connected to node u will be selected. After mask $\mathcal{M}$ is learned, we use threshold to remove small $E_c \odot \mathcal{M}$ and isolated nodes. Our proposed optimization methods to optimize $\mathcal{M}$ maximizing mutual information (Eq. (11)) under above constrains is shown in Algorithm 1.

4.3 Guided Gradient (GGD) Salience

Guided gradient-based explanation methods [19] is perhaps the most straight forward and easiest approach. By calculating the differentiate of the output w.r.t the model input then applying norm, a score can be obtained. The gradient-based score can be used to indicate the relative importance of the input feature since it represents the change in input space which corresponds to the maximizing positive rate of change in the model output. Since edge weights are variables in GNN, we can obtain the edge mask as

$$g_{vu}^E = ReLU\left(\frac{\partial \hat{y}_u^c}{\partial e_{vu}}\right) \tag{15}$$

where $c \in \{0, \ldots, C-1\}$ is the correct class of node u, and y_c^u is the score for class c before softmax layer, where $\mathbf{x}_v$ is node v's feature. We normalize g_{vu}^E by dividing $max(g_{vu}^E)$ to be bound it to $[0,1]$. Here, we select the edges whose g^E is in the top k largest ones and their connecting nodes. The advantage of contrasting gradient salience method is easy to compute.

5 Node Feature Importance

Node's features information play an important role in computing messages between nodes. That data contribute to the message passing among nodes in the message layer (see Eq. (1)). Therefore, the explanation for the classification task (or others, like regression) must take into account the feature information. In this section, we will discuss three approaches to define node feature importance in the case that the node attribute $X_u \in \mathbb{R}^d$ is a vector containing multiple features.

5.1 Maximal Mutual Information (MMI) Mask

Following GNNExplainer [22], in addition to learning a mask on edge to maximize mutual information, we also can learn a mask on node attribute to filter features given G_S. The filtered node feature $X_S^T = X_S \odot \mathcal{M}_T$, where $\mathcal{M}_T$ is a feature selection mask matrix to be learned, is optimized by

$$\min_{M_T} - \sum_{c=1}^{C} \mathbb{I}[y = c] \log P_\Phi(Y|G_S, X_S \odot \mathcal{M}_T))$$

In order to calculate the output given G_S but without feature T and also guarantee propagation, a reparametrization on X is used in paper [22]:

$$X = Z + (X_S - Z) \odot \mathcal{M}_T, \quad s.t. \sum_j \mathcal{M}_{Tj} < k \tag{16}$$

where Z is a matrix with the same dimension of X_S and each column i is sampled from the Gaussian distribution with mean and std of the i_{th} row of X_S. To minimize the objective function, when i_{th} dimension is not important; that is, any sample of Z will pull the corresponding mask value $\mathcal{M}_{Ti}$ towards 0; if i_{th} dimension is very important, the mask value $\mathcal{M}_{Ti}$ will go towards 1. Again, we set constrain:

$$0 \leq \mathcal{M}_{Ti} \leq 1, \tag{17}$$

and perform projected gradient decent optimization.

However, before performing optimization on $\mathcal{M}_T$, Z is only sampled once. Different samples of Z may affect the optimized $\mathcal{M}_T$, resulting in unstable results. Performing multiple sampling of Z will be time-consuming since each sample is followed by optimization operation on $\mathcal{M}_T$.

5.2 Prediction Difference Analysis (PDA)

We propose using PDA for node features importance, which can cheaply perform multiple random sampling with GNN testing time. The importance of a nodal feature, towards the correct prediction, can be measured as the drop of prediction score to its actual class after dropping a certain nodal feature. We denote by $X \backslash i$

the subset of the feature set X where we removed feature x_i. The prediction score of the corrupted node is $P_\Phi(y = y_u|G = G_S, X = X_S\backslash i)$. To compute $P_\Phi(y = y_u|G = G_S, X = X_S\backslash i)$, we need to marginalize out the feature x_i:

$$\bar{P} = \mathbb{E}_{\hat{x}_i \sim p(x_i|X_S\backslash i)} P_\Phi(y = y_u|G = G_S, X = \{X_S\backslash i, \hat{x}_i\}), \tag{18}$$

Modeling $p(x_i|X_S\backslash i)$ by a generative model can be computationally intensive and may not be feasible. We empirically sample $\hat{x}_i$ from training data. Noting that the training data maybe unbalance, to reduce sampling bias we should have $p(x_i \in K|X_S\backslash i) \propto 1/N_k$, where K is the features space of class k and N_k is the number of training instance in class k. Explicitly, $p(x_i \in K|X_S\backslash i) \propto 1/N_k$. We define the importance score for i_{th} node feature as the difference of original prediction score

$$PDA_i = ReLU(P_\Phi(y = y_u|G = G_S, X = X_S) - \bar{P}). \tag{19}$$

Naturally, PDA_i is bounded in $[0, 1]$. The larger the PDA_i indicates a more important the i_{th} feature.

5.3 Guided Gradient (GGD) Node Feature Salience

Similar to the guided gradient method in detecting explainable components, we calculate the differentiate of the output with respect to the node under prediction and its neighbors in its computation graph $G_c(u)$ on the i_{th} feature for $i \in I_C$:

$$g_v^i = ReLU\left(\frac{\partial \hat{y}_u^c}{\partial x_v^i}\right), \quad v \in G_c(u). \tag{20}$$

The larger the g_i is, the more important the i_{th} feature is.

6 Evaluation Metrics and Methods

For synthetic data, we can compare explanation with data generation rules. However, for real data, we do not have ground truth for the explanation. In order to evaluate the results, we propose the evaluation metrics for quantitatively measuring the explanation results and propose the correlation methods to validate if edge connection pattern or node feature is the crucial factor for classification.

6.1 Evaluation Metrics

We define metrics *consistency*, *contrastivity* and sparsity (Here, definition of *contrastivity* andsparsity are different from the ones in [16]) to measure informative component detection results. Firstly, To measure the similarity between graphs, we introduce graph edit distance (GED) [2], which is a graph similarity measure analogous to Levenshtein distance for strings. It is defined as minimum cost of edit path (sequence of node and edge edit operations) transforming graph G1

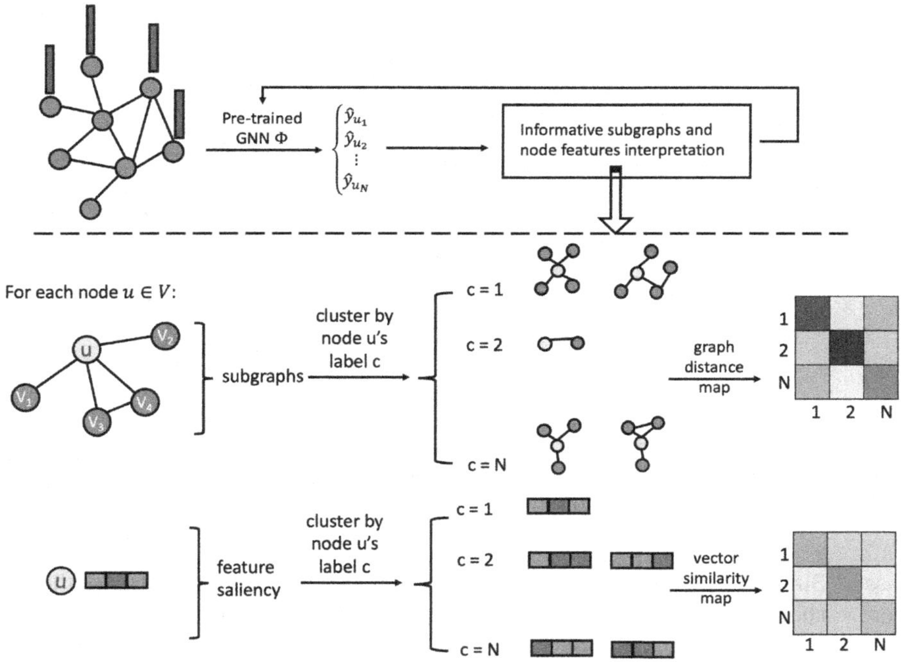

Fig. 2. Disentangle informative subgraphs and node features

to graph isomorphic to G2. In case the structure is isomorphic but edge weights are different. If GED=0, Jensen-Shannon Divergence (JSD) [15], is added on GED to further compare the two isomorphic subgraphs. Specifically, we design consistency as the GED between the informative subgraphs of the node in the same class, as and whether the informative components detected for the node in the same class are consist; and design contrastivity as the GED across the informative subgraphs of the node in the same class, as and whether the informative components detected for the node in the different class are contrastive; Sparsity is defined as the density of mask $\sum_{e_{vw} \in G_c(u)} \Upsilon_{vw}/Q, \Upsilon \in \{\mathcal{M}, g^E\}$, as the density of component edge importance weights.

6.2 Important Features Disentanglement

We follow the pipeline described in Fig. 2. Hence, after training a GNN, we perform informative component detection and node importance analysis on each of the nodes $u \in V$. Furthermore, we get the local topology $G_S(u)$ that explains the labeling of that node. After, for each label $c \in I_C$, we collect all the subgraphs that explain that label, $\{G_S(w)\}_{w \in c}$, where $c \in I_C$ means that node w is classified as class c. Then, we measure the distance, using the predefined GED, from all the subgraphs in each label c to all the subgraphs in all labels $j \in I_C$. So, we obtain a set of distances between the instance within the class and across

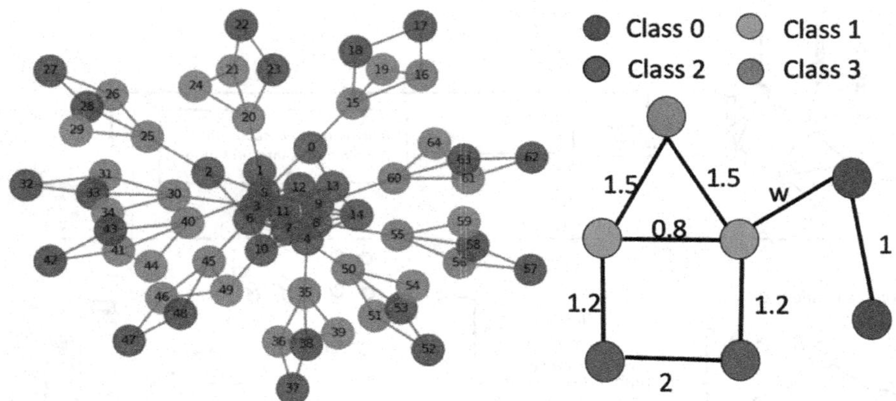

Fig. 3. Synthetic BA-house graph data and corresponding edge weights, each BA node belongs to class "0," and each "house" shape node belongs labeled "1–3" based on its motif. The node orders are denoted

classes. Similarly, for each label $c \in I_C$, we collect all the node feature saliency vectors that explain that label, $\{\mathcal{F}(w)\}_{w \in c}$, where $c \in I_C$ means that node w is classified as class c ,and $\mathcal{F} \in \{\mathcal{M}_T, PDA, g\}$. We then measure the similarity using predefined Pearson correlation of all the feature saliency vectors in each label $c \in I_C$, so that we obtain a set of correlations between the instance within the class and across classes.

As the last step, we group the distance and correlations by class-pairs and take the average of the instance in each class pair. Therefore, we generate a $C \times C$ distance map for informative components and a $C \times C$ similarity map for node feature salience. The key features should have high consistency within the groups and contrastivity across different classes. Therefore, we examine the distance map and similarity map of the given graph and GNN classifier. If topology information contributes significantly to the GNN, the diagonal entries of distance maps should be small, while the other entries should be large. When node features are key factors for node labeling, the diagonal entries of distance maps should be large, while the other entries should be small. From those maps, not only we can examine if the detected informative components or the node features are meaningful for node classification, but also we find which classes have similar informative components or important node features.

7 Experiments

The topic that we addressed in this work of model-agnostic GNN post-hoc explaination was quite new. Few previous studies could be compared to our work. For example, Pope et al. [16] formulated GNN differently, which replied on adjacent matrix, and the attention method in [22] is model-specific. Therefore, those methods were not easily adopted. We mainly compared with the original MMI Mask proposed in GNNExplainer [22]. Furthermore, to our knowledge, graph feature importance disentangle pipeline is first proposed here. We simulated synthetic data and compared the results with human interpretation to demonstrate the feasibility of our methods. Note that, the color codes for all the figures below follow the on denoted in Fig. 3. The red node is the node we try to classify and explain.

7.1 Synthetic Data 1 - SynComp

Following [22], we generated a Barabási–Albert (BA) graph with 15 nodes and attached 10 five-node house-structure graph motifs are attached to random nodes, ended with 65 nodes in Fig. 3. We created a small graph for visualization purpose. However, the experiment results held for large graphs. Several natural and human-made systems, including the Internet, citation networks, social networks, and banking payment system can be thought to be approximately a BA graph, which certainly contains few nodes (hubs) with unusually high degree and a big number of nodes poorly connected. The edges connecting with different node pairs were assigned different weights denoted in Fig. 3 as well, where w was an edge weight we will discuss later. Then, we added noise to synthetic data by uniformly randomly adding $0.1N$ edges, where N was the number of nodes in the graph. In order to constrain the node label is determined by motif only, all the node feature $\mathbf{x}_i$ was designed the 2-D node attributes with the same constant.

We use $g = \bar{e}_{vu}\mathbf{m}_{vu}^{(l)}$ in Eq. (5). The parameters setting are *input_dim = 2, hidden_dim = 8, num_layers = 3 and epoch =300.* We randomly split 60% of the nodes for training and the rest for testing. GNN achieved 100% and 96.7% accuracy on training and testing dataset correspondingly. We performed informative component detection (kept top 6 edges) and compare them with human interpretation – the 'house shape,' which can be used as a reality check (Table 1). The GNNExplainer [22] performed worse in this case, because it ignored the weights on the edge so that the blue nodes were usually included into the informative subgraphs. In Fig. 4, we showed the explanation results of the node in the same place but has different topology structure (row a & b) and compared how eight weights affected the results (row a & d). We also showed the results generated by different methods (row a & c).

Table 1. Saliency component compared with 'house' shape.

(*Measuring on all the nodes in class 1 with* $w = 0.1$)

Method	MMI mask	GGD	GNNExplainer [22]
AUC	**0.932**	0.899	0.804

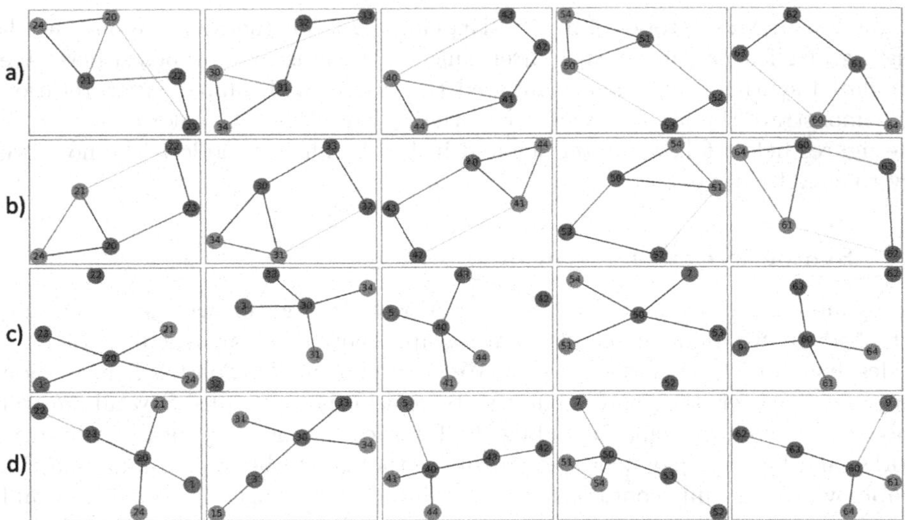

Fig. 4. Informative Components. Row a)-c), $w = 0.1$. Row a) is for the node in class one not connecting to class 0 nodes using MMI mask. Row b) is for the node in class one connecting to class 0 nodes using MMI mask. Row c) is for the node in class one connecting to class 0 nodes using GGD. Row d) is for the node in class one connecting to class 0 nodes using MMI mask, but $w = 2$.

We compared our proposed MMI mask edge with GNNExplainer [22] for weighed graph informative components detection. Given the pretrained GNN Φ, GNNExplainer learned a mask on edges and used a sigmoid function to bound each entry of the mask to $[0, 1]$. Then the mask weights were used as edge weights inputted to Φ.

Remind that we created SynComp dataset by generating a Barabasi–Albert (BA) graph with 15 nodes and attaching 10 five-node house-structure graph motifs to 10 random BA nodes. Each BA node belongs to class"0" and colored in blue. Each node on "house" belongs to class "1–3" based on its motif, and we define: the nodes on the house shoulder (colored in green) belong to class "1"; the nodes on the house bottom (colored in purple) belong to class "2"; and the node on house top (colored in orange) belong to class "3". We performed the detection of the informative components for all the nodes on the house shoulder, which connect to a BA graph node as well. We set the connection with a small edge weights $w = 0.1$ in SynComp dataset (shown in Fig. 5a) with all edge weights denoted), which meant the connection was not important compared to other edges.

The informative components detection results are shown in Fig. 5c) and d) for our proposed method and GNNExplainer correspondingly. We used human interpretation that a node on the house shoulder should belong to class "1" as ground truth. Therefore, the ground truth of the informative components to

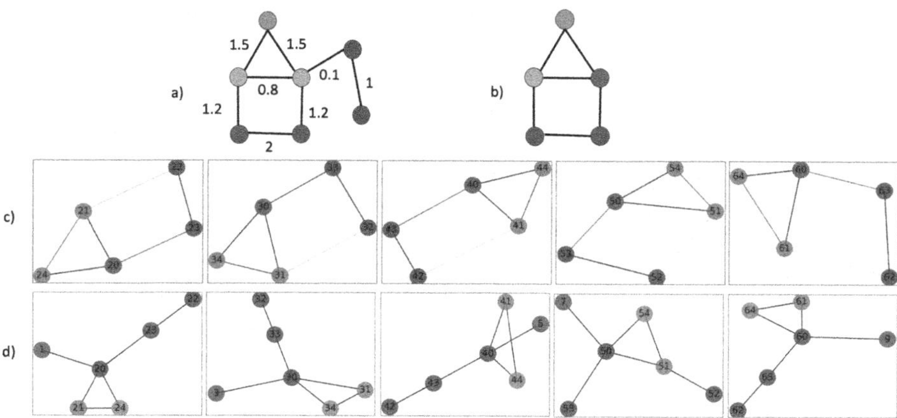

Fig. 5. Comparing with GNNExplainer [22] on SynComp dataset: a) the motif and corresponding edge weights; b) the human interpretation of the informative component to classify a node (colored in red) as class "1"; c) informative components of nodes classified as class "1" detected by our proposed MMI mask, which correctly detects the house structure; d) and informative components of nodes classified as class "1" detected by GNNExplainer [22], which wrongly includes the unimportant connection to BA graph. Node orders are denoted in c) and d). (Color figure online)

classify a node in class "1" should be a "house" structure (shown as Fig. 5b), the node we try to classify is colored in red). Because no matter the node connects to a BA node or not, once it is on the "house" shoulder, it belongs to class "1". Obviously, our methods could accurately detect the 'house' structure, while directly applied GNNExplainer on weighted graph resulted in wrongly including the edge to BA nodes, as GNNExplainer ignore edge weights.

7.2 Synthetic Data 2 - SynNode

In order to constrain the node labels were determined by node features only, we constructed a graph with BA topology and designed the 2D node attributes for each node on the graph. We generated a random normal distributed noise s_u for each node u, where $s_u \sim N(0, 0.1)$. The 1_{st} entry of the node attribute vector was assigned as s_u. For the 2_{nd} entry, the value is $s_u + (y_u + 1) * 0.2$, where y_u is the real label of u. We constructed a graph containing 60 nodes and randomly removed half of the edges to make it sparse. We used the same training model and methods in SynComp. For the quantitative measurement on node importance, we calculated the accuracy of classifying the 2_{nd} entry as the important features. Then we applied softmax function on the node feature importance vectors and calculated their mean square error (MSE) with $[0, 1]^\intercal$. Last, we theoretically listed the computation complexity estimation. We show the measurements on one example node in Table 2, where k is number of sampling times.

Table 2. Compare importance score with ground truth.

(Repeating 10 times, mean ± std)

Method	MMI mask	PDA	GGD
Accuracy	$100 \pm 0\%$	$100 \pm 0\%$	$100 \pm 0\%$
MSE	0.29 ± 0.03	$0.30 \pm 4e^{-4}$	0.17 ± 0.00
Time cost	Train	kTest	Test

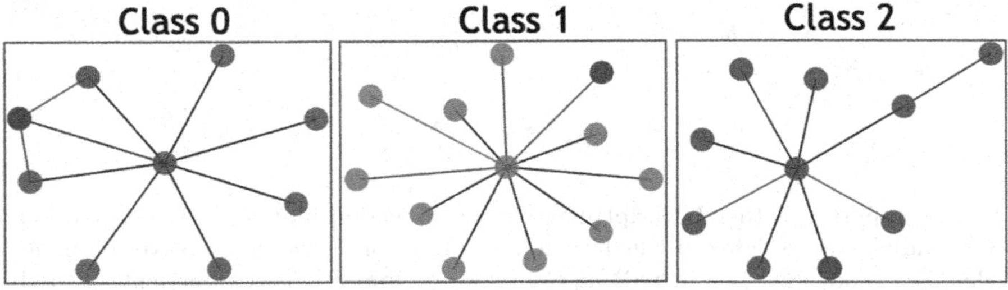

Fig. 6. Overlapping informative components detected by MMI mask and GGD for the examples of each class.

7.3 Citation Network Data

PubMed dataset [1] contains 19717 scientific publications pertaining to diabetes classified into one of three classes, "Diabetes Mellitus, Experimental," "Diabetes Mellitus Type 1", "Diabetes Mellitus Type 2". The citation network built on PubMed consists of 44338 links. Each publication in the dataset is described by a TF/IDF weighted word vector from a dictionary which consists of 500 unique words. Edge attribute is defined as a positive Pearson correlation of the node attributes. We randomly split 80% of the nodes as training data and rest as testing dataset. GNN used edge as filtering and $g = \bar{e}_{vu}\mathbf{m}_{vu}^{(l)}$. The parameters setting are *hidden_dim = 32, num_layers = 3 and epoch =1000.* Learning rate was initialized as 0.1, and decreased half per 100 epochs. We achieved an accuracy of 0.786 and 0.742 on training and testing data separately. We selected top 20 edges in both MMI and GGD, show the overlapping informative component detection results of an example in each class in Fig. 6. Obviously, we can find the pattern that those nodes were correctly classified since they connect to the nodes in the same class.

For the selected examples, we used above three node feature importance methods to vote the top 10 important features. Specifically, we first ranked the feature (keywords in the publications) importance by each method. Different nodes' feature might have different ranks by different methods. Then we summed the rank of each feature over the three methods. The smaller the summed rank number is, the more important the feature is. The top 10 ranked keywords are *"children", "type 2", "iddm", "type 1", "insulindepend", "noninsulindepend",*

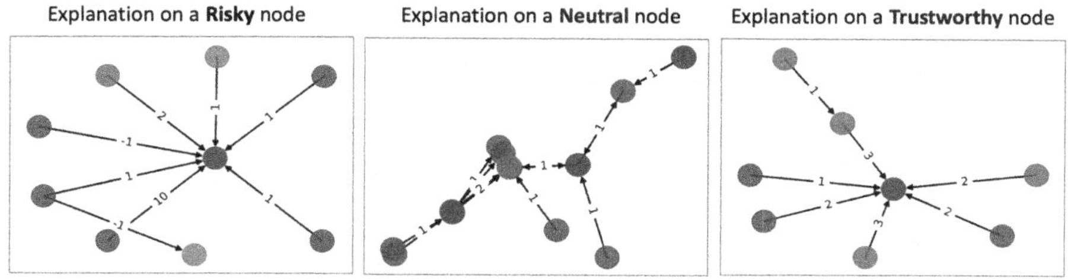

Fig. 7. Informative subgraph detected by MMI mask (showing the original rating scores on the edges).

"autoimmun", *"hypoglycemia"*, *"oral"*, *"fast"*. We consulted 2 diabetes experts and got the validation that *"type 2"*, *"iddm"*, *"noninsulindepend"* were directly related to publications of class "Diabetes Mellitus Type 2"; *"autoimmune"*, *"children"*, *"hypoglycemia"*, *"insulindepend"*, *"type 1"* are closely associated to class "Diabetes Mellitus Type 1"; and *"oral"*, *"fast"* are the common experment methods in class "Diabetes Mellitus, Experimental".

7.4 Bitcoin OTC Data

Bitcoin is a cryptocurrency that is used for trading anonymously. There is counterparty risk due to anonymity. We use Bitcoin dataset ([13]) collecting in one month, where Bitcoin users rate the level of trust to the users they made transactions to. The rating scales are from -10 to $+10$ (except for 0). According to OTC's guideline, the higher the rating, the more trustworthy. We labeled the users whose rating score had at list one negative score as risky; the users whose more than half received ratings were greater than one as trustworthy users; the users who did not receive any rating scores as an unknown group; and the rest of the users were assigned to the neural group. We chose the rating network data at a time point, which contained 1447 users, 5739 rating records. We renormalized the edge weights to $[0, 1]$ by $\tilde{e}_{ij} = e_{ij}/20 + 1/2$. Then we trained a GNN on 90% unknown, neutral and trustworthy node, 20% risky node, those nodes only, and perform classification on the rest of the nodes. We chose g as a *GRU* gate and the other settings are setting are *hidden_dim = 32, num_layers = 3 and epoch =1000.* Learning rate was initialized as 0.1, and decreased half per 100 epochs. We achieved accuracy 0.730 on the training dataset and 0.632 on the testing dataset. Finally, we showed the explanation result using MMI mask since it is more interpretable (see Fig. 7) and compared them with possible human reasoning ones. The pattern of the informative component of the risky node contains negative rating; the major ratings to a trustworthy node are greater than 1; and for the neutral node, it received lots of rating score 1. The informative components match the rules of how we label the nodes.

Using both real datasets, we measured consistency, contrastivity, and sparsity by selecting the top 4 important edges. The results on the two real datasets are listed in Table 3.

Table 3. Evaluate informative components.

(Average on 50 random correctly classified nodes in each class)

	Dataset	Consistency	Contrastivity	Sparsity
MMI	PubMed	2.00	1.99	0.022
	BitCoin	1.81	2.45	0.132
GGD	PubMed	2.14	2.07	0.049
	BitCoin	2.05	2.60	0.151

7.5 Feature Importance Disentanglement

We performed the disentanglement experiment on SynComp ($w = 0.1$), SynNode and Pubmed datasets, because these datasets have both node and edge features. For the Pubmed dataset, we randomly selected 50 correctly classified nodes in each class to calculate the stats. Since we had different explanation methods, we calculated the distance maps and similarity maps for each method and performed averaging over different methods. The distance map calculating on the subgraph

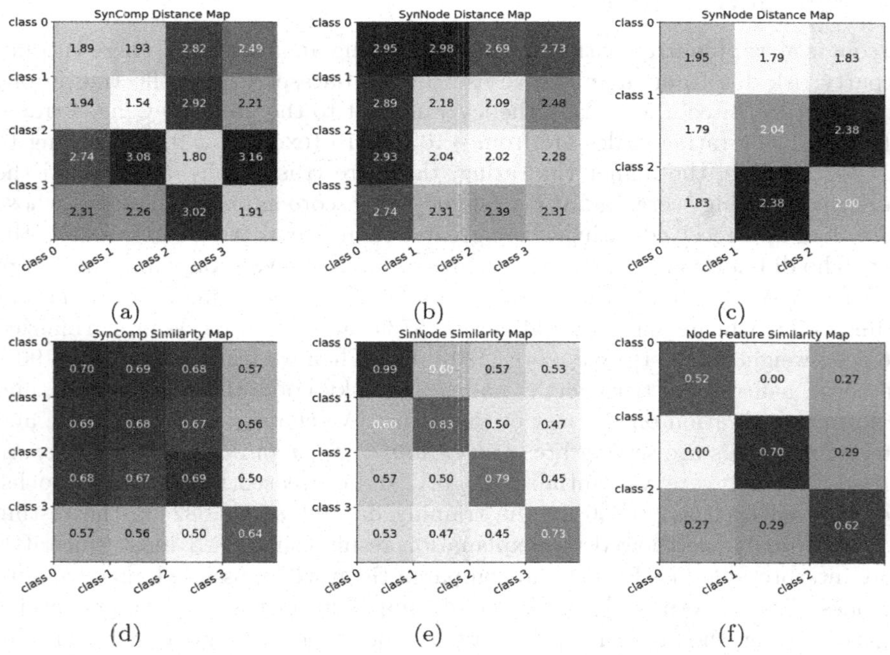

Fig. 8. Explanation disentangle using maps: (a) SynComp informative subgraphs distance map; (b) SynNode informative subgraphs distance map; (c) PubMed informative subgraphs distance map; (d) SynComp node salience similarity map; (e) SynNode node salience similarity map; (f) PubMed node salience similarity map.

with top 4 informative edges is shown in Fig. 8a and 8b. From the distance map, we can examine the connecting pattern is a key factor for classifying the nodes in SynComp, but not in SynNode. For the SynComp dataset, in-class distances were smaller than cross-class distances. Whereas, the distance map for SynNode and PubMed did not contain the pattern. Also, from the distance map, we could see the node in class 2 and 3 had the most distinguishable informative component, but classes 0 and 1's are similar. For the similarity maps (Fig. 8d, Fig. 8e, and 8f), SynNode and PubMed datasets had much more significant similarities within the class compared with the similarities across the classes. Combining distance maps and similarity maps for each dataset, we could understand that topology was the critical factor for SynComp dataset, and node feature was the key factor for SynNode and PubMed dataset for node classification in GNNs.

8 Conclusion

In this work, we formulate the explanation on weighted graph features used in GNN for node classification task as two perspectives: *Components Detection* and *Node Feature Importance*, that can provide subjective and comprehensive explanations of feature patterns used in GNN. We also propose evaluation metrics to validate the explanation results and a pipeline to find whether topology information or node features contribute more to the node classification task. The explanations may help debugging, feature engineering, informing human decision-making, building trust, increase transparency of using graph neural networks, among others. Our future work will include extending the explanation to graphs with multi-dimensional edge features and explaining different graph learning tasks, such as link prediction and graph classification.

References

1. Pubmed dataset downloading address. https://linqs.soe.ucsc.edu/data. Accessed 11 Aug 2019
2. Abu-Aisheh, Z., Raveaux, R., Ramel, J.Y., Martineau, P.: An exact graph edit distance algorithm for solving pattern recognition problems (2015)
3. Adadi, A., Berrada, M.: Peeking inside the black-box: a survey on explainable artificial intelligence (XAI). IEEE Access **6**, 52138–52160 (2018)
4. Baldassarre, F., Azizpour, H.: Explainability techniques for graph convolutional networks. arXiv preprint arXiv:1905.13686 (2019)
5. Battaglia, P.W., et al.: Relational inductive biases, deep learning, and graph networks. arXiv preprint arXiv:1806.01261 (2018)
6. Cover, T.M., Thomas, J.A.: Elements of Information Theory. Wiley, Hoboken (2012)
7. Goebel, R., et al.: Explainable AI: the new 42? In: Holzinger, A., Kieseberg, P., Tjoa, A.M., Weippl, E. (eds.) CD-MAKE 2018. LNCS, vol. 11015, pp. 295–303. Springer, Cham (2018). https://doi.org/10.1007/978-3-319-99740-7_21
8. Gong, L., Cheng, Q.: Exploiting edge features for graph neural networks. In: Proceedings of the IEEE Conference on Computer Vision and Pattern Recognition, pp. 9211–9219 (2019)

9. Gunning, D.: Explainable artificial intelligence (XAI). Defense Advanced Research Projects Agency (DARPA), nd Web 2, 2 (2017)
10. Hamilton, W., Ying, Z., Leskovec, J.: Inductive representation learning on large graphs. In: Advances in Neural Information Processing Systems, pp. 1024–1034 (2017)
11. Holzinger, A., Carrington, A., Müller, H.: Measuring the quality of explanations: the system causability scale (SCS). KI - Künstl. Intell. **34**(2), 193–198 (2020). https://doi.org/10.1007/s13218-020-00636-z
12. Kipf, T.N., Welling, M.: Semi-supervised classification with graph convolutional networks. arXiv preprint arXiv:1609.02907 (2016)
13. Kumar, S., Hooi, B., Makhija, D., Kumar, M., Faloutsos, C., Subrahmanian, V.: Rev2: fraudulent user prediction in rating platforms. In: Proceedings of the Eleventh ACM International Conference on Web Search and Data Mining, pp. 333–341. ACM (2018)
14. Mittelstadt, B., Russell, C., Wachter, S.: Explaining explanations in AI. In: Proceedings of the Conference on Fairness, Accountability, and Transparency, pp. 279–288 (2019)
15. Nielsen, F.: A family of statistical symmetric divergences based on Jensen's inequality. arXiv preprint arXiv:1009.4004 (2010)
16. Pope, P.E., Kolouri, S., Rostami, M., Martin, C.E., Hoffmann, H.: Explainability methods for graph convolutional neural networks. In: Proceedings of the IEEE Conference on Computer Vision and Pattern Recognition, pp. 10772–10781 (2019)
17. Schlichtkrull, M., Kipf, T.N., Bloem, P., van den Berg, R., Titov, I., Welling, M.: Modeling relational data with graph convolutional networks. In: Gangemi, A., et al. (eds.) ESWC 2018. LNCS, vol. 10843, pp. 593–607. Springer, Cham (2018). https://doi.org/10.1007/978-3-319-93417-4_38
18. Shang, C., et al.: Edge attention-based multi-relational graph convolutional networks. arXiv preprint arXiv:1802.04944 (2018)
19. Simonyan, K., Vedaldi, A., Zisserman, A.: Deep inside convolutional networks: Visualising image classification models and saliency maps (2013)
20. Veličković, P., et al.: Graph attention networks. In: ICLR (2018)
21. Yang, H., et al.: Interpretable multimodality embedding of cerebral cortex using attention graph network for identifying bipolar disorder. In: Shen, D., et al. (eds.) MICCAI 2019. LNCS, vol. 11766, pp. 799–807. Springer, Cham (2019). https://doi.org/10.1007/978-3-030-32248-9_89
22. Ying, R., Bourgeois, D., You, J., Zitnik, M., Leskovec, J.: GNN explainer: a tool for post-hoc explanation of graph neural networks. arXiv preprint arXiv:1903.03894 (2019)
23. Zhang, Z., Cui, P., Zhu, W.: Deep learning on graphs: a survey (2018)
24. Zhou, J., et al.: Graph neural networks: a review of methods and applications (2018)

Explainable Reinforcement Learning: A Survey

Erika Puiutta(✉) and Eric M. S. P. Veith

OFFIS – Institute for Information Technology,
Escherweg 2, 26121 Oldenburg, Germany
{erika.puiutta,eric.veith}@offis.de

Abstract. Explainable Artificial Intelligence (XAI), i.e., the development of more transparent and interpretable AI models, has gained increased traction over the last few years. This is due to the fact that, in conjunction with their growth into powerful and ubiquitous tools, AI models exhibit one detrimental characteristic: a performance-transparency trade-off. This describes the fact that the more complex a model's inner workings, the less clear it is how its predictions or decisions were achieved. But, especially considering Machine Learning (ML) methods like Reinforcement Learning (RL) where the system learns autonomously, the necessity to understand the underlying reasoning for their decisions becomes apparent. Since, to the best of our knowledge, there exists no single work offering an overview of Explainable Reinforcement Learning (XRL) methods, this survey attempts to address this gap. We give a short summary of the problem, a definition of important terms, and offer a classification and assessment of current XRL methods. We found that a) the majority of XRL methods function by mimicking and simplifying a complex model instead of designing an inherently simple one, and b) XRL (and XAI) methods often neglect to consider the human side of the equation, not taking into account research from related fields like psychology or philosophy. Thus, an interdisciplinary effort is needed to adapt the generated explanations to a (non-expert) human user in order to effectively progress in the field of XRL and XAI in general.

Keywords: Machine learning · Explainable · Reinforcement Learning · Human-computer interaction · Interpretable

1 Introduction

Over the past decades, AI has become ubiquitous in many areas of our everyday lives. Especially Machine Learning (ML) as one branch of AI has numerous fields of application, be it transportation [57], advertisement [46], or medicine [38]. Unfortunately, the more powerful and flexible those models are, the more opaque they become, essentially making them black boxes (see Fig. 1). This trade-off is

Published by Springer Nature Switzerland AG 2020
A. Holzinger et al. (Eds.): CD-MAKE 2020, LNCS 12279, pp. 77–95, 2020.
https://doi.org/10.1007/978-3-030-57321-8_5

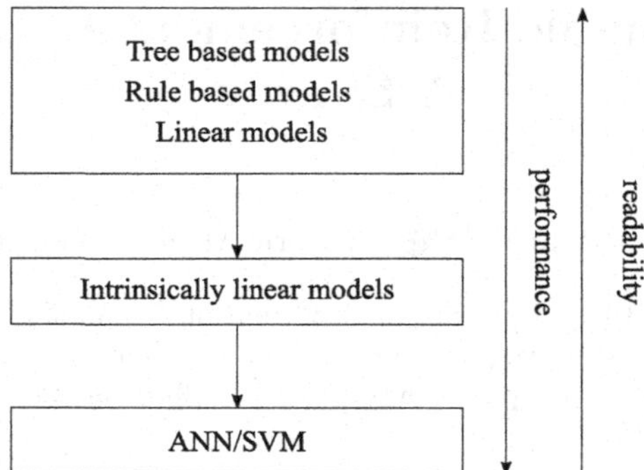

Fig. 1. Schematic representation of the performance-readability trade-off. Simpler, linear models are easy to understand and interpret, but suffer from a lack of performance, while non-linear, more flexible models are too complex to be understood easily. Adopted from Martens et al. [41].

referred to by different terms in the literature, e.g. readability-performance trade-off [12], accuracy-comprehensibility trade-off [16], or accuracy-interpretability trade-off [49]. This work aims to, first, establish the need for eXplainable Artificial Intelligence (XAI) in general and eXplainable Reinforcement Learning (XRL) specifically. After that, the general concept of RL is briefly explained and the most important terms related to XAI are defined. Then, a classification of XAI models is presented and selected XRL models are sorted into these categories. Since there already is an abundance of sources on XAI but less so about XRL specifically, the focus of this work lies on providing information about and presenting sample methods of XRL models[1]. Thus, we present one method for each category in more detail and give a critical evaluation over the existing XRL methods. We will especially emphasize the need for XAI/XRL models that are adapted to a human (non-expert) end-user since that is what many XRL models are lacking but which we deem crucial.

1.1 The Importance of Explainability

Why is explainability so crucial? First, there is one obvious psychology-related reason: ‘if the users do not trust a model or a prediction, they will not use it’ [48, p. 1]. Trust can be defined as ‘the attitude that an agent will help achieve an individual’s goals in a situation characterized by uncertainty and vulnerability’ [32] and is an essential prerequisite of using a model or system [12,28]. Bearing in mind the fact that transparency has been identified as one key component both in increasing users’ trust [18,67], as well as users’ acceptance of a system [24], the interest in ‘trustworthy AI’ is not surprising, especially in the context

[1] Please note that, while there is a distinction between Reinforcement Learning and Deep Reinforcement Learning (DRL), for the sake of simplicity, we will refer to both as just Reinforcement Learning going forward.

of uncertainty [66]. Thus, in order to confidently use a system, it needs to be trusted, and in order to be trusted, it needs to be transparent and its decisions need to be justifiable (for a formal definition of transparency and related terms, see Sect. 1.3).

Second, AI technologies have become an essential part in almost all domains of Cyber-Physical Systems (CPSs). Reasons include the thrive for increased efficiency, business model innovations, or the necessity to accommodate volatile parts of today's critical infrastructures (e.g. a high share of renewable energy sources). In time, AI technologies evolved from being an additional input to an otherwise soundly defined control system, over fully decentralized, but still rule-governed systems (e.g. the *Universal Smart Grid Agent* [60]), to a system where all behavior originates from ML (e.g. *AlphaGo Zero* and *MuZero* [51]). For CPS analysis and operation, however, Adversarial Resilience Learning (ARL) has emerged as a novel methodology based on DRL [15,59]. It is specifically designed to analyse and control critical infrastructures; obviously, explainability is tantamount here.

There is also a legal component to be considered; the EU General Data Protection Regulation (GDPR) [14], which came into effect in May 2018, aims to ensure a 'right to explanation' [19, p. 1] concerning automated decision-making and profiling. It states that '[...] such processing should subject to suitable safeguards, which should include [...] the right to obtain human intervention [...] [and] an explanation of the decision reached after such assessment' [14, recital 71]. Additionally, the European Commission set out an AI strategy with transparency and accountability as important principles to be respected [55], and in their Guidelines on trustworthy AI [56] they state seven key requirements, with transparency and accountability as two of them.

Finally, there are important practical reasons to consider; despite the increasing efficiency and versatility of AI, its incomprehensibility reduces its usefulness, since 'incomprehensible decision-making can still be effective, but its effectiveness does not mean that it cannot be faulty' [33, p. 1]. For example, in [54], neural nets successfully learnt to classify pictures but could be led to misclassification by (to humans) nearly imperceptible perturbations, and in [45], deep neural nets classified unrecognizable images with >99% certainty. This shows that a high level of effectiveness (under standard conditions) or even confidence does not imply that the decisions are correct or based on appropriately-learnt data. There exists a number of 'AI explainability toolkits'[2] that have common explainability methods implemented and enable their (easy) use with a pre-built framework, but, as far as we know, there is none specifically for RL.

Bearing this in mind, and considering the fact that, nowadays, AI can act increasingly autonomous, explaining and justifying the decisions is now more crucial than ever, especially in the domain of RL where an agent learns by itself, without human interaction.

[2] E.g. the AI Explainability 360 (AIX360) as the currently most comprehensive one [4] (see also for a list of other toolkits).

1.2 Reinforcement Learning

Reinforcement Learning is a trial-and-error learning algorithm in which an autonomous agent tries to find the optimal solution to a problem through automated learning [52]. It is usually introduced as a Markov Decision Process (MDP) if it satisfies the Markov property: the next state depends only on the current state and the agent's action(s), not on past states [30].

The learning process is initiated by an agent randomly performing an action which leads to a certain environmental state. This state has a reward assigned to it depending on how desirable this outcome is, set by the designer of the task. The algorithm will then learn a policy, i.e., an action-state-relation, in order to maximize the cumulative reward and be able to select the most optimal action in each situation. For more information on RL, see also [34,52].

1.3 Definition of Important Terms

As already mentioned in Sect. 1, the more complex a systems becomes, the less obvious its inner workings become. Additionally, there is no uniform term for this trade-off in the literature; XAI methods use an abundance of related, but distinct terms like transparency, reachability, etc. This inconsistency can be due to one or both of the following reasons: a) different terms are used in the same sense due to a lack of official definition of these terms, or b) different terms are used because the authors (subjectively) draw a distinction between them, without an official accounting of these differences. In any case, a uniform understanding and definition of what it means if a method is described as 'interpretable' or 'transparent' is important in order to clarify the potential, capacity and intention of a model. This is not an easy task, since there is no unique definition for the different terms to be found in the literature; even for 'interpretability', the concept which is most commonly used, 'the term [...] holds no agreed upon meaning, and yet machine learning conferences frequently publish papers which wield the term in a quasi-mathematical way' [35]. In Doshi-Velez and Kim [11, p. 2], interpretability is 'the ability to explain or to present in understandable terms to a human', however, according to Kim et al. [31, p. 7] 'a method is interpretable if a user can correctly and efficiently predict the method's result'. Some authors use transparency as a synonym for interpretability [35], some use comprehensibility as a synonym [16], then again others draw a distinction between the two [10] (for more information on how the different terms are used in the literature, we refer the reader to [8,10,11,16,31,35,36,44]). If we tackle this issue in a more fundamental way, we can look at the definition of 'to interpret' or 'interpretation'. The Oxford Learners Dictionary[3] defines it as follows:

- to explain the meaning of something
- to decide that something has a particular meaning and to understand it in this way
- to translate one language into another as it is spoken

[3] https://www.oxfordlearnersdictionaries.com/.

- the particular way in which something is understood or explained

Seeing that, according to the definition, interpretation contains an explanation, we can look at the definition for 'to explain'/'explanation':

- to tell somebody about something in a way that makes it easy to understand
- to give a reason, or be a reason, for something
- a statement, fact, or situation that tells you why something happened
- a statement or piece of writing that tells you how something works or makes something easier to understand

Both definitions share the notion of conveying the reason and meaning of something in order to make someone understand, but while an explanation is focused on *what* to explain, an interpretation has the additional value of considering *how* to explain something; it translates and conveys the information in a way that is more easily understood. And that is, in our opinion, essential in the frame of XAI/XRL: not only extracting the necessary information, but also presenting it in an appropriate manner, translating it from the 'raw data' into something humans and especially laypersons can understand.

So, because we deem a shared consensus on the nomenclature important, we suggest the use of this one uniform term, *interpretability*, to refer to the ability to not only extract or generate explanations for the decisions of the model, but also to present this information in a way that is understandable by human (non-expert) users to, ultimately, enable them to predict a model's behaviour.

2 XAI Taxonomy

While there are slight differences between the different taxonomy approaches [2,4,7], XAI methods can be broadly categorized based on two factors; first, based on when the information is extracted, the method can be intrinsic or post-hoc, and second, the scope can be either global or local (see Fig. 2, and Fig. 3 for examples).

Global and local interpretability refer to the scope of the explanation; global models explain the entire, general model behaviour, while local models offer explanations for a specific decision [43]. Global models try to explain the whole logic of a model by inspecting the structures of the model [2,13]. Local explanations try to answer the question: 'Why did the model make a certain prediction/decision for an instance/for a group of instances?' [2,43]. They also try to identify the contributions of each feature in the input towards a specific output [13]. Additionally, global interpretability techniques lead to users trusting a model, while local techniques lead to trusting a prediction [13].

Intrinsic vs. post-hoc interpretability depend on the time when the explanation is extracted/generated; An intrinsic model is a ML model that is constructed to be inherently interpretable or self-explanatory at the time of training by restricting the complexity of the model [13]. Decision trees, for example, have a simple structure and can be easily understood [43]. Post-hoc interpretability, in

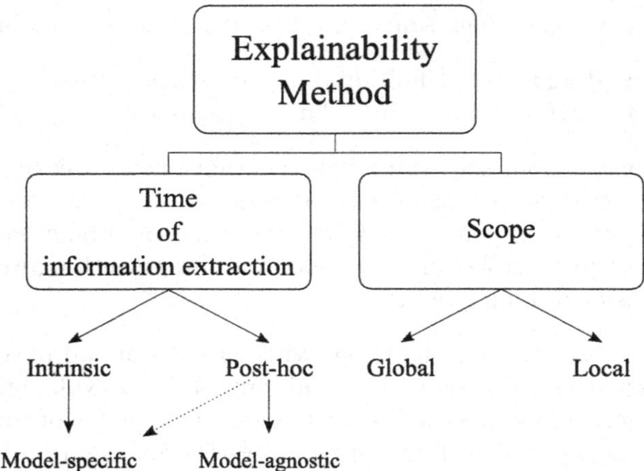

Fig. 2. A pseudo ontology of XAI methods taxonomy. Adapted from Adadi and Berrada [2].

contrast, is achieved by analyzing the model after training by creating a second, simpler model, to provide explanations for the original model [13,43]. Surrogate models or saliency maps are examples for this type [2]. Post-hoc interpretation models can be applied to intrinsic interpretation models, but not necessarily vice versa. Just like the models themselves, these interpretability models also suffer from a transparency-accuracy-trade-off; intrinsic models usually offer accurate explanations, but, due to their simplicity, their prediction performance suffers. Post-hoc interpretability models, in contrast, usually keep the accuracy of the original model intact, but are harder to derive satisfying and simple explanations from [13].

Another distinction, which usually coincides with the classification into intrinsic and post-hoc interpretability, is the classification into model-specific or model-agnostic. Techniques are model-specific if they are limited to a specific model or model class [43], and they are model-agnostic if they can be used on any model [43]. As you can also see in Fig. 2, intrinsic models are model-specific, while post-hoc interpretability models are usually model-agnostic.

Adadi and Berrada [2] offer an overview of common explainability techniques and their rough (i.e., neither mutually exclusive nor exhaustive) classifications into these categories. In Sect. 3, we follow their example and provide classifications for a list of selected XRL method papers.

3 Non-exhaustive List of XRL Methods

A literature review was conducted using the database Google Scholar. Certain combinations of keywords were used to select papers; first, 'explainable reinforcement learning', and 'XRL' together with 'reinforcement learning' and 'machine

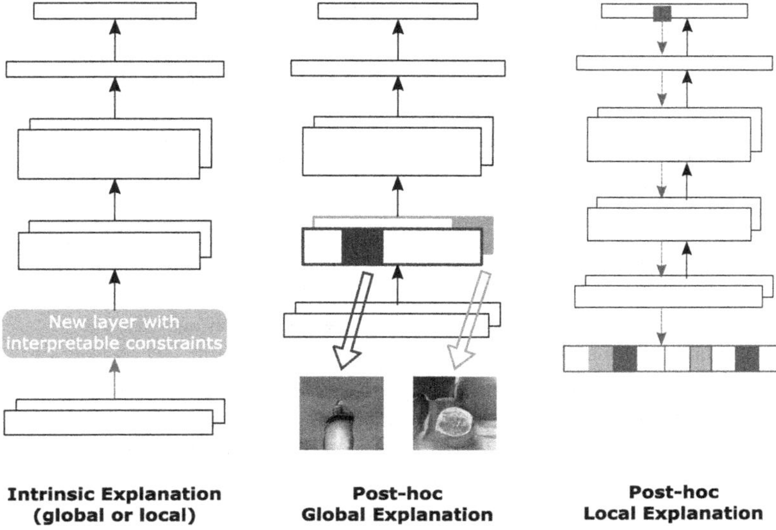

Fig. 3. An illustration of global vs. local, and intrinsic vs. post-hoc interpretable machine learning techniques, with a deep neural network as an example. On the left, the model and the layers' constraints are built in a way that is inherently interpretable (intrinsic interpretability). The middle and right column show post-hoc interpretability, achieved by a global and local explanation, respectively. The global explanation explains the different representations corresponding to the different layers in general, while the local explanation illustrates the contribution of the different input features to a certain output. Adopted from Du et al. [13].

learning' were used. Then, we substituted 'explainable' for common variations used in literature like 'explainable', 'transparent', and 'understandable'. We then scanned the papers for relevance and consulted their citations and reference lists for additional papers. Because we only wanted to focus on current methods, we restricted the search to papers from 2010–2020. Table 1 shows the list of selected papers and their classification according to Sect. 2 based on our understanding.

For a more extensive demonstration of the different approaches, we chose the latest paper of each quadrant[4] and explain them in more detail in the following sections as an example for the different XRL methods.

[4] With the exception of method C in Sect. 3.3, where we present a Linear Model U-Tree method although another paper with a different, but related method was published slightly later. See the last paragraph of that section for our reasoning for this decision.

Table 1. Selected XRL methods and their categorization according to the taxonomy described in Sect. 2.

Time	Scope	
	Global	Local
Intrinsic	• **PIRL** (Verma et al. [61]) • Fuzzy RL policies (Hein et al. [22])	• **Hierarchical Policies** (Shu et al. [53])
Post-hoc	• Genetic Programming (Hein et al. [23])	
	• Reward Decomposition (Juozapaitis et al. [29])	• Interestingness Elements (Sequeira and Gervasio [52])
	• Expected Consequences (van der Waa et al. [62])	• Autonomous Self-Explanation (Fukuchi et al. [17])
	• Soft Decision Trees (Coppens et al. [9])	• **Structural Causal Model** (Madumal et al. [40])
	• Deep Q-Networks (Zahavy et al. [64])	• Complementary RL (Lee [33])
	• Autonomous Policy Explanation (Hayes and Shah [21])	• Expected Consequences (van der Waa et al. [62])
	• Policy Distillation (Rusu et al. [50])	• Soft Decision Trees (Coppens et al. [9])
	• **Linear Model U-Trees** (Liu et al. [37])	• **Linear Model U-Trees** (Liu et al. [37])

Notes. Methods in bold are presented in detail in this work.

3.1 Method A: Programmatically Interpretable Reinforcement Learning

Verma et al. [61] have developed 'PIRL', a Programmatically Interpretable Reinforcement Learning framework, as an alternative to DRL. In DRL, the policies are represented by neural networks, making them very hard (if not impossible) to interpret. The policies in PIRL, on the other hand, while still mimicking the ones from the DRL model, are represented using a high-level, human-readable programming language. Here, the problem stays the same as in traditional RL (i.e., finding a policy that maximises the long-term reward), but in addition, they restrict the vast amount of target policies with the help of a *(policy) sketch*. To find these policies, they employ a framework which was inspired by imitation learning, called *Neurally Directed Program Search (NDPS)*. This framework first uses DRL to compute a policy which is used as a neural 'oracle' to direct the policy search for a policy that is as close as possible to the neural oracle. Doing this, the performances of the resulting policies are not as high than the ones from the DRL, but they are still satisfactory and, additionally, more easily interpretable. They evaluate this framework by comparing its performance with, among others, a traditional DRL framework in The Open Racing Car Simulator (TORCS) [63].

Here, the controller has to set five parameters (acceleration, brake, clutch, gear and steering of the car) to steer a car around a race track as fast as possible. Their results show that, while the DRL leads to quicker lap time, the NDPS still outperforms this for several reasons: it shows much smoother driving (i.e., less steering actions) and is less perturbed by noise and blocked sensors. It also is easier to interpret and is better at generalization, i.e., it performs better in situations (in this case, tracks) not encountered during training than a DRL model. Concerning restrictions of this method, it is worth noting that the authors only considered environments with symbolic inputs, not perceptual, in their experiments. They also only considered deterministic policies, not stochastic policies.

3.2 Method B: Hierarchical and Interpretable Skill Acquisition in Multi-task Reinforcement Learning

Shu et al. [53] proposed a new framework for multi-task RL using hierarchical policies that addressed the issue of solving complex tasks that require different skills and are composed of several (simpler) subtasks. It is based on and extends multi-task RL with modular policy design through a two-layer hierarchical policy [3] by incorporating less assumptions, and, thus, less restrictions. They trained and evaluated their model with object manipulation tasks in a Minecraft game setting (e.g. finding, getting, or stacking blocks of a certain color), employing advantage actor-critic as policy optimization using off-policy learning. The model is hierarchical because each top-level policy (e.g., 'stack x') consists of several lower levels of actions ('find x' → 'get x' → 'put x', see also Fig. 4). The novelty of this method is the fact that each task is described by a human instruction (e.g. 'stack blue'), and agents can only access learnt skills through these descriptions, making its policies and decisions inherently human-interpretable.

Additionally, a key idea of their framework is that a complex task could be decomposed into several simpler subtasks. If these sub-tasks could be fulfilled by employing an already learnt 'base policy', no new skill had to be learnt; otherwise, it would learn a new skill and perform a different, novel action. To boost efficiency and accuracy, the framework also incorporated a stochastic temporal grammar model that was used to model temporal relationships and priorities of tasks (e.g., before stacking a block on top of another block, you must first obtain said block).

The resulting framework could efficiently learn hierarchical policies and representations in multi-task RL, only needing weak human supervision during training to decide which skills to learn. Compared to a flat policy that directly maps the state and instruction to an action, the hierarchical model showed a higher learning efficiency, could generalize well in new environments, and was inherently interpretable.

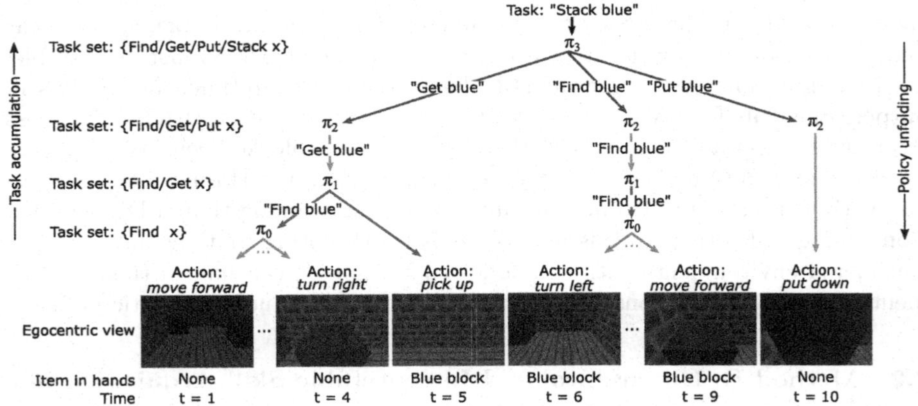

Fig. 4. Example for the multi-level hierarchical policy for the task to stack two blue boxes on top of each other. The top-level policy (π_3, in red) encompasses the high-level plan 'get blue' → 'find blue' → 'put blue'. Each step (i.e., arrow) either initiates another policy (marked by a different color) or directly executes an action. Adopted from Shu et al. [53]. (Color figure online)

3.3 Method C: Toward Interpretable Deep Reinforcement Learning with Linear Model U-Trees

In Liu et al. [37], a mimic learning framework based on stochastic gradient descent is introduced. This framework approximates the predictions of an accurate, but complex model by mimicking the model's Q-function using Linear Model U-Trees (LMUTs). LMUTs are an extension of Continuous U-Trees (CUTs) which were developed to approximate continuous functions [58]. The difference between CUTs and LMUTs is that, instead of constants, LMUTs have a linear model at each leaf node which also improves its generalization ability. They also generally have fewer leaves and are therefore simpler and more easily understandable. The novelty of this method lies in the fact that other tree representations used for interpretations were only developed for supervised learning, not for DRL.

The framework can be used to analyze the importance of input features, extract rules, and calculate 'super-pixels' ('contiguous patch[es] of similar pixels' [48, p. 1]) in image inputs (see Table 2 and Fig. 5 for an example). It has two approaches to generate data and mimic the Q-function; the first one is an *experience training setting* which records and generates data during the training process for batch training. It records the state-action pairs and the resulting Q-values as 'soft supervision labels' [37, p. 1] during training. In cases where the mimic learning model cannot be applied to the training process, the second approach can be used: *active play setting*, which generates mimic data by applying the mature DRL to interact with the environment. Here, an online algorithm is required which uses stochastic gradient descent to dynamically update the linear models as more data is generated.

Table 2. Examples of feature influences in the Mountain Car and Cart Pole scenario, extracted by the LMUTs in Liu et al. [37]

	Feature	Influence
Mountain Car	Velocity	376.86
	Position	171.28
Cart Pole	Pole angle	30541.54
	Cart velocity	8087.68
	Cart position	7171.71
	Pole velocity at tip	2953.73

a)

velocity ε [-∞, -0.018]
position ε [-0.86, -0.83]
Q =< -25.2, -26.2,-28.0>

b)

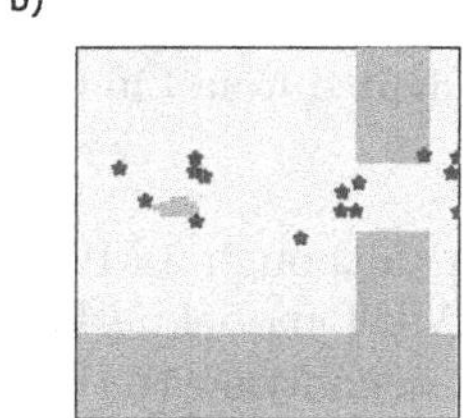

Fig. 5. Examples of a) rule extraction, and b) super-pixels extracted by the LMUTs in Liu et al. [37]. a) Extracted rules for the mountain Cart scenario. Values at the top are the range of velocity and position and a Q vector ($Q_{move\_left}, Q_{no\_push}, Q_{move\_right}$) representing the average Q-value). In this example, the cart is moving to the left to the top of the hill. The car should be pushed left (Q_{move_left} is highest) to prepare for the final rush to the target on the right side. b) Super-pixels for the Flappy Bird scenario, marked by red stars. This is the first of four sequential pictures where the focus lies on the location of the bird and obstacles (i.e., pipes). In later pictures the focus would shift towards the bird's location and velocity.

They evaluate the framework in three benchmark environments: Mountain Car, Cart Pole, and Flappy Bird, all simulated by the OpenAI Gym toolkit [6]. Mountain Car and Cart Pole have a discrete action space and a continuous feature space, while Flappy Bird has two discrete actions and four consecutive images as inputs which result in 80 × 80 pixels each, so 6400 features. The LMUT method is compared to five other tree methods: a CART regression tree [39], M5 trees [47] with regression tree options (M5-RT) and with model tree options (M5-MT), and Fast Incremental Model Trees (FIMT, [27]) in the basic version, and in the advanced version with adaptive filters (FIMT-AF). The two parameters *fidelity* (how well the predictions of the mimic model match those from the mimicked model) and *play performance* (how well the average return in the mimic model matches that of the mimicked model) are used as evaluation metrics. Compared to CART and FIMT (-AF), the LMUT model showed higher fidelity with fewer leaves. For the Cart Pole environment, LMUT showed the highest fidelity, while the M5 trees showed higher performance for the other two

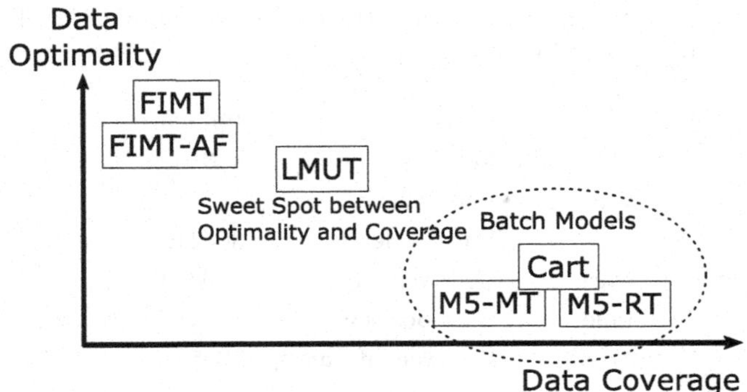

Fig. 6. Placement of the different tree models on the axes data coverage vs. data optimality. Adapted from Liu et al. [37].

environments, although LMUT was comparable. Concerning the play performance, the LMUT model performs best out of all the models. This was likely due to the fact that, contrary to the LMUTs, the M5 and CART trees fit equally over the whole training experience which includes sub-optimal actions in the beginning of training, while the FIMT only adapts to the most recent input and thus cannot build linear models appropriately. In their work, this is represented by sorting the methods on an axis between 'data coverage' (when the mimic model matches the mimicked model on a large section of the state space) and 'data optimality' (when it matches the states most important for performance) with the LMUT at the, as they call it, 'sweet spot between optimality and coverage' (see also Fig. 6).

There is a similar, newer tree method that uses Soft Decision Trees (SDTs) to extract DRL polices [9]. This method was not presented in this paper because, for one thing, it is less versatile (not offering rule extraction, for example), and for another, it was not clear whether the SDTs actually adequately explained the underlying, mimicked policy for their used benchmark.

3.4 Method D: Explainable RL Through a Causal Lens

According to Madumal et al. [40], not only is it important for a RL agent to explain itself and its actions, but also to bear in mind the human user at the receiving end of this explanation. Thus, they took advantage of the prominent theory that humans develop and deploy causal models to explain the world around them, and have adapted a structural causal model (SCM) based on Halpern [20] to mimic this for model-free RL. SCMs represent the world with random exogenous (external) and endogenous (internal) variables, some of which might exert a causal influence over others. These influences can be described with a set of structural equations.

Since Madumal et al. [40] focused on providing explanations for an agent's behaviour based on the knowledge of how its actions influence the environment, they extend the SCM to include the agent's actions, making it an *action influence model*. More specifically, they offer 'actuals' and 'counterfactuals', that is, their explanations answer 'Why?' as well as 'Why not?' questions (e.g. 'Why (not) action A?'). This is noticeable because, contrary to most XAI models, it not only considers actual events occurred, but also hypothetical events that did not happen, but could have.

In more detail, the process of generating explanations consists of three phases; first, an action influence model in the form of a directed acyclic graph (DAG) is required (see Fig. 7 for an example). Next, since it is difficult to uncover the true structural equations describing the relationships between the variables, this problem is circumvented by only approximating the equations so that they are exact enough to simulate the counterfactuals. In Madumal et al. [40], this is done by multivariate regression models during the training of the RL agent, but any regression learner can be used. The last phase is generating the explanations, more specifically, *minimally complete contrastive explanations*. This means that, first, instead of including the vectors of variables of ALL nodes in the explanation, it only includes the absolute minimum variables necessary. Moreover, it explains the actual (e.g. 'Why action A?') by simulating the counterfactual (e.g. 'Why not action B?') through the structural equations and finding the differences between the two. The explanation can then be obtained through a simple NLP template (for an example of an explanation, again, see Fig. 7).

Madumal et al. [40]'s evaluations of the action influence model show promising results; in a comparison between six RL benchmark domains measuring accuracy ('Can the model accurately predict what the agent will do next?') and performance (training time), the model shows reasonable task prediction accuracy and negligible training time. In a human study, comparing the action influence model with two different models that have learnt how to play Starcraft II (a real-time strategy game), they assessed task prediction by humans, explanation satisfaction, and trust in the model. Results showed that the action influence model performs significantly better for task prediction and explanation satisfaction, but not for trust. The authors propose that, in order to increase trust, further interaction might be needed. In the future, advancements to the model can be made including extending the model to continuous domains or targeting the explanations to users with different levels of knowledge.

4 Discussion

In this paper, inspired by the current interest in and demand for XAI, we focused on a particular field of AI: Reinforcement Learning. Since most XAI methods are tailored for supervised learning, we wanted to give an overview of methods employed only on RL algorithms, since, to the best of our knowledge, there is no work present at the current point in time addressing this.

First, we gave an overview over XAI, its importance and issues, and explained related terms. We stressed the importance of a uniform terminology and have thus suggested and defined a term to use from here on out. The focus, however,

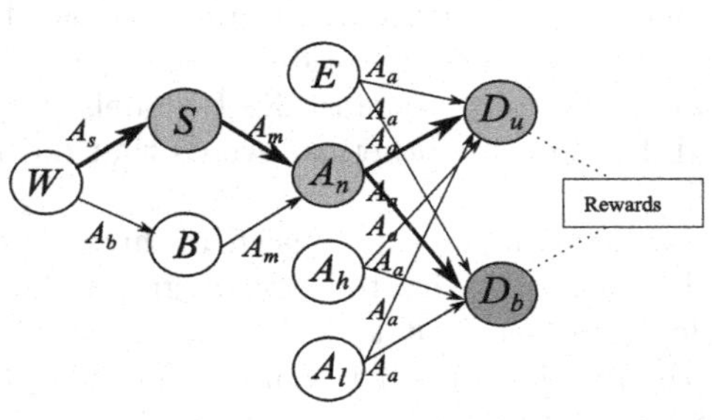

State variables:
W - Worker number
S - Supply depot number
B - Barracks number
E - Enemy location
A_n - Ally unit number
A_h - Ally unit health
A_l - Ally unit location
D_u - Destroyed units
D_b - Destroyed buildings
Actions:
A_s - Build supply depot
A_b - Build barracks
A_m - Train offensive unit
A_a - Attack

Fig. 7. Action influence graph of an agent playing Starcraft II, a real-time strategy game with a large state and action space, reduced to four actions and nine state variables for the purpose of generating the explanations. In this case, the causal chain for the actual action 'Why A_s?' is shown in bold, and the chain for the counterfactual action 'Why not A_b?' would be $B \rightarrow A_n \rightarrow [D_u, D_b]$. The explanation to the question 'Why not build_barracks (A_b)?' would be 'Because it is more desirable to do action build_supply_depot (A_s) to have more Supply Depots (S) as the goal is to have more Destroyed Units (D_u) and Destroyed buildings (D_b)'. Adapted from Madumal et al. [40].

lay on collecting and providing an overview over the aforementioned XRL methods. Based on Adadi and Berrada [2]'s work, we have sorted selected methods according to the scope of the method and the time of information extraction. We then chose four methods, one for each possible combination of those categorizations, to be presented in detail.

Looking at the collected XRL methods, it becomes clear that post-hoc interpretability models are much more prevalent than intrinsic models. This makes sense, considering the fact that RL models were developed to solve tasks without human supervision that were too difficult for un-/supervised learning and are thus highly complex; it is, apparently, easier to simplify an already existing, complex model than it is to construct it to be simple in the first place. It seems that the performance-interpretability trade-off is present not only for the AI methods themselves, but also for the explainability models applied to them.

The allocation to global vs. local scope, however, seems to be more or less balanced. Of course, the decision to develop a global or a local method is greatly dependent on the complexity of the model and the task being solved, but one should also address the question if one of the two is more useful or preferable to human users. In van der Waa et al.'s study [62], for example, 'human users tend to favor explanations about policy rather than about single actions' (p. 1).

In general, the form of the explanation and the consideration of the intended target audience is a very important aspect in the development of XAI/XRL methods. Holzinger et al. [26] emphasize the need for *causability*: a combination of causality - referring to the human reliance on causal models for explanations - and usability - a term from the area of human-computer interaction defined as 'a function of the ease of use [...] and the acceptability of the product' [5, p. 2]. Just as usability measures the 'quality of use', causability measures the 'quality of explanation'. In Holzinger et al. [25], they have developed a *System Causability Scale*, an explanation interface evaluating explanations along specific dimensions such as efficiency and completeness. XAI methods also need to exhibit *context-awareness*: adapting to environmental and user changes like the level of experience, cultural or educational differences, domain knowledge, etc., in order to be more human-centric [2]. The form and presentation of the explanation is essential as XAI 'can benefit from existing models of how people define, generate, select, present, and evaluate explanations' [42, p. 59]. For example, research shows that (causal) explanations are contrastive, i.e., humans answer a 'Why X?' question through the answer to the – often only implied – counterfactual 'Why not Y instead?'. This is due to the fact that a complete explanation *for* a certain event (instead of an explanation *against* the counterevent) involves a higher cognitive load [42]. Not only that, but a layperson also seems to be more receptive to a contrastive explanation, finding it 'more intuitive and more valuable' [42, p. 20]. While there are some XAI studies focusing on the human side of the equation (e.g. [41,65–67]), especially in XRL, this is often neglected [1].

Out of the papers covered in this work, we highlight Madumal et al.'s work [40], but also Sequeira and Gervasio [52] and van der Waa et al. [62]; of all thirteen selected XRL methods, only five evaluate (non-expert) user satisfaction and/or utility of a method [17,29,40,52,62], and only three of these offer contrastive explanations [40,52,62]. So, of *all* selected papers, only these free provide a combination of both, not only offering useful contrastive explanations, but also explicitly bearing in mind the human user at the end of an explanation.

4.1 Conclusion

For practical, legal, and psychological reasons, XRL (and XAI) is a quickly advancing field in research that has to address some key challenges to prove even more beneficial and useful. In order to have a common understanding about the goals and capabilities of an XAI/XRL model, a ubiquitous terminology is important; due to this, we suggest the term *interpretability* to be used from here on out and have defined it as 'the ability to not only extract or generate explanations for the decisions of the model, but also to present this information in a way that is understandable by human (non-expert) users to, ultimately, enable them to predict a model's behaviour'. This is closely related to *Causability*, referring to the quality of an explanation [26]. Different approaches are possible to achieve interpretability, depending on the scope (global vs. local) and the time of information extraction (intrinsic vs. post-hoc). Due to the complexity of a RL model, post-hoc interpretability seems to be easier to achieve than intrinsic interpretability: simplifying the original model (for example with the use of a surrogate model) instead of developing a simple model in the first place seems to be easier to achieve, but comes at the cost of accuracy/performance.

However, despite some existing research, especially XRL models often lack to consider the human user at the receiving end of an explanation and to adapt the model to them for maximum benefit. Research shows that contrastive explanations are more intuitive and valuable [42], and there is evidence that human users favor a global approach over a local one [62]. A context-aware system design is also important in order to cater to users with different characteristics, goals, and needs [2]. Especially considering the growing role of AI in critical infrastructures (for example analyzing and controlling power grids with models such as ARL [15,59]), where the AI model might have to act autonomously or in cooperation with a human user, being able to explain and justify the model's decisions is crucial.

To achieve this and be able to develop human-centered models for optimal and efficient human-computer interaction and cooperation, a bigger focus on interdisciplinary work is necessary, combining efforts from the fields of AI/ML, psychology, philosophy, and human-computer interaction.

Acknowledgements. This work was supported by the German Research Foundation under the grant GZ: JI 140/7-1. We thank our colleagues Stephan Balduin, Johannes Gerster, Lasse Hammer, Daniel Lange and Nils Wenninghoff for their helpful comments and contributions.

References

1. Abdul, A., Vermeulen, J., Wang, D., Lim, B.Y., Kankanhalli, M.: Trends and trajectories for explainable, accountable and intelligible systems. In: Proceedings of the 2018 CHI Conference on Human Factors in Computing Systems - CHI 2018. ACM Press (2018)
2. Adadi, A., Berrada, M.: Peeking inside the black-box: a survey on explainable artificial intelligence (XAI). IEEE Access **6**, 52138–52160 (2018). https://doi.org/10.1109/access.2018.2870052
3. Andreas, J., Klein, D., Levine, S.: Modular multitask reinforcement learning with policy sketches. In: Proceedings of the 34th International Conference on Machine Learning, ICML 2017, vol. 70, pp. 166–175. JMLR.org (2017)
4. Arya, V., et al.: One explanation does not fit all: a toolkit and taxonomy of AI explainability techniques (2019). arXiv:1909.03012
5. Bevana, N., Kirakowskib, J., Maissela, J.: What is usability. In: Proceedings of the 4th International Conference on HCI. Citeseer (1991)
6. Brockman, G., Cheung, V., Pettersson, L., Schneider, J., Schulman, J., Tang, J., Zaremba, W.: OpenAI gym (2016). arXiv:1606.01540
7. Carvalho, D.V., Pereira, E.M., Cardoso, J.S.: Machine learning interpretability: a survey on methods and metrics. Electronics **8**(8), 832 (2019). https://doi.org/10.3390/electronics8080832
8. Chakraborty, S., et al.: Interpretability of deep learning models: a survey of results. In: 2017 IEEE SmartWorld, Ubiquitous Intelligence & Computing, Advanced & Trusted Computed, Scalable Computing & Communications, Cloud & Big Data Computing, Internet of People and Smart City Innovation (SmartWorld/SCALCOM/UIC/ATC/CBDCom/IOP/SCI). IEEE (2017)
9. Coppens, Y., et al.: Distilling deep reinforcement learning policies in soft decision trees. In: Proceedings of the IJCAI 2019 Workshop on Explainable Artificial Intelligence, pp. 1–6 (2019)

10. Doran, D., Schulz, S., Besold, T.R.: What does explainable AI really mean? A new conceptualization of perspectives (2017). arXiv:1710.00794
11. Doshi-Velez, F., Kim, B.: Towards a rigorous science of interpretable machine learning (2017). arXiv:1702.08608
12. Dosilovic, F.K., Brcic, M., Hlupic, N.: Explainable artificial intelligence: a survey. In: 2018 41st International Convention on Information and Communication Technology, Electronics and Microelectronics (MIPRO). IEEE (2018). https://doi.org/10.23919/mipro.2018.840004
13. Du, M., Liu, N., Hu, X.: Techniques for interpretable machine learning. Commun. ACM **63**(1), 68–77 (2019). https://doi.org/10.1145/3359786
14. European Commission, Parliament: Regulation (EU) 2016/679 of the European parliament and of the council of 27 April 2016 on the protection of natural persons with regard to the processing of personal data and on the free movement of such data, and repealing Directive 95/46/EC (General Data Protection Regulation). OJ L 119, 1–88 (2016)
15. Fischer, L., Memmen, J.M., Veith, E.M., Tröschel, M.: Adversarial resilience learning–towards systemic vulnerability analysis for large and complex systems. In: The Ninth International Conference on Smart Grids, Green Communications and IT Energy-aware Technologies (ENERGY 2019), vol. 9, pp. 24–32 (2019)
16. Freitas, A.A.: Comprehensible classification models. ACM SIGKDD Explor. Newsl. **15**(1), 1–10 (2014)
17. Fukuchi, Y., Osawa, M., Yamakawa, H., Imai, M.: Autonomous self-explanation of behavior for interactive reinforcement learning agents. In: Proceedings of the 5th International Conference on Human Agent Interaction - HAI 2017. ACM Press (2017)
18. Glass, A., McGuinness, D.L., Wolverton, M.: Toward establishing trust in adaptive agents. In: Proceedings of the 13th International Conference on Intelligent User Interfaces - IUI 2008. ACM Press (2008)
19. Goodman, B., Flaxman, S.: European union regulations on algorithmic decision-making and a "right to explanation". AI Mag. **38**(3), 50–57 (2017)
20. Halpern, J.Y.: Causes and explanations: a structural-model approach. Part II: explanations. Br. J. Philos. Sci. **56**(4), 889–911 (2005)
21. Hayes, B., Shah, J.A.: Improving robot controller transparency through autonomous policy explanation. In: Proceedings of the 2017 ACM/IEEE International Conference on Human-Robot Interaction - HRI 2017. ACM Press (2017)
22. Hein, D., Hentschel, A., Runkler, T., Udluft, S.: Particle swarm optimization for generating interpretable fuzzy reinforcement learning policies. Eng. Appl. Artif. Intell. **65**, 87–98 (2017). https://doi.org/10.1016/j.engappai.2017.07.005
23. Hein, D., Udluft, S., Runkler, T.A.: Interpretable policies for reinforcement learning by genetic programming. Eng. Appl. Artif. Intell. **76**, 158–169 (2018)
24. Herlocker, J.L., Konstan, J.A., Riedl, J.: Explaining collaborative filtering recommendations. In: Proceedings of the 2000 ACM Conference on Computer Supported Cooperative Work - CSCW 2000. ACM Press (2000)
25. Holzinger, A., Carrington, A., Müller, H.: Measuring the quality of explanations: the system causability scale (SCS). KI - Künstliche Intelligenz **34**(2), 193–198 (2020). https://doi.org/10.1007/s13218-020-00636-z
26. Holzinger, A., Langs, G., Denk, H., Zatloukal, K., Müller, H.: Causability and explainability of artificial intelligence in medicine. WIREs Data Min. Knowl. Disc. **9**(4) (2019). https://doi.org/10.1002/widm.1312
27. Ikonomovska, E., Gama, J., Džeroski, S.: Learning model trees from evolving data streams. Data Min. Knowl. Disc. **23**(1), 128–168 (2010)

28. Israelsen, B.W., Ahmed, N.R.: "Dave...I can assure you...that it's going to be all right..." a definition, case for, and survey of algorithmic assurances in human-autonomy trust relationships. ACM Comput. Surv. **51**(6), 1–37 (2019)
29. Juozapaitis, Z., Koul, A., Fern, A., Erwig, M., Doshi-Velez, F.: Explainable reinforcement learning via reward decomposition. In: Proceedings of the IJCAI 2019 Workshop on Explainable Artificial Intelligence, pp. 47–53 (2019)
30. Kaelbling, L.P., Littman, M.L., Moore, A.W.: Reinforcement learning: a survey (1996). arXiv:cs/9605103
31. Kim, B., Khanna, R., Koyejo, O.O.: Examples are not enough, learn to criticize! criticism for interpretability. In: Lee, D.D., Sugiyama, M., Luxburg, U.V., Guyon, I., Garnett, R. (eds.) Advances in Neural Information Processing Systems 29, pp. 2280–2288. Curran Associates, Inc. (2016). http://papers.nips.cc/paper/6300-examples-are-not-enough-learn-to-criticize-criticism-for-interpretability.pdf
32. Lee, J.D., See, K.A.: Trust in automation: designing for appropriate reliance. Hum. Fact. J. Hum. Fact. Ergon. Soc. **46**(1), 50–80 (2004). https://doi.org/10.1518/hfes.46.1.50_30392
33. Lee, J.H.: Complementary reinforcement learning towards explainable agents (2019). arXiv:1901.00188
34. Li, Y.: Deep reinforcement learning (2018). arXiv:1810.06339
35. Lipton, Z.C.: The mythos of model interpretability (2016). arXiv:1606.03490
36. Lipton, Z.C.: The mythos of model interpretability. Commun. ACM **61**(10), 36–43 (2018)
37. Liu, G., Schulte, O., Zhu, W., Li, Q.: Toward interpretable deep reinforcement learning with linear model U-Trees. In: Berlingerio, M., Bonchi, F., Gärtner, T., Hurley, N., Ifrim, G. (eds.) ECML PKDD 2018. LNCS (LNAI), vol. 11052, pp. 414–429. Springer, Cham (2019). https://doi.org/10.1007/978-3-030-10928-8_25
38. Liu, Y., et al.: Detecting cancer metastases on gigapixel pathology images (2017). arXiv:1703.02442
39. Loh, W.Y.: Classification and regression trees. WIREs Data Min. Knowl. Disc. **1**(1), 14–23 (2011)
40. Madumal, P., Miller, T., Sonenberg, L., Vetere, F.: Explainable reinforcement learning through a causal lens (2019). arXiv:1905.10958
41. Martens, D., Vanthienen, J., Verbeke, W., Baesens, B.: Performance of classification models from a user perspective. Decis. Support Syst. **51**(4), 782–793 (2011)
42. Miller, T.: Explanation in artificial intelligence: insights from the social sciences. Artif. Intell. **267**, 1–38 (2019)
43. Molar, C.: Interpretable machine learning (2018). https://christophm.github.io/interpretable-ml-book/. Accessed 31 Mar 2020
44. Montavon, G., Samek, W., Müller, K.R.: Methods for interpreting and understanding deep neural networks. Digit. Signal Proc. **73**, 1–15 (2018)
45. Nguyen, A., Yosinski, J., Clune, J.: Deep neural networks are easily fooled: high confidence predictions for unrecognizable images. In: The IEEE Conference on Computer Vision and Pattern Recognition (CVPR) (2015)
46. Nguyen, T.T., Hui, P.M., Harper, F.M., Terveen, L., Konstan, J.A.: Exploring the filter bubble. In: Proceedings of the 23rd International Conference on World Wide Web - WWW 2014. ACM Press (2014)
47. Quinlan, J.R., et al.: Learning with continuous classes. In: 5th Australian Joint Conference on Artificial Intelligence, vol. 92, pp. 343–348. World Scientific (1992)
48. Ribeiro, M.T., Singh, S., Guestrin, C.: "Why should I trust you?". In: Proceedings of the 22nd ACM SIGKDD International Conference on Knowledge Discovery and Data Mining - KDD 2016. ACM Press (2016)

49. Rudin, C.: Stop explaining black box machine learning models for high stakes decisions and use interpretable models instead. Nat. Mach. Intell. **1**(5), 206–215 (2019)
50. Rusu, A.A., et al.: Policy distillation (2015). arXiv:1511.06295
51. Schrittwieser, J., et al.: Mastering ATARI, go, chess and shogi by planning with a learned model (2019)
52. Sequeira, P., Gervasio, M.: Interestingness elements for explainable reinforcement learning: understanding agents' capabilities and limitations (2019). arXiv:1912.09007
53. Shu, T., Xiong, C., Socher, R.: Hierarchical and interpretable skill acquisition in multi-task reinforcement learning (2017)
54. Szegedy, C., et al.: Intriguing properties of neural networks (2013). arXiv:1312.6199
55. The European Commission: Communication from the Commission to the European Parliament, the European Council, the Council, the European Economic and Social Committee and the Committee of the Regions. The European Commission (2018). https://ec.europa.eu/digital-single-market/en/news/communication-artificial-intelligence-europe. Article. Accessed 27 Mar 2020
56. The European Commission: Independent High-Level Expert Group on Artificial Intelligence set up by the European Commission. The European Commission (2018). https://ec.europa.eu/digital-single-market/en/news/communication-artificial-intelligence-europe. Article. Accessed 27 Apr 2020
57. Tomzcak, K., et al.: Let Tesla park your Tesla: driver trust in a semi-automated car. In: 2019 Systems and Information Engineering Design Symposium (SIEDS). IEEE (2019)
58. Uther, W.T., Veloso, M.M.: Tree based discretization for continuous state space reinforcement learning. In: AAAI/IAAI, pp. 769–774 (1998)
59. Veith, E., Fischer, L., Tröschel, M., Nieße, A.: Analyzing cyber-physical systems from the perspective of artificial intelligence. In: Proceedings of the 2019 International Conference on Artificial Intelligence, Robotics and Control. ACM (2019)
60. Veith, E.M.: Universal Smart Grid Agent for Distributed Power Generation Management. Logos Verlag Berlin GmbH, Berlin (2017)
61. Verma, A., Murali, V., Singh, R., Kohli, P., Chaudhuri, S.: Programmatically interpretable reinforcement learning. PMLR **80**, 5045–5054 (2018). arXiv:1804.02477
62. van der Waa, J., van Diggelen, J., van den Bosch, K., Neerincx, M.: Contrastive explanations for reinforcement learning in terms of expected consequences. In: IJCAI 2018 Workshop on Explainable AI (XAI), vol. 37 (2018). arXiv:1807.08706
63. Wymann, B., Espié, E., Guionneau, C., Dimitrakakis, C., Coulom, R., Sumner, A.: TORCS, the open racing car simulator, vol. 4, no. 6, p. 2 (2000). Software http://torcs.sourceforge.net
64. Zahavy, T., Zrihem, N.B., Mannor, S.: Graying the black box: understanding DQNs (2016). arXiv:1602.02658
65. Zhou, J., Chen, F. (eds.): Human and Machine Learning. HIS. Springer, Cham (2018). https://doi.org/10.1007/978-3-319-90403-0
66. Zhou, J., Chen, F.: Towards trustworthy human-AI teaming under uncertainty. In: IJCAI 2019 Workshop on Explainable AI (XAI) (2019)
67. Zhou, J., Hu, H., Li, Z., Yu, K., Chen, F.: Physiological indicators for user trust in machine learning with influence enhanced fact-checking. In: Holzinger, A., Kieseberg, P., Tjoa, A.M., Weippl, E. (eds.) CD-MAKE 2019. LNCS, vol. 11713, pp. 94–113. Springer, Cham (2019). https://doi.org/10.1007/978-3-030-29726-8_7

A Projected Stochastic Gradient Algorithm for Estimating Shapley Value Applied in Attribute Importance

Grah Simon[1(✉)] and Thouvenot Vincent[1,2(✉)]

[1] Thales SIX GTS, 4 Avenue des Louvresses, Gennevilliers, France
{simon.grah,vincent.thouvenot}@thalesgroup.com
[2] SINCLAIR AI Lab, 7, boulevard Gaspard Monge, Palaiseau, France

Abstract. Machine Learning is enjoying an increasing success in many applications: medical, marketing, defence, cyber security, transportation. It is becoming a key tool in critical systems. However, models are often very complex and highly non-linear. This is problematic, especially for critical systems, because end-users need to fully understand the decisions of an algorithm (e.g. why an alert has been triggered or why a person has a high probability of cancer recurrence). One solution is to offer an interpretation for each individual prediction based on attribute relevance. Shapley Values allow to distribute fairly contributions for each attribute in order to understand the difference between a predicted value for an observation and a base value (e.g. the average prediction of a reference population). They come from cooperative game theory. While these values have many advantages, including their theoretical guarantees, they are however really hard to calculate. Indeed, the complexity increases exponentially with the dimension (the number of variables). In this article, we propose two novel methods to approximate these Shapley Values. The first one is an optimization of an already existing Monte Carlo scheme. It reduces the number of prediction function calls. The second method is based on a projected gradient stochastic algorithm. We prove for the second approach some probability bounds and convergence rates for the approximation errors according to the learning rate type used. Finally, we carry out experiments on simulated datasets for a classification and a regression task. We empirically show that these approaches outperform the classical Monte Carlo estimator in terms of convergence rate and number of prediction function calls, which is the major bottleneck in Shapley Value estimation for our application.

Keywords: Attribute importance · Interpretability · Shapley value · Monte Carlo · Projected stochastic gradient descent

---

Supported by SPARTA project.

A. Holzinger et al. (Eds.): CD-MAKE 2020, LNCS 12279, pp. 97–115, 2020.
https://doi.org/10.1007/978-3-030-57321-8_6

1 Introduction

Nowadays, Machine Learning models are used for various applications with already successful or promising results. Unfortunately, a common criticism is the lack of transparency associated with these algorithm decisions. This is mainly due to a greater interest in performance (measurable on specific tasks) at the expense of a complete understanding of the model. This results in a lack of knowledge of the internal working of the algorithm by the developer and the end user. The most obvious consequences are firstly a difficulty to correct the algorithm by an expert (different assumptions, removing outliers, adding new variables or diverse samples). Secondly, limiting its adoption by operational staff. There is even an urgent need for an explainable Artificial Intelligence (AI). Indeed, beyond these first reasons, the European Commission has imposed by legal means, with the General Data Protection Regulation, this transparency constraint on companies whose algorithms learn from personal data coming from European citizens. The challenge that companies are facing today is to bring AI into production. The transition from conclusive laboratory tests (Proof of Concept) to a production environment is not easy. To ensure that the model generalizes well on new data, a good human/machine interaction is highly appreciated.

There is no single definition of interpretability or explainability concerning model prediction (e.g. see the excellent introductory book [19]). Therefore, there are several ways to proceed. Assessing them objectively is a real problem because we do not have unanimous criteria. Most studies analyze the feedback from a panel of individuals, expert or not, to demonstrate the contribution of a method in terms of understanding. Methods are rarely compared directly with each other, but rather against a lack of interpretation of algorithm decisions. However, some references try to create quantitative indicators to evaluate the complexity of a model [18].

We can however separate methods into two dimensions [3]. If the method is local or global, and if its approach is model agnostic or on the contrary inherent to it. A global method aims at explaining the general behaviour of a model, whereas a local method focuses on each decision of a model. The agnostic category (also called post-hoc explanation) considers the model as a black box. On the other hand, inherent or non-agnostic methods can modify the structure of a model or the learning process to create intrinsically transparent algorithms. Naturally, the best strategy is to find a model that is both completely transparent by design and sufficient in terms of accuracy. Unfortunately, the most effective machine learning models tend to be less transparent because their degrees of complexity are high (e.g. gradient boosting trees, deep learning, kernel methods).

In this study, the method that we improve is agnostic and local. This approach makes it possible to create a reusable and generic module for different use cases (this is the agnostic aspect). On the other hand, the complexity of such approaches is more important and therefore hinders applications where transparent decision making is done in real time. The objective of this work is precisely to speed up calculation of these explanations.

For local explanations in Machine Learning, many methods have been proposed but the one based on Shapley Values [23] is becoming more and more

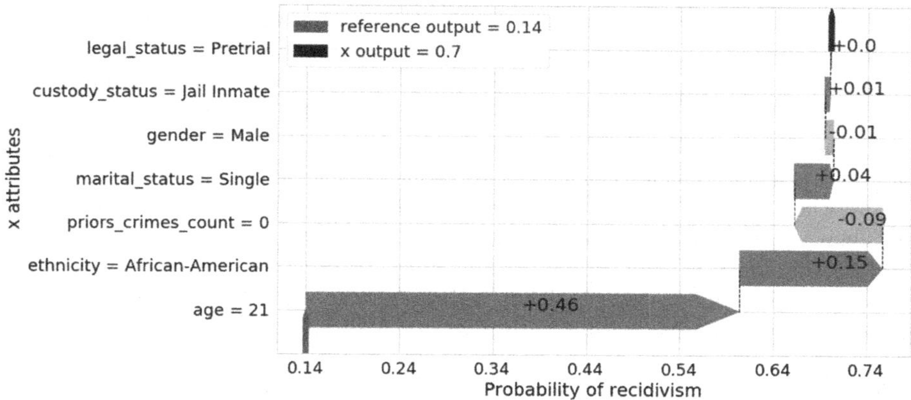

Fig. 1. Illustration of how are used Attribute Importance on a particular prediction. Here is the COMPAS dataset [5]. A machine learning has been trained to predict whether an individual will re-offend (giving the estimated probability associated). The importance of individual attributes give an interpretation of the difference between the probability of that individual (70% here) and the mean probability of a reference group (14%). It is relevant to choose non predicted recidivist individual references as element of comparison. We observe that the age of the individual (21 years old) has increased the probability by 46% while the absence of priors crimes has reduced it by 9%. The prediction is thus decomposed into an additive model where each attribute has a main effect.

popular. This is largely explained by the well-established theory behind these values, with the guarantee that they respect a number of interesting properties in our context, as explain in Sect. 2. In addition, there is no assumption made about feature independence. Shapley Values are derived from cooperative game theory and depend on the definition of a game (Fig. 1). This is why we encounter several slightly different versions of Shapley Values in the context of attribute importance [17]; [12]. However, Shapley Values have an unpleasant drawback: the computation cost grows exponentially with the number of features. For instance, if the dimension is 30, that is to say 30 features, we must take into account 2^{30} coalitions and for each coalition perform 2 evaluations of the reward function. A dimension greater than 30 is common for Machine Learning problems. Several approaches have been proposed to approximate Shapley Values. Most of them are stated in articles from the Operational Research and Game Theory communities in different contexts. In this study, we will be focus only on methods related to attribute importance in Machine Learning. [8] worked on the estimation of Shapley Values when the data is structured (e.g. images, sentences, etc.). This relationship can look like chains or grids for example. The authors propose two approaches they call L-Shapley and C-Shapley. Because the features can be represented by a graph, we can use the notion of neighbor to limit the number of coalitions to be considered for the calculation of a Shapley Value per player. In L-Shapley, we consider all coalitions with entities whose distance is less than k from the given feature, k being a parameter chosen. With C-Shapley, coalitions are taken into account if their distance is less than k but also if they have a direct link with the player. Other authors have proposed algorithm-specific approaches. For instance, [9] and [14] present DeepSHAP, a Shapley Value approximation for Deep Learning. It is an adaptation of Deep LIFT [24]. In [15], authors propose an approximation to compute Shapley Value for tree based model (e.g. Random Forest [4], Gradient Tree Boosting [11]). In the context of Federated Learning, [29] give another Shapley Value approximation technique. We use Federated Learning when several entities collaborate together to train a model on distributed datasets, but do not want to share their data. In [29], they focus on a process where each member of the coalition train a model, and then a meta-model is learned. They are also dealing with Vertical Federated Learning, where there are many overlapped instances but few overlapped features (e.g. insurer and online retailers). Their objective is twofold: find the importance of each feature and preserve the confidential information of each partner. Their article propose an adaptation of [14] in this context. [27] formalize the use of Shapley Value for Machine Learning, in particular individual prediction explanation. All these previous approximation approaches have been used in specific contexts (Federated Learning, structured dataset) or models (Deep Learning, Tree-based model). We are interested in more generic cases. [25] propose an approach based on a Monte Carlo estimator which has a solid theoretical background. [14] and [1] rewrite Shapley Value computation as a weighted least square problem.

After having defined Shapley Values in Sect. 2, we propose two novel techniques for approximating Shapley Values, based on the works from [25] and [14]. In Sect. 3, we define a method based on an optimization trick of the Monte Carlo estimator of [25]. In Sect. 4, we use a projected stochastic gradient algorithm to solve the weighted least square problem of [1] and [14]. We give the theoretical properties in term of approximation errors for the second algorithm. Finally, in Sect. 5, we compare these two approaches with the classical Monte Carlo estimator [25] on simulated examples. Empirically, we observe that the time spent by calling the machine learning model prediction is often the bottleneck of estimation methods (in an agnostic approach). That is why the number of reward function evaluations, which relies on model predictions, is a good element of comparison between these methods. This point drives us for the theoretical and empirical studies. Moreover, since the true Shapley Values are intractable in many cases, theoretical guarantees such as upper bounds with high probability are essential.

2 Shapley Values in Machine Learning

2.1 Shapley Values Definition

In Collaborative Game Theory, Shapley Values [23] can distribute a reward among players in a fairly way according to their contribution to the win in a cooperative game. We note $\mathcal{M}$ a set of d players. Moreover, we note $v : P(\mathcal{M}) \rightarrow R_v$ a reward function such that $v(\emptyset) = 0$. The range R_v can be $\Re$ or a subset of $\Re$. We express R_v in the context of Machine Learning in Sect. 2.2. $P(\mathcal{M})$ is a family of sets over $\mathcal{M}$. If $S \subset \mathcal{M}$, $v(S)$ is the amount of wealth produced by coalition S when they cooperate.

The Shapley Value of a player j is a fair share of the global wealth $v(\mathcal{M})$ produced by all players together:

$$\phi_j(\mathcal{M}, v) = \sum_{S \subset \mathcal{M} \backslash \{j\}} \frac{(d - |S| - 1)!|S|!}{d!} \left(v(S \cup \{j\}) - v(S)\right),$$

with $|S|$ = cardinal(S), i.e. the number of players in coalition S. The Shapley Values are the only values which respect the four following properties:

- Additivity: $\phi_j(\mathcal{M}, v + w) = \phi_j(\mathcal{M}, v) + \phi_j(\mathcal{M}, w)$ for all j, with $v : P(\mathcal{M}) \to R_v$ and $w : P(\mathcal{M}) \to R_v$;
- Null player: if $v(S \cup \{j\}) = v(S)$ for all $S \subset \mathcal{M} \backslash \{j\}$ then $\phi_j(\mathcal{M}, v) = 0$;
- Symmetry: $\phi_{\Pi j}(\Pi \mathcal{M}, \Pi v) = \phi_j(\mathcal{M}, v)$ for every permutation Π on $\mathcal{M}$;
- Efficiency: $\sum_{j \in \mathcal{M}} \phi_j(\mathcal{M}, v) = v(\mathcal{M})$.

When there is no risk of confusion, we will simply write ϕ_j instead of $\phi_j(\mathcal{M}, v)$ in the rest of document.

2.2 Shapley Values as Contrastive Local Attribute Importance in Machine Learning

In this study we consider the context described in [17] but all the estimation methods presented hereafter can be extended. Let be $X^* \subset \Re^d$ a dataset of individuals where a Machine Learning model f is trained and/or tested and d the dimension of X^*. $d > 1$ else we do not need to compute Shapley Value. We consider the attribute importance of an individual $\mathbf{x}^* = \{x_1^*, \dots, x_d^*\} \in X^*$ according to a given reference $\mathbf{r} = \{r_1, \dots, r_d\} \in X^*$. We're looking for $\boldsymbol{\phi} = (\phi_j)_{j \in \{1,\dots,d\}} \in \Re^d$ such that:

$$\sum_{j=1}^{d} \phi_j = f(\mathbf{x}^*) - f(\mathbf{r}),$$

where ϕ_j is the attribute contribution of feature indexed j. We loosely identify each feature by its column number. Here the set of players $\mathcal{M} = \{1, \dots, d\}$ is the feature set.

The local explanation is then contrastive because attribute relevance depends on a reference. For Machine Learning purposes, the range R_v of wealth v could be any real number, namely the output of a regression model, the maximum probability estimated or the individual likelihood in a classification task, anomaly score for outliers detection, and so on. It could also be a discrete number, for instance the predicted rank in a ranking problem, a one-loss function for binary or multi-class classification which means that the reward equals 1 if two instances are in the same class and 0 otherwise.

In Machine Learning, a common choice for the reward is $v(S) = \mathbb{E}[f(X)|X_S = \mathbf{x}^*_\mathbf{S}]$, where $\mathbf{x}^*_\mathbf{S} = (x^*_j)_{j\in S}$ and X_S the element of X for the coalition S.

For any $S \subset \mathcal{M}$, let's define $z(\mathbf{x}^*, \mathbf{r}, S)$ such that $z(\mathbf{x}^*, \mathbf{r}, \emptyset) = \mathbf{r}$, $z(\mathbf{x}^*, \mathbf{r}, \mathcal{M}) = \mathbf{x}^*$ and

$$z(\mathbf{x}^*, \mathbf{r}, S) = (z_1, ..., z_d) \text{ with } z_i = \begin{cases} x^*_i \text{ if } i \in S \\ r_i \text{ if } i \notin S \end{cases}.$$

As explain in [17], each reference $\mathbf{r}$ sets a single-game with $v(S) = f(z(\mathbf{x}^*, \mathbf{r}, S)) - f(\mathbf{r})$, $v(\emptyset) = 0$ and $v(\mathcal{M}) = f(\mathbf{x}^*) - f(\mathbf{r})$. If we sample many references from a dataset with one distribution D^{pop}, we can recover the more classical definition of attribute contributions according to a base value $\mathbb{E}_{r\sim D^{pop}}[f(r)]$ like in [14], [25] and [26] by averaging all the Shapley Values of each single game obtained on individuals from the reference population.

Out of direct interest, estimating $\mathbb{E}[f(X)|X_S = \mathbf{x}^*_\mathbf{S}]$ is not an easy task. In [12], the authors exhibit two popular ways using conditional or interventional distributions. Both techniques have their own pro and cons which lead to different definitions of what attribute relevance should be. When we use a reference $\mathbf{r}$ and create a new instance $z(\mathbf{x}^*, \mathbf{r}, S)$, we are in the second family. The main drawback is that we assume feature independence (only for the calculation of $v(S)$) which can produce out-of-distribution samples. On the other hand, the conditional approach could give non zero contribution to attributes which do not impact the reward function. It happens when an irrelevant attribute is correlated to relevant ones. Anyway, the methods that we present here are agnostic to the chosen approach, it can be conditional or interventional. Even if we use the interventional approach as an illustration, the same techniques will also work by changing the reward function or the way we estimate $v(S)$.

3 Estimation of Shapley Values by Monte Carlo

The Monte Carlo method and its variants are by far the most commonly used techniques for estimating Shapley Values. In its classical form, this approach samples random permutations between players (e.g. [16,25,26]). Our goal is to reduce the number of times the costly reward function is asked. We propose in Algorithm 1 an optimized version of the algorithm proposed by [25] which divides by two the use of the reward function v. To the best of our knowledge, this optimization trick has not been explicitly stated in any article dealing with Shapley Values. Moreover, this strategy can be combined with stratified sampling (e.g. [7,16]) in order to reduce the number of iterations required. Indeed, estimated variances of each player are updated online. Let $\pi(\{1,\ldots,d\})$ be the set of all ordered permutations of $\{1,\ldots,d\}$ in Algorithm 1.

Data: instance $\mathbf{x}^*$ and $\mathbf{r}$, the reward function v and the number of iterations T.
Result: The Shapley Values $\widehat{\boldsymbol{\phi}} \in \Re^d$
initialization $\widehat{\boldsymbol{\phi}} = \{0, \ldots, 0\}$ and $\widehat{\boldsymbol{\sigma^2}} = \{0, \ldots, 0\}$;
for *t=1,...,T* **do**
  Choose the subset resulting of an uniform permutation $O \in \pi(\{1, \ldots, d\})$ of the features values ;
  $v^{(1)} = v(\mathbf{r})$;
  $\mathbf{b} = \mathbf{r}$;
  for *j in O* **do**
    $\mathbf{b} = \begin{cases} x_i^* & \text{if } i = j \\ b_i & \text{if } i \neq j \end{cases}$, with $i \in \{1, \ldots, d\}$;
    $v^{(2)} = v(\mathbf{b})$;
    $\phi_j = v^{(2)} - v^{(1)}$;
    if t > 1, $\widehat{\sigma_j^2} = \frac{t-2}{t-1}\widehat{\sigma_j^2} + (\phi_j - \widehat{\phi_j})^{2/t}$;
    $\widehat{\phi_j} = \frac{t-1}{t}\widehat{\phi_j} + \frac{1}{t}\phi_j$;
    $v^{(1)} = v^{(2)}$;
  end
end

Algorithm 1: Optimized version of Monte Carlo algorithm.

[16] demonstrate that the estimation error could be bounded with high probability regarding some assumptions. These results are still valid for the optimized version.

4 Estimation of Shapley Values by a Projected Stochastic Gradient Algorithm

An alternative way to Monte Carlo is to use the equivalence between the initial formulation of the Shapley values and an optimization problem. Indeed, these values are the only solution of a weighted linear regression problem with an equality constraint (see [14,22] and [1]). The convex optimization problem is given by Eq. (1).

$$\begin{aligned} &\underset{\phi \in \Re^d}{\text{argmin}} \quad \sum_{S \in \mathcal{M}, S \neq \{\emptyset, \mathcal{M}\}} w_S \, [v(S) - \sum_{j \in S} \phi_j]^2 \\ &\text{subject to} \quad \sum_{i=j}^{d} \phi_j = v(\mathcal{M}) \end{aligned} \tag{1}$$

where the weights $w_S = \dfrac{(d-1)}{\binom{d}{|S|}|S|(d-|S|)}$.

There are few resources that specifically address that problem. [14] only mention very briefly its estimation by a debiased version of Least Absolute Shrinkage and Selection Operator (LASSO, see [28]) without further details. [1] formalize more finely the resolution of this weighted linear regression. The weighted sum takes into account all the coalitions, including therefore $\mathcal{M}$ and $\emptyset$ with infinite weights $w_{\mathcal{M}} = w_{\emptyset} = \infty$ (in practice these weights are set by a high constant). There is no equality constraint since it is ensured by the infinite weight $w_{\mathcal{M}}$. The function to be minimized is reformulated as a weighted least square problem, which basically has a unique solution. Because of the high dimension, exponential with the number of features, [1] propose to sample the coalitions used according to coalition weights to reduce the dimension. Unfortunately, we have no information on the error made by considering only a sub-sample of all coalitions. The authors recommend the largest possible value for that sub-sample size, however this results in a costly computation. The new method that we propose and detail in this paper aims to continue the work initiated by these authors on the estimation of Shapley Values by solving this weighted linear regression problem.

4.1 Solving by a Projected Stochastic Gradient Algorithm

Our goal is to reduce the number of coalitions used and then the reward function evaluations while controlling the estimation error. The function we want to minimize is:

$$F(\boldsymbol{\phi}) = (X\boldsymbol{\phi} - Y)^T W (X\boldsymbol{\phi} - Y) = \frac{1}{n}\sum_{i=1}^{n} n w_i (y_i - \mathbf{x_i}^T\boldsymbol{\phi})^2 = \frac{1}{n}\sum_{i=1}^{n} g_i(\boldsymbol{\phi}),$$

where $n = 2^d - 2$ is the number of all coalitions except the full and the empty coalitions, $W = \text{diag}(w_S)$ is a diagonal matrix of size $n \times n$ whose diagonal elements are the weights w_S without $S = \emptyset$ or $\mathcal{M}$. X is a binary matrix of size $n \times d$ representing all coalitions (except null and full coalitions): each element in the column j of the row i is equal to 1 if the player j is in the coalition i, 0 otherwise. $\mathbf{x_i}$ corresponds to the i-th row of X. $\mathbf{Y} = (y_i)_{i\in\{1,\dots,n\}}$ is a vector of size n with $y_i = v(S)$ where S is the i-th coalition. We assume that for all $i \in \{1,\dots,n\}$, $|y_i| < C$, with $C > 0$ a constant. In our configuration $v(S) = v(z(\mathbf{x}^*, \mathbf{r}, S)) - v(\mathbf{r})$, each coalition S is indexed by an integer i.

We denote $K_1 = \{\boldsymbol{\phi}; \sum_{j=1}^{d} \phi_j = v(\mathcal{M})\}$ and $K_2 = \{\boldsymbol{\phi};\ \|\boldsymbol{\phi}\| \leq D\}$ two convex sets. $D > 0$ is a constant which is required to demonstrate the theoretical performance in Sect. 4.2, but in practice it can be large enough. This allows to avoid large gradient norm, but it can be removed by using a small learning rate. The convex set K_1 ensures that the solution respects the equality constraint $\sum_{j=1}^{d} \phi_j = v(\mathcal{M})$. F is a μ-strongly convex function defined on a convex set:

$$K = \{\boldsymbol{\phi}; \sum_{j=1}^{d} \phi_j = v(\mathcal{M})\ ;\ \|\boldsymbol{\phi}\| \leq D\} = K_1 \cap K_2.$$

This optimization problem has a unique solution $\boldsymbol{\phi}^*$ which is the Shapley Values if D is chosen such that $||\boldsymbol{\phi}^*|| \leq D$.

We denote $\boldsymbol{\phi_t} = (\phi_i^t)_{i \in \{1,...,d\}}$ the Shapley Values estimator at the iteration t. We also define $i_t \sim U_n(\{1,\ldots,n\})$, with $U_n(\{1,\ldots,n\})$ a discrete uniform distribution with support $\{1,\ldots,n\}$, the coalition randomly draw for the iteration t. To find the unique minimum of F on K, the Projected Stochastic gradient algorithm at each iteration t follows the rules:

$$
\begin{aligned}
&i_t \sim U_n(\{1,\ldots,n\}),\\
&\boldsymbol{\phi_t} = \mathrm{Proj}_K(\boldsymbol{\phi_{t-1}} - \gamma_t \nabla g_{i_t}),
\end{aligned}
$$

where

- γ_t is a constant or decreasing step-size (also called the learning rate). $\forall t, \gamma_t > 0$;
- Proj_K is the orthogonal projection on K;
- $\mathbb{E}[\nabla g_{i_t} | \mathcal{F}_{t-1}]$ is the gradient of F at $\boldsymbol{\phi_{t-1}}$. $\mathcal{F}_{t-1}$ is the σ-field generated by $x_1, y_1, ..., x_{t-1}, y_{t-1}$;
- $\mathbb{E}[\|\nabla g_{i_t}\|^2] \leq B^2$ (finite variance condition). $B > 0$.

For each iteration t, we need to find the orthogonal projection of $\boldsymbol{\phi_t} \in \Re^d$ onto the convex set $K_1 \cap K_2 = K$ where K_1, K_2 are convex sets. Dykstra's algorithm ([6], Algorithm 2) can be used because we know how to project onto the sets K_1 and K_2 separately. For $\boldsymbol{\phi_t} \in \Re^d$, if $\boldsymbol{\phi_t}$ does not belong to either K_1 or K_2:

$$
\mathrm{Proj}_{K_1}(\boldsymbol{\phi_t}) = \boldsymbol{\phi_t} - \frac{\sum_j \phi_j^t - v(\mathcal{M})}{d},
$$

$$
\mathrm{Proj}_{K_2}(\boldsymbol{\phi_t}) = \boldsymbol{\phi_t} \times \frac{D}{\|\boldsymbol{\phi_t}\|}.
$$

```
Data: instance φ_t ∈ ℜ^d, Proj_{K_1} and Proj_{K_2} and the maximum number of
      iterations L.
Result: the orthogonal projection of φ_t onto K
initialization: α_1 = φ and p_1 = q_1 = 0;
for l=1,...,L do
    β_l = Proj_{K_2}(α_l + p_l);
    p_{l+1} = α_l + p_l − β_l;
    if Proj_{K_1}(β_l + q_l) = α_l then
        break;
    else
        α_l = Proj_{K_1}(β_l + q_l);
        q_{l+1} = β_l + q_l − α_l;
    end
end
return α_l
```

Algorithm 2: Dykstra's Algorithm 2.

4.2 Convergence Rate and High-Probability Bounds

Upper Bound B of Stochastic Gradient Norm. Considering $\nabla g_{i_t} = 2n(w_{i_t} < \mathbf{x_{i_t}}, \boldsymbol{\phi}_{t-1} > \mathbf{x_{i_t}} - w_{i_t} y_{i_t} \mathbf{x_{i_t}})$ and applying triangle inequality leads to:

$$\begin{aligned} \|\nabla g_{i_t}\| &\leq 2n \left(\|w_{i_t} < \mathbf{x_{i_t}}, \boldsymbol{\phi}_{t-1} > \mathbf{x_{i_t}}\| + \|w_{i_t} y_{i_t} \mathbf{x_{i_t}}\|\right) \\ &\leq 2n \left(|w_{i_t}| \, \|\boldsymbol{\phi}_{t-1}\| \, \|\mathbf{x_{i_t}}\|^2 + |w_{i_t}| |y_{i_t}| \, \|\mathbf{x_{i_t}}\|\right) \\ &\leq 2n w_{i_t} \|\mathbf{x_{i_t}}\| \left(D \|\mathbf{x_{i_t}}\| + C\right). \end{aligned} \tag{2}$$

We introduce L_{i_t} such that $L_{i_t} = 2nw_{i_t} \|\mathbf{x_{i_t}}\| (D \|\mathbf{x_{i_t}}\| + C)$. L_{i_t} only depends on the chosen coalition i_t and $\|x_{i_t}\|^2$ equals the number of players for that coalition. Hence L_{i_t} is maximum when the number of players is $d-1$ with $w_{i_t} = \frac{1}{d}$. That is why:

$$\mathbb{E}\big[\, \|\nabla g_{i_t}\|^2 \,\big] \leq \mathbb{E}[L_{i_t}^2] \leq \big[2n \, \frac{\sqrt{d-1}}{d} (\sqrt{d-1} D + C)\big]^2.$$

This upper bound can be improved by using Importance Sampling. If we consider a discrete distribution p on $[0,1]^n$:

$$F(\boldsymbol{\phi}) = (X\boldsymbol{\phi} - Y)^T W (X\boldsymbol{\phi} - Y) = \frac{1}{n} \sum_{i=1}^{n} g_i(\boldsymbol{\phi}) = \sum_{i=1}^{n} p_i \, (np_i)^{-1} g_i(\boldsymbol{\phi}),$$

Then, $\forall t > 0$:

$$\nabla F(\boldsymbol{\phi}_{t-1}) = \sum_{i=0}^{n} p_i \, (np_i)^{-1} \nabla g_i(\boldsymbol{\phi}_{t-1}) = \mathbb{E}_{i_t \sim p}\big[(np_{i_t})^{-1} \nabla g_{i_t}\big].$$

We want to find a distribution p such that $\mathbb{E}_{i_t \sim p}\big[\, \|(np_{i_t})^{-1} \nabla g_{i_t}\|^2 \,\big]$ is better bounded (e.g.[30]). As we already showed in Eq. (2), $\|\nabla g_{i_t}\| \leq L_{i_t}$ and a suggested distribution is:

$$p_i = \frac{L_i}{\sum_{j=1}^{n} L_j}, \forall i = 1, \ldots, n.$$

For each coalition i, $L_i = 2nw_i\sqrt{l_i}(D\sqrt{l_i} + C)$ where l_i is the number of attributes in that coalition. Then we get:

$$\begin{aligned} \mathbb{E}_{i_t \sim p}\big[\, \|(np_{i_t})^{-1} \nabla g_{i_t}\|^2 \,\big] &= \frac{1}{n^2} \sum_{i=1}^{n} (p_i)^{-1} \, \|\nabla g_i\|^2 \\ &\leq \frac{1}{n^2} \sum_{i=1}^{n} \frac{\sum_j L_j}{L_i} L_i^2 \\ &\leq \frac{\left(\sum_j L_j\right)^2}{n^2}. \end{aligned}$$

Actually, we do not have to compute L_i for all coalitions because L_i only depends on the size of the ith coalition. For all i^{th} coalitions whose size is $l \in \{1, ..., d-1\}$, $L_i = 2n\frac{(d-1)}{\binom{d}{l}l(d-l)}\sqrt{l}(D\sqrt{l}+C)$. By denoting $L^l = 2n\frac{(d-1)}{\binom{d}{l}l(d-l)}\sqrt{l}(D\sqrt{l}+C)$ for every size l, we get $\sum_j L_j = \sum_{l=1}^{d-1}\binom{d}{l}L^l$.

$$\sum_j L_j = 2n\sum_{l=1}^{d-1}\binom{d}{l}\frac{(d-1)}{\binom{d}{l}l(d-l)}\sqrt{l}(\sqrt{l}D+C) = 2n\sum_{l=1}^{d-1}\frac{d-1}{\sqrt{l}(d-l)}(\sqrt{l}D+C).$$

Finally, let's define B such that $B^2 = \frac{\left(\sum_j L_j\right)^2}{n^2} = 4\left[\sum_{l=1}^{d-1}\frac{d-1}{\sqrt{l}(d-l)}(\sqrt{l}D+C)\right]^2$. We have found an upper bound for the stochastic gradient norm:

$$\mathbb{E}_{i_t\sim p}\left[\left\|(np_{i_t})^{-1}\nabla g_{i_t}\right\|^2\right] \le B^2$$

Note that we have removed n from the previous upper bound of gradient norm. We will use this new estimator of gradient F and then the Projected Stochastic gradient algorithm becomes:

$$\begin{aligned} &i_t \sim p, \\ &\boldsymbol{\phi}_t = \text{Proj}_K(\boldsymbol{\phi}_{t-1} - \gamma_t\,(np_{i_t})^{-1}\nabla g_{i_t}), \end{aligned}$$

at each iteration t with p the chosen distribution above.

Strongly Convex Constant μ. F is a μ-strongly convex function. We know that μ is the smallest eigenvalues of the Hessian of F: $\nabla^2 F = X^TWX$ which does not rely on $\boldsymbol{\phi}$. We can demonstrate that $\mu = 1 - 1/d$.

$$X^TWX_{(d,d)} = \begin{pmatrix} a & c & \cdots & c \\ c & a & \cdots & c \\ \vdots & \vdots & \ddots & \vdots \\ c & c & \cdots & a \end{pmatrix} = (a-c)\begin{pmatrix} 1 & 0 & \cdots & 0 \\ 0 & 1 & \cdots & 0 \\ \vdots & \vdots & \ddots & \vdots \\ 0 & 0 & \cdots & 1 \end{pmatrix} + c\begin{pmatrix} 1 & 1 & \cdots & 1 \\ 1 & 1 & \cdots & 1 \\ \vdots & \vdots & \ddots & \vdots \\ 1 & 1 & \cdots & 1 \end{pmatrix} = (a-c)I_d + cJ_d,$$

where $a = \sum_{k=1}^{d-1}\binom{d-1}{k-1}w_k$ and $c = \sum_{k=2}^{d-1}\binom{d-2}{k-2}w_k$.

The eigenvalues of J_d are 0 (order $d-1$) and d (order 1). If z is an eigenvector of J_d associated to the eigenvalue λ, then $X^TWXz = ((a-c)I_d + cJ_d)z = ((a-c)+c\lambda)z$. That is why eigenvalues of X^TWX are $(a-c)$ and $(a-c)+cd$. The smallest one is $a-c$ and thus by definition $\mu = a-c$. We can then prove that $a - c = 1 - 1/d$. Full details of that demonstration are given in Appendix 7.1.

Convergence Rate. For the sake of clarity, we will denote $\kappa = \frac{B}{\mu} = 4\sum_{l=1}^{d-1}\frac{d}{\sqrt{l}(d-l)}(\sqrt{l}D+C)$.

It has been proved in [13] that if we choose an inverse decreasing step-size $\gamma_t = \frac{2}{\mu(t+1)}$, with $t \in \{1,\dots,T\}$, T being the number of iterations, we get the following convergence rate:

$$F(\bar{\phi}_T) - F(\phi^*) \leq \frac{2B^2}{\mu T},$$

where $\bar{\phi}_T = \frac{2}{(T+1)(T+2)} \sum_{t=0}^{T}(t+1)\phi_t$. In practice, these averaging is updated online with:

$$\bar{\phi}_T = (1-\rho_t)\bar{\phi}_{T-1} + \rho_t\phi_t, \text{ where } \rho_t = \frac{2}{(t+2)}$$

As F is μ-strongly convex, we have the following inequality for all $\mathbf{x}, \mathbf{y} \in \Re^d$:

$$F(\mathbf{y}) \geq F(\mathbf{x}) + \nabla F(\mathbf{x})^T(\mathbf{y}-\mathbf{x}) + \frac{\mu}{2}\|\mathbf{y}-\mathbf{x}\|^2.$$

In particular if $\mathbf{x} = \phi^*$, the unique solution, $\nabla F(\phi^*) = 0$ and $\|\mathbf{y} - \phi^*\|^2 \leq \frac{2}{\mu}(F(\mathbf{y}) - F(\phi^*))$ for any $\mathbf{y} \in \mathbf{R}^d$.

That is why:

$$\mathbb{E}\Big[\|\bar{\phi}_T - \phi^*\|^2\Big] \leq \frac{4B^2}{\mu^2 T} = \frac{4\kappa^2}{T} = \mathcal{O}(\frac{1}{T}).$$

With a square root decreasing step-size $\gamma_t = \frac{2D}{B\sqrt{t}}$ and $\bar{\phi}_T = \frac{1}{T}\sum_{t=0}^{T}\phi_t$ (e.g. [2]): $F(\bar{\phi}_T) - F(\phi^*) \leq \frac{2DB}{\sqrt{T}}$.

Then

$$\mathbb{E}\Big[\|\bar{\phi}_T - \phi^*\|^2\Big] \leq \frac{4DB}{\mu\sqrt{T}} = \frac{4D\kappa}{\sqrt{T}} = \mathcal{O}(\frac{1}{\sqrt{T}}).$$

For a constant step size $\gamma < \frac{1}{\mu} = \frac{d}{d-1}$ (see [10]), we get:

$$\mathbb{E}\Big[\|\phi_T - \phi^*\|^2\Big] \leq (1-\gamma\mu)^T\|\phi_0 - \phi^*\|^2 + \frac{\gamma B^2}{\mu} = \mathcal{O}(\rho^T) + \mathcal{O}(\gamma),$$

where $\rho = 1 - \gamma\mu$ and ϕ_0 the initial value used for the stochastic gradient algorithm. It is a fast convergence towards an imprecise solution that we can control.

High-Probability Bounds. In order to obtain high-probability bounds for projected stochastic gradient descent algorithm (SGD), we can use either the Markov inequality: $\forall a \geq 0,\ \mathbb{P}(Z \geq a) \leq \frac{\mathbb{E}[Z]}{a}$, with Z being a random variable, or the deviation inequality: $\forall a, A \geq 0,\ \mathbb{E}[Z] \leq A \Rightarrow \mathbb{P}(Z \geq A(2+4a)) \leq 2e^{-a^2}$ (see [2,20,21]). In the following we use Markov inequality and let the results obtained by the deviation inequality in Appendix 7.2.

For the inverse decreasing step-size, we obtain (with the appropriate $\bar{\phi}_{\mathbf{T}}$ defined before):

$$\mathbb{P}\Big(\|\bar{\phi}_T - \phi^*\|^2 \geq \epsilon \Big) \leq \frac{4\kappa^2}{\epsilon T}, \quad \text{for all } \epsilon > 0.$$

In a same manner, with the square root decreasing step-size we get:

$$\mathbb{P}\Big(\|\bar{\phi}_T - \phi^*\|^2 \geq \epsilon \Big) \leq \frac{4D\kappa}{\epsilon\sqrt{T}}, \quad \text{for all } \epsilon > 0.$$

Considering a constant step-size leads to:

$$\mathbb{P}\Big(\|\phi_T - \phi^*\|^2 \geq \epsilon \Big) \leq \frac{(1-\gamma\mu)^T}{\epsilon} \|\phi_0 - \phi^*\|^2 + \frac{\gamma B^2}{\epsilon\mu}, \quad \text{for all } \epsilon > 0.$$

A well suited element of comparison between this method and the Monte Carlo presented in Sect. 3, is to consider the number of reward function evaluations. According to this criteria, performing T iterations of Monte Carlo is equivalent to $T \times d$ iterations of stochastic gradient.

5 Experimental Evaluation

5.1 Simulated Dataset

Classification. We will use the simulated dataset introduced [11], page 339. The features $X_1, \ldots, X_d$ are standard independent Gaussian, and the deterministic target Y is defined by:

$$Y = \begin{cases} 1 \text{ if } \sum_{j=1}^{d} X_j^2 > \chi_d^2(0.5) \\ 0 \text{ otherwise} \end{cases},$$

where $\chi_d^2(0.5)$ is the median of a chi-squared random variable with d degrees of freedom (the sum of d standard Gaussian squared follows a χ^2 probability law). We denote by f_{class} a classification function that returns 1 if the predicted score is greater than 0.5 and 0 otherwise. For a reference $\mathbf{r}^*$ and a target $\mathbf{x}^*$, we define the reward function $v_c^{\mathbf{r}^*,\mathbf{x}^*}$ such that for each coalition S, $v_c^{\mathbf{r}^*,\mathbf{x}^*}(S) = \mathbb{1}_{f_{class}(\mathbf{z}(\mathbf{x}^*,\mathbf{r}^*,S))=f_{class}(\mathbf{x}^*)}$. This reward function is one choice among others. Here, all the contributions sum to 1. Moreover, using an uncommon reward function in Machine Learning illustrates that the techniques used are agnostic of that reward function.

Regression. We will also use a simulated dataset from the same book ([11], page 401, the Radial example). $X_1, \ldots, X_d$ are standard independent Gaussian. The model is determined by:

$$Y = \prod_{j=1}^{d} \rho(X_j),$$

where ρ: $t \rightarrow \sqrt{(0.5\pi)} \exp(-t^2/2)$. The regression function f_{regr} is deterministic and simply defined by f_r: $\mathbf{x} \rightarrow \prod_{j=1}^{d} \rho(x_j)$. For a reference $\mathbf{r}^*$ and a target $\mathbf{x}^*$, we define the reward function $v_r^{\mathbf{r}^*,\mathbf{x}^*}$ such as for each coalition S, $v_r^{\mathbf{r}^*,\mathbf{x}^*}(S) = f_{regr}(\mathbf{z}(\mathbf{x}^*, \mathbf{r}^*, S)) - f_{regr}(\mathbf{r}^*)$.

Procedure. We select at random 50 couple of instances $\mathbf{x}^*$ and $\mathbf{r}^*$. For each one, the true Shapley Values are calculated and estimation errors of the methods under study are stored for several iterations. Some graphs will sum up the experiments by displaying the mean estimation errors per iteration. For the classification problem, the instances are sampled from separate classes. Finally, let's remember that our goal is to use the fewest number of reward function evaluations as possible while having a good estimation error. The code is available here: https://github.com/ThalesGroup/shapkit.

5.2 Comparison Between All Methods

For the gradient based methods, the initial value ϕ_0 is $\text{Proj}_{K_1}(\mathbf{0}) = \left\{\frac{f_p(\mathbf{x}^*) - f_p(\mathbf{r}^*)}{d}, \ldots, \frac{f_p(\mathbf{x}^*) - f_p(\mathbf{r}^*)}{d}\right\}$, with $p = class$ or $regr$ according to the fact we work on the classification or regression task. Furthermore, we select interesting decreasing step size strategies on out-of-experiment samples $(\mathbf{x}^*, \mathbf{r}^*)$ and only display the best ones found.

Dimension 16. We choose at first a dimension d of 16 features which allows us to compute the true Shapley Values in a reasonable time. The total number of coalitions is 65 534. Figure 2 shows the results obtained for that dimension. All the proposed methods outperform the classical Monte Carlo algorithm both in classification and regression. The stochastic gradient methods displayed use a constant step size of 0.01 and a decreasing step size following $\gamma_t = 0.1/\sqrt{t}$ at each iteration t.

Dimension 300. We would like to test the behavior of these approaches when the dimension is quite high. That is why we generate 300 features. A dimension higher than this is not so frequent for tabular datasets. Due to computational constraints we will only study the classification problem. Indeed Shapley Values collapse towards zero in the regression settings. Because the true Shapley Values

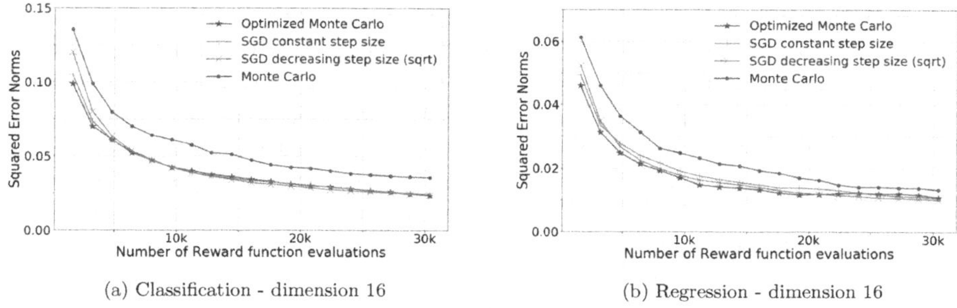

(a) Classification - dimension 16

(b) Regression - dimension 16

Fig. 2. Evolution of the mean squared error norms with the number of reward function evaluations.

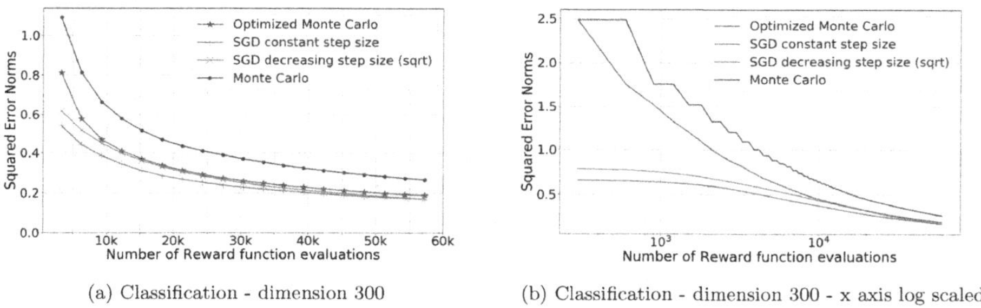

(a) Classification - dimension 300

(b) Classification - dimension 300 - x axis log scaled

Fig. 3. Evolution of the mean squared error norms with the number of function evaluations. The right plot log scales the x axis.

are intractable, we estimate it with the optimized Monte Carlo technique and a large number of iterations. We performed 5000 iterations which represent $5000 \times d$ reward evaluations.

The mean squared error norms can be observed on Fig. 3. The constant step size is 0.001 and the decreasing step size follows $\gamma_t = \dfrac{0.01}{\sqrt{t}}$. By its design, Monte Carlo techniques update each Shapley Value component sequentially during one iteration of d reward evaluations. In the meantime gradient based methods could update several Shapley Values components at each iteration. Empirically, we find that when there are strong interactions between features and when the link is strongly non-linear between the features and the target, the method of Monte Carlo approaches need more time to decrease their estimation error compared to the others.

6 Conclusion

In this article, we propose two novel methods for approximating Shapley Values when we want to interpret individual predictions of a Machine Learning model. The first one is based on an optimization trick applied to the classical

Monte Carlo estimator of Shapley Values. The second one uses a rewrite in the form of a weighted optimization problem of the Shapley's value approximation problem, which is solved by projected stochastic gradient descent algorithm. These estimates offer theoretical guarantees on the error made. Empirically, we show that these approaches outperform the classical Monte Carlo estimator. We have observed during experiments that when features interact less with each other according to the model (that is to say the estimated model tends to an additive model), then the Monte Carlo methods are better suited while having less hyper-parameters. But when the model output depends more strongly on attribute associations (like in the previous simulated classification task), gradient based alternatives offer interesting results. It might be useful in the future to study the contribution of mini-batch approaches for the stochastic gradient. We could later study the use of Shapley Values for global explanation. Indeed, Shapley values can be estimated for a significant sub-sample of individuals and then draw several graphs: all Shapley Values as a function of one feature, mean absolute value of the shapley values for each feature, and so much more.

Acknowledgement. This work is supported by the SPARTA project, which has received funding from the European Union's Horizon 2020 research and innovation programme under grant agreement No 830892.

7 Appendix

7.1 Strongly convex constant μ

F is a μ-strongy convex function. We know that μ is the smallest eigenvalues of the Hessian of F: $\nabla^2 F(\phi) = X^T W X$ which does not rely on ϕ. We can prove that $\mu = 1 - 1/d$. At first, one can observe that:

$$X^T W X_{(d,d)} = \begin{pmatrix} a & c & \cdots & c \\ c & a & \cdots & c \\ \vdots & \vdots & \ddots & \vdots \\ c & c & \cdots & a \end{pmatrix} = (a-c) \begin{pmatrix} 1 & 0 & \cdots & 0 \\ 0 & 1 & \cdots & 0 \\ \vdots & \vdots & \ddots & \vdots \\ 0 & 0 & \cdots & 1 \end{pmatrix} + c \begin{pmatrix} 1 & 1 & \cdots & 1 \\ 1 & 1 & \cdots & 1 \\ \vdots & \vdots & \ddots & \vdots \\ 1 & 1 & \cdots & 1 \end{pmatrix} = (a-c)I_d + cJ_d,$$

where $a = \sum_{k=1}^{d-1} \binom{d-1}{k-1} w_k$ and $c = \sum_{k=2}^{d-1} \binom{d-2}{k-2} w_k$.

Indeed, $X^T W X$ is a $d \times d$ matrix whose (i,j) term is $\sum_{l=1}^{n} \sum_{k=1}^{n} (\mathbf{x}^T)_{ik} w_{kl} x_{lj} = \sum_{l=1}^{n} x_{li} w_{ll} x_{lj}$ because $w_{kl} = 0$ if $k \neq l$. For each coalition l, value of w_{ll} only depends of the size of that coalition and the product $x_{li} \times x_{lj}$ equals 1 if features i and j are present in coalition l. Therefore if we denote k the size of one coalition l, it exists two cases: when $i = j$ we have $\binom{d-1}{k-1}$ possible coalitions of size k which contain feature i $(= j)$. And if $i \neq j$ there are $\binom{d-2}{k-2}$ coalitions. That is why $a = \sum_{k=1}^{d-1} \binom{d-1}{k-1} w_k$ and $c = \sum_{k=2}^{d-1} \binom{d-2}{k-2} w_k$.

The eigenvalues of J_d are 0 (order $d-1$) and d (order 1). If $\mathbf{z_e}$ is an eigenvector of J_d associated to the eigenvalue λ, then $X^T W X \mathbf{z_e} = ((a-c)I_d + cJ_d)\mathbf{z_e} = ((a-c) + c\lambda)\mathbf{z_e}$. That is why eigenvalues of $X^T W X$ are $(a-c)$ and $(a-c) + cd$.

The smallest one is $a - c$ and thus by definition $\mu = a - c$. We can then prove that $a - c = 1 - 1/d$.

$$
\begin{aligned}
a - c &= \sum_{k=1}^{d-1} \binom{d-1}{k-1} w_k - \sum_{k=2}^{d-1} \binom{d-2}{k-2} w_k \\
&= w_1 + \sum_{k=2}^{d-1} [\binom{d-1}{k-1} - \binom{d-2}{k-2}] w_k \\
&= w_1 + \sum_{k=2}^{d-1} \binom{d-2}{k-1} w_k \\
&= \sum_{k=1}^{d-1} \binom{d-2}{k-1} w_k \\
&= \sum_{k=1}^{d-1} \binom{d-2}{k-1} \frac{(d-1)}{\binom{d}{k} k(d-k)} \\
&= \sum_{k=1}^{d-1} \frac{(d-2)!(d-1)}{(k-1)!(d-k-1)!\binom{d}{k} k(d-k)} \\
&= \sum_{k=1}^{d-1} \frac{(d-1)!}{(k)!(d-k)!\binom{d}{k}} \\
&= \sum_{k=1}^{d-1} \frac{(d-1)!}{d!} \\
&= \sum_{k=1}^{d-1} \frac{1}{d} \\
&= \frac{d-1}{d} \\
&= 1 - 1/d.
\end{aligned}
$$

7.2 High-Probability bounds with a deviation inequality

In order to obtain high-probability bounds for projected stochastic gradient descent algorithm (SGD), we can use the deviation inequality: $\forall a, A \geq 0$, $\mathbb{E}[Z] \leq A \Rightarrow \mathbb{P}(Z \geq A(2 + 4a)) \leq 2e^{-a^2}$ (see [2,20,21]).

For the inverse decreasing step-size, we obtain (with the appropriate $\bar{\phi}_{\mathbf{T}}$ defined before):

$$\mathbb{P}\Big(\|\bar{\phi}_T - \phi^*\|^2 \geq \epsilon \Big) \leq 2 \exp\Big(-\frac{1}{16} [\frac{\epsilon T}{4\kappa^2} - 2]^2 \Big) \text{ for all } \epsilon > 0.$$

In a same manner, with the square root decreasing step-size we get:

$$\mathbb{P}\Big(\|\bar{\phi}_T - \phi^*\|^2 \geq \epsilon \Big) \leq 2 \exp\Big(-\frac{1}{16} [\frac{\epsilon\sqrt{T}}{4D\kappa} - 2]^2 \Big) \text{ for all } \epsilon > 0.$$

Considering a constant step-size leads to:

$$\mathbb{P}\Big(\|\phi_T - \phi^*\|^2 \geq \epsilon \Big) \leq 2\exp\Big(- \frac{1}{16}\big[\epsilon/\big(\rho^T \|\phi_0 - \phi^*\|^2 + \frac{\alpha B^2}{\mu}\big) - 2\big]^2 \Big) \text{ for all } \epsilon > 0.$$

References

1. Aas, K., Jullum, M., Løland, A.: Explaining individual predictions when features are dependent: more accurate approximations to Shapley values (2019)
2. Bach, F.: https://www.di.ens.fr/fbach/orsay2020.html, https://www.di.ens.fr/~fbach/fbach_orsay_2020.pdf
3. Barredo Arrieta, A., et al.: Explainable artificial Intelligence (XAI): concepts, taxonomies, opportunities and challenges toward responsible AI. J. Inf. Fusion **58**, 82–115 (2020)
4. Breiman, L., Random, F.: Machine Learning **45**, 5–32 (2001)
5. https://www.propublica.org/datastore/dataset/compas-recidivism-risk-score-data-and-analysis
6. Boyle, J.P., Dykstra, R.L.: A method for finding projections onto the intersection of convex sets in Hilbert spaces (1986). Lecture Notes in Statistics. 37, pp. 28–47
7. Castro, J., Gómez, D., Molina, E., Tejada, J.: Improving polynomial estimation of the Shapley value by stratified random sampling with optimum allocation. Comput. Oper. Res. **82**, 180–188 (2017)
8. Chen, J., Le, S., Wainwright, M.J., Jordan, M.I.: L-Shapley and C-Shapley: Efficient Model Interpretation for Structured Data (2018)
9. Chen, H., Lundberg, S., Lee, S.-I.: Explaining Models by Propagating Shapley Values (2019). https://arxiv.org/abs/1911.11888
10. Gower, R.M.: https://perso.telecom-paristech.fr/rgower/pdf/M2_statistique_optimisation/grad_conv.pdf
11. Hastie, T., Tibshirani, R., Friedman, J.: The Elements of Statistical Learning: Data Mining, Inference, and Prediction, 2nd edn. Springer Series in Statistics (2009)
12. Elizabeth Kumar, I., Venkatasubramanian, S., Scheidegger, C., Friedler, S.: Problems with Shapley-value-based explanations as feature importance measures (2020)
13. Lacoste-Julien, S., Schmidt, M., Bach, F.: A simpler approach to obtaining an O(1/t) convergence rate for the projected stochastic subgradient method (2012)
14. Lundberg, S.M., Lee, S.-I.: A unified approach to interpreting model predictions. Advances in Neural Information Processing Systems (2017)
15. Lundberg, S.M., Lee, S.-I.: Consistent feature attribution for tree ensembles (2017). https://arxiv.org/abs/1706.06060
16. Maleki, S., Tran-Thanh, L., Hines, G., Rahwan, T., Rogers, A.: Bounding the Estimation Error of Sampling-based Shapley Value Approximation With/Without Stratifying (2013)
17. Merrick, L., Taly, A.: The Explanation Game: Explaining Machine Learning Models with Cooperative Game Theory (2019)
18. Molnar, C., Casalicchio, G., Bischl, B.: Quantifying Model Complexity via Functional Decomposition for Better Post-Hoc Interpretability (2019)
19. Molnar, C.: Interpretable Machine Learning, A Guide for Making Black Box Models Explainable (2019). https://christophm.github.io/interpretable-ml-book/
20. Nemirovski, A., Juditsky, A., Lan, G., Shapiro, A.: Robust stochastic approximation approach to stochastic programming. SIAM J. Optim. **19**(4), 1574–1609 (2009)

21. Nesterov, Y., Vial, J.P.: Confidence level solutions for stochastic programming. Automatica **44**(6), 1559–1568 (2008)
22. Ruiz, L.M., Valenciano, F., Zarzuelo, J.M.: The Family of Least Square Values for Transferable Utility Games, Games and Economic Behavior (1998)
23. Shapley, L.S.: A value for n-person games. In: Contributions to the Theory of Games. 2.28, pp. 307–317 (1953)
24. Shrikumar, A., Greenside, P., Shcherbina, A., Kundaje, A.: Not Just a Black Box: Learning Important Features Through Propagating Activation Differences (2016). https://arxiv.org/abs/1605.01713
25. Štrumbelj, E., Kononenko, I.: Explaining prediction models and individual predictions with feature contributions. Knowl. Inf. Syst. **41**(3), 647–665 (2013). https://doi.org/10.1007/s10115-013-0679-x
26. Mach, J., Strumbelj, E., Kononenko, I.: An efficient explanation of individual classifications using game theory. Mach. Learn. Res. **11**, 1–18 (2010)
27. Sundararajan, M., Najmi, A.: The many Shapley values for model explanation (2019)
28. Tibshirani, R.: Regression shrinkage and selection via the lasso. J. Roy. Stat. Soc. Ser. B **58**(1), 267–288 (1996)
29. Wang, G.: Interpret Federated Learning with Shapley Values (2019)
30. Zhao, P., Zhang, T.: Stochastic optimization with importance sampling for regularized loss minimization. In: Proceedings of the 32nd International Conference on Machine Learning, vol. 37, pp. 1–9 (2015)

Explaining Predictive Models with Mixed Features Using Shapley Values and Conditional Inference Trees

Annabelle Redelmeier(✉), Martin Jullum(✉), and Kjersti Aas

Norwegian Computing Center, P.O. Box 114, Blindern, 0314 Oslo, Norway
{annabelle.redelmeier,jullum,kjersti}@nr.no

Abstract. It is becoming increasingly important to explain complex, black-box machine learning models. Although there is an expanding literature on this topic, Shapley values stand out as a sound method to explain predictions from any type of machine learning model. The original development of Shapley values for prediction explanation relied on the assumption that the features being described were independent. This methodology was then extended to explain dependent features with an underlying continuous distribution. In this paper, we propose a method to explain mixed (i.e. continuous, discrete, ordinal, and categorical) dependent features by modeling the dependence structure of the features using conditional inference trees. We demonstrate our proposed method against the current industry standards in various simulation studies and find that our method often outperforms the other approaches. Finally, we apply our method to a real financial data set used in the 2018 FICO Explainable Machine Learning Challenge and show how our explanations compare to the FICO challenge Recognition Award winning team.

Keywords: Explainable AI · Shapley values · Conditional inference trees · Feature dependence · Prediction explanation

1 Introduction

Due to the ongoing data and artificial intelligence (AI) revolution, an increasing number of crucial decisions are being made with complex automated systems. It is therefore becoming ever more important to understand how these systems make decisions. Such systems often consist of 'black-box' machine learning models which are trained to predict an outcome/decision based on various input data (i.e. features). Consider, for instance, a model that predicts the price of car insurance based on the features age and gender of the individual, type of car, time since the car was registered, and number of accidents in the last five years. For such a system to work in practice, the expert making the model, the insurance brokers communicating the model, and the policyholders vetting the model should know which features drive the price of insurance up or down.

Published by Springer Nature Switzerland AG 2020
A. Holzinger et al. (Eds.): CD-MAKE 2020, LNCS 12279, pp. 117–137, 2020.
https://doi.org/10.1007/978-3-030-57321-8_7

Although there are numerous ways to explain complex models, one way is to show how the individual features contribute to the overall predicted value for a given individual[1]. The Shapley value framework is recent methodology to calculate these contributions [15,20,21]. In the framework, a Shapley value is derived for each feature given a prediction (or 'black-box') model and the set of feature values for the given individual. The methodology is such that the sum of the Shapley values for the individual equals their prediction value so that the features with the largest (absolute) Shapley values are the most important.

The Shapley value concept is based on economic game theory. The original setting is as follows: Imagine a game where N players cooperate in order to maximize the *total gains* of the game. Suppose further that each player is to be given a certain payout for his or her efforts. Lloyd Shapley [19] discovered a way to distribute the total gains of the game among the players according to certain desirable axioms. For example, players that do not contribute anything get a payout of 0; two players that contribute the same regardless of other players get the same payout; and the sum of the payouts equals the total gains of the game. A player's payout is known as his or her *Shapley value*.

[15,20,21] translate Shapley values from the game theory setting to a machine learning setting. The cooperative game becomes the individual, the total gains of the game become the prediction value, and the players become the feature values. Then, analogous to game theory, the Shapley value of one of the features (called the *Shapley value explanation*) is how the feature contributes to the overall prediction value.

Figure 1 shows how such Shapley value explanations can be visualized for two examples of the aforementioned car insurance scenario. For the individual on the left, 'number of accidents' pulls the predicted insurance price up (its Shapley value is positive) whereas 'gender' and 'age' pull it down. The features 'type of car' and 'time since registration' only minimally affect the prediction. For the individual on the right, 'gender' and 'type of car' pull the predicted insurance price up whereas 'age', 'time since registration', and 'number of accidents' pull it marginally down. The sum of the Shapley values of each individual gives the predicted price of insurance (123.5 and 229.9 USD/month, respectively). Note that 'none' is a fixed average prediction contribution not due to any of the features in the model.

As we demonstrate in Sect. 2, calculating Shapley values is not necessarily straightforward or computationally simple. To simplify the estimation problem, [15,20,21] assume the features are independent. However, [1] shows that this may lead to severely inaccurate Shapley value estimates and, therefore, incorrect explanations when the features are not independent. [1] extends [15]'s methodology to handle dependent *continuously* distributed features by modeling/estimating the dependence between the features. However, as exemplified by the aforementioned car insurance example, practical modeling scenarios often involve a mixture of different feature types: continuous (age and time since the

[1] Here, 'individual' could be an individual person or an individual non-training observation - not necessarily a person.

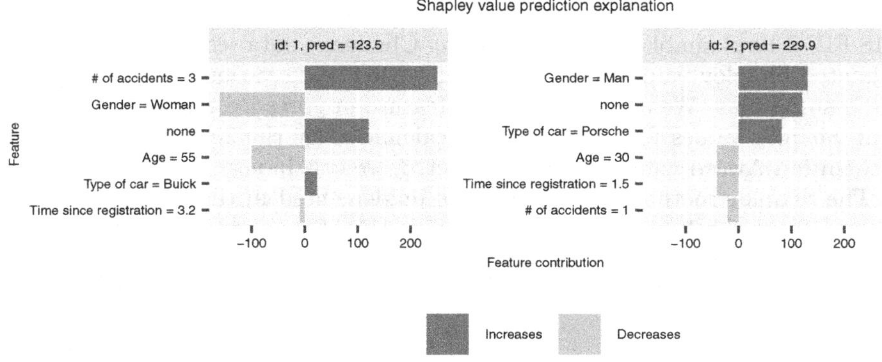

Fig. 1. An example of using Shapley values to show how the predicted price of car insurance can be broken down into the respective features.

car was registered), discrete (number of accidents in the last five years), and categorical (gender and type of car). Thus, there is a clear need to extend the Shapley value methodology to handle dependent mixed (i.e. continuous, discrete, ordinal, categorical) features.

While it is, in principle, possible to naively apply some of the methods proposed by [1] to discrete or categorical features, it is unlikely that they will function well. This will typically require encoding categorical features with L different categories into $L - 1$ new indicator features using one-hot encoding. The main drawback of this approach is that the feature dimension increases substantially unless there are very few categories. Computational power is already a non-trivial issue with the Shapley value framework (see [1]), so this is not a feasible approach unless the number of categories or features is very small.

The aim of this paper is to show how we can extend the Shapley value framework to handle mixed features without assuming the features are independent. We propose to use a special type of tree model, known as conditional inference trees [12], to model the dependence between the features. This is similar to [1]'s extension of [15]'s work but for mixed features. We use tree models since they are inherently good at modeling both simple and complex dependence structures in mixed data types [8]. The conditional inference tree model has the additional advantage of naturally extending to multivariate responses, which is required in this setting. Since conditional inference trees handle categorical data, this approach does not require one-hot encoding any features resulting in a much shorter computation time. In addition, we do not run the risk of estimating one-hot encoded features using a method not designed for the sort.

The rest of the paper is organized as follows. We begin by explaining the fundamentals of the Shapley value framework in an explanation setting in Sect. 2 and then outline how to extend the method to mixed features using conditional inference trees in Sect. 3. In Sect. 4, we present various simulation studies for both continuous and categorical features that demonstrate that our method works in a variety of settings. Finally, in Sect. 5, we apply our method to the 2018 FICO Explainable Machine Learning Challenge data set and show how the estimated Shapley values differ when calculated using various feature distribution assumptions. We also compare the feature importance rankings calculated using Shapley values with the rankings calculated by the 2018 FICO challenge Recognition Award winning team. In Sect. 6, we conclude.

The Shapley methodology from [1] is implemented in the software package `shapr` [18] in the `R` programming language [17]. Our new approach is implemented as an extension to the `shapr` package. To construct the conditional inference trees in `R`, we use the packages `party` and `partykit` [12,13].

2 Shapley Values

2.1 Shapley Values in Game Theory

Suppose we are in a cooperative game setting with M players, $j = 1, \dots, M$, trying to maximize a payoff. Let $\mathcal{M}$ be the set of all players and $\mathcal{S}$ any subset of $\mathcal{M}$. Then the Shapley value [19] for the jth player is defined as

$$\phi_j = \sum_{\mathcal{S} \subseteq \mathcal{M} \setminus \{j\}} \frac{|\mathcal{S}|!(M - |\mathcal{S}| - 1)!}{M!} (v(\mathcal{S} \cup \{j\}) - v(\mathcal{S})). \tag{1}$$

$v(\mathcal{S})$ is the contribution function which maps subsets of players to real numbers representing the worth or contribution of the group $\mathcal{S}$ and $|\mathcal{S}|$ is the number of players in subset $\mathcal{S}$.

In the game theory sense, each player receives ϕ_j as their payout. From the formula, we see that this payout is just a weighted sum of the player's marginal contributions to each group $\mathcal{S}$. Lloyd Shapley [19] proved that distributing the total gains of the game in this way is 'fair' in the sense that it obeys certain important axioms.

2.2 Shapley Values for Explainability

In a machine learning setting, imagine a scenario where we fit M features, $\boldsymbol{x} = (x_1, \dots, x_M)$, to a univariate response y with the model $f(\boldsymbol{x})$ and want to explain the prediction $f(\boldsymbol{x})$ for a specific feature vector $\boldsymbol{x} = \boldsymbol{x}^*$. [15,20,21] suggest doing this with Shapley values where the predictive model replaces the cooperative game and the features replace the players. To use (1), [15] defines the contribution function $v(\mathcal{S})$ as the following expected prediction

$$v(\mathcal{S}) = \mathbb{E}[f(\boldsymbol{x}) | \boldsymbol{x}_{\mathcal{S}} = \boldsymbol{x}^*_{\mathcal{S}}]. \tag{2}$$

Here $\boldsymbol{x}_{\mathcal{S}}$ denotes the features in subset $\mathcal{S}$ and $\boldsymbol{x}^*_{\mathcal{S}}$ is the subset $\mathcal{S}$ of the feature vector $\boldsymbol{x}^*$ that we want to explain. Thus, $v(\mathcal{S})$ denotes the expected prediction given that the features in subset $\mathcal{S}$ take the value $\boldsymbol{x}^*_{\mathcal{S}}$.

Calculating the Shapley value for a given feature x_j thus becomes the arduous task of computing (1) but replacing $v(\mathcal{S})$ with the conditional expectation (2). It is clear that the sum in (1) grows exponentially as the number of features, M, increases. [15] cleverly approximates this weighted sum in a method they call Kernel SHAP. Specifically, they define the Shapley values as the optimal solution to a certain weighted least squares problem. They prove that the Shapley values can explicitly be written as

$$\phi = (\boldsymbol{Z}^T \boldsymbol{W} \boldsymbol{Z})^{-1} \boldsymbol{Z}^T \boldsymbol{W} \boldsymbol{v}, \tag{3}$$

where $\boldsymbol{Z}$ is the $2^M \times (M+1)$ binary matrix representing all possible combinations of the M features, $\boldsymbol{W}$ is the $2^M \times 2^M$ diagonal matrix containing Shapley weights, and $\boldsymbol{v}$ is the vector containing $v(\mathcal{S})$ for every $\mathcal{S}$. The full derivation is described in [1].

To calculate (3), we still need to compute the contribution function $v(\mathcal{S})$ for different subsets of features, $\mathcal{S}$. When the features are continuous, we can write the conditional expectation (2) as

$$\mathbb{E}[f(\boldsymbol{x})|\boldsymbol{x}_{\mathcal{S}} = \boldsymbol{x}^*_{\mathcal{S}}] = \mathbb{E}[f(\boldsymbol{x}_{\bar{\mathcal{S}}}, \boldsymbol{x}_{\mathcal{S}})|\boldsymbol{x}_{\mathcal{S}} = \boldsymbol{x}^*_{\mathcal{S}}] = \int f(\boldsymbol{x}_{\bar{\mathcal{S}}}, \boldsymbol{x}^*_{\mathcal{S}}) p(\boldsymbol{x}_{\bar{\mathcal{S}}}|\boldsymbol{x}_{\mathcal{S}} = \boldsymbol{x}^*_{\mathcal{S}})\, d\boldsymbol{x}^*_{\bar{\mathcal{S}}}, \tag{4}$$

where $\boldsymbol{x}_{\bar{\mathcal{S}}}$ is the vector of features not in $\mathcal{S}$ and $p(\boldsymbol{x}_{\bar{\mathcal{S}}}|\boldsymbol{x}_{\mathcal{S}} = \boldsymbol{x}^*_{\mathcal{S}})$ is the conditional distribution of $\boldsymbol{x}_{\bar{\mathcal{S}}}$ given $\boldsymbol{x}_{\mathcal{S}} = \boldsymbol{x}^*_{\mathcal{S}}$. Note that in the rest of the paper we use $p(\cdot)$ to refer to both probability mass functions and density functions (made clear by the context). We also use lower case x-s for both random variables and realizations to keep the notation concise.

Since the conditional probability function is rarely known, [15] replaces it with the simple (unconditional) probability function

$$p(\boldsymbol{x}_{\bar{\mathcal{S}}}|\boldsymbol{x}_{\mathcal{S}} = \boldsymbol{x}^*_{\mathcal{S}}) = p(\boldsymbol{x}_{\bar{\mathcal{S}}}). \tag{5}$$

The integral then becomes

$$\mathbb{E}[f(\boldsymbol{x})|\boldsymbol{x}_{\mathcal{S}} = \boldsymbol{x}^*_{\mathcal{S}}] = \int f(\boldsymbol{x}_{\bar{\mathcal{S}}}, \boldsymbol{x}^*_{\mathcal{S}}) p(\boldsymbol{x}_{\bar{\mathcal{S}}})\, d\boldsymbol{x}^*_{\bar{\mathcal{S}}}, \tag{6}$$

which is estimated by randomly drawing K times from the full training data set and calculating

$$v_{\text{KerSHAP}}(\mathcal{S}) = \frac{1}{K} \sum_{k=1}^{K} f(\boldsymbol{x}^k_{\bar{\mathcal{S}}}, \boldsymbol{x}^*_{\mathcal{S}}), \tag{7}$$

where $\boldsymbol{x}^k_{\bar{\mathcal{S}}}$, $k = 1, \ldots, K$ are the samples from the training set and $f(\cdot)$ is the estimated prediction model.

Unfortunately, when the features are not independent, [1] demonstrates that naively replacing the conditional probability function with the unconditional one leads to very inaccurate Shapley values. [1] then proposes multiple methods for estimating $p(\boldsymbol{x}_{\bar{S}}|\boldsymbol{x}_S = \boldsymbol{x}_S^*)$ without relying on the naive assumption in (5). However, these methods are only constructed for continuous features. In the next section we demonstrate how we can use conditional inference trees to extend the current Shapley framework to handle mixed features.

3 Extending the Shapley Framework with Conditional Inference Trees

Conditional inference trees (ctree) [12] is a type of recursive partitioning algorithm like CART (classification and regression trees) [4] and C4.5 [16]. Just like these algorithms, ctree builds trees recursively, making binary splits on the feature space until a given stopping criterion is fulfilled. The difference between ctree and CART/C4.5 is how the feature/split point and stopping criterion are chosen. CART and C4.5 solve for the feature and split point simultaneously: each feature and split point is tried together and the best pair is the combination that results in the smallest error (often based on the squared error loss or binary cross-entropy loss depending on the response). Ctree, on the other hand, proceeds sequentially: the splitting feature is chosen using statistical significance tests and then the split point is chosen using any type of splitting criterion [12]. According to [12], choosing the splitting feature without first checking for the potential split points avoids being biased towards features with many split points. In addition, unlike CART and C4.5, ctree is defined independently of the dimension of the response variable. This is advantageous since proper handling of multivariate responses is crucial for our problem.

3.1 Conditional Inference Tree Algorithm

Suppose that we have a training data set with p features, a q dimensional response, and n observations: $\{\boldsymbol{y}_i, \boldsymbol{x}_i\}_{i=1,\ldots,n}$ with $\boldsymbol{y}_i = (y_{i1}, \ldots y_{iq})$ and $\boldsymbol{x}_i = (x_{i1}, \ldots, x_{ip})$. Suppose further that the responses come from a sample space $\mathcal{Y} = \mathcal{Y}_1 \times \cdots \times \mathcal{Y}_q$ and the features come from a sample space $\mathcal{X} = \mathcal{X}_1 \times \cdots \times \mathcal{X}_p$. Then conditional inference trees are built using the following algorithm:

1. For a given node in the tree, test the global null hypothesis of independence between all of the p features and the response $\boldsymbol{y}$. If the global hypothesis cannot be rejected, do not split the node. Otherwise, select the feature x_j that is the least independent of $\boldsymbol{y}$.
2. Choose a splitting point in order to split $\mathcal{X}_j$ into two disjoint groups.

Steps 1 and 2 are repeated until no nodes are split.

The global null hypothesis can be written as

$$H_0 : \cap_{j=1}^p H_0^j,$$

where the p partial hypotheses are

$$H_0^j : F(\boldsymbol{Y}|X_j) = F(\boldsymbol{Y}),$$

and $F(\cdot)$ is the distribution of $\boldsymbol{Y}$.

Specifically, we calculate the p P-values for the partial hypotheses and combine them to form the global null hypothesis P-value. If the P-value for the global null hypothesis is smaller than some predetermined level α, we reject the global null hypothesis and assume that there is some dependence between the features and the response. The feature that is the least independent of the response (i.e. has the smallest partial P-value) becomes the splitting feature. If the global null hypothesis is not rejected, we do not split the node. The size of the tree is controlled using the parameter α. As α increases, we are more likely to reject the global null hypothesis and therefore split the node. This results in deeper trees. However, if α is too large, we risk that the tree overfits the data.

Step 2 can be done using any type of splitting criterion, specifically it can be done with the permutation test framework devised by [12]. Note that this method is not tied to a specific feature type and can be used with mixtures of continuous, discrete, ordinal, and categorical features. We refer the reader to the original paper [12] for more details on how to form the test statistic, associated distribution, and P-values.

3.2 Extending the Shapley Value Framework with Conditional Inference Trees

As already mentioned, one of the main limitations with the Shapley value framework is estimating the contribution function (2) when the conditional distribution of the features is unknown but the features are assumed dependent. [1] estimates (2) by modeling the conditional probability density function

$$p(\boldsymbol{x}_{\bar{\mathcal{S}}}|\boldsymbol{x}_{\mathcal{S}} = \boldsymbol{x}^*_{\mathcal{S}}) \tag{8}$$

using various approaches. Then, [1] samples K times from this modeled conditional distribution function and uses these samples to estimate the integral (4) using (7).

We extend this approach to mixed features by modeling the conditional distribution function (8) using conditional inference trees. We fit a tree to our training data where the features are $\boldsymbol{x}_{\mathcal{S}}$ and the response is $\boldsymbol{x}_{\bar{\mathcal{S}}}$ with the algorithm described in Sect. 3.1. Then for a given $\boldsymbol{x}^*_{\mathcal{S}}$, we find its leaf in the tree and sample K times from the $\boldsymbol{x}_{\bar{\mathcal{S}}}$ part of the training observations in that node to obtain $\boldsymbol{x}^k_{\bar{\mathcal{S}}}$, $k = 1, \ldots, K$. Finally, we use these samples to estimate (4) using the approximation (7).

We fit a new tree to every combination of features $\boldsymbol{x}_{\mathcal{S}}$ and response $\boldsymbol{x}_{\bar{\mathcal{S}}}$. Once $v(\mathcal{S})$ is estimated for every $\mathcal{S}$, we follow [14]'s steps and estimate the Shapley value of this feature with (3). Since conditional inference trees handle continuous, discrete, ordinal, and categorical features; univariate and multivariate responses; and any type of dependence structure, using conditional inference trees to estimate (8) is a natural extension to [1]'s work. Below, we use the term *ctree* to refer to estimating Shapley value explanations using conditional inference trees.

4 Simulation Studies

In this section, we discuss two simulation studies designed to compare different ways to estimate Shapley values. Specifically, we compare our ctree estimation approach with [15]'s independence estimation approach (below called *independence*) and [1]'s empirical and Gaussian estimation approaches. A short description of each approach is in Table 1.

Table 1. A short description of the approaches used to estimate (8) in the simulation studies.

Method	Citation	Description
independence	[14]	Assume the features are independent. Assume (2) is (6) and estimate it with (7) where $x_{\bar{S}}^{k}$ are sub-samples from the training data set.
empirical	[1]	Calculate the distance between the set of features being explained and every training instance. Use this distance to calculate a weight for each training instance. Approximate (2) using a function of these weights.
Gaussian (100)	[1]	Assume the features are jointly Gaussian. Estimate the mean/covariance of this conditional distribution and then sample 100 times from this distribution. Estimate (2) with (7) using this sample.
Gaussian (1000)	[1]	The same as Gaussian (100), but we sample 1000 times.
ctree		See Sect. 3.2. Set $\alpha = 0.5$.
ctree-onehot		Convert the categorical features into one-hot encoded features and then apply the algorithm in Sect. 3.2 to these binary features. This approach is used only as a reference.

The independence, empirical, and Gaussian approaches are all implemented in the `R` package `shapr` [18]. We implement the ctree method in the `shapr` package as an additional method. Building the conditional inference trees for each combination of features is done using either the `party` package or `partykit` package in `R` [12,13]. Although `party` is faster than `partykit`, it sometimes runs into a convergence error related to the underlying linear algebra library in `R` (error code 1 from Lapack routine 'dgesdd'). We therefore fall back to `partykit` when this error occurs. Both packages typically give identical results.

In the first simulation study, we simulate only categorical features and in the second, we simulate both categorical and continuous features. Then, we estimate the Shapley values of each test observation with the methods in Table 1 and compare them against the truth using a mean absolute error type of performance measure.

For simplicity, in both situations we restrict ourselves to a linear predictive function of the form

$$f(\boldsymbol{x}) = \alpha + \sum_{\{j:j\in\mathcal{C}_{\text{cat}}\}} \sum_{l=2}^{L} \beta_{jl}\mathbf{1}(x_j = l) \quad + \sum_{\{j:j\in\mathcal{C}_{\text{cont}}\}} \gamma_j x_j, \tag{9}$$

where $\mathcal{C}_{\text{cat}}$ and $\mathcal{C}_{\text{cont}}$ denote, respectively, the set of categorical and continuous features, L is the number of categories for each of the categorical features, and $\mathbf{1}(x_j = l)$ is the indicator function taking the value 1 if $x_j = l$ and 0 otherwise. α, β_{jl} for $j \in \mathcal{C}_{\text{cat}}$, $l = 2, \ldots, L$, and γ_j for $j \in \mathcal{C}_{\text{cont}}$ are the parameters in the linear model. We define $M = |\mathcal{C}_{\text{cat}}| + |\mathcal{C}_{\text{cont}}|$, where $|\mathcal{C}_{\text{cat}}|$ and $|\mathcal{C}_{\text{cont}}|$ denote the number of categorical and continuous features, respectively.

The empirical and Gaussian methods cannot handle categorical features. For these methods, we transform the categorical features into one-hot encoded features. If the categorical feature originally has L categories, the one-hot encoded transformation creates $L-1$ binary features representing the second, third (etc) categories. The first category is represented by the intercept. The Shapley value of each categorical feature is then the sum of the Shapley values of the corresponding one-hot encoded features.

4.1 Evaluation Method

We measure the performance of each method based on the mean absolute error (MAE), across both the features and sample space. This is defined as

$$\text{MAE}(\text{method } q) = \frac{1}{M}\sum_{j=1}^{M}\sum_{i=1}^{T} p(\boldsymbol{x}_i)|\phi_{j,\text{true}}(\boldsymbol{x}_i) - \phi_{j,q}(\boldsymbol{x}_i)|, \tag{10}$$

where $\phi_{j,q}(\boldsymbol{x})$ and $\phi_{j,\text{true}}(\boldsymbol{x})$ denote, respectively, the Shapley value estimated with method q and the corresponding true Shapley value for the prediction $f(\boldsymbol{x})$. In addition, M is the number of features and T is the number of test observations. For the case with only categorical features, the set $\{\boldsymbol{x}_i : i = 1, \ldots, T\}$ corresponds to all the unique combinations of features and $p(\boldsymbol{x}_i)$ is the probability mass function of $\boldsymbol{x}$ evaluated at $\boldsymbol{x}_i$[2]. In the case where we have both categorical and numerical features, the set $\{\boldsymbol{x}_i : i = 1, \ldots, T\}$ is sampled from the distribution of $\boldsymbol{x}$ and $p(\boldsymbol{x}_i)$ is set to $1/T$ for all i.

4.2 Simulating Dependent Categorical Features

To simulate M dependent categorical features with L categories each, we first simulate an M-dimensional Gaussian random variable with a specified mean $\boldsymbol{\mu}$ and covariance $\boldsymbol{\Sigma}$

$$(\tilde{x}_1, \ldots, \tilde{x}_M) \sim N_M(\boldsymbol{\mu}, \boldsymbol{\Sigma}). \tag{11}$$

[2] If there are many categorical features or number of categories, we instead use a subset of the most likely combinations and scale the probabilities such that they sum to 1 over those combinations.

We then transform each feature, $\tilde{x}_j$, into a categorical feature, x_j, using the following transformation:

$$x_j = l, \text{ if } v_l < \tilde{x}_j \le v_{l+1}, \text{ for } l = 1, \dots, L \text{ and } j = 1, \dots, M, \tag{12}$$

where $v_1, \dots, v_{L+1}$ is an increasing, ordered set of cut-off values defining the categories with $v_1 = -\infty$ and $v_{L+1} = +\infty$. We redo this n_{train} times to create a training data set of M dependent categorical features. The strength of the dependencies between the categorical features is controlled by the correlations specified in $\boldsymbol{\Sigma}$. Note that the actual value of x_j is irrelevant – the features are treated as non-ordered categorical features.

For the simulation setting in Sect. 4.5 where there are both categorical and continuous features, we first sample $M = |\mathcal{C}_{\text{cat}}| + |\mathcal{C}_{\text{cont}}|$ features using (11). Then we transform the features $\tilde{x}_j$ where $j \in \mathcal{C}_{\text{cat}}$ to categorical ones using (12), and leave the remaining features untouched (i.e letting $x_j = \tilde{x}_j$, when $j \in \mathcal{C}_{\text{cont}}$). This imposes dependence both within and between all feature types.

4.3 Calculating the True Shapley Values

To evaluate the performance of the different methods with the MAE from Sect. 4.1, we need to calculate the true Shapley values, $\phi_{j,\text{true}}(\boldsymbol{x}^*)$, $j = 1, \dots, M$, for all feature vectors where $\boldsymbol{x}^* = \boldsymbol{x}_i$, $i = 1, \dots, T$. This requires the true conditional expectation (2) for all feature subsets $\mathcal{S}$. We compute these expectations differently depending on whether the features are all categorical or whether there are both categorical and continuous features. The linearity of the predictive function (9) helps to simplify the computations for the latter case. Since there is no need of it in the former case, we present that case more generally.

When the features are all categorical, the desired conditional expectation can be written as

$$\mathbb{E}[f(\boldsymbol{x})|\boldsymbol{x}_{\mathcal{S}} = \boldsymbol{x}_{\mathcal{S}}^*] = \sum_{\boldsymbol{x}_{\bar{\mathcal{S}}} \in \mathcal{X}_{\bar{\mathcal{S}}}} f(\boldsymbol{x}_{\mathcal{S}}^*, \boldsymbol{x}_{\bar{\mathcal{S}}}) p(\boldsymbol{x}_{\bar{\mathcal{S}}}|\boldsymbol{x}_{\mathcal{S}} = \boldsymbol{x}_{\mathcal{S}}^*),$$

where $\mathcal{X}_{\bar{\mathcal{S}}}$ denotes the feature space of the feature vector $\boldsymbol{x}_{\bar{\mathcal{S}}}$ which contains $|\bar{\mathcal{S}}|^L$ unique feature combinations. Thus, all we need is the conditional probability $p(\boldsymbol{x}_{\bar{\mathcal{S}}}|\boldsymbol{x}_{\mathcal{S}} = \boldsymbol{x}_{\mathcal{S}}^*)$ for each combination of $\boldsymbol{x}_{\bar{\mathcal{S}}} \in \mathcal{X}_{\bar{\mathcal{S}}}$. Using standard probability theory, this conditional probability can be written as

$$p(\boldsymbol{x}_{\bar{\mathcal{S}}}|\boldsymbol{x}_{\mathcal{S}}) = \frac{p(\boldsymbol{x}_{\bar{\mathcal{S}}}, \boldsymbol{x}_{\mathcal{S}})}{p(\boldsymbol{x}_{\mathcal{S}})},$$

and then evaluated at the desired $\boldsymbol{x}_{\mathcal{S}}^*$. Since all feature combinations correspond to hyperrectangular subspaces of Gaussian features, we can compute all joint probabilities exactly using the cut-offs $v_1, \dots, v_{L+1}$:

$$p(x_1 = l_1, \dots, x_M = l_M) = P(v_{l_1} < \tilde{x}_1 \le v_{l_1+1}, \dots, v_{l_M} < \tilde{x}_M \le v_{l_M+1}),$$

for $l_j = 1, \dots, L$, $j = 1, \dots, M$. Here $p(\cdot)$ denotes the joint probability mass function of $\boldsymbol{x}$ while $P(\cdot)$ denotes the joint continuous distribution function of

$\tilde{\boldsymbol{x}}$. The probability on the right is easy to compute based on the cumulative distribution function of the multivariate Gaussian distribution (we used the `R` package `mvtnorm` [11]). The marginal and joint probability functions based on only a subset of the features are computed analogously based on a subset of the full Gaussian distribution, which is also Gaussian.

For the situation where some of the features are categorical and some are continuous, the computation of the conditional expectation is more arduous. However, due to the linearity of the predictive function (9), the conditional expectation reduces to a linear combination of two types of univariate expectations. Let $\mathcal{S}_{\text{cat}}$ and $\bar{\mathcal{S}}_{\text{cat}}$ refer to, respectively, the $\mathcal{S}$ and $\bar{\mathcal{S}}$ part of the categorical features, $\mathcal{C}_{\text{cat}}$, with analogous sets $\mathcal{S}_{\text{cont}}$ and $\bar{\mathcal{S}}_{\text{cont}}$ for the continuous features. We then write the desired conditional expectation as

$$\begin{aligned}\mathbb{E}[f(\boldsymbol{x})|\boldsymbol{x}_{\mathcal{S}}=\boldsymbol{x}_{\mathcal{S}}^*] &= \mathbb{E}\left[\alpha+\sum_{j\in\mathcal{C}_{\text{cat}}}\sum_{l=2}^{L}\beta_{jl}\mathbf{1}(x_j=l)+\sum_{j\in\mathcal{C}_{\text{cont}}}\gamma_k x_j\,\middle|\,\boldsymbol{x}_{\mathcal{S}}=\boldsymbol{x}_{\mathcal{S}}^*\right]\\
&=\alpha+\sum_{j\in\mathcal{C}_{\text{cat}}}\sum_{l=2}^{L}\beta_{jl}\mathbb{E}[\mathbf{1}(x_j=l)|\boldsymbol{x}_{\mathcal{S}}=\boldsymbol{x}_{\mathcal{S}}^*]+\sum_{j\in\mathcal{C}_{\text{cont}}}\gamma_j\mathbb{E}[x_j|\boldsymbol{x}_{\mathcal{S}}=\boldsymbol{x}_{\mathcal{S}}^*]\\
&=\alpha+\sum_{j\in\bar{\mathcal{S}}_{\text{cat}}}\sum_{l=2}^{L}\beta_{jl}\mathbb{E}[\mathbf{1}(x_j=l)|\boldsymbol{x}_{\mathcal{S}}=\boldsymbol{x}_{\mathcal{S}}^*]+\sum_{j\in\mathcal{S}_{\text{cat}}}\sum_{l=2}^{L}\beta_{jl}\mathbf{1}(x_j^*=l)\\
&+\sum_{j\in\bar{\mathcal{S}}_{\text{cont}}}\gamma_j\mathbb{E}[x_j|\boldsymbol{x}_{\mathcal{S}}=\boldsymbol{x}_{\mathcal{S}}^*]+\sum_{j\in\mathcal{S}_{\text{cont}}}\gamma_j x_j^*.\end{aligned}$$

Then, we just need expressions for the two conditional expectations: $\mathbb{E}[\mathbf{1}(x_j = l)|\boldsymbol{x}_{\mathcal{S}} = \boldsymbol{x}_{\mathcal{S}}^*]$ for $j \in \bar{\mathcal{S}}_{\text{cat}}$ and $\mathbb{E}[x_j|\boldsymbol{x}_{\mathcal{S}} = \boldsymbol{x}_{\mathcal{S}}^*]$ for $j \in \bar{\mathcal{S}}_{\text{cont}}$. To calculate them, we use results from [3] on selection (Gaussian) distributions in addition to basic probability theory and numerical integration. Specifically, the conditional expectation for the continuous features takes the form

$$\mathbb{E}[x_j|\boldsymbol{x}_{\mathcal{S}}] = \int_{-\infty}^{\infty} x g(x)\frac{p(\boldsymbol{x}_{\mathcal{S}}|x_j = x)}{p(\boldsymbol{x}_{\mathcal{S}})}\,dx, \tag{13}$$

where $g(x)$ denotes the density of the standard normal (Gaussian) distribution, $p(\boldsymbol{x}_{\mathcal{S}}|x_j = x)$ is the conditional distribution of $\boldsymbol{x}_{\mathcal{S}}$ given x_j, and $p(\boldsymbol{x}_{\mathcal{S}})$ is the marginal distribution of $\boldsymbol{x}_{\mathcal{S}}$. The latter two are both Gaussian and can be evaluated at the specific vector $\boldsymbol{x}_{\mathcal{S}}^*$ using the `R` package `mvtnorm` [11]. Finally, the integral is solved using numerical integration.

For the second expectation, recall that $x_j = l$ corresponds to the original Gaussian variable $\tilde{x}_j$ falling in the interval $(v_l, v_{l+1}]$. Then, the conditional expectation for the categorical features takes form

$$\begin{aligned}\mathbb{E}[\mathbf{1}(x_j = l)|\boldsymbol{x}_{\mathcal{S}}] &= P(v_l < \tilde{x}_j \le v_{l+1}|\boldsymbol{x}_{\mathcal{S}})\\
&= \int_{v_l}^{v_{l+1}} g(x)\frac{p(\boldsymbol{x}_{\mathcal{S}}|\tilde{x}_j = x)}{p(\boldsymbol{x}_{\mathcal{S}})}\,dx,\end{aligned}$$

which can be evaluated similarly to (13) and solved with numerical integration. Once we have computed the necessary conditional expectations for each of the 2^M feature subsets $\mathcal{S}$, we compute the Shapley values using (3). This goes for both the pure categorical case and the case with both categorical and continuous features.

4.4 Simulation Study with only Categorical Features

We evaluate the performance of the different Shapley value approximation methods in the case of only categorical features with six different experimental setups. Table 2 describes these different experiments.

In each experiment, we sample $n_{\text{train}} = 1000$ training observations using the approach from Sect.4.2, where the mean $\boldsymbol{\mu}$ is $\mathbf{0}$ and the covariance matrix is constructed with $\Sigma_{j,j} = 1$, $j = 1, \dots, M$, $\Sigma_{i,j} = \rho$, for $i \neq j$, where $\rho \in \{0, 0.1, 0.3, 0.5, 0.8, 0.9\}$. We set the response to

$$y_i = \alpha + \sum_{j=1}^{M} \sum_{l=2}^{L} \beta_{jl} \mathbf{1}(x_{ij} = l) + \varepsilon_i, \tag{14}$$

where x_{ij} is the jth feature of the ith training observation, ε_i, $i = 1, \dots, n_{\text{train}}$, are i.i.d. random variables sampled from the distribution $N(0, 0.01)$, and α, β_{jl}, $j = 1, \dots, M$, $l = 1, \dots, L$ are parameters sampled from $N(0, 1)$, which are fixed for every experiment. The predictive model, $f(\cdot)$, takes the same form without the noise term (i.e. (9) with $\mathcal{C}_{\text{cont}} = \emptyset$), where the parameters are fit to the n_{train} training observations using standard linear regression. Then, we estimate the Shapley values using the different methods from Table 1.

Table 2 shows that only ctree and the independence method are used when $M > 4$. This is because for $M > 4$, the methods that require one-hot encoding are too computationally expensive. In the same three cases, the number of unique feature combinations (M^L) is so large that a subset of the $T = 2000$ most likely feature combinations are used instead – see the discussion related to (10).

Table 2. An outline of the simulation study when using only categorical features. M denotes the number of features, L denotes the number of categories, and T denotes the number of unique test observations used to compute (10).

M	L	T	Categorical cut-off values	Methods used
3	3	27	$(-\infty, 0, 1, \infty)$	all
3	4	81	$(-\infty, -0.5, 0, 1, \infty)$	all
4	3	64	$(-\infty, 0, 1, \infty)$	all
5	6	2000	$(-\infty, -0.5, -0.25, 0, 0.9, 1, \infty)$	ctree, independence
7	5	2000	$(-\infty, -0.5, -0.25, 0, 1, \infty)$	ctree, independence
10	4	2000	$(-\infty, -0.5, 0, 1, \infty)$	ctree, independence

The results of these experiments are shown in Table 3. When the dependence between the features is small, the performance of each method is almost the same. Note that when the correlation, ρ, is 0 (i.e. the features are independent) and $M \leq 4$, the ctree and independence methods perform equally in terms of MAE, and, in fact, give identical Shapley values. This is because when $\rho = 0$, ctree never rejects the hypothesis of independence when fitting any of the trees. As a result, ctree weighs all training observations equally which is analogous to the independence method. This ability to adapt the complexity of the dependence modeling to the actual dependence in the data is a major advantage of the ctree approach. When $M > 4$, the results of the independence and ctree methods for $\rho = 0$ are slightly different. The reason is that when the dimension is large, ctree tests many more hypotheses and therefore is more likely to reject some of the hypotheses. Since the independence method performs better than ctree in these cases, this suggests that the parameter α could be reduced for higher dimensions to improve the performance in low-correlation settings. This remains to be investigated, however.

As expected, the ctree method outperforms the independence method unless the dependence between the features is very small. The ctree approach also always outperforms (albeit marginally) the empirical, Gaussian, and ctree-onehot approaches. In addition, a major advantage of using ctree is that it does not require one-hot encoding. Since the computational complexity of computing Shapley values grows exponentially in the number of features (one-hot encoded or not), the computation time for methods requiring one-hot-encoding grows quickly compared to ctree. In Table 4, we show the average run time (in seconds) per test observation of each method. The average is taken over all correlations since the computation times are almost the same for each correlation.

The empirical method is the fastest amongst the one-hot encoded methods and is still between two and five times slower than the ctree method. This means that if the number of features/categories is large, using one-hot encoding is not suitable. For the Gaussian method we calculate (7) using both 100 and 1000 samples from the conditional distribution. Table 3 shows that the MAE is slightly smaller in the latter case but from Table 4, we see that it is nearly three times slower. Such a small performance increase is probably not worth the extra computation time.

4.5 Simulation Study with both Categorical and Continuous Features

We also perform a simulation study with both categorical and continuous features. Because we need to use numerical integration to calculate the true Shapley values (see Sect. 4.3), the computational complexity is large even for lower-dimensional settings. Therefore, we restrict ourselves to an experiment with two categorical features with $L = 4$ categories each and two continuous features. Unless otherwise mentioned, the simulation setup follows that of Sect. 4.4. As described in Sect. 4.2, we simulate dependent categorical/continuous data by only transforming two of the four original Gaussian features. The cut-off vector

Table 3. The MAE of each method and correlation, ρ, for each experiment. The bolded numbers denote the smallest MAE per experiment and ρ.

M	L	Method	ρ					
			0	0.1	0.3	0.5	0.8	0.9
3	3	empirical	0.0308	0.0277	0.0358	0.0372	0.0419	0.0430
		Gaussian (100)	0.0308	0.0237	0.0355	0.0330	0.0320	0.0384
		Gaussian (1000)	0.0307	0.0236	0.0354	0.0327	0.0318	0.0383
		ctree-onehot	0.0278	0.0196	0.0345	0.0363	0.0431	0.0432
		ctree	**0.0274**	**0.0191**	**0.0302**	**0.0310**	**0.0244**	**0.0259**
		independence	**0.0274**	**0.0191**	0.0482	0.0777	0.1546	0.2062
3	4	empirical	0.0491	0.0465	0.0447	0.0639	0.0792	0.0659
		Gaussian (100)	0.0402	0.0350	0.0358	0.0620	0.0762	0.0724
		Gaussian (1000)	0.0403	0.0353	0.0361	0.0624	0.0763	0.0738
		ctree-onehot	0.0324	0.0244	0.0429	0.0617	0.0808	0.0680
		ctree	**0.0318**	0.0331	**0.0369**	**0.0422**	**0.0416**	**0.0291**
		independence	**0.0318**	**0.0283**	0.0774	0.1244	0.2060	0.2519
4	3	empirical	0.0385	0.0474	0.0408	0.0502	0.0473	0.0389
		Gaussian (100)	0.0312	0.0381	0.0327	0.0459	0.0475	0.0409
		Gaussian (1000)	0.0312	0.0385	0.0330	0.0453	0.0480	0.0410
		ctree-onehot	0.0234	0.0305	0.0402	0.0530	0.0484	0.0397
		ctree	**0.0223**	0.0414	**0.0387**	**0.0453**	**0.0329**	**0.0253**
		independence	**0.0223**	**0.0355**	0.0961	0.1515	0.2460	0.2848
5	6	ctree	0.0237	0.0492	**0.0621**	**0.0760**	**0.0767**	**0.0899**
		independence	**0.0222**	**0.0469**	0.1231	0.1803	0.2835	0.3039
7	5	ctree	0.0209	**0.0333**	**0.0402**	**0.0542**	**0.0530**	**0.0559**
		independence	**0.0193**	0.0345	0.0794	0.1294	0.1908	0.2397
10	4	ctree	0.0169	**0.0505**	**0.0617**	**0.0607**	**0.0627**	**0.0706**
		independence	**0.0153**	0.0544	0.1593	0.2180	0.3017	0.3412

for the categorical features is set to $(-\infty, -0.5, 0, 1, \infty)$. Similarly to (14), the response is given by

$$y_i = \alpha + \sum_{j=1}^{2}\sum_{l=2}^{4} \beta_{jl}\mathbf{1}(x_{ij} = l) + \sum_{j=3}^{4} \gamma_j x_{ij} + \varepsilon_i,$$

for which we fit a linear regression model of the same form without the error term to act as the predictive model $f(\cdot)$.

Then, we estimate the Shapley values using the methods from Table 1 except for the Gaussian method with 1000 samples. This method is excluded since Sect. 4.4 showed that its performance was very similar to that of the Gaussian method with 100 samples but significantly more time consuming. To compare the

Table 4. The mean run time (in seconds) per test observation, T, where the mean is taken over all correlations, ρ.

M	L	T	Method	Mean time per test obs
3	3	27	empirical	0.086
			Gaussian (100)	4.833
			Gaussian (1000)	13.295
			ctree-onehot	0.338
			ctree	0.040
			independence	0.013
3	4	64	empirical	0.553
			Gaussian (100)	8.041
			Gaussian (1000)	29.160
			ctree-onehot	1.807
			ctree	0.023
			independence	0.007
4	3	81	empirical	0.293
			Gaussian (100)	3.845
			Gaussian (1000)	12.983
			ctree-onehot	0.841
			ctree	0.052
			independence	0.012
5	6	2000	ctree	0.118
			independence	0.030
7	5	2000	ctree	0.590
			independence	0.158
10	4	2000	ctree	6.718
			independence	2.066

performance of the different methods, we sample $T = 500$ observations from the joint distribution of the features and compute the MAE using (10) as described in Sect. 4.1.

The results are displayed in Table 5. The Gaussian method is the best performing method when $\rho = 0.1, 0.3, 0.5$ while the empirical and ctree methods are the best performing when $\rho = 0.8$ and $\rho = 0.9$, respectively. The results are not surprising since we only have two categorical features. With more categorical features or categories, we expect that the ctree method would outperform the other ones when ρ is not small. We also show the run time of each method in Table 6. The one-hot encoded methods are between nine and 75 times slower than the ctree method. This demonstrates, again, the value of using the ctree method when estimating Shapley values with categorical features.

Table 5. The MAE of each method and correlation, ρ, for the experiment with two continuous and two categorical features ($L = 4$ categories each). The bolded numbers denote the smallest MAE per ρ.

M	L	Method	ρ					
			0	0.1	0.3	0.5	0.8	0.9
2 cont/2 cat	4	empirical	0.0853	0.0852	0.0898	0.0913	**0.0973**	0.1027
		Gaussian (100)	0.0570	**0.0586**	**0.0664**	**0.0662**	0.1544	0.2417
		ctree-onehot	0.0266	0.0714	0.1061	0.1024	0.1221	0.1188
		ctree	**0.0093**	0.0848	0.1073	0.1060	0.0977	**0.0917**
		independence	**0.0093**	0.0790	0.2178	0.3520	0.5524	0.6505

Table 6. The mean run time (in seconds) per test observation, T, where the mean is taken over all correlations, ρ. The simulation study has two continuous features and two categorical features ($L = 4$ categories each).

M	L	T	Method	Mean time per test obs
4	4	500	empirical	0.758
			Gaussian (100)	5.914
			ctree-onehot	1.514
			ctree	0.082
			independence	0.057

5 Real Data Example

Although there is a growing literature of how to explain black-box models, there are very few studies that focus on quantifying the relevance of these methods [2]. This makes it difficult to compare different explainability methods on a real data set since there is no ground truth. One partial solution is to compare how different explainability models rank the same features for predictions based on specific test observations.

In this section, we use a data set from the 2018 FICO Explainable Machine Learning Challenge [9] aimed at motivating the creation of explainable predictive models. The data set is of Home Equity Line of Credit (HELOC) applications made by homeowners. The response is a binary feature called RiskPerformance that takes the value 1 ('Bad') if the customer is more than 90 days late on his or her payment and 0 ('Good') otherwise. 52% of customers have the response 'Bad' and 48% have the response 'Good'. There are 23 features: 21 continuous and two categorical (with eight and nine categories, respectively) which can be used to model the probability of being a 'Bad' customer. Features with the value –9 are assumed missing. We remove the rows where all features are missing.

We first use this data set to compare the Shapley values calculated using the independence approach with those calculated with our ctree approach. Then, for a few test observations, we see how the Shapley explanations compare with the explanations from the 2018 FICO challenge Recognition Award winning team from Duke University [5] (hereafter referred to as just 'Duke').

After removing the missing data and a test set of 100 observations, we use the remaining 9,765 observations to train a 5-fold cross validation (CV) model using xgboost [6] and then average these to form the final model. Our model achieves an accuracy of 0.737 (compared to Duke's accuracy of 0.74). In our experience, explanation methods often behave differently when there is dependence between the features. As a measure of dependence, we use the standard Pearson correlation for all continuous features, Cramer's V correlation measure [7] for categorical features, and the correlation ratio [10] for continuous and categorical features. The feature 'MSinceMostRecentInqexcl7days' is the least correlated with the rest of the features with correlations between –0.109 and 0.07. The 22 other features are strongly correlated with at least one other feature (max absolute correlations between 0.4 and 0.99).

Turning to the Shapley value comparisons, we estimate the Shapley values of the features belonging to the 100 test observations using the independence approach and the ctree approach. Then, we plot the Shapley value estimates against each other for a selection of four features in Fig. 2. The top left panel shows the Shapley values of one of the two categorical features ('MaxDelq2PublicRecLast12M'). Both methods give Shapley values fairly close to 0 for this feature, but there are some differences. The top right panel shows an example of a feature ('ExternalRiskEstimate') where the two methods estimate quite different Shapley values. Since these are some of the largest (absolute) Shapley values, this is one of the most influential features. We also see that for most test observations, the independence method estimates more extreme Shapley values than the ctree method.

The bottom left panel shows a feature ('MSinceMostRecentInqexcl7days') where the two methods estimate relatively similar Shapley values. As noted above, this feature is the least correlated with the rest of the features. We believe the two methods behave similarly because the independence method performs best when dealing with nearly independent features. Finally, the bottom right panel shows a feature ('NumTrades90Ever2DerogPubRec') where the independence method assigns most test observations a Shapley value very close to 0 while the ctree method does not. Although not plotted, we see this trend for 6 out of the 23 features. We notice that each of these 6 features are highly correlated with at least one other feature (max absolute correlation between 0.46 and 0.99). We suspect that the methods behave differently because of the independence method's failure to account for dependence between features. We also colour three random test observations to show that for some test observations (say 'green'), all Shapley values are estimated very similarly for the two methods, while for others (say 'blue'), the methods are sometimes quite different.

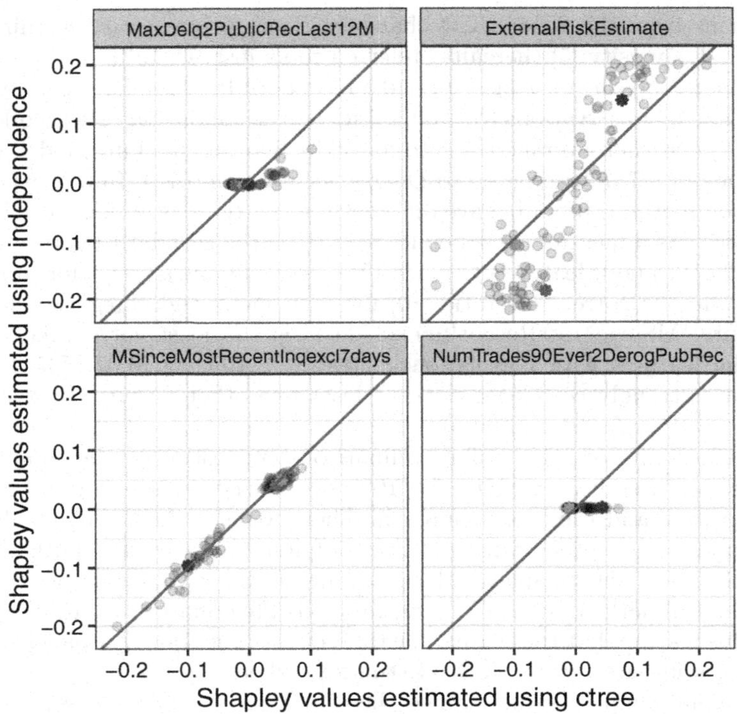

Fig. 2. The Shapley values of 100 test observations calculated using both the independence and the ctree method for four of the 23 features. (Color figure online)

We also attempt to compare explanations based on Shapley values (estimated with either the independence or ctree method) with those based on Duke's approach [5] We reinforce that there is *no ground truth* when it comes to explanations and that Duke does not use Shapley values in their solution. Therefore, we only compare how these three methods *rank* feature importance for specific test observations.

Duke's explainability approach is based on 10 smaller regression models fit to 10 partitions (below called 'groups') of the features. They use a combination of learned weights and risks to calculate the most influential group for each customer/test observation. Based on our understanding, if the customer has a large predicted probability of being 'Bad', the largest weight × risk is the most influential group (given rank 1), while for small predicted probabilities, the largest weight divided by risk is given rank 1. It is not clear how they rank medium-range predictions.

We speculate that Duke does not properly account for feature dependence since they fit 10 independent models that only interact using an overall learned risk for each model. To test this hypothesis, we compare the group rankings of a few[3] customers/test observations calculated by 1. Duke, 2. The Shapley approach under the independence assumption, and 3. Our new Shapley approach that uses conditional inference trees.

To calculate group importance based on Shapley values for a given test observation, we first estimate the Shapley values of each feature either either the independence or ctree approach. Then, we sum the Shapley values of the features belonging to the same group. This gives 10 new grouped Shapley values. Finally, we rank the grouped Shapley values by giving rank 1 to the group with the largest absolute grouped Shapley value. While the prediction models being compared here are different (we use an xgboost model while Duke does not), the two models have very similar overall performance and give similar predictions to specific test observations. We believe this validates the rough comparison below.

We observe that for test observations with a large predicted probability of being 'Bad', there is little pattern among the rankings calculated by the three explanation methods. However, when Duke and independence give a group the same ranking out of 10 (and ctree does not), we notice that this group includes at least one feature that is very correlated with a feature in another group. On the other hand, for test observations with a small predicted probability of being 'Bad', we notice that all three explanation methods rank the groups similarly. Again, the only time ctree ranks a group differently than Duke and independence (but Duke and independence rank similarly), the group includes at least one feature highly correlated with a feature in another group.

6 Conclusion

The aim of this paper was to extend [14] and [1]'s Shapley methodology to explain mixed dependent features using conditional inference trees [12]. We showed in two simulation studies that when the features are even mildly dependent, it is advantageous to use our ctree method over the traditional independence method. Although ctree often has comparable accuracy to some of [1]'s methods, those methods require transforming the categorical features to one-hot encoded features. We demonstrated that such one-hot encoding leads to a substantial increase in computation time, making it infeasible in high dimensions.

We also demonstrated our methodology on a real financial data set. We first compared the Shapley values of 100 test observations calculated using the independence and ctree approaches. We noticed that the methods performed similarly for an almost independent feature but otherwise performed quite differently.

Then, we compared explanations based on the independence/ctree Shapley approaches with those based on Duke's approach [5]. We had to fall back to comparing how the different methods ranked features rather than the explanations themselves because there is no ground truth when it comes to explainability.

[3] Duke's explanations were not readily available. For a given test observation, we had to manually input 23 feature values into a web application to get an explanation. Therefore, it was too time consuming to compare many test observations.

It was difficult to argue for one explanatory approach over another; however, Duke's rankings seemed to agree more with the rankings based on Shapley values calculated under independence (which we saw was inaccurate in simulation studies), than with our proposed ctree based Shapley value estimation method.

References

1. Aas, K., Jullum, M., Løland, A.: Explaining individual predictions when features are dependent: More accurate approximations to shapley values (2019). arXiv preprint arXiv:1903.10464
2. Adadi, A., Berrada, M.: Peeking inside the black-box: a survey on explainable artificial intelligence (xai). IEEE Access **6**, 52138–52160 (2018)
3. Arellano-Valle, R.B., Branco, M.D., Genton, M.G.: A unified view on skewed distributions arising from selections. Can. J. Stat. **34**(4), 581–601 (2006)
4. Breiman, L., Friedman, J., Olshen, R., Stone, C.: Classification and Regression Trees. Chapman and Hall, London (1984)
5. Chen, C., Lin, K., Rudin, C., Shaposhnik, Y., Wang, S., Wang, T.: An interpretable model with globally consistent explanations for credit risk (2018). arXiv preprint arXiv:1811.12615
6. Chen, T., Guestrin, C.: XGBoost: a scalable tree boosting system. In: Proceedings of the 22nd ACM SIGKDD International Conference on Knowledge Discovery and Data Mining (KDD), pp. 785–794. ACM (2016)
7. Cramir, H.: Mathematical Methods of Statistics, p. 500. Princeton University Press, Princeton (1946)
8. Elith, J., Leathwick, J.R., Hastie, T.: A working guide to boosted regression trees. J. Anim. Ecol. **77**(4), 802–813 (2008)
9. FICO: Explainable machine learning challenge (2018). https://community.fico.com/s/explainable-machine-learning-challenge
10. Fisher, R.A.: Statistical methods for research workers. In: Kotz, S., Johnson, N.L. (eds.) Breakthroughs in Statistics, pp. 66–70. Springer, Heidelberg (1992). https://doi.org/10.1007/978-1-4612-4380-9_6
11. Genz, A., Bretz, F.: Computation of Multivariate Normal and t Probabilities. Lecture Notes in Statistics. Springer, Heidelberg (2009). https://doi.org/10.1007/978-3-642-01689-9
12. Hothorn, T., Hornik, K., Zeileis, A.: Unbiased recursive partitioning: a conditional inference framework. J. Comput. Graph. Stat. **15**(3), 651–674 (2006)
13. Hothorn, T., Zeileis, A.: partykit: A modular toolkit for recursive partytioning in R. J. Mach. Learn. Res. **16**, 3905–3909 (2015)
14. Lundberg, S.M., Erion, G.G., Lee, S.I.: Consistent individualized feature attribution for tree ensembles (2018). arXiv preprint arXiv:1802.03888
15. Lundberg, S.M., Lee, S.I.: A unified approach to interpreting model predictions. In: Advances in Neural Information Processing Systems. pp. 4768–4777. Curram Associates Inc., New York (2017)
16. Quinlan, J.R.: C4.5: Programs for Machine Learning. Morgan Kaufmann Publishers Inc., Burlington (1993)
17. Team, R.C.: R: A Language and Environment for Statistical Computing. R Foundation for Statistical Computing, Vienna, Austria (2019)
18. Sellereite, N., Jullum, M.: shapr: an r-package for explaining machine learning models with dependence-aware shapley values. J. Open Source Softw. **5**(46), 2027 (2020)

19. Shapley, L.S.: A value for N-person games. Contrib. Theory Games **2**, 307–317 (1953)
20. Štrumbelj, E., Kononenko, I.: An efficient explanation of individual classifications using game theory. J. Mach. Learn. Res. **11**, 1–18 (2010)
21. Štrumbelj, E., Kononenko, I.: Explaining prediction models and individual predictions with feature contributions. Knowl. Inf. Syst. **41**(3), 647–665 (2013). https://doi.org/10.1007/s10115-013-0679-x

Explainable Deep Learning for Fault Prognostics in Complex Systems: A Particle Accelerator Use-Case

Lukas Felsberger[1,3(✉)], Andrea Apollonio[3], Thomas Cartier-Michaud[3], Andreas Müller[2], Benjamin Todd[3], and Dieter Kranzlmüller[1]

[1] MNM-Team, Ludwig-Maximilians-Universität Muenchen, Oettingenstr. 67, 80538 München, Germany
[2] Hochschule Darmstadt, Haardtring 100, 64295 Darmstadt, Germany
[3] CERN, Route de Meyrin, 1211 Genève, Switzerland
lukas.felsberger@cern.ch

Abstract. Sophisticated infrastructures often exhibit misbehaviour and failures resulting from complex interactions of their constituent subsystems. Such infrastructures use alarms, event and fault information, which is recorded to help diagnose and repair failure conditions by operations experts. This data can be analysed using explainable artificial intelligence to attempt to reveal precursors and eventual root causes. The proposed method is first applied to synthetic data in order to prove functionality. With synthetic data the framework makes extremely precise predictions and root causes can be identified correctly. Subsequently, the method is applied to real data from a complex particle accelerator system. In the real data setting, deep learning models produce accurate predictive models from less than ten error examples when precursors are captured. The approach described herein is a potentially valuable tool for operations experts to identify precursors in complex infrastructures.

Keywords: Prognostics and diagnostics · Explainable AI · Deep learning · Multivariate time series

1 Introduction

Technical infrastructures are becoming increasingly complex while demands on availability are constantly rising. Failures of simple systems can often be manually analyzed in a relatively straight-forward manner by experts, whereas systems with increasing complexity and dependencies between infrastructures render manual failure analysis largely infeasible. This is primarily due to the sheer amount of potentially relevant failure precursors that must be considered.

This work has been sponsored by the German Federal Ministry of Education and Research (grant no. 05E12CHA).

Published by Springer Nature Switzerland AG 2020
A. Holzinger et al. (Eds.): CD-MAKE 2020, LNCS 12279, pp. 139–158, 2020.
https://doi.org/10.1007/978-3-030-57321-8_8

In this study, modern particle accelerators are taken as example of complex infrastructures. Complete analytical models of failures and abnormal behaviors of particle accelerators are usually impossible; accelerators have numerous inter-operating subsystems, recording large amounts of diverse data, which is difficult to analyse. In addition, the operational modes of particle accelerators can change over time, influencing the reliability and operating margins of sub-systems (e.g. an accelerator may operate as both an ion mode or a proton mode, with significant operating margins in one mode, and limited margins in the other). Moreover, an accelerator is a continuously evolving infrastructure, maintenance is carried out, sub-systems are upgraded and evolved, modes of operation are tuned, and adjusted. All combined, this makes traditional modelling approaches inadequate.

In general, operation data, such as system alarms, events, faults, physical measurements, etc., are abundant and are logged at rates and dimensionalities which are impossible to analyze in real time by a human operator. Hence, automated data driven analyses are required to assist human operators in diagnosis of system operation.

For application in particle accelerator environments, data driven methods need to handle heterogeneous data sources (e.g. binary alarms, discrete logged settings, continuous monitoring values), function with raw data and extract features automatically, learn from few observed failures and many observed non-failures (imbalanced data), and scale to several hundreds of input signals.

A data driven prognostics and diagnostics framework should reveal both (a) prediction of failures and alarms in advance and (b) clear insights for the interpretation of failure predictions. This would allow operators to increase infrastructure availability by preventive and pro-active actions to mitigate or remove failure conditions.

Related Work. Methods to predict faults have been reviewed extensively in the fields of prognostics and diagnostics [14,28,34], system health management [18] and predictive maintenance [26]. They are commonly classified as model driven, when a-priori modeling of the system behaviour is employed, or data driven, when the system behaviour is inferred from data. As model driven approaches are becoming infeasible when prior knowledge on the infrastructure behaviour is limited, only data driven methods are considered here.

Within data driven approaches, a distinction can be made between classical Machine Learning (ML) (e.g. support vector machine, k-nearest neighbour, decision tree), deep learning (e.g. deep belief networks, convolutional neural networks, recurrent neural networks) and probabilistic reasoning (e.g. Hidden Markov models, Gaussian Processes, Bayesian Graphical Networks) methods.

Further possible classifications are based on the field of application (e.g. mechanical systems, electronics, software), the complexity of the studied system (e.g. component, unit, system, system of system, human interaction), the type of learning (supervised, semi-supervised, unsupervised) and the kind of data used (univariate, multivariate, binary, numeric, discrete, text, raw data, features). Methods are usually not classified by the interpretability and explainability of their predictions, which is an important criterion for the considered use case and for many other applications [1]. In the following, related work will be grouped by choice of modeling approach.

Support-Vector Machines (SVMs) play a large role within traditional ML approaches. Zhu et al. [35] and Fulp et al. [13] developed SVM based methods to predict the failures of hard drives based on features indicating system health. Leahy et al. [19] predicted wind turbine failures based on features of data from Supervisory Control and Data Acquisition (SCADA) systems in wind turbines. Fronza et al. [12] extended the approach to systems of systems by predicting failures in large software systems. SVMs would allow interpretation of trained models, especially with linear Kernel functions. However, none of the authors considered investigating the structure of the learned models in order to gain insights into the failure mechanisms of the systems.

L1 regularized Granger causality was developed by Qiu et al. [25] to detect root causes of anomalies in industrial processes. They reported interpretable results, scalability and robust performance. However, the method was not used to predict faults.

Association rule mining based methods were used by Vilalta et al. [31] and Serio et al. [30] to identify failure mechanisms in complex infrastructures using interpretable models. Vilalta et al. detected anomalies in computer networks. The class imbalance problem is overcome by learning only from the minority class representing anomalies. They reported good accuracy but limited applicability of the method. The work by Serio et al. represents the only relevant application in the particle accelerator domain. The authors successfully extracted expert verified fault dependencies between subsystems from logging data. However, time dependence between events were not considered and fault predictions are therefore not possible.

As an example of probabilistic reasoning methods, Mori et al. [22] proposed a Bayesian graphical model approach to perform root cause diagnosis in industrial processes. The method is interpretable and accurate. At the overlap of probabilistic modeling and deep learning is the work of Liu et al. [20]. The framework combines ideas from state space modeling with Restricted Boltzmann Machines or Deep Neural Networks to identify root causes of anomalies in industrial processes. High accuracy and scalability were reported.

With deep learning methods Saeki et al. [27] classified wind turbine generator anomalies from spectral data. On a test data set, a visual explanation technique attributed importance to the same failure precursors as human experts. They noted that the data set used was not representative for real world scenarios. Amarsinghe et al. [2] detected Denial of Service attacks in computer networks using a Deep Neural Network and a so called Layer-wise Relevance Propagation (LRP) introduced by Bach et al. [4] to highlight relevant inputs for classification decisions. High classification accuracy was reported and explanations were intuitive to interpret. However, the method used features generated from raw data. Bach-Andersen et al. [5] performed an extensive study of early fault precursor detection for ball bearings in wind turbines using raw spectral data. They compared logistic regression, fully connected neural networks and deep convolutional neural networks across three classification tasks. The deep network was found to perform the best. Using a visualization technique of higher layers of the trained deep network, the strong performance of the network could be explained and insights about the failure behaviour were derived. The method yielded accurate results, handled class imbalance and scaled well.

Demonstrating performance advantage and universality, explainable deep learning frameworks seem promising for fault prediction in the accelerator domain. The work of Bach-Andersen et al. provides a strong baseline but it was optimized for a different application domain and used a data structure which is not compatible with the particle accelerator use case. Moreover, the LRP mechanism by Bach et al. was more intuitive to the authors of this study than the high level feature visualization used in Andersen et al. Furthermore, LRP is based on a more firmly established theory [21,29]. A recent extensive review by Fawaz et al. [10] on deep learning architectures for time series problems reveals that convolutional neural network structures outperform traditional methods across a variety of multivariate time series classification tasks. Similar findings were previously reported by Wang et al. [32] for univariate time series. Therefore, we chose neural network architectures as suggested in Fawaz et al. for failure prediction and LRP by Bach et al as the explanation mechanism for the framework presented in this study. The goal is to evaluate whether such a framework can successfully be applied as fault prognostics and diagnostics tool in the accelerator domain and whether it provides significant advantages over classical ML methods. The main contribution of this work is the first application of state-of-the-art deep learning for multivariate time series combined with explainable AI methods in the particle accelerator domain.

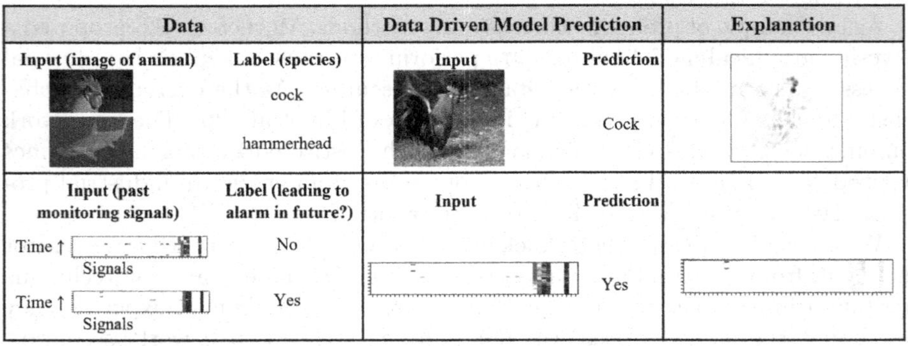

Fig. 1. Upper Row: Machine learning algorithms are able to identify animal species based on labeled images. Explanation techniques help to understand which pixels contribute the most to assign a certain species to an input image. [4] Lower Row: In the same way, a machine learning algorithm can learn a model to predict infrastructure failures based on time series data of monitoring signals. Here explanation techniques provide information about the most relevant signals leading to the failure.

The idea of the proposed framework is illustrated in Fig. 1. Time series of data are obtained during the operation of complex infrastructures, such as particle accelerators. Operational alarms or anomalies lead to specific fault events in the data. A sliding window approach can extract snapshots of the machine behaviour before the occurrence of fault events and snapshots during normal operation. Thereby, a supervised training data set is generated without manual labeling effort. From such data, a discriminator, such as a deep neural network, can learn general rules to predict when certain system faults occur. If such a fault is predicted, LRP highlights the most relevant fault precursors. This helps system experts understand the expected fault mechanism. With this knowledge they can take preventive measures to avoid the fault before it happens. For complex infrastructures effective use of such a method can help to reduce unexpected downtime and increase system availability.

For example, the algorithm could predict a critical failure leading to interruption of operations, such as power converter preventive shut down in a particle accelerator. Power converters supply precise electrical currents to magnets to focus and bend the particle beam. Without knowing the relevant precursors, system experts cannot identify how to prevent the shut down due to the sheer amount of potentially relevant monitoring signals. However, if the LRP highlights that the relevant signal is a noisy measurement of the particle beam position, the experts can simply replace the faulty beam position monitor. If successful, the power converter will not shut down due to erroneous beam position measurements and operations will not be interrupted.

The framework is introduced in Sect. 2. In Sect. 3 the effectiveness and the suitability of the framework are evaluated in experiments with synthetically generated time series data. Then, the method is applied to real world logging data sets of a particle accelerator to verify its suitability for the accelerator domain. Throughout, the deep learning frameworks are compared to classical machine learning methods, such as support-vector machines, random forests, and k-nearest-neighbor classifiers. Summary, Conclusions and Outlook are given in Sect. 4.

2 Methodology

Definitions and Overview. The subject of study is an infrastructure $\mathbf{I}$ which can be composed of multiple sub-systems. A range of N observable signals, monitors the behaviour of the infrastructure and its environment over time, forming a multivariate time series, $\mathbf{S} = \{\mathbf{S}_{i,t} : i \in [1 : N] \text{ and } t \in \mathbb{N}\}$. These can include logged continuous and discrete parameters, event- and alarm-logs, input- and output-signals, etc. The infrastructure has a range of failure modes which indicate certain malfunctions. These failure modes are observable in a subset of signals.

An autoregressive model predicts the future behaviour of a system based on its current and past states. For a complex infrastructure, it can be expected that failures may appear without announcing themselves in advance by precursors.

Even for situations with advance precursors, not all relevant processes might be monitored. Therefore, an autoregressive model can only approximate future failures based on time-discrete monitoring signals of complex infrastructures,

$$\mathbf{S}^F_{N,[t+t_p\delta t\ :\ t+(t_p+n_o)\delta t]} \approx \mathbf{\Phi}(\mathbf{S}^P_{[1:N],[t-n_i\delta t\ :\ t]})$$

with

- $\mathbf{S}^F_{N,[t+t_p\delta t\ :\ t+(t_p+n_o)\delta t]} = 1$, if a failure occurs between time $t+t_p\delta t$ and time $t+(t_p+n_o)\delta t$, and zero otherwise,
- $\mathbf{S}^P_{[1:N],[t-n_i\delta t\ :\ t]}$ being finite histories of observed signals covering the time stamps $t-n_i\delta t$ to t and being considered as possible precursors,
- δt being the discretization time,
- t_p the prediction- or lead-time,
- n_o the number of time steps chosen to capture the future failure behaviour,
- n_i the number of discrete time steps chosen to capture the history of the observed signals and
- $\mathbf{\Phi}$ an auto-regressive model,

as illustrated in Fig. 2.

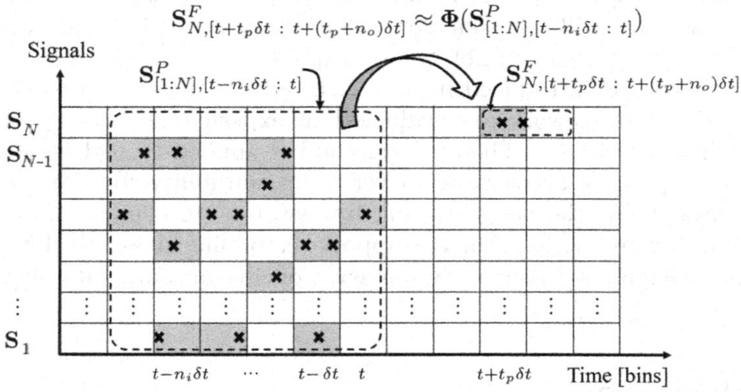

Fig. 2. Time discrete model formulation. The x-axis represents discrete time and the y-axis monitoring signals of the investigated infrastructure. Crosses mark events which could be faults, alarms, changes in monitoring values, etc. Events of the signal $\mathbf{S}_N$ represent infrastructure faults that the model $\mathbf{\Phi}(\cdot)$ predicts.

In a few simple cases, the model $\mathbf{\Phi}(\cdot)$ can be obtained from first principles. In the case of complex infrastructure, the model needs to be determined in a data driven fashion using machine learning or time series analysis techniques. Models can learn the system behaviour from time series data in a supervised fashion by supplying pairs of input-data, $\mathbf{S}^P_{[1:N],[t-n_i\delta t\ :\ t]}$, and output- or target-data, $\mathbf{S}^F_{N,[t+t_p\delta t\ :\ t+(t_p+n_o)\delta t]}$, of the observed history of the studied infrastructure.

Once such a model has been trained, it can predict failures when supplied with observed data of the infrastructure. However, acting as black box it is not able to provide operators of the infrastructure any further information concerning the predicted failures. Such information could be used for actions to prevent the reoccurence of the failure observed.

To address this, the framework provides a relevance measure, $\rho(\mathbf{S}^P) \in \mathbb{R}^{(n_i,N)}$, of each of the observed signals at each time step, which signifies the most relevant input signals for model predictions. This helps infrastructure operators to focus their attention on a small range of potential precursors. The framework does not search for causality but temporal precedence of correlated failure precursors [9]. However, it helps experts to verify causal dependencies and generate model based descriptions of causal failure behaviour [11].

The framework can be used as a real-time analysis tool, acquiring data continuously from the infrastructure as an input, predict imminent failures as an output. In this manner it could advise operators to take preventive measures. These actions require a certain lead-time, $t_p > 0$, to allow the system operators time to preemptively act on predicted failures. As a post-mortem tool, the framework could be used without lead-time constraints, in the analysis and explanation of complex failure mechanisms, which could then be investigated by system experts to mitigate reoccurrence. All of these considerations are particularly relevant for future generations of high-energy particle accelerators, for which the increasing size (order of 100 km), are expected to set unprecedented challenges in terms of maintainability of the infrastructures.

Machine Learning Pipeline. This Subsection describes in more detail how predictive models $\mathbf{\Phi}(\cdot)$ are learned from observed monitoring data.

Data Collection. The observable signals $\mathbf{S}$ of the studied infrastructure are stored in time series format in a data-set $\mathcal{D}$. Based on a-priori expert knowledge, a preselection of potentially relevant signals can reduce the required storage capacities. Further details on the data collection will be given for the use cases 3.

Model Selection and Evaluation. The problem formulation contains a range of hyperparameters to be optimized, e.g. $[\delta T, n_i, n_o, t_p]$, some of which are introduced later in this Section. To do so, a K-fold validation strategy is adopted for the studied use-cases [7]. It is performed by splitting the overall data-set, $\mathcal{D}$, in a training set, $\mathcal{D}_{train}$ up to time t_{split}, and a final test set, $\mathcal{D}_{test}$ after time t_{split}. The K-folds for hyperparameter selection are obtained by a further splitting of the training set into K sub-training sets at splitting times $t_{sub-split,k}, k = 1, ..., K$.

Subsampling. As failures in the considered infrastructures are rare, the target data $\mathbf{S}_N^F$ will contain few failures and many more '0's (no failures) than '1's (failures). The resulting class imbalance depends on the number of faults in the target variable, the discretization time δt, the number of time steps to capture failure behaviour n_o, and the length of the time series available for training.

Depending on the parameters, imbalances up to $1:10^4$ are obtained. Such a data-set requires balancing of the classes to ensure good performance of classifiers.

This is primarily achieved by randomly subsampling the majority class until a certain target ratio $p_{0,targ} = freq(cl_0)/freq(cl_1)$, is reached. Here, $freq(cl_x)$ denotes the number of class 'x' instances in the data set.[1]

More advanced sampling strategies were not tested in this initial study. They are often based on transformations of the data. Due to the complexity of the data structure suitable transformations could not be identified a priori and would have added optimization hyperparameters. Nevertheless, advanced subsampling strategies should be subject of future investigations.

After subsampling, data n_{cov} time-steps before and after each class '1' instance are added to the training set as it leads to better performance of the learned models. This can be seen as an oversampling method of class '0' to increase 'contrast' in the class '1' neighbourhood.

Choosing the output representation window length $n_o > 1$ also leads to an artificial oversampling of class '1' because a discretized fault can be captured n_o times within the representation window. As can be seen in the results Section, this can lead to improved classification performance at reduced time resolution.

Input Filtering and Normalization. Input signals having values non-equal to zero less than α_{min}[2] times or having a variance smaller or equal to σ_{min}[3] are automatically removed. After the filtering, the input signals of the training data are normalized to the range $[0, 1]$.

Model Learning Algorithms. To learn a model $\mathbf{\Phi}(\cdot)$, from pairs of historical input- and output-data of the infrastructure, deep learning algorithms and classical machine learning algorithms were used. The target variables take values '0' and '1'. Hence, the failure forecasting problem is formulated as binary classification.

Based on recent studies of deep learning for multivariate time series classification, fully-convolutional neural networks are chosen as main classification architecture. They reach state-of-the-art performance while being faster to train than recurrent neural networks [10,32]. These deep networks were compared against SVM, Random-Forest, and K-Nearest-Neighbour classifiers, representing classical ML techniques. Overall, the following algorithms were used:

[1] Both the training and test data set are subsampled for computational performance reasons. Keeping the full data set would lead to slow out-of-memory-computations due to the size of the input data. Subsampling the test set is normally avoided as it could induce a bias in the generalization performance estimation [15]. However, tests with different subsampling ratios showed no influence on the generalitzation performance estimation for the studied scenarios. Hence, the subsampling of the test set does not bias the performance estimation but allows faster computation here.

[2] Unless stated otherwise, $\alpha_{min} = 4$, as it was the minimal number of examples from which the selected algorithms could learn from [3].

[3] Unless stated otherwise, $\sigma_{min} = 0$, to only remove constant signals which do not contain any discriminatory information.

- FCN: The classifier is based on an architecture proposed by Wang et al. [32]. It consists of three convolutional blocks with three operations in each: a convolution is followed by a batch normalization [17] and fed into a ReLU activation. The output of the last convolutional block is averaged over the whole time-dimension in a Global Average Pooling layer (GAP). Lastly, the GAP's output is fully connected to a traditional softmax classifier.
  The convolutions are characterised by having a stride of 1 with zero padding to conserve the shape of the input data. The three convolution layers contain 128, 256, and 128 filters with a filter length of 8, 5, and 3, respectively. It was selected as it achieved the highest accuracy across 13 multivariate time series datasets in the review by Fawaz et al. [10]. The implementation of the review paper is used with minor modifications. The number of training epochs is set to 2000. An early stop criterion ensures that training is terminated if the validation loss is not decreasing by more than 0.001 after 200 epochs, with the loss function set to categorical cross-entropy.
- FCN2drop: This is the same classifier as FCN, except with dropout applied to two layers in the network. Dropout is applied on the second convolution and on the GAP layer with a dropout probability of $p_{drop} = 0.5$. Due to the scarcity of class '1' items in the learning data, dropout regularization is expected to prevent overfitting of the network.
- FCN3drop: This is the same classifier as FCN, except with dropout applied to three layers in the network. Dropout is applied on the second and third convolution and on the GAP layer with $p_{drop} = 0.7$.
- tCNN: As proposed by Zhao et al. [33], the network consists of two convolutional layers with 6 and 12 filters, respectively. The final layer is a traditional fully-connected layer with sigmoid activation function. It uses the mean-squared error instead of cross-entropy as loss function. The implementation from Fawaz et al. is taken using the same early stopping criterion as for the FCN models.
- SVM: A support vector machine with linear kernel functions. The implementation from [24] is used with default parameters.
- RF: A random forest classifier is a meta classifier of many decision trees. The implementation from [24] is used with default parameters except for the number of features to consider for optimal splitting set to the square-root of the number of features.
- kNN: A k-Nearest-Neighbour classifier based on the implementation from [24] using default parameters except for $n = 7$ neighbours.

The classifier parameters were manually pre-selected based on recommendations in the Scikit-learn user guide [24] and preliminary experiments on data-sets as described in Sect. 3. SVM, RF and kNN classifiers require the input to be one-dimensional. Therefore, the 2D multivariate time series input data is flattened to one dimension when fed into the classifier for training and prediction.

To evaluate the performance of the classifiers, the accuracy and the F1 score on the test-set is examined. Due to the imbalance of classes, the accuracy might be misleading. Hence, additionally the fraction of the majority class in the test-set is reported for reference.

Explaining Predictions. In order to help operation experts interpreting predictions of the framework and discovering failure mechanisms, the relevance of each input at discrete time steps in the observed history, $\rho(\mathbf{S}^P) \in \mathbb{R}^{(n_i,N)}$, is quantified and reported.

For deep learning methods, several such relevance reporting techniques have been developed. The so-called LRP was chosen for implementation as it provides best-in-class explanations [29]. It is based on a backward pass within the neural network which is layer-wise relevance conserving. Neurons contributing the most to the following layer receive most relevance from it during its backwards pass.

Testing the Gradient x Input [21], LRP-0, and LRP-ϵ rules [4], the LRP-0 rule showed a better omission of irrelevant failure precursors with synthetic test data.

For the classical machine learning methods, the input relevance for the SVM classifier was calculated by evaluating the input feature weight vector [24]. Input activations for kNN and RF are not calculated as these classifiers were solely used as classification performance benchmarks. The input relevance is depicted as 2D heatmaps with more relevant inputs being represented in darker colours.

The quality and usefulness of explanations for its users should be assessed as proposed in the literature (e.g. Holzinger et al. [16]). Since the proposed method is currently a proof of concept, the quality of explanations could only be assessed by assuming the conditions of actual usage scenarios. This is carried out by qualitatively evaluating three criteria (inspired by [16]) for the use cases in Sect. 3: The completeness of the provided explanation factors, the ease of understanding, and the degree of causality within the studied processes that can be derived from the explanation. The timeliness of explanations is not discussed as it can always be ensured, depending on the choice of the prediction lead time t_p and the intended usage as either predictive or post-mortem explanation.

3 Numerical Experiments

The method described above is applied to several use-cases, which are briefly introduced. Implementations are available on github[4].

Synthetic Data Experiments. The framework is tested with synthetically generated data. In comparison to the real-world data-sets it has the advantage of a known ground truth. This allows to verify if the framework predicts faults accurately and identifies the correct failure precursors.[5]

Noise Robustness. In this experiment, an infrastructure is modeled by n_{rand} systems firing precursors randomly and one system firing two consequent failure precursors which are always followed by an infrastructure failure S_s^F. The timing

[4] https://github.com/lfelsber/alarmsMining.

[5] It has to pointed out that the performance of the methods on synthetic data can not directly be generalized to real world data due to differences in data distributions.

of the alarms is illustrated in Fig. 3. The goal is to study the ability of the framework to filter and explain the deterministic pattern at increasing numbers n_{rand} of randomly firing systems despite being provided only less than ten failures to learn from.

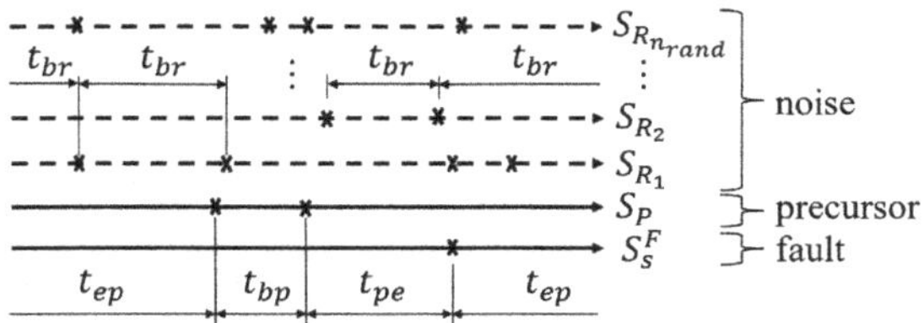

Fig. 3. Parameters of synthetic pattern.

The synthetic data is generated with a time $t_{br} \sim \mathcal{N}(\mu = 14.61d,\ \sigma = 14.61d)$ between randomly firing precursors, S_{R_l}, $l = 1, 2, ..., n_{rand}$, a time $t_{bp} \sim \mathcal{N}(\mu = 1d,\ \sigma = 1d/24)$ between deterministic precursors S_p, a time $t_{pe} \sim \mathcal{N}(\mu = 10d/24,\ \sigma = 1d/24)$ between deterministic precursors S_p and infrastructure failures S_s^F, and a time $t_{ep} \sim \mathcal{N}(\mu = 36.525d,\ \sigma = 36.525d)$ between infrastructure failure S_s^F and deterministic precursors S_p with d being a day of 24 h. It covers a time range of 2.7 years and n_{rand} being $[2^0, 2^1, ..., 2^9]$.

The method is applied with sampling times $\delta t = [2h, 3h]$ (h for hours), an input range $n_i = 40$, a lead-time $t_p = 0$, an output range of $n_o = [1, 2, 3, 4]$, a sub-sampling target ratio $p_{0,targ} = 0.8$, and a class '1' neighbourhood coverage $n_{cov} = 2$. The data is split at times t_{split} chosen so that 80% of the data-set are used for training and model-selection and 20% for final testing. Training and model selection is performed by a 7-fold validation for sub-splitting times $t_{sub-split}$ chosen so that $[50, 55, 60, 65, 70, 75, 80]$ percent of the training data set are used for training and $[50, 45, 40, 35, 30, 25, 20]$ percent for validation. On average 7 (13) infrastructure failures were in the training data of the validation folds (the whole data-set). Hence, a small data scenario is investigated.

Of the 4480 trained models, the results for $\delta t = 3$ h and $n_o = 2$ led to good results for all classifiers and are presented. In Fig. 4a and 4b, the performance metrics are plotted as a function of the number of randomly firing signals, n_{rand}. Evidently, for higher numbers of random signals the performance is decreasing. Nevertheless, the correct patterns can be identified out of up to 100 random signals from as little as 7 examples in the training sets with the chosen parametrization. This suggests that in a real-data scenario, less than 10 training examples can be sufficient to detect failure patterns.

Further characteristics of the framework have been studied in [3]. It was found that increasing n_o by one or two can lead to accuracy improvements especially when the duration between precursors and failures has a high variance. The input relevance highlights the precursors with the lowest timing variance, and patterns are identified from as few as four failure examples.

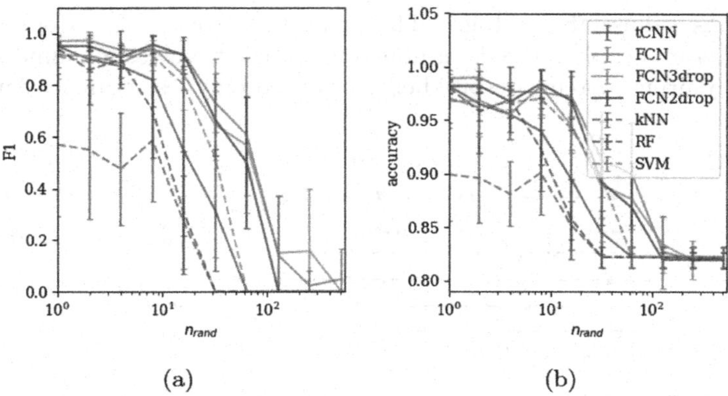

Fig. 4. Dependency of the predictive performance on the number of randomly firing signals. The line depicts the mean and the error bar plus and minus one standard deviation calculated over the 7 validation sets. Solid lines represent deep models which perform on average better than the classical models (dashed). (a) The F1 score. Note that the predictors level out at 0.0 for large n_{rand}, which is the binary F1 score when always predicting the majority class ('0'). (b) The accuracy. The predictors level out at 0.82 for large n_{rand}, which is the accuracy when always predicting the majority class ('0').

Recovering Fault Tree Structure. Often faults in infrastructures are due to the interaction of multiple sub-systems. This experiment tests if the framework is able to identify failures due to interaction of sub-systems and if it can be explained by a system operator.

To do so, synthetic data is generated by simulating multiple sub-system interactions leading to infrastructure failures as illustrated in Fig. 5. An infrastructure failure, S_b^F, occurs after two precursor signals, S_{P_1} and S_{P_2}, fulfill either a Boolean AND, OR, or XOR condition. Four additional noise signals, $S_{R_{1-4}}$, are added to simulate non-interacting parts of the infrastructure. Time delays between signals are chosen to represent realistic scenarios.

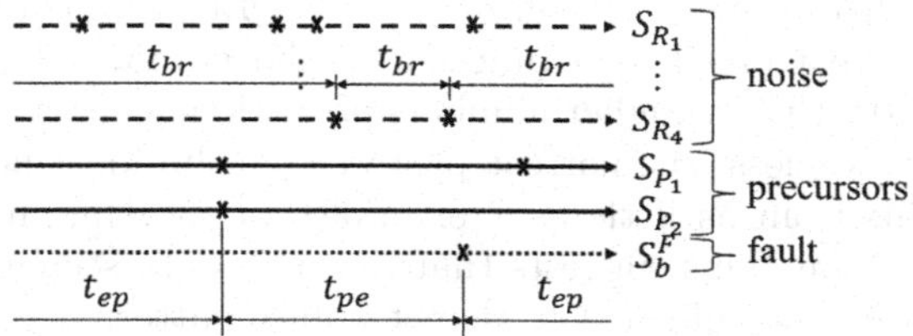

Fig. 5. Parameters of synthetic pattern.

The results for data generation parameters $t_{br} \sim \mathcal{N}(\mu = 23\,\text{min}, \sigma = 24\,\text{min})$, $t_{pe} = 71\,\text{min}$, $t_{ep} = 120\,\text{min}$ are shown in Fig. 6. The framework is applied with sampling time $\delta t = 12\,\text{min}$ (min for minutes), an input range $n_i = 5$, a lead-time $t_p = 5$, an output range of $n_o = 1$, a sub-sampling target ratio $p_{0,targ} = 0.8$, and a class '1' neighbourhood coverage $n_{cov} = 2$. The data set was split in an equally sized training and testing set without additional K-fold validation as no hyperparameter selection was performed. The input data contain less than 20 examples of infrastructure failures. Deep networks and traditional ML algorithms perform well, consistently reaching $F1 > 0.97$. The results for the FCN2drop network are detailed below.

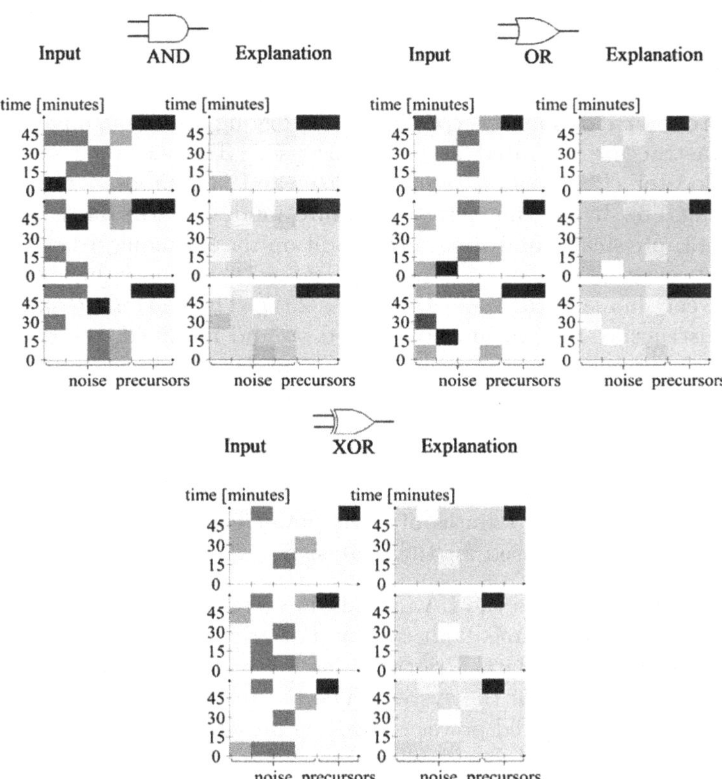

Fig. 6. Illustration of AND, OR and XOR fault logic extraction. Left columns show three randomly selected input windows before failure occurrence. Right columns show the relevant precursors obtained with the FCN2drop network (darker colours indicate higher relevance). Comparing the relevant precursors (right columns), allows to distinguish different Boolean rules and recover the fault logic of the system.

Figure 6 shows three randomly selected input windows from the test data set with subsequent infrastructure failures for the AND, OR, and XOR scenario. Left columns show the unfiltered input window and right columns show the explanations with relevant signals as obtained from the FCN2drop network. Clearly, the correct precursors, S_{P_1} and S_{P_2}, could be identified by the framework and the noise, S_{R_1-4}, filtered. Comparing the groups of three input windows, the Boolean logic can be reconstructed. However, this relies on comparing different situations and is not possible from a single image. Still, the results confirm that the framework can identify failures due to interaction of multiple subsystems and allows system operators to explain the interactions. The inputs (left columns) would not expose the fault logic without the filtering by the explanation framework (right columns). Hence the explanation can be considered complete if different system behaviours are presented. The ease of understanding largely depends on the complexity of the studied system. For this simple case it is straightforward to disentangle different system behaviour. The causality cannot be assessed for this synthetic example.

Particle Accelerator Data Experiments. Logging data from a particle accelerator infrastructure operated at CERN is used. The so-called Proton Synchrotron Booster (PSB) has a radius of 25 m and is composed of four superimposed rings [6]. It continuously logs failure modes, alarm data, operational settings data, physical monitoring and condition data, among others. The goal is to learn predictive models of failure modes and their mechanisms from data stored between January 2015 and December 2017. The learning task is difficult as the infrastructure is continuously worked on and modified, the data logging mechanisms have not been designed for historical data analysis, and failure data are rare [23]. As for any real-world infrastructure, only a subset of all relevant processes leading to failures can be observed. Furthermore, only system operators and experts can verify if the framework highlights the correct relevant precursors.

The goal is to forecast failures of eight power converters used in the PSB. The following signals are used for the analysis:

- Alarm logging data from the LASER alarm system [8]. The alarms are characterised by a system name, fault code and priority. The priority can be either 2 or 3 for the selected data. Priority 2 leads to a warning, whereas, priority 3 leads to a shutdown of the system. The ten most frequent priority 3 fault types of the 8 investigated power converters are selected as the target failure signals $\mathbf{S}_{O,F}$. The alarms are logged with a rising and falling flag indicating the beginning and the end of the alarm state, respectively. Only the rising flag is used as data. Data is grouped by system name for the input. This leads to eight input signals.
- Interlock signals register external and internal disturbances which potentially lead to the shut-down of the infrastructure. Based on operations experts' recommendations 27 signals were taken.
- The beam destination variable is an indicator of the operational mode of the PSB. The eight different beam destinations are hot encoded and added to the input data.

Time periods in which the PSB is switched off for maintenance were removed, as the alarm data is not valid during these periods of time.

Mixing Synthetic and Real Data. In a first attempt, the goal is to test if a known pattern can be isolated from real-world data. Therefore, the noise robustness experiment was repeated with the randomly firing systems being replaced by real-world data containing 8 LASER alarm signals, 27 interlock signals, and 8 beam destination signals from the PSB.

The framework was applied to the data with sampling times δt =[2 h,3 h] (h for hours), an input range $n_i = 40$, a lead-time $t_p = 0$, an output range of $n_o = [1, 2, 3, 4]$, a sub-sampling target ratio $p_{0,targ} = 0.8$, and a class '1' neighbourhood coverage $n_{cov} = 2$. The same model validation strategy is chosen as for the synthetic data experiment. All classifiers were trained and evaluated.

Table 1. Performance metrics for mixing synthetic and real data experiments. $\mathbf{frac_{maj}}$ stands for the fraction of the majority class and is shown as reference for the accuracy of a trivial predictor always predicting the majority class. v and $\sigma_{\mathbf{v}}$ stand for the mean and standard deviation over the 7 validation folds, respectively, and t for results on the test set.

	FCN			FCN3drop			FCN2drop			tCNN			kNN			RF			SVM			frac maj		
	v	σ_v	t	v	σ_v	t	v	σ_v	t	v	σ_v	t	v	σ_v	t	v	σ_v	t	v	σ_v	t	v	σ_v	t
acc	0.97	0.03	0.98	0.93	0.06	0.95	0.97	0.02	0.98	0.83	0.03	0.95	0.84	0.03	0.87	0.83	0.03	0.89	0.91	0.05	0.94	0.83	0.03	0.89
F1	0.89	0.11	0.93	0.79	0.22	0.80	0.92	0.05	0.93	0.00	0.00	0.80	0.12	0.16	0.20	0.00	0.00	0.00	0.73	0.15	0.71			

Of the 448 trained models, the results for $\delta t = 3$ h and $n_o = 3$ achieved high F1 and accuracy and are presented in Table 1. The *FCN* networks show a strong performance in this experiment reaching F1 close to 1 based on only 7 training examples. This indicates that artificial patterns within the real-world data can be detected from less than ten examples. Figure 7a shows the input activation for the FCN and SVM, respectively. Both correctly identify the relevant precursor out of 43 signals. As the explanation highlights a single precursor signal, it can be considered easy to understand. Completeness and causality cannot be assessed for this synthethic example.

Real Data. The framework is tested to determine whether it can predict and explain critical priority 3 failures in the PSB accelerator power converters using the data introduced above. All signals are chosen as input data and the ten most active failure signals within the data set ($[\mathbf{S}_{F_0}, ..., \mathbf{S}_{F_9}]$) are predicted.

The framework is applied with sampling times δt =[10 min, 30 min, 2 h] (h for hours, min for minutes), input ranges $n_i = [16, 32, 64]$, lead-times $t_p = [0, 1]$, output ranges of $n_o = [1, 2, 4, 16]$, a sub-sampling target ratio $p_{0,targ} = 0.8$, and a class '1' neighbourhood coverage $n_{cov} = 2$. The same model validation strategy is chosen as for the synthetic data experiment.

Of the 11520 trained models, the results for δt =30 min, $n_i = [16, 32]$, $t_p = [0, 1]$, and $n_o = 4$ when predicting fault code $\mathbf{S}_{F_4}$ (malfunction of a power

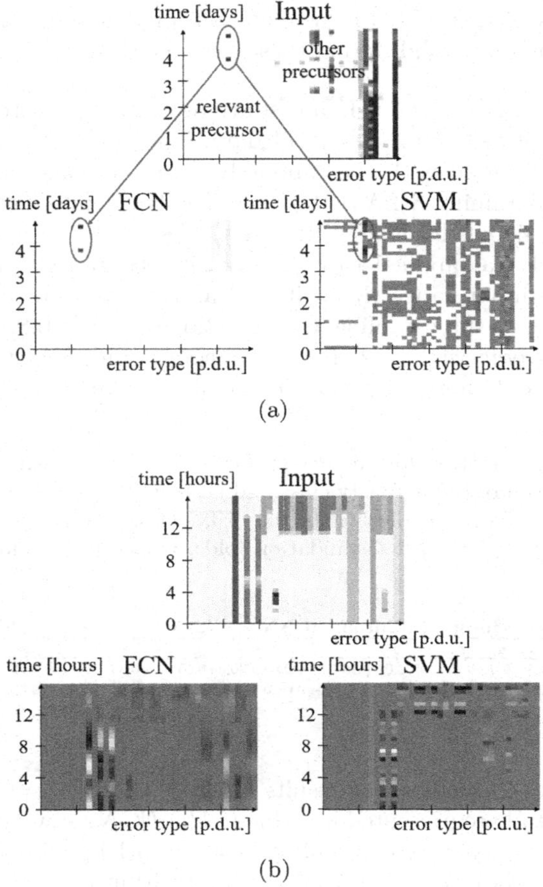

Fig. 7. (a) Upper: Input data for a single example of class '1' in the test set (not shown, occuring shortly after day 5). Lower left: Correctly identified relevant failure precursors by FCN network. Lower right: Correctly identified failure precursors by SVM network across all class '1' examples in the test set. Note that FCN and SVM evaluate non-relevant error messages differently in their models (darker colours in the heatmap signify higher relevance). (b) Input relevance for real data snapshot with $\delta t = 30\,\text{min}$, $n_i = 32$, $t_p = 0$, $n_o = 4$ and $\mathbf{S}_{F_0}$. The relevance in the upper region is higher for SVM. System experts could identify that certain combinations of external interlock signals and operational modes leading to infrastructure failures.

converter controller) and $\mathbf{S}_{F_7}$ (failure of a current measurement device) are presented in Table 2. It shows high accuracy for both on-line ($t_p = 1$) and post-mortem ($t_p = 0$) use.

The FCN networks show F1 close to 1. Note that the models were trained with as few as 17 class '1' examples on average for both the validation folds and the final training on the whole data-set. The F1 for the tCNN networks ranges

Table 2. Performance metrics for real data experiments. $\mathbf{frac_{maj}}$ stands for the fraction of the majority class and is shown as reference for the accuracy of a trivial predictor always predicting the majority class. v and $\sigma_{\mathbf{v}}$ stand for the mean and standard deviation over the 7 validation folds, respectively, and t for results on the test set.

	$s_{F,i}$	n_i	t_p	FCN			FCN3drop			FCN2drop			tCNN			kNN			RF			SVM			frac maj		
				v	σ_v	t	v	σ_v	t	v	σ_v	t	v	σ_v	t	v	σ_v	t	v	σ_v	t	v	σ_v	t	v	σ_v	t
acc	4	16	0	0.95	0.03	1.00	0.95	0.03	1.00	0.95	0.03	1.00	0.91	0.06	0.92	0.90	0.02	0.92	0.90	0.04	0.92	0.89	0.04	0.92	0.87	0.04	0.92
F1	4	16	0	0.81	0.12	1.00	0.84	0.09	1.00	0.84	0.09	1.00	0.36	0.50	0.00	0.68	0.10	0.67	0.35	0.33	0.00	0.13	0.30	0.67			
acc	7	16	0	0.95	0.03	1.00	0.95	0.03	0.83	0.92	0.06	0.96	0.87	0.03	0.92	0.91	0.03	0.92	0.87	0.03	0.96	0.89	0.04	0.96	0.86	0.03	0.92
F1	7	16	0	0.84	0.09	1.00	0.84	0.09	0.33	0.71	0.27	0.80	0.00	0.00	0.00	0.74	0.03	0.67	0.00	0.00	0.67	0.17	0.38	0.80			
acc	4	32	0	0.98	0.03	1.00	0.97	0.02	0.92	0.98	0.03	1.00	0.98	0.03	0.92	0.89	0.01	0.92	0.88	0.03	0.92	0.85	0.04	0.96	0.88	0.04	0.92
F1	4	32	0	0.94	0.09	1.00	0.90	0.05	0.00	0.92	0.11	1.00	0.93	0.10	0.00	0.57	0.09	0.67	0.18	0.25	0.00	0.33	0.10	0.80			
acc	7	32	0	0.97	0.03	1.00	0.95	0.03	0.92	0.97	0.02	0.92	0.93	0.05	0.92	0.87	0.04	0.96	0.88	0.03	0.92	0.85	0.04	1.00	0.86	0.03	0.92
F1	7	32	0	0.89	0.07	1.00	0.84	0.09	0.00	0.89	0.07	0.00	0.68	0.39	0.00	0.53	0.14	0.80	0.46	0.29	0.00	0.38	0.21	1.00			
acc	4	16	1	0.94	0.06	1.00	0.92	0.03	1.00	0.97	0.03	1.00	0.88	0.05	0.92	0.91	0.03	0.92	0.88	0.03	1.00	0.94	0.02	0.96	0.86	0.04	0.92
F1	4	16	1	0.75	0.26	1.00	0.74	0.06	1.00	0.89	0.10	1.00	0.16	0.36	0.00	0.74	0.06	0.67	0.08	0.18	1.00	0.66	0.24	0.80			
acc	7	16	1	0.95	0.01	1.00	0.91	0.03	1.00	0.96	0.01	1.00	0.86	0.03	0.91	0.91	0.03	0.96	0.86	0.03	0.91	0.94	0.02	1.00	0.83	0.00	0.91
F1	7	16	1	0.85	0.06	1.00	0.77	0.06	1.00	0.88	0.01	1.00	0.00	0.00	0.00	0.76	0.04	0.80	0.00	0.00	0.67	0.67	0.25	1.00			
acc	4	32	1	0.92	0.03	1.00	0.93	0.02	0.92	0.96	0.01	0.96	0.88	0.04	0.92	0.88	0.02	0.96	0.91	0.05	0.92	0.87	0.03	0.96	0.86	0.03	0.92
F1	4	32	1	0.62	0.18	1.00	0.68	0.19	0.00	0.84	0.06	0.80	0.16	0.36	0.00	0.55	0.12	0.80	0.72	0.18	0.00	0.40	0.15	0.80			
acc	7	32	1	0.92	0.03	1.00	0.96	0.01	0.91	0.97	0.02	0.96	0.88	0.04	0.91	0.86	0.05	0.96	0.89	0.05	0.91	0.84	0.04	1.00	0.84	0.02	0.91
F1	7	32	1	0.68	0.23	1.00	0.86	0.04	0.00	0.90	0.05	0.80	0.17	0.38	0.00	0.53	0.14	0.80	0.33	0.45	0.00	0.38	0.21	1.00			

from zero to close to one for different problem parameters. Its performance might be improved by additional tuning of the network parameters. The F1 of classical models is mostly smaller than 0.5 which is evidence that for infrastructures with discrete data deep networks outperform traditional machine learning classifiers. Applying dropout does not significantly improve the performance.

Overall, the framework demonstrates good performance in predicting system failures. However, only a subset of failures are predictable. Most likely this is due to insufficient observability of relevant processes within the logged data, which was neither conceived nor stored with the goal of using it for failure predictions. Furthermore, in all systems there are randomly occurring errors that do not necessarily have precursors.

An input relevance example is shown in Fig. 7b. The FCN filters less inputs as relevant than the SVM. Still both have comparable predictive performance. Analyzing the input relevance plots with system experts, the system behaviour could be recovered and non-trivial insights obtained. In terms of quality of explanations, it was concluded that the explanations are partially complete as additional sources needed to be consulted. The ease of understanding dropped quickly with the number of highlighted signals in the input activation plots. The explanation helped to postulate causal chains but a degree of uncertainty remained. However, system experts confirmed that the input relevance provides useful insights for failure analysis, which gives confidence in the method and approach for future analyses.

4 Summary, Conclusions and Outlook

Our data driven framework identifies failure mechanisms in complex infrastructures, such as particle accelerators. Using multivariate time series data from infrastructure monitoring signals, a predictive model is learned with deep convolutional neural networks and classical machine learning algorithms. Explainable AI methods, such as layer wise relevance propagation, identify the most relevant failure precursors in the monitoring data. This has the potential to allow a more focused trouble-shooting of operational incidents.

The framework is applied to synthetic and real world data-sets. With synthetic data, the framework correctly isolates relevant failure precursors from up to hundred time series with as few as ten examples of failures to learn from and is able to recover interactions between multiple sub-systems. With real-world data, deep neural networks predict failures with F1 scores close to 1 for particle accelerator problems at a bare minimum of data pre-processing and problem-adaptation. Non-trivial system behaviour could be identified from the explanation mechanism. Fully Convolutional Neural Networks outperform classical ML methods in our experiments. Explainable deep learning proves to be a promising tool for future fault prognostics applications in particle accelerators.

For future research, the quality of explanations should be further surveyed in actual usage settings with system operators and experts. The experimental verification should be extended within and outside the particle accelerator domain. Since the framework does not rely upon specific insights from particle accelerators, it can be assumed that it performs well in other fields of application. To solve the limitations due to the lack of failure data, transfer learning and few-shot learning could be investigated. Changes in the infrastructure causing concept drifts could be tackled by re-learning approaches.

References

1. Abdul, A., Vermeulen, J., Wang, D., Lim, B.Y., Kankanhalli, M.: Trends and trajectories for explainable, accountable and intelligible systems: an HCI research agenda. In: Proceedings of the 2018 CHI Conference on Human Factors in Computing Systems, pp. 1–18 (2018)
2. Amarasinghe, K., Kenney, K., Manic, M.: Toward explainable deep neural network based anomaly detection. In: 2018 11th International Conference on Human System Interaction (HSI), pp. 311–317. IEEE (2018)
3. Apollonio, A., Cartier-Michaud, T., Felsberger, L., Müller, A., Todd, B.: Machine learning for early fault detection in accelerator systems (2020). http://cds.cern.ch/record/2706483
4. Bach, S., Binder, A., Montavon, G., Klauschen, F., Müller, K.R., Samek, W.: On pixel-wise explanations for non-linear classifier decisions by layer-wise relevance propagation. PloS one **10**(7), e130140 (2015)
5. Bach-Andersen, M., Rømer-Odgaard, B., Winther, O.: Deep learning for automated drivetrain fault detection. Wind Energy **21**(1), 29–41 (2018)
6. Benedikt, M., Blas, A., Borburgh, J.: The ps complex as proton pre-injector for the lhc-design and implementation report. Technical Report, European Organization for Nuclear Research (2000)
7. Bergmeir, C., Benítez, J.M.: On the use of cross-validation for time series predictor evaluation. Inf. Sci. **191**, 192–213 (2012)

8. Calderini, F., Stapley, N., Tyrell, M., Pawlowski, B.: Moving towards a common alarm service for the lhc era. Technical Report (2003)
9. Eichler, M.: Causal inference with multiple time series: principles and problems. Phil. Trans. Roy. Soc. A Math. Phys. Eng. Sci. **371**(1997), 20110613 (2013)
10. Ismail Fawaz, H., Forestier, G., Weber, J., Idoumghar, L., Muller, P.-A.: Deep learning for time series classification: a review. Data Min. Knowl. Disc. **33**(4), 917–963 (2019). https://doi.org/10.1007/s10618-019-00619-1
11. Felsberger, L., Todd, B., Kranzlmüller, D.: Power converter maintenance optimization using a model-based digital reliability twin paradigm. In: 2019 4th International Conference on System Reliability and Safety (ICSRS), pp. 213–217. IEEE (2019)
12. Fronza, I., Sillitti, A., Succi, G., Terho, M., Vlasenko, J.: Failure prediction based on log files using random indexing and support vector machines. J. Syst. Softw. **86**(1), 2–11 (2013)
13. Fulp, E.W., Fink, G.A., Haack, J.N.: Predicting computer system failures using support vector machines. WASL **8**, 5–5 (2008)
14. Guo, J., Li, Z., Li, M.: A review on prognostics methods for engineering systems. IEEE Transactions on Reliability (2019)
15. Hastie, T., Tibshirani, R., Friedman, J.: The Elements of Statistical Learning: Data Mining, Inference, and Prediction. Springer, New York (2009). https://doi.org/10.1007/978-0-387-84858-7
16. Holzinger, A., Carrington, A., Müller, H.: Measuring the quality of explanations: the system causability scale (scs). In: KI-Künstliche Intelligenz, pp. 1–6 (2020)
17. Ioffe, S., Szegedy, C.: Batch normalization: Accelerating deep network training by reducing internal covariate shift (2015). arXiv preprint arXiv:1502.03167
18. Khan, S., Yairi, T.: A review on the application of deep learning in system health management. Mech. Syst. Signal Process. **107**, 241–265 (2018)
19. Leahy, K., Hu, R.L., Konstantakopoulos, I.C., Spanos, C.J., Agogino, A.M., O'Sullivan, D.T.: Diagnosing and predicting wind turbine faults from scada data using support vector machines. Int. J. Prognostics Health Manag. **9**(1), 1–11 (2018)
20. Liu, C., Lore, K.G., Sarkar, S.: Data-driven root-cause analysis for distributed system anomalies. In: 2017 IEEE 56th Annual Conference on Decision and Control (CDC), pp. 5745–5750. IEEE (2017)
21. Montavon, G.: Gradient-based vs. propagation-based explanations: an axiomatic comparison. In: Samek, W., Montavon, G., Vedaldi, A., Hansen, L.K., Müller, K.-R. (eds.) Explainable AI: Interpreting, Explaining and Visualizing Deep Learning. LNCS (LNAI), vol. 11700, pp. 253–265. Springer, Cham (2019). https://doi.org/10.1007/978-3-030-28954-6_13
22. Mori, J., Mahalec, V., Yu, J.: Identification of probabilistic graphical network model for root-cause diagnosis in industrial processes. Comput. Chem. Eng. **71**, 171–209 (2014)
23. Niemi, A., Apollonio, A., Ponce, L., Todd, B., Walsh, D.J.: CERN Injector Complex Availability 2018 (2019). https://cds.cern.ch/record/2655447
24. Pedregosa, F., et al.: Scikit-learn: machine learning in Python. J. Mach. Learn. Res. **12**, 2825–2830 (2011)
25. Qiu, H., Liu, Y., Subrahmanya, N.A., Li, W.: Granger causality for time-series anomaly detection. In: 2012 IEEE 12th International Conference on Data Mining, pp. 1074–1079. IEEE (2012)
26. Ran, Y., Zhou, X., Lin, P., Wen, Y., Deng, R.: A survey of predictive maintenance: Systems, purposes and approaches (2019). arXiv preprint arXiv:1912.07383

27. Saeki, M., Ogata, J., Murakawa, M., Ogawa, T.: Visual explanation of neural network based rotation machinery anomaly detection system. In: 2019 IEEE International Conference on Prognostics and Health Management (ICPHM), pp. 1–4. IEEE (2019)
28. Salfner, F., Lenk, M., Malek, M.: A survey of online failure prediction methods. ACM Comput. Surv. (CSUR) **42**(3), 1–42 (2010)
29. Samek, W., Binder, A., Montavon, G., Lapuschkin, S., Müller, K.R.: Evaluating the visualization of what a deep neural network has learned. IEEE Trans. Neural Netw. Learn. Syst. **28**(11), 2660–2673 (2016)
30. Serio, L., Antonello, F., Baraldi, P., Castellano, A., Gentile, U., Zio, E.: A smart framework for the availability and reliability assessment and management of accelerators technical facilities. In: Journal of Physics: Conference Series, vol. 1067, p. 072029. IOP Publishing (2018)
31. Vilalta, R., Ma, S.: Predicting rare events in temporal domains. In: 2002 IEEE International Conference on Data Mining, 2002, Proceedings, pp. 474–481. IEEE (2002)
32. Wang, Z., Yan, W., Oates, T.: Time series classification from scratch with deep neural networks: A strong baseline. In: 2017 International Joint Conference on Neural Networks (IJCNN), pp. 1578–1585. IEEE (2017)
33. Zhao, B., Lu, H., Chen, S., Liu, J., Wu, D.: Convolutional neural networks for time series classification. J. Syst. Eng. Electron. **28**(1), 162–169 (2017)
34. Zhao, G., Zhang, G., Ge, Q., Liu, X.: Research advances in fault diagnosis and prognostic based on deep learning. In: 2016 Prognostics and System Health Management Conference (PHM-Chengdu), pp. 1–6. IEEE (2016)
35. Zhu, B., Wang, G., Liu, X., Hu, D., Lin, S., Ma, J.: Proactive drive failure prediction for large scale storage systems. In: 2013 IEEE 29th Symposium on Mass Storage Systems and Technologies (MSST), pp. 1–5. IEEE (2013)

eXDiL: A Tool for Classifying and eXplaining Hospital Discharge Letters

Fabio Mercorio[1], Mario Mezzanzanica[1], and Andrea Seveso[2(✉)]

[1] Department of Statistics and Quantitative Methods - CRISP Research Centre, University of Milano-Bicocca, Milan, Italy

[2] Department of Informatics, Systems and Communication, University of Milano-Bicocca, Milan, Italy

andrea.seveso@unimib.it

Abstract. Discharge letters (DiL) are used within any hospital Information Systems to track diseases of patients during their hospitalisation. Such records are commonly classified over the standard taxonomy made by the World Health Organization, that is the International Statistical Classification of Diseases and Related Health Problems (ICD-10). Particularly, classifying DiLs on the right code is crucial to allow hospitals to be refunded by Public Administrations on the basis of the health service provided. In many practical cases the classification task is carried out by hospital operators, that often have to cope under pressure, making this task an error-prone and time-consuming activity. This process might be improved by applying machine learning techniques to empower the clinical staff. In this paper, we present a system, namely `eXDiL`, that uses a two-stage Machine Learning and XAI-based approach for classifying DiL data on the ICD-10 taxonomy. To skim the common cases, we first classify automatically the most frequent codes. The codes that are not automatically discovered will be classified into the appropriate chapter and given to an operator to assess the correct code, in addition to an extensive explanation to help the evaluation, comprising of an explainable local surrogate model and a word similarity task. We also show how our approach will be beneficial to healthcare operators, and in particular how it will speed up the process and potentially reduce human errors.

Keywords: eXplainable AI · Machine learning · Healthcare · Text classification

1 Introduction

A large amount of medical examinations are carried out every day at hospitals and emergency rooms. For every visit, many bureaucratic documents must be compiled. One of these is the *discharge letter* (DiL). A DiL is a document issued to the patient at time of discharge from a hospital. It is the summary of the information contained in the medical record - of which it is an integral part - and contains the advice for any checks or therapies to be carried out. The

Published by Springer Nature Switzerland AG 2020
A. Holzinger et al. (Eds.): CD-MAKE 2020, LNCS 12279, pp. 159–172, 2020.
https://doi.org/10.1007/978-3-030-57321-8_9

information contained in the document is therefore intended to be useful to the doctor who will follow the patient in the future.

To be correctly classified according to international standards, at least one International Statistical Classification of Diseases and Related Health Problems code (ICD [27]) must be associated with each visit. ICD-10 is a medical classification taxonomy created by the World Health Organization. It contains codes for diseases, signs and symptoms, abnormal findings, complaints, social circumstances, and external causes of injury or diseases.

Responsibility for the correct completion of the letter of discharge lies with the doctor responsible for discharge. The ICD code must be assigned manually by the attending physician, who however is not always available to manually enter data, mainly due to the fast-paced environment of hospitals and first aid centers. Therefore, the code is often missing or entered as a placeholder.

We would like to investigate the following three research questions:

Q1: How can machine learning techniques support the clinical staff classifying the text data and help avoiding human errors?
Q2: Can such a system provide explanations to users for supporting transparency and trustworthiness?
Q3: Is there a way to discover lexical similarities and relationships between medical terms?

1.1 Motivating Example

To elaborate on our research question, next we introduce a concrete example, which allows the reader to understand the problem and shows why and for whom the system is useful to. We investigate the scenario of a particular Italian medical center, where the number of visits without ICD is very high ($\frac{1}{3}$ of visits). Assigning the right ICD code to a DL is a crucial and beneficial task for the hospital, for many practical reasons: getting reimbursements from the regional health service provider, assessment of fund allocation and so on. If the code is not assigned, it is necessary to manually read the DiLs, which contain all the information necessary to trace the specific ICD of the visit. This process is error-prone and time-consuming; however, it could be improved by applying text mining techniques such as text classification.

This particular medical center only treats a subset of possible diseases, those that are specific to Italy and to the expertise of the center. As an application paper, we would like to focus on this specific domain for our analyses.

1.2 Contribution

The contribution of this project is the following:

- Realisation of a XAI-based prototype to healthcare for classifying and explaining Discharge Letter (DiL) data, in order to answer the research questions Q1 and Q2. A demonstrative video of the prototype realised is also provided.

- The XAI module is beneficial to healthcare operators to understand the rationale behind the classification process as well as to speed-up the classification process as a whole;
- The trained italian Word Embeddings, specific to the healthcare domain, support word similarities and classification tasks and are required for the research task Q3.

We begin by discussing the technical backgrounds in Sect. 2. Then, we show the "eXplainable Discharge Letters" (`eXDiL`) system in Sect. 3 and its performances in Sect. 4. Section 5 concludes the paper with the discussion of pros and cons, conclusions and future work we intend to carry on.

2 Backgrounds and Related Work

In this section we introduce some background notions on word embeddings and XAI, as well as previous articles that explored this research area in the past.

Diagnosis code assignment is a well-known classification problem. In recent years it has been tackled with rule based methods as well as statistical and machine learning approaches.

One of the first to approach this task was [16] and [7] using rule based methods. Such methods are not easily created, and require extensive domain expertise in order to create the appropriate classification rules. However, the interpretability of this kind of models is the highest, as you can explain perfectly how a prediction was made.

In [17], the authors used machine learning methods such as Support Vector Machine (SVM) and Bayesian Ridge Regression (BRR). They include only the five most frequent ICD codes, and their classification performance is not very high. The upside of machine learning methods in classification tasks is that a lesser amount of domain expertise is needed, and the performance is in many cases higher than rule based systems.

More recent works include [26], who use a novel Convolutional Neural Network (CNN) model with attention. They select a subsection of the 50 most frequent codes, and perform a multilabel classification. They also conduct an human evaluation on the attention explanations. In [2] authors use multiple models; SVM, Continuous Bag of Words (CBOW), CNN and an hierarchical model, HA-GRU. The performance of more complex and deep models is superior to a model such as SVM. They interpret their results with an attention mechanism. Unlike other works presented, they include all the labels present in the dataset, using both the full 5 character codes and rolled up codes at 3 characters. The latter two works both use the publicly available MIMIC II and III datasets for training and testing their models.

2.1 Word Embeddings

Vector representation of words belongs to the family of neural language models [3], where each word of a given lexicon is mapped to a unique vector in the corresponding N-dimensional space (with a fixed N).

In our application, each word can be considered as the text content of an DiL. Here, an important contribution comes from the *Word2Vec* algorithm [22,23], that computes the vector representations of words by looking at the context where these words are used. Intuitively, given a word w and its context k (i.e., m words in the neighbourhood of w), it uses k as a feature for predicting the word w. This task can be expressed as a machine learning problem, where the representation of m context words is fed into a neural network trained to predict the representation of w, according to the *Continuous Bag of Words* (CBOW) model proposed by [22][1].

Consider two different words w_1 and w_2 having very similar *contexts*, k_1 and k_2 (e.g., synonyms are likely to have similar though different contexts), a neural network builds an internal (abstract) representations of the input data in each internal network layer. If the two output words have similar input contexts (namely, k_1 and k_2) then, the neural network is motivated to learn similar internal representations for the output words w_1 and w_2. For more details, see [23].

After the Word2vec training on the lexicon, words with similar meanings are mapped to a similar position in the vector space. For example, "powerful" and "strong" are close to each other, whereas "powerful" and "Paris" are farther away. The word vector differences are also meaningful. For example, the word vectors can be used to answer analogy questions using simple vector algebra: "King" - "man" + "woman" $\approx$ "Queen" [24].

As one might note, this approach allows representing a specific word in the N-dimensional space, while our task is to compute the vector space of *documents* (i.e., research products), rather than words. We therefore apply the *Doc2Vec* approach [15], an unsupervised algorithm that learns fixed-length feature representations from variable-length pieces of texts, such as sentences, paragraphs, and documents as well. As a consequence, a vector is now the N-dimensional representation of documents.

In our framework, the use of word-embedding allows computing the similarities between DiLs, improving the effectiveness of the result.

2.2 XAI

There is a growing interest in the use of AI algorithms in many real-life scenarios and applications. However, many AI algorithms - as in the case of machine learning - rarely provide explanations or justifications to allow users understanding what the system really learnt, and this might affect the reliability of the algorithms' outcomes when these are used for taking decisions. In order to engender trust in AI, humans must understand what an AI system is trying to achieve, and which criteria guided its decision. A way to overcome this problem requests the underlying AI process must produce explanations that are transparent and

[1] A similar (but reversed problem) is the *Skip-n-gram model* i.e., to train a neural network to predict the representation of n context words from the representation of w. The Skip-n-gram approach can be summarised as "predicting the context given a word" while the CBOW, in a nutshell, is "predicting the word given a context".

comprehensible to the final user, so that she/he can consider the outcome generated by the system as *believable*[2] taking decisions accordingly. Not surprisingly, an aspect that still plays a key role in machine learning relies on the quality of the data used for training the model. In essence, we may argue that the well-known principle *"garbage-in, garbage-out"* that characterizes the data quality research field, also applies to machine learning ,and AI in general, that is used to evaluated data quality on big data (see, e.g. [1,4,20,21]) and perform cleaning tasks as well (see, e.g. [6,18,19]).

Given the success and spread of AI systems, all these concerns are becoming quite relevant enabling a wide branch of AI to emerge, with the aim of making AI algorithms explainable for getting an improved trustability and transparency (*aka* Explainable AI (XAI)). Though some research on explainable AI had already been published before DARPA's program that launched a call for XAI in 2016 (see, e.g., [28,31]) XAI [5,8,25], effectively encouraged a large number of researchers to take up this challenge. In the last couple of years, several publications have appeared that investigate how to explain the different areas of AI, such as machine learning [12,30], robotics and autonomous systems [11], constraint reasoning [10], and AI planning [9], just to cite a few. Furthermore, as recently argued in [5], a key element of an AI system relies on the ability to explain its decisions, recommendations, predictions or actions as well as the process through which they are made. Hence, explanation is closely related to the concept of interpretability: systems are interpretable if their operations can be understood by a human, either through introspection or through a produced explanation.

3 The eXDiL System

The "eXplainable Discharge Letters" system (**eXDiL**) intends to help the clinical staff identifying the main ICD code related to each visit in order to significantly lighten human workload. It would act at operational-level of the hospital to support operators in assigning the correct ICD code to each visit (i.e., operational-level information system). We propose a two-step system for semi-real time classification with an *human in the loop* approach. A visual representation of the workflow can be seen in Fig. 4.

In order to let the reader easily understand the workflow, we also present an operative example in this section. A video walkthrough of this example is available at https://youtu.be/u0UJnp4RyQQ. The following working example should clarify the matter.

Working Example. Let us consider the following DiL: "*Reason for visit*: Low back pain in patients with osteoporosis not under drug treatment. *Diagnosis*: lumbar pain in patient with osteoporosis, deformation in L1 with lowering of the limiting upper in outcomes, anterograde slipping of L3-L4 and L5-S1 with

[2] Here the term believability is inherited from the definition of [32] intended as "the extent to which data are accepted or regarded as true, real and credible".

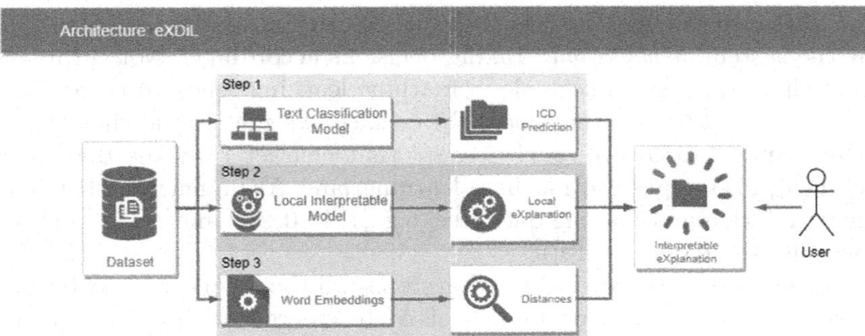

Fig. 1. A representation of the eXDiL workflow, highlighting the main modules.

reduction in amplitude of the interbody spaces." The true ICD class of this example is *Dorsalgia*. Assigning the correct ICD class to the letter is crucial to allow the hospitals to be refunded according to the health service really provided. To this end, in the following we discuss how eXDiL works (Fig. 1).

3.1 Step 1: ICD Prediction

After the doctor finishes writing the letter, the system uses the text data to automatically classify the most common ICDs, as to perform a first skimming. If the classification is successful, then the clinician can accept or reject the suggestion.

In the prototype, the doctor must type a reason for visit and diagnosis in a free text format, or choose an example from a predefined list. Then, the eXDiL system will attempt to classify the data using the workflow described in Fig. 4.

In the other case, if the reason for the visit is not found among the most common cases, then the most relevant chapter is proposed, but the single ICD is not provided. The doctor can use this suggestion to input manually the correct code.

3.2 Step 2: Local eXplanation

After the prediction, a visual explanation of the result is displayed in order to make the clinician aware of the main reasons why certain classes are assigned to certain visits. Moreover, this part is fundamental to establish a relationship of trust between man and algorithm.

Using the LIME [30] approach, we propose a first visualization that explains quantitatively how much a particular term is in favour or against w.r.t. the aforementioned classification (see Fig. 2).

This visualization is accompanied by a second one, in which the terms in question are highlighted directly in the text in such a way as to easily identify the context of use and determine whether or not they are significant according to the judgment of the domain expert, who in this case is the doctor of reference.

Fig. 2. Example of explainable output from the eXDiL prototype.

3.3 Step 3: Word Similarity

In addition, a Word2Vec [22–24] system is offered to suggest words similar to those already inserted, in order make the clinician more aware of similar cases. A word cloud generated by the model is printed on the screen in order to generate immediate cues. The size of the related words is related to the similarity degree. The aforementioned is accompanied by a more detailed outline of the similarity of the suggested words w.r.t. the starting one. An example of the visualization can be seen in Fig. 3.

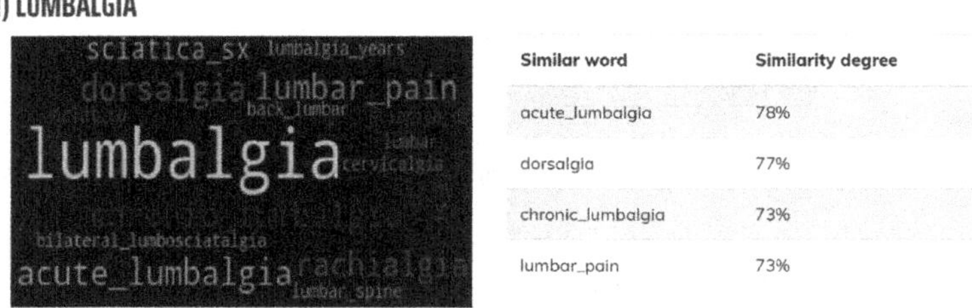

Fig. 3. Example of most similar words from the eXDiL prototype.

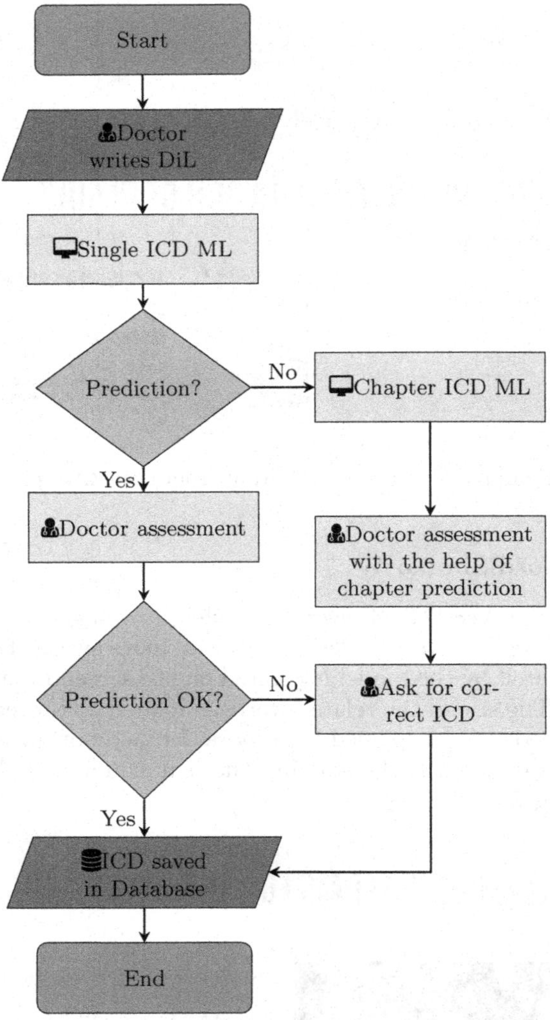

Fig. 4. Semi-real time ML assisted ICD classification workflow.

4 Experimental Results

4.1 Dataset Description and Characteristics

The dataset is composed by 168.925 individual visits, collected from 2011 to 2018 in an Italian Hospital.[3] Notice that the ICD taxonomy is built to include *any disease*, including eradicated ones. For this reason and due to the massive amount

[3] The name of the Hospital is omitted due to non-disclosure agreements.

of existing classes (around 10,000), the classification task should concentrate only on diseases that are more likely to be treated by a given hospital.

Following the example of [14], the codes are truncated at the three character level; as an example, code M54.1 (*Radiculopathy*) is converted to M54 (*Dorsalgia*). We also chose to restrict the dataset to the 5 most common specialities described in Table 1. For each speciality, the top-2 most common ICD classes were chosen for the single ICD classifier, as seen in Table 2.

Table 1. Count of selected ICD chapters.

Chapter	Chapter label	N	Percent
XIII	Diseases of the musculoskeletal system and connective tissue	32051	38.9%
XIV	Diseases of the genitourinary system	14650	17.8%
XII	Diseases of the skin, subcutaneous tissue	12400	15.0%
V	Mental and behavioural disorders	11907	14.4%
X	Diseases of the respiratory system	11431	13.9%

Table 2. Count of most frequent ICD classes.

Code	Label	N	Percent
M54	Dorsalgia	9009	29.9%
J30	Vasomotor and allergic rhinitis	3705	12.3%
M77	Other enthesopathies	3002	10.0%
N76	Other inflammation of vagina and vulva	2806	9.3%
F41	Other anxiety disorders	2692	8.9%
N94	Pain and other conditions associated with female genital organs and menstrual cycle	2692	8.9%
F60	Specific personality disorders	2496	8.3%
L70	Acne	1484	4.9%
L50	Urticaria	1115	3.7%
J45	Asthma	1085	3.6%

After filtering for only the five chosen specialities and applying the preprocessing pipeline, 82.439 letters remain (49% of total data). For the single ICD prediction task, the two most common ICD classes were chosen for each speciality, obtaining 30.086 letters (36% of the 5 specialities, 18% of total data).

For each visit, the DiL describes many features of the patient, such as: reason for the visit, free text doctor diagnosis, medical history, therapy and clinical tests to be carried out, specialization of the practitioner and other information related to the DiL, such as clinical indications, allergies, follow-up instructions.

Out of these features, reason for the visit and free text doctor diagnosis have been chosen to make a prediction, as they are most informative for this task.

4.2 Classification Pipelines

Free text data is not eligible to use as-is. A pre-processing step is required in order to clean the data, according to the following steps: (i) fix character encoding issues, (ii) remove punctuation, isolated numbers and stop words, (iii) lower casing, (iv) remove domain-specific common words, such as "visit" and "control". After pre-processing, we can use the text data to train the classifiers. The mean word count of each note was 16 words is of 15.6 words, with a high standard deviation of 28.7. The longest note in the dataset contains 1124 words. The data set was then separated in two sets: the training set, with 67% of the data, and the test set, with 33% of the data.

In order to create a classification model, a text representation, classifier and set of hyperparameters must be chosen. We have considered the following text representations: (i) Bag of Words (BoW), (ii) Tf-Idf with only Unigrams, (iii) Tf-Idf with Bigrams.

We also considered the Word2Vec Skipgram, Continuous Bag Of Words (CBoW) and GloVe [29] text representations. However, these embeddings did not provide sufficient performances on the classification tasks. As such, they were not included in the results, and the embeddings were used exclusively for the word similarity task.

The following models and hyperparameters sets were considered:

1. SVC with $C \in \{1, 0\}$
2. Random Forest with number of estimators $\in \{10, 100\}$
3. Naive Bayes with $\alpha \in \{0.1, 0.01, 0.001\}$
4. Logistic regression with mode $\in$ {multinomial, sag} $\times$ $C \in \{1, 10\}$

A 5-fold cross-validated grid search on the text representations, models and hyperparameters was conducted in order to find the best models for classification of single and chapter ICD. Also, in order to test the hypothesis that the system will improve with additional data from human input, we started by training the models with only 50% of the available training data, then increasing to 67% and finally using all the training data. The test set was not changed between tests to ensure results consistency.

Similarly to [2], the main metric for model evaluation was chosen as the F1 micro average score.

4.3 Evaluation of Single ICD Model

Figure 5 shows the performances of the models on the test set. Each point in the violin plot represents the F1 score for a tuple (model type, text representation, hyperparameters). The y axis represents the F1 score, ranging between [0.7, 1.0], while the X axis represents the ICD class. For a complete list of the ICD classes, see Table 2. The average performance increases slightly when increasing the available training data. This suggests that increasing the training set size might lead to better performances, however the impact of this increase might is not statistically significant.

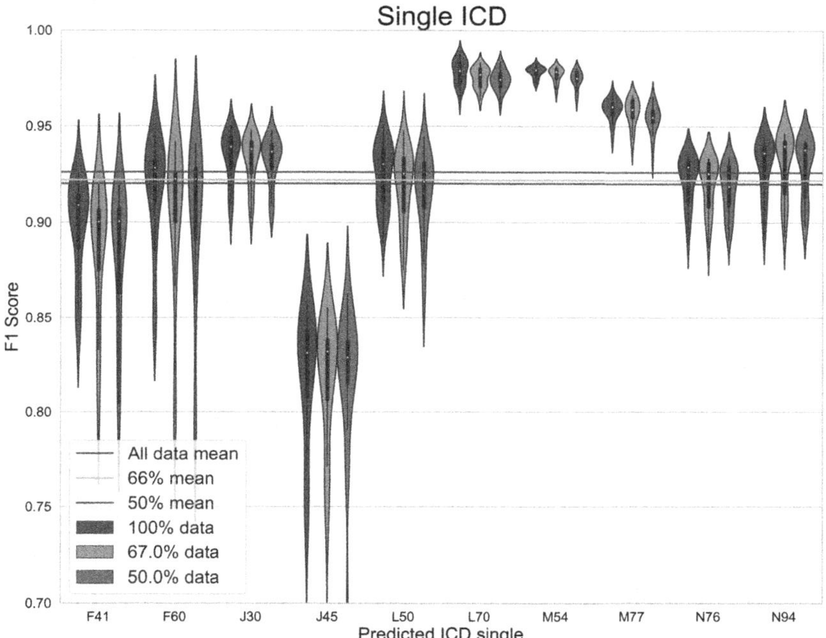

Fig. 5. Visualization of single ICD classification models performance.

The best model out of all the possible combinations is a logistic regression with mode = OVR and C = 1 on the BoW representation. This model reaches an average F1 score of 0.952. The highest percentage of errors is between ICD classes *vasomotor and allergic rhinitis* and *asthma*. This might be induced by the semantic similarity between the two concepts, and also the fact that a patient might be affected by both conditions at the same time.

4.4 Evaluation of Chapter ICD Model

In this higher granularity of classification the performance is higher compared to the third character level. The classes are semantically different between each other, and this distance is reflected on the more accurate results in the classifiers. In Fig. 6 we show the results for each classifier trained. In order to properly show the differences between classes, we restricted the y axis between [0.8, 1.0]. In this case, the models performances do not decrease nor increase with different amounts of training data.

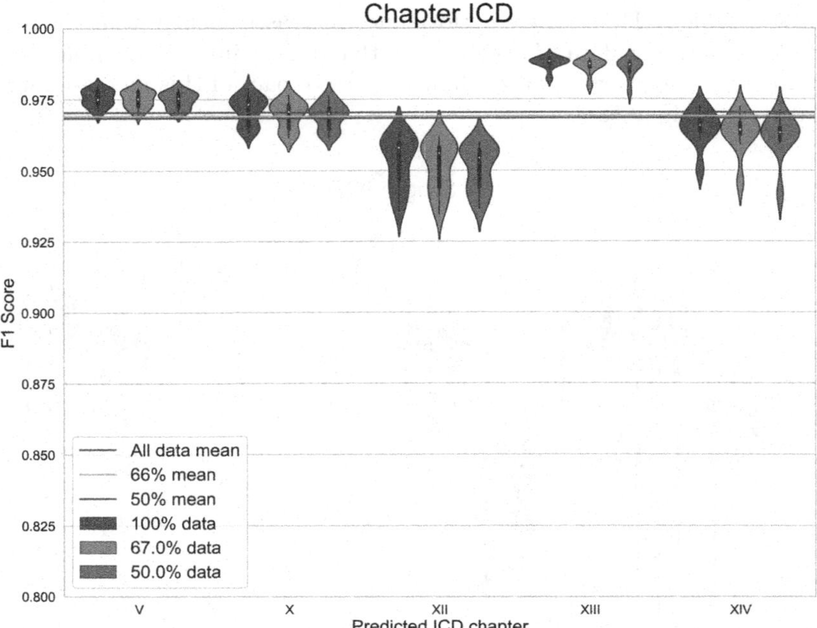

Fig. 6. Visualization of chapter ICD classifications models performance.

The best performing model is a SVC classifier with $C = 1$ on Tf-Idf Bigrams text representation. This model reaches an average F1 score of 0.983.

5 Discussion and Conclusion

Considering the *Pros*, the resulting classifications have excellent performances on both the chapter and single ICD levels. In particular, the chapter level can be trusted with high confidence (F1 Micro = 0.983). It seems that increasing the collected data helps improve performance by a small amount, however the increase does not seem to be significant. The system may therefore help the doctor save time and better classify the DiLs.

Evaluating the *Cons*, a major issue is that this procedure cannot be done on all ICD classes at once. It is firstly advised to choose specific specialties, since without filtering, classifying most of the over 10,000 classes would be infeasible with our dataset. Therefore the scope must be restricted to certain specialties, and, as shown in [14], the granularity should be set at the third character level, as in our case it is not possible to distinguish accurately between the subtle differences at the fourth character level.

In conclusion, we have shown that the `eXDiL` system is an accurate XAI system for classifying hospital discharge letters. Future work can be conducted to improve and assess the whole procedure to finally bring it to life in a real world environment providing an hopefully useful service. Firstly, it has to be tested in the hospital field to check for real world usefulness. Secondly, it is to be understood if the "human in the loop" works as it has been conceived.

To date, `eXDiL` has been trained on Italian DLs provided by an Italian Hospital. We have been working on applying `eXDiL` on the well-known benchmark MIMIC-III [13], a widely known and used dataset. It comprises a larger amount of data, with more labels and variety, and importantly it is in english, meaning it would create a classifier with a broader use case.

DEMO. A demonstration video of the system has been also provided.[4]

References

1. Amato, F., et al.: Multimedia story creation on social networks. Fut. Gener. Comput. Syst. **86**, 412–420 (2018). https://doi.org/10.1016/j.future.2018.04.006
2. Baumel, T., Nassour-Kassis, J., Cohen, R., Elhadad, M., Elhadad, N.: Multi-label classification of patient notes: case study on ICD code assignment. In: Workshops at the Thirty-Second AAAI Conference on Artificial Intelligence (2018)
3. Bengio, Y., Ducharme, R., Vincent, P., Jauvin, C.: A neural probabilistic language model. J. Mach. Learn. Res. **3**(Feb), 1137–1155 (2003)
4. Bergamaschi, S., et al.: Big data research in Italy: a perspective. Engineering **2**(2), 163–170 (2016). https://doi.org/10.1016/J.ENG.2016.02.011
5. Biran, O., Cotton, C.: Explanation and justification in machine learning: a survey. In: IJCAI-17 Workshop on Explainable AI (XAI), p. 8 (2017)
6. Boselli, R., Cesarini, M., Mercorio, F., Mezzanzanica, M.: Inconsistency knowledge discovery for longitudinal data management: a model-based approach. In: Human-Computer Interaction and Knowledge Discovery in Complex, Unstructured, Big Data - Third International Workshop, HCI-KDD, pp. 183–194 (2013)
7. Crammer, K., Dredze, M., Ganchev, K., Talukdar, P.P., Carroll, S.: Automatic code assignment to medical text. In: Proceedings of the Workshop on Bionlp 2007: Biological, Translational, and Clinical Language Processing, pp. 129–136. Association for Computational Linguistics (2007)
8. DARPA: Explainable artificial intelligence (xai) program. http://www.darpa.mil/program/explainable-artificial-intelligence. full solicitation at http://www.darpa.mil/attachments/DARPA-BAA-16-53.pdf (2016)
9. Fox, M., Long, D., Magazzeni, D.: Explainable planning (2017). arXiv preprint arXiv:1709.10256
10. Freuder, E.C.: Explaining ourselves: human-aware constraint reasoning. In: AAAI, pp. 4858–4862 (2017)
11. Hayes, B., Shah, J.A.: Improving robot controller transparency through autonomous policy explanation. In: 12th ACM/IEEE International Conference on Human-Robot Interaction (HRI), pp. 303–312. IEEE (2017)
12. Hendricks, L.A., Akata, Z., Rohrbach, M., Donahue, J., Schiele, B., Darrell, T.: Generating visual explanations. In: Leibe, B., Matas, J., Sebe, N., Welling, M. (eds.) ECCV 2016. LNCS, vol. 9908, pp. 3–19. Springer, Cham (2016). https://doi.org/10.1007/978-3-319-46493-0_1
13. Johnson, A.E., et al.: Mimic-iii, a freely accessible critical care database. Sci. Data **3**, 160035 (2016)

[4] https://youtu.be/u0UJnp4RyQQ.

14. Koopman, B., Zuccon, G., Nguyen, A., Bergheim, A., Grayson, N.: Automatic icd-10 classification of cancers from free-text death certificates. Int. J. Med. Inf. **84**(11), 956–965 (2015)
15. Le, Q., Mikolov, T.: Distributed representations of sentences and documents. In: International Conference on Machine Learning, pp. 1188–1196 (2014)
16. de Lima, L.R., Laender, A.H., Ribeiro-Neto, B.A.: A hierarchical approach to the automatic categorization of medical documents. In: International Conference on Information and Knowledge Management, pp. 132–139. ACM (1998)
17. Lita, L.V., Yu, S., Niculescu, S., Bi, J.: Large scale diagnostic code classification for medical patient records. In: Proceedings of the Third International Joint Conference on Natural Language Processing: Volume-II (2008)
18. Mezzanzanica, M., Boselli, R., Cesarini, M., Mercorio, F.: Data quality through model checking techniques. In: Advances in Intelligent Data Analysis X - 10th International Symposium, IDA, pp. 270–281 (2011)
19. Mezzanzanica, M., Boselli, R., Cesarini, M., Mercorio, F.: Data quality sensitivity analysis on aggregate indicators. In: International Conference on Data Technologies and Applications, pp. 97–108 (2012)
20. Mezzanzanica, M., Boselli, R., Cesarini, M., Mercorio, F.: Automatic synthesis of data cleansing activities. In: Proceedings of the 2nd International Conference on Data Technologies and Applications, pp. 138–149 (2013)
21. Mezzanzanica, M., Boselli, R., Cesarini, M., Mercorio, F.: A model-based approach for developing data cleansing solutions. J. Data Inf. Qual. **5**(4), 13:1–13:28 (2015)
22. Mikolov, T., Chen, K., Corrado, G., Dean, J.: Efficient estimation of word representations in vector space (2013). arXiv preprint arXiv:1301.3781
23. Mikolov, T., Sutskever, I., Chen, K., Corrado, G.S., Dean, J.: Distributed representations of words and phrases and their compositionality. In: Advances in Neural Information Processing Systems, pp. 3111–3119 (2013)
24. Mikolov, T., Yih, W.t., Zweig, G.: Linguistic regularities in continuous space word representations. In: Hlt-naacl, vol. 13, pp. 746–751 (2013)
25. Miller, T., Howe, P., Sonenberg, L.: Explainable AI: Beware of inmates running the asylum. In: IJCAI-17 Workshop on Explainable AI (XAI), p. 36 (2017)
26. Mullenbach, J., Wiegreffe, S., Duke, J., Sun, J., Eisenstein, J.: Explainable prediction of medical codes from clinical text. In: Proceedings of the 2018 Conference of the North American Chapter of the Association for Computational Linguistics: Human Language Technologies, Volume 1 (Long Papers), pp. 1101–1111 (2018)
27. Organization, W.H., et al.: The ICD-10 classification of mental and behavioural disorders: clinical descriptions and diagnostic guidelines. World Health Organization, Geneva (1992)
28. Papadimitriou, A., Symeonidis, P., Manolopoulos, Y.: A generalized taxonomy of explanations styles for traditional and social recommender systems. Data Min. Knowl. Disc. **24**(3), 555–583 (2012)
29. Pennington, J., Socher, R., Manning, C.: Glove: Global vectors for word representation. In: Proceedings of the 2014 Conference on Empirical Methods in Natural Language Processing (EMNLP), pp. 1532–1543 (2014)
30. Ribeiro, M.T., Singh, S., Guestrin, C.: Why should i trust you?: explaining the predictions of any classifier. In: ACM SIGKDD, pp. 1135–1144. ACM (2016)
31. Swartout, W., Paris, C., Moore, J.: Explanations in knowledge systems: design for explainable expert systems. IEEE Expert **6**(3), 58–64 (1991)
32. Wang, R.Y., Strong, D.M.: Beyond accuracy: what data quality means to data consumers. J. Manag. Inf. Syst. **12**(4), 5–33 (1996)

Cooperation Between Data Analysts and Medical Experts: A Case Study

Judita Rokošná[1], František Babič[1](✉), Ljiljana Trtica Majnarić[2,3], and L'udmila Pusztová[1]

[1] Department of Cybernetics and Artificial Intelligence, Faculty of Electrical Engineering and Informatics, Technical University of Košice, 042 01 Košice, Slovakia
judita.rokosna@student.tuke.sk,
{frantisek.babic,ludmila.pusztova.2}@tuke.sk

[2] Department of Internal Medicine, Family Medicine and the History of Medicine, Faculty of Medicine, Josip Juraj Strossmayer University of Osijek, Josipa Huttlera 4, 31000 Osijek, Croatia
ljiljana.majnaric@mefos.hr

[3] Department of Public Health, Faculty of Dental Medicine and Health, Josip Juraj Strossmayer University of Osijek, Crkvena 21, 31000 Osijek, Croatia

Abstract. The medical diagnosis and determine a correct medical procedure represent a comprehensive process that consists of many input information and potential associations. This information can lead to clinical reasoning to resolve a patient's health problem and set the treatment. Effective communication between the medical expert and data analyst can support this process more effectively, dependent on the available data. It is essential to create a shared vocabulary for this cooperation to reduce possible misunderstandings and unnecessary experiments. In our work, we performed exploratory data analysis, statistical tests, correlation analysis, and logistic regression in close cooperation with the participated expert thanks to whom we could verify the achieved results of our models. The collaboration between the medical expert and data analytic requires a lot of communication and explanation from the medical expert because of the correct interpretation of the medical data and its resulting associations. On the other hand, it requires a proper understanding of the task from the data analyst's point of view, a lot of iterations of graphs, and other models, which must be modified to be easy to read and interpret.

Keywords: Medical expert · Data analysts · Collaboration · Thyroid

1 Introduction

The medical diagnosis and determine a correct medical procedure represent a comprehensive process, where it is necessary to consider some variables and relationships among them. The medical record consists of a quantity of information about the patient, such as necessary information (age, year of born, weight, height, etc.), its results of

Published by Springer Nature Switzerland AG 2020
A. Holzinger et al. (Eds.): CD-MAKE 2020, LNCS 12279, pp. 173–190, 2020.
https://doi.org/10.1007/978-3-030-57321-8_10

tests, disease data and its development, and so on. All the medical records' information is useful because of the determination of the right medical treatment of particular diseases. Based on them, the physician can find hidden dependencies between identifiable symptoms and potential definite diagnosis.

Among the critical skills of all physicians belong to constructing diagnosis, choosing diagnostic tests, and interpreting the results. These skills are essential in the diagnosis process. The diagnosis process [1] is a process like any other. The process is particularly complex patient-centered because it includes many handoffs of information or materials and clinical reasoning to determine a patient's health problem. The diagnostic process draws on an adaptation of a decision-making model that describes the cyclical process of information gathering, integration, and interpretation, and forming a diagnosis. This process and decision making can be particularly complicated when caring for older patients with aging diseases, such as hypertension. Aging diseases typically appear as multiple comorbidities, which imply complex, often non-linear relationships between disorders [2]. Little is known about these relationships. Patients' classification into smaller, more homogeneous groups would be necessary to help decision making.

Thyroid diseases can occur at different ages, and the type of disorder is somewhat age and sex-related. The most common thyroid disorder in older people, prevalently women, is subclinical hypothyroidism [3]. It is prevalent in persons with hypertension and with decreased renal function. Although without overt clinical symptoms, this disorder is associated with an increased risk of CVD and cognitive impairment. The relationships between the TSH hormone levels and BMI and other CV risk factors, depending on different stages of renal function decline, in persons with hypertension are poorly known. In this critical area of clinical decision making, there may be the benefit of data analytics methods and collaboration between a data analyst and the medical expert.

1.1 Thyroid Disease and Hypothyroidism

Thyroid gland diseases are the most prevalent endocrine disorders. They have a relatively high incidence in the general population, and these diseases occurred more often in women. Thyroid disease may occur in 5–10% of the general population and in women in middle-aged to older age 10–15%. The regions with iodine-deficient constitute a third of the world population, what it can be an essential risk factor for the onset of goiter and hypothyroidism. The prevalence of hypothyroidism and hyperthyroidism is different between women and men. Hyperthyroidism is prevalent in 0.5–2% of women and 0.1–0.2% of men, whereas hypothyroidism occurs in 0.06–1.2% in women and 0.1–0.4% in men [4].

Hypothyroidism [5] is a common endocrine disorder, and it affects hundreds of millions around the world. This disorder is resulting from a deficiency of thyroid hormones or by the complete loss of its function. About 95% of hypothyroidism cases occur as a result of primary gland failure. One of the grades of hypothyroidism is subclinical hypothyroidism [6]. This disorder is a prevalent disorder among middle-aged and elderly patients. It represents a state with increased thyroid-stimulating hormone - TSH and typical values of thyroxine – T4 and triiodothyronine – T3. If the values of TSH are above 4.0 mU/l, it represents increased levels. By their increase, the subclinical hypothyroidism can be divided into a mild form (values from 4.0–10.0 mU/l) and a more severe form (values above 10.0 mU/l). Most patients with subclinical hypothyroidism have no symptoms that would indicate this disorder. So, the diagnosis of this hypothyroidism is made based on laboratory findings. Among the general symptoms of hypothyroidism can include [7]: less energy, more fatigue, drier and itchier skin, drier and more brittle hair and more hair loss, loss of appetite, weight gain, slow thought and speech, muscle cramps and joint aches, slowing of heart rate, slightly higher blood pressure, higher cholesterol level, hoarse voice or depression. The only way to know whether you have hypothyroidism is with a blood test. The complete cure of hypothyroidism is cannot possible, but it can be treated by wholly controlled. Hypothyroidism is treated by replacing the amount of hormone that thyroid can no longer make to bring T4 and TSH levels back to normal levels. T4 replacement can restore the body's thyroid hormone levels and the body's function if the thyroid gland cannot work right.

1.2 Related Works

Data analytics is becoming a strategically important tool for many organizations, including the healthcare sector. The goal is to search for new patterns and knowledge, which are not visible sometimes for the first look or to confirm an assumption of the physician on more large data samples. This process requires intensive collaboration between analysts and relevant domain experts. In this section, we present some works related to this crucial aspect of the analytical process and some existing studies related to thyroid disease.

The research group of professor Andreas Holzinger propose a concept called an interactive machine learning with a human-in-the-loop, i.e. "algorithms that can interact with agents and can optimize their learning behavior through these interactions, where the agents can also be human." [8, 9]. Mao et al. investigated various aspects of the collaboration between data scientist and domain experts through the interviews with bio-medical experts collaborating with data scientists. They identified bottlenecks like collaboration and technology readiness or coupling of work dimensions [10]. Jeanquartier and Holzinger applied a visual analytics process in cell physiology [11]. Experts in this domain are using their domain knowledge in combination with both automatic and visual analysis together. They need to be guided by computer science experts to improve the choice of tools that are used. They point out that it is a gap between free available visualization tools and their usability for the experts.

Ionita I and Inoina L, in their study, used for experiments the dataset provided by UCI Machine Learning Repository containing data about clinical history patients with thyroid disorders [12]. The authors applied four types of classifications methods: Naïve Bayes, Decision Trees, Multilayer Perceptron, and RBF Network (Radial Basis Function Network). The best accuracy was obtained by the Decision tree (97.35%). Sidiq et al. worked with a clinical dataset from one of the leading diagnostic labs in Kashmir [13]. The authors generated several classification models based on the following methods: K-Nearest Neighbor, Support Vector Machine, Decision Tree, and Naïve Bayes to diagnose thyroid diseases. They used a programming language, Python, and 10-fold cross-validation. The best accuracy of 98.89% was achieved again by the Decision Tree approach. Logistic regression was used by the collective of authors to predict the patients without thyrotoxicosis and with thyrotoxicosis [14]. The outcomes demonstrate that the logistic regression obtains promising results in classifying regression on thyroid disease diagnosis 98.92%

2 Methods

Typically, the analytical process contains in the modeling phase (according to the CRISP-DM methodology) an application of suitable machine learning, artificial intelligence, or statistical methods. We have experience with all these methods, and sometimes it isn't easy to apply them based on the data quality or data range. On the other hand, the data analytics domain offers other unusual methods like EDA to meet the domain experts' expectations.

John W. Tukey defined exploratory data analysis (EDA) as "detective work – or more precisely numerical detective work" [15]. It is mainly the philosophy of data analysis. EDA's primary goal is to examine the data for distribution, outliers, and anomalies to direct specific testing of the hypothesis. The EDA gives analysts unparalleled power for gaining insight into the data and their visualizations [16].

The Chi-square test (also known as the Pearson Chi-square test) is the most useful a nonparametric statistical test that measures the association between two categorical variables [17]. This test utilizes a contingency table to analyse the data, where each row represents a category for one variable, and each column represents a category for the other variable. Each cell of the contingency table reflects the total count of cases for a specific pair of classes.

The most popular methods among normality tests are the Kolmogorov – Smirnov test, the Anderson – Darling test, and the Shapiro – Wilk normality test [18]. The Shapiro – Wilk test tests the null hypothesis on the significance level α that a sample $x_1, x_2, \ldots, x_n$ comes from a normally distributed population *norm* (μ, σ) with unspecified parameters μ and σ, where μ is median, and σ is the standard deviation [19].

Students' t-test is one of the most commonly used methods of statistical hypothesis testing. This test is a parametric test, and it is used to compare samples of normally distributed data. There are several types of t-test: one-sample t-test, paired-samples t-test, unpaired two-sample t-test. Unpaired two samples t-test, also called independent t-test, is a parametric test, which compares the means of two independent groups [20]. This test aims to determine whether there is statistical evidence that the associated population means are significantly different. The main requirements for the independent t-test are that two groups of samples are normally distributed, and the variances of the two groups are equal.

Mann-Whitney U test is a nonparametric test, which is an alternative to the independent sample t-test [21]. This test is used to compare two population means that come from the same population. It can also apply to test whether two population means are equal or not. The test is used when the data fails the normality assumption or if the sample sizes in each group are too small to assess normality.

ROC curve or a Receiver operating characteristics curve is a useful technique for visualizing, organizing, and selecting classifier based on performance [22]. The receiver operating characteristics curve is computed by comparing a binary outcome with a continuous variable. Each observed level of a continuous variable is evaluated as a candidate cut point discriminating observed positive from negative [23]. Positive observations concerning the continuous measurement are these, exceeding the cut point, while those less than or equal to the cut point are classified negatively (Fig 1).

		PREDICTED CONDITION	
		Positive	**Negative**
TRUE CONDITION	**Positive**	True positive (TP) (Sensitivity)	False negative (FN)
	Negative	False positive (FP)	True negative (TN) (Specificity)

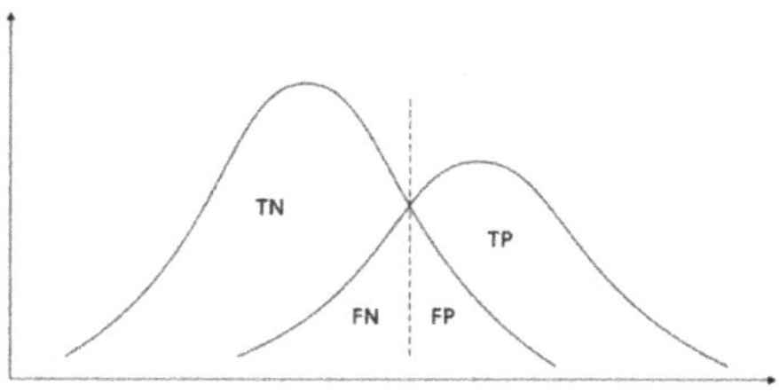

Fig. 1. Example of the contingency table.

As shown in the table, sensitivity is defined as a probability that observation with a positive outcome is correctly classified by a continuous measurement above a candidate cut point.

$$sensitivity = \frac{true\ positive}{true\ positive + false\ negative}$$

And specificity is defined as the probability that a continuous measurement correctly classifies an observed negative outcome at or below the candidate cut point.

$$specificity = \frac{true\ negative}{true\ negative + false\ positive}$$

The coordinates for the ROC curve are computed where the x-axis is $1 -$ specificity ($=$ false positive rate; FPR), and the y-axis is sensitivity ($=$ true positive rate; TPR). The best cut point given the data may be identified from the ROC curves coordinates with a criterion that maximizes TPR (True Positive Rate) and minimizes FPR (False Positive Rate).

To evaluate the ROC curve can be used the AUC (Area Under Curve), also known as the c-statistics [24]. The AUC metric varies between 0.5 and 1.00 (Ideal value), where values above 0.80 is an indication of a good classifier.

Logistic regression is a method of modelling the probability of an outcome that can only have two values [25]. The main is to find the best fitting model that described the relationship between the dichotomous variable (dependent variable – it contains data coded as 1/0, TRUE/FALSE, yes/no, etc.) and asset of independent variables. The final logistic regression generates the coefficients (standard errors, significance levels) of a formula to predict the logit transformation of the probability of the presence of the characteristic of interest.

3 Analytical Process

This study was motivated by previous successful cooperation between Slovak data analysts and medical experts from Croatia. This research team cooperated on several preliminary studies or experiments focused on effective diagnostics of Metabolic syndrome, Mild Cognitive Impairment, hypertension, or frailty within suitable analytical methods.

We used these experiences to support the medical diagnostics in the case of Hypothyroidism disease. The analytical process was interactive and iterative. The medical expert proposed the initial set of research questions (tasks). This set was continuously updated based on obtained results and their verification. The success of the proposed solution was evaluated not only by the novelty and correctness of new knowledge but also by the simple, understandable form of visualization for domain experts. All experiments were performed within the R programming language.

3.1 Data Description

The medical experts described all three datasets. Their deeper understanding required intensive communication, and the exchange of information resulted in a comprehensive overview. The first dataset contained 70 patients characterized by 32 variables like older than 50 years, with hypertension and diagnosed hypothyroidism (Table 1 and Table 2).

Table 1. Description of the numerical variables (dataset 1).

Variable	Minimum	Maximum	Median (interquartile range)	Mean (standard deviation)
TSH (mlU/L)	0.2	10.10	2.1 (1.25)	2.37 (1.55)
Age (years)	48	86	63.5 (13.75)	64.7 (9.69)
Menop (years)	0	35	0 (13.75)	7.45 (10.05)
Hy dur (years)	1	20	9 (8)	9.91 (5.35)
All drugs (count)	0	10	3 (3)	3.67 (2.23)
BMI (kg/m^2)	19	44	29 (6)	29.41 (4.92)
Wc (cm)	70.00	135.00	103.50 (13.75)	103.50 (12.60)
CRP (mg/L)	0.40	17.80	2.30 (1.47)	2.68 (2.41)
Erythro	3.68	5.83	4.72 (0.55)	4.76 (0.49)
Hct	0.297	1.74	0.43 (0.04)	0.47 (0.22)
Hgb (g/L)	90	173	144 (16.5)	144.10 (13.34)
MCV (fl)	72.9	101	90.00 (7.65)	90.09 (5.25)
F Glu (mmol/L)	4	16.9	5.6 (1.87)	6.46 (2.46)
Creatin (umol/L)	55	120	80 (16.75)	79.81 (14.18)

(continued)

Table 1. (*continued*)

Variable	Minimum	Maximum	Median (interquartile range)	Mean (standard deviation)
Gfr (ml/min/1.73 m^2)	48	135	74.5 (22.25)	78.67 (15.27)
Chol (mmol/L)	2.1	8.1	5.25 (1.57)	5.317 (1.26)
LDL (mmol/L)	1	5.6	2.95 (1.6)	2.93 (1.10)
HDL (mmol/L)	0.7	10	1.4 (0.5)	1.523 (1.15)
Triglycer (mmol/L)	0.51	6.56	1.79 (1.10)	1.94 (1.09)
Dm dur (years)	0	15	0 (0)	1.84 (4.09)
All dg (count)	0	6	2 (1)	2.28 (1.34)
Cogn	0	16	8 (4)	6.81 (3.35)

Table 2. Description of the categorical variables (dataset 1).

Variable	Value	Number of values (%)
Gender	1 - Man	30 (42.89%)
	2 - Woman	40 (57.14%)
Hipolip drugs	0 - No	45 (64.29%)
	1 - Yes	25 (35.71%)
Phys act	0 - No	40 (57.14%)
	1 - Yes	30 (42.86%)
dm 2	0 - No	53 (75.71%)
	1 - Yes	17 (24.29%)
coronar	0 - No	61 (87.14%)
	1 - Yes	9 (12.86%)
fibril altri	0 - No	66 (94.29%)
	1 - Yes	4 (5.71%)
myocard	0 - No	62 (88.57%)
	1 - Yes	8 (11.43%)
walking	0 - No	19 (27.14%)
	1 - Yes	51 (72.86%)
Anxy depr	0–2 (Normal)	41 (58.58%)
	3–5 (Mild)	13 (18.57%)
	6–8 (Moderate)	12 (17.14%)
	9–12 (Severe)	4 (5.72%)

The second dataset contained 197 records about women between 50–59, characterized by 22 variables (Table 3 and Table 4).

Table 3. Description of the numerical variables (dataset 2).

Variable	Minimum	Maximum	Median (interquartile range)	Mean (standard deviation)
age (years)	50	59	52 (1.96)	52.6 (3)
FGlu (mmol/L)	4	13	5.50 (0.9)	5.723 (0.91)
TG (mmol/L)	0.42	4.49	1.68 (0.52)	1.77 (0.55)
Cho (mmol/L)	3.5	8.2	6.1 (1.7)	5.94 (0.98)
LDL (mmol/L)	1.02	5.79	3.00(1.72)	3.07 (1.03)
HDL (mmol/L)	0.80	7.20	1.20 (0.49)	1.45 (0.85)
Cre (mmol/L)	43	110	78 (19)	78.4(12.07)
GFR (ml/min/1.73 m^2)	40.91	143.29	69.99 (19.04)	72.56 (14.12)
CRP (mg/L)	0.20	11.50	2.80 (2)	3.07 (1.49)
Hb (g/L)	106	155	137 (8)	135.4 (8.67)
Wc (cm)	78	120	90 (11)	90.57 (8.69)
BMI (kg/m^2)	21.11	38.28	26.89 (5.32)	27.56 (3.89)
chdi	1	10	5 (2)	4.91 (1.51)

Table 4. Description of the categorical variables (dataset 2).

Variable	Value	Number of values (%)
Hypdu	<5	28 (14.21%)
	>10	56 (28.43%)
	>5	113 (57.36%)
DGDM	No	147 (74.62%)
	Yes	50 (25.38%)
CHD	No	184 (93.4%)
	Yes	13 (6.6%)
CoHD	No	181 (91.88%)
	Yes	16 (8.12%)
cogn	No	172 (87.31%)
	Yes	25 (12.69%)

(*continued*)

Table 4. (*continued*)

Variable	Value	Number of values (%)
depr	No	27 (13.71%)
	Yes	170 (86.29%)
psy	No	195 (98.98%)
	Yes	2 (1.02%)
sta	No	91 (46.19%)
	Yes	106 (53.81%)
MeSy	No	67 (34.01%)
	Yes	130 (65.99%)

The last dataset also contained women (135 records) but between 60–89, characterized by 20 variables (Table 5 and Table 6).

Table 5. Description of the numerical variables (dataset 3).

Variable	Minimum	Maximum	Median (interquartile range)	Mean (standard deviation)
age (years)	60	89	72 (10)	71.21 (6.46)
bmi (kg/m^2)	14.33	47.05	30.49 (6.67)	30.89 (4.97)
wc (cm)	50	148	98 (16)	98.39 (12.76)
glu_f (mmol/L)	3.9	16.2	5.7 (1.6)	6.24 (1.85)
chol (mmol/L)	2.9	9.3	5.96 (1.65)	5.96 (1.22)
ldl (mmol/L)	1.2	6.8	3.68 (1.4)	3.68 (1.10)
hdl (mmol/L)	0.8	2.3	1.5 (0.4)	1.47 (0.30)
Trig (mmol/L)	0.6	7.0	1.7 (0.85)	1.76 (0.91)
cre (mmol/L)	42	205	66 (17)	69.78 (22.96)
gfr (ml/min/1.73 m^2)	24	191	86 (38.5)	86.32 (27.51)
hb (g/L)	68	158	133.4 (12.5)	133.4 (11.81)
erit	2.7	5.87	4.57 (0.42)	4.54 (0.42)
hct	0.22	0.48	0.41 (0.03)	0.41 (0.03)
som_com	1	8	3 (2)	3.48 (1.61)

Table 6. Description of the categorical variables (dataset 3).

Variable	Value	Number of values (%)
gender	f - female	135 (100%)
hyp	no	1 (0.74%)
	yes	134 (99.26%)
hyp_dur	less	53 (39.26%)
	more	79 (58.52%)
	no	3 (2.22%)
dm	no	102 (75.56%)
	yes	33 (24.44%)
chd-nyha	higher	1 (0.74%)
	lower	6 (4.44%)
	no	128 (94.81%)
coron	no	123 (91.11%)
	yes	12 (8.89%)

The first step provided by the data analysts was to explore data characteristics through suitable visualization techniques like histograms or within correlation analysis or statistical tests. All outputs were consulted within the expert to find possible adequate information for the research task solving. Also, we used them to identify potential outliers or incorrect or incomplete patient records. Based on a relatively large total number of variables, we present only one figure as an illustration. Also, we can state that sometimes it is necessary to generate them iteratively based on the expert's recommendations (description of axes, accurate scales).

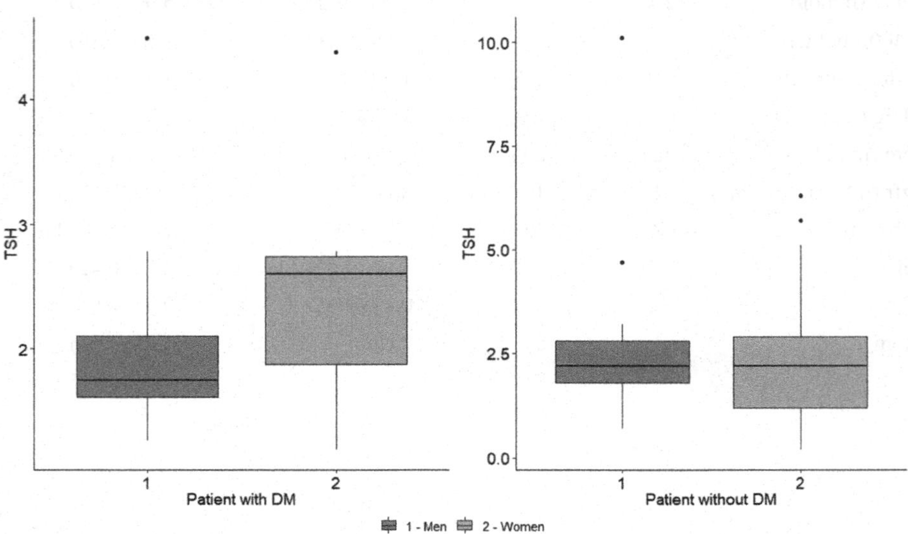

Fig. 2. Boxplots of TSH range in patients with DM and without DM by gender.

Figure 2 shows the range of TSH in patients with Diabetes mellitus (DM) and patients without Diabetes mellitus separately for men and women. The analysis shows that the average values of TSH in patients with DM and without DM are about the same. The average value of TSH in men with Diabetes mellitus is 2.09 while in men without Diabetes mellitus is a little higher at 2.59. The analysis shows that the average value of TSH in women with Diabetes mellitus is higher than in men in the same group.

In the case of numerical variables, we performed a correlation analysis:

- strong correlation: *Creatinine* (a waste product in a blood, which is removed from blood by kidneys) – *Glomerular filtration rate* in the second dataset and *Haemoglobin – Hematocrit, Cholesterol and LDL* in the third dataset.
- moderate correlation: *Cholesterol and LDL* and *BMI – Waist circumference* in the first and second datasets; *All drugs – All diagnoses, Age – Menopause* in the first dataset; *Cholesterol – waist circumference* in the second *and Erythrocytes – Hematocrit, Haemoglobin – Erythrocytes, Creatinine – Glomerular filtration rate, BMI – Waist circumference, Age – Glomerular filtration rate.*

In the case of nominal variables, we applied the Pearson's Chi-squared test (a dependency exists):

- 1st dataset: *Gender – Physical activity, Hipolip drugs – diabetes mellitus 2, Physical activity – Walking, Cardiomyopathy – Fibrillation atriorum.*
- 2nd dataset: *almost half of the variables.*
- 3rd dataset: *Gender with Hypertension, Hypertension duration, Diabetes mellitus, Stages of chronic heart disease* and *coronary artery disease, Hypertension duration – Diabetes mellitus, Hypertension.*

Finally, we performed selected statistical tests within numerical variables. We started with the Shapiro-Wilk normality test: *Waist circumference, Erythrocytes, Mean corpuscular volume, Creatin, Cholesterol,* and *LDL.* Based on these results, we choose a statistical test – if variables were normally distributed, we used the Two-Sample t-test (Welch test), but if variables were not normally distributed, we used a Mann-Whitney test. The results show that the dependency exists between almost all the variables besides combinations: *Duration of menopause* with *Hematocrit, HDL, Triglycerides, C-reactive protein, All drugs, All diagnoses.*

Some of these results have a logical basis like total cholesterol and low-density lipoproteins or hypertension and its duration. The expert confirmed some of them based on the existing knowledge base and her experience. In general, we used them for features reduction, improving the data quality.

3.2 Task 1

The first experiment aimed on investigation of the possible differences in variable TSH (*test for thyroid stimulating hormone*) according different cut-off values for *Glomerular filtration rate*, such as $> = 60$ or <60 and $> = 80$ (Fig. 3, right) or <80 (Fig. 3, left).

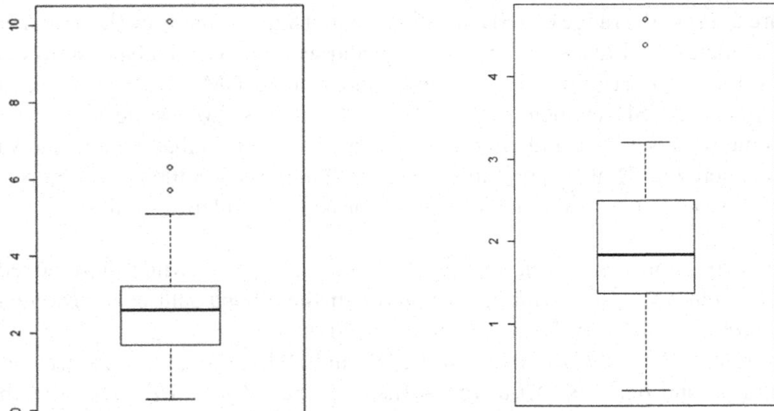

Fig. 3. The comparison of TSH distribution according to the Gfr cut-off value 80.

All combinations were evaluated by the expert to investigate a sign of mild kidney impairment. It means that the kidney is not able to excrete enough waste substances and redundant water from the blood and it is very often in older people with hypertension or diabetes.

3.3 Task 2

The second task focused on the investigation of the possible differences in other input variables according to the following condition: below the reference range (left), reference range (middle), and above the reference range of the *TSH* variable (right). The reference range of *thyroid stimulating hormone* is 0.46–4.68 lU/ml). As an illustration, we present a comparison of gender balance (Fig. 4).

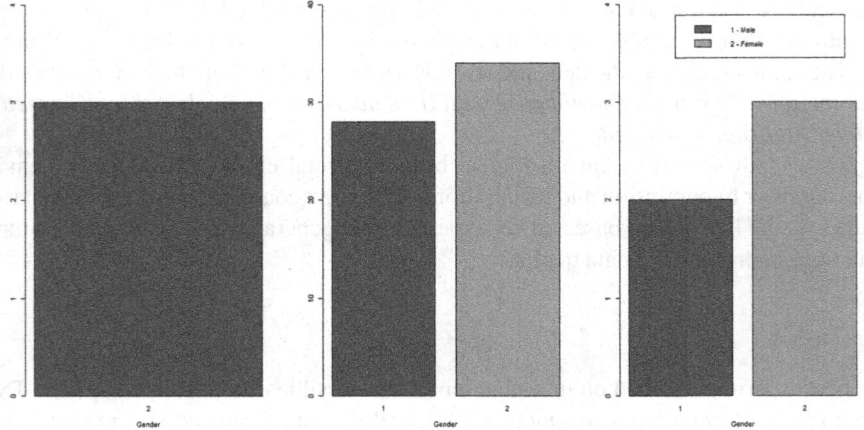

Fig. 4. The comparison of gender distribution according to three TSH levels.

The set of graphs showed several interesting findings evaluated by the expert. If *TSH* is below the reference range, it can indicate hyperthyroidism associated with more cardiac arrhythmias. But if *TSH* is within the reference range and above the reference range, it indicates hypothyroidism, and it may be related to the decreased renal function (low *Gfr*) and is known to be associated with higher *cholesterol, LDL* and *triglycerides.* Paradoxically, due to decreased renal function and associated frailty, is tends to be lower *BMI*.

3.4 Task 3

In 3rd task, we investigated collaborative possible trends between TSH and other variables like *age, glomerular filtration rate, waist circumference, BMI* (Fig. 5), *total cholesterol, LDL, HDL, triglycerides, fasting blood glucose* and *c-reactive protein.* The results showed that *TSH* values increase as the metabolism increases until the point when the level of insulin resistance becomes high. It is the case at high *BMI* values and very high waist circumference values indicating obesity. That is also following with increased *triglycerides* and *LDL* values. Or when renal function (*Gfr*) becomes decreased - at the cut-off of 60, then because of malnutrition *BMI* may fall. But a high level of insulin resistance (the barrier for the action of insulin on cells – that is slowing down metabolism) causes that TSH trends become decreasing.

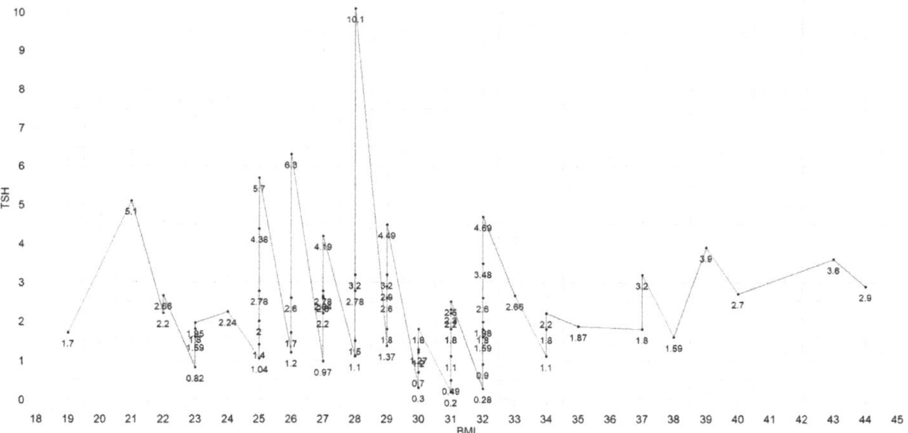

Fig. 5. Line chart visualizing a relation between variables TSH and BMI.

3.5 Task 4

This task was specified based on the outputs from previous ones. We aimed to estimate the significance of differences trough suitable statistical tests like Shapiro-Wilk normality test, two-sample t-test (Welch test), or Mann-Whiney test. The results confirmed the expert's expectations like *TSH* increases in parallel with increasing *age* and decreasing renal function (*Gfr*). Paradoxically when *TSH* increases, the variables *BMI*, *waist circumference,* and *fasting blood glucose* decrease. If *TSH* decreases in parallel with reducing *haemoglobin, LDL,* and *triglycerides*, these factors are in accordance with hypermetabolism.

3.6 Task 5

The fifth task dealt with an experimental calculation of new cut-off values for variables *TSH* according to several target binary conditions like *Gfr* (<60, >= 60), *BMI* (<30, >= 30) or (<25, >= 25), *waist circumference* (<80, >= 80) or (<88, > = 88), *fasting blood glucose* (<6.1, >= 6.1), etc. For this purpose, we used Receiver operating characteristics (ROC) as simple understandable visualisation technique for the domain expert. The ROC analysis showed that hypothyroid patients had significantly lower *Gfr* (median 66.5, interquartile range 64.2–72.5) than *euthyroid* ones (median 78, interquartile range 68–91), as well as *BMI* (median 25.5, interquartile range 23–27 vs median 29, interquartile range 26–32).

Figure 6 shows the cut-off value 2.55 for *Gfr* indicating patients with mild renal impairment (AUC 0.62, sensitivity 0.53, specificity 0.77). In hypertensive patients, an increase in *TSH* values, already within the reference range, contributes to variations in cardiovascular risk factors if there is a mild renal impairment.

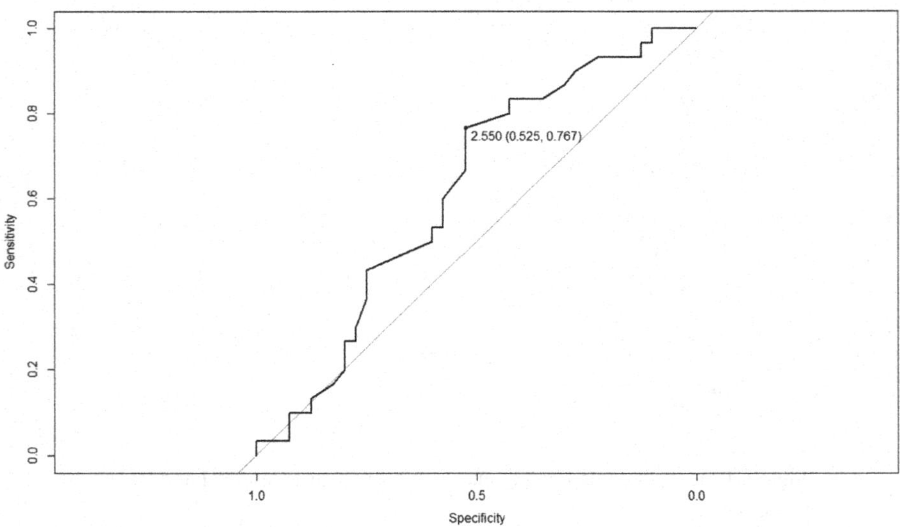

Fig. 6. ROC curve of variables TSH and Gfr.

The second ROC curves were generated from the new sample combining the second and third datasets. Anthropometric measures of obesity moderately depend on good renal function (*Gfr* > 90) and obviously on other factors such as age, the time after menopause. Many patients with *Gfr* > 90 (good renal function) have high cholesterol

(Chol > 6). Patients with older age of around 76 have a low renal function (*Gfr* < 45). *BMI* indicating overweight (26–29) well correlates with low renal function but is not exclusive for low renal function, because it may also be a characteristic of older patients with preserved renal function (*Gfr* > 90). It means that patients have not been obese and did not get diabetes (15.7%) at higher rates. The relationship between low *Gfr* and *waist circumference* is a complex one because *waist circumference* is increased moderately.

3.7 Task 6

Finally, we decided to apply multiple logistic regressions on the joined dataset with women older than 50 years; one example is visualized in Fig. 7.

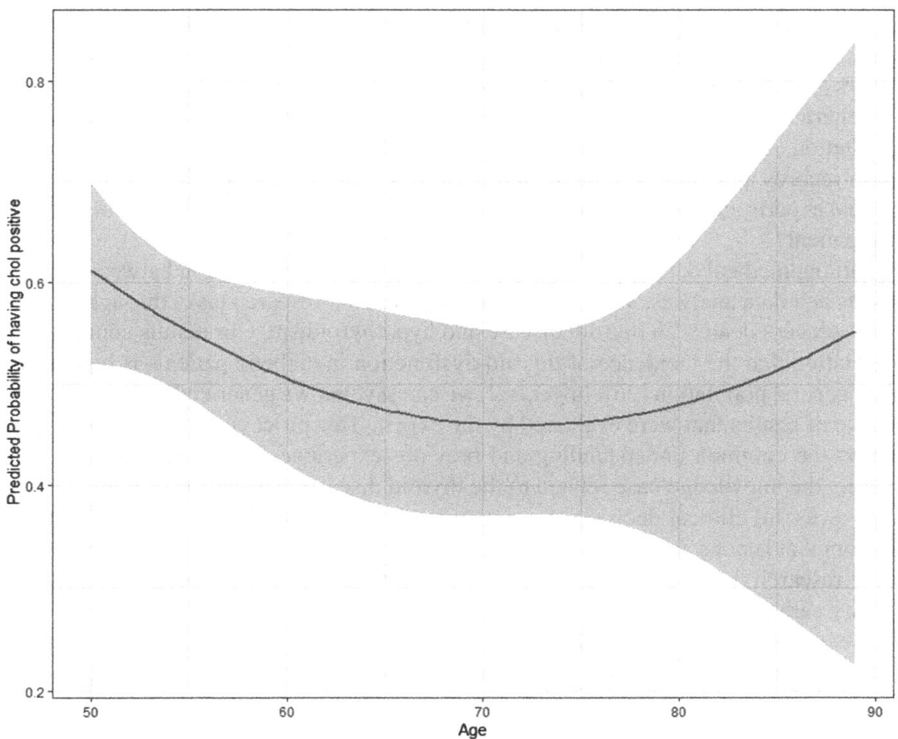

Fig. 7. Logistic regression of the variable age and total cholesterol.

The results show that there are two groups of women with the diagnosis of *hypertension*. The first group is younger (50–59 years old) and a higher prevalence of *diabetes*. The presence of *diabetes*, in combination with *hypertension*, in the *age* of 54–55 years, is associated with a mildly reduced renal function (*Gfr* = 89–60 or 59–45). These women are usually overweight – *BMI* 26–30 (*BMI* > 26. and *waist circumference* > 100). The second group represents older women, and their age is higher than 65 and may be divided into two subgroups, according to the *Gfr* range values. The first subgroup is women *age* around 65 with good renal function (*Gfr* > 90), but women in this subgroup may be obese, their *BMI* may be higher than 30 or with the normal weight (*BMI* < 26). The second subgroup is women age around 76 with a low renal function (*Gfr* < 45). It can associate with a low weight (*BMI* < 26), which indicates the frailty status, because of *low renal function* and high *age*. *Low renal function* is an insulin-resistant state and is associated with high *waist circumference* (>90), which is, typically, a characteristic of obesity for women with *age* from 50 to 60 years - years after post-menopause. But if women are in *age* higher than 76 years, their high *waist circumference* falls more intensively depending on advanced age that it increases with a drop of *Gfr*.

4 Conclusion

The practicing doctors mention two significant limitations of their decision/diagnostic process: existing literature and case studies contain a large volume of information, and doctors often lack time to find, consider, and use it all. The second constraint is sometimes too generic method, procedure, or recommendation not focused on the specific patient or situation. This situation is changing step by step with the deployment of electronic health records and suitable analytical approaches. Correctly set collaboration between medical experts and data analysts can answer the age-old question: what is truly best for each patient?

Mining medical data requires intensive and effective collaboration between medical experts and data analysts. We experimentally solved six research tasks through the analytical process dealt with thyroid disease and hypothyroidism. Our results confirmed an expectation that the incidence of thyroid dysfunction in diabetic patients is higher than in the general population [26]. In general, we can say that we generated a relatively large volume of results that were evaluated by the expert. This process was improved step by step by the common understanding and previous experience. The next step should be creating the knowledge base related to the thyroid disease as a basis for future development. A useful clinical decision support system will represent the final stage. But this development is not a simple task. It requires more resources and a broader collaboration of the research teams around the world, including data analysts, medical experts, and primary care doctors.

We have several recommendations for effective collaboration within domain experts: at first, have clearly defined tasks that reduce the risk of mutual misunderstanding; regular communication and joint decision; the easy-to-understand form of results and detailed explanations; state-of-the-art analysis to identify suitable methods; verification of the obtained results with existing literature or expert knowledge.

Acknowledgements. The work was partially supported by The Slovak Research and Development Agency under grants no. APVV-16-0213 and no. APVV-17-0550.

References

1. Balogh, E.P., Miller, B.T., Ball, J.R.: Improving Diagnosis in Health Care. The National Academies Press, Washington, DC (2015)

2. Onder, G., Palmer, K., Navickas, R., et al.: Time to face the challenge of multimorbidity. a European perspective from the joint action on chronic diseases and promoting healthy ageing across the life cycle (JA-CHRODIS). Eur. J. Intern. Med. **26**, 157–159 (2015)
3. Paul, L., Jeemon, P., Hewwit, J., McCallum, L., Higgins, P., Walters, M., et al.: Hematocrit predicts long-term mortality in a nonlinear and sex-specific manner in hypertensive adults. Hypertension **60**(3), 631–638 (2012)
4. Silva, N.O., Ronsoni, M.F., Colombo, Bda.S., Correa, C.G., Hatanaka, S.A., et al.: Clinical and laboratory characteristics of patients with thyroid diseases with and without alanine aminotransferase levels above the upper tertile – cross-sectional analytical study. Arch. Endocrinol. Metab. **60**(2), 101–107 (2016)
5. Ahmed, O.M., Ahmed, R.G.: Hypothyroidism. A New Look at Hypothyroidism, pp. 1–20. InTech, Lagos (2012)
6. Cojić, M., Cvejanov-Kezunović, L.: Subclinical hypothyroidism – whether and when to start treatment? Open Access Maced J. Med. Sci. **5**(7), 1042–1046 (2017)
7. Carlé, A., Pedersen, I.B., Knudsen, N., Perrild, H., Ovesen, L., Laurberg, P.: Hypothyroid symptoms and the likelihood of overt thyroid failure: a population-based case-control study. Eur. J. Endocrinol. **171**(5), 593–602 (2014)
8. Girardi, D., Kueng, J., Holzinger, A.: A domain-expert centered process model for knowledge discovery in medical research: putting the expert-in-the-loop. In: Guo, Y., Friston, K., Aldo, F., Hill, S., Peng, H. (eds.) BIH 2015. LNCS (LNAI), vol. 9250, pp. 389–398. Springer, Cham (2015). https://doi.org/10.1007/978-3-319-23344-4_38
9. Holzinger, A.: Interactive machine learning for health informatics: when do we need the human-in-the-loop? Brain Inf. **3**(2), 119–131 (2016). https://doi.org/10.1007/s40708-016-0042-6
10. Mao, Y., Wang, D., Muller, M.J., Varshney, K.R., Baldini, I., et al.: How data scientists work together with domain experts in scientific collaborations: to find the right answer or to ask the right question? Proc. ACM Hum. Comput. Interact. **237**, 1–23 (2019)
11. Jeanquartier, F., Holzinger, A.: On visual analytics and evaluation in cell physiology: a case study. In: Cuzzocrea, A., Kittl, C., Simos, Dimitris E., Weippl, E., Xu, L. (eds.) CD-ARES 2013. LNCS, vol. 8127, pp. 495–502. Springer, Heidelberg (2013). https://doi.org/10.1007/978-3-642-40511-2_36
12. Ioniţă, I., Ioniţă, L.: Prediction of thyroid disease using data mining techniques. Brain. Artif. Intell. Neurosci. **7**(3), 115–124 (2016)
13. Sidiq, U., Aaqib, S.M., Khan, R.A.: Diagnostic of various thyroid ailments using data mining classification techinques. Int. J. Sci. Res. Comput. Sci. Eng. Inf. Technol. **5**(1), 131–135 (2019)
14. Gurram, D., Rao, M.R.N.: A comparative study of support vector machine and logistic regression for the diagnosis of thyroid dysfunction. Int. J. Eng. Technol. **7**(1.1), 326–328 (2018)
15. Cox, V.: Exploratory data analysis. Translating Statistics to Make Decisions A Guide for the Non-Statistician, pp. 47–74. Apress, Berkeley, CA (2017). https://doi.org/10.1007/978-1-4842-2256-0_3
16. Komorowski, M., Marshall, Dominic C., Salciccioli, J.D., Crutain, Y.: Exploratory data analysis. Secondary Analysis of Electronic Health Records, pp. 185–203. Springer, Cham (2016). https://doi.org/10.1007/978-3-319-43742-2_15
17. Franke, T.M., Ho, T., Christie, C.H.A.: The chi-square test: often used and more often misinterpreted. Am. J. Eval. **33**(3), 448–458 (2012)
18. Ghasemi, A., Zahedias, S.: Normality tests for statistical analysis: a guide for non-statisticians. Int. J. Endocrinol. Metab. **10**(2), 486–489 (2012)

19. Oztuna, D., Elhan, A.H., Tuccar, E.: Investigation of four different normality tests in terms of type 1 error rate and power under different distributions. Turk. J. Med. Sci. **36**(3), 171–176 (2006)
20. Rice, J.A.: Mathematical Statistics and Data Analysis, 3rd edn. Duxbury Advanced, Duxbury (2006)
21. Mann, H.B., Whitney, D.R.: On a test of whether one of two random variables is stochastically larger than the other. Ann. Math. Stat. **18**(1), 50–60 (1947)
22. Hajian-Tilaki, K.: Receiver Operating Characteristic (ROC) curve analysis for medical diagnostic test evaluation. Caspian J. Intern. Med. **4**(2), 627–635 (2013)
23. deCASTRO, B.R.: Cumulative ROC curves for discriminating three or more ordinal outcomes with cutpoints on a shared continuous measurement scale. PLoS ONE **14**(8), e0221433 (2019)
24. Carter, J.V., Pan, J., Rai, S.N., Galandiuk, S.: ROC-ing along: evaluation and interpretation of receiver operating characteristic curves. Surgery **159**(6), 1638–1645 (2016)
25. Tolles, J., Meurer, W.J.: Logistic regression relating patient characteristics to outcomes. JAMA **316**(5), 533–534 (2016)
26. Mohamed, G.A., Elsayed, A.M.: Subclinical hypothyroidism ups the risk of vascular complications in type 2 diabetes. Alexandria J. Med. **53**(3), 285–288 (2017)

A Study on the Fusion of Pixels and Patient Metadata in CNN-Based Classification of Skin Lesion Images

Fabrizio Nunnari(✉), Chirag Bhuvaneshwara, Abraham Obinwanne Ezema, and Daniel Sonntag

German Research Center for Artificial Intelligence (DFKI), Saarbrücken, Germany
{fabrizio.nunnari,chirag.bhuvaneshwara,abraham_obinwanne.ezema, daniel.sonntag}@dfki.de

Abstract. We present a study on the fusion of pixel data and patient metadata (age, gender, and body location) for improving the classification of skin lesion images. The experiments have been conducted with the ISIC 2019 skin lesion classification challenge data set. Taking two plain convolutional neural networks (CNNs) as a baseline, metadata are merged using either non-neural machine learning methods (tree-based and support vector machines) or shallow neural networks. Results show that shallow neural networks outperform other approaches in all overall evaluation measures. However, despite the increase in the classification accuracy (up to +19.1%), interestingly, the average per-class sensitivity decreases in three out of four cases for CNNs, thus suggesting that using metadata penalizes the prediction accuracy for lower represented classes. A study on the patient metadata shows that age is the most useful metadatum as a decision criterion, followed by body location and gender.

Keywords: Skin lesion classification · Convolutional neural network · Machine learning · Patient metadata · Data fusion

1 Introduction

The skin cancer death rate has escalated sharply in the USA, Europe and Australia. However, with proper early detection, the survival rate after surgery (wide excision) increases a lot. For this reason, the research community has put a significant effort in the early detection of skin cancer through the inspection of images. In order to increase their diagnostic accuracy, dermatologists use *dermascopes* (or dermatoscope) for the visual inspection of the skin. A dermascope is typically a cylinder containing a magnifying lens and a light emitter, helping the analysis of the substrate of the skin (see Fig. 1 for an example).

The use of deep convolutional neural networks (CNN) for the classification of skin lesions has significantly increased in the last years [2,5,13,15]. The breakthrough work of Esteeva et al. [9] being one of the most representative use cases,

Published by Springer Nature Switzerland AG 2020
A. Holzinger et al. (Eds.): CD-MAKE 2020, LNCS 12279, pp. 191–208, 2020.
https://doi.org/10.1007/978-3-030-57321-8_11

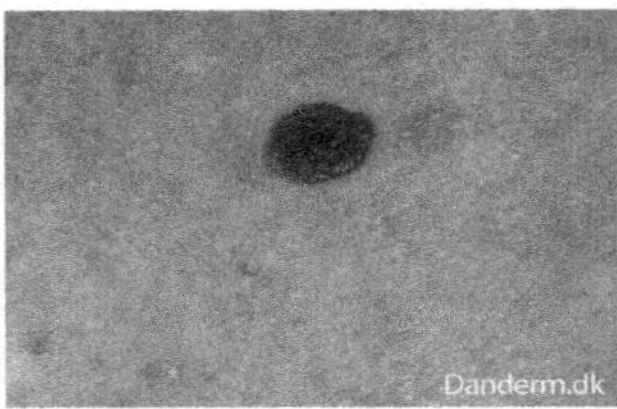

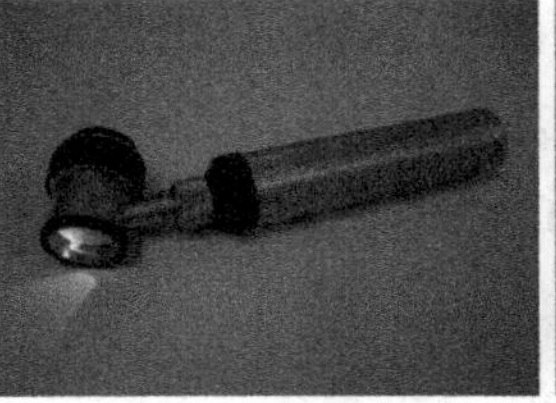
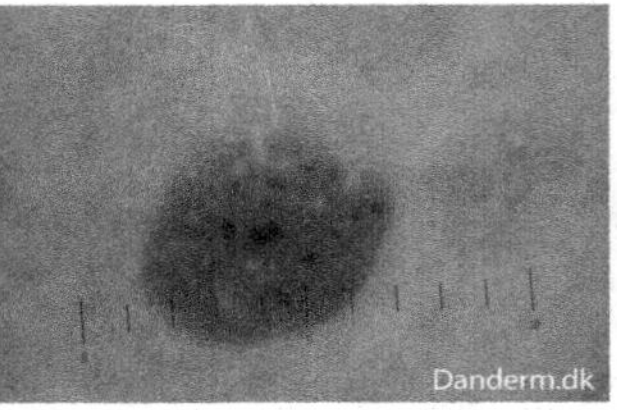

Fig. 1. Left: a skin lesion as seen from a normal camera and, right, through a dermatoscope (source: http://danderm.dk/). Transparent rulers are often added to give a size reference. In the middle, we see such a dermatoscope with an ergonomic handle (source: Wikipedia).

where a CNN matched the accuracy of expert dermatologists in the diagnosis of skin lesions from image analysis. While this result was achieved through the use of a private dataset, in the Skincare project[1] we work on several extensions [16,20] using image material from the scientific community.

In the context of dermatoscopy, the most popular dataset is provided since 2016 by the Society for Digital Imaging of the Skin, which organizes the ISIC (International Skin Imaging Collaboration[2]) challenge. In all its editions, the ISIC challenge includes a classification task, which increased from the 2 classes of the first edition in 2016 (Nevus vs. Melanoma) to the 8 classes of the 2019 edition[3].

The 2019 challenge is enriched by two elements. In Task 1 (classification using only images) the test set used to evaluate the performances also contains images *not* belonging to any of the 8 classes present in the training set; the so called UNK (unknown) class. In other words, participating machine learning experts can only train models on 8 classes, but must predict 9 classes in the evaluation set. This should resemble actual clinical diagnostic conditions more and hence provide better decision support. In Task 2, participants should use additional patient *metadata* (age, gender, and location of the lesion on the body) to improve the prediction accuracy, and this is the focus of this study.

As pointed by Kawahara et al. [13], the comparison in performance between man vs. machine is often unfair. In most of the literature, machines (either classic Machine Learning algorithms or recent Deep Learning architectures) infer their diagnosis solely from image pixel information, and the comparison with human practitioners is done by providing the same material to both of them. However, in practice, doctors complement visual information with other *metadata*, which is usually collected by medical experts during their daily interactions with patients. Hence, to better match the diagnosis conditions, the data source of the ISIC 2019 challenge, namely the BCN20000 dataset [4], includes information available in clinical routine.

1 https://medicalcps.dfki.de/?page_id=1056.
2 https://isdis.org/isic-project/.
3 https://challenge2019.isic-archive.com/.

Table 1. Participants of ISIC 2019 Task 2, and their scores in the first (images-only) and the second task (images + metadata).

Team	Task 1		Task 2		Gain
	Rank	Acc.	Rank	Acc.	
DAISYLab	1	0.636	1	0.634	−0.31%
Torus actions	6	0.563	2	0.597	6.04%
DermaCode	4	0.578	3	0.56	−3.11%
BGU_hackers	11	0.543	4	0.541	−0.37%
BITDeeper	7	0.558	5	0.534	−4.30%
offer_show	14	0.532	6	0.532	0.00%
Tencent	16	0.525	7	0.527	0.38%
VisinVis	21	0.513	8	0.517	0.78%
MGI	31	0.489	9	0.5	2.25%
Le-Health	36	0.469	10	0.488	4.05%
MMU-VCLab	26	0.502	11	0.481	−4.18%
SY1	38	0.464	12	0.47	1.29%
IML-DFKI	40	0.445	13	0.445	0.00%
Panetta's vision	39	0.461	14	0.431	−6.51%
KDIS	44	0.429	15	0.417	−2.80%
mvlab-skin	59	0.258	16	0.324	25.58%

It has been observed that the use of metadata leads to higher accuracy [12, 17, 23]. However, out of the 64 teams participating to the ISIC 2019 challenge, only 16 participants followed up with a submission on the images+metadata task. As can be seen in Table 1, the challenge obtains unexpected surprising results: when introducing metadata into the predictors, out of 16 teams, only seven increased their performance, with a relative increase between less than 1% to about 6%, with only one team able to boost performance of 25%, but starting from a relatively low initial score. Two teams did not achieve any performance increase. More surprisingly, seven teams decreased their accuracy. These results suggest that the integration of metadata in CNN-based architectures is still not a well-known practice. Additionally, it is worth noticing that, from the point of view of evaluating the usefulness of metadata, the reported scores are biased by the presence of the extra UNK class in the test set, and by the need to handle missing metadata for some samples.

To the best of our knowledge, there is no prior work of systematically comparing the performance of pixel-only skin lesion classification with pixel+metadata conditions. Hence, in this paper we present a post-challenge study focusing on the use of metadata to improve the performance of skin lesion classification in the ISIC 2019 dataset. We compare several fusion techniques, some of them used by participants of the challenge, and measure their relative increase in perfor-

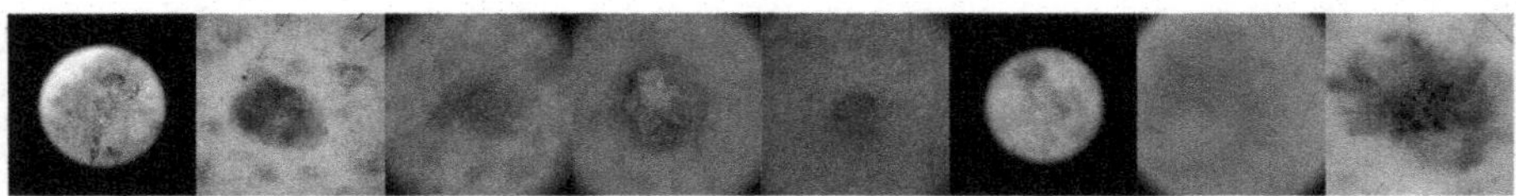

Fig. 2. A sample for each of the eight classes in the ISIC 2019 dataset. From left to right: Melanoma, Melanocytic nevus, Basal cell carcinoma, Actinic keratosis, Benign keratosis, Dermatofibroma, Vascular lesion, and Squamous cell carcinoma.

mance for each of the available metadata. The comparison is performed while using two different CNN baseline architectures.

The paper is structured as follows: Sect. 2 gives more details about the ISIC challenge and presents an analysis of the training material. Section 3 describes related work on the use of metadata for skin lesion diagnosis and our ISIC evaluation. Section 4 describes the methodology used in our experiments. Section 5 presents the results of our tests. Section 6 summarizes the results of the experiments, and finally Sect. 7 concludes.

2 The ISIC 2019 Challenge

The ISIC 2019 dataset (courtesy of [3,7,22], License (CC-BY-NC) https://creativecommons.org/licenses/by-nc/4.0/) provides ground truth for training (25331 samples), while the test set ground truth remains undisclosed. Hence, for our tests, we used a split of the ISIC 2019 training set. Figure 2 shows a sample for each class.

Image *metadata* consist of patient gender (male/female), age, and the general location of the skin lesion on the body. Not all of the images are associated with full metadata info. Since the management of missing metadata would increase the complexity of the deep learning architecture (as in [12]), for this work, we used only the subset of 22480 images for which all metadata are present. As can be seen in Table 2, the dataset is strongly unbalanced; this issue has been addressed by applying weightings to the loss function used to train the CNN models (see Sect. 4.1).

Table 2. Class distribution in our ISIC 2019 training subset.

Class	MEL	NV	BCC	AK	BKL	DF	VASC	SCC	Tot
Count	4346	10632	3245	845	2333	235	222	622	22480
Pct	17.8%	50.8%	13.1%	3.4%	10.4%	1.0%	1.0%	2.5%	100%

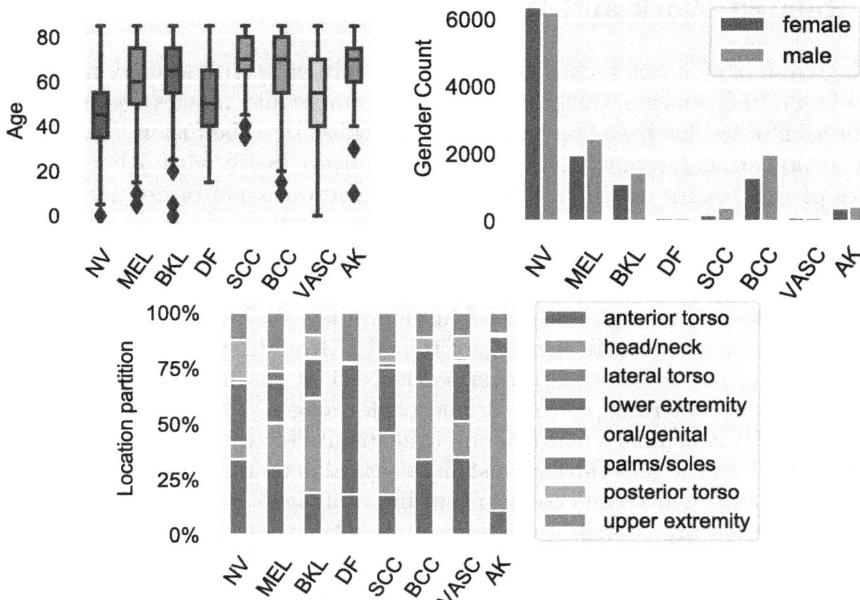

Fig. 3. Metadata distribution divided by class for age (left), gender (right), and body location (down).

Age (Fig. 3, left) is subdivided into groups with bin size 5. The mean value is 54, and the minimum and maximum age bins are 0 (less than 5-year old children) and 85, respectively. Gender (Fig. 3, right) denotes 11950 male and 10530 female patients. The location of the skin lesion in the body has 8 possible options (Fig. 3, down). The samples are not evenly distributed, as categories lateral torso, oral/genital, and palms/soles have only about a hundred samples each, while the others have about 2300.

The ISIC challenge measures the performance of a classifier by "Normalized (or balanced) multi-class accuracy"[4]. It can be computed by considering the diagonal of the confusion matrix. Each element of the diagonal (correctly classified class) is normalized according to the number of samples for that class. The elements of the diagonal are then averaged together, regardless of the number of samples per class, as to give the same importance to each class regardless of their observed frequency. This is equivalent to the average of the per-class sensitivities. In reporting the classification performances, we will use the term *accuracy* as the usual proportion of correctly classified samples, while the term *(average) sensitivity* as equivalent to the ISIC 2019 evaluation metric.

[4] https://challenge2019.isic-archive.com/evaluation.html.

3 Related Work and ISIC 2019 Evaluation

In the realm of skin lesion classification, Kawahara et al. [12] already integrated pixel-based information (macroscopic and dermoscopic images) with human annotation of lesions based on the 7-point checklist [1]. The fusion is performed by concatenating internal CNN features of images [8,18] with 1-hot encoded scores of the 7-point method. The final classification is performed by an additional fully connected layer plus a final softmax. They report an increase of accuracy from 0.618 to 0.737 (+19.2%) using Inception V3 as base CNN. In particular, their work addresses the problem of dealing with missing or partial metadata information through a combination of ad-hoc loss functions.

Yap et al. [23] report an increase of the AUC from 0.784 to 0.866 (+10.5%) when merging patient metadata over a RESNET50 baseline. Again, the input is a mixture of macroscopic and dermoscopic images. They used an internal layer of the CNN as image features and concatenated it with the metadata. The concatenated vector goes through a shallow neural network of 2 dense layers and a final softmax. Their results confirm that internal layers activation of CNNs are useful image feature representations, as it has been seen in other application domains [8,18].

The participants of the ISIC 2019 challenge Task 2 however addressed the problem of metadata fusion using a variety of different approaches.

Among the first five best performers, DAISYLab (1st) fed the metadata to a 2-layer shallow neural network (sNN). The result is concatenated with internal image features and fed to a final dense layer + softmax. Metadata were encoded with 1-hot, but missing metadata were left to 0s and missing age to an arbitrary −5. The final score is slightly worse than using no metadata. Torus Actions (2nd) saw an increase of 6.04% when using metadata, but did not report any detail. Also BGUHackers (4th) and BITDeeper (5th) did not report any detail, but their score worsened.

DermaCode (3rd) used a manually engineered set of rules derived from a visual inspection on metadata analysis. They report having preferred rules since tests using small NNs gave negative results. However, their official score decreased, too, in Task 2 (−3.11%).

Among good performers, MGI (9th) was able to increase their accuracy (+2.25%) by concatenating the final softmax output with a shallow NN of 2x dense layers plus softmax. Le-Health (10th) increased accuracy (+4.05%) following the principle: "To combine image data with meta-data, we first use one-hot encoding to encode meta-data and then concatenate them with the image feature extracted from the layer before the first fully-connected layer". No more details are given. Finally, mvlab-skin used a first shallow NN to reduce the number of features from the convolution output. The result is concatenated with metadata and fed to another sequence of two dense layers + softmax. They achieved a remarkable increase in accuracy of +25.58%, but starting from a low initial accuracy of 0.258.

Given the variety of strategies and baselines it is difficult to objectively state what is the best approach for metadata integration, especially in presence of the

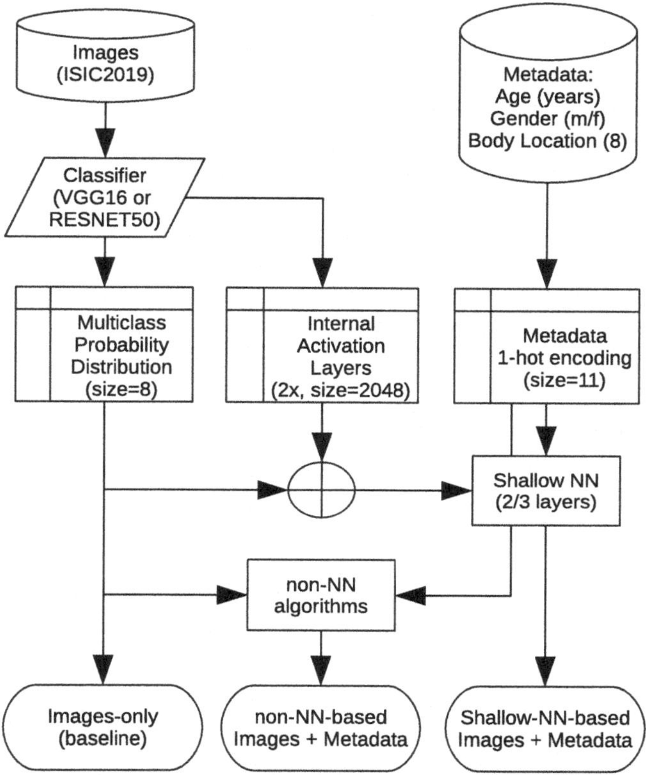

Fig. 4. The data flow of our experiments, concatenating the output of a CNN (either final predictions or internal layer activation values) with metadata to improve prediction.

UNK class influencing the final scores and the lack of details on how to handle partial metadata information.

In this paper, we replicate existing approaches, we add new ones based on classic ML algorithms, and compare them all over the same baseline CNNs, without the biases of unknown class samples and missing metadata information in the test set.

4 Method

Figure 4 depicts the methods used for integrating metadata together with pixel-based image classification. The pipeline starts with an initial training of a deep CNN for the classification of an image across the eight ISIC 2019 categories (softmax output). We repeated the same procedure for two CNN architectures, VGG16 [19] and RESNET50 [11] (details can be found in Sect. 4.1), to monitor the difference in the relative improvement given by metadata on two baselines. In parallel, metadata are encoded as 1-hot vectors of 11 values (details in Sect. 4.2).

The fusion with metadata is then performed in two ways. In the first fusion method (non-NN, Sect. 4.3), the output of the CNN classification (softmax, size 8) is concatenated with the metadata. The resulting feature vector (size 19) is passed to several well-known learning methods (either tree-based or SVM). In the second fusion method, (sNN, Sect. 4.4), we take, from the CNN, either the softmax output (size 8), or the activation values of the two fully connected layers (size 2048, each) located between the last convolution stage and the final softmax. Each fusion vector is then the concatenation of the softmax output (or the activation values for that matter) and the metadata vector. The concatenated vector is passed through a shallow neural network of two or three layers.

The following sections give more details about the metadata encoding and the training procedures.

4.1 Baseline CNN Classifier

Figure 5 shows the architectures for the VGG16 and RESNET50 baseline classifiers, the main differences being the resolution of the input image and the size of

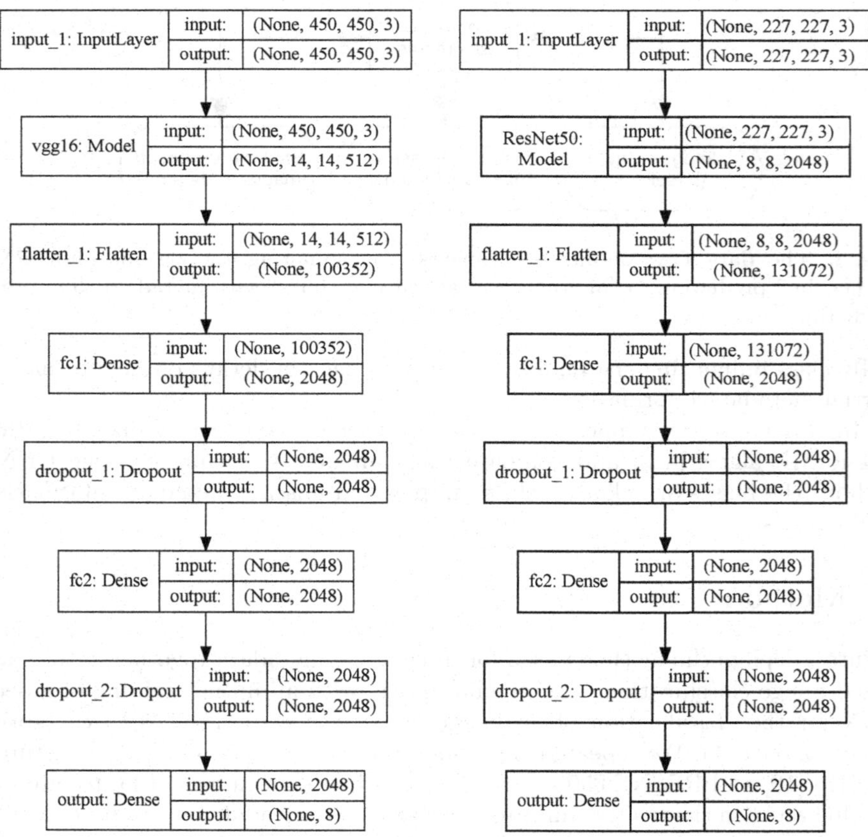

Fig. 5. Architecture of the baseline classifier for VGG16 (left) and RESNET50 (right).

the flattened layer. The architecture was implemented using the Keras framework (https://keras.io/). We follow a transfer learning approach [21] by first initializing the weights of the original VGG16/RESNET50 of a pre-trained model from ImageNet [6] and then substituting the final part of the architecture. The last convolution layer is flattened into a vector of size 100352/131072, followed by 2 fully connected layers of size 2048. Each fully connect layer is followed by a dropout layer with probability 0.5. The network ends with an 8-way softmax output. For VGG16, we set the input resolution to 450×450 pixels, instead of the original 224×224, to improve accuracy by introducing more details on the images.

The 22480 samples of the ISIC2019 subset arew randomly split in 19490 samples for training and 2×1495 samples for validation and testing. The sample selection is performed by ensuring the same between-class proportion on all of the three subsets. This means that in all three sets (train, development, and test), for example the nevus class represents about 50% of the samples, melanoma 20%, and so on for the remaining 6 classes. The same split is used for all further experiments that include metadata information.

The class unbalance is compensated by providing a class weight vector (size 8) as parameter `class_weight` to the method `Sequential.fit()`. The weight vector is used to modulate the computation of the loss for each sample in a training batch, and it is computed by counting the occurrences of each class in the training set and then normalizing the most frequent class to 1.0. For our training set, this translates into a base identity weight (1.0) for class NV and a maximum weight (47,89) for class VASC.

We trained our VGG16/RESNET50 baseline models for 10/30 epochs, batch size 8/32, SGD optimizer, lr = 1E-5, with a $48 \times$ augmentation factor (each image is flipped and rotated 24 times at 15° steps, as in Fujisawa et al. [10]). Training takes about 3/5 days on an NVIDIA RTX 2080Ti GPU.

4.2 Metadata Preprocessing

In our scheme, the extracted high-level image features are continuous, in contrast to the age approximation (discrete), anatomical location (categorical), and gender (categorical) from the metadata. We normalized the age range [0,100] to the range [0,1], and applied one-hot encoding to the categorical metadata. Hence, for each image in the dataset, a corresponding metadata information vector of size eleven is generated. Our choices in representation are influenced by the needs to have a uniform representation (allowing for the encoding of all data into a single 1D feature vector) and to reduce the variation in the different input sources.

4.3 Data Fusion Using Classical ML

In this approach, we concatenate the final probability density from our baseline networks with the metadata information.

We experimented with several well established Machine Learning algorithms like Support Vector Machines (SVM), Gradient Boosting and Random Forest from the scikit-learn library (https://scikit-learn.org/), and XG Boost from the xgboost library (https://xgboost.readthedocs.io). All of these models were trained with a train, development, and test split of the data with the hyperparameters being tuned on the train data w.r.t. the development data. Hyperparameter exploration was conducted using a grid approach. The final results are reported on the test data set, which was not included in the training nor in the hyperparameter tuning.

SVM (Support Vector Machines) is a supervised discriminative classifier based on generating separating hyperplanes between the different classes. Hyperplanes can be generated using different kernels. We experimented with several hyperparameters and found the best ones to be regularization parameter C = 1000 and kernel coefficient $\gamma = 0.1$ with the Radial Basis Function Kernel.

XGBoost and **Gradient Boosting** are similar, the former works on the second derivative of the formulated loss function and the latter works on the first derivative. XGBoost uses advanced regularization which helps achieve better regularization. In the case of XGBoost, we found the best hyperparameters to be colsample bytree (Subsample ratio of columns when constructing each tree) = 1.0, gamma = 3, learning rate = 0.05, max depth = 6, minimum child weight = 10, number of estimators = 500, subsample = 0.6. For Gradient Boosting, the best hyperparameters are learning rate = 0.1, maximum depth = 6, maximum features = 2, minimum samples per leaf = 9, number of estimators = 500, subsample = 1.

Finally, we use the ensemble learning method of **Random Forests** which is a decision tree algorithm that trains multiple trees and, for classification problems, picks the class with the highest mode during testing. This ensemble learning method prevents overfitting on training data, which is a common problem for decision trees. In the case of Random Forests model, we found the best hyperparameters to be bootstrap = False, class weight = balanced, maximum depth = 100, maximum features = 1, minimum samples per leaf = 1, minimum samples per split = 2, number of estimators = 500.

To address the problem of class imbalance in the data, we used the same class weights computed for the baseline CNN classifiers. The weights were directly fed into the Random Forests and SVM classifiers. As Gradient Boosting and XG Boost functions only support sample weights, we assigned to each sample the weight of its true class.

Each of these models contain multiple other hyperparameters, which were left at their default settings as provided in the scikit-learn and xgboost libraries. All of the four approaches can be trained in a few minutes.

4.4 Data Fusion Using Shallow NN

In this approach, we concatenate different feature vectors from our baseline networks with the metadata information. The concatenated vectors are then forwarded to stacks of uniform Glorot-initiliazed dense layers, terminated by a softmax, to predict disease classes.

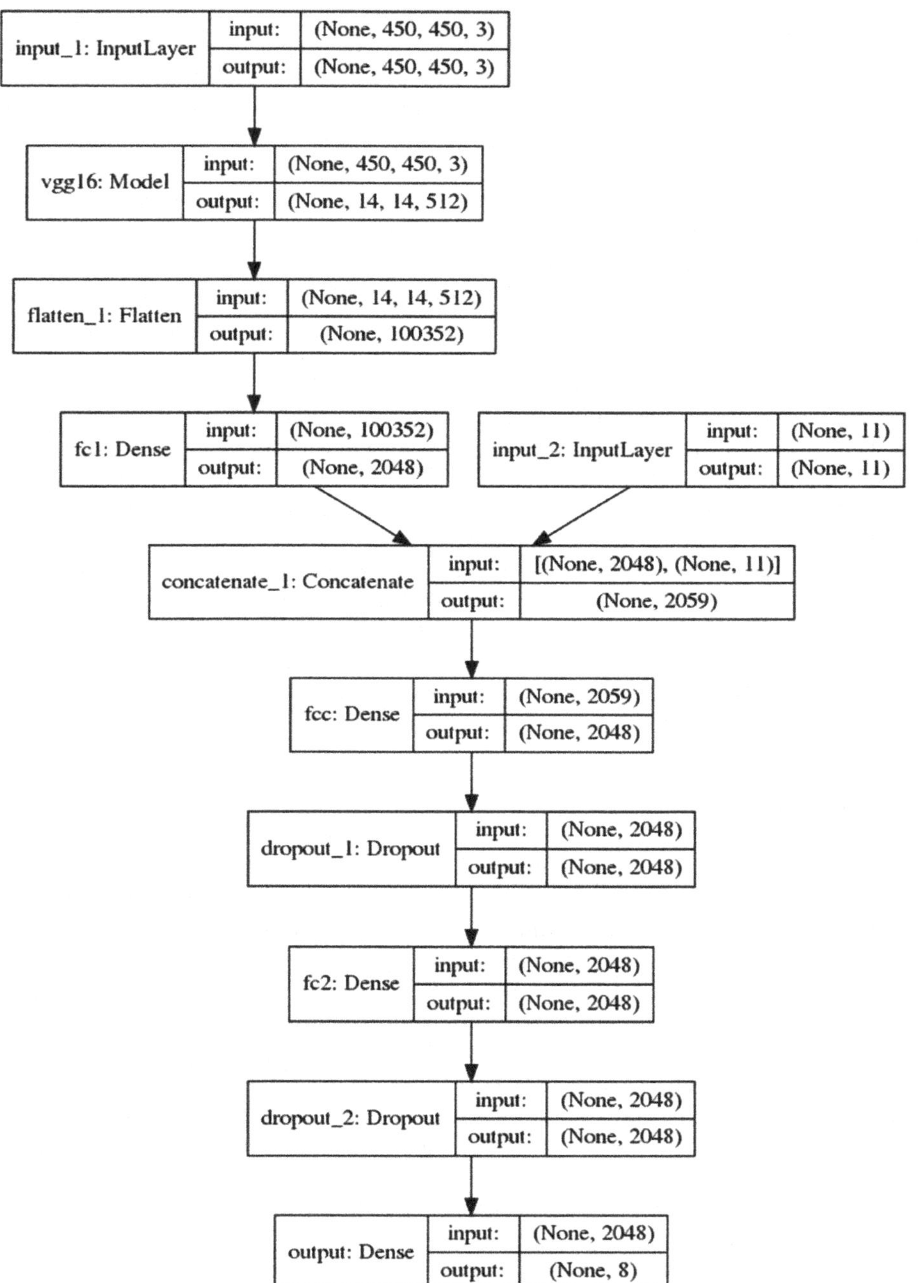

Fig. 6. Architecture for configuration `fc1_fc+doX2`, where fc1, concatenated with metadata, is followed by two blocks of dense and dropout layers. `input_2` is the 1-hot encoded metadata.

As feature vectors, we utilize the activation values of the internal layers (`fc1` and `fc2`) as well as the output softmax layer. We experimented with different combinations of `fc1`, `fc2`, and `prediction` probabilities followed by one or two dense layers (size 2048) coupled with dropout layers (p = 0.5). Figure 6 shows an example for the configuration `fc1_fc+doX2`. We tested using a sampling search approach.

When utilising internal layers, after the concatenation layer, a dense layer follows in the network, contrary to a dropout layer from our baseline models. This design decision was made to avoid masking out some metadata input values during Bernoulli sampling, which is peculiar to the inverted dropout method.

Among our experiments, we also considered concatenating the metadata directly to the `flatten_1` layer, just after the convolution (see Fig. 5), which means concatenating a vector of size 100352 (VGG16) or 131072 (RESNET50) to only 11 elements. Intermediate experimental results showed that this configuration gives no improvements with respect to the baseline. This is likely due to the significant difference between the sizes of the two feature vectors, which leads to the metadata being "obscured" by the high amount of other features. To overcome this issue, strategies that perform size-dependent output normalization do exist [14]. However, this would require the manual tuning of an extra equalization parameter. Hence, we did not further investigate in this direction and left the "flatten+metadata" configuration for future work.

For all configurations, we froze the whole base convolution model and trained the remaining layers for an average of 19 epochs, with lr = 1E-4, using adam (default) or SGD optimizers. On average, training one epoch takes 5 min.

5 Results

We applied the two fusion methods (cML and sNN) to the two baseline CNNs (VGG16 and RESNET50) in several configurations, where each configuration is either a different ML algorithm or shallow NN architecture. For each of the four combinations between CNN+method, we report i) the performance of each configuration, followed by ii) an analysis on the contribution of each metadata (age, gender, location) in the best performing configuration.

As for the metrics, we report the overall classification accuracy together with class-averaged specificity, sensitivity, and F1 score. The three last scores are computed by considering each class separately, measuring the metric as class-vs-others, and finally averaging the eight results. The so-computed sensitivity is hence equal to the scoring metric used in the ISIC 2019 challenge.

Among all metrics, sensitivity is the most important in practical, medical terms, as it represents the number of lesions correctly predicted in the specific class, for which a correct treatment would follow. However, while trying to obtain the best configuration, we choose accuracy, as it is the metric normally used to optimize the predictors. It is worth noting that the specificity is strongly influenced by the highly unbalanced dataset. A misclassification of a few samples in a lower-represented class doesn't affect global accuracy but can lower the average sensitivity significantly.

In all tables, **bold** font marks the highest value in a metric as well as the configuration with highest accuracy, while *italic* marks the highest value in a metadata group.

VGG16+cML. As reported in Table 3, top, random forest gave the best accuracy followed by SVM, while gradboost worsened the predictions. In some configurations, average sensitivity even decreases with respect to the baseline. A closer look to the per-class results shows that sensitivity lowers for classes with a low number of samples: BKL, VASC, and SCC.

Table 3, bottom, shows that *age* gives the best accuracy boost and disrupts sensitivity the least, followed by location and gender. The combination age+location gives the best performances.

VGG16+sNN. Table 4, top, shows that, in contrast to classical ML, with sNN all the metric performances are increasing with respect to the baseline. Configurations using the image features from the internal layer fc1 gives the best results, and clearly surpasses classical ML methods. The simplest neural network, composed of only 1 dense layer (size 2048) followed by a dropout (p = 0.5) performs the best in terms of accuracy (nonetheless, also using 2 dense layers gives similar accuracy).

Table 4, bottom, shows the same pattern as in VGG16+cML: best metadata are in order age, location, and gender. Curiously enough, the combination of only gender and location gives better sensitivity than using all metadata.

RESNET50+cML. When switching to RESNET50 as a baseline, integration through classic ML (Table 5) shows nearly the same behavior as for VGG16+cML: random forest and SVM give the best performance but SVM's performance is marginally better in this case, and age, location, and gender improve performance with the same order of efficiency. Again, the combination age+location gives the best performances.

RESNET50+sNN. Finally, when using RESNET50+sNN (Table 6) the best configuration still uses the input from fc1, followed by two dense layers. It is worth noticing that the configurations using class predictions as input data (pred_fc+...) are able to increase sensitivity over the baseline, even though the overall accuracy isn't as good as when using internal layers. Among metadata, age is still the most useful as a decision criterion, but location and gender switch positions.

Table 3. Performances of VGG16 + classical ML.

Algorithm comparison				
Method	Accuracy	Specificity	Sensitivity	F1
None	0.6676	0.9477	0.6597	0.5597
Gradboost	0.5920	0.9342	0.5236	0.4293
rf	**0.7679**	**0.9592**	0.6728	**0.6754**
svm	0.7532	0.9563	0.6543	0.6463
xgboost	0.7338	0.9577	**0.6730**	0.6420
Details for random forest				
Metadata	Accuracy	Specificity	Sensitivity	F1
None	0.6676	0.9477	0.6597	0.5597
Age	*0.7478*	*0.9562*	*0.6340*	*0.6370*
Gender	0.7090	0.9482	0.5958	0.6016
Location	0.7311	0.9521	0.6280	0.6326
Age+Gender	0.7492	0.9564	0.6416	0.6455
Age+Location	*0.7579*	*0.9573*	*0.6572*	*0.6591*
Gender+Location	0.7324	0.9523	0.6360	0.6415
All	**0.7679**	**0.9592**	**0.6728**	**0.6754**

Table 4. Performances of VGG16 + shallow NN.

Architecture comparison				
Architecture	Accuracy	Specificity	Sensitivity	F1
None	0.6676	0.9477	0.6597	0.5597
fc1_fc+do	**0.7953**	**0.9646**	0.7184	**0.7087**
fc1_fc+doX2	0.7913	0.9639	**0.7248**	0.7020
fc2_fc+do	0.7833	0.9631	0.7059	0.6916
fc2_fc+doX2	0.7672	0.9616	0.7004	0.6664
pred_fc+bnX2_adam	0.7304	0.9573	0.6913	0.6431
pred_fc+bnX2_sgd	0.7304	0.9572	0.6723	0.6232
Details for fc1_fc+do				
Metadata	Accuracy	Specificity	Sensitivity	F1
None	0.6676	0.9477	0.6597	0.5597
Age	*0.7726*	*0.9618*	0.6954	0.6709
Gender	0.7525	0.9574	0.6890	0.6787
Location	0.7579	0.9588	*0.7054*	*0.6802*
Age+Gender	0.7732	0.9613	0.6905	0.6736
Age+Location	*0.7759*	*0.9626*	0.7184	0.6855
Gender+Location	0.7679	0.9613	***0.7259***	*0.6963*
All	**0.7953**	**0.9646**	0.7184	**0.7087**

Table 5. Performance of RESNET50 + classical ML.

Algorithm comparison				
Method	Accuracy	Specificity	Sensitivity	F1
None	0.7833	0.9645	**0.7849**	0.7569
gradboost	0.7010	0.9501	0.6733	0.6137
rf	0.8100	0.9664	0.7623	0.7728
svm	**0.8127**	**0.9669**	0.7626	**0.7785**
xgboost	0.7926	0.9659	0.7634	0.7652
Details for random forest				
Metadata	Accuracy	Specificity	Sensitivity	F1
None	0.7833	0.9645	**0.7849**	0.7569
Age	*0.8094*	*0.9662*	*0.7642*	0.7737
Gender	0.8020	0.9644	0.7608	0.7711
Location	0.8027	0.9651	0.7618	*0.7749*
Age+Gender	0.8087	0.9660	0.7622	0.7730
Age+Location	*0.8120*	*0.9667*	0.7629	*0.7782*
Gender+Location	0.8033	0.9651	*0.7631*	0.7751
All	**0.8127**	**0.9669**	0.7626	**0.7785**

Table 6. Performance of RESNET50 + shallow NN.

Architecture comparison				
Architecture	Accuracy	Specificity	Sensitivity	F1
None	0.7833	0.9645	0.7849	0.7569
fc1_fc+do	0.8194	0.9684	0.7672	0.7806
fc1_fc+doX2	**0.8334**	**0.9700**	0.7718	**0.7908**
fc2_fc+do	0.8194	0.9681	0.7447	0.7691
fc2_fc+doX2	0.8167	0.9677	0.7600	0.7729
pred_fc+bnX2_adam	0.8074	0.9678	0.7868	0.7880
pred_fc+bnX2_sgd	0.8100	0.9686	**0.7904**	0.7859
Details for fc1_fc+doX2				
Metadata	Accuracy	Specificity	Sensitivity	F1
None	0.7833	0.9645	**0.7849**	0.7569
Age	*0.8201*	*0.9680*	0.7586	0.7796
Gender	0.8167	0.9665	0.7400	0.7655
Location	0.8147	0.9675	*0.7742*	*0.7846*
Age+Gender	0.8167	0.9665	0.7400	0.7655
Age+Location	0.8221	0.9678	0.7550	0.7744
Gender+Location	*0.8274*	*0.9687*	*0.7611*	***0.7915***
All	**0.8334**	**0.9700**	0.7718	0.7908

6 Discussion

VGG16 represent a baseline with relatively low performance (accuracy = 0.66). In VGG16 + rf accuracy increases (+0.1003, +15.0%), but sensitivity is quite the same (0.0131, +2.0%). In VGG16 + sNN both accuracy (+0.1278, +19.1%) and sensitivity (+0.0587, +8.9%) increase.

When using a baseline with better starting performance (accuracy = 0.78), there are only slight improvements in accuracy, and a decrease in sensitivity occurs more often. In RESNET50 + SVM accuracy increases +0,0294 (3,8%), while sensitivity decreases −0.0223 (−2.8%). In RESNET50 + sNN accuracy increases +0,0502 (6,4%), while sensitivity decreases −0,0131 (−1,7%).

In general, it seems that, when applied to poorly performing baselines, metadata help the classification in both accuracy and sensitivity. However, when the CNN are already well performing, the gain in accuracy is marginal and sensitivity generally decreases. This means that metadata can help increase the overall number of correctly classified samples, but compromises the recognition of samples belonging to lower-represented classes. Among the three metadata, age is most useful in increasing accuracy, followed by location and gender.

Among the fusion techniques, random forests and SVM are the best for non-neural techniques, which can be used to merge only predictions and metadata, and offer a fast computation. However, best results are obtained by merging metadata with the activation values of the first fully connected layer.

7 Conclusions

Motivated by the observation of a lack of active participation, together with the surprisingly negative results in the Task 2 of the ISIC 2019 challenge, we presented a detailed study on the fusion between pixels and metadata for the improvement of the accuracy in the classification of images of skin lesions. In general, our experiments confirm (and quantify) the superiority of shallow neural networks over SVM and tree-based ML algorithms. The experiments suggest that internal CNN activation values are the best option for an integration with metadata.

Concerning the ISIC 2019 challenge, from our overview, it appears that some teams chose suboptimal strategies to merge metadata. But more interestingly, "good" strategies (increasing accuracy) are always associated with a decrease in the average sensitivity, the evaluation metric used in the ISIC challenges.

Trying to explain the unexpected reduction in performance in Task 2 when compared to Task 1, the reason of this behaviour might be the fact that Age, Gender, Location have been added to the dataset (by the designers) because it was known that they correlate with the higher-represented classes in the dataset (Nevus and Melanoma). Possibly, this doesn't hold for lower-represented classes (e.g., VASC) which were only recently added to the ISIC challenge dataset. Further data analysis is needed to confirm this hypothesis.

Another possible explanation for the divergence between accuracy and average sensitivity might be related to the optimization goal (loss function) of our baseline models, which aim at maximizing accuracy. Another set of experiments should be conducted to check if the decrease in sensitivity still emerges when directly training a network to maximize for average sensitivity.

We hope that this work will give an overview of the techniques and solution that are worth pursuing when including metadata to pixel-based classification of skin images and the challenges that might occur.

It is still to be validated how our findings generalize to other medical contexts, different metadata, or to non-medical contexts, where images and metadata pertain to very different domains (e.g., the use of age and nationality in the detection of emotion from facial expressions).

References

1. Argenziano, G., et al.: Seven-point checklist of dermoscopy revisited: seven-point checklist of dermoscopy revisited. Br. J. Dermatol. **164**(4), 785–790 (2011)
2. Emre Celebi, M., Codella, N., Halpern, A.: Dermoscopy image analysis: overview and future directions. IEEE J. Biomed. Health Inf. **23**(2), 474–478 (2019)
3. Codella, N.C.F., et al.: Skin Lesion Analysis Toward Melanoma Detection: A Challenge at the 2017 International Symposium on Biomedical Imaging (ISBI), Hosted by the International Skin Imaging Collaboration (ISIC). arXiv:1710.05006 [cs], October 2017
4. Combalia, M., et al.: BCN20000: Dermoscopic Lesions in the Wild. arXiv:1908.02288 [cs, eess], August 2019
5. Curiel-Lewandrowski, C., et al.: Artificial intelligence approach in melanoma. In: Fisher, D.E., Bastian, B.C. (eds.) Melanoma, pp. 1–31. Springer, New York (2019)
6. Deng, J., Dong, W., Socher, R., Li, L.-J., Li, K., Fei-Fei, L.: ImageNet: large-scale hierarchical image database. In: 2009 IEEE Conference on Computer Vision and Pattern Recognition, pp. 248–255. IEEE, Miami, June 2009
7. Hospital Clínic de Barcelona Department of Dermatology. Bcn_20000 dataset
8. Donahue, J., et al.: DeCAF: a deep convolutional activation feature for generic visual recognition. In: Xing, E.P., Jebara, T. (eds.) Proceedings of the 31st International Conference on Machine Learning. Proceedings of Machine Learning Research, Bejing, China, vol. 32, pp. 647–655, June 2014. PMLR
9. Esteva, A., et al.: Dermatologist-level classification of skin cancer with deep neural networks. Nature **542**, 115 (2017)
10. Fujisawa, Y., et al.: Deep-learning-based, computer-aided classifier developed with a small dataset of clinical images surpasses board-certified dermatologists in skin tumour diagnosis. Br. J. Dermatol. **180**(2), 373–381 (2018)
11. He, K., Zhang, X., Ren, S., Sun, J.: Deep residual learning for image recognition. In: The IEEE Conference on Computer Vision and Pattern Recognition (CVPR), June 2016
12. Kawahara, J., Daneshvar, S., Argenziano, G., Hamarneh, G.: Seven-point checklist and skin lesion classification using multitask multimodal neural nets. IEEE J. Biomed. Health Inf. **23**(2), 538–546 (2019)
13. Kawahara J., Hamarneh, G.: Visual diagnosis of dermatological disorders: human and machine performance. arXiv:1906.01256 [cs], June 2019
14. Komura, T., Holden, D., Saito, J.: Phase-functioned neural networks for character control. ACM Trans. Graph. **36**(4), 1–13 (2017). Siggraph 2017; Conference date: 30–07-2017 Through 03–08-2017

15. Mishra, N.K., Emre Celebi, M.: An Overview of Melanoma Detection in Dermoscopy Images Using Image Processing and Machine Learning. arXiv:1601.07843 [cs, stat], January 2016
16. Nunnari, F., Sonntag, D.: A CNN toolbox for skin cancer classification (2019). https://arxiv.org/abs/1908.08187. DFKI Technical report
17. Pacheco, A.G.C., Krohling, R.A.: The impact of patient clinical information on automated skin cancer detection. arXiv:1909.12912 [cs, eess, stat], September 2019
18. Razavian, A.S., Azizpour, H., Sullivan, J., Carlsson, S.: CNN features off-the-shelf: an astounding baseline for recognition. In: The IEEE Conference on Computer Vision and Pattern Recognition (CVPR) Workshops, June 2014
19. Simonyan, K., Zisserman, A.: Very Deep Convolutional Networks for Large-Scale Image Recognition. arXiv:1409.1556 [cs], September 2014
20. Sonntag, D., Nunnari, F., Profitlich, H.: The Skincare project, an interactive deep learning system for differential diagnosis of malignant skin lesions. Technical report (2020). https://arxiv.org/abs/2005.09448
21. Tan, C., Sun, F., Kong, T., Zhang, W., Yang, C., Liu, C.: A survey on deep transfer learning. In: Kůrková, V., Manolopoulos, Y., Hammer, B., Iliadis, L., Maglogiannis, I. (eds.) ICANN 2018. LNCS, vol. 11141, pp. 270–279. Springer, Cham (2018). https://doi.org/10.1007/978-3-030-01424-7_27
22. Medical University of Vienna ViDIR Group, Department of Dermatology. Ham10000 dataset. https://doi.org/10.1038/sdata.2018.161
23. Yap, J., Yolland, W., Tschandl, P.: Multimodal skin lesion classification using deep learning. Exp. Dermatol. **27**(11), 1261–1267 (2018)

The European Legal Framework for Medical AI

David Schneeberger[1,2](✉), Karl Stöger[1], and Andreas Holzinger[2]

[1] University of Graz, Universitätsstrasse 15, 8010 Graz, Austria
{david.schneeberger,karl.stoeger}@uni-graz.at
[2] Medical University of Graz, Auenbruggerplatz 2, 8036 Graz, Austria
andreas.holzinger@medunigraz.at

Abstract. In late February 2020, the European Commission published a White Paper on Artificial Intelligence (AI) and an accompanying report on the safety and liability implications of AI, the Internet of Things (IoT) and robotics. In its White Paper, the Commission highlighted the "European Approach" to AI, stressing that "it is vital that European AI is grounded in our values and fundamental rights such as human dignity and privacy protection". It also announced its intention to propose EU legislation for "high risk" AI applications in the nearer future which will include the majority of medical AI applications.

Based on this "European Approach" to AI, this paper analyses the current European framework regulating medical AI. Starting with the fundamental rights framework as clear guidelines, subsequently a more in-depth look will be taken at specific areas of law, focusing on data protection, product approval procedures and liability law. This analysis of the current state of law, including its problems and ambiguities regarding AI, is complemented by an outlook at the proposed amendments to product approval procedures and liability law, which, by endorsing a human-centric approach, will fundamentally influence how medical AI and AI in general will be used in Europe in the future.

Keywords: Anti-discrimination · EU legal framework · Explainability · Fundamental rights · GDPR · Human dignity · Human in the loop · Informed consent · Liability · Medical AI · Product approval · Right to explanation

1 Fundamental Rights as Legal Guidelines for Medical AI

1.1 Some Basic Information on Fundamental Rights in the EU

(European) fundamental rights (a.k.a. human rights) constitute part of the highest "layer" of EU legislation ("primary law") and provide already today an important legal (and not merely ethical) basic framework for the development and application of medical AI. Lower layers of EU law ("secondary and tertiary law") have to respect the guidelines of this framework which is – in contrast

Published by Springer Nature Switzerland AG 2020
A. Holzinger et al. (Eds.): CD-MAKE 2020, LNCS 12279, pp. 209–226, 2020.
https://doi.org/10.1007/978-3-030-57321-8_12

to these lower layers – not very likely to change substantially in the coming years. The main source of this framework is the European Charter of Fundamental Rights (CFR), which is in its entirety applicable to the use of medical AI because the provision of medical services is covered by the freedom to provide services under European law. For its part, the CFR is strongly modelled on the European Convention on Human Rights (ECHR), which is also applicable in all EU states. In spite of the diversity of national legislation in the EU Member States, these two instruments ensure a rather uniform level of protection of fundamental rights across the EU. As medical AI can affect a person's physical and mental integrity in a very intense way and any malfunction could have serious consequences, it is a particularly relevant field of AI in terms of fundamental rights.

In this context, it should be stressed that fundamental rights not only protect individuals from state intervention, but also oblige the state to protect certain freedoms from interference by third parties. The state can fulfil these so-called "obligations to protect" by, for example, enacting appropriate legislation that applies to relations between private individuals or by creating specific approval procedures for placing goods or services on the market that could endanger the fundamental rights of its users. This is why "obligations to protect" are of particular importance in medicine: For example, the European Court of Human Rights has repeatedly stated that fundamental rights entail an obligation on the state to regulate the provision of health services in such a way that precautions are taken against serious damage to health due to poorly provided services [33]. On this basis, the state must, for example, oblige providers of health services to implement quality assurance measures and to respect the due "standard of care". To sum up, fundamental rights constitute a binding legal framework for the use of AI in medicine which is not only relevant for EU Member States, but for all developers and providers of medical AI.

1.2 Human Oversight as a Key Criterion

It has already been emphasized by the Ethics Guidelines of the HLEG that "European AI" has to respect human dignity, one of the key guarantees of European fundamental rights, (Art. 1 CFR) [34], which means that medical AI must never regard humans as mere objects [15]. Every human being therefore has a right that the state respects and protects his or her individuality, also towards third persons. Humans must therefore "never be completely or irrevocably subjected to technical systems" [13], which also applies to the use of medical AI. Since AI works on the basis of correlations, complex AI applications in particular must always be monitored by human beings to ensure that they do not miss any special features of human thinking or decision-making. From this, it can be deduced that the demands for human oversight expressed in computer science [20] are also required by EU fundamental rights. Decisions of medical AI require human assessment before any significant action is taken on their basis. The European Union has also implemented this fundamental requirement in the much-discussed provision of Art. 22 General Data Protection Regulation (henceforth GDPR), which allows "decisions based solely on automated processing" only with considerable restrictions (discussed in further detail in the following Sect. 2.2 about the GDPR). In other words: European medical AI legally requires human oversight (a.k.a. "a human in the loop" [35]).

1.3 Medical AI and Anti-discrimination Law

There is a rich body of fundamental rights provisions requiring equality before the law and nondiscrimination, including gender, children, the elderly and disabled persons in the CFR (Arts. 20–26). From these provisions, further requirements for the development and operation of European medical AI can be deduced: Not only must training data be thoroughly checked for the presence of bias, also the ongoing operation of AI must be constantly monitored for the occurrence of bias. If medical AI is applied to certain groups of the population that were not adequately represented in the training data, the usefulness of the results must be questioned particularly critically [27,29]. At the same time, care must be taken to ensure that useful medical AI can nevertheless be made available to such groups in the best possible way. In other words: European medical AI must be available for everyone. The diversity of people must always be taken into account, either in programming or in application, in order to avoid disadvantages.

1.4 Obligation to Use Medical AI?

However, fundamental rights not only set limits to the use of AI, they can also promote it. If a medical AI application meets the requirements just described, it may also be necessary to use it. European fundamental rights – above all the right to protection of life (Art. 2 CFR) and private life (Art. 7 CFR) – give rise to an obligation on the part of the state, as already mentioned above, to ensure that work in health care facilities is carried out only in accordance with the respective medical due "standard of care" (a.k.a. "state of the art") [57]. This also includes the obligation to prohibit medical treatment methods that can no longer be provided in the required quality without the involvement of AI [53]. This will in the near future probably hold true for the field of medical image processing.

2 Some Reflections on Four Relevant Areas of "Secondary" EU Law

2.1 Introduction

While the European fundamental rights described above constitute a basic legal foundation for the use of medical AI, the details of the relevant legal framework need to be specified by more detailed legislation known as "secondary law" (e.g.

directives and regulations) or by "tertiary law" (which specifies secondary law even further). The main purpose of this legislation is to create a more or less uniform legal framework across all EU Member States either by replacing national legislation (in particular through regulations) or by harmonizing its contents (in particular through directives). Hence, while the picture we have presented so far has been painted with a broad brush, we will now take a more in-depth look at the finer details of three areas of EU "secondary law", which are of specific importance for the use of medical AI: the GDPR, product approval procedures and the question of liability. Some conclusions we have already drawn in the section about fundamental laws (e.g. human oversight as a key criterion) are further strengthened and expanded through this more detailed overview.

2.2 The General Data Protection Regulation (GDPR) and the "Right to an Explanation"

The GDPR establishes transparency as a key principle for data processing and links it with lawfulness and fairness (Art. 5 para 1(a) GDPR) which both are important parts of the principle of accountability (Art. 5 para 2 GDPR). This focus on transparency as a basic requirement for data processing should be kept in mind when discussing the GDPR.

The presentation of the first draft of the GDPR marked the starting point of an extensive "right to explanation" debate in legal academia (e.g. [6,7,9,11,18,19,28,38,42,43,55,58,59]) the implications of which were also felt in computer sciences [40]. To (mostly) circumnavigate this intricate and complicated debate, which is muddled in semantics, we will not enter into the academic discussion about what constitutes or does not constitute an explanation - which is still a point of contention [41,44,46] - but we will try to clarify the duties to provide information without too much speculation.

Prohibition of Decisions Based Solely on Automated Processing. As stated above, the aim of Art. 22 GDPR is to prevent that individuals will be regarded as mere objects in an automated decision-making process determined solely by machines. Such a situation would result in the loss of their autonomy and hence the loss of human control and responsibility [9]. Therefore Art. 22 para 1 GDPR provides for a prohibition of autonomous decision-making without human assessment ("solely based on automated processing"), the final decision should always remain in human hands.

Decision-support systems are not affected by this prohibition, as long as the human in the loop has substantial powers of assessment and can change the outcome (e.g. doctor who decides based on an AI recommendation). However, if the human does not have any real authority to question the outcome (e.g. nurse who is obliged to strictly follow the AI recommendations) this equals to prohibited fully automated decision-making [2].

If an AI-system is designed for a fully autonomous approach, it will only be prohibited if the decision has serious consequences (a legal effect or a similarly significant effect) [2]. In the context of medical AI for diagnosis or treatment this threshold will almost certainly be reached, therefore medical AI without a human in the loop is generally prohibited under the GDPR regime. However, there are a few exceptions. The most important exception in the context of medical AI is the documented (e.g. written/electronic) explicit consent of the "data subject" (that is the patient) to the fully automated processing of their health data (data related to physical or mental health [Art. 22 para 4 GDPR]) [23]. As the principle of "informed consent" is (also outside the scope of data protection law) one of the pillars of medical law not only in EU law, but also in the law of EU Member States, there is only one further exception to the requirement of "informed consent" which is, however, to be interpreted narrowly: Automated processing of health data may take place in the reasons of substantial public interest, e.g. public health. Under this exception, it would e.g. be conceivable to identify persons that are particularly vulnerable to a pandemic disease like COVID-19 by means of a fully automated AI system. However, it should be stressed again that this exception is only applicable if a substantial public interest shall be protected. Consequently, it must not be used as a blanket exception to easily circumvent the prohibition stated by Art. 22 para 1 GDPR (Recital 71 lists fraud and tax-evasion monitoring and prevention purposes as example cases) [10,31].

Human in the Loop as a Necessary Safeguard. Even if explicit consent was gained, additional safeguards to protect the rights and freedoms of the data subject must be implemented. The GDPR does not state an exhaustive list of such safeguards, it only lists three examples of these, which constitute a bare minimum standard: a. the right to obtain human intervention, b. to express one's point of view and c. to contest the decision. Accordingly, even in cases where fully automated decision-making is in principle permissible, human intervention and human assessment are still required. Furthermore, the processing of health data as a particularly sensitive category of data requires a higher standard and the implementation of additional safeguards (e.g. frequent assessments of the data to rule out bias, to prevent errors etc.) [2]. Therefore, the GDPR necessitates human oversight a.k.a a human in the loop for medical AI, irrespective of whether it is designed as a decision-support or a fully automated system.

Is There a "Right to an Explanation"? The accompanying so-called recitals of the GDPR, which function as interpretative guidelines [43], also mention additional safeguards for the fully automated processing of health data, among them "The right to obtain an explanation of the decision reached after such assessment" (Recital 71). At the first look this clearly seems to be a right to an explanation of an individual decision, but as recitals are primarily interpretative in nature, this "right" is (according to the current reading) more or less a recommendation and not an obligation. The "controller" (the natural or legal person responsible for the processing of data) is free to choose the safeguards it deems necessary as long as three basic safeguards (possibility of human intervention, expression of the data subject's point of view, contestation of the decision) are upheld, compliance with the GDPR is present [30,58]. While the implementation of a "right to an explanation" ultimately is not obligatory, it is seen as a good practice to foster trust and is recommended in the GDPR guidelines [2].

Consequently the answer to the question "Is there a right to an explanation?" depends on the definition of "explanation". If "explanation" is defined as "information about basic system functionality" (see the following paragraph), the answer is in the affirmative, if explanation is interpreted broadly in the sense of "explain the causes/internal processes which lead to an individual decision", the answer is in the negative. As long as either the European Court of Justice does not clarify and expand the "right to an explanation" (e.g. the "right to be forgotten" was also created primarily through interpretation by the court [26]) or the GDPR is amended, it seems to only be a recommendation (and, as stated above, mere decision-support systems do not fall under the scope of such a right).

Duty to Provide Information/Right to Access. Even if there is no obligation to explain a specific decision, any controller of an AI-system based solely on automated processing nevertheless has, according to Arts. 13 and 14 GDPR, to provide the subject - in addition to basic information - with information about 1. the existence of automated decision-making, 2. meaningful information about the logic involved (comprehensive information about the reasoning/system functionality, e.g. models, features, weights etc.) and 3. about the significance and the envisaged consequences of such processing (e.g. use for detection of melanoma). Even outside the scope of fully automated decision-making, where there is no obligation to provide this information, it should nevertheless be provided voluntarily as a good practice to ensure fairness and transparency. Independently of the duty of the designer/user to provide information, Art. 15 GDPR grants the data subject a symmetrical right of access to the information defined in Arts. 13 and 14 GDPR (logic involved, significance and envisaged consequences) [2]. Art. 12 GDPR clarifies that this information must be provided in a concise, transparent, intelligible and easily accessible form, using clear and plain language, in particular for any information addressed specifically to a child (if it is already required to give "informed consent"). The information should normally be provided in a written form (including electronic means), free of charge and without undue delay (maximum within one month) [3]. Therefore, the provision of mere technical details, which are not understandable for a lay person, will not suffice to satisfy this duty, the information should enable the subject to make use of the GDPR rights [9]. Hence it is a question of balancing expectations: while a detailed model description is not required, information must not be simplified to an extent that makes it worthless for the data subject.

Summary. To summarise, there are (broadly) three possible scenarios:

1. *Scenario 1:* If a medical AI system does not fall in the category "based solely on automated processing" (e.g. decision-support), Arts. 13–15 (duty to

provide information) and Art. 22 GDPR (limitation on automated processing) are not applicable (although providing information is recommended as good practice).

2. *Scenario 2:* If the medical AI system does per se fall under the prohibition of Art. 22 para 1 GDPR, its use is only permissible if it falls under one of the exceptions of this prohibition, the most important for medical AI being explicit (informed) consent. Even if explicit consent is given, the fully automated processing of special categories of data (including health data) requires additional safeguards, the bare minimum being the possibility of human intervention, the expression of the data subject's point of view and the possible contestation of the decision (Art. 22 paras 3 and 4 GDPR). Finally, it is obligatory to provide the necessary information according to Arts. 13 to 15 GDPR (1. The data subject (patient) is informed that automated decision-making takes place 2. provision of meaningful information about the logic involved and 3. explanation of the envisaged significance and consequences of the processing).
3. *Scenario 3:* If an AI system is fully automated and hence falls under the prohibition of Art. 22 para 1 GDPR, and there is no exception applicable, this type of AI system is illegal under the regime of the GDPR. This result confirms that the inclusion of a "human in the loop" is a key design criterion necessary for compliance with European "AI law".

2.3 Additional GDPR Requirements: Privacy by Design and Data Protection Impact Assessment

As stated above, transparency is a basic requirement of the GDPR. The guarantees we have just described are just one aspect of transparency. The GDPR also tries to foster an environment where better AI systems are developed already from the design-stage onwards, e.g. through risk based accountability (Art. 24 GDPR: technical and organisational countermeasures corresponding to the scope and risk of the intended processing) in combination with a privacy by design (Art. 25 GDPR) approach to ensure that data protection issues are already parts of the design and planning process and integrated directly into the data processing (e.g. pseudonymisation, technical transparency measures etc.) [8].

Before the implementation of medical AI, a so-called data protection impact assessment (DPIA; Art. 35 GDPR) will have to be provided: If processing (in particular by means of new risky technologies like AI) is likely to result in a high risk to the rights and freedoms of natural persons, a prior assessment has to be carried out. This assessment must contain a systematic description of the envisaged processing operations and the purposes (e.g. medical AI based on neural networks for melanoma diagnosis), an assessment of the necessity and proportionally of the processing in relation to the envisaged purposes (e.g. processing of health data for the purposes of treatment), and an assessment of the risk to the rights and freedoms of data subjects (risk of harming physical/mental health, privacy etc.). Furthermore, a description of the measures to address these risks (e.g. the use of XAI, restriction of features, anonymization etc.) is required.

Lastly, a possibility for the persons who are affected by the processing operations to provide feedback shall be established. As a matter of good practice, a DPIA should be continuously reviewed and regularly re-assessed. While there is no obligation to publish the DPIA, parts of it (e.g. a summary) should be accessible to the public (and especially to the data subjects) in order to foster trust and transparency [1].

2.4 Product Safety Law

The concept of privacy by design as well as the general assessment needed for a DPIA can also be thematically linked with general product safety procedures which are another key component of the EU secondary law framework for (medical) AI. In both cases, prior assessment is required before the implementation or the market approval of AI systems in order to secure their compliance with basic safety standards. While the DPIA is focused on risks for privacy, product safety regulations want to minimise the risk of harm by a faulty product, i.e. aim at securing a high level of safety for goods. Product safety and product liability provisions function as two complementary regimes, therefore these two mechanisms will be disscussed discussed in the following Sects. 2.4 and 2.5 [21].

Most medical AI applications will, if they are intended by the manufacturer to be used for human beings for specific medical purposes, qualify as medical devices under EU law. Product approval procedures for medical devices are in a state of transition and will soon be fully harmonized by two European regulations (Regulations 2017/745 and 2017/746). While the regulations were intended to enter into force by May 2020/2022, the Commission has recently proposed to postpone this date to May 2021/2022 due to the COVID-19-pandemic. Both regulations aim at securing a uniform standard for quality and safety for medical products to reduce barriers for entry for such devices caused by divergent national legislation. However, even these recent EU regulations do, somewhat surprisingly, not really address medical AI specifically and do not include AI as a special product category. However, most medical AI applications qualify as software intended by the manufacturer to be used for human beings for specific medical purposes and hence as a medical device (or part of a medical device). Based on the risk classification of these applications, conformity assessment procedures may be required (certification, review, clinical evidence to prove accuracy and reliability etc.). It has been noted that - at the current moment - the definition of software and its associated risk is relatively inflexible and does not differentiate between static and machine learning systems, thereby failing to address specific risks of ML (explainability, dynamic nature, false positives/negatives etc. [50]). In the USA the FDA has recognized this dynamic nature and the opacity of ML as sources of potential problems and presented a vision of appropriately tailored regulatory oversight to control the specific risks of ML [25,45] which the EU still lacks (though, as the above-mentioned White Paper shows [22], it is aware of this problem).

Medical AI used as therapeutic or diagnostic tool is at least associated with a medium (potential) risk and will therefore in any cases require market access approval ("CE-marking") granted by private companies (so-called notified bodies), which is followed by a post market-entry assessment by national authorities (e.g. through collection and assessment of risk data by means of audits). To gain a CE-marking, (medical) devices must conform with the general safety requirements (mitigation of risks and a positive balance of benefit over risk). Explainability is not a core aspect in the assessment of general safety and performance (through a clinical/performance evaluation), but transparency of the system may be necessary to sufficiently demonstrate that it does not mistake mere correlations within data for causality [50].

Software should be designed according to the state of the art, which is specified by so-called harmonised standards. Verification and validation procedures are part of these standards, they require proper data management (bias avoidance), assurance of accuracy, ability to generalize etc. Again, explainability is not a specific part of this process, but it could be important for proper risk management, therefore as the PHG Foundation states convincingly: "Verification and validation may require some machine learning models to be made somewhat intelligible" [50]. Besides product safety law, it has also been convincingly argued that some degree of explainability of medical AI may also be required to avoid liability [30]; we will return to this later when assessing liability law. Because of the specific dangers of ML systems, continuous risk assessment (post-market surveillance, periodical safety reviews) by notified bodies have been proposed as a necessity if there is a substantial change to the product [37,50].

Future Developments in Product Safety Law. The need to properly address the risks of AI as medical devices has been recognized by the European Commission and the American FDA. The American FDA proposed that ML systems, which are not "locked" but continue to adapt, will require constant monitoring through their life-cycle, including additional review of modifications, and states that "Transparency about the function and modifications of medical devices is a key aspect of their safety." [25]

This assessment is shared by the Commission in the above-mentioned report [21] which enumerates the specific risks of AI which need to be addressed by the new legal framework. Among these risks are connectivity, complexity and the "autonomy" of AI-systems (i.e. the ability to learn) which could - when future outcomes cannot be determined in advance - make re-assessment during the life-cycle of the product necessary. Requirements for human oversight throughout the life-cycle of an AI-system and data quality standards have also been announced as part of planned new EU legislation. The Commission Report also addresses the problem of algorithmic opacity and states that product safety legislation does not explicitly address this risk at the moment, therefore making it necessary to implement transparency requirements (as well as requirements for robustness, accountability, human oversight and unbiased outcomes) to build trust in AI applications (e.g. by an obligation to disclose the design parameters and metadata of datasets). In the words of the Commission: "Humans may not need to understand every single step of the decision making process, but as AI algorithms grow more advanced and are deployed into critical domains, it is decisive that humans can be able to understand how the algorithmic decisions of the system have been reached." [21]

2.5 Liability

While law is generally (relatively) flexible when addressing new technologies like AI, there seems to be one important blindspot: Questions of liability law. Although liability law is generally ambiguous by design because it has to cover many different scenarios, it remains silent in relation to AI, therefore it lacks necessary considerations, which leads to considerable legal uncertainty. Pertinent questions particularly unsettle the AI community. Who will be legally responsible when medical AI malfunctions? The software developer, the manufacturer, the maintenance people, the IT provider, the hospital, the clinician? Even a short analysis shows that many questions about "Who is liable?" and how can liability be proved cannot be answered conclusively or satisfactory by the current legal doctrine. While it would be an option to leave the questions to be answered by the courts and their case-law, this would nevertheless create considerable legal uncertainty (including differences between individual EU Member States) for at least some period of time. This is why the European Commission, for good reasons, plans to fill the void with a new and uniform European legal framework on (civil, not criminal) liability for AI.

European liability law broadly consists of national, non-harmonized civil liability and harmonized product liability law. Both these liability regimes have many ambiguities and problems when addressing AI. Civil liability (based on a contract, e.g. a medical treatment contract or on tort [=non-contractual liability]) is mostly fault-based, therefore normally the fault of the liable person, the damage and the causality between the fault and the damage must be proved [21]. Besides fault-based liability there is also strict-liability in specified areas (e.g. use of dangerous objects like motor vehicles): liability for a risk is attributed to a specific person by law (e.g. holder of a car) and the proof of fault (or causality between fault and damage) is not necessary. One idea behind strict liability is that while the use of the dangerous object is socially acceptable or even desirable, its operator should bear the liability irrespective of any fault on their part [39]. Fault-based and strict liability often overlap and function in parallel. With regards to the complexity and opacity of ML algorithms, it is questionable whether the burden of proof should lie with the victim. It will be hard to trace the damage back to human behaviour and to establish a causal link [21] (discussing this problem with regard to the national law of Austria [52], Germany [14] or the UK [53]). The concept of burden of proof therefore has been described as an nearly insurmountable hurdle. Due to this, many lawyers argue that when using AI the operator and/or the producer (e.g. the medical service provider [physician, hospital etc.]/designer) should carry the burden of proof [53]. Others go further than this and propose the introduction of a strict liability regime for AI [56,60]. The often mentioned possible downside to this strict liability approach is, that it could stifle innovation [5,14].

Liability for Treatment Errors. According to medical malpractice law a medical service provider (e.g. physician, hospital) could be held liable for treatment errors or for the absence of "informed consent". Normally, the health service provider is not responsible for the success of the treatment, only for providing a professional treatment according to the due standard of care which must be in accordance with current medical scientific knowledge (see above in the section on fundamental rights). Therefore, liability could for example be established if a doctor - who is by professional standards required to independently assess an AI recommendation using his expertise - realizes that the AI recommendation is incorrect but still bases a medical decision on it. However, the opacity of ML could it make it hard to assess 1. whether it was a reasonable decision to use AI, 2. whether the doctor was right or wrong (in the sense of adhering to the required medical standard) to deviate from an AI recommendation and 3. whether he hence is liable or not [47,53]. However, liability law not only addresses the (mis-)use of AI, it is also relevant as to the non-use of AI: If AI-assisted medical treatment reached higher accuracy than treatments without the involvement of AI, its use would constitute the (new) "due standard of medical care", making health care providers liable if they do not use AI for treatment or diagnosis [30,51,53]. Such an obligation cannot only result from liability law, but also from the European fundamental rights framework (see Sect. 1.4 above).

"Informed Consent". We already concluded that the lack of "informed consent" can also lead to liability. Consequently, the duties to provide information and to respect the autonomy of the patient are an integral part of contemporary medicine (and medical law). Already at the level of fundamental rights, Art. 3 para 2(a) CFR states that "informed consent" must be respected. This results in the concept of a "shared decision-making" by doctor and patient where the patient has the ultimate say, hence the patient and the doctor are seen as equal partners. The patient must have the autonomy to make a free informed decision, this implicitly requires sufficient information. This duty to provide information about the use and possible malfunctions of medical AI will depend on the risk associated with a particular AI system [47]. This implies that the patient must not necessarily be informed about each particular use of medical AI. It is interesting to note that a comparable approach can also be found in the American legal literature. While it has been argued, that there is no general duty to disclose the use of medical AI to patients, two factors have been identified which could establish an obligation to disclose its use to the patient: first, the opacity and second, the (increased) operational risk of an AI system [12].

The relation between "informed consent" and "explainability" is already being intensively discussed in legal literature. Various opinions on this question are expressed: Rather pragmatically, some authors point out that medical processes with and without the use of AI already reach a complexity today that obliges medical personnel to explain with "appropriately reduced complexity" [16,17]. Consequently, the idea of "informed consent" does not require that an AI decision is comprehensible in detail or that an explanation is given how a specific decision has been reached through internal processes. According to this approach, it is sufficient if information is given in rough terms on how a medical AI application works and which type of mistakes can occur during its operation. It is interesting to note that there is a certain congruency between this (civil law) approach and the rather restrained reading of a "right to explanation" for automated processing of data under the GDPR (see Sect. 2.2. above). In other words: If health care providers use approved AI systems with a critical eye and point out possible errors of the system to patients, then they should – in case the patient has given consent - not be liable for errors that occur nevertheless (at best, the manufacturer might be liable [53]). Other opinions assume that medical personnel must be fully satisfied with the functioning of AI-based systems and otherwise must not use them (see note [51] where the author argues for risk-based validation; similarly, albeit more cautiously [47]) - which, consequently, should also enable them to inform patients comprehensively about the functioning of the AI-based system. According to this approach, medical AI can only be used if patients have been informed about its essential functions beforehand – admittedly in an intelligible form. These conflicting opinions clearly show that a legal regulation of this aspect would indeed be advisable to ensure legal certainty for health service providers.

Informed consent is a subject-matter which also shows the difference between "law in the books" and "law in practice". In real life, a patient's choice of a health care provider and a treatment method will often mainly depend on highly subjective aspects (e.g. the institution, the manufacturer of an AI system or the doctor is perceived as trustworthy) and not on the objective content of the information provided. However, as personal impressions can be misleading, the provision of scientifically sound facts as a base for informed decision-making remains, from a legal point of view, a cornerstone of the concept of "informed consent". Admittedly, this somewhat idealized concept of "informed consent" has sometimes been characterized as unnecessary complex and practically unattainable by health care providers. However, this criticism is not limited to the use of AI in medicine but part of the general discussion about the pros and cons of "informed consent" in medicine [16,17]. Furthermore, "informed consent" is not a monolithic concept, but has different manifestations. Routinely, the necessary information has to be provided by the health care provider in a personal consultation, however, in case of medication a package insert is (in addition to a prescription) regarded as satisfactory from a legal point of view. Building on this approach, the provision of a comparable "AI package insert" has also been sometimes been proposed as a means to meet the necessary transparency standards for AI [61].

Product Liability. Harm caused by a defective medical device is normally also addressed by European product liability legislation (in form of a directive), which holds the producers/designer liable for defects of the product even without fault. However, product liability primarily addresses "tangible" products (e.g. embedded software as part of a composite product), not "intangibles" like non-embedded standalone software [49,53]. Therefore, medical AI - as long as it is not a composite part of a physical product - will be outside the scope of current product liability of manufacturers (this mirrors the situation in the American legal doctrine [32]). Furthermore, current European product liability law addresses neither AI's ability of continued learning and the resulting regular modifications of its models in a satisfying way as it focuses on the time of placing on the market and does not cover subsequent errors. It can be very challenging to prove that the defect of a ML algorithm had already been present at this point in time and could also have been detected [47].

Future Developments in Liability Law. Comparable to the legal framework on product safety procedures, the European Commission is well aware of the severe challenges in regard to civil and product liability for AI applications and announced several (including legislative) measures in the above-mentioned report on liability [21]. This should also contribute to a more harmonized legal regime across all EU Member States. In civil liability law the burden of proof concerning causation and fault will probably be adapted to mitigate the complexity of AI (e.g. shift of burden of proof from the patient to the doctor/health care provider concerning damage caused by medical AI).

With regards to product liability law the Commission will in the near future evaluate the introduction of a strict liability system, combined with compulsory insurance for particularly hazardous AI applications (that is, systems which may cause significant harm to life, health and property, and/or expose the public at large to risks). Such a system will presumably cover most medical AI applications - the use of which would also be affected by the proposed changes to the rules on the burden of proof. This new legal framework will probably also further address the difficult question of software as a product or as a service as the Commission has already announced that a clarification of the Product Liability Directive in this respect will be necessary [21,24]. Furthermore, the important concept of placing on the market as the reference point for liability could be changed to take account of the adaptability of ML; after-market assessment and monitoring therefore could become part of liability law [54]. Such an enhanced dual liability system (civil and product liability) would certainly help to eliminate many existing ambiguities regarding the liability of medical AI applications.

3 Conclusion

The European Commission stated in its White Paper [22] that "[...] while a number of the requirements are already reflected in existing legal or regulatory regimes, those regarding transparency, traceability and human oversight are not specifically covered under current legislation in many economic sectors." As shown in this paper, this conclusion does not fully hold true for medical AI. As medical AI is closely intertwined with questions of fundamental rights, data protection and autonomy, it is a field of AI where the current state of legislation provides more answers to open questions than in other areas of the application of artificial intelligence. It must not be forgotten that legal provisions are a technologically-neutral instrument, which can also (at least to a considerable extent) be applied to the use of (medical) AI even if it was not enacted with AI in mind.

As to the use of medical AI, fundamental rights and the GDPR both prescribe clear duties to provide information to enable "informed consent" and also require a "human in the loop" as an essential element of oversight. Even if it is doubtful that there is an outright "right to an explanation" of specific decisions, the patient must be provided with enough information to understand the pros and cons associated with medical AI and can therefore participate in the shared-decision-making process or make use of his privacy rights stated in the GDPR (e.g. Art. 22 para 3 GDPR). European AI must be developed and operated in accordance with the requirements of fundamental rights, including the protection of data and privacy (Arts. 8 and 7 CFR). We conclude: European medical AI requires human oversight and explainability.

We also showed that the current framework for product approval procedures and liability for AI has not so far addressed the use of AI in a satisfactory way, however, the EU took note of these inadequacies and plans to amend its legislation. In this regard, the Commission has announced that it will soon provide clarity by proposing market approval procedures which address the specific risks of AI (e.g. need for constant re-assessment) and a strict liability approach combined with an obligatory insurance scheme for malfunctions of AI. These proposed changes will also strengthen the focus on transparency. Furthermore, new legislation will possibly bring along changes in the burden of proof for product approval procedures and in case of damages allegedly caused by AI. Hence the new regulation will probably nudge AI developers to use explainable AI (XAI) to comply with its requirements more easily [30].

This European approach which is already visible in current legislation will be further substantiated by the work of the Commission which - in contrast to other nations - expressly pursues a "human-centric" approach to AI, which should be integrated in an "ecosystem of trust" [22], thereby necessitating transparency of AI applications. Therefore, the future of AI envisioned by the EU isn't a future where humans are mere cogs in a mechanical decision-making machinery, but a vision where AI still remains an important tool - but a tool only - to shape a future for humans. This seems particular relevant for medical AI which in many ways touches upon the very essence of a human being. In this respect, exaggerated fears of "Dr. Robot" [4] are not appropriate: The European legal framework for medical AI basically requires the use of explainable AI in medicine, thereby being well in line recent medical research on XAI [36,48].

Acknowledgements. The authors declare that there are no conflicts of interests and the work does not raise any ethical issues. Parts of this work have been funded by the Austrian Science Fund (FWF), Project: P-32554 "A reference model of explainable Artificial Intelligence for the Medical Domain".

References

1. Article 29 Data Protection Working Group: Guidelines on Data Protection Impact Assessment (DPIA) and determining whether processing is "likely to result in a high risk" for the purposes of Regulation 2016/679, WP248rev.01 (2017). https://ec.europa.eu/newsroom/article29/item-detail.cfm?item_id=611236
2. Article 29 Data Protection Working Group: Guidelines on Automated individual decision-making and Profiling for the purposes of Regulation 2016/679, WP251rev.01 (2018). https://ec.europa.eu/newsroom/article29/item-detail.cfm?item_id=612053
3. Article 29 Data Protection Working Group: Guidelines on transparency under Regulation 2016/679, WP260.rev.01 (2018). https://ec.europa.eu/newsroom/article29/item-detail.cfm?item_id=622227
4. Bambauer, J.R.: Dr. Robot. UC Davis Law Rev. **51**, 383–398 (2017)
5. Bathaee, Y.: The artificial intelligence black box and the failure of intent and causation. Harv. J. Law Technol. **31**, 889–938 (2018)
6. Brkan, M.: Do algorithms rule the world? Algorithmic decision-making and data protection in the framework of the GDPR and beyond. Int. J. Law Inf. Technol. **27**, 91–121 (2019). https://doi.org/10.1093/ijlit/eay017
7. Brkan, M., Bonnet, G.: Legal and technical feasibility of the GDPR's quest for explanation of algorithmic decisions: of black boxes, white boxes and Fata Morganas. Eur. J. Risk Regul. **11**, 18–50 (2020). https://doi.org/10.1017/err.2020.10
8. Bygrave, L.: Data protection by design and by default: deciphering the EU's legislative requirements. Oslo Law Rev. **4**, 105–120 (2017). https://doi.org/10.18261/issn.2387-3299-2017-02-03
9. Bygrave, L.: Minding the machine v2.0. The EU general data protection regulation and automated decision-making. In: Yeung, K., Lodge, M. (eds.) Algorithmic Regulation, pp. 248–262. Oxford University Press, Oxford (2019). https://doi.org/10.1093/oso/9780198838494.001.0001
10. Bygrave, L.: Article 22. In: Kuner, C., Bygrave, L., Docksey, C., Drechsler, L. (eds.) The EU General Data Protection Regulation (GDPR). A Commentary. Oxford University Press, Oxford (2020)
11. Casey, B., Farhangi, A., Vogl, R.: Rethinking explainable machines: the GDPR's 'right to explanation' debate and the rise of algorithmic audits in enterprise. Berkeley Technol. Law J. **34**, 143–188 (2019)
12. Cohen, I.G.: Informed consent and medical artificial intelligence: what to tell the patient? Georgetown Law J. (2020). https://papers.ssrn.com/sol3/papers.cfm?abstract_id=3529576
13. Datenethikkommission: Gutachten der Datenethikkommission (2019). https://www.bmi.bund.de/SharedDocs/downloads/DE/publikationen/themen/it-digitalpolitik/gutachten-datenethikkommission.html
14. Denga, M.: Deliktische Haftung für künstliche Intelligenz. Computer und Recht **34**, 69–78 (2018). https://doi.org/10.9785/cr-2018-0203
15. Dupré, C.: Article 1. In: Peers, S., Hervey, T., Kenner, J., Ward, A. (eds.) The EU Charter of Fundamental Rights. A Commentary. C.H. Beck - Hart - Nomos, Baden-Baden - München - Oxford (2014). https://doi.org/10.5771/9783845259055
16. Eberbach, W.: Wird die ärztliche Aufklärung zur Fiktion? (Teil 1). Medizinrecht **37**, 1–10 (2019). https://doi.org/10.1007/s00350-018-5120-8
17. Eberbach, W.: Wird die ärztliche Aufklärung zur Fiktion? (Teil 2). Medizinrecht **37**, 111–117 (2019). https://doi.org/10.1007/s00350-019-5147-5

18. Edwards, L., Veale, M.: Slave to the algorithm? Why a ‘right to explanation’ is probably not the remedy you are looking for. Duke Law Technol. Rev. **16**, 18–84 (2017)
19. Edwards, L., Veale, M.: Enslaving the algorithm: from a “right to an explanation” to a “right to better decisions”? IEEE Secur. Priv. **16**, 46–54 (2018). https://doi.org/10.1109/MSP.2018.2701152
20. Etzioni, A., Etzioni, O.: Designing AI systems that obey our laws and values. Commun. ACM **59**, 29–31 (2016). https://doi.org/10.1145/2955091
21. European Commission: Report on the safety and liability implications of Artificial Intelligence, the Internet of Things and robotics (2020). https://ec.europa.eu/info/sites/info/files/report-safety-liability-artificial-intelligence-feb2020_en_1.pdf
22. European Commission: White Paper On Artificial Intelligence - A European approach to excellence and trust (2020). https://ec.europa.eu/info/sites/info/files/commission-white-paper-artificial-intelligence-feb2020_en.pdf
23. European Data Protection Board: Guidelines 05/2020 on consent under Regulation 2016/679, Version 1.1 (2020). https://edpb.europa.eu/sites/edpb/files/files/file1/edpb_guidelines_202005_consent_en.pdf
24. Expert Group on Liability and New Technologies - New Technologies Formation: Liability for artificial intelligence and other emerging digital technologies (2019). https://ec.europa.eu/transparency/regexpert/index.cfm?do=groupDetail.groupMeetingDoc&docid=36608
25. FDA: Proposed Regulatory Framework for Modifications to Artificial Intelligence/Machine Learning (AI/ML)-Based Software as a Medical Device (SaMD) - Discussion Paper and Request for Feedback (2019). https://www.fda.gov/medical-devices/software-medical-device-samd/artificial-intelligence-and-machine-learning-software-medical-device
26. Fosch Villaronga, E., Kieseberg, P., Li, T.: Humans forget, machines remember: artificial intelligence and the right to be forgotten. Comput. Law Secur. Rev. **34**, 304–313 (2018). https://doi.org/10.1016/j.clsr.2017.08.007
27. FRA: Data quality and artificial intelligence - mitigating bias and error to protect fundamental rights (2019). https://fra.europa.eu/sites/default/files/fra_uploads/fra-2019-data-quality-and-ai_en.pdf
28. Goodman, P., Flaxman, S.: European Union regulations on algorithmic decision-making and a “right to explanation”. AI Mag. **38**, 50–57 (2017). https://doi.org/10.1609/aimag.v38i3.2741
29. Hacker, P.: Teaching fairness to artificial intelligence: existing and novel strategies against algorithmic discrimination under EU law. Common Market Law Rev. **55**, 1143–1186 (2018). https://kluwerlawonline.com/JournalArticle/Common+Market+Law+Review/55.4/COLA2018095
30. Hacker, P., Krestel, R., Grundmann, S., Naumann, F.: Explainable AI under contract and tort law: legal incentives and technical challenges. Artif. Intell. Law **16** (2020). https://doi.org/10.1007/s10506-020-09260-6
31. Haidinger, V.: Art 22 DSGVO. In: Knyrim, R. (ed.) Der DatKomm Praxiskommentar zum Datenschutzrecht - DSGVO und DSG. Manz, Wien, rdb.at (2018)
32. Harned, Z., Lungren, M.P., Rajpurkar, P.: Machine vision, medical AI, and malpractice. Harv. J. Law Technol. Digest (2019). https://jolt.law.harvard.edu/digest/machine-vision-medical-ai-and-malpractice
33. Harris, D., O’Boyle, M., Bates, E., Buckley, C.: Law of the European Convention on Human Rights, 4th edn. Oxford University Press, Oxford (2018)

34. High-Level Expert Group on Artificial Intelligence: Ethics Guidelines for trustworthy AI (2019). https://ec.europa.eu/digital-single-market/en/news/ethics-guidelines-trustworthy-ai
35. Holzinger, A.: Interactive machine learning for health informatics: when do we need the human-in-the-loop? Brain Inform. **3**, 119–131 (2016). https://doi.org/10.1007/s40708-016-0042-6
36. Holzinger, A., Langs, G., Denk, H., Zatloukal, K., Müller, H.: Causability and explainability of artificial intelligence in medicine. Wiley Interdiscip. Rev. Data Min. Knowl. Discov. **59**, 29–31 (2019). https://doi.org/10.1002/widm.1312
37. Jabri, S.: Artificial intelligence and healthcare: products and procedures. In: Wischmeyer, T., Rademacher, T. (eds.) Regulating Artificial Intelligence, pp. 307–335. Springer, Cham (2020). https://doi.org/10.1007/978-3-030-32361-5_14
38. Kaminski, M.E.: The right to explanation, explained. Berkeley Technol. Law J. **34**, 189–218 (2019). https://doi.org/10.15779/Z38TD9N83H
39. Koziol, H.: Comparative conclusions. In: Koziol, H. (ed.) Basic Questions of Tort Law from a Comparative Perspective, pp. 685–838. Jan Sramek Verlag, Vienna (2015)
40. Lapuschkin, S., Wäldchen, S., Binder, A., Montavon, G., Samek, W., Müller, K.R.: Unmasking Clever Hans predictors and assessing what machines really learn. Nat. Commun. **10**(1) (2019). https://doi.org/10.1038/s41467-019-08987-4
41. Lipton, Z.C.: The mythos of model interpretability. ACM Queue **16**, 1–27 (2018). https://doi.org/10.1145/3236386.3241340
42. Malgieri, G., Comandé, G.: Why a right to legibility of automated decision-making exists in the general data protection regulation. Int. Data Priv. Law **7**, 243–265 (2017). https://doi.org/10.1093/idpl/ipx019
43. Mendoza, I., Bygrave, L.: The right not to be subject to automated decisions based on profiling. In: Synodinou, T.E., Jougleux, P., Markou, C., Prastitou, T. (eds.) EU Internet Law. Regulation and Enforcement, pp. 77–98. Springer, Cham (2017). https://doi.org/10.1007/978-3-319-64955-9_4
44. Miller, T.: Explanation in artificial intelligence: insights from the social sciences. Artif. Intell. **267**, 1–38 (2019). https://doi.org/10.1016/j.artint.2018.07.007
45. Minssen, T., Gerke, S., Aboy, M., Price, N., Cohen, G.: Regulatory responses to medical machine learning. J. Law Biosci. 1–18 (2020). https://doi.org/10.1093/jlb/lsaa002
46. Mittelstadt, B., Russell, C., Wachter, S.: Explaining explanations in AI. In: FAT* 2019: Proceedings of the Conference on Fairness, Accountability, and Transparency, January 2019. pp. 279–288. ACM (2019). https://doi.org/10.1145/3287560.3287574
47. Molnár-Gábor, F.: Artificial intelligence in healthcare: doctors, patients and liabilities. In: Wischmeyer, T., Rademacher, T. (eds.) Regulating Artificial Intelligence, pp. 337–360. Springer, Cham (2020). https://doi.org/10.1007/978-3-030-32361-5_15
48. O'Sullivan, S., et al.: Legal, regulatory, and ethical frameworks for development of standards in artificial intelligence (AI) and autonomous robotic surgery. Int. J. Med. Robot. Comput. Assist. Surg. **15**, 1–12 (2019). https://doi.org/10.1002/rcs.1968
49. PHG Foundation: Legal liability for machine learning in healthcare (2018). https://www.phgfoundation.org/briefing/legal-liability-machine-learning-in-healthcare
50. PHG Foundation: Algorithms as medical devices (2019). https://www.phgfoundation.org/documents/algorithms-as-medical-devices.pdf

51. Price, N.W.: Medical malpractice and black box medicine. In: Cohen, G., Fernandez Lynch, H., Vayena, E., Gasser, U. (eds.) Big Data, Health Law and Bioethics, pp. 295–306. Cambridge University Press, Cambridge (2018). https://doi.org/10.1017/9781108147972
52. Reinisch, F.: Künstliche Intelligenz - Haftungsfragen 4.0. Österreichische Juristen-Zeitung, pp. 298–305 (2019)
53. Schönberger, D.: Artificial intelligence in healthcare: a critical analysis of the legal and ethical implications. Int. J. Law Inf. Technol. **27**, 171–203 (2019). https://doi.org/10.1093/ijlit/eaz004
54. Seehafer, A., Kohler, J.: Künstliche Intelligenz: Updates für das Produkthaftungsrecht? Europäische Zeitschrift für Wirtschaftsrecht **31**, 213–218 (2020)
55. Selbst, A.D., Powles, J.: Meaningful information and the right to explanation. Int. Data Priv. Law **7**, 233–242 (2017). https://doi.org/10.1093/idpl/ipx022
56. Spindler, G.: Roboter, Automation, künstliche Intelligenz, selbst-steuernde Kfz - Braucht das Recht neue Haftungskategorien? Computer und Recht **31**, 766–776 (2015). https://doi.org/10.9785/cr-2015-1205
57. Topol, E.: Deep Medicine. Basic Books, New York (2019)
58. Wachter, S., Mittelstadt, B., Floridi, L.: Why a right to explanation of automated decision-making does not exist in the general data protection regulation. Int. Data Priv. Law **7**, 76–99 (2017). https://doi.org/10.1093/idpl/ipx005
59. Wachter, S., Mittelstadt, B., Russell, C.: Counterfactual explanations without opening the black box: automated decisions and the GDPR. Harv. J. Law Technol. **31**, 841–887 (2018)
60. Zech, H.: Künstliche Intelligenz und Haftungsfragen. Zeitschrift für die gesamte Privatrechtswissenschaft **5**, 198–219 (2019)
61. Zweig, K.A.: Wo Maschinen irren können (2018). https://www.bertelsmann-stiftung.de/fileadmin/files/BSt/Publikationen/GrauePublikationen/WoMaschinenIrrenKoennen.pdf

An Efficient Method for Mining Informative Association Rules in Knowledge Extraction

Parfait Bemarisika(✉) and André Totohasina

Laboratoire de Mathématiques et Informatique ENSET, Université d'Antsiranana, Antsiranana, Madagascar
bemarisikap7@yahoo.fr, andre.totohasina@gmail.com

Abstract. Mining association rules is an important problem in Knowledge Extraction (KE). This paper proposes an efficient method for mining simultaneously informative positive and negative association rules, using a new selective pair support-M_{GK}. For this, we define four new bases of positive and negative association rules, based on Galois connection semantics. These bases are characterized by frequent closed itemsets, maximal frequent itemsets, and their generator itemsets; it consists of the non-redundant exact and approximate association rules having minimal premise and maximal conclusion, i.e. the informative association rules. We introduce NONRED algorithm allowing to generate these bases and all valid informative association rules. Results experiments carried out on reference datasets show the usefulness of this approach.

Keywords: Knowledge Extraction · Minimal generators · Frequent closed itemsets · Maximal frequent itemsets · Informative basis of rules

1 Introduction and Motivations

Mining association rules is an important problem in Knowledge Extraction (KE). This paper focuses on informative basis for association rules which is a subset of non-redundant from which we can derive all valid rules. Given $\mathcal{I}$ a set of items from a context, an association rule is an implication of the form $X \rightarrow Y$, where $X, Y \subseteq \mathcal{I}$ and $X \cap Y = \emptyset$. The itemsets X and Y are called premise (or antecedent) and conclusion (or consequent) of this rule, respectively. An association rule is called *exact* if its intensity (M_{GK}) is equal to 1 and *approximate*, otherwise. An *informative* association rule is one that, from the minimal premise, provides the maximal consequent. A rule r_1 is said to be redundant with respect to r_2 if (i) it shares the same information as r_2, (ii) its premise (resp. conclusion) is superset of premise (resp. subset of conclusion) of the r_2.

In KE concept, the concept of bases for association rules has developed by several approaches [8,9,11,12]. However, most of them are not based on nega-

Published by Springer Nature Switzerland AG 2020
A. Holzinger et al. (Eds.): CD-MAKE 2020, LNCS 12279, pp. 227–247, 2020.
https://doi.org/10.1007/978-3-030-57321-8_13

tive rules[1] but rather based on positive rules, and this, with less selective pair support-confidence [1]. However, the positive rules exclusively cannot cover all interest of mining association rules in databases, it also needs the negative rules. To tackle these notable limitations, we propose an efficient method for mining simultaneously positive and negative informative rules, based on Galois connetion, and this, with a selective pair support-M_{GK}. For this, we define four new bases: Informative Basis for Positive Exact Association Rules (IBE^{+}), Informative Basis for Positive Approximate Association Rules (IBA^{+}), Informative Basis for Negative Exact Association Rules (IBE^{-}), and Informative Basis for Negative Approximate Association Rules (IBA^{-}). Different optimizations for searching space are then developed. Based on these optimizations, we introduce NonRed algorithm for mining these bases and all valid informative association rules.

The rest of this paper is organized as follows. Section 2 discusses the related works. Section 3 gives the preliminaries, where we formally introduce the basic concepts relative to Galois connection and association rules, and the main properties of M_{GK} [10,16,18]. Section 4 details our approach. Section 5 describes the experimental evaluation. A conclusion and perspectives are given in Sect. 6.

2 Related Works

In KE concept, mining association rules is structured on two lines of research: (1) Bases of positive association rules, and (2) Bases of negative association rules.

In base of positive association rules, we present Duquenne-Guigues basis [9]. Without going into the details of its calculation, the Duquenne-Guigues basis is not informative because the premises are chosen from to pseudo-closed that is incompatible of minimality. Bastide et al. [2,15] adapts this Duquenne-Guigues basis. In order to derive the redundant approximate association rules, it uses the closure mechanism based on Galois lattices [7]. However, it has been shown in Kryszkiewicz [11] that this concept of closures mechanism is invalid and the Duquenne-Guigues basis [9] is not informative. To address this problem, Kryszkiewicz extends this same Duquenne-Guigues basis of exact and approximate association rules. However, this approach presents a significant number of association rules, especially for dense contexts, making it difficult to manipulate the result. Zaki [19] defines a generic basis for non-redundant association rules where it uses the transitivity axiom. However, the proposed definition of redundancy is not very appropriate, which is not conform of informative concept. Recently, [12] offers a new generic basis. However, the definition of a redundant association rules adopted does not guarantee the absolute minimal premise. This approach is then inappropriate on concept of the informative association rules.

The concept of negative basis is introduced in [6]. Despite its notable interest, this approach is not informative, because it selects the premises on pseudo-closed [9] which intuitively returns the maximal elements, so incompatible of

[1] An association of the form $X \rightarrow \overline{Y}$, $\overline{X} \rightarrow Y$ and $\overline{X} \rightarrow \overline{Y}$, where $\overline{I} = \neg I = \mathcal{I} \backslash I$.

minimality. In addition, its formulation of exact negative association rules is not appropriate, which can present a high memory for searching space.

From this quick literature, mining informative association rules is still a major challenge, for several reasons. On the one hand, the majority of existing approaches are limited on positive association rules which are not sufficient to guarantee the interest of knowledge extraction. On the other hand, these approaches are also limited on classic pair support-confidence [1] which produces a high number of association rules whose interest is not always guaranteed.

3 Basic Notions

Table 1. Context $\mathcal{B}$

TID	Items
1	ACD
2	BCE
3	ABCE
4	BE
5	ABCE
6	BCE

In KE concept, a formal context (cf. Table 1) is a triplet $\mathcal{B} = (\mathcal{T}, \mathcal{I}, \mathcal{R})$. $\mathcal{T}$ and $\mathcal{I}$ are finite sets of transactions and items respectively. $\mathcal{R} \subseteq \mathcal{T} \times \mathcal{I}$ is a binary relation between $\mathcal{T}$ and $\mathcal{I}$. A relation $i\mathcal{R}t$ denotes that the item i satisfies the transaction t. Let $X \subseteq \mathcal{I}$, $\overline{X} = \neg X = \{t \in \mathcal{T} | \exists i \in X : (i,t) \notin \mathcal{R}\}$ is complementary set of X (i.e. $\mathcal{I} \backslash X$). A subset $X \subseteq \mathcal{I}$ with $k = |X|$ is called k-itemset, where $|\ell|$ denotes the cardinality of ℓ. For $I \subseteq \mathcal{I}$, the set $\phi(I) = I' = \{t \in \mathcal{T} | i\mathcal{R}t, \forall i \in I\}$ is called extension of I, it is the set of transactions that satisfy all items in I. Similarly, for $T \subseteq \mathcal{T}$, the set $\psi(T) = T' = \{i \in \mathcal{I} | i\mathcal{R}t, \forall t \in T\}$ is intension of T. Both functions ϕ and ψ form a Galois connection between $\mathcal{P}(\mathcal{I})$ and $\mathcal{P}(\mathcal{T})$ [7], where $\mathcal{P}(\ell)$ is a powerset lattice of ℓ. The support of $X \subseteq \mathcal{I}$ is $supp(X) = P(X') = \frac{|\phi(X)|}{|\mathcal{T}|}$ where P is the discrete probability on $(\mathcal{T}, \mathcal{P}(\mathcal{T}))$. X is frequent if $supp(X) \geqslant minsup$ where $minsup \in]0,1]$ is a minimum support. Let $\mathcal{F}$ be the set of all frequent on $\mathcal{B}$, i.e. $\mathcal{F} = \{X \subseteq \mathcal{I} | supp(X) \geqslant minsup\}$. $\gamma(X) = \psi o \phi(X)$ is called Galois closure operator. Formally, a rule $X \rightarrow Y$ is said to be exact if $X \subseteq Y$ and $\gamma(X) = \gamma(Y)$. It is approximate if $X \subseteq Y$ and $\gamma(X) \subset \gamma(Y)$. Two itemsets $X, Y \subseteq \mathcal{I}$ are said to be equivalent, denoted by $X \cong Y$, iff $supp(X) = supp(Y)$. The set of itemsets that are equivalent to an itemset X is denoted by $[X] = \{Y \subseteq \mathcal{I} \mid X \cong Y\}$.

Property 1 (Antimonotonicity). $\forall X, Y \subseteq \mathcal{I}$, we have $X \subseteq Y \Rightarrow \phi(X) \supseteq \phi(Y)$.

Definition 1 (Closed itemset). *An itemset $X \subseteq \mathcal{I}$ is closed iff $X = \gamma(X)$.*

Property 2 ([2,15,19]). For all $X, Y \subseteq \mathcal{I}$, we have $X \subset Y \Rightarrow \gamma(X) \subset \gamma(Y)$.

Definition 2 (Generators). *An itemset G is said to be generator of a closed itemset $\mathcal{C}$ iff $\gamma(G) = \mathcal{C}$ and $\nexists g \subseteq \mathcal{I}$ with $g \subseteq G$ such that $\gamma(g) = \mathcal{C}$. Consider $0 < minsup \leqslant 1$, we define the set $\mathcal{G}_\mathcal{C}$ of all frequent generator itemsets in $\mathcal{B}$ as:*

$$\mathcal{G}_\mathcal{C} = \{G \in [\mathcal{C}] | \mathcal{C} \in \mathcal{FC},\ \nexists g \subset G,\ supp(G) \geqslant minsup\}$$

An itemset $G \in [\gamma(G)]$ is called a generator, if G has no proper subset (ordered by $\subseteq$) in $[\gamma(G)]$ given by $[\gamma(G)] = \{Y \subseteq \mathcal{I} | \gamma(Y) = \gamma(G)\}$. In other words, it has no proper subset with the same support (i.e. the same closure).

Property 3 ([2,15,19]). For all $X \subseteq \mathcal{I}$ from the context $\mathcal{B}$, $supp(X) = supp(\gamma(X))$.

Definition 3 (Frequent closed itemsets). *The closed itemset $\mathcal{C}$ is said to be frequent if $supp(\mathcal{C}) \geqslant minsup$. We define the set $\mathcal{FC}$ of all frequent closed as:*

$$\mathcal{FC} = \{\mathcal{C} \in \mathcal{I} | \mathcal{C} = \gamma(\mathcal{C}),\ supp(\mathcal{C}) \geqslant minsup\}$$

Definition 4 (Maximal frequent closed itemsets). *Let $\mathcal{FC}$ be the set of all frequent closed. We define $\mathcal{MC}$ the set of all maximal frequent closed in $\mathcal{B}$ as:*

$$\mathcal{MC} = \{\mathcal{C} \in \mathcal{FC} \mid \nexists \widetilde{\mathcal{C}} \supset \mathcal{C},\ \widetilde{\mathcal{C}} \in \mathcal{FC}\}$$

For all $X, Y \subseteq \mathcal{I}$, the support and confidence of $X \to Y$ are respectively defined by $supp(X \cup Y) = \frac{|\phi(X \cup Y)|}{|\mathcal{T}|}$ and $P(Y'|X') = \frac{P(X' \cap Y')}{P(X')}$. Despite its notable contribution, the pair support-confidence generates a large number of rules many of which are uninteresting and redundant (see [3,4]). So, we use the selective pair support-M_{GK}. We define M_{GK} [16] of a rule $X \to Y$ as:

$$M_{GK}(X \to Y) = \begin{cases} \frac{P(Y'|X') - P(Y')}{1 - P(Y')}, \text{ if } P(Y'|X') > P(Y'),\ P(Y') \neq 1 \\ \frac{P(Y'|X') - P(Y')}{P(Y')}, \text{ if } P(Y'|X') \leqslant P(Y'),\ P(Y') \neq 0. \end{cases} \quad (1)$$

M_{GK} varies in $[-1, 1]$. When $-1 \leqslant M_{GK}(X \to Y) < 0$, then $P(Y'|X') \leqslant P(Y')$ (i.e. X disfavors Y) means that Y is negatively dependent on X. In this case, $X \to Y$ is not interesting rule. When $M_{GK}(X \to Y) = 0$, then $P(Y'|X') = P(Y')$ means that X and Y are independent. In this case, $X \to Y$ is also not interesting rule. When $M_{GK}(X \to Y) > 0$, then $P(Y'|X') > P(Y')$ (i.e. X favors Y) means that Y is positively dependent on X, so $X \to Y$ is interesting.

Formally, a rule $X_2 \to Y_2$ is redundant with respect to $X_1 \to Y_1$ iff (*i*) ($X_1 \subseteq X_2$ and $Y_1 \supset Y_2$) and (*ii*) ($supp(X_1 \cup Y_1) = supp(X_2 \cup Y_2)$, $M_{GK}(X_1 \to Y_1) = M_{GK}(X_2 \to Y_2)$). A rule $X \to Y$ is informative if $X \in \mathcal{G}_{\gamma(X)}$ and $Y \in \mathcal{FC}$.

Property 4. Given X and Y two itemsets of $\mathcal{I}$, if (X, Y) is a stochastically independent pair, so $(\overline{X}, Y)$, $(X, \overline{Y})$, ($\overline{X}$ and $\overline{Y}$) are also independent.

Proof. Let $X, Y \subseteq \mathcal{I}$. We have $P(\overline{X'})P(Y') - P(\overline{X'} \cap Y') = (1 - P(X'))P(Y') - (P(Y') - P(X' \cap Y')) = P(X' \cap Y') - P(X')P(Y')$. So, if $P(X' \cap Y') = P(X')P(Y')$, then $P(\overline{X'})P(Y') = P(\overline{X'} \cap Y')$. We have the same result for $(X, \overline{Y})$ and $(\overline{X}, \overline{Y})$, then replacing Y with $\overline{Y}$. □

Then, no rule can be interesting if (X, Y) is stochastically independent.

Property 5. For all $X, Y \subseteq \mathcal{I}$, we have $M_{GK}(X \to Y) = -M_{GK}(X \to \overline{Y})$.

Proof. (1) If $P(Y'|X') > P(Y')$, we have $P(Y'|X') + P(\overline{Y}|X) = 1 \Leftrightarrow P(\overline{Y}|X) = 1 - P(Y'|X') \leqslant 1 - P(Y') = P(\overline{Y})$. So, $M_{GK}(X \to Y) + M_{GK}(X \to \overline{Y}) = \frac{P(Y'|X') - P(Y')}{1 - P(Y')} + \frac{P(\overline{Y}|X) - P(\overline{Y})}{P(\overline{Y})} = \frac{P(Y'|X') - P(Y')}{1 - P(Y')} + \frac{1 - P(Y'|X') - 1 + P(Y')}{1 - P(Y')} = 0.$ (2)
If $P(Y'|X') \leqslant P(Y')$, we have $P(Y'|X') + P(\overline{Y'}|X') = 1 \Leftrightarrow P(\overline{Y}|X) = 1 - P(Y'|X') \geq 1 - P(Y') = P(\overline{Y'})$. Thus, $M_{GK}(X \to Y) + M_{GK}(X \to \overline{Y}) = \frac{P(Y'|X') - P(Y')}{P(Y')} + \frac{P(\overline{Y'}|X') - P(\overline{Y'})}{1 - P(\overline{Y'})} = \frac{P(Y'|X') - P(Y')}{1 - P(Y')} + \frac{1 - P(Y'|X') - 1 + P(Y')}{P(Y')} = 0.$ □

It follows that if the value of M_{GK} for the rule $X \to Y$ is strictly negative, we conclude that it is the rule $X \to \overline{Y}$ which will be pertinent and we have the value of this rule without having to recalculate it thanks to this notable property.

Property 6. For all $X, Y \subseteq \mathcal{I}$, we have: (1) $P(Y'|X') > P(Y') \Rightarrow 0 < M_{GK}(X \to Y) \leqslant 1$, and (2) $P(Y'|X') \leqslant P(Y') \Rightarrow -1 \leqslant M_{GK}(X \to Y) \leqslant 0$.

Proof. (1) Since $P(Y'|X') > P(Y')$ we have $P(Y'|X') - P(Y') > 0 \overset{P(Y')\neq 1}{\Leftrightarrow} \frac{P(Y'|X')-P(Y')}{1-P(Y')} > 0$. For each $X, Y \subseteq \mathcal{I}$: $P(Y'|X') \leqslant 1 \Leftrightarrow P(Y'|X') - P(Y') \leqslant 1 - P(Y') \overset{P(Y')\neq 1}{\Leftrightarrow} \frac{P(Y'|X')-P(Y')}{1-P(Y')} \leqslant 1$. So, $0 < M_{GK}(X \to Y) \leqslant 1$. (2) Since $P(Y'|X') \leqslant P(Y')$ we have $P(Y'|X') - P(Y') \leqslant 0 \Rightarrow -P(Y') \leqslant P(Y'|X') - P(Y') \leqslant 0 \overset{P(Y')\neq 0}{\Leftrightarrow} -1 \leqslant \frac{P(Y'|X')-P(Y')}{P(Y')} \leqslant 0 \Leftrightarrow -1 \leqslant M_{GK}(X \to Y) \leqslant 0$. □

From this Property 6, we conclude that M_{GK} offers a robust and efficient tool to prune systematically the uninteresting association rules (i.e. $-1 \leqslant M_{GK} \leqslant 0$). Note that the first component of M_{GK} (cf. Eq. (1)) is implicative but the second not, only the first will be active. This procedure is thus more consistent with the classic causal interpretation of an association rule. Let $n = |\mathcal{T}|$, $n_X = |\phi(X)|$, $n_Y = |\phi(Y)|$, $n_{X\wedge Y} = |\phi(X \cup Y)|$ and $n_{X\wedge\overline{Y}} = |\phi(X \cup \overline{Y}|$. Also, $N_{X\wedge\overline{Y}}$ indicates the random variable which generates $n_{X\wedge\overline{Y}}$, and $N_{X\wedge Y}$ that which generates $n_{X\wedge Y}$. For any association rule $X \to Y$, we define M_{GK} as:

$$M_{GK}(X \to Y) \overset{P(\overline{Y'})\neq 0}{=} 1 - \frac{P(\overline{Y'}|X')}{P(\overline{Y'})} = 1 - \frac{n n_{X\wedge\overline{Y}}}{n_X n_{\overline{Y}}} \tag{2}$$

In principle, such an association rule $X \to Y$ will be all the better if it contains large examples $N_{X\wedge Y}$ and relatively few counter-examples $N_{X\wedge\overline{Y}}$.

4 Mining Informative Association Rules

Our approach is based on the same theoretical basis as the approach proposed by [2]. However, our extraction strategy is different in terms of the measure used and the rules extracted. Indeed, our approach uses the selective couple support-M_{GK}, and simultaneously extracts the positive and negative rules. The current version [17] of the support-M_{GK} approach uses the critical value $\sqrt{\frac{1}{n}\frac{n-n_X}{n_X}\frac{n_Y}{n-n_Y}\chi^2(\alpha)}$, i.e. a rule $X \to Y$ will be valid if $M_{GK}(X \to Y) \geqslant \sqrt{\frac{1}{n}\frac{n-n_X}{n_X}\frac{n_Y}{n-n_Y}\chi^2(\alpha)}$ where $\chi^2(\alpha)$, at the risk of error $\alpha \in]0,1]$, is the statistic of Chi-square to a degree of freedom. Despite its indisputable interest, this critical value can nevertheless present some faults. A low value (natural choice) of α leads to a high critical value which exponentially exceeds the real value of M_{GK}. This rejects the robust association rules. Conversely, a relatively large value of α leads to a very low critical value. This accepts the very bad rules.

In order to overcome these limits, we introduce a new technique which consists in modeling the number $N_{X\wedge\overline{Y}}$ of counter-examples of this rule $X \to Y$.

In principle, such a rule is all the better when the number $N_{X\wedge\overline{Y}}$ of counter-examples to its formal validity is zero or sufficiently small. To do this, it should be noted that $\dfrac{\partial M_{GK}}{\partial n_{X\wedge\overline{Y}}} = -\dfrac{1}{\frac{n_X n_{\overline{Y}}}{n}}$ (cf. Eq. 2), which shows that M_{GK} decreases if the counter-examples $n_{X\wedge\overline{Y}}$ increase and all the more quickly as the $\frac{n_X n_{\overline{Y}}}{n}$ is relatively small. It would therefore be reasonable to compare the counter-examples $n_{X\wedge\overline{Y}}$ to the $\frac{n_X n_{\overline{Y}}}{n}$. For lack of space, we were unable to detail our technique and only present here a very abstract way. Therefore, consider M_{GK} (cf. Eq. (2) as the realization of a random variable $\mathcal{K}$ defined by $\mathcal{K} = 1 - \dfrac{nN_{X\wedge\overline{Y}}}{N_X N_{\overline{Y}}}$. The latter takes its values in $[0,1]$. Its values are therefore fractions of the integer values whose numerators are Poissonian, and we obtain:

$$P(\mathcal{K} \geqslant \alpha) = P\left(1 - \frac{nN_{X\wedge\overline{Y}}}{N_X N_{\overline{Y}}} \geqslant \alpha\right) = P\left(N_{X\wedge\overline{Y}} \leqslant \frac{N_X N_{\overline{Y}}}{n}(1-\alpha)\right) \tag{3}$$

However in the contingency, the random variable N_X (resp. $N_{\overline{Y}}$) takes the fixed value and equal to n_X (resp. $n_{\overline{Y}}$), which brings the (3) to the Eq. (4):

$$P(\mathcal{K} \geqslant \alpha) = P\left(N_{X\wedge\overline{Y}} \leqslant \frac{n_X n_{\overline{Y}}}{n}(1-\alpha)\right) \tag{4}$$

We then establish the formula of $N_{X\wedge\overline{Y}}$ under the assumption H_0 of independence. Let $U, Z \subseteq \mathcal{I}$ be chosen randomly and independently of the same cardinals of X and Y respectively. The modeling of $N_{X\wedge\overline{Y}}$ depends on the distribution of $|\phi(Z \cup \overline{U})|$ which follows a Poisson distribution of parameter $\frac{n_X n_{\overline{Y}}}{n}$ [13]. We center and reduce the $N_{X\wedge\overline{Y}}$ into the variable $Q(X,\overline{Y})$ called contingent observation, we get $Q(X,\overline{Y}) = \dfrac{N_{X\wedge\overline{Y}} - \frac{n_X n_{\overline{Y}}}{n}}{\sqrt{\frac{n_X n_{\overline{Y}}}{n}}} \sim \mathcal{N}(0,1)$. From where we get $P\left(N_{X\wedge\overline{Y}} \leqslant \frac{n_X n_{\overline{Y}}}{n}(1-\alpha)\right) = P\left(Q(X,\overline{Y})\sqrt{\frac{n_X n_{\overline{Y}}}{n}} + \frac{n_X n_{\overline{Y}}}{n} \leqslant \frac{n_X n_{\overline{Y}}}{n}(1-\alpha)\right)$. Let $q(X,\overline{Y}) = \dfrac{\frac{n_X n_{\overline{Y}}}{n}(1-\alpha) - \frac{n_X n_{\overline{Y}}}{n}}{\sqrt{\frac{n_X n_{\overline{Y}}}{n}}}$, contingent realization of $Q(X,\overline{Y})$. So,

$$\begin{aligned} P(\mathcal{K} \geqslant \alpha) = P\left(Q(X,\overline{Y}) \leqslant q(X,\overline{Y})\right) = \Phi(q(X,\overline{Y})) \\ = \frac{1}{\sqrt{2\pi}} \int_{-\infty}^{q(X,\overline{Y})} e^{-\frac{t^2}{2}}\,\mathrm{d}t, \end{aligned} \tag{5}$$

where Φ is the normal distribution function $\mathcal{N}(0,1)$. This result (Eq. (5)) is called M_{GK} **Gaussianized**. It will be used especially in the evaluation of approximate association rules but also in that of the exact ones. If we want $X \to Y$ to be likely to be significant, it is necessary that the number $N_{X\wedge\overline{Y}}$ of counterexamples is not greater than the corrective factor $\frac{n_X n_{\overline{Y}}}{n}(1-\alpha)$ and will be all the better as the probability $P\left(N_{X\wedge\overline{Y}} \leqslant \frac{n_X n_{\overline{Y}}}{n}(1-\alpha)\right)$ will be close to 1. More formally, once we have specified the degree of dependence $(P(Y'|X') - P(Y'))$ of the candidate association rule $X \to Y$ and the different thresholds ($0 < minsup \leqslant 1$ and $0 < \alpha \leqslant 1$) the proposed approach must generate the set:

$$\left\{X \to Y \text{ informative sur } \mathcal{B} \mid \begin{cases} (i)\ supp(X \cup Y) \geqslant minsup \\ (ii)\ N_{X\wedge\overline{Y}} \leqslant \frac{n_X n_{\overline{Y}}}{n}(1-\alpha) \end{cases}\right\}$$

This task will be carried out in two stages: (*i*) Extraction of all frequent itemsets on a context $\mathcal{B}$, (*ii*) Generation of all informative association rules of the type $X \to Y$ from these frequent itemsets whose number $N_{X\wedge\overline{Y}}$ of counter-examples is not greater than the corrective factor $\frac{n_X n_{\overline{Y}}}{n}(1-\alpha)$ for a α chosen in $]0,1]$.

4.1 Mining All Frequent Itemsets

From a context $\mathcal{B}$, this first phase consists in determining $\mathcal{G}_\mathcal{C}$, $\mathcal{FC}$ and $\mathcal{MC}$. Our main motivation lies in the absence of an autonomous algorithm to determine these three subsets. So, we propose GCM (GeneratorClosedMaximal), an autonomous algorithm allowing to collect these three subsets simultaneously. Close algorithm [15] partly solves this problem: it returns the closed ones while here we want to list all the frequent ones, whether they are generators, closed or maximal closed. We therefore modified Close by adding the concepts of maximal frequent and their generators. These two concepts can be derived from a frequent closed using the Definitions 2 and 4. In addition, we introduce an efficient technique to calculate the supports that the following Theorem 1 exposes.

Theorem 1. *The support of a k-nongenerator ($k \geqslant 3$) is a minimum support of its ($k-1$)-itemsets: if X is a k-nongenerator, then* $supp(X) = min\{supp(\widetilde{X}) | \widetilde{X} \subset X\}$.

Proof. Let X and Z two itemset of $\mathcal{I}$ such that $Z \subseteq X$. Since $Z \subseteq X$, we have $\phi(Z) \supseteq \phi(X) \Rightarrow supp(Z) \geqslant supp(X)$. If X is not generator, it exists $\widetilde{X} \subseteq X$ such that $supp(\widetilde{X}) = supp(X)$. However, $supp(Z)$ is minimal in $\mathcal{I}$, so $supp(Z) \leqslant supp(\widetilde{X})$. Finally, $supp(X) = supp(Z) = min\{supp(\widetilde{X}) | \widetilde{X} \subset X\}$. □

Thus, the support of a k-nongenerator ($k \geqslant 3$) can be derived from ($k-1$) subsets (proofs are omitted due to lack of space, we can consult [3,4]). From Table 1, we have $supp(ABC) = min(\{sup(AB), sup(AC), sup(BC)\}) = min\{2/6, 3/6, 4/6\} = 2/6$. This Theorem 1 is therefore very central: it avoids systematic access in a context made by existing approaches. GCM browses by level the search space where the enumeration follows the Theorems 2 and 3 below.

Corollary 1. *Let X a frequent itemset on formal context $\mathcal{B}$. The itemset X is a generator iff* $supp(X) \neq min\{supp(\widetilde{X}) | \widetilde{X} \subset X\}$.

Proof. Let X be a generator. Let $\widetilde{X}$ be a frequent itemset of length $k-1$ with minimum support and a subset of X. Then, $\widetilde{X} \subset X \Rightarrow \phi(\widetilde{X}) \supseteq \phi(X)$. If $\phi(\widetilde{X}) =$

$\phi(X)$, then $supp(\widetilde{X}) = supp(X)$ and X is not a generator. Moreover, it is not the element with the smallest support, whose closure is $\gamma(X)$. This concludes that $\phi(\widetilde{X}) \supseteq \phi(X)$ and hence, $supp(X) \neq min\{supp(\widetilde{X}) | \widetilde{X} \subset X\}$. On the other hand, if $supp(X) \neq min\{supp(\widetilde{X}) | \widetilde{X} \subset X\}$, the itemset X is then the smallest element of the closure $\gamma(X)$. Hence, X is a generator. □

Theorem 2 (Intuitive in [1]). *(1) All subsets of a frequent itemset are frequent. (2) All supersets of an infrequent itemset are infrequent.*

Proof. (1) Let $X, Y \subseteq \mathcal{I}$ such that $X \in \mathcal{F}$ and $Y \subseteq X$. Since $Y \subseteq X$, we have (by antimonotonicity of support) $\phi(Y) \supseteq \phi(X) \Rightarrow supp(Y) \geqslant supp(X) \geqslant minsup \Rightarrow Y \in \mathcal{F}$. (2) Let $X, Y \subseteq \mathcal{I}$ such that $X \notin \mathcal{F}$ and $Y \supseteq X$. Since $Y \supseteq X$, we have $\phi(Y) \subseteq \phi(X) \Rightarrow supp(Y) \leqslant supp(X) \leqslant minsup \Rightarrow Y \notin \mathcal{F}$. □

Theorem 3. *Given an itemset $X \subseteq \mathcal{I}$. If X is generator, then $\forall Y \subseteq X$ is also generator. If X is not generator, then Z is not generator, $\forall Z \supseteq X$.*

Proof. Let $X, Z \subseteq \mathcal{I}$ such that $X \subseteq Z$. It exists $Y \subseteq \mathcal{I}$ such that $X \cap Y = \emptyset$ and $Z = X \cup Y$. Consider X is not generator, it admits then a proper subset T which is equivalent to $T \subseteq X$ and $T \approx X$ implies that $T \cup Y \approx X \cup Y$. By hypothesis, $X \cap Y = \emptyset$, so $T \cup Y \subseteq X \cup Y$, The itemset Z is equivalent to a proper subset $T \cup Y$, so it is not generator. The contrapose gives the result. □

These results will be synthesized in the Algorithm 1 below. The GCM algo-

Algorithm 1. GCM

Require: A formal context $\mathcal{B}$, A minimum support threshold $minsup \in]0, 1]$.
Ensure: $\mathcal{G}_\mathcal{C}$ all frequent generators, $\mathcal{FC}$ all frequent closed, $\mathcal{MC}$ all maximal closed.
1: $\mathcal{FCC}_1$.GENERATORS $\leftarrow$ {1-itemsts}
2: **for all** $(k \leftarrow 1; \mathcal{FCC}_k.\text{GENERATORS} \neq \emptyset; k++)$ **do**
3: $\quad\mathcal{FCC}_k.closure \leftarrow \emptyset$; $\mathcal{FCC}_k.support \leftarrow 0$;
4: $\quad\mathcal{FCC}_k \leftarrow$ GENERATECLOSURES($\mathcal{FCC}_k$)
5: $\quad$**for all** (candidate itemsets $c \in \mathcal{FCC}_k$) **do**
6: $\quad\quad$**if** $(supp(c) \geqslant minsup)$ **then**
7: $\quad\quad\quad\mathcal{FC}_k \leftarrow \mathcal{FC}_k \cup \{c\}$
8: $\quad\quad$**end if**
9: $\quad$**end for**
10: $\quad\mathcal{FCC}_{k+1} \leftarrow$ GENERATEGENERATORS($\mathcal{FC}_k$)
11: $\quad\mathcal{FCC}_{k+1} \leftarrow$ GENERATEMAXIMAL($\mathcal{FC}_k$)
12: **end for**
13: $\mathcal{FC} \leftarrow \bigcup_{j=1}^{k-1}\{\mathcal{FC}_j.\text{CLOSURE}, \mathcal{FC}_j.\text{support}\}$
14: **return** $\mathcal{FC}$

rithm takes as input a context $\mathcal{B}$ and a minimum support *minsup*. It simultaneously returns three subsets $\mathcal{G}_\mathcal{C}$, $\mathcal{FC}$ and $\mathcal{MC}$ in three recursive procedures. This choice of decomposition of the algorithms is motivated by the parallelization of these three procedures during the implementation to get these three types of frequent itemsets. Due to lack of space, we could not detail this Algorithm 1 and only present a very global way. Thus, the procedure GENERATECLOSURES (line 4) takes as input $\mathcal{FCC}_k$ the k-frequent closed candidates, and generates the

Scan $\mathcal{B}$ ⟶

$\mathcal{FCC}_1$		supp
A	AC	3/6
B	BE	5/6
C	C	5/6
D	ACD	min(3/6,1/6,1/6)=1/6
E	BE	5/6

Pruning the infrequent ⟶

$\mathcal{G}_C$	$\mathcal{FC}$	$\mathcal{MC}$	supp
A	AC	-	3/6
B	BE	-	5/6
C	C	-	5/6
E	BE	-	5/6

Scan $\mathcal{B}$ ⟶

$\mathcal{FCC}_2$		supp
AB	ABCE	min(2/6,2/6,2/6,4/6)=2/6
AE	ABCE	min(2/6,2/6,2/6,4/6)=2/6
BC	BCE	min(4/6,5/6,4/6)=4/6
CE	BCE	min(4/6,5/6,4/6)=4/6

Pruning infr. ⟶

$\mathcal{G}_C$	$\mathcal{FC}$	$\mathcal{MC}$	supp
AB	ABCE	ABCE	2/6
AE	ABCE	ABCE	2/6
BC	BCE	-	4/6
CE	BCE	-	4/6

Fig. 1. Example of execution of GCM on context $\mathcal{B}$ with a $minsup = 2/6$

frequent closed ones. The procedure GenerateGenerators (line 10) takes as input $\mathcal{FC}_k$ the k-frequent closed itemsets, and generates all frequent generators. The GenerateMaximal procedure (line 11) also takes $\mathcal{FC}_k$ as input, and generates all maximal frequent itemsets. Figure 1 shows its example of execution with a small context from Table 1 and $minsup = 2/6$. The set $\mathcal{FCC}_1$ initialized with the list of all 1-itemsets. The 1-itemset D is pruned from $\mathcal{FCC}_1$ to $\mathcal{FC}$ because it is not frequent. The 1-itemset C is also own closure, it's added in $\mathcal{FC}$. Six candidates AB, AC, AE, BC, BE and CE are created. Thus, AC and BE are closures of A and, B and E, so added to $\mathcal{FC}$. ABE is created but it's pruned because its subset $BE \notin \mathcal{FCC}_2$. BCE is closure of BC and CE, so added to $\mathcal{FC}$. BC and CE are then generators, so added in $\mathcal{G}_C$. Finally, $ABCE$ is both closed and maximal of AB and AE, so it is added both in $\mathcal{FC}$ and $\mathcal{MC}$.

4.2 Mining All Informative Association Rules

From three subsets $\mathcal{G}_C$, $\mathcal{FC}$ and $\mathcal{MC}$, the second phase of our approach allows us to extract the set of all informative association rules of the form $X \to Y$ where $X \in \mathcal{G}_C$ and $Y \in \mathcal{FC}$ (or $\mathcal{MC}$). During the selection phase of association rules, many uninteresting and redundant rules can be generated. Fortunately, using Property 6, the uninteresting association rules are systematically pruned. It remains to study in the following the redundant association rules. For this, we rely on a new concept called *bases of rules*. We propose a new concept in which we define the four informative bases IBE^+, IBA^+, IBE^- and IBA^-.

From each base, we first identify the degree of dependence of the itemsets, and then measure its intensity using the measure M_{GK}. For any rule $X \to Y$, the degree of dependence is obtained by measuring the difference in confidence $P(Y'|X')$ to the probability $P(Y')$, i.e. $P(Y'|X') - P(Y')$. If the difference is positive (i.e. $P(Y'|X') > P(Y')$), then Y is positively dependent on X, this means that $X \to Y$ is interesting rule. Otherwise, $X \to Y$ is not interesting because we have more counter-examples than examples. In this case, the negative rule $X \to \overline{Y}$ which could be interesting. This avoids the independence of 8 rules (total number) $X \to Y$, $Y \to X$, $\overline{X} \to \overline{Y}$, $\overline{Y} \to \overline{X}$, $X \to \overline{Y}$, $\overline{X} \to Y$, $\overline{Y} \to X$ and $Y \to \overline{X}$, and leads the algorithm into two recursives substeps. Indeed, if X and Y are positively dependent, then these are the four rules $X \to Y$, $\overline{X} \to \overline{Y}$, $Y \to X$ and $\overline{Y} \to \overline{X}$ which will be evaluated. Otherwise, these are the four opposite rules $X \to \overline{Y}$, $\overline{X} \to Y$, $Y \to \overline{X}$ and $\overline{Y} \to X$ which will be evaluated.

As we demonstrated in [4], we only retain 4/8 rules $X \to Y$, $\overline{X} \to \overline{Y}$, $X \to \overline{Y}$ and $\overline{X} \to Y$, the other four rules are semantically redundant. Among these four retained, we study only two $X \to Y$ and $X \to \overline{Y}$ because $\overline{X} \to \overline{Y}$ (resp. $\overline{X} \to Y$) can be derived from $X \to Y$ (resp. $X \to \overline{Y}$) [4]. This gives a 75% reduction of the search space. Based on two rules, we then formalize our four informative bases. The first concerns a base of positive exact association rules. The similar approaches has been developed in [2,6]. However, these approaches are not informative. Thus, we propose the new base IBE^+ which selects the premise (resp. consequent) in $\mathcal{G}_\mathcal{C}$ set of generators (resp. $\mathcal{FC}$ set of frequent closed).

Definition 5. *Let $\mathcal{FC}$ be the set of all frequent closed and, for each frequent closed itemset $\mathcal{C}$, $\mathcal{G}_\mathcal{C}$ denotes the set of generators of closed $\mathcal{C}$, we have:*

$$IBE^+ = \{G \to \mathcal{C}\backslash G \mid G \in \mathcal{G}_\mathcal{C},\ \mathcal{C} \in \mathcal{FC},\ G \neq \mathcal{C}\} \tag{6}$$

From Table 1, finded that $A \subset AC$ and $\gamma(A) = \gamma(AC)$ implies that $A \to C$ is candidate. We recall, if $P(Y'|X') > P(Y')$ then, because $P(Y'|X') = 1 \Leftrightarrow P(Y'|X') - P(Y') = 1 - P(Y') \Leftrightarrow \frac{1-P(Y')}{1-P(Y')} = 1 \Leftrightarrow M_{GK}(X \to Y) = 1$. Therefore, $P(C'|A') = \frac{|\phi(A \cup C)|}{|\phi(A)|} = \frac{|\phi(A)|}{|\phi(A)|} = 1 \Leftrightarrow M_{GK}(A \to C) = 1$, hence $A \to C \in IBE^+$.

Like any (informative) basis, the IBE^+ basis is a minimal. In order to derive the other informative association rules, we propose the Theorem 4 below.

Theorem 4. *(i) All valid positive exact rules and their supports can be derived from the IBE^+ basis. (ii) All rules in the IBE^+ are non-redundant exact rules.*

Proof. (*i*) Let $r_1 : X_1 \to Y_1\backslash X_1$ be a positive exact rule between two frequent itemsets with $X_1 \subset Y_1$. Since $M_{GK}(r_1) = 1$, we have $supp(X_1) = supp(Y_1)$. By Property 5, we derived that $supp(\gamma(X_1)) = supp(\gamma(Y_1)) \Rightarrow \gamma(X_1) = \gamma(Y_1) = \mathcal{C}$. The itemset $\mathcal{C}$ is a frequent closed itemset (i.e. $\mathcal{C} \in \mathcal{FC}$) and, Obviously, there exists a rule $r_2 : G \to \mathcal{C}\backslash G \in IBE^+$ such that G is a generator of $\mathcal{C}$ for which $G \subseteq X_1$ and $G \subseteq Y_1$. We show that the rule r_1 and its supports can be derived from the rule r_2 and its supports. From $\gamma(X_1) = \gamma(Y_1) = \mathcal{C}$, we deduce that $supp(r_1) = supp(\gamma(X_1)) = supp(\gamma(Y_1)) = supp(\mathcal{C}) = supp(r_2)$. Since $G \subseteq X_1 \subset Y_1 \subseteq \mathcal{C}$, then the rule r_1 can be derived from the rule r_2.

(*ii*) Let $r_2 : G \to \mathcal{C}\backslash G \in IBE^+$. According to Definition 5, we have $G \in \mathcal{G}_\mathcal{C}$ and $\mathcal{C} \in \mathcal{FC}$. We demonstrate that there is no other rule $r_3 : X_3 \to Y_3\backslash X_3 \in IBE^+$ such as $supp(r_3) = supp(r_2)$, $M_{GK}(r_3) = M_{GK}(r_2)$, $X_3 \subseteq G$ and $\mathcal{C} \subseteq Y_3$. If $X_3 \subseteq G$ then, according to Definition 2, we have $\gamma(X_3) \subseteq \gamma(G) = \mathcal{C} \Rightarrow X_3 \notin \mathcal{G}_\mathcal{C}$ and then $r_3 \notin IBE^+$. If $\mathcal{C} \subseteq Y_3$, we have $\mathcal{C} = \gamma(\mathcal{C}) = \gamma(G) \subset Y_3 = \gamma(Y_3)$. From Definition 2, we deduce that $G \notin \mathcal{G}_{Y_3}$ and conclude that $r_3 \notin IBE^+$. □

The second base is the base of positive approximate rules (i.e. $0 < M_{GK}(X \rightarrow Y) < 1$). The existing bases [2,6] using the pseudo-closed [2,9,15] are not informative. Thus, we propose the new informative base IBA^+, which selects the premise in $\mathcal{G}_\mathcal{C}$ and the conclusions in other $\mathcal{FC}$ containing this current closed F.

Definition 6. *Let $\mathcal{FC}$ the set of frequent closed and, for each frequent closed $\mathcal{C}$, $\mathcal{G}_\mathcal{C}$ indicates the set of generators of $\mathcal{C}$. Consider $0 < \alpha \leqslant 1$, we have:*

$$IBA^+ = \{G \rightarrow \mathcal{C}\backslash G | (G, \mathcal{C}) \in \mathcal{G}_{\gamma(G)} \times \mathcal{FC}, \gamma(G) \subset \mathcal{C}, \frac{n_G n_{\overline{\mathcal{C}}}}{n}(1-\alpha) \geqslant N_{G\overline{\mathcal{C}}}\} \quad (7)$$

Since $BE \subset ABCE$, then $B \rightarrow ACE$ and $E \rightarrow ABC$ are candidates. Here, $n = 6$, $n_B = n_E = 5$, $n_{\overline{ACE}} = n_{\overline{ABE}} = 4$, $n_{B\overline{ACE}} = n_{E\overline{ACE}} = 5 - 2 = 3$, and $\sqrt{\frac{n_E n_{\overline{ABC}}}{n}} = 1.82$. Consider $\alpha = 1\%$, we have $\frac{n_B n_{\overline{ACE}}}{n}(1-\alpha) = \frac{n_E n_{\overline{ABC}}}{n}(1-\alpha) = 3.3 > 3 = n_{B\overline{ACE}}$ and $P\left(N_{B\wedge\overline{ACE}} \leqslant \frac{n_B n_{ACE}}{n}(1-\alpha)\right) = 0.49 \Rightarrow \{B \rightarrow ACE, E \rightarrow ABC\} \in IBA^+$, i.e. the association rules $B \rightarrow ACE$ and $E \rightarrow ABC$ are valid (99% likely) in IBA^+ basis with probability 0.49.

Lemma 1. *For all $X, Y, T, Z \subseteq \mathcal{I}$, such that X favors Y and Z favors T, and $X \cap Y = Z \cap T = \emptyset$, and $X \subset Z \subseteq \gamma(X)$, and $Y \subset T \subseteq \gamma(Y)$. Then, $supp(X \cup Y) = supp(Z \cup T)$ and $M_{GK}(X \rightarrow Y) = M_{GK}(Z \rightarrow T)$.*

Proof. $\forall X, Y, T, Z \subseteq \mathcal{I}$, $supp(X \cup Y) = \frac{|\phi(X \cup Y)|}{|\mathcal{T}|} = \frac{|\phi(X) \cap \phi(Y)|}{|\mathcal{T}|}$ and $supp(Z \cup T) = \frac{|\phi(X \cup T)|}{|\mathcal{T}|} = \frac{|\phi(Z) \cap \phi(T)|}{|\mathcal{T}|}$. Since $X \subset Z \subseteq \gamma(X)$ and $Y \subset T \subseteq \gamma(Y)$, we have $supp(X) = supp(Z)$ and $supp(Y) = supp(T)$ implies $supp(X \cup Y) = supp(Z \cup T)$. From $supp(X) = supp(Z)$ and $supp(Y) = supp(T)$, we have $P(Y'|X') = P(T'|Z') \Leftrightarrow P(Y'|X') - P(Y') = P(T'|Z') - P(Y')$ equivalent to $\frac{P(Y'|X') - P(Y')}{1 - P(Y')} = \frac{P(T'|Z') - P(T')}{1 - P(T')} \Leftrightarrow M_{GK}(X \rightarrow Y) = M_{GK}(Z \rightarrow T)$. □

Theorem 5 below is proposed in order to derive the other valid rules.

Theorem 5. *(i) All valid positive approximate association rules, their supports and M_{GK}, can be derived from the rules of IBA^+. (ii) All association rules in the IBA^+ basis are non-redudant positive approximate association rules.*

Proof. (*i*) Let $r_1 : X_1 \rightarrow Y_1 \backslash X_1$ be a valid positive approximate rule between two frequent itemsts with $X_1 \subset Y_1$. Since $M_{GK}(r_1) < 1$, we also have $\gamma(X_1) \subset \gamma(Y_1)$. For any frequent itemsets X_1 and Y_1, there is a generator G_1 such that $G_1 \subset X_1 \subseteq \gamma(X_1) = \gamma(G_1)$ and a generator G_2 such that $G_2 \subset Y_1 \subseteq \gamma(Y_1) = \gamma(G_2)$. Since $X_1 \subset Y_1$, we have $X_1 \subseteq \gamma(G_1) \subset Y_1 \subseteq \gamma(G_2)$ and the rule $r_2 : G_1 \rightarrow (\gamma(G_2)) \backslash G_1 \in IBA^+$. We show that the rule r_1 and its support can be derived from the rule r_2, its support and its M_{GK}. Since $G_1 \subset X_1 \subseteq \gamma(X_1) = \gamma(G_1)$ and $G_2 \subset Y_1 \subseteq \gamma(Y_1) = \gamma(G_2)$, we have (cf. Lemma 1), $supp(G_1) = supp(X_1)$ and $supp(G_2) = supp(Y_1) = supp(\gamma(G_2))$. According to Lemma 1, we have $supp(X_1 \cup Y_1) = supp(G_1 \cup \gamma(G_2))$ (i.e. $supp(r_1) = supp(r_2)$) and we thus deduce that $M_{GK}(X_1 \rightarrow Y_1) = M_{GK}(G_1 \rightarrow \gamma(G_2))$ (i.e. $M_{GK}(r_1) = M_{GK}(r_2)$).

(*ii*) Let $r_2 : G \rightarrow \mathcal{C}\backslash G \in IBA^+$. According to Definition 6, we have $\mathcal{C} \in \mathcal{FC}$ and $G \in \mathcal{G}_C$ such as $C \subset \mathcal{C}$. We demonstrate that there is no other rule $r_3 : X_3 \rightarrow Y_3\backslash X_3 \in IBA^+$ such as $supp(r_3) = supp(r_2)$, $M_{GK}(r_3) = M_{GK}(r_2)$, $X_3 \subseteq G$ and $\mathcal{C} \subseteq Y_3$. If $X_3 \subseteq G$ then, by Definition 2, we have $\gamma(X_3) \subset \gamma(G) = C$ and then $X_3 \notin \mathcal{G}_C$. We deduce that $supp(X_3) > supp(G)$ and then $M_{GK}(r_3) < M_{GK}(r_2)$. If $\mathcal{C} \subseteq Y_3$, we have (by Definition 1) $\mathcal{C} = \gamma(\mathcal{C}) \subset Y_3 = \gamma(Y_3)$. We deduce that $supp(\mathcal{C}) > supp(Y_3)$ and conclude that $M_{GK}(r_2) > M_{GK}(r_3)$. □

The third model concerns a base of negative exact association rules (i.e. $M_{GK}(X \rightarrow \overline{Y}) = 1$). A reference approach [6] for this is not appropriate: it selects a premise from to maximal elements which is not adapted of minimality concept, so it's not informative. Thus, we propose an informative base IBE^- which selects a premise in generator of a maximal frequent itemset $\mathcal{M} \in \mathcal{MC}$ and a consequent from to dualization in $\mathcal{I}$ of this maximal $\mathcal{M}$ (i.e. $\mathcal{I}\backslash\mathcal{M}$).

Definition 7. *Given* $\mathcal{MC}$ *the set of maximal frequent itemset and, for each* $\mathcal{M} \in \mathcal{MC}$, $\mathcal{G}_{\mathcal{M}}$ *denotes the set of generators of* $\mathcal{M}$*, we have:*

$$IBE^- = \{G \rightarrow \{\overline{y}\} \mid G \in \mathcal{G}_{\mathcal{M}},\ \mathcal{M} \in \mathcal{MC},\ y \in \mathcal{I}\backslash\mathcal{M}\} \tag{8}$$

For example from Table 1 if $minsup = 0.2$, we finded $\mathcal{MC} = \{ABCE\}$ and $\mathcal{I}\backslash\mathcal{M} = \{\overline{ABCE}\} = \{D\}$. We see that AB and AE are generators of $ABCE$ implies that $AB \rightarrow \overline{D}$ and $AE \rightarrow \overline{D}$ are candidates. Indeed, $supp(AB\overline{D}) = supp(AB) - supp(ABD) = 2/6 - 0 \Rightarrow P(\overline{D'}|\{AB\}') = \frac{2/6}{2/6} = 1$ equivalent to $M_{GK}(AB \rightarrow \overline{D}) = 1 \Rightarrow AB \rightarrow \overline{D} \in IBE^-$. Likewise for rule $AE \rightarrow \overline{D}$.

Corollary 2. *For all* $X, Y \subseteq \mathcal{I}$: $supp(X \cup Y) = 0 \Leftrightarrow M_{GK}(X \rightarrow \overline{Y}) = 1$.

Proof. Since $supp(X \cup Y) = 0$, we have $|\phi(X \cup Y)| = 0$ (because $|\phi(X)| \neq 0$) equivalent to $P(Y'|X') = 0 \Leftrightarrow P(\overline{Y}|X) = 1$ equivalent to $P(\overline{Y}|X) - P(\overline{Y}) = 1 - P(\overline{Y})$ equivalent to $\frac{P(\overline{Y}|X) - P(\overline{Y})}{1 - P(\overline{Y})} = 1$ equivalent to $M_{GK}(X \rightarrow \overline{Y}) = 1$ □

Theorem 6. *(i) All valid negative exact association rules, their supports and* M_{GK}*, can be derived from the rules of the* IBE^- *basis. (ii) All association rules in the* IBE^- *basis are non-redudant negative exact association rules.*

Proof. (*i*) Let $r_1 : X_1 \rightarrow \overline{Y}_1\backslash X_1$ be a valid negative exact rule between two frequent itemsts with $X_1 \subset \overline{Y_1} \subseteq \mathcal{M}$ (i.e. $Y_1 = \mathcal{I}\backslash\mathcal{M}$), where $\mathcal{M}$ is a frequent maximal itemset. Since $M_{GK}(r_1) = 1$, we have, according to Corollary 2, $supp(X_1 \cup Y_1) = 0 \Rightarrow supp(X_1 \cup \overline{Y}_1) = supp(X_1) = supp(\overline{Y_1})$. By Property 5, we derived that $supp(\gamma(X_1 \cup \overline{Y_1})) = supp(\gamma(X_1)) = supp(\gamma(\overline{Y_1})) \Rightarrow \gamma(X_1 \cup \overline{Y}_1) = \gamma(X_1) = \gamma(\overline{Y_1}) = \mathcal{M}$ (*a*). Obviously, there exists a rule $r_2 : G \rightarrow \overline{y}\backslash G \in IBE^+$ such that G is a generator of $\mathcal{M}$ for which $G \subseteq X_1$ and $G \subseteq \overline{Y_1}$, and thus, according to Definition 7, $G \subseteq \overline{y}$. We show that the rule r_1 and its supports can be derived from the rule r_2 and its supports. Since $G \rightarrow \overline{y}\backslash G \in IBE^+$, we have, according to Corollary 2, $supp(G \cup \overline{y}) = supp(G)$. By Property 5, we deduced that $supp(\gamma(G \cup \overline{y})) = supp(\gamma(G)) = supp(\gamma(\overline{y})) \Rightarrow \gamma(G \cup \overline{y}) = \gamma(G) = \gamma(\overline{y}) = \mathcal{M}$ (*a'*).

From (a) and (a'), we have $\gamma(G\cup\overline{y}) = \gamma(X_1\cup\overline{Y_1}) \Rightarrow supp(G\cup\overline{y}) = supp(X_1\cup\overline{Y_1})$. Since $G \subseteq X_1 \subset \overline{Y_1} \subset \overline{y} \subseteq \gamma(G) = \mathcal{M}$, we have $supp(G) = supp(X_1) = supp(\overline{Y_1}) = supp(\overline{y}) = supp(\mathcal{M})$ and thus $M_{GK}(X_1 \to \overline{Y_1}) = M_{GK}(G \to \overline{y})$.

(ii) Let $r_2 : G \to \overline{y}\backslash G \in IBE^-$ be a valid negative exact rule. According to Definition 7, we have $G \in \mathcal{G}_{\mathcal{M}}$ and $y \in \mathcal{I}\backslash\mathcal{M}$. We demonstrate that there is no other rule $r_3 : X_3 \to \overline{Y}_3\backslash X_3 \in IBE^-$ such as $supp(r_3) = supp(r_2)$, $M_{GK}(r_3) = M_{GK}(r_2)$, $X_3 \subseteq G$ and $\overline{y} \subseteq \overline{Y_3}$. If $X_3 \subseteq G$ then, according to Definition 2, we have $\gamma(X_3) \subseteq \gamma(G) \subset \gamma(\overline{y}) = \mathcal{M} \Rightarrow X_3 \notin \mathcal{G}_{\mathcal{M}}$ and then $r_3 \notin IBE^-$. If $\overline{y} \subseteq \overline{Y_3}$ then, according to Definition 1, we have $\gamma(G) \subset \gamma(\overline{y}) \subseteq \gamma(\overline{Y_3}) = \mathcal{M}$. From Definition 2, we deduce that $G \notin \mathcal{G}_{\overline{Y}_3}$ and conclude that $r_3 \notin IBE^-$. □

The fourth model address on negative approximate association rules (i.e. $M_{GK}(X \to \overline{Y}) < 1$). A similar approach is the one defined in [6]. However, this approach uses the pseudo-closed [2,15] which is not informative. To tackle this notable limitation, we propose the new informative base IBA^- which selects both premise and conclusion in generator of incomparable closed itemsets.

Definition 8. *Let $\mathcal{FC}$ be the set of frequent closed itemsets and, for each frequent closed $\mathcal{C}$, $\mathcal{G}_{\mathcal{C}}$ is the set of generators of $\mathcal{C}$. Consider $0 < \alpha \leqslant 1$, we have:*

$$IBA^- = \{G \to \overline{g} | (G, g) \in \mathcal{G}_{\gamma(G)} \times \mathcal{G}_{\gamma(g)}, \gamma(G) \subsetneq \gamma(g), \frac{n_G n_{\overline{g}}}{n}(1-\alpha) \geqslant N_{G\overline{g}}\} \quad (9)$$

For example from Table 1 if $minsup = 0.2$, we have $[AC] = \{A, AC\}$ and $[BE] = \{B, E, BE\}$. We see that $AC \not\subseteq BE$ and mutually disfavors (i.e. AC favors $\overline{BE}$), so $A \to \overline{B}$ and $A \to \overline{E}$ are candidates. Here, $n = 6$, $n_A = 3$, $n_B = n_E = 5$, $n_{AB} = n_{AE} = 2$ and $\sqrt{\frac{n_A n_B}{n}} = 1.58$. Consider $\alpha = 1\%$, we have $\frac{n_A n_B}{n}(1-\alpha) = \frac{n_A n_E}{n}(1-\alpha) = 2.5 > 2 = n_{AB}$ and $P\left(N_{A\wedge B} \leqslant \frac{n_A n_B}{n}(1-\alpha)\right) = 0.49 \Rightarrow \{A \to \overline{B}, A \to \overline{E}\} \in IBA^-$, i.e. the association rules $A \to \overline{B}$ and $A \to \overline{E}$ are valid (99% likely) in IBA^- basis with probability 0.49.

Lemma 2. *$\forall X, Y, T, Z \subseteq \mathcal{I}$ such that X disfavors Y, Z disfavors T, $Z \subseteq \gamma(X)$, $T \subseteq \gamma(Y)$: (i) $supp(X \cup Y) = supp(Z \cup T)$; (ii) $M_{GK}(X \to \overline{Y}) = M_{GK}(Z \to \overline{T})$.*

Proof. (i) Because $Z \subseteq \gamma(X)$ and $T \subseteq \gamma(Y)$, we have $supp(X) = supp(Z)$ and $supp(Y) = supp(T)$. Thus, $supp(X \cup Y) = \frac{|\phi(X\cup Y)|}{|\mathcal{T}|} = \frac{|\phi(X)\cap\phi(Y)|}{|\mathcal{T}|} = \frac{|\phi(Z)\cap\phi(T)|}{|\mathcal{T}|} = \frac{|\phi(Z\cup T)|}{|\mathcal{T}|} = supp(Z \cup T)$. (ii) Since $supp(X) = supp(Z)$, $supp(Y) = supp(T)$ and $supp(X \cup Y) = supp(Z \cup T)$, we have $P(Y'|X') = P(T'|Z') \Leftrightarrow P(\overline{Y}|X) = P(\overline{T}|Z)$ equivalent to $P(\overline{Y}|X) - P(\overline{Y}) = P(\overline{T}|Z) - P(\overline{Y})$ equivalent to $\frac{P(\overline{Y}|X)-P(\overline{Y})}{1-P(\overline{Y})} = \frac{P(\overline{T}|Z)-P(\overline{T})}{1-P(\overline{T})}$, hence $M_{GK}(X \to \overline{Y}) = M_{GK}(Z \to \overline{T})$. □

Theorem 7. *(i) All valid negative approximate association rules, their supports and M_{GK}, can be derived from the rules of IBA^-. (ii) All association rules in the IBA^- basis are non-redudant negative approximate association rules.*

Proof. (i) Let $r_1 : X_1 \to \overline{Y_1}\backslash X_1$ be a valid negative approximate rule between two frequent itemsts with $X_1 \subset \overline{Y_1}$. Since $0 < M_{GK}(r_1) < 1$, we also have

$\gamma(X_1) \subset \gamma(\overline{Y_1})$. For any frequent itemsets X_1 and Y_1, there is a generator G_1 such that $G_1 \subset X_1 \subseteq \gamma(X_1) = \gamma(G_1)$ and a generator G_2 such that $G_2 \subset Y_1 \subseteq \gamma(Y_1) = \gamma(G_2)$. Since $X_1 \subset \overline{Y_1}$, we have $X_1 \subseteq \gamma(G_1) \subset \overline{Y_1} \subset \overline{G_2} \subseteq \gamma(\overline{Y_1}) = \gamma(\overline{G_2})$ and the rule $r_2 : G_1 \rightarrow \overline{G_2} \backslash G_1 \in IBA^-$. We show that the rule r_1 and its support can be derived from the rule r_2, its support and its M_{GK}. Since $G_1 \subset X_1 \subseteq \gamma(G_1)$ and $G_2 \subset Y_1 \subseteq \gamma(G_2)$, we have, according to Lemma 2, $supp(X_1 \cup Y_1) = supp(G_1 \cup G_2)$ implies $|\phi(X_1) \cap \phi(Y_1)| = |\phi(G_1) \cap \phi(G_2)|$ (a). Since $G_1 \subset X_1 \subseteq \gamma(G_1) \subset \overline{Y_1} \subset \overline{G_2} \subseteq \gamma(\overline{Y_1})$, we have $supp(G_1) = supp(X_1) = supp(\gamma(G_1)) = supp(\overline{Y_1}) = supp(\overline{G_2})$. Therefore, we have from (a), $|\phi(X_1) \cap \phi(\overline{Y_1})| = |\phi(G_1) \cap \phi(\overline{G_2})| \Leftrightarrow |\phi(X_1 \cup \overline{Y_1})| = |\phi(G_1 \cup \overline{G_2})|$ implies $supp(X_1 \cup \overline{Y_1}) = supp(G_1 \cup \overline{G_2})$, and thus $M_{GK}(X_1 \rightarrow \overline{Y_1}) = M_{GK}(G_1 \rightarrow \overline{G_2})$.

(*ii*) Let $r_2 : G \rightarrow \overline{g} \backslash G \in IBA^-$. According to Definition 8, we have $G \in \mathcal{G}_C$ and $g \in \mathcal{G}_C$ and $C \subsetneq \mathcal{C}$. We demonstrate that there is no other rule $r_3 : X_3 \rightarrow \overline{Y_3} \backslash X_3 \in IBA^-$ such that $supp(r_3) = supp(r_2)$, $M_{GK}(r_3) = M_{GK}(r_2)$, $X_3 \subset G$ and $Y_3 \subset g$ (i.e. $\overline{Y_3} \supset \overline{g}$). If $X_3 \subset G$ then, according to Definition 2, we have $\gamma(X_3) \subset \gamma(G) = C$ and then $X_3 \notin \mathcal{G}_C$. We deduce that $supp(X_3) > supp(G)$ and then $M_{GK}(r_3) < M_{GK}(r_2)$. If $\overline{g} \subset \overline{Y_3}$, we have $\gamma(\overline{g}) \subset \gamma(\overline{Y_3})$. We deduce that $supp(\overline{g}) > supp(\overline{Y_3})$ and conclude that $M_{GK}(r_2) > M_{GK}(r_3)$. □

4.3 NONRED Algorithm

NonRed algorithm is composed of four algorithms (Algorithm 1, Algorithm 2, Algorithm 3 and Algorithm 4). The principal procedure (Algorithm 2) takes as input the minimal generators $\mathcal{G}_C$, the frequent closed $\mathcal{FC}$, the maximal frequent itemsets $\mathcal{MC}$ and, the minimum thresholds $minsup$ and α. It returns all informative positive and negative association rules containing exact and approximate rules, denoted $\mathcal{IB}$. Its efficiency mainly stems from the economic calculation of the M_{GK} of all candidate rules as explained by the following Theorem 8.

Theorem 8 (Pruning space). *Let* $X_1 \rightarrow Y \backslash X_1$ *and* $X_2 \rightarrow Y \backslash X_2$ *be two rules, we have:* $X_2 \subseteq X_1 \subseteq Y \Rightarrow M_{GK}(X_2 \rightarrow Y \backslash X_2) \leqslant M_{GK}(X_1 \rightarrow Y \backslash X_1)$.

Proof. By antimonotonicity of support, we have $X_2 \subseteq X_1 \Rightarrow supp(X_1) \leqslant supp(X_2)$ (i.e. $|\phi(X_1)| \leqslant |\phi(X_2)|$). Since $X_2 \subseteq X_1 \subseteq Y$, we have $P(Y'|X_1') = \frac{|\phi(X_1 \cup Y)|}{|\phi(X_1)|} = \frac{|\phi(X_1) \cap \phi(Y)|}{|\phi(X_1)|} = \frac{|\phi(Y)|}{|\phi(X_1)|} \geqslant \frac{|\phi(Y)|}{|\phi(X_2)|} = P(Y'|X_2)$. From $P(Y'|X_2') \leqslant P(Y'|X_1')$, we have $P(Y'|X_2') - P(Y') \leqslant P(Y'|X_1') - P(Y') \Leftrightarrow \frac{P(Y'|X_2') - P(Y')}{1 - P(Y')} \leqslant \frac{P(Y'|X_1') - P(Y')}{1 - P(Y')}$ equivalent to $M_{GK}(X_2 \rightarrow Y \backslash X_2) \leqslant M_{GK}(X_1 \rightarrow Y \backslash X_1)$. □

Theorem 8 infers that, for all $\widetilde{X} \subseteq X$, if $X \rightarrow Y \backslash X$ does not valid, neitheir does $\widetilde{X} \rightarrow Y \backslash \widetilde{X}$. And, if $X \rightarrow \overline{Y} \backslash X$ is not valid, then $\widetilde{X} \rightarrow \overline{Y} \backslash \widetilde{X}$ will not be. For example, if $A \rightarrow BCD$ is valid, then $AB \rightarrow CD$ and $ABC \rightarrow D$ are valid. If $A \rightarrow \overline{BCD}$ is not valid, then $AB \rightarrow \overline{CD}$ and $ABC \rightarrow \overline{D}$ will not be valid.

These optimizations are summarized in Algorithm 2. The latter consists of two main parts. The first part (lines 2–16) generates the IBE^+ basis the IBA^+ basis. The second part (lines 17–32) corresponds to the generation of IBE^-

Algorithm 2. NonRedBase

```
Require: $\mathcal{G}_C$, $\mathcal{FC}$, $\mathcal{MC}$, minimum threshold $minsup$ and $\alpha$.
Ensure: Base, a set of Informative basis of association rules.
1: Base = $\emptyset$;
2: for all ($C \in \mathcal{FC}$) do
3:    for all ($G \in \mathcal{G}_C$) do
4:       if ($P(C'|G') > P(C')$) then
5:          if ($\gamma(G) = C$) then
6:             if ($G \neq \gamma(G)$ && $supp(G \cup C) \geq minsup$) then
7:                Base ← Base ∪ $\{G \to C \backslash G\}$;            /* Positive Exact Rules-$IBE^+$ */
8:             end if
9:          else
10:            for all ($\mathcal{C} \in \mathcal{FC} \mid \mathcal{C} \supset \gamma(G)$) do
11:               if ($supp(G \cup \mathcal{C}) \geq minsup$ && $\frac{n_G n_{\overline{\mathcal{C}}}}{n}(1-\alpha) \geq N_{G\overline{\mathcal{C}}}$) then
12:                  Base ← Base ∪ $\{G \to \mathcal{C} \backslash G\}$;     /* Positive Approximate Rules-$IBA^+$ */
13:               end if
14:            end for
15:         end if
16:      else
17:         for all ($\mathcal{M} \in \mathcal{MC}$) do
18:            $\mathcal{G}_{\mathcal{M}} = generator(\mathcal{M})$;
19:            for all ($G \in \mathcal{G}_{\mathcal{M}}$) do
20:               for all ($y \in \mathcal{I} \backslash \mathcal{M}$) do
21:                  if ($supp(G \cup \{\overline{y}\}) \geq minsup$) then
22:                     Base ← Base ∪ $\{G \to \{\overline{y}\} \backslash G\}$;     /* Negative Exact Rules-$IBE^-$ */
23:                  end if
24:               end for
25:            end for
26:         end for
27:         for all ($g \in \mathcal{G}_{\gamma(g)} | \gamma(G) \subsetneq \gamma(g)$) do
28:            if ($supp(G \cup \overline{g}) \geq minsup$ && $\frac{n_G n_{\overline{g}}}{n}(1-\alpha) \geq N_{G\overline{g}}$) then
29:               Base ← Base ∪ $\{G \to \overline{g} \backslash G\}$;     /* Negative Approximate Rules-$IBA^-$ */
30:            end if
31:         end for
32:      end if
33:   end for
34: end for
35: PruneRedRules(Base)
36: return Base
```

basis and IBA^- basis. For all closed C (line 2) and generator G of this closed C (line 3) which respectively represent the premise and the consequence of the rule, we check if these two itemsets are positively dependent (line 4). We also check if they belong to the same equivalence class (line 5). From line 6, we check that the generator G is not a single element in its equivalence class (i.e. $\gamma(G) \neq G$), and also check if an itemset $G \cup C$ of a candidate rule $G \to C$ is frequent. All elements of Base (line 7) must satisfy these conditions, so this candidate is eligible for giving the exact positive rule. If these two itemsets are not in the same equivalence class (line 9), we generate the approximate positive rules (lines 10–14). We collect another closed $\mathcal{C}$ containing the closure of G (i.e. $\gamma(G)$) (line 10), and then check if the candidate satisfies the constraints $minsup$ and α (line 11). If so, the candidate is eligible and added in Base (line 12). This completes the first part. The second part also consists of two sub-parts. The first sub-part (lines 17–26) corresponds to the procedure for mining the exact negative association rules. The second sub-part corresponds to the procedure for mining approximate negative rules (lines 27–31). So, for a maximal $\mathcal{M}$ (line 17),

Algorithm 3. PRUNEREDRULES

Require: BASE Base of informative rules
1: BASE=BASE;
2: **for all** ($X \rightarrow Y\backslash X \in$ BASE) **do**
3:   **for all** ($\widetilde{X} \rightarrow Y\backslash\widetilde{X} \in$ BASE) **do**
4:     **if** ($\widetilde{X} \subset X$) **then**
5:       BASE $\leftarrow$ BASE$\backslash\{X \rightarrow Y\backslash X\}$
6:     **end if**
7:   **end for**
8: **end for**
9: **for all** ($X \rightarrow \overline{Y}\backslash X \in$ BASE) **do**
10:   **for all** ($\widetilde{X} \rightarrow \overline{Y}\backslash\widetilde{X} \in$ BASE) **do**
11:     **if** ($\widetilde{X} \subset X$) **then**
12:       BASE $\leftarrow$ BASE$\backslash\{X \rightarrow \overline{Y}\backslash X\}$
13:     **end if**
14:   **end for**
15: **end for**
16: **return** BASE

we generate its generator $\mathcal{G}_{\mathcal{M}}$ (line 18). For a dual y (dual of $\mathcal{M}$) (line 20), we check if the support of the rule $G \rightarrow \overline{y}$ is frequent (line 21). If this is the case, the BASE will be updated (line 22). Finally, for a generator g which does not belong to the same equivalence class of G (line 27), we check if the support and M_{GK} of a candidate rule $G \rightarrow \overline{g}$ are frequent (line 28). If so, this rough rule is valid and added in BASE (line 29). The procedure PRUNEREDRULES (cf. Algorithm 3) removes the redundancies. So, after initialization (line 1), consider two association rules $X \rightarrow Y\backslash X$ et $\widetilde{X} \rightarrow Y\backslash\widetilde{X}$ (lines 2–3). We check if $\widetilde{X} \subseteq X$, then $X \rightarrow Y\backslash X$ is redundant with respect to $\widetilde{X} \rightarrow Y\backslash\widetilde{X}$, so pruned (line 5). Next, consider two negative rules $X \rightarrow \overline{Y}\backslash X$ et $\widetilde{X} \rightarrow \overline{Y}\backslash\widetilde{X}$ (lines 9–10). We then check if $\widetilde{X} \subseteq X$, then $X \rightarrow Y\backslash X$ is redundant, therefore pruned in BASE (line 12). ALLVALIDRULES algorithm (Algorithm 4) derives *all valid informative rules*. It first derives the rules of type $X \rightarrow Y\backslash X$. Indeed, if $X \rightarrow Y\backslash X$ is valid, then $\overline{X} \rightarrow \overline{Y}\backslash\overline{X}$ is also valid (concept of derivability [4]) and added in All_{RUL} (Algorithm 4 line 4). The last step address for deriving the rules of type $X \rightarrow \overline{Y}\backslash X$ (Algorithm 4 lines 7–11). For this, if $X \rightarrow \overline{Y}\backslash X$ is valid, then $\overline{X} \rightarrow Y\backslash\overline{X}$ is also valid (derivability [4]), and added in All_{RUL} (Algorithm 4 line 9).

We present the complexity of the principal algorithm NONREDBASE. Its complexity remains linear in $|\mathcal{FC}| \times |\mathcal{G}_{\mathcal{C}}|$, and is in $\mathcal{O}(|\mathcal{FC}||\mathcal{G}_{\mathcal{C}}|(5^m - 2(3^m)))$. Indeed, the line 2 (resp. line 3) is in $\mathcal{O}(|\mathcal{FC}|)$ (resp. $\mathcal{O}(|\mathcal{G}_{\mathcal{C}}|)$). It has two recursives tests. The first test (lines 4–15) is in $C_1 = \mathcal{O}(|\mathcal{FC}||\mathcal{G}_{\mathcal{C}}|)$, and the second test (lines 17–31) in $C_2 = \mathcal{O}(|\mathcal{MC}| + |\mathcal{G}_{\mathcal{C}}|)$. C_1 is more complex than C_2 (i.e. $C_2 \leqslant C_1$). For a m-itemset, the cardinality of association rules is equal to $2^{2m} - 2^{m+1}$. Which gives $C_m^{m-1}(2^{2(m-1)} - 2^m)$ for a $(m-1)$-itemset, $C_m^{m-2}(2^{2(m-2)} - 2^{(m-1)})$ for a $(m-2)$-itemset, and so an. In sum, $\sum_{k=2}^{m} C_m^k(2^{2k} - 2^{k+1}) = \sum_{k=2}^{m} C_m^k 4^k - 2\sum_{k=2}^{m} C_m^k 2^k = \left[\sum_{k=0}^{m} C_m^k 4^k - (1+4m)\right] - 2\left[\sum_{k=0}^{m} C_m^k 2^k - (1+2m)\right]$. For all $x \in \mathbb{R}$, $\sum_{k=0}^{m} C_m^k x^k = (1+x)^m$, then $\sum_{k=2}^{m} C_m^k(2^{2k} - 2^{k+1}) = \mathcal{O}(5^m - 2(3^m))$. Finally, the time complexity of NONREDBASE is in $\mathcal{O}(|\mathcal{FC}||\mathcal{G}_{\mathcal{C}}|(5^m - 2(3^m)))$.

Algorithm 4. ALLVALIDRULES

Require: BASE Base of informative rules, and *minsup*.
Ensure: All_{RUL} (*All Valid Association Rules*).
All_{RUL} = BASE;
for all ($X \rightarrow Y \backslash X \in$ BASE) **do**
    if ($supp(\overline{X} \cup \overline{Y}) \geqslant minsup$) **then**
        $All_{RUL} \leftarrow All_{RUL} \cup \{\overline{X} \rightarrow \overline{Y} \backslash \overline{X}\}$
    end if
end for
for all ($X \rightarrow \overline{Y} \backslash Y \in$ BASE) **do**
    if ($supp(\overline{X} \cup Y) \geqslant minsup$) **then**
        $All_{RUL} \leftarrow All_{RUL} \cup \{\overline{X} \rightarrow Y \backslash \overline{X}\}$
    end if
end for
return All_{RUL}

5 Experimental Evaluation

In this section, we present the performance of NONRED algorithm with respect to Bastide [2] and Feno [6] approaches. Our approach is implemented in a PC with an Intel Core i3 processor running at 4 GB, under Windows (64bit), conducted on four reference databases (or datasets) (cf. Table 2): T10I4D100K[2] and T20I6D100K (cf. footnote 4), C20D10K[3] and MUSHROOMS (cf. footnote 5). The

Table 2. Database characteristics

Database	Number of transaction	Number of items	Average size of transaction
T10I4D100K	100 000	1 000	10
T20I6D100K	100 000	1 000	20
C20D10K	10 000	386	20
MUSHROOMS	8 416	128	23

Table 2 represents the variation of the number of association rules obtained by our algorithm with respect to those of Bastide and Feno approaches on different datasets for various *minsup* at fixed $\alpha = 0.05$ (for NONRED and Feno approach) and $minconf = 0.8$ (Bastide approach). We also denote by "–" a subset which could not generated. Recall that Bastide contains no negative rules. So, the exact negative rules E^- (resp. approximate rules A^-) are absent, which gives a notable loss of information for Bastide. For each algorithm, no exact positive E^+ (resp. approximate A^-) association rule is generated from sparse database T10I4D100K since, for $minsup \leq 30\%$. The reason is that all frequent itemsets are frequent closed itemsets. On the other databases, we can observe that the total number of exact positive and exact negative rules is very reasonable, for all *minsup*. For this, Feno represents number smaller than Bastide and NONRED.

[2] http://www.almaden.ibm.com/cs/quest/syndata.html.
[3] http://kdd.ics.uci.edu/.

Table 3. Number of all valide informative association rules

Dataset	*minsup*	Bastide et al.				Feno et al.				NonRed			
		$\|E^+\|$	$\|A^+\|$	$\|E^-\|$	$\|A^-\|$	$\|E^+\|$	$\|E^-\|$	$\|A^+\|$	$\|A^-\|$	$\|E^+\|$	$\|E^-\|$	$\|A^+\|$	$\|A^-\|$
T10I4D100K	10%	0	11625	–	–	0	0	20555	1256	0	0	725	52
	20%	0	8545	–	–	0	0	15656	1058	0	0	545	34
	30%	0	3555	–	–	0	0	12785	954	0	0	355	25
T20I6D100K	10%	115	71324	–	–	95	98	71899	3897	115	103	1804	56
	20%	76	57336	–	–	66	91	45560	2705	76	95	1403	38
	30%	58	45684	–	–	43	63	41784	1887	58	63	1175	27
C20D10K	10%	1125	33950	–	–	975	255	34588	11705	1125	285	1856	182
	20%	997	23821	–	–	657	135	25582	8789	997	185	1453	123
	30%	967	18899	–	–	567	98	19581	4800	967	101	1221	97
Mushrooms	10%	958	4465	–	–	758	289	4150	3887	958	304	1540	89
	20%	663	3354	–	–	554	178	2944	2845	663	198	1100	78
	30%	543	2961	–	–	444	109	2140	1987	543	115	998	39

The explanation is that Feno uses the pseudo-closed which returns a reduced number of itemsets and thus, it is the same for the association rules, but it's not informative. Whereas Bastide and NonRed algorithms generate the informative association rules. In this case, the premise is selected from to the set of generator itemset which is more dense with respect to the set of pseudo-closed.

On the dense and strongly correlated datasets (C20D10K and Mushrooms), it is very visible that our algorithm, NonRed, is much more selective than Bastide and Feno, for all *minsup*. For example, with the dense database C20D10K at good *minsup* (1%), NonRed only extracts $|A^+| = 1856$ against $|A^+| = 33950$ and $|A^+| = 34588$ for Bastide and Feno respectively (cf. Table 3), let a difference of more than 32000 approximate rules. The main reason is associated with a pruning strategy. Using the pruning strategy (cf. Property 6), NonRed can prune the uninteresting rules, this is not the case for Bastide. In addition, NonRed includes an efficient technique for pruning weakly correlated rules (i.e. close to independence), based on the constraint of M_{GK} minimal, this is not the case for Feno approach. The latter uses a strategy based on critical value, while this critical value is not very selective, it accepts often weakly correlated rules.

We present in the following the execution times of our algorithm, compared to those of literature (Bastide and Feno approaches, in particular). However, this comparison is still very difficult, for several reasons. First, Feno approach, only approach (to our knowledge) for informative basis of positive and negative association rules, does not take into account the frequent itemsets mining, while this step considerably affects the execution times. For this, the frequent itemsets are extracted in other algorithms, which are not taken into account in its cursus. Thus, Feno approach is not comparable of our approach. On the other hand, Bastide approach could not integrate the negative exact and approximate association rules (E^- and A^-), while these subsets could to give very high complexity. For this situation, we partially compare NonRed and Bastide. More precisely,

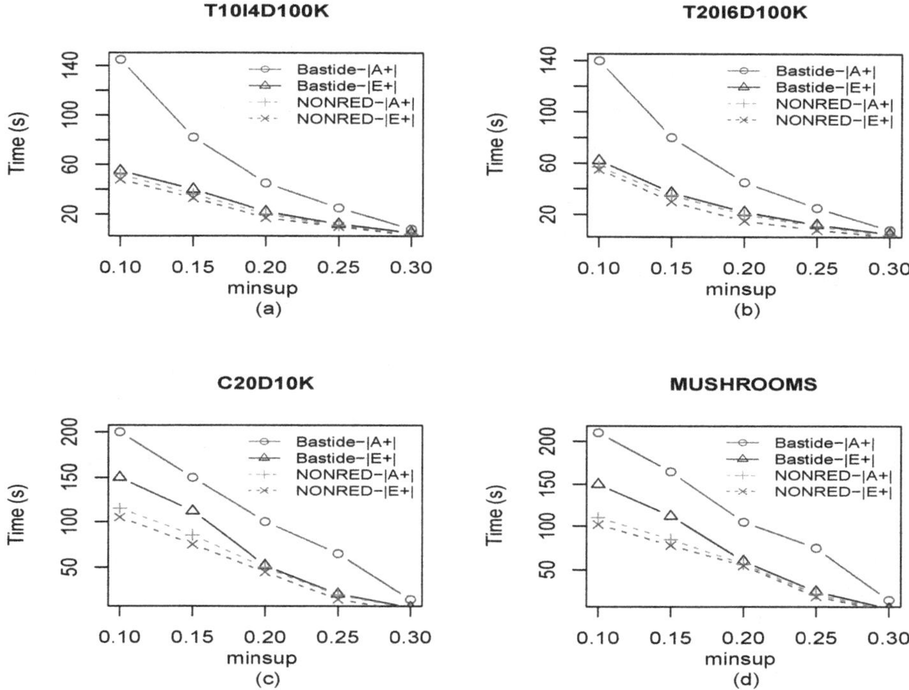

Fig. 2. Response times by varying *minsup* at fixed $\alpha = 0.05$ and $minconf = 0.6$

this comparative study only concerns execution times for positive exact E^+ and approximate A^+ association rules. The results of this will be represented in Fig. 2 by varying the *minsup* at fixed $\alpha = 0.05$ and $minconf = 0.6$. On sparse datasets (T10I4D100K and T20I6D100K), the execution times of NonRed and Bastide algorithms are almost identical for positive exact association rules E^+, at the lowest *minsup* (cf. Fig. 2a and b). On approximate association rules A^+, it is very obvious that our algorithm, NonRed, is better than Bastide approach (cf. Fig. 2a, b). The explanation is that all frequent itemsets are frequent closed itemsets, which complicates the task of Bastide who performs more operations than NonRed algorithm to determine the closures and approximate rules. Even if NonRed algorithm is linear on the number of frequent closed, it benefits a significant reduction for number of accesses to the datasets to determine the supports and frequent closed itemsets, its execution time is then low.

On dense and strongly correlated datasets (C20D10K and Mushrooms), NonRed algorithm is once again better than Bastide, for approximate association rules (cf. Fig. 2c and d). The main reason is also associated with the pruning strategy. Using the pruning strategies (cf. Property 6, Theorems 4, 5, 6 and 7), NonRed can reduce considerably the search space, this is not the case for Bastide, and NonRed ends quickly (cf. Fig. 2c and d). Bastide obtains the less performance: there is also no pruning strategy for uninteresting association rules, while variations of these rules affect execution times, considerably. As a result, the search space can be browsed in its entirety, which considerably penalizes the execution times for Bastide. This is no longer the case for exact association rules E^+ where Bastide joins NonRed, for *minsup* of 20% to 30%.

6 Conclusion

We presented and evaluated our approach for mining informative association rules. This approach simultaneously generates both the positive and negative association rules using the frequent closed itemsets and maximal itemsets, and their generators. Experiments have shown that this approach is more efficient than the existing approaches of the literature. The prospective for future work relate to the interactive visualization of the association rules extracted. Another perspective would be to extend this work in paradigm of multidimensional rules.

References

1. Agrawal, R., Srikant, R.: Fast algorithms for mining association rules. In: Proceedings of 20th VLDB Conference, Santiago Chile, pp. 487–499 (1994)
2. Bastide, Y., Pasquier, N., Taouil, R., Stumme, G., Lakhal, L.: Mining minimal non-redundant association rules using frequent closed itemsets. In: Lloyd, J., et al. (eds.) CL 2000. LNCS (LNAI), vol. 1861, pp. 972–986. Springer, Heidelberg (2000). https://doi.org/10.1007/3-540-44957-4_65
3. Bemarisika, P.: Extraction de règles d'association selon le couple support-M_{GK}: Graphes implicatifs et Applications en didactique des mathématiques. Ph.D. thesis, Université d'Antananarivo (Madagasar) (2016)
4. Bemarisika, P., Ramanantsoa, H., Totohasina, A.: An efficient approach for extraction positive and negative association rules from big data. In: Proceedings of International Cross Domain Conference for Machine Learning & Knowledge Extraction (CD-MAKE 2018), pp. 79–97 (2018)
5. Durand, N., Quafafou, M.: Approximation of frequent itemset border by computing approximate minimal hypergraph transversals. In: Bellatreche, L., Mohania, M.K. (eds.) DaWaK 2014. LNCS, vol. 8646, pp. 357–368. Springer, Cham (2014). https://doi.org/10.1007/978-3-319-10160-6_32
6. Diatta, J., Feno, D.R., Totohasina, A.: Galois lattices and bases for M_{GK}-valid association rules. In: Yahia, S.B., Nguifo, E.M., Belohlavek, R. (eds.) CLA 2006. LNCS (LNAI), vol. 4923, pp. 186–197. Springer, Heidelberg (2008). https://doi.org/10.1007/978-3-540-78921-5_12
7. Ganter, B., Wille, R.: Formal Concept Analysis. Springer, Heidelberg (1999). https://doi.org/10.1007/978-3-642-59830-2
8. Giacomo, K., Alexandre B.: Average size of implicational bases. In: Ignatov, D.I., Nourine, L. (eds.) CLA 2018, pp. 37–45 (2018)
9. Guigues, J.L., Duquenne, V.: Familles minimales d'implications informatives résultant d'un tableau de donnés binaires. Maths et Sci. Humaines **95**, 5–18 (1986)
10. Guillaume, S.: Traitement des données volumineuses. Mesures et algorithmes d'extraction des règles d'association et règles ordinales. Ph.D. thesis, Universté de Nantes (France) (2000)

11. Kryszkiewicz, M.: Concise representations of association rules. In: Hand, D.J., Adams, N.M., Bolton, R.J. (eds.) Pattern Detection and Discovery. LNCS (LNAI), vol. 2447, pp. 92–109. Springer, Heidelberg (2002). https://doi.org/10.1007/3-540-45728-3_8
12. Latiri, C., Haddad, H., Hamrouni, T.: Towards an effective automatic query expansion process using an association rule mining approach. J. Intell. Inf. Syst. **39**, 209–247 (2012). https://doi.org/10.1007/s10844-011-0189-9
13. Lerman, I.C.: Classification et analyse ordinale des données. Dunod (1981)
14. Mannila, H., Toivonen, H.: Levelwise search and borders of theories in knowledge discovery. Data Min. Knowl. Disc. **1**, 241–258 (1997)
15. Pasquier, N.: Extraction de Bases pour les Règles d'Association à partir des Itemsets Fermés Fréquents. CNRS (2000)
16. Totohasina, A., Ralambondrainy, H.: ION, a pertinent new measure for mining information from many types of data. In: IEEE, SITIS, pp. 202–207 (2005)
17. Totohasina, A., Feno, D.R.: De la qualité de règles d'association: Etude comparative des mesures M_{GK} et Confiance. In: CARI (2008)
18. Wu, X., Zhang, C., Zhang, S.: Efficient mining of both positive and negative association rules. ACM Trans. Inf. Syst. **3**, 381–405 (2004)
19. Zaki, M.J.: Mining non-redundant association rules. Data Min. Knowl. Disc. **9**, 223–248 (2004). Proc. of KDDM

Interpretation of SVM Using Data Mining Technique to Extract Syllogistic Rules

Exploring the Notion of Explainable AI in Diagnosing CAD

Sanjay Sekar Samuel[1], Nik Nailah Binti Abdullah[1(✉)], and Anil Raj[2(✉)]

[1] Monash University, Kuala Lumpur, Malaysia
mail@sanjaysekarsamuel.com, nik.nailah@monash.edu
[2] IHMC, Pensacola, FL, USA
araj@ihmc.us

Abstract. Artificial Intelligence (AI) systems that can provide clear explanations of their behaviors have been suggested in many studies as a critical feature for human users to develop reliance and trust when using such systems. Medical Experts (ME) in particular while using an AI assistant system must understand how the system generates disease diagnoses before making patient care decisions based on the AI's output. In this paper, we report our work in progress and preliminary findings toward the development of a human-centered explainable AI (XAI) specifically for the diagnosis of Coronary Artery Disease (CAD). We applied syllogistic inference rules based on CAD Clinical Practice Guidelines (CPGs) to interpret the data mining results using a Support Vector Machine (i.e., SVM) classification technique—which forms an early model for a knowledge base (KB). The SVM's inference rules are then explained through a voice system to the MEs. Based on our initial findings, we discovered that MEs trusted the system's diagnoses when the XAI described the chain of reasoning behind the diagnosis process in a more interpretable form—suggesting an enhanced level of trust. Using syllogistic rules alone, however, to interpret the classification of the SVM algorithm lacked sufficient contextual information—which required augmentation with more descriptive explanations provided by a medical expert.

Keywords: Explainable AI · Coronary Artery Disease · Support Vector Machine · Data mining · Medical expert · Artificial intelligence · Human-centered

1 Introduction and Motivation

Explainable artificial intelligence (XAI) or Interpretable AI seeks to make expert systems more transparent by ensuring the understandability of the design's complexities and operations of the AI, thereby promoting trust to those who use the systems [1]. Explanation capabilities are not just desirable, but also crucial for the success of an expert system [2]. These explanations will enable users to understand the contents and limitations of the system's knowledge base (KB) and its chain of reasoning process across that KB

Published by Springer Nature Switzerland AG 2020
A. Holzinger et al. (Eds.): CD-MAKE 2020, LNCS 12279, pp. 249–266, 2020.
https://doi.org/10.1007/978-3-030-57321-8_14

[3]. Machine learning (ML), a branch of AI which includes pattern identification from input streams and predict the outputs [4] can be classified as supervised, unsupervised and semi-supervised learning techniques. A Support Vector Machine (SVM), one of the well-known supervised ML approaches, can use data mining techniques to classify the data into categorical class labels while supporting visual representations of how the ML algorithm categorized the processed data [5]. Currently, SVM methods are being used to improve diagnosis of diseases like Coronary Artery Disease (CAD) in clinical settings [6, 7]. They have also demonstrated high performance in solving classification problems in bioinformatics [8, 9]. Though analogous ML algorithms like neural networks (NNs) have also shown remarkable performance while classifying outcomes in CAD, they lack direct support for visualization capabilities like SVM algorithm. Decision trees on the other hand have also demonstrated excellent performance in visualizing their tree branching. However, subject matter experts or medical experts (ME) in particular, have found the visual explanation approach given by the SVM algorithm's graphs more accordant compared to the complex neural network and decision tree graphs. SVM also come handy in representing cases that are similar through the visualization of shared patient characteristics [10]. Moreover, SVM also allows the use of syllogisms, a form of deductive reasoning where one infers a conclusion 'C' through a rule-based examination of two other premises 'A & B' which can be given as A + B = C [11]. Resultantly, since SVM algorithms comes right after neural networks in the interpretability and accuracy graph, this swayed us to choose SVM as the ML model for our initial work to build the components of an XAI model to accommodate the ME's request.

In the domain of healthcare, ML solutions must provide an explanation of the AI's rationale for the resultant classifications or predictions to enable Medical Experts (ME) to understand it themselves and explain the information to their patients [12]. The provided explanation develops trust in the ML by both the MEs and patients. Moreover, when MEs were asked to rank in the order of importance the top fifteen computer-based consultation systems that develops trust in them, they ranked the "ability to explain their diagnostic and treatment decisions to ME users" as the most essential [13]. At our initial stage of work, we define XAI as an AI model that can provide an accurate and contextualized explanation that can establish the aspect of trust with MEs. To explore the notion of XAI, we use SVM that used inference data mining techniques to extract syllogistic rules from unseen data. The syllogistic inference rules were then validated with MEs and accepted Clinical Practice Guidelines (CPGs) from the American College of Cardiology [14]. CPGs or commonly known as Medical guidelines are universally accepted documents that are accepted by all the members of the medical community. CPGs have guided decisions and criteria regarding diagnosis, management and treatment in specific areas of health care [14]. Because of their universal standardization and accepted diagnostic rules that have been used and updated for many years, these CPG rules were additionally used to validate the MEs inference of the syllogisms extracted from the data mining results of SVM's classification through graphs. The model then used text-to-speech to explain the MEs which factors in the KB inference rules contributed to the CAD classification. The synthetic voice method was used to evaluate goodness and satisfaction of the MEs mental models of the XAI. Once the goodness and satisfaction are evaluated by the MEs, we can then calculate the precision and performance score of the complete XAI model.

With that, we organize this chapter as follows: First, we will discuss the problem statement and related work briefly. Then we introduce our research methodology. Next, we elaborate on our experiments using data mining techniques and syllogistic inference rules to interpret SVM's classification. Lastly, we conclude with a discussion of the results and future work.

2 Problem Statement

CAD manifests as narrowing of the lumen of the coronary arteries of the heart—which can impair or block blood flow to the cardiac tissue. CAD has risen to be one of the greatest scourges of the human population since the industrial revolution [15]. The multifactorial causes of CAD (elevated cholesterol, smoking, diabetes, aging, etc.,) can make early diagnosis challenging without using invasive coronary catheterization, or costly computed tomography (CT), angiography [16]. Applying XAI in the context of early CAD diagnosis could provide recommendations for the CPG-recommended tests based on model outputs for each patient. Deployment of an XAI model that can address these challenges could result in significant cost savings in developing countries such as Malaysia and India, where the government heavily subsidizes patient care [17]. In light of these challenges, our research study seeks to explore the components required to develop an XAI model that can assist MEs in the diagnosis of CAD by focusing on outlier cases.

Thus, at the initial stage, we focus on two objectives:

1. Interpreting SVM-based classification, and the modeling of syllogistic rules in a KB.
2. Communicating the interpretation to MEs in a manner that develops trust.

Therefore, the preliminary aim of our project is to answer the following research question—how do we represent the classification provided by a ML algorithm to help MEs understand how the XAI arrived at a specific diagnostic output?

3 Related Work

Prior implementations have shown the potential of data mining techniques on SVM-based CAD diagnostic systems [18–21]. Though other ML methods, like decision tree and neural network models, can demonstrate significant performance in classifying heart disease patients, SVM-approaches are compatible with large and complex data (e.g., "omic" data) and can process data with higher accuracy than other supervised learning algorithmic approaches [22]. Omic data in this context refers to genomics, metabolomics, proteomics, and data from standardized electronic health records (EHRs) or precision medicine platforms. In light of the ML algorithms mentioned earlier, NN-based AI assistants have also shown effective performance in the diagnoses of CAD and other chronic diseases in many medical studies [23]. However, compared to the hidden layers in NNs, SVM algorithm provide a direct pathway to visualize the underlying AI model feature characteristics through graphs while reaching similar or higher levels of accuracy [24]. Additionally, we see that decision tree ML algorithms also support design tools useful for explaining and interpreting predictions derived by the ML algorithms [25]. Representing algorithmic predictions through human-machine[1] explanatory dialogue systems that employ contrastive explanations and exemplar-based explanations can provide transparency and improve trust in XAI [26]. In this context, the XAI uses contrastive rather than direct explanations to illustrate the cause of an event concerning some other event. This is because, with contrastive explanation, the AI has ability to explain itself by identifying the chain of reasoning it went through to reach the diagnostic outcome [27]. Such explanations are a major requirement when a ME evaluates a patient.

When users accept an explanation as good and relatively complete, they can develop a representative mental model, which in turn, fosters appropriate trust towards the AI system [28]. Moreover, these explanations are key contributor to trust because enhancing the explanatory power of an AI systems can result in systems that are easier to use with improved decision-making and problem-solving performance [29]. In our proposed work, we aim to explore the components needed for an XAI model by using SVM and a data mining technique through which we extract syllogistic rules that support transparency to the MEs for CAD diagnosis. We will use voice communication as a tool to explain the interpretation of the classification with contextual information to enhance the level trust while using the XAI. In the next section, we will elaborate more on the methodology involved in discovering and building our early components of an XAI.

4 Research Methodology

For this study, we undertook a combination of constructive and a human-centered methodology which was iteratively conducted in two stages. The "constructive" methodology here refers to a new concept, theory or model being developed in a research [30], which will then be evaluated by the target user population. And a "human-centered" approach involves an iterative development process where a target user population (MEs in our case) were involved in the loop. These target user population play an important role in this research to make improvements iteratively and identify inconspicuous components required to construct an XAI model [31, 32]. Human-centered approach is crucial for this research as these data sets may contain missing data, unwanted data, dirty data noisy data and most importantly data that has missing contextual information [33, 34]. Thereby, with the integration of experienced MEs in the loop, we can ensure an enhanced level of knowledge discovery process pipeline. This is because, these MEs will have the tacit knowledge required to fill the missing links in these data sets which is critical for an XAI to make its diagnosis for a given condition.

During the first stage of our research we used a constructive approach by using real-world datasets specifically to identify the components needed to construct an early XAI model for the diagnosis of CAD. In the second stage, we applied a human-centered approach, using questionnaires to get qualitative feedback from MEs regarding any improvements needed for the model throughout the iterative stages. The following sections will detail our early model construction and research results.

[1] Human-machine system is a system in which the functions of a human user and a machine are integrated.

5 A Syllogistic Approach for Interpreting SVM's Classifications

In this section, we will present the steps involved in designing our early XAI model and its different components, starting with an analysis of the data used to develop the model.

5.1 Data Selection

The data selected for this project was obtained from the University of California-Irvine (UCI) Cleveland heart disease database and the Framingham Heart Study Repository [35, 36]. The UCI repository has 304 records (patients) with 22 attributes (physiological condition). The Framingham heart study database includes 4241 records (patients) with 17 attributes (physiological condition). The attributes/features used for our experiment from the UCI data set are Max heart rate, ST-depression, Number of blood vessels highlighted by fluoroscopy, typical angina, exercise-induced angina, cholesterol level, age, and non-anginal pain. Whereas the attributes/features used for our experiment from the Framingham data set are: SysBP, DiaBP, age, sex, cholesterol level, cigsPerday, diabetes, prevalent hypertension, and glucose level. CPGs and MEs inputs were used to validate the selected attributes, which represent the top ten results given by the univariate feature selection method. Univariate feature selection method is used here because of its unique ability to examine each feature independently by using Pearson correlation to identify the strength of each feature with the target variable [37].

5.2 Analyzing and Interpreting the Information from SVM by Using Syllogistic Rules

When analyzing the data as a whole using the SVM algorithm, the interpretation behind the chain of reasoning used by the algorithm tend to get complicated and hard to process because of the vast number of attributes involved in the prediction. However, breaking down the data and analyzing the visualization of the predictions one at a time reduces complexity and simplifies interpretation. To accomplish this, we used classification techniques to interpret information from the SVM algorithm output. Classification technique is a technique where the algorithm parts the data into their respective dependencies depending upon their internal relations. Classification is also one of the most important techniques for data mining [10]. In order to easily extract syllogistic rules, the attributes from the selected data (as detailed from the previous section) were individually classified by the SVM algorithm in the form of visual graphs (see Fig. 2 for a detailed excerpt). Both the datasets have a target column that indicates if a patient has heart disease or not (1 for yes and 0 for no). A single attribute selected from the dataset will then be correlated with the target to identify the correlation coefficient as seen in (Fig. 1). Correlation coefficient here refers to the numerical measurement of the statistical relationship between two variables [38]. With this correlation coefficient number illustrated on a graph, we were able to identify and extract syllogistic rules from the hyperplane's division.

To delineate this in reference to Fig. 1, selected attributes from the dataset (blood pressure, cholesterol, etc.,) placed in variable "X" were individually evaluated to find its correlation coefficient with the target variable "Y" (CAD $\pm$). The inferred outcomes from the correlation coefficient graph are then used to develop the rules manually in the form of syllogisms.

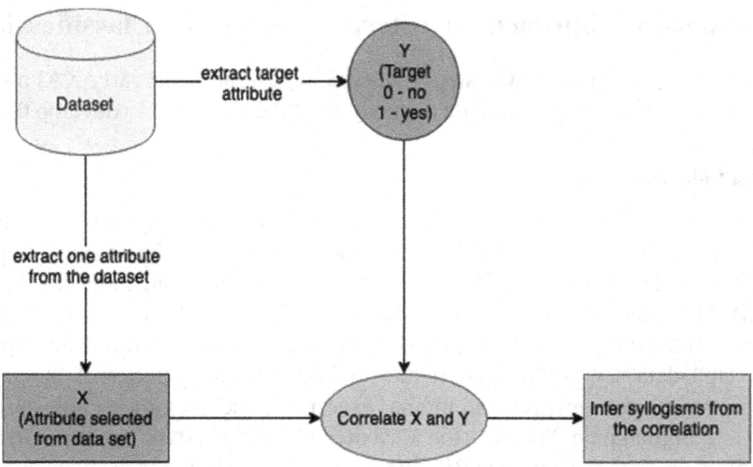

Fig. 1. Overview of the SVM process workflow

5.3 Modelling of Syllogistic Inference Rules

In this section, we illustrate the process of building syllogistic rules through the interpretation of the individual features from the SVM's classification output.

First, we define the following:

$$\mathrm{X} = (X_{f1},\ X_{f2},\ X_{f3}, \ldots .X_{fn}) \text{ Set of all features available in the dataset.} \tag{1}$$

$$\mathrm{Y} = \text{Target} \tag{2}$$

First, to simplify the complexity of the SVM algorithm and make it more interpretable, we extract multiple subsets from the main feature set $X\ (X_{f1},\ X_{f2},\ X_{f3} \ldots .\ X_{fn})$ and find the correlation coefficient of them individually on the target Y. Next, we visualize each of these coefficient values on a graph, which will correspond to the visual reasoning task that is decomposed into a small set of primitives that facilitate the interpretability of the model. Thus, by applying this principle, we know that each subset$(X_{f1},\ X_{f2})$ extracted and visualized from the main feature set X on the target Y will represent a portion of the interpretable classification from the original feature set X. Thereby, with all these subsets combined $[(X_1,\ X_2),\ (X_2,\ X_3)\ldots]$ on the target Y will attain the complete transparent output of the set X. Thus, extracting a syllogism A_n from each of these subsets and combining these syllogisms together will correspond to have complete interpretation of the classification outcome given by the SVM algorithm.

This can be formulated as follows:

$$\sum (X_{f1},\ X_{f2},\ X_{f3}, \ldots .X_{fn}) \rightarrow \mathrm{Y} \tag{3}$$

$$(X_{f1} + X_{f2}) \rightarrow \mathrm{Y} \Rightarrow A_n(X_{f1} + X_{f2}) \Rightarrow Z \tag{4}$$

Table 1. Variables explanation

Variable	Representation
X_{f1}	Feature 1
X_{f2}	Feature 2
Y	Target
$A_n(X_{f1} + X_{f2})$	The rule generated with two selected features on the target variable
Z	Interpretable output from the selected features

Table 1 (below) defines the variables and symbolic representations used in the syllogism.

An Excerpt of Extracting Syllogistic Rules from SVM

To illustrate the above-mentioned method graphically, we use the example of cholesterol

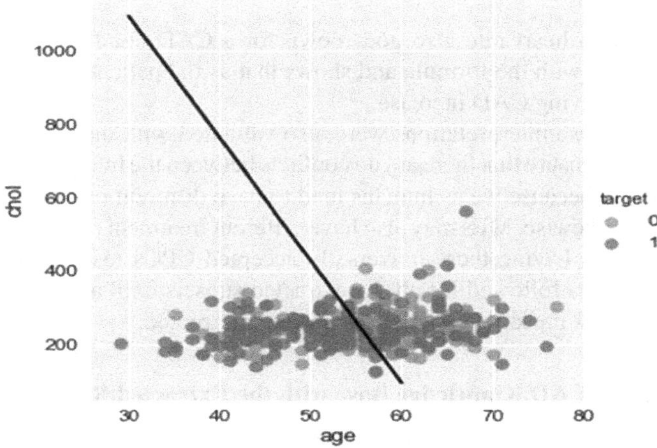

Fig. 2. SVM graphical classification with hyperplane on Cholesterol VS Age

vs age in Fig. 2 as the two features extracted from the main feature set. Using the data mining approach on Age vs. Cholesterol as the first result iteration, we observe the effect each selected feature Xage and Xchol (X_{f1}, X_{f2}) has on the target Y. From the hyperplane's division of the plotted points, we could easily interpret that patients below the age of 60 with a cholesterol level of over 200 are more prone to have CAD.

Let's take another example with maximum heart rate vs age in Fig. 3. From this hyperplane's division we noticed that there is high coagulation of data points in between 140–200 beats per minute. A maximum heart rate a person can have is 220 subtracted from the patient's age. This formula signifies that as the patient gets older, their maximum heart rate decreases. Additionally, we can observe from the graph that as the patient gets

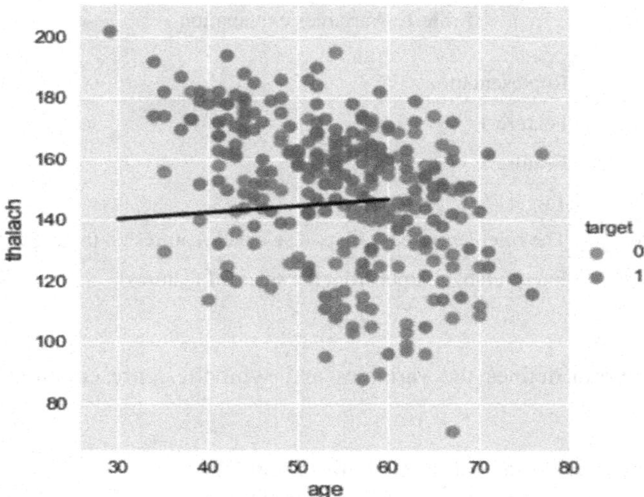

Fig. 3. SVM graphical classification with hyperplane on maximum heart rate vs Age

older, the maximum heart rate also goes down for a CAD condition to persist. This inference correlates with the formula and shows that as the patient's heart gets weaker, the probability of having CAD increase.

Additionally, these interpretations were also validated with the MEs and also with CPGs in the loop to ensure that there are no conflicts between the interpretations provided by the ME. This is because we as humans tend to have different opinions based on our tacit knowledge. Likewise, MEs may also have different treatment regimens for different symptoms. Thereby, having these universally accepted CPGs resolves such conflicts. Similar approach was followed for all the extracted subsets until a satisfactory number of syllogistic rules as prescribed by the MEs were interpreted.

5.4 Updating the CAD Knowledge Base with the Extracted Rules from SVM

The syllogistic rules extracted from the SVM algorithm's output are then used to build an early KB. In our work, we do not apply a complete KB with every representation of events. Instead, the KB here stores background information extracted from the SVM algorithm to provide an interpretation of its classification. This information is then used by XAI to generate inferences about a specific CAD condition in rule-based form.

The diagnosis of CAD is highly complex due to the additive and synergistic effects of the multifactorial underlying disease variables. Therefore, constructing a complete KB with all the possible inference rules is not tractable. We were, however, able to make incremental improvements to the KB by integrating interactions with MEs in the iterative development cycle and merging their interpretations with the SVM's output. With this approach, we were able to develop a XAI which was robust enough to diagnose CAD patients in a more precise manner than the original SVM's classifications. More on how the XAI was able to perform better than SVM will be explained in the testing and results section.

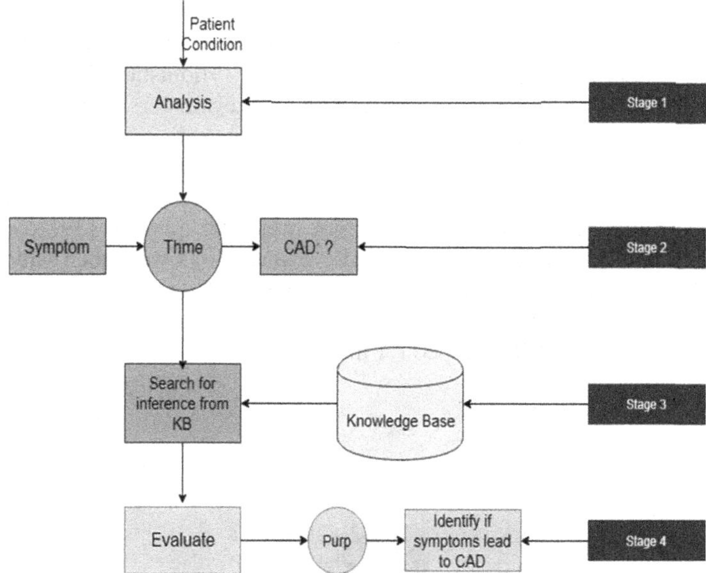

Fig. 4. Workflow for the development of an early KB

Figure 4 adapted from the workflow of Sowa [11] gives an illustrative representation of the stages involved on how an XAI uses its KB to infer diagnosis for a particular patient condition. In stage 1, the anonymized patient's data is fed to the algorithm for analysis. In stage 2, the algorithm identifies if the anonymized patient condition has symptoms of CAD by going through the syllogisms stored in the KB. Here the symbol "Theme" refers to the symptoms that match the theme of CAD. And finally, in stage 3, the XAI evaluates the inference from the KB to identify if the given patient condition may lead to CAD.

5.5 Validation by MEs in the Loop for Early Experiment Output

In this section, we describe the iterative process of integrating MEs in-the-loop when building the components of our XAI. A total of five MEs from the Cardiovascular department of well acclaimed medical institutions were involved in this stage. Additionally, we also involved two MEs from different medical department to ensure that the XAI's outcome can be understood and trusted by them who have less experience in this particular field.

First, we use SVM algorithm's data mining technique to classify the data in the database in the form of graphs to determine if a given patient has CAD or not for a given physiological condition. Second, we use syllogistic approach to interpret rules from the SVM's classification in graphs by analyzing how the hyperplane divides the data. Third, MEs were involved to evaluate the syllogistic rules interpreted from the SVM's hyperplane division to identify any missing contextual information that may be vital for diagnosis based on their tacit knowledge. Contextual information here refers to the hidden information within the data that are usually excluded by the algorithm. Some examples of contextual information for a patient are medication record, innate physiological conditions and demographic data. These syllogistic rules were also then validated with CPGs because when it comes to human evaluators, there will always be biases in their evaluations. Hence, by the use of a universally accepted gold standard CPGs, we were able to nullify such dissentions. Lastly, these validated syllogistic rules with the necessary contextual information are then transformed into explainable outcomes by using a voice system that was implemented with "pytsx3" [39] to explain the diagnosis in a natural dialogue manner. These explanations were then validated with MEs in iterative stages to measure the level of goodness and satisfactoriness of each of these explanations. Figure 5 shows a pictorial representation of the workflow consisting of the different components developed for the XAI.

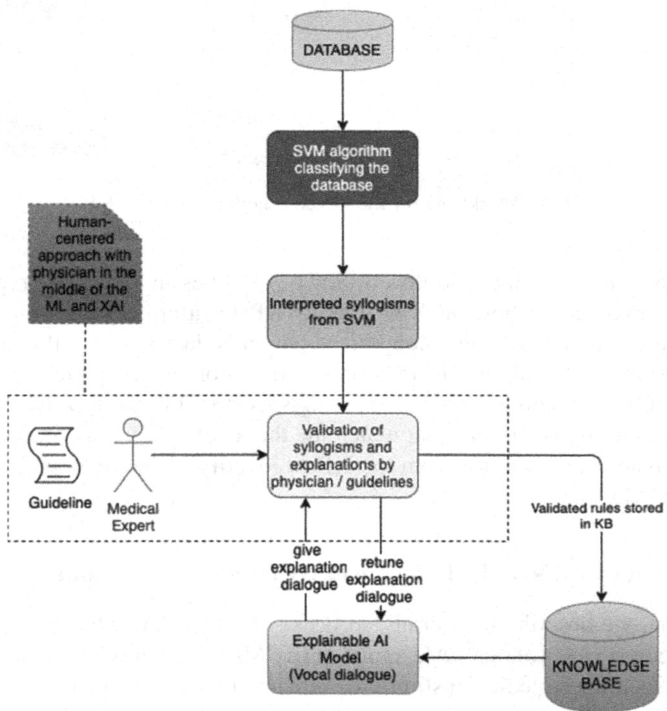

Fig. 5. XAI model components and workflow with ME in loop

6 Preliminary Results from Testing

In this section, we describe the results of applying our process experimentally to the UCI and Framingham datasets. We partitioned the repositories into training sets of (80%) and reserved 20% for testing and provide a representative excerpt of the syllogistic rules interpreted as our preliminary results. The symbol ∃ here represents the existence of a specific type of risk.

```
Blood pressure:
(SystolicBloodPressure > 140) ∧ (DiastolicBloodPressure > 90)
→(∃:x(HighBloodPressure))

Cholesterol:
(ch_LDL_lev(x) > 160) ∧ (age(x) > 21) ∧ (ch_HDL_lev(x) < 40
→(∃:x(cholesterol_risk_high))

Blood sugar:(blood_sugar(x) > 4) ∧ (blood_sugar(x) <= 5.4) →
¬(∃:x(DiabeticRisk))

Chest pain risk:(anginal_cp) ∨ (atypical_anginal_cp) ∨
(non_anginal_cp) → (∃:x(chest_pain_risk)
```

Physiological Triggering Factors (KB Inference Engine)

```
Rule 1: if there exists a high cholesterol risk, and diabetic risk,
and high blood pressure risk, then CAD is present:
(∃:x(cholesterol_risk_high)) ∧ (∃:x(DiabeticRisk)) ∧
(∃:x(HighBloodPressure)) →(∃:x(CoronaryArteryDisease))

Rule 2: if the patient's age is between 30 and 33 years old and dias-
tolic blood pressure falls between: 60 and 110 mmHg, then CAD is
present:
((age(x) > 30 ∧ age(x) < 33) ∧ (DiastolicBloodPressure(x) > 60 ∧
DiastolicBloodPressure(x) < 110)) →(∃:x(CoronaryArteryDisease))

Rule 3: if there exists diabetic risk and a body-mass index (BMI)
risk, then CAD is present:(∃:x(DiabeticRisk)) ∧ (∃:x(BMI_risk)) →
(∃:x(CoronaryArteryDisease))
```

The syllogistic rules generated above represent only a small portion of the knowledge background for the early KB. When a specific patient condition is given to the model, the XAI analyzes the condition based on stored syllogistic information in the KB to determine if a CAD condition can be warranted. We incrementally improved the explainability of this reasoning process during the study by verbalizing the rules via the voice system for MEs to understand and validate the syllogisms. Given below is an excerpt of the incremental development of the dialogues given by the XAI model.

For the explanation dialogues used in Phase I testing (13 April 2019), the XAI model only reported the risk factors in the rules without the incorporation of any contextual information:

A

"Male, and has cholesterol level risk, blood pressure risk, smoking risk. Prone to have CAD"

B

"Patient has normal glucose level. Prone to have CAD"

Explanation dialogues used in Phase II testing (7 May 2019), utilized a more natural language dialogue to represent the XAI model's output with the incorporation of the missing links from the contextual data:

A

"Since the patient is Male, and males have a higher chance of attaining CAD, and patient's test results show that they have high cholesterol, high blood pressure, and high diabetic risk. This infers that the patient has a high probability risk for CAD"

B

"The patient seems to be on glucose medication which normalizes blood glucose level. This infers why patient may have high potential risk for CAD though they have a normal glucose level"

From the above two iterative excerpts, we can infer how the inclusion of ME's contextual information within the explanation has drastically improved the level of reasoning given by the XAI. We will see more on how we measured the level of trust and understandability of the XAI's explanations in the next section.

6.1 Using Questioners to Evaluate the Precision and Performance

To measure the trust and understandability of the XAI, we performed qualitative analysis with 5 MEs to evaluate the precision and performance of the XAI model using a human-machine work system analysis approach. The MEs used checklist-based questionnaires to evaluate the goodness and satisfactoriness of the explanations generated by the XAI model [28]. The evaluators must have extensive experience in the specific disease process supported by the XAI. With their expert understanding of CAD and general patient care we were able to evaluate and validate the XAI model's explanations.

The testing of performance and precision of the XAI model were conducted in two phases using Robert Hoffman's chart [28] as described below. The score attained in each phase represents the precision, performance and trustworthiness of the XAI model. Phase I represents preliminary stage testing where the MEs qualitatively assessed the dialogues given by the XAI model. While, the Phase II testing incorporated Phase I MEs feedback and recommendations to improve the model's explanation (Fig. 6).

Phase I

An excerpt of comment given by ME for testing Phase I, iteration 1:

Explanatory goodness and satisfaction test

For each of the statements listed below, on a scale of 1-5 (where 1 being very bad and 5 being very good), please indicate how well the AI was able to explain its diagnosis to you by circling one of the numbers from 1-5 below.

No.	Statement					
1.	I understand the explanation of how the AI works.	1	2	3	4	5
2.	The explanation given by the AI is satisfying.	1	2	3	4	5
3.	The explaining given by the AI has sufficient details.	1	2	3	4	5
4.	The explanation lets me judge when I can trust and not trust the AI.	1	2	3	4	5
5.	The explanation says how accurate the AI is.	1	2	3	4	5
6.	The explanation will aid me in diagnosis.	1	2	3	4	5

Fig. 6. Phase I. Iteration 1. XAI model testing results

"The explanation could be made more versatile. Will be more helpful if it could help me in identifying the special cases in CAD"

Precision & performance score I.1:

$$\frac{\text{Attained Score from (Fig 5)}}{\text{Total scorefrom (Fig 5)}} = \frac{5+4+4+3+5+5}{5+5+5+5+5+5} = \frac{26}{30} = 86\%$$

An excerpt of comment given by ME for testing Phase I, iteration 2:

"Needs more explanation and contextual information about patient is necessary to be convincing and trustworthy. Naming the factors that caused the patient to acquire CAD is not enough. With better explanation, it can perform better than scorecards"

Precision & performance score I.2: 83% (calculated using the same formula shown in Phase I.1).

Phase II

In Phase II of the development, we modified the dialogues and added in more contextual information about the patient's conditions like medication intake, daily routine etc. as per the feedback given by the ME. With the incorporation of these information into the model, there was a drastic improvement in the diagnostic performance of the model and enabled phase 2 to score better on the precision and performance test (Fig. 7).

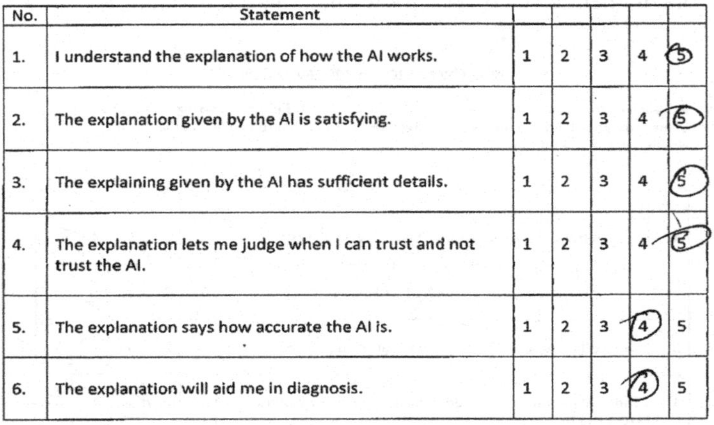

No.	Statement					
1.	I understand the explanation of how the AI works.	1	2	3	4	5
2.	The explanation given by the AI is satisfying.	1	2	3	4	5
3.	The explaining given by the AI has sufficient details.	1	2	3	4	5
4.	The explanation lets me judge when I can trust and not trust the AI.	1	2	3	4	5
5.	The explanation says how accurate the AI is.	1	2	3	4	5
6.	The explanation will aid me in diagnosis.	1	2	3	4	5

Fig. 7. Phase II XAI model's precision and performance testing result

An excerpt from a comment given by a ME for testing Phase II:

"Explanations have been improved to be more trustworthy and precise. Additionally, we were able to get more insights through the explanations. Yet, fails to identify the anomaly cases in CAD."

Precision & performance score II by ME 1: 93%
Precision & performance score II by ME 2: 95%
Precision & performance score II by ME 3: 89%
Precision & performance score II by ME 4: 96%
Precision & performance score II by ME 5: 92%

(calculated using the same formula shown in Phase I.1).

7 Results

Through the two iterative testing phases, we observed that the MEs rated Phase I XAI performance and precision lower than the Phase II version. This is likely due to the incompleteness and lack of narrative of the explanations given by the Phase I model. The Phase I model lacked the type of information the MEs felt necessary for understanding and trusting the XAI model. The second iterative phase, however, through the iterative involvement of MEs in every stage returned a much more comprehensive model explanation. This model included the qualitative and contextual information presented in a natural dialogue form which the MEs felt necessary for a more trustworthy and understandable interaction with the model's outputs. As seen from the score given by five MEs, the Phase II explanations were rated as more satisfactory by the MEs as it enabled them to develop complete and trustworthy mental models about the XAI's diagnosis compared to the simple explanations given by the Phase I model. The subjective effectiveness of the XAI model for MEs is based on these ratings which demonstrates the degree to which a person could gain understanding from the explanations [40].

Additionally, an interesting finding we observed was that the final phase of our early XAI model scored 96% (according to the precision and performance chart given by Robert Hoffman, IHMC) from the MEs which is considerably better than the 86% scored by the SVM algorithm standing alone with a training and testing cohort of 80% and 20% from its respective records. Since the XAI was built through the interpretation of the individual feature sets on SVM algorithm as illustrated in Sect. 5.2, it should score approximately the same accuracy rating as the SVM algorithm. However, with the incorporation of the human-centered approach and integrating contextual information (e.g., treatment regimens, demographic data, pharmaceutical history, etc.), the XAI was able to perform considerably better than the original SVM algorithm.

8 Conclusion and Future Work

Our preliminary work in exploring the notion of Explainable AI by the use of SVM and data mining techniques using syllogistic rules revealed two main findings. Firstly, we showed the importance of employing a human-centered approach iteratively when developing and interpreting the SVM output. By including MEs in the process, we found that data lacked the contextual, demographic and treatment information from the patients' records. The significance of contextual information can be illustrated by a finding whereby some of the interpretations from the SVM algorithm's graph gave contradicting results when validated against the CPGs. For example, blood glucose results from the Framingham dataset showed that patients with normal blood glucose are more prone to have CAD. However, the MEs inferred that blood glucose level is one of the most important factors contributing to CAD. In this case, the MEs surmised that most of these CAD patients were compliant with their diabetes treatment, and, thus, they maintained target therapeutic levels (i.e., normal range blood glucose) despite being diagnosed with CAD. Therefore, this proposed method will rely on MEs to discover the hidden rules and patterns within the data (i.e., specific types of CAD). While ML algorithms exhibit a hard to interpret behavior, the XAI provides an alternative pathway (through data visualization and natural language dialogue) to iteratively decode the inherent complexity of how risk factor variables interactions affect patient health, disease progression and outcomes. Although intelligent assistants often apply KBs, we employed a novel technique to improve the KB quality and precision using syllogistic rules to interpret SVM classification coupled with integral, iterative human-in-the-loop feedback during the development process.

Secondly, we observed that the XAI model's diagnostic capacity improved with more contextual information. With this, the MEs found the diagnosis performed by the XAI model to be more reliable than other conventional ML algorithms (Neural Networks, Decision Trees etc.) they have worked with before. Additionally, it also improves MEs assessment of the XAI model by enabling them to have a better understanding and trust with the model's chain of reasoning for a particular output (diagnoses). Moreover, the MEs trust in a the XAI model improved by employing a voice-based natural language dialogue system rather than a text-based output. Perhaps this may be due to the voice-based dialogue system providing the explanations of the XAI's decision-making process when proposing a diagnosis. The trust and confidence of the AI assistant is increased by providing more specific details and contextual information with explanations that employ natural language dialogue. Hence with this, the XAI was able to accomplish something a ML algorithm could not do on its own.

In the near future, we plan to explore the following two potential directions. First, we will investigate how to apply multiagent system techniques to automate the acquisition and integration of the multivariate contextual information needed to develop fully automated XAI systems. With this automation, the need for human technical support to integrate newly discovered contextual information would not be necessary anymore. Second, we would investigate the use of this automated XAI system to identify various forms of cardiovascular anomalies, which are generally deemed to be difficult for MEs to diagnose. Apart from that, these anomalies are also often misdiagnosed by ML algorithms due to the lack of requisite contextual information, which again strains the crucial need for the automation of XAI system.

With this proposed XAI model, we conclude this study with hopes to inspire and convince other researches to join and invest their experience and expertise in this emerging research field and transform the field of health care for multitudes around the world.

References

1. Core, M., Lane, C., Lent, M.V., Gomboc, D., Solomon, S., Rosenberg, M.: Building explainable artificial intelligence systems. In: Proceedings of the 18th Conference On Innovative Applications of Artificial Intelligence. (IAAI 2006), vol. 2, pp. 1766–1773. AAAI Press (2006)
2. Moore, J., Swartout, W.: Explanation in Expert Systems-A Survey. University of Southern California. Information Sciences Institute. Technical report ISI/RR-88-228 (1988)
3. Buchanan, B., Shortliffe, E.: Rule Based Expert Systems the MYCIN Experiments of the Stanford Heuristic Programming Project. Addison-Wesley, Boston (1984)
4. Bishop, C.: Pattern Recognition and Machine Learning. Springer, New York (2006)
5. Liu, B., Hsu, W., Ma, Y.: Integrating classification and association rule mining, vol. 98, pp. 80–86. KDD Publication (1998)
6. Maglogiannis, I., Loukis, E., Zafiropoulos, E., Stasis, A.: Support vectors machine-based identification of heart valve diseases using heart sounds. Comput. Methods Programs Biomed. **95**(1), 47–61 (2009)
7. Thurston, R., Matthews, K., Hernandez, J., Torre, F.D.L.: Improving the performance of physiologic hot flash measures with support vector machines. Psychophysiology **46**(2), 285–292 (2009)
8. Adrienne, C., et al.: A decision support system to facilitate management of patients with acute gastrointestinal bleeding. Artif. Intell. Med. **42**(3), 247–259 (2008)
9. Rice, S., Nenadic, G., Stapley, B.: Mining protein function from text using term-based support vector machines. BMC Bioinf. **6**(1), S22 (2005)

10. Lamy, J.B., Sekar, B., Guezennec, G., Bouaud, J., Séroussi, B.: Explainable artificial intelligence for breast cancer: a visual case-based reasoning approach. Artif. Intell. Med. **94**, 42–53 (2019)
11. Sowa, J.: Knowledge Representation: Logical, Philosophical, and Computational Foundations. PWS Publishing Company, Boston (2000)
12. London, A.J.: Artificial intelligence and black-box medical decisions: accuracy versus explainability. Hastings Cent. Rep. **49**(1), 15–21 (2019)
13. Teach, R., Shortliffe, E.: An analysis of physician attitudes regarding computer-based clinical consultation systems. Comput. Biomed. Res. **14**(6), 542–558 (1981). https://doi.org/10.1016/0010-4809(81)90012-4
14. American College of Cardiology Homepage. https://www.acc.org/guidelines#doctype=Guidelines. Accessed 28 Dec 2019
15. Cohn, P.: Diagnosis and Therapy of Coronary Artery Disease. Springer Science & Business Media, Berlin (2012)
16. Shavelle, D.: Almanac 2015: coronary artery disease. Heart **102**(7), 492–499 (2016)
17. Abdullah, N., Clancey, W., Raj, A., Zain, A., Khalid, K.F., Ooi, A.: Application of a double loop learning approach for healthcare systems design in an emerging market. In: IEEE/ACM International Workshop on Software Engineering in Healthcare Systems (SEHS), pp. 10–13. IEEE (2018)
18. Babaoğlu, I., Fındık, O., Bayrak, M.: Effects of principle component analysis on assessment of coronary artery diseases using support vector machine. Expert Syst. Appl. **37**(3), 2182–2185 (2010)
19. Hongzong, S., et al.: Support vector machines classification for discriminating coronary heart disease patients from non-coronary heart disease. West Indian Med. J. **56**(5), 451–457 (2007)
20. Xing, Y., Wang, J., Zhao, Z.: Combination data mining methods with new medical data to predicting outcome of coronary heart disease. In: International Conference on Convergence Information Technology. (ICCIT 2007), pp. 868–872 (2007)
21. Zhu, Y., Wu, Z., Fang, Y.: Study on application of SVM in prediction of coronary heart disease. J. Biomed. Eng. **30**(6), 1180–1185 (2013)
22. Krittanawong, C., Zhang, H.J., Wang, Z., Aydar, M., Kitai, T.: Artificial intelligence in precision cardiovascular medicine. J. Am. Coll. Cardiol. **69**(21), 2657–2664 (2017)
23. Çolak, M.C., Çolak, C., Kocatürk, H., Sagiroglu, S., Barutçu, I.: Predicting coronary artery disease using different artificial neural network models. AKD **8**(4), 249 (2008)
24. Guidi, G., Pettenati, M.C., Melillo, P., Iadanza, E.: A machine learning system to improve heart failure patient assistance. IEEE J. Biomed. Health Inf. **18**(6), 1750–1756 (2014). IEEE
25. Sokol, K., Flach, P.: Conversational explanations of machine learning predictions through class-contrastive counterfactual statements, pp. 5785–5786. IJCAI Publication (2018)
26. Miller, T.: Explanation in artificial intelligence: insights from the social sciences. arXiv 1706.07269 (2018)
27. Mittelstadt, B., Russell, C., Wachter, S.: Explaining explanations in AI. In: Proceedings of the Conference On Fairness, Accountability, and Transparency. ACM Library (2019)
28. Hoffman, R., Mueller, S., Klein, G., Litman, J.: Metrics for explainable AI: challenges and prospects. arXiv 1812.04608 (2018)
29. Nakatsu, R.: Explanatory power of intelligent systems. In: Intelligent Decision-making Support Systems, pp. 123–143. Springer (2006). https://doi.org/10.1007/1-84628-231-4_7
30. Lehtiranta, L., Junnonen, J.M., Kärnä, S., Pekuri, L.: The constructive research approach: problem solving for complex projects. Designs, Methods and Practices for Research of Project Management, pp. 95–106. Routledge, London (2015)

31. Trentesaux, D., Millot, P.: A human-centred design to break the myth of the magic human in intelligent manufacturing systems. In: Borangiu, T., Trentesaux, D., Thomas, A., McFarlane, D. (eds.) Service Orientation in Holonic and Multi-Agent Manufacturing. SCI, vol. 640, pp. 103–113. Springer, Cham (2016). https://doi.org/10.1007/978-3-319-30337-6_10
32. Kass, R., Finin, T.: The need for user models in generating expert system explanations: Int. J. Expert Syst. **1**(4), 11–14 (1988)
33. Clark, P., Niblett, T.: Induction in Noisy Domains. (EWSL 1987), pp. 11–30 (1987)
34. Holzinger, A.: Interactive machine learning for health informatics: when do we need the human-in-the-loop? Brain Inf. **3**(2), 119–131 (2016). https://doi.org/10.1007/s40708-016-0042-6
35. Heart Disease UCI. Kaggle. https://www.kaggle.com/ronitf/heart-disease-uci. Accessed 12 Aug 2019
36. Framingham heart study dataset. Kaggle. https://www.kaggle.com/amanajmera1/framingham-heart-study-dataset. Accessed 12 Aug 2019
37. Scikit learn homepage. https://scikit-learn.org/stable/auto_examples/feature_selection/plot_feature_selection.html. Accessed 28 Dec 2019
38. Benesty, J., Chen, J., Huang, Y., Cohen, I.: Pearson correlation coefficient. In: Noise Reduction in Speech Processing, pp. 1–4. Springer, Heidelberg (2009). https://doi.org/10.1007/978-3-642-00296-0_5
39. PyPI Homepage. https://pypi.org/project/pyttsx3/. Accessed 28 Dec 2019
40. Keil, F.: Explanation and understanding. Annu. Rev. Psychol. **57**, 227–254 (2006)

Non-local Second-Order Attention Network for Single Image Super Resolution

Jiawen Lyn(✉) and Sen Yan

Trinity College Dublin, Dublin 2, D02PN40, Ireland
linj1@tcd.ie

Abstract. Single image super-resolution is a ill-posed problem which aims to characterize the texture pattern given a blurry and low-resolution image sample. Convolution neural network recently are introduced into super resolution to tackle this problem and further bringing forward progress in this field. Although state-of-the-art studies have obtain excellent performance by designing the structure and the way of connection in the convolution neural network, they ignore the use of high-order data to train more power model. In this paper, we propose a non-local second-order attention network for single image super resolution, which make the full use of the training data and further improve performance by non-local second-order attention. This attention scheme does not only provide a guideline to design the network, but also interpretable for super-resolution task. Extensive experiments and analyses have demonstrated our model exceed the state-of-the-arts models with similar parameters.

Keywords: Super resolution · Deep neural network · Deep learning

1 Introduction

Because the rapid growth of the video and image data, super-resolution (SR) has enjoyed the current advances in deep learning and has attracted more attention in recent years. In real life, super-resolution techniques can be applied to many applications such as satellite and medical image processing [17], facial image improvement [2] and aerial imaging [34], etc. Obtaining high-resolution images given low-resolution images can be an ill-posed problem, but convolution neural network had a huge impact in this field, making the result images detailed and natural. In this work, we mainly tackle single image super-resolution task.

Considering the successful experience of convolutional neural network (CNN) in high-level vision tasks such as images segmentation, Dong et al. [7] proposed CNN based SR algorithm namely SRCNN. So from then on CNN have attract more attention for researchers to tackle super-resolution tasks [8,19,20,23,26,31]. Although the performance is largely improved, exist some problems. Firstly, and most importantly, previous researches focus on introducing deeper convolutional neural network to improve performance and ignore the

Published by Springer Nature Switzerland AG 2020
A. Holzinger et al. (Eds.): CD-MAKE 2020, LNCS 12279, pp. 267–279, 2020.
https://doi.org/10.1007/978-3-030-57321-8_15

computation overhead. A large number of calculations make the algorithm difficult to be applied in practice. Secondly, with the depth of network increasing, the training procedure will become more unstable [23,25], which means that need more training tricks to train network for improving performance. Thirdly, most of the previous methods did not make full use of the training data to reconstruct the super-resolution image. Practically, we have some train data did not use in training.

To tackle the above problems, we propose applying non-local second-order attention mechanism to super-resolution network designs. First, we focus on the non-local block to make the network to learn self-attention by capturing long-range dependency. Second, we develop the network to make full use of the training data for reconstructing super-resolution image. To the best of our knowledge, this is the first proposed non-local second-order training strategy into single image super-resolution network design, providing a special viewpoint of the data enhancement for deep learning and a extraordinary guidance on network design. In this work, we propose a both lightweight and efficient networks using the proposed schemes to design. Experimental results on benchmark datasets demonstrate our methods is superior most of state of the art models.

2 Related Work

2.1 Single Image Super-Resolution

Single image super resolution is a low-level computer vision task. The popular method in our literatures is learning the mapping function from low-resolution images to high-resolution images to reconstruct. Traditional machine learning techniques are widely applied in super-resolution, including kernel method[4], PCA [3], sparse-coding [30], learning embedding [5], etc. There are a powerful method take full sue of the image self-similarity without extra data. In order to obtain a super-resolution image, [11] use the patch redundancy to produce. Freedam et al. [9] further develop a localized searching method. [14] extend this algorithm to guide the patch search through using detected perspective geometry.

Current advances in SISR make full use of the powerful representation capability of convolution neural network. Dong et al. [7] first proposed SRCNN to recovery high-resolution image. They interpret the architecture in CNN as extraction layer, non-linear mapping layer, and reconstruction layer, corresponding these steps in sparse coding [30]. DRCN [19] further these steps through firstly interpolating the low-resolution image to the desired size so that suffers from the huge computational complexity and some detail lost. Kim et al. [18,19] adopt the deep residual convolutional neural network to achieve better performance, which use the bicubic interpolation to upsample the low-resolution image to the desired size and then fed in network to output super-resolution image. Since then, the deeper CNN-based super resolution models is a trend to obtain superior performance, such as LapSRN [20], DRRN [26], SRResNet [21], EDSR [23] and RCAN [31].

Nevertheless, the depth of the network bring a huge amount of the computation and increase the process time. In order to solve this problem, Dong et al. adopt smaller filter sizes and a deeper network namely FSRCNN [8], which remove the bicubic interpolation layer in SRCNN and embedding the deconvolution layer at the tail of the FSRCNN. To reduce parameters, DRRN [26] proposed the combination of the residual skip connection and the recursive so that compromise the runtime speed. Currently, CARN [1] exploit the multiple shortcut connections and multiple-level representation to obtain a cascading mechanism upon a residual network. In order to utilize the multi-scale feature, [22] proposed MSRN model to capture the multi-scale feature at different scale size. In order to improve the performance, Dai et al. proposed SAN [6] and He et al. proposed ODE-inspired network [12], which both introduced high-order feature extractor to capture high-order statistic, but they ignored the operate of the convolution layer is local so we combined both the non-local operate and high-order statistic extractor to improve our network.

Although most of the CNN-based super-resolution methods strongly promote progress in this field, most of the advanced model blindly increase the depth and parameters of the network and they ignore the operate of the convolution is local. It is clear that these method increase the running time and not necessarily improve accuracy.

2.2 Attention Model

To human perception, attention generally means human visual systems focus on salient areas [16] and adaptively process visual information. Currently, several study have proposed embedding attention mechanism processing to improve the performance of CNNs for different tasks, such as image segmentation, image and video classification [13,29]. Wang et al. proposed non-local neural network [29] for video classification, which incorporate non-local process to spatially attention long range feature. Hu et al. proposed SENet [13] to capture channel-wise feature relationships to obtain better performance for image classification. Li et al. proposed expectation-maximization attention network for semantic segmentation, which borrowed EM algorithm to iteratively optimize parameters and decrease the complex of the operation in non-local block. Huang et al. proposed criss-cross attention [15] for semantic segmentation, which can efficiently capture contextual pattern from long-range dependencies. Fu et al. proposed a dual attention network (DANet) [10], which mainly consists of the position attention module and the channel attention module. They use position attention module to learn the spatial interdependencies. The channel attention module is designed to model channel interdependencies. It largely improves the segmentation results through capturing rich contextual dependencies. Zhang et al. proposed residual channel attention network (RCAN) [31] for single image super resolution, which adopt channel attention (CA) mechanism to adaptively capture channel-wise pattern information through considering interdependencies among channels. Zhang et al. is first introduce non-local block in single image super resolution. They proposed residual non-local attention learning [32] to capture more detailed information through preserving more low-level features, being more suitable for super resolution image reconstruction. The network pursue better network representational ability and achieve high-quality image reconstruction results. Dai et al. proposed non-locally enhanced residual group (NLRG) [6] to capture spatial contextual information so that hugely improve the performance of the model.

3 Non-local Second-Order Attention Network

3.1 Network Framework

As show in Fig. 1, our NSAN mainly consists of four parts: shallow feature extractor, high-order enhanced group (HEG) based deep feature extraction, up-scale layer and reconstruction layer. Give I_{LR} and I_{SR} as the input and output of our NSAN. Following the [6,23], we apply one convolution layer to capture the shallow feature F_0 from the LR input

$$F_0 = H_{SF}(I_{LR}) \tag{1}$$

where H_{SF} represents the convolution operation. Then the shallow feature F_0 fed in HEG based deep feature extraction, which thus obtains the deep feature as

$$F_{DF} = H_{HEG}(I_0) \tag{2}$$

where H_{HEG} stands for the HEG based non-local enhanced feature extraction module, which consists of two RL-NL modules to capture the long-range information and G residual channel attention groups. So our proposed HEG achieve very deep depth and can capture more information. Then the extracted deep feature F_{DF} is upsample through the upsacale module via

$$F_{\uparrow} = H_{\uparrow}(I_{LR}) \tag{3}$$

where $H_{\uparrow}$ and $F_{\uparrow}$ are a upsample layer and upsampled feature respectively. In the previous works, there are several choices to perform as upscale part, such as transposed convolution [8], ESPCN [24]. Embedding upscaling feature in the last few layers achieve a good trade off between performance and computational burden, thus is preferable in recent SR models [6,8,23]. Then upscaled feature is through one convolution layer

$$I_{SR} = H_R(F_{\uparrow}) = H_{NSAN}(I_{LR}) \tag{4}$$

where H_R, $H_{\uparrow}$ and H_{NSAN} are the reconstruction layer, upsample layer and the function of NSAN, respectively.

Then NSAN will be optimized with a loss function. Some loss functions have been widely used, such as L2, L1, perceptual losses. In order to verify the effectiveness of our NSAN, we adopt the L1 loss functions followed previous works. Given a training set with N low-resolution images and high-resolution images denoted by $\{I_{HR}, I_{HR}\}^N$, the purpose of the NSAN is to optimize the loss function:

$$L(\Theta) = \frac{1}{N}\sum_{i=1}^{N} ||I_{HR} - I_{SR}||_1 \tag{5}$$

where θ represents the parameter set of NSAN. We choose Adam algorithm to optimize the loss function.

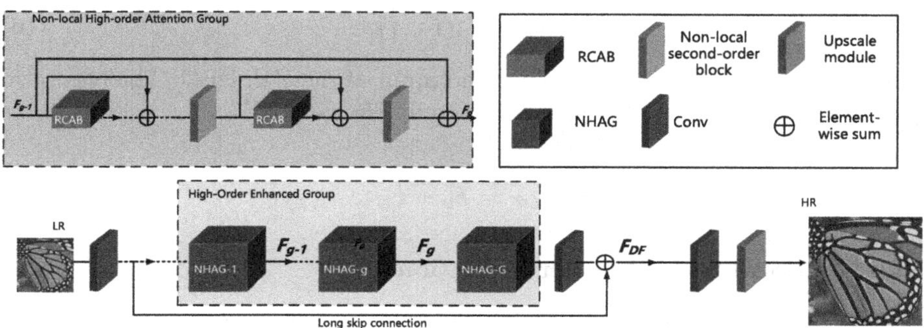

Fig. 1. Framework of the proposed non-local second-order attention network (NSAN).

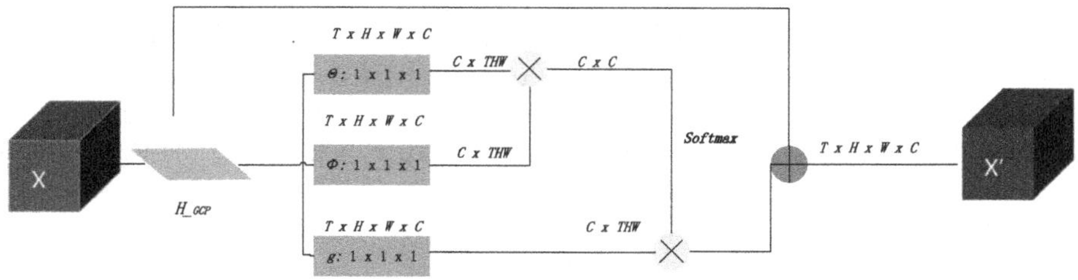

Fig. 2. Framework of the proposed non-local second-order attention module (NSA).

3.2 High-Order Enhanced Group (HEG)

We now describe our edge enhanced (HEG) (see Fig. 1), which can be divided into the main branch and the edge enhanced branch. The main branch consists of two region-level non-local (RL-NL) modules [6] and G non-local residual channel attention groups (NRCAG) structure. The RL-NL can capture the long-range information. Each NRCAG further contains M simplified residual channel blocks with local skip connection, followed by a non-local channel attention (NCA) module to exploit feature interdependencies. The edge enhanced branch consists of the padding module and V NRCAG, which can make full use of the edge information and use edge information to enhance channel feature attention.

Stacking residual blocks has been verified that is helpful way to form a deep network in [6,22,23]. Nevertheless, deeper network built in such way would lead in performance bottleneck and training difficulty during the problem of gradient vanishing and exploding in deep network. It is known simply stacking repeated block may not to obtain better performance. In order to address this issue, we introduce the NHAG to not only to bypass abundant low-frequency information from LR images, but also facilitate the training of our deep network. Then a HEG in the g-th group is represented as:

$$F_g = H_g(F_{g-1}) \tag{6}$$

where F_g, F_{g-1} denote the output and input of the g-th HEG. The bias term is omitted for simplicity. H_g is the function of the g-th HEG.

Then deep feature is obtained as:

$$F_{DF} = F_0 + F_G \tag{7}$$

3.3 Non-local Second-Order Attention

Most previous CNN-based SR models ignore the feature interdependencies. In order to take full use of these information, SENet [13] introduced CNNs to rescale the channel-wise features for image SR. Nevertheless, SENet only exploits first-order statistics features through global average pooling, while ignoring non-local statistics more rich than local, thus hindering the discriminative ability of the network.

Inspired by the above works, we propose a non-local second-order attention (NSA) module (see Fig. 2) to capture high-order feature interdependencies through considering non-local features. Now we will describe how to exploit such non-local information. We reshape the feature map $\mathrm{F} = [\mathrm{f}_1, \cdots, \mathrm{f}_C]$ with C feature maps with size of $H \times W$ to a feature matrix X with $s = WH$ features of C-dimension. Then compute the sample covariance matrix as

$$\Sigma = \mathrm{X}\bar{I}\mathrm{X}^T$$

where $\bar{I} = \frac{1}{s}(\mathrm{I} - \frac{1}{s}\mathrm{1})$, I and 1 are the $s \times s$ identity matrix and manix of all ones, respectively.

It is shown that covariance normalization plays a critical role for more discriminative representations. For this reason, we first perform covariance normalization for the obtained covariance matrix Σ, which is symmenic positive semi-definite and thus has eigenvalue decomposition (EIG) as follows

$$\Sigma = \mathrm{U}\Lambda\mathrm{U}^T$$

where U is an orthogonal matrix and $\Lambda = \mathrm{diag}(\lambda_1, \cdots, \lambda_C)$ is diagonal matrix with eigenvalues in non-increasing order. Then covariance normalization can be converted to the power of eigenvalues:

$$\hat{\mathrm{Y}} = \Sigma^\alpha = \mathrm{U}\Lambda^\alpha\mathrm{U}^T$$

where α is a positive real number, and $\Lambda^{\alpha} = \mathrm{diag}(\lambda_1^{\alpha}, \cdots, \lambda_C^{\alpha})$. When $\alpha = 1$, there is no normalization; when $\alpha < 1$, it nonlinearly shrinks the eigenvalues larger than 1.0 and stretches those less than 1.0. As explored in [13], $\alpha = 1/2$ works well for more discriminative representations. Thus, we set $\alpha = 1/2$ in the following.

The normalized covariance manix characterizes the correlations of channel-wise features. We then take such normalized covariance matrix as a channel descriptor by global covariance pooling. As illustrated in Fig. 2, let $\hat{\mathrm{Y}} = [\mathrm{y}_1, \cdots, \mathrm{y}_C]$, the channel-wise statistics $\mathrm{z} \in R^{C\times 1}$ can be obtained by shrinking $\hat{\mathrm{Y}}$. Then the c-th dimension of z is computed as

$$z_c = H_{GCP}(\mathrm{y}_c) = \frac{1}{C}\sum_{i}^{C}\mathrm{y}_c(i)$$

where H_{GCP} denotes the global covariance pooling function. Compared with the commonly used first-order pooling (*e.g.*, global average pooling), our global covariance pooling explores the feature distribution and captures the feature statistics higher than first-order for more discriminative representations.

To fully exploit feature interdependencies from the aggregated information by global covariance pooling, we also introduce non-local block to capture long range pattern. Inspire [10], which proposed non-local channel attention block to extract more useful feature, but it do not use second-order feature. In our network, we combine the second order extractor and non-local attention, which can extract second-order feature and then obtain non-local attention map

$$\mathrm{X}^{'} = H_{NSB}(z)$$

where H_{NSB} denote the non-local second-order block. The detail of the second-order block can see Fig. 2.

4 Experiments

4.1 Setup

Following [23,32], we train on 800 training images in DIV2K dataset [28]. In order to verify the effectiveness of our network, we choose 5 benchmark datasets: Set5, Set14, BSD100, Urban100 and Manga109. For the degradation model, we adopt Matlab resize function with bicubic operation. For the metrics, we use PSNR and SSIM to evaluate SR result.

For the training, the low-resolution images are augmented through horizontally flipping and randomly rotating $90°, 180°, 270°$. For the each min-batch, we set 16 low resolution image patches with size 48×48 as inputs. We use ADAM algorithm to optimize our model with $\beta_1 = 0.9, \beta_2 = 0.99$, and $\epsilon = 10^{-8}$ and initialize learning rate as 10^{-4} and then reduced to half every 200 epochs. We use Pytorch framework to train our proposed NSAN on an Nvidia 1080Ti GPU.

4.2 Ablation Study

As show in Fig. 1, our NSAN contains two main components, including High-order Enhanced Group (HEG) and non-local second-order attention module (NSA). In order to test the effectiveness of the various modules, we train and test NSAN with its variants on the Set5 dataset for comparison. Specific performance is shown in Table 1.

We set R_{BASE} as a basic baseline, which only contains the convolutional layer containing 20 NHAG and 10 remaining blocks in each NHAG. Following the [33], we also added long skip and short skip connections to the base model. R_a and R_b mean embedding second-order feature extractor and non-local block in base structure, respectively. R_c means that the result of combining second-order feature extractor and non-local block. It can be found that both of R_c obtain better performance than methods of R_a to R_b.

Table 1. Effect of different module. We report the result in Set5 dataset on 200 epoch

	Base	Ra	Rb	Rc
Second-order Feature		True		
Non-local Block			True	
Non-local Block with Non-local Block				True
PSNR	31.97	32.04	32.08	32.23

4.3 Results with Bicubic Degradation (BI)

We set up a comparison test with model 12 state-of-the-art CNN-based SR methods: SRCNN [7], FSRCNN [8], VDSR [18], LapSRN [20], MemNet [27], EDSR [23], RDN [33] and RCAN [31] for verifying the effectiveness of the NSAN. The quantitative results of each scale factor are shown in Fig. 3. Compared to other methods, our NSAN performed best on all datasets, with different scaling factors. Without self-integration, NSAN and SAN can achieve very similar results and are superior to other approaches. This is mainly because both of them use high-order feature to learn the interdependence between features, which makes the network pay more attention to information features (Fig. 5).

Compared to RCAN, our NSAN got satisfactory performance for data sets with rich texture information, such as Set5, Set14, and BSD100, and slightly worse results for data sets, such as Manga109 and BSD100 with rich reprocessing edge information. As we all know, texture is a higher-order pattern with more complex statistical properties, while edge is a first-order pattern that can be extracted by a first-order operator. Therefore, our NSA based on second-order feature statistics and non-local operator works better on images with more higher-order information like texture.

Method	Scale	Set5	Set14	BSD100	Urban100	Manga109
Bicubic	2	33.66/.9299	30.24/.8688	SSIM	26.88/.8403	30.80/.9339
SRCNN	2	36.66/.9542	32.45/.9067	31.36/.8879	29.50/.8946	35.60/.9663
FSRCNN	2	37.05/.9560	32.66/.9090	31.53/.8920	29.88/.9020	36.67/.9710
VDSR	2	37.53/.9590	33.05/.9130	31.90/.8960	30.77/.9140	37.22/.9750
LapSRN	2	37.52/.9591	33.08/.9130	31.08/.8950	30.41/.9101	37.27/.9740
MemNet	2	37.78/.9597	33.28/.9142	32.08/.8978	31.31/.9195	37.72/.9740
EDSR	2	38.11/.9602	33.92/.9195	32.32/.9013	32.93/.9351	39.10/.9773
SRMD	2	37.79/.9601	33.32/.9159	32.05/.8985	31.33/.9204	38.07/.9761
DBPN	2	38.09/.9600	33.85/.9190	32.27/.9000	32.55/.9324	38.89/.9775
RDN	2	38.24/.9614	34.01/.9212	32.34/.9017	32.89/.9353	39.18/.9780
RCAN	2	38.27/.9614	34.11/.9216	32.41/.9026	33.34/.9384	39.43/.9786
SAN	2	38.31/.9620	34.07/.9213	32.42/.9028	33.10/.9370	39.32/.9792
NSAN	2	38.43/.9634	34.17/.9233	32.47/.9038	33.12/.9350	39.42/.9893
Bicubic	3	39.32/.9792	27.55/.7742	27.21/.7385	24.46/.7349	26.95/.8556
SRCNN	3	32.75/.9090	29.30/.8215	28.41/.7863	26.24/.7989	30.48/.9117
FSRCNN	3	33.18/.9140	29.37/.8240	28.53/.7910	26.43/.8080	31.10/.9210
VDSR	3	33.67/.9210	29.78/.8320	28.83/.7990	27.14/.8290	32.01/.9340
LapSRN	3	33.82/.9227	29.87/.8320	28.82/.7980	27.07/.8280	32.21/.9350
MemNet	3	34.09/.9248	30.01/.8350	28.96/.8001	27.56/.8376	32.51/.9369
EDSR	3	34.65/.9280	3.52/ .8462	29.25/.8093	28.80/.8653	34.17/.9476
SRMD	3	34.12/.9254	30.04/.8382	28.97/.8025	27.57/.8398	33.00/.9403
RDN	3	34.71/.9296	30.57/.8468	29.26/.8093	28.80/.8653	34.13/.9484
RCAN	3	34.74/.9299	30.64/.8481	29.32/.8111	29.08/.8702	34.43/.9498
SAN	3	34.75/.9300	30.59/.8476	29.33/.8112	28.93/.8671	34.30/.9494
NSAN	3	34.85/.9321	30.63/.8576	29.54/.8121	28.99/.8771	34.41/.9497
Bicubic	4	28.42/.8104	26.00/.7027	25.96/.6675	23.14/.6577	24.89/.7866
SRCNN	4	30.48/.8628	27.50/.7513	26.90/.7101	24.52/.7221	27.58/.8555
FSRCNN	4	30.72/.8660	27.61/.7550	26.98/.7150	24.62/.7280	27.90/.8610
VDSR	4	31.35/.8830	28.02/.7680	27.29/.0726	25.18/.7540	28.83/.8870
LapSRN	4	31.54/.8850	28.19/.7720	27.32/.7270	25.21/.7560	29.09/.8900
MemNet	4	31.74/.8893	28.26/.7723	27.40/.7281	25.50/.7630	29.42/.8942
EDSR	4	32.46/.8968	28.80/.7876	27.71/.7420	26.64/.8033	31.02/.9148
SRMD	4	31.96/.8925	28.35/.7787	27.49/.7337	25.68/.7731	30.09/.9024
DBPN	4	32.47/.8980	28.82/.7860	27.72/.7400	26.38/.7946	30.91/.9137
RDN	4	32.47/.8990	28.81/.7871	27.72/.7419	26.61/.8028	31.00/.9151
RCAN	4	32.62/.9001	28.86/.7888	27.76/.7435	26.82/.8087	31.21/.9172
SAN	4	32.64/.9003	28.92/.7888	27.78/.7436	26.79/.8068	31.18/.9169
NSAN	4	32.67/.90021	28.95/.7894	27.81/.7456	26.87/.8087	31.23/.9188

Fig. 3. Quantitative results with BI degradation model.

	EDSR	MemNet	NLRG	DBPN	RDN	RCAN	NSAN
Para.	43M	677k	330k	10M	22.3M	16M	15.5M
PSNR	38.11	37.78	38.00	38.09	38.24	38.27	38.43

Fig. 4. Computational and parameter comparison (2X) Set5).

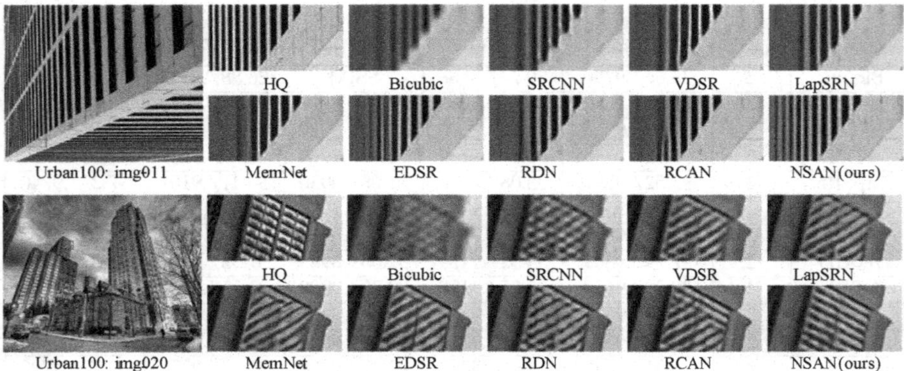

Fig. 5. Visual comparison for 4x SR with BI model on Urban100 dataset.

We also show the visual results of different methods as shown in Fig. 2. We find that most SR models cannot accurately reconstruct the lattices and have severe fuzzy artifacts. On the contrary, our NSAN achieve clearer results and reconstruct more high-frequency details such as high contrast and sharp edges. In the case of "img011", most of the comparison methods output heavily fuzzy artifacts. The early developments of bicubic, SRCNN, FSRCNN and LapSRN even lost their main structures.

Compared with the ground-truth, NSAN gets more reliable results and restores more image detail. Although reconstructing high frequency information is hard during the limited input information of LR, our NSAN can still take full advantage of the limited LR information through second-order non-local attention, while taking advantage of the spatial feature of both high-order characteristics associated with more powerful pattern representation, resulting in more refined results.

4.4 Model Size Analyses

The Fig. 4 shows the model size and performance of current CNN SR models. In these methods, MemNet and NLRG contain far fewer parameters for the cost of performance degradation. Not only NSAN had fewer parameters than RDN, RCAN and SAN, but also achieved better performance, which means NSAN could have a great performance trade-off between model complexity and performance.

5 Conclusions

We propose a deep non-local second-order attention network (NSAN) for SISR. Specifically, the high-order enhanced group allows NSAN to capture the structural information and long-range dependencies through embedding non-local operations. Meanwhile, NHAG allows abundant low-frequency information from the LR images to be bypassed through local skip connections. Not only NSAN exploiting the spatial feature correlations, but also learn high-order feature interdependencies by global covariance pooling for more discriminative representations through second-order non-local attention (NSA) module. Extensive experiment on SR with BI demonstrate the effectiveness of our NSAN in terms of quantitative and visual results.

References

1. Ahn, N., Kang, B., Sohn, K.-A.: Fast, accurate, and lightweight super-resolution with cascading residual network. In: Ferrari, V., Hebert, M., Sminchisescu, C., Weiss, Y. (eds.) ECCV 2018. LNCS, vol. 11214, pp. 256–272. Springer, Cham (2018). https://doi.org/10.1007/978-3-030-01249-6_16
2. Bo, L., Hong, C., Shan, S., Chen, X.: Low-resolution face recognition via coupled locality preserving mappings. IEEE Signal Process. Lett. **17**(1), 20–23 (2009)
3. Capel, D., Zisserman, A.: Super-resolution from multiple views using learnt image models. In: Proceedings of the 2001 IEEE Computer Society Conference on Computer Vision and Pattern Recognition, CVPR 2001, vol. 2, p. II. IEEE (2001)
4. Chakrabarti, A., Rajagopalan, A., Chellappa, R.: Super-resolution of face images using kernel PCA-based prior. IEEE Trans. Multimedia **9**(4), 888–892 (2007)
5. Chang, H., Yeung, D.Y., Xiong, Y.: Super-resolution through neighbor embedding. In: Proceedings of the 2004 IEEE Computer Society Conference on Computer Vision and Pattern Recognition, CVPR 2004, vol. 1, p. I. IEEE (2004)
6. Dai, T., Cai, J., Zhang, Y., Xia, S.T., Zhang, L.: Second-order attention network for single image super-resolution. In: Proceedings of the IEEE Conference on Computer Vision and Pattern Recognition, pp. 11065–11074 (2019)
7. Dong, C., Loy, C.C., He, K., Tang, X.: Image super-resolution using deep convolutional networks. IEEE Trans. Pattern Anal. Mach. Intell. **38**(2), 295–307 (2015)
8. Dong, C., Loy, C.C., Tang, X.: Accelerating the super-resolution convolutional neural network. In: Leibe, B., Matas, J., Sebe, N., Welling, M. (eds.) ECCV 2016. LNCS, vol. 9906, pp. 391–407. Springer, Cham (2016). https://doi.org/10.1007/978-3-319-46475-6_25
9. Freedman, G., Fattal, R.: Image and video upscaling from local self-examples. ACM Trans. Graph. (TOG) **30**(2), 12 (2011)
10. Fu, J., et al.: Dual attention network for scene segmentation. In: Proceedings of the IEEE Conference on Computer Vision and Pattern Recognition, pp. 3146–3154 (2019)
11. Glasner, D., Bagon, S., Irani, M.: Super-resolution from a single image. In: 2009 IEEE 12th International Conference on Computer Vision, pp. 349–356. IEEE (2009)
12. He, X., Mo, Z., Wang, P., Liu, Y., Yang, M., Cheng, J.: Ode-inspired network design for single image super-resolution. In: Proceedings of the IEEE Conference on Computer Vision and Pattern Recognition, pp. 1732–1741 (2019)
13. Hu, J., Shen, L., Sun, G.: Squeeze-and-excitation networks. In: Proceedings of the IEEE Conference on Computer Vision and Pattern Recognition, pp. 7132–7141 (2018)

14. Huang, J.B., Singh, A., Ahuja, N.: Single image super-resolution from transformed self-exemplars. In: Proceedings of the IEEE Conference on Computer Vision and Pattern Recognition, pp. 5197–5206 (2015)
15. Huang, Z., Wang, X., Huang, L., Huang, C., Wei, Y., Liu, W.: CCNET: criss-cross attention for semantic segmentation. In: Proceedings of the IEEE International Conference on Computer Vision, pp. 603–612 (2019)
16. Itti, L., Koch, C., Niebur, E.: A model of saliency-based visual attention for rapid scene analysis. IEEE Trans. Pattern Anal. Mach. Intell. **11**, 1254–1259 (1998)
17. Kennedy, J.A., Israel, O., Frenkel, A., Bar-Shalom, R., Azhari, H.: Super-resolution in pet imaging. IEEE Trans. Med. Imaging **25**(2), 137–147 (2006)
18. Kim, J., Kwon Lee, J., Mu Lee, K.: Accurate image super-resolution using very deep convolutional networks. In: Proceedings of the IEEE Conference on Computer Vision and Pattern Recognition, pp. 1646–1654 (2016)
19. Kim, J., Kwon Lee, J., Mu Lee, K.: Deeply-recursive convolutional network for image super-resolution. In: Proceedings of the IEEE Conference on Computer Vision and Pattern Recognition, pp. 1637–1645 (2016)
20. Lai, W.S., Huang, J.B., Ahuja, N., Yang, M.H.: Deep Laplacian pyramid networks for fast and accurate super-resolution. In: Proceedings of the IEEE Conference on Computer Vision and Pattern Recognition, pp. 624–632 (2017)
21. Ledig, C., et al.: Photo-realistic single image super-resolution using a generative adversarial network. In: Proceedings of the IEEE Conference on Computer Vision and Pattern Recognition, pp. 4681–4690 (2017)
22. Li, J., Fang, F., Mei, K., Zhang, G.: Multi-scale residual network for image super-resolution. In: Ferrari, V., Hebert, M., Sminchisescu, C., Weiss, Y. (eds.) ECCV 2018. LNCS, vol. 11212, pp. 527–542. Springer, Cham (2018). https://doi.org/10.1007/978-3-030-01237-3_32
23. Lim, B., Son, S., Kim, H., Nah, S., Mu Lee, K.: Enhanced deep residual networks for single image super-resolution. In: Proceedings of the IEEE Conference on Computer Vision and Pattern Recognition Workshops, pp. 136–144 (2017)
24. Shi, W., et al.: Real-time single image and video super-resolution using an efficient sub-pixel convolutional neural network. In: Proceedings of the IEEE Conference on Computer Vision and Pattern Recognition, pp. 1874–1883 (2016)
25. Szegedy, C., Ioffe, S., Vanhoucke, V., Alemi, A.A.: Inception-v4, inception-resnet and the impact of residual connections on learning. In: Thirty-First AAAI Conference on Artificial Intelligence (2017)
26. Tai, Y., Yang, J., Liu, X.: Image super-resolution via deep recursive residual network. In: Proceedings of the IEEE Conference on Computer Vision and Pattern Recognition, pp. 3147–3155 (2017)
27. Tai, Y., Yang, J., Liu, X., Xu, C.: MemNet: a persistent memory network for image restoration. In: Proceedings of the IEEE International Conference on Computer Vision, pp. 4539–4547 (2017)
28. Timofte, R., Agustsson, E., Van Gool, L., Yang, M.H., Zhang, L.: Ntire 2017 challenge on single image super-resolution: methods and results. In: Proceedings of the IEEE Conference on Computer Vision and Pattern Recognition Workshops, pp. 114–125 (2017)
29. Wang, X., Girshick, R., Gupta, A., He, K.: Non-local neural networks. In: Proceedings of the IEEE Conference on Computer Vision and Pattern Recognition, pp. 7794–7803 (2018)
30. Yang, J., Wright, J., Huang, T.S., Ma, Y.: Image super-resolution via sparse representation. IEEE Trans. Image Process. **19**(11), 2861–2873 (2010)

31. Zhang, Y., Li, K., Li, K., Wang, L., Zhong, B., Fu, Y.: Image super-resolution using very deep residual channel attention n etworks. In: Ferrari, V., Hebert, M., Sminchisescu, C., Weiss, Y. (eds.) ECCV 2018. LNCS, vol. 11211, pp. 294–310. Springer, Cham (2018). https://doi.org/10.1007/978-3-030-01234-2_18
32. Zhang, Y., Li, K., Li, K., Zhong, B., Fu, Y.: Residual non-local attention networks for image restoration. arXiv preprint arXiv:1903.10082 (2019)
33. Zhang, Y., Tian, Y., Kong, Y., Zhong, B., Fu, Y.: Residual dense network for image super-resolution. In: Proceedings of the IEEE Conference on Computer Vision and Pattern Recognition, pp. 2472–2481 (2018)
34. Zhang, Y.: Problems in the fusion of commercial high-resolution satelitte as well as landsat 7 images and initial solutions. Int. Arch. Photogrammetry Remote Sens. Spat. Inf. Sci. **34**(4), 587–592 (2002)

ML-ModelExplorer: An Explorative Model-Agnostic Approach to Evaluate and Compare Multi-class Classifiers

Andreas Theissler[1](✉), Simon Vollert[1], Patrick Benz[1], Laurentius A. Meerhoff[2], and Marc Fernandes[1]

[1] Aalen University of Applied Sciences, 73430 Aalen, Germany
andreas.theissler@hs-aalen.de

[2] Leiden Institute of Advanced Computer Sciences (LIACS), Leiden University, Leiden, The Netherlands

Abstract. A major challenge during the development of Machine Learning systems is the large number of models resulting from testing different model types, parameters, or feature subsets. The common approach of selecting the best model using one overall metric does not necessarily find the most suitable model for a given application, since it ignores the different effects of class confusions. Expert knowledge is key to evaluate, understand and compare model candidates and hence to control the training process. This paper addresses the research question of how we can support experts in the evaluation and selection of Machine Learning models, alongside the reasoning about them. ML-ModelExplorer is proposed – an explorative, interactive, and model-agnostic approach utilising confusion matrices. It enables Machine Learning and domain experts to conduct a thorough and efficient evaluation of multiple models by taking overall metrics, per-class errors, and individual class confusions into account. The approach is evaluated in a user-study and a real-world case study from football (soccer) data analytics is presented.

ML-ModelExplorer and a tutorial video are available online for use with own data sets: www.ml-and-vis.org/mex

Keywords: Multi-class classification · Model selection · Feature selection · Human-centered machine learning · Visual analytics

1 Introduction

During the development of Machine Learning systems a large number of model candidates are generated in the training process [27] by testing different model types, hyperparameters, or feature subsets. The increased use of Deep Learning [19] further aggravates this problem, as the number of model candidates is very large due to the enormous number of parameters. This paper is motivated by the following observations for multi-class classification problems:

Published by Springer Nature Switzerland AG 2020
A. Holzinger et al. (Eds.): CD-MAKE 2020, LNCS 12279, pp. 281–300, 2020.
https://doi.org/10.1007/978-3-030-57321-8_16

1. Automatically selecting the best model based on a single metric does not necessarily find the model that is best for a specific application, e.g. different per-class errors have different effects in applications.
2. In applications with uncertain relevance and discriminative power of the given input features, models can be trained on different feature subsets. The results of the models are valuable for drawing conclusions about the feature subsets, since the level of contribution of a feature to the classification performance is unknown a priori.

We argue that expert knowledge is key to evaluate, understand and compare model candidates and hence to control the training process. This yields the research question: *How can we support experts to efficiently evaluate, select and reason about multi-class classifiers?*

This paper proposes ML-ModelExplorer which is an explorative and interactive approach to evaluate and compare multi-class classifiers, i.e. models assigning data points to $N > 2$ classes. ML-ModelExplorer is model-agnostic, i.e. works for any type of classifier and does not evaluate the inner workings of the models. It solely uses the models' confusion matrices and enables the user to investigate and understand the models' results. It allows to take different overall metrics, the per-class errors, and the class confusions into account and thereby enables a thorough and efficient evaluation of models.

We believe that in a multi-class problem – due to the high number of errors per model, per class and class confusions – interactively analysing the results at different levels of granularity, is more efficient and will yield more insights than working with raw data. This hypothesis is evaluated with a user study and a real-world case study. In the case study on football data, we examine how successful attacking sequences from different parts of the pitch can best be modelled using a broad range of novel football-related metrics.

This paper makes the following contributions:

1. Provision of a brief review of the state-of-the-art in visual analysis of multi-class classifier results (Sect. 2).
2. Proposal of a data- and model-agnostic approach for the evaluation, comparison and selection of multi-class classifiers (Sect.3, Sect. 4).
3. Evaluation with a user study (Sect. 5).
4. Validation of real-world relevance with a case study (Sect. 6).
5. Supply of ML-ModelExplorer for use with own data sets.

2 Related Work

The general interplay of domain experts and Machine Learning has been suggested in literature, for example in [3,10,14,30]. Closely related to the problem discussed in this paper, approaches to interactively analyse the results in multi-class problems have been proposed and are briefly surveyed in the following.

In [29] the authors proposed Squares which integrates the entire model evaluation workflow into one visualisation. The core element is a sortable parallel coordinates plot with the per-class metrics, enhanced by boxes showing the classification results of instances and the thumbnails of the images themselves. ConfusionWheel [1] is a radial plot with classes arranged on an outer circle, class confusions shown by chords connecting the classes, and histograms on the circle for the classification results of all classes. ComDia+ [23] uses the models' metrics to rank multiple image classifiers. The visualization is subdivided into a performance ranking view resembling parallel coordinates, a diagnosis matrix view showing averaged misclassified images, and a view with information about misclassified instances and the images themselves. Manifold [33] contrasts multiple models, showing the models' complementarity and diversity. Therefor it uses scatter plots to compare models in a pairwise manner. A further view indicates the differences in the distributions of the models at the feature level. INFUSE [16] is a dashboard for the selection of the most discriminative features in a high-dimensional feature space. The different feature rankings across several feature ranking methods can be interactively compared.

The idea from [1] of using a radial plot was used in one visualisation in ML-ModelExplorer. While Squares [29] and ConfusionWheel [1] are designed for the evaluation of a single classifier, ML-ModelExplorer has the focus of contrasting multiple models. ComDia+ [23] and Manifold [33] allow to compare multiple models, where the view of averaged images constrains ComDia+ to (aligned) images. Manifold is a generic approach which in addition to classification is applicable to regression. While the mentioned approaches allow to refine the analyses to instance or feature level, they require the input data. ML-ModelExplorer solely works on the models' confusion matrices and is hence applicable to the entire range of classification problems, not constrained to data types like images or feature vectors. A further reason not to incorporate the data set itself is, that having to upload their data into an online tool will discourage practitioners and researchers from testing the approach. In addition, in contrast to some of the aforementioned approaches, ML-ModelExplorer is made publicly available.

3 Problem Analysis: Evaluating Multi-class Classifiers

For a multi-class classification problem the approach incorporates all tested models M into the user-driven analysis. The output of a multi-class classification problem with $|C|$ classes denoted as C_i can be presented as a confusion matrix of dimension $|C| \times |C|$ (see e.g. [15]). The $|C|$ elements on the diagonal show the correct classifications, the remaining elements show the $|C| \times (|C| - 1)$ different confusions between classes. An example is shown in Table 1, where in this paper columns correspond to class labels and rows show the predictions.

Table 1. A confusion matrix of an imbalanced three-class classification problem with absolute numbers and percentages (0...1).

	Class label C_1	Class label C_2	Class label C_3
Prediction C_1	70 (0.7)	30 (0.15)	0 (0.0)
Prediction C_2	20 (0.2)	150 (0.75)	50 (0.1)
Prediction C_3	10 (0.1)	20 (0.1)	450 (0.9)

From the confusion matrix, a variety of metrics can be deduced [6,15]. In the following, the metrics relevant for this paper are introduced. The absolute number of correctly classified instances of class C_i is referred to as true predictions and denoted as TP_{C_i}. The true prediction rate – also termed recall or true positive rate – for class C_i is denoted as TPR_{C_i} and is the percentage of correctly classified instances of class C_i:

$$TPR_{C_i} = \frac{TP_{C_i}}{|C_i|} \tag{1}$$

The per-class error E_{C_i} is given by:

$$E_{C_i} = 1 - TPR_{C_i} \tag{2}$$

The overall accuracy acc refers to the percentage of correctly classified instances of all classes C_i

$$acc = \frac{1}{N} \sum_{i=1}^{|C|} TP_{C_i} \tag{3}$$

Taking into account potential class imbalance in the data set, can be achieved with the macro-average recall $recall_{avg}$ which is the average percentage of correctly classified instances of all classes C_i:

$$recall_{avg} = \frac{1}{|C|} \sum_{i=1}^{|C|} TPR_{C_i} \tag{4}$$

The common approach of model selection based on a single metric, e.g. overall or weighted accuracy, does not necessarily find the most suitable model for an application, where different class confusions have different effects [11]. For example a model might be discarded due to a low accuracy caused by frequently confusing just two of the classes, while being accurate in detecting the remaining ones. This model can be of use for (a) building an ensemble [25,32], (b) by refining it with regard to the two confused classes, or (c) to uncover mislabelling in the two classes.

Target users of ML-ModelExplorer are (1) *Machine Learning experts* for evaluation, refinement, and selection of model candidates, and (2) *domain experts*[1] for the selection of appropriate models for the underlying application and for reasoning about the discriminative power of feature subsets.

Based on the authors' background in Machine Learning projects and the discussion with further experts, Scrum user stories were formulated. These user stories guided the design of ML-ModelExplorer.

- **User story #1 (Overview)**: As a user I want an overview that contrasts the results of all $|M|$ models, so that I can find generally strong or weak models as well as similar and outlier models.

[1] domain experts are assumed to have a basic understanding of classification problems, i.e. understand class errors and class confusions.

- **User story #2 (Model and class query)**: As a user I want to query for models based on their per-class errors, so that I can understand which classes lead to high error rates over all $|M|$ models and which classes cause problems only to individual models.
- **User story #3 (Model drill-down)**: As a user I want to drill-down into the details of one model M_k, so that I can conduct a more detailed analysis e.g. regarding individual class confusions.
- **User story #4 (Model comparison)**: As a user I want to be able to select one model M_k and make a detailed comparison with a reference model M_r or the average of all models M_{avg}, so that I can understand where model M_k needs optimization.

4 The Approach: ML-ModelExplorer

ML-ModelExplorer provides an overview of all models and enables interactive detailed analyses and comparisons. Starting with contrasting different models based on their overall metrics, more detailed analyses can be conducted by goal-oriented queries for models' per-class results. A model's detailed results can be investigated and compared to selected models.

ML-ModelExplorer uses a variety of interactive visualisations with highlighting, filtering, zooming and comparison facilities that enable users to (1) select the most appropriate model for a given application, (2) control the training process in a goal-oriented way by focusing on promising models and further refining them, and (3) reason about the effect of features, in the case where the models were trained on different feature subsets.

The design was governed by the goal to provide an approach that does not require specific knowledge in data visualisation or the familiarisation with new visualisation approaches, since domain experts do not necessarily have a Data Science background. Consequently a combination of well-known visualisations, that can be reasonably assumed to be known by the target users, are used as key elements. Examples are easily interpretable scatter plots, box plots, bar charts, tree maps, and chord diagrams. In addition some more advanced – but common – interactive visualisations were utilised, i.e. parallel coordinates or the hierarchical sun burst diagram. In order to compensate differing prior knowledge or preferences of users, the same information is redundantly communicated with different visualisations, i.e. there are multiple options to conduct an analysis.

ML-ModelExplorer is implemented in R [26] with shiny [4] and plotly [12] and can be used online[2] with own data sets and a tutorial video[3] is available. Different characteristics of the models' results are emphasized with complementary views. The design follows Shneiderman's information seeking mantra [31], where *overview first* is achieved by a model overview pane. In order to incrementally refine the analysis, *zoom + filter* is implemented by a filtering facility for models and classes and by filtering and zooming throughout the different visualisations.

[2] ML-ModelExplorer online: www.ml-and-vis.org/mex.

[3] ML-ModelExplorer video: https://youtu.be/IO7IWTUxK_Y.

Details-on-demand is implemented by views on different detail levels, e.g. model details or the comparison of models. The design was guided by the user stories in Sect. 3, the mapping of these user stories to visualisations is given in Table 2.

Table 2. Mapping of user stories to interactive visualisations.

User story	Implemented by
User story #1 (Overview)	Per-model metrics plot model similarity plot
User story #2 (Model and class query)	Per-class errors query view class error radar chart
User story #3 (Model drill-down)	Error hierarchy plot confusion matrix view confusion circle bilateral confusion plot confusion tree map
User story #4 (Model comparison)	Delta confusion matrix delta radar chart

In the following, the views are introduced where screenshots illustrate an experiment with 10 convolutional neural networks (CNN) [28] on the MNIST data set [18], where the task is to classify the handwritten digits 0...9. CNNs with a convolution layer with 32 filters, a 2×2 max pooling layer, and a dropout of 0.2 were trained. The hyperparameters kernel size k, which specifies the size of the filter moved over the image, together with the stride were varied from $k = 2$ to $k = 11$, resulting in 10 model candidates denoted by $\text{M1\_CNN}_{k=2}...\text{M10\_CNN}_{k=11}$.

4.1 Model Overview Pane

The *model overview pane* (Fig. 1) is subdivided into three horizontal subpanes starting with (1) a coarse overview on the top showing the summarised metrics of all models, e.g. the overall accuracy and the dispersion of the true prediction rates TPR_{C_i} over all classes C_i. The middle subpane (2) contrasts and allows to query the per-class errors E_{C_i}. On the bottom (3), a detailed insight can be interactively gained by browsing the models' class confusions:

Model Metrics Subpane (1):

- *Per-model metrics plots:* This set of plots gives an overview of generally good or weak models (Fig. 1, 1), hence serving as a starting point to detect potential model candidates for further refinement or for the exclusion from the training process. The per-model metrics can be viewed at different levels of granularity with the following subplots: a list of ranked and grouped models, a line plot with the model accuracies, and a box plot with the dispersions of recall, precision and F1-score.

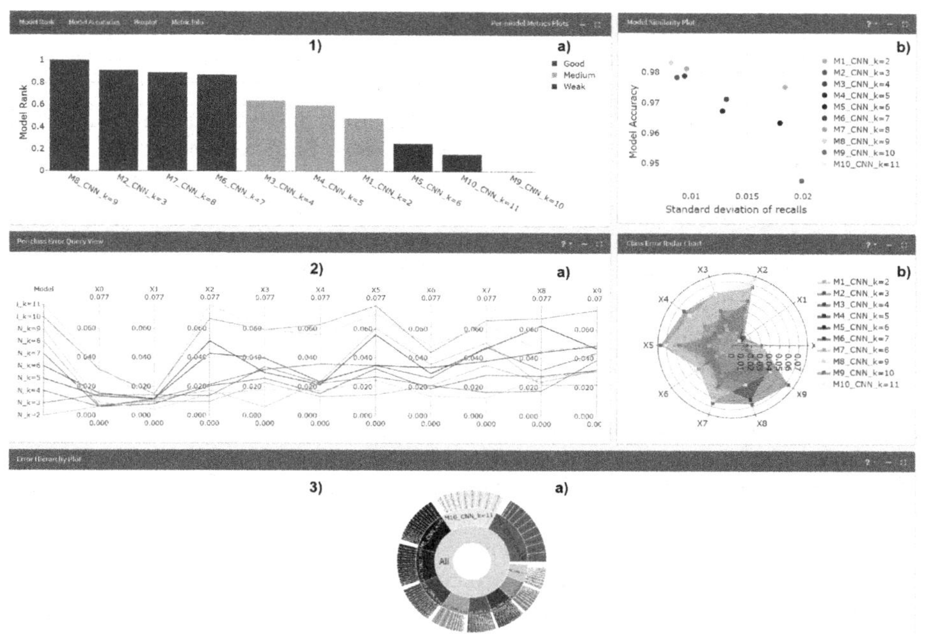

Fig. 1. Model overview pane contrasting the results of ten multi-class classifiers on the MNIST data set. The models are ranked according to their accuracy and classification imbalance in 1) a). The non-monotonic effect of the varied kernel size in the used convolutional neural networks can be seen in 2) a).

In the model rank subplot (Fig. 1, 1 a), the models are ranked and grouped into strong, medium and weak models. For the ranking of the models, the underlying assumption is, that a good model has a high accuracy and a low classification imbalance, i.e. all classes have a similarly high detection rate. In the following, a metric to rank the models is proposed. In a first step, the classification imbalance *CI* is defined as Eq. (5), which is the mean deviation of the true prediction rates TPR_{C_i} from the model's macro-average recall, where $CI = 0$ if TPR_{C_i} is identical for all C_i:

$$CI = \frac{1}{|C|}\sum_{i=1}^{|C|} |\, TPR_{C_i} - recall_{avg}| \tag{5}$$

Each model M_k is described by the vector $\gamma_k = (recall_{avg}, CI)$. To ensure equal influence of both metrics, the components of γ_k are min-max scaled over all models, i.e. $\gamma'_k = (recall'_{avg}, CI')$ with $recall'_{avg} = [0, 1]$ and $CI' = [0, 1]$. To assign greater values to more balanced models, CI' is substituted by $1 - CI'$ and the L1-norm is then used to aggregate the individual metrics into a model rank metric:

$$M_{rank_k} = \frac{1}{2}|recall'_{avg} + (1 - CI')| \tag{6}$$

where $\frac{1}{2}$ scales M_{rank_k} to a range of $[0, 1]$, allowing for direct interpretation of M_{rank_k}. The models are ranked by M_{rank_k}, where $M_{rank_k} \rightarrow 1$ correspond to stronger models.
In addition to ranking, the models are grouped into *good*, *medium*, *weak*, which is beneficial for a high number of models. Since the categorization of good and weak models is not absolute, but rather dependent on the complexity of the problem, i.e. the data set, the grouping is conducted using reference models from M. From the $|M|$ models, the best model M_b and the weakest model M_w are selected as reference models utilizing M_{rank_k}. In addition a medium model M_{med} is selected, which is the median of the ranked models. Following that, the $|M|$ models are classified as any of *good*, *medium*, *weak* using a 1-nearest neighbour classifier on M_{rank_k}, encoded with green, yellow, and red (see Fig. 1, 1 a)).
In the second subplot the models' accuracies are contrasted with each other in order to a allow a coarse comparison of the models. In addition the accuracies are shown in reference to a virtual random classifier, randomly classifying each instance with equal probability for each class, and to a baseline classifier, assigning all instances to the majority class.
In the third subplot, the models are contrasted using box plots showing the dispersions of the per-class metrics. Box plots positioned at the top indicate stronger models while the height indicates a model's variability over the classes. For the MNIST experiment, the strong and non-monotonic effect of the kernel size is visible, with 7, 8, and 9 yielding the best results and a kernel size of 6 having a high variability in the classes' precisions.
- *Model similarity plot:* This plot shows the similarities between models (Fig. 1, 1b). For each model the overall accuracy and the standard deviation of the true prediction rates $TPR_{C_i} \forall C_i$ are extracted, and presented in a 2D-scatter plot. Similar models are thereby placed close to each other, where multiple similar models might reveal clusters. Weak, strong, or models with highly different results become obvious as outliers. For the MNIST data set, the plot reveals a group of strong models, with high accuracies and low variability over the classes: M6_CNN$_{k=7}$, M7_CNN$_{k=8}$, M8_CNN$_{k=9}$, and M2_CNN$_{k=3}$.

Per-Class Errors Subpane (2):

- *Per-class errors query view:* This view shows the errors E_{C_i} and allows to query for models and classes (Fig. 1, 2a). The errors are mapped to parallel coordinates [13] which show multi-dimensional relations with parallel axes and allow to highlight value ranges. The first axis shows the models, each class is mapped to one axis with low E_{C_i} at the bottom. For each model, line segments connect the errors. For the MNIST data, the digits 0 and 1 have the lowest errors, while some of the models have high errors on 2 and 5.

- *Class error radar chart:* The per-class errors E_{C_i} can be interactively analysed in a radar chart, where the errors are mapped to axes (Fig. 1, 2b). The models' results can be rapidly contrasted, larger areas showing high E_{C_i}, and the shape indicating high or low errors on specific classes. The analysis can be incrementally refined by deselecting models. In the MNIST experiment, models with general weak performance are visible by large areas and it reveals that all models have high detection rates TPR_{C_i} on digit 0 and 1.

Class Confusions Subpane (3):

- *Error hierarchy plot:* This plot allows to navigate through all errors per model and class in one view (Fig. 1, 3a). The hierarchy of the overall errors for each model ($1 - recall_{avg}$), the per-class errors E_{C_i}, and the class confusions are accessible in a sun burst diagram. The errors at each level are ordered clockwise allowing to see the ranking. One finding in the MNIST experiment is, that the model with the highest accuracy (M8_CNN$_{k=9}$) has its most class confusions on digit 9, which is most often misclassified with 7, 4, and 1.

4.2 Model Details Pane

The *model details pane* shows different aspects of one selected model, here M3_CNN$_{k=4}$ (see Fig. 2). The following four plots are contained:

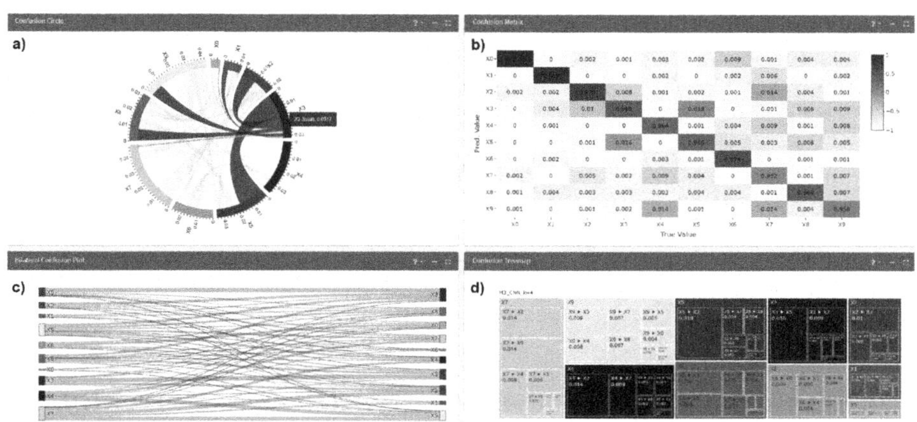

Fig. 2. Model details pane showing one selected model. Per-class errors and class confusions can be investigated.

- *Confusion circle:* This plot (Fig. 2, a) is a reduced version of the confusion wheel proposed in [1]. The $|C|$ classes are depicted by circle segments in one surrounding circle. The class confusions are shown with chords connecting the circle segments. The chords' widths encode the error between the classes. Individual classes can be highlighted and the detailed errors are shown on demand. For the MNIST experiment, the class confusions of M3_CNN$_{k=4}$ reveal that e.g. digit 3 is most often misclassified as 5, 8, and 9. On the other hand, of all digits misclassified as 3, digit 5 is the most frequent one.

- *Confusion matrix:* The model's confusion matrix is shown in the familiar tabular way, with a colour gradient encoding the class confusions (Fig. 2, b).
- *Bilateral confusion plot:* In an interactive Sankey diagram (Fig. 2), misclassifications can be studied (class labels on the left, predictions on the right), c). By rearranging and highlighting, the focus can be put on individual classes.
- *Confusion tree map:* A model's per-class errors E_{C_i} are ranked in a tree map allowing to investigate how E_{C_i} is composed of the individual class confusions, where larger areas correspond to higher errors (Fig. 2, d). If class C_i is selected, the ranked misclassifications to $C_1...C_{|C|}$ are shown. In the MNIST experiment, for M3_CNN$_{k=4}$ the weakness is digit 7, which in turn is most frequently misclassified as 9 and 2.

4.3 Model Comparison Pane

In the *model comparison pane* a model M_k can be selected and compared to a selected reference model M_r or to the average over all models M_{avg} (Fig. 3).

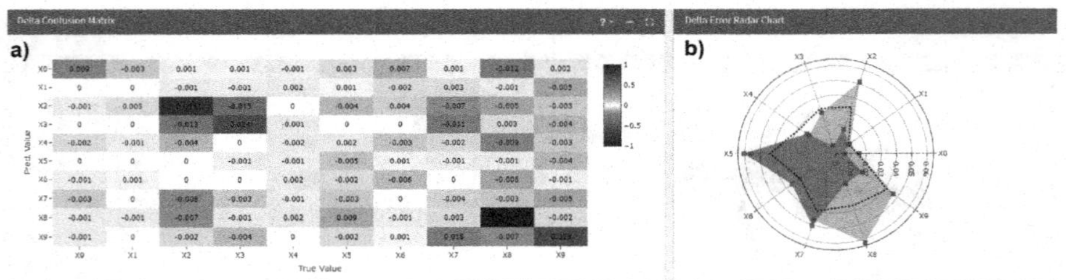

Fig. 3. Model comparison pane: a selected model can be compared with a selected reference model and with the average of all models.

- *Delta confusion matrix:* The class confusions of M_k can be contrasted to a reference model M_r showing where M_k is superior and where it needs optimization (Fig. 3, a). The difference between the class confusions is visible per cell with shades of green encoding where M_k is superior to M_r and red where M_r is superior, respectively. In the MNIST experiment, while M5_CNN$_{k=6}$ is in general the weaker model compared to M1_CNN$_{k=2}$, it less frequently misclassifies e.g. 7 as 9 and 5 as 8.
- *Delta error radar chart:* The differences in the per-class errors of a model M_k w.r.t. a reference model M_r and the average M_{avg} is illustrated in a radar chart (Fig. 3, b). The area and shape in the radar chart allows to

rapidly draw conclusions about weak or strong accuracies on certain classes and about differences between the models. While in the MNIST experiment M1_CNN$_{k=2}$ has slightly higher errors on digits 5, 6, 7 and approximately similar errors on 0 and 1, it performs significantly better than M5_CNN$_{k=6}$ and the overall average on the remaining digits.

5 Evaluation: User Study

A user study was conducted in order to compare ML-ModelExplorer to the common approach of working on a Machine Learning library's raw output. Python's scikit-learn [24] was used as a reference. Two typical activities were tested:

1. evaluation and selection of a single model
2. controlling the training process by identifying weak models to be discarded, strong models to be optimised, and by uncovering optimisation potential

For these two activities, hypotheses H1 and H2 were formulated and concrete typical tasks were defined in Table 3. The tasks were solved by two disjoint groups of users using either Python (group A) or ML-ModelExplorer (group B). While using two disjoint groups halves the sample size, it avoids a learning effect which is to be expected in such a setting. The efficiency is measured by the number of correct solutions found in a given time span, i.e. [correct solutions/minute].

Eighteen students with industrial background, enrolled in an extra occupational master course, participated in the user study. The participants had just finished a machine learning project with multi-class classification and had no specific knowledge about data visualisation. The 18 participants were randomly assigned to group A and B resulting in a sample size of $N = 9$ for a paired test. Group A was given a jupyter-notebook with the raw output pre-loaded into Python's pandas data structures and additionally text file with all confusion matrices and metrics. These participants were allowed to use the internet and a pandas cheat sheet was handed out. Group B used ML-ModelExplorer and a one-page documentation was handed out.

As a basis for the user study, the results of 10 different models on the MNIST data set [18] were used, as shown in Sect. 4. Prior to the study, the data, the supplied Python code and ML-ModelExplorer were briefly explained. A maximum of 25 min for the tasks of H1 and 15 min for H2 was set. The tasks were independently solved by the test participants, without intervention. No questions were allowed during the user study. The individual performances of the students are shown in Fig. 4. Note that the maximum possible score for the tasks within H1 was 3, whereas the maximum possible score for the tasks within H2 was 16. Therefore the efficiency of the students is calculated using the number of correct answers as well as the required time to solve the tasks.

The distribution of the efficiencies is shown in Fig. 5, indicating that participants using ML-ModelExplorer were more efficient. In addition there appears to be a learning effect: for the tasks connected with hypothesis H2 the participants of both groups were more efficient than for H1.

Table 3. Hypotheses and typical tasks to be solved in the user study.

$\mathbf{H1}_{\mathbf{Null}}$	With ML-ModelExplorer the selection of the best model is *not* more efficient than with a ML library's raw output
$\mathbf{H1}_{\mathbf{Alternative}}$	With ML-ModelExplorer ... is more efficient
$T1_1$	Find the model with the highest overall accuracy
$T1_2$	Find the model with the lowest error on class 8
$T1_3$	For model M8 find the two classes that class 8 is most frequently misclassified as
$\mathbf{H2}_{\mathbf{Null}}$	With ML-ModelExplorer controlling the training process is *not* more efficient than with a ML library's raw output
$\mathbf{H2}_{\mathbf{Alternative}}$	With ML-ModelExplorer ... is more efficient
$T2_1$	Find the 3 models with the highest and the 3 with the lowest accuracies
$T2_2$	For model M8, find the 3 classes with the highest per-class errors
$T2_3$	For model M8, find the 3 pairs of classes most frequently confused
$T2_4$	Find the classes, where M8 has a higher error than M6
$T2_5$	Compare M8 and M6 and from the class confusions where M8 has a higher error, find the 2 with the highest differences

The hypotheses $H1_{Null}$ and $H2_{Null}$ state that there is no statistically significant difference in the efficiencies' mean values between group A (raw output and python code) and group B (ML-ModelExplorer). One-sided paired t-tests were conducted with a significance level of $\alpha = 0.05$. The resulting critical values are $c_{H1} = 0.191$ and $c_{H2} = 0.366$. The observed differences in the user study are $\overline{x}_{B_{H1}} - \overline{x}_{A_{H1}} = 0.376$ and $\overline{x}_{B_{H2}} - \overline{x}_{A_{H2}} = 0.521$, where all values are given as [correct solutions/minute].

Hence, due to $(\overline{x}_{B_{H1}} - \overline{x}_{A_{H1}}) > c_{H1}$ and $(\overline{x}_{B_{H2}} - \overline{x}_{A_{H2}}) > c_{H2}$, both null hypotheses $H1_{Null}$ and $H2_{Null}$ were rejected, i.e. ML-ModelExplorer was found to be more efficient for both of the typical activities (1) evaluation and selection of a single best model and (2) controlling of the training process.

6 Case Study: Analysing Tactics in Football

In the following case study, the applicability of ML-ModelExplorer to real-world problems is evaluated with a multi-class classification problem on tracking data from football (soccer). In football, a recent revolution has been unchained with the introduction of position tracking data [22]. With the positions of all the players and the ball, it is possible to quantify tactics using the players' locations over time [21]. Machine Learning techniques can be adopted to fully exploit the opportunities tracking data provides to analyse tactical behaviour [9]. Although without a doubt Machine Learning will be a useful addition to the tactical analyses, one of the major challenges is to involve the domain experts (i.e., the

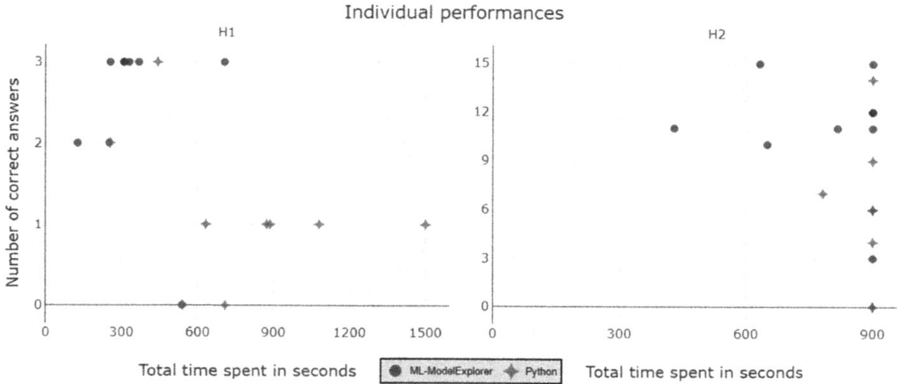

Fig. 4. The distribution of individual performances across both hypotheses.

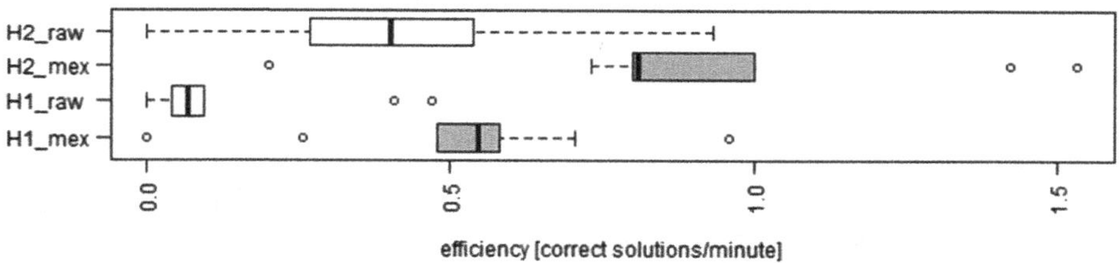

Fig. 5. The distribution of [correct solutions/minute] when analysing raw output with Python (H1_raw, H2_raw) and with ML-ModelExplorer (H1_mex, H2_mex).

coaching staff) in the decision-making process. Engaging the domain expert in the model selection process is crucial for (fine-) tuning the models. Specifically, the domain expert can play an important role in identifying the least disruptive class confusions. With better models, and models that are more supported by the domain experts, Machine Learning for analysing tactics in football will be more quickly embraced.

Football is an invasion-based team sport where goals are rare events, typically 2–4 goals out of the 150–200 offensive sequences in a 90 min match [2]. It is thus important to find the right balance between creating a goal-scoring opportunity without weakening the defence (and giving the opponents a goal-scoring opportunity). For example, a team could adopt a compact defence (making it very difficult for the opponents to score, even if they outclass the defending team) and wait for the opponent to lose the ball to start a quick counter-attack. If the defence is really compact, the ball is usually recovered far away from the attacking goal, whereas a team that puts a lot of pressure across the whole pitch might recover the ball in a promising position close to the opponent's goal. To formulate an effective tactic, analysts want to know the consequences of losing (or regaining) the ball in specific parts of the pitch. This raises the question:

How can successful and unsuccessful attacks that started in different parts of the pitch (see Fig. 6) be modelled?

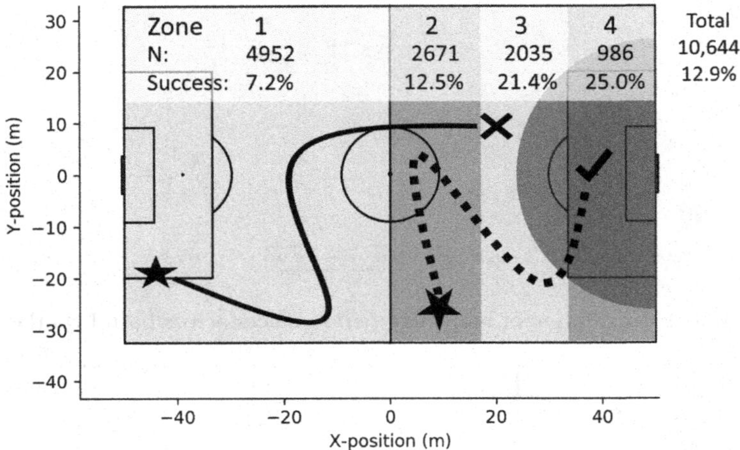

Fig. 6. Visualisation of the 8 classes based on a combination of zone (1–4) and attack outcome (success, fail, that is in-/outside green area, respectively). Example trajectories of the ball demonstrate an unsuccessful attack from zone 1 ($Z1_{fail}$, solid line) and a successful attack from zone 2 ($Z2_{success}$, dotted line). (Color figure online)

6.1 Procedure

The raw data contain the coordinates of each player and the ball recorded at 10 Hz with an optical tracking system (SportsVU, STATS LLC, Chicago, IL, USA). We analysed 73 matches from the seasons 2014–2018 from two top-level football clubs in the Dutch premier division ('Eredivisie'). For the current study, we analysed attacking sequences, which were defined based on team ball possession. Each attacking sequence was classed based on *where an attack started* and *whether it was successful.* The starting locations were binned into 4 different zones (see the 'stars' in Fig. 6). To deal with the low number of truly successful attacks (i.e., goals scored), we classed each event using the distance to the goal at the end of an attack as a proxy for success: Successful attacks ended within 26 m to the centre of the goal (see the green shaded area in Fig. 6).

For each event, we computed 72 different metrics that capture football tactics [21]. Some of these metrics describe the spatial distribution of the players on the pitch [7]. Other metrics capture the disruption of the opposing team (i.e., how much they moved in response to an action of the other team) [8]. Lastly, we created a set of metrics related to the ball carrier's danger on the pitch (i.e., *"Dangerousity"* [20]), which is a combination of four components. *Control* measures how much control the player has over the ball when in possession. *Density* quantifies how crowded it is between the ball carrier and the goal. *Pressure* captures how closely the ball carrier is defended. Lastly, *Zone*, refers to where on the pitch the ball carrier is, where players closer to the goal get a higher value than players further away. Note that the metric *Zone* only has values for the last part of the pitch, which corresponds to zone 4 of zones used for the target.

Finally, we combined the classed events (i.e., attacking sequences) with the tactical metrics by aggregating the temporal dimension by, for example, averaging across various windows prior to the end of the event. The resulting feature vectors were grouped based on whether the metrics described the *Spatial* distribution of the players on the pitch (n = 1092), *Disruption* (n = 32), *Control* (n = 46), *Density* (n = 46), *Pressure* (n = 46), *Zone* (n = 46), *Dangerousity* (n = 46), and all *Link*'s Dangerousity-related metrics combined (n = 230). Subsequently, we trained five different classifiers (decision tree, linear SVC, k-NN, extra trees, and random forest) with each of the eight feature vectors, yielding 40 different models to evaluate with ML-ModelExplorer.

6.2 Model Evaluation with ML-ModelExplorer

An exploration of all models reveals the large variation in accuracy (see Fig. 7). The difficulty of modelling tactics in football is apparent given how many of the models are under Baseline Accuracy (i.e., majority class). Particularly the Random Forests do well in this Machine Learning task. Next to the modelling techniques, the different features subsets also yield varying model accuracies. The Random Forests with *Density*, *Zone*, *Dangerousity*, *Link* and *Spatial* clearly outperform the other subsets.

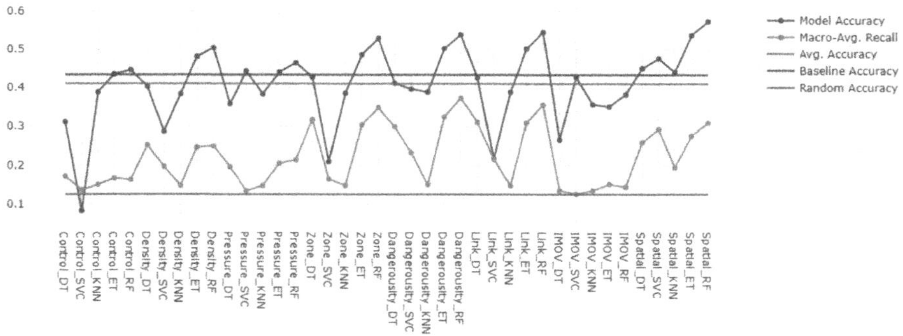

Fig. 7. An overview of the quality of all 40 models where an accuracy above baseline indicates that the model performed better than simply taking the majority class.

By selecting the models with the highest accuracies, the per-class errors can be easily compared (see Fig. 8). Two of the models, *Spatial RF* and *Density RF* have more class confusions with the successful attacking sequences. Here, the class-imbalance seems to play a role: the more interesting successful attacking sequences occur much less frequently than the unsuccessful attacking sequences.

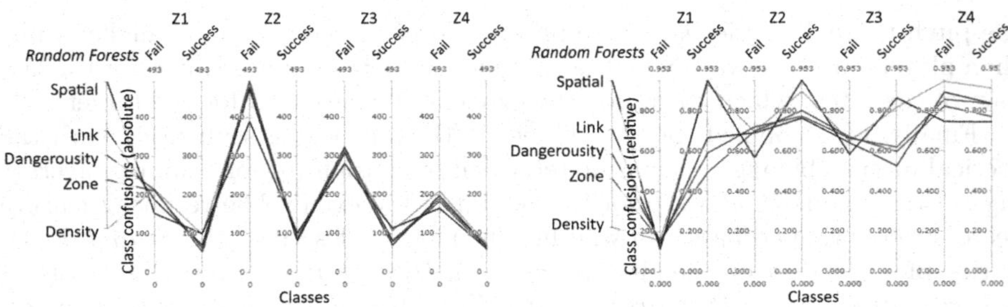

Fig. 8. Absolute (left) and relative (right) class confusions of the most promising models.

This becomes even more evident when using the built-in function to switch to relative numbers (see Fig. 8, left and right panel, respectively).

In fact, a domain expert might put more or less importance to specific classes. In this case, a football analyst would not be interested in unsuccessful attacks starting in zone 1 (which also happens to be the bulk of the data). Using another of the ML-Explorer's built-in functions, the domain expert can deselect 'irrelevant' classes. By excluding the unsuccessful attacks from zone 1 (i.e., "$Z1_{fail}$"), a clear difference in the best performing models becomes apparent: the *Spatial*-related models perform worse than average when the least interesting class is excluded (see Fig. 9). For a domain expert this would be a decisive difference to give preference to a model that might not have the highest overall accuracy.

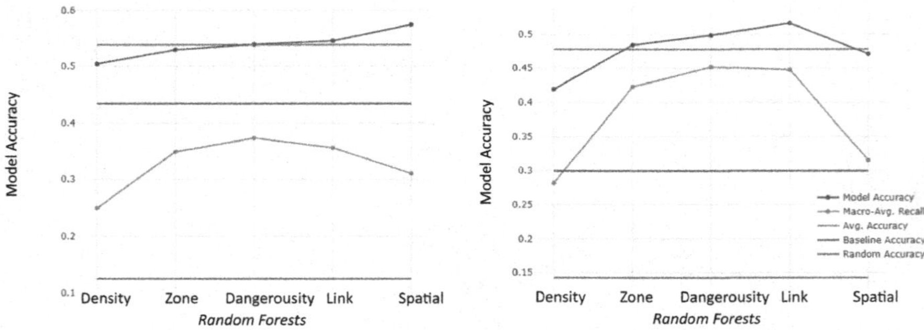

Fig. 9. The model qualities for the 5 most promising models with all classes included (left) and the less relevant class $Z1_{fail}$ excluded (right).

By now, it is clear that the models have different strengths and weaknesses. Some of the models perform well on the unsuccessful attacking sequences starting further away from the opponent's goal (i.e., $Z1_{fail}$, but also $Z2_{fail}$ and $Z3_{fail}$). These instances occur most frequently, but are not always the focus for the coaching staff. In Fig. 10, two of these distinct models are compared with and without the least interesting class ($Z1_{fail}$) excluded (left and right panel, respectively).

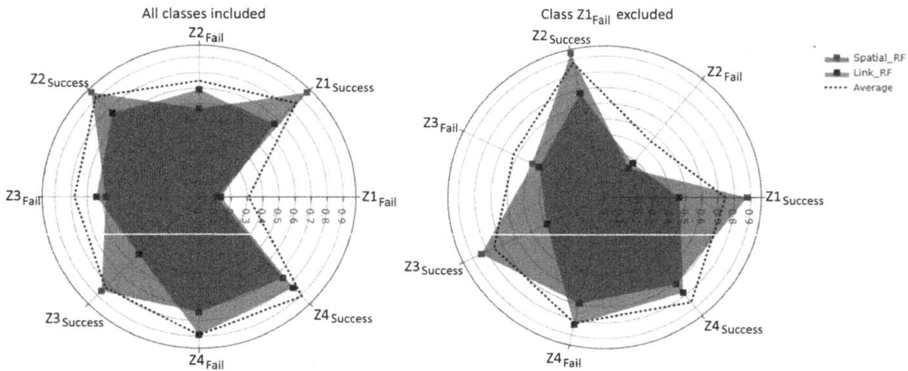

Fig. 10. A direct comparison of the *Spatial*- and *Link*- related models. Compared to including all classes (left panel), excluding the least interesting class gives a more nuanced insight into the relevant differences between the two models (right panel).

Looking at all classes, it stands out that $Z1_{fail}$ is predicted correctly more often than all other classes (see Fig. 10, left panel). As this is also the least interesting class, it clouds the accuracy for the other classes. After excluding $Z1_{fail}$ (see Fig. 10, right panel), it becomes clear that the *Spatial*-related model outperforms the *Link*-related model in the classes related to zone 4 ($Z4_{success}$ and $Z4_{fail}$). As these are attacking sequences starting from close to the opponent's goal, predicting these right is often less interesting than predicting the (successful) attacking sequences correct that start further away from the goal. Therefore, the use of all *Link*'s Dangerousity-related metrics is the most promising to examine how attacking sequences starting in different zones yield successful attacks.

7 Conclusion and Future Work

When selecting suitable Machine Learning models, the involvement of the expert is indispensable for evaluation, comparison and selection of models. This paper contributes to this overall goal by having proposed ML-ModelExplorer, involving the expert in the explorative analysis of the results of multiple multi-class classifiers. The design goals were deduced from typical, recurring tasks in the model evaluation process. In order to ensure a shallow learning curve, a combination of well-known visualisations together with some more advanced visualisations was proposed. A user study was conducted where the participants were statistically significantly more efficient using ML-ModelExplorer than working on raw classification results from scikit-learn. Note, that the authors believe that scikit-learn is one of the most powerful libraries. However, for the recurring analysis of multiple models, approaches like ML-ModelExplorer can be powerful supplements in the toolchain of Machine Learning experts.

While the usefulness was experimentally shown, there is potential for further work. After performing the mentioned user stories, there is a possibility that no single model is sufficient to fulfil the requirements of the given application. This could be the case if the investigated models are strongly diverse in their decisions, which would lead to different patterns in their class confusions. So for example one model could have a very low accuracy on class C_1 but a high accuracy on class C_2, while another model acts vice versa. In this case, taking the diversity of the investigated models and classes into account, the composition of multiple models could be used to improve the classification performances through means of ensembles [5]. This would propose a useful addition to ML-ModelExplorer, especially in cases where the formulation of diversity of the classes and their respective confusions is not easily quantified [17]. Additionally, the mentioned user stories are not all encompassing. A scenario that is not covered, is the discovery of classes that seem to be not properly defined or labelled. Consequences could be the removal of that class, the separation into multiple classes or the merging with other classes. In order to compare the new class definitions with the existing one would require the comparison of differently sized confusion matrices.

ML-ModelExplorer enables domain experts without programming knowledge to reason about model results to some extent. Yet, there are open research questions, like how to derive concrete instructions for actions regarding goal-oriented model hyperparameter adjustment, i.e. letting the expert pose *what if*-questions in addition to *what is*-questions.

References

1. Alsallakh, B., Hanbury, A., Hauser, H., Miksch, S., Rauber, A.: Visual methods for analyzing probabilistic classification data. IEEE Trans. Visual Comput. Graphics **20**(12), 1703–1712 (2014)
2. Armatas, V., Yiannakos, A., Papadopoulou, S., Skoufas, D.: Evaluation of goals scored in top ranking soccer matches: Greek "superleague" 2006–08. Serbian J. Sports Sci. **3**, 39–43 (2009)
3. Bernard, J., Zeppelzauer, M., Sedlmair, M., Aigner, W.: VIAL: a unified process for visual interactive labeling. Vis. Comput. **34**(9), 1189–1207 (2018). https://doi.org/10.1007/s00371-018-1500-3
4. Chang, W., Cheng, J., Allaire, J., Xie, Y., McPherson, J.: shiny: web application framework for R. r package version 1.0.5 (2017). https://CRAN.R-project.org/package=shiny
5. Dietterich, T.G.: Ensemble methods in machine learning. In: Kittler, J., Roli, F. (eds.) MCS 2000. LNCS, vol. 1857, pp. 1–15. Springer, Heidelberg (2000). https://doi.org/10.1007/3-540-45014-9_1
6. Fawcett, T.: ROC graphs: notes and practical considerations for researchers. Technical report, HP Laboratories (2004)
7. Frencken, W., Lemmink, K., Delleman, N., Visscher, C.: Oscillations of centroid position and surface area of soccer teams in small-sided games. Eur. J. Sport Sci. **11**(4), 215–223 (2011). https://doi.org/10.1080/17461391.2010.499967
8. Goes, F.R., Kempe, M., Meerhoff, L.A., Lemmink, K.A.P.M.: Not every pass can be an assist: a data-driven model to measure pass effectiveness in professional soccer matches. Big Data **7**(1), 57–70 (2019). https://doi.org/10.1089/big.2018.0067

9. Goes, F.R., et al.: Unlocking the potential of big data to support tactical performance analysis in professional soccer: a systematic review. Eur. J. Sport Sci. (2020, to appear). https://doi.org/10.1080/17461391.2020.1747552
10. Holzinger, A., et al.: Interactive machine learning: experimental evidence for the human in the algorithmic loop. Appl. Intell. **49**(7), 2401–2414 (2018). https://doi.org/10.1007/s10489-018-1361-5
11. Huang, W., Song, G., Li, M., Hu, W., Xie, K.: Adaptive weight optimization for classification of imbalanced data. In: Sun, C., Fang, F., Zhou, Z.-H., Yang, W., Liu, Z.-Y. (eds.) IScIDE 2013. LNCS, vol. 8261, pp. 546–553. Springer, Heidelberg (2013). https://doi.org/10.1007/978-3-642-42057-3_69
12. Inc., P.T.: Collaborative data science (2015). https://plot.ly
13. Inselberg, A.: The plane with parallel coordinates. Vis. Comput. **1**(2), 69–91 (1985)
14. Jiang, L., Liu, S., Chen, C.: Recent research advances on interactive machine learning. J. Vis. **22**(2), 401–417 (2018). https://doi.org/10.1007/s12650-018-0531-1
15. Kautz, T., Eskofier, B.M., Pasluosta, C.F.: Generic performance measure for multiclass-classifiers. Pattern Recogn. **68**, 111–125 (2017). https://doi.org/10.1016/j.patcog.2017.03.008
16. Krause, J., Perer, A., Bertini, E.: Infuse: interactive feature selection for predictive modeling of high dimensional data. IEEE Trans. Visual Comput. Graph. **20**(12), 1614–1623 (2014)
17. Kuncheva, L.I., Whitaker, C.J.: Measures of diversity in classifier ensembles and their relationship with the ensemble accuracy. Mach. Learn. **51**(2), 181–207 (2003)
18. LeCun, Y.: The MNIST database of handwritten digits (1999). http://yann.lecun.com/exdb/mnist/
19. LeCun, Y., Bengio, Y., Hinton, G.: Deep learning. Nature **521**, 436–444 (2015). https://doi.org/10.1038/nature14539
20. Link, D., Lang, S., Seidenschwarz, P.: Real time quantification of dangerousity in football using spatiotemporal tracking data. PLoS ONE **11**(12), 1–16 (2016). https://doi.org/10.1371/journal.pone.0168768
21. Meerhoff, L.A., Goes, F., de Leeuw, A.W., Knobbe, A.: Exploring successful team tactics in soccer tracking data. In: MLSA@PKDD/ECML (2019)
22. Memmert, D., Lemmink, K.A.P.M., Sampaio, J.: Current approaches to tactical performance analyses in soccer using position data. Sports Med. **47**(1), 1–10 (2016). https://doi.org/10.1007/s40279-016-0562-5
23. Park, C., Lee, J., Han, H., Lee, K.: ComDia+: an interactive visual analytics system for comparing, diagnosing, and improving multiclass classifiers. In: 2019 IEEE Pacific Visualization Symposium (PacificVis), pp. 313–317, April 2019
24. Pedregosa, F., et al.: Scikit-learn: machine learning in Python. J. Mach. Learn. Res. **12**, 2825–2830 (2011)
25. Polikar, R.: Ensemble based systems in decision making. IEEE Circuits Syste. Mag. **6**, 21–45 (2006)
26. R Core Team: R: A Language and Environment for Statistical Computing. R Foundation for Statistical Computing, Vienna, Austria (2017). https://www.R-project.org/
27. Raschka, S.: Model evaluation, model selection, and algorithm selection in machine learning. CoRR abs/1811.12808 (2018)
28. Rawat, W., Wang, Z.: Deep convolutional neural networks for image classification: a comprehensive review. Neural Comput. **29**(9), 2352–2449 (2017)
29. Ren, D., Amershi, S., Lee, B., Suh, J., Williams, J.D.: Squares: supporting interactive performance analysis for multiclass classifiers. IEEE Trans. Visual Comput. Graphics **23**(1), 61–70 (2017)

30. Sacha, D., et al.: What you see is what you can change: human-centered machine learning by interactive visualization. Neurocomputing **268**, 164–175 (2017). https://doi.org/10.1016/j.neucom.2017.01.105
31. Shneiderman, B.: The eyes have it: a task by data type taxonomy for information visualizations. In: In Proceedings of Visual Languages, pp. 336–343. IEEE Computer Science Press (1996)
32. Theissler, A.: Detecting known and unknown faults in automotive systems using ensemble-based anomaly detection. Knowl. Based Syst. **123**(C), 163–173 (2017). https://doi.org/10.1016/j.knosys.2017.02.023
33. Zhang, J., Wang, Y., Molino, P., Li, L., Ebert, D.S.: Manifold: a model-agnostic framework for interpretation and diagnosis of machine learning models. IEEE Trans. Visual Comput. Graph. **25**(1), 364–373 (2019)

Subverting Network Intrusion Detection: Crafting Adversarial Examples Accounting for Domain-Specific Constraints

Martin Teuffenbach(✉), Ewa Piatkowska(✉), and Paul Smith

AIT Austrian Institute of Technology, Vienna, Austria
{martin.teuffenbach,ewa.piatkowska,paul.smith}@ait.ac.at

Abstract. Deep Learning (DL) algorithms are being applied to network intrusion detection, as they can outperform other methods in terms of computational efficiency and accuracy. However, these algorithms have recently been found to be vulnerable to adversarial examples – inputs that are crafted with the intent of causing a Deep Neural Network (DNN) to misclassify with high confidence. Although a significant amount of work has been done to find robust defence techniques against adversarial examples, they still pose a potential risk. The majority of the proposed attack and defence strategies are tailored to the computer vision domain, in which adversarial examples were first found. In this paper, we consider this issue in the Network Intrusion Detection System (NIDS) domain and extend existing adversarial example crafting algorithms to account for the domain-specific constraints in the feature space. We propose to incorporate information about the difficulty of feature manipulation directly in the optimization function. Additionally, we define a novel measure for attack cost and include it in the assessment of the robustness of DL algorithms. We validate our approach on two benchmark datasets and demonstrate successful attacks against state-of-the-art DL network intrusion detection algorithms.

Keywords: Network intrusion detection · Deep neural networks · Adversarial examples · Adversarial robustness

1 Introduction

A Network Intrusion Detection System (NIDS) can be used to monitor network traffic and detect suspicious patterns that could be part of an attack. To address the challenges of modern network architectures, researchers have investigated the use of machine learning techniques for network intrusion detection [5,14]. In particular, Deep Learning (DL) methods, such as Deep Neural Networks (DNNs), are receiving substantial interest as they outperform shallow networks in accuracy. Several DL algorithms have been proposed for network intrusion detection, some reaching an average accuracy score up to 99% for specific datasets [11,20].

Published by Springer Nature Switzerland AG 2020
A. Holzinger et al. (Eds.): CD-MAKE 2020, LNCS 12279, pp. 301–320, 2020.
https://doi.org/10.1007/978-3-030-57321-8_17

However, DL algorithms have been found to be vulnerable to so-called *adversarial examples* [21] – inputs that are crafted to cause a misclassification. A great deal of research on this issue has been performed for DL algorithms that are used for image recognition. The aim is to introduce a small perturbation, imperceptible to a human, that causes an algorithm to misclassify an image. In a white-box setting, in which the architecture and gradients of a model are known, adversarial example attacks reach misclassification rates that are close to 100%. Considering the use of DL in computer vision for self-driving cars, adversarial examples are a serious threat, as they can cause misclassification of street signs.

In this work, we consider the concept of adversarial examples in the NIDS domain. Unlike in computer vision, in which features are independent from each other and can be changed somewhat arbitrarily, network-flow data has underlying compliance constraints [9]. Nevertheless, we show how an adversary can craft adversarial examples, even when constraints are placed on how network flow features can be manipulated. We reproduce state-of-the-art DL models and formulate restrictions for attacking them in a NIDS setting. To ensure comparability over different datasets and models, we provide a rule-set for the grouping of features. Building on this, we derive a novel crafting algorithm that preserves compliance with these rules. An evaluation has been performed that examines how effective these attacks are under a given budget. We demonstrate that by perturbing less than 10% of the features used by the classifier by less than an average of 0.2 we can achieve up to 100% success rate for an attack.

The remainder of this paper is structured as follows: In Sect. 2, we review state-of-the art models, attacks and metrics on the topic of adversarial examples. Section 3 describes the models that we have used in our studies and a threat model. In Sect. 4, we propose our approach to attack the models and the metrics we will use for evaluation; in Sect. 5, we present the results of our attacks.

2 Related Work

Initial research that investigated adversarial examples for NIDSs, e.g. the work by Yang *et al.* [24], often considered network traffic datasets arbitrarily – i.e. they do not constrain the perturbations that can be introduced to craft an adversarial example. Consequently, adversarial capabilities [2] – constraints on permitted perturbations – were not thoroughly considered for most of the proposed attacks. This is appropriate for attacking an image-based input, but not for network traffic-based input – unlike pixels, which can take any value from 0–255 and be independently changed, features in network flow-datasets contain dependencies and have compliance constraints. Recently, Zhang *et al.* [25] investigated a reinforcement learning approach to match IDS dataset-specific restrictions. The action space of their algorithm only contains valid actions, meaning those actions that would not degrade the validity of the instance. Hashemi *et al.* [9] introduced the idea of treating features differently, based on their properties, when crafting adversarial examples for flow-based NIDSs. They also take dependencies between features into account. We have extended this research by assigning weights to feature groupings, which reflect perturbation constraints, and incorporating these weights into the optimization function that is used to craft the adversarial example.

There are several approaches to measuring the robustness of algorithms against adversarial examples. As the concept of adversarial examples for image recognition algorithms involves imperceptibility from the original image for a human observer, most robustness metrics use a distance metric, using the L1/L2 norm. This is appropriate in this domain, because the distance between the original image input and adversarial example is correlated with the visible difference. Moosavi *et al.* [15] define the expectation value of the *minimal perturbation* over a test dataset as a measure of robustness. Using a theoretical approach, Weng *et al.* [23] have developed the 'CLEVER' score, which is also an estimation for the minimal distance required to subvert a neural network classifier. Papernot *et al.* [16] have proposed the *adversarial distance*, which measures distances between different labels using gradient information to indicate the risk of misclassification between classes. Meanwhile, in the NIDS domain, Hartl *et al.* [8] have developed the *Adversarial Risk Score (ARS)*, which is a distance-based robustness score for classifiers against adversarial examples. In their work, they use a Recurrent Neural Network (RNN) for classification, and investigate the feature sensitivity of their classifier. We argue that without considering the properties of features, e.g. to what extent they can be manipulated, a distance-based approach for measuring the effectiveness of adversarial examples against NIDSs does not accurately reflect the threat. We will elaborate an empirical score for robustness that is based on the relative number of adversarial examples within a given (constrained) feature subspace.

3 Preliminaries

Based on previous research, we present a taxonomy for adversarial examples. We use this taxonomy to define the threat model that we have used in our work. Subsequently, we introduce network intrusion detection using DL algorithms and summarize the algorithms that we have used.

3.1 Adversarial Example Threat Model

The following taxonomy, which describes a threat model for adversarial examples, is adopted from previous work by Carlini *et al.* [2]. The threat model of an adversarial attack can be defined by the *adversarial goal*, *adversarial knowledge*, and *adversarial capabilities*. Based on this taxonomy, the *goal* of the adversary is to perform a network attack that is known (correct classification with high confidence) to the NIDS and change its features to remain undetected (a source/target misclassification problem). It is assumed that the adversary has *white-box knowledge*. Specifically, the type of attack that is performed is one contained in the training dataset of the NIDS, as these instances are known to the model and have higher accuracy. Furthermore, the adversary has full access to the gradient information of the model. We consider two restrictions regarding *adversarial capabilities*: *(i)* the feature space is reduced to a subset of features (referred to as 'considered features') that an attacker can perturb; and *(ii)* a maximum distance δ_{max} to the original sample (L1-norm) is imposed. We use the L1-norm for the maximum distance constraint, as this norm reflects the average absolute change per feature. With this approach, we want to show the worst-case vulnerability of a given NIDS.

3.2 Deep Learning Algorithms

To get a representative sample of DL algorithms for our experiments, we use several state-of-the-art models: a Deep Neural Network (DNN) for binary and multi-class classification [18], in a supervised and semi-supervised fashion; a Deep Belief Network (DBN) for multi-class classification (semi-supervised) [6]; and an Auto Encoder (AE) that is trained to perform outlier detection for unsupervised anomaly detection [10].

Deep Neural Network. To extend the functionality of a regular DNN, which usually works as a supervised classifier, Rezvy *et al.* [18] proposed the idea to stack an Auto Encoder on top of a two-layer classifier network. This algorithm trains the model in three stages: *(i)* the AE is trained unsupervised; *(ii)* the classifier is trained with the output of the AE as input to perform a classification, in a supervised fashion; and *(iii)* the network as a whole is tuned with a few training samples, also supervised. We use this DNN to perform binary classification, to get a comparable result to the AE-based outlier detection (see below).

Deep Belief Network. A model with a similar approach to the AE-DNN is a Deep Belief Network, which is a perceptron network that consists of several layers of Restricted Boltzmann Machines (RBMs). RBMs are often used for dimensionality reduction or feature extraction, which is similar to the algorithm proposed by Gao *et al.* [6]. The model consists of several layers of RBMs with a single-layer classifier stacked on top. The RBMs are trained unsupervised, the classifier then supervised, using the output of the final RBM as input. The idea is that the RBMs in sequence reduce the input dimension to achieve a better representation of the features.

Auto Encoder. Hawkins *et al.* first proposed the use of an AE to perform outlier detection [10]. The approach is to train an AE on benign data (train the network to reproduce the input, unsupervised) and then use the reconstruction error to measure for outliers. The Outlier Factor (OF) of a record i is defined as the average of the squared reconstruction error. To get a more general outlier detection, we extended this concept with a method proposed by Azami *et al.*, which converts distance-based outlier detection methods to probabilities using a sigmoid function [1]:

$$P(\text{i is outlier}) = (1 + exp(\frac{\text{OF}_i - \gamma}{\sigma}))^{-1} \tag{1}$$

where γ is the anomaly threshold ($\text{OF}_i \geq \gamma \Rightarrow \text{P(i is outlier)} \geq 50\%$) and σ a scaling constant. We define the threshold as the 95-percentile and σ as the standard derivation of the outlier factors of the training dataset.

4 Methodology

The majority of work on adversarial examples has targeted computer vision algorithms – specifically, classifiers that take raw images as an input. Applying crafting algorithms that are designed for image processing to other domains might not be appropriate. There are several domain-specific aspects to be considered when crafting adversarial examples for NIDS. First, the features extracted from network traffic are heterogeneous, including flows, context, statistical and categorical features. The dependencies between features imposes additional limitations on how their values can be modified. Second, adversarial perturbations should be crafted considering the way the attack will be implemented, e.g. via the modification of network flows. Therefore, perturbations should render correct flows and ensure compliance with protocols. Third, the concept of *imperceptibility*, which is applicable in the image domain, does not readily apply in the NIDS domain. Nevertheless, minimising perturbation may help to ensure that the original malicious intent of the network attack is preserved. In addition, restrictions on perturbation magnitude could also be important to remain stealthy, i.e. introducing high perturbation to some features might trigger alerts. For instance, increasing packet numbers to hide one attack could result in it being detected as another, either by a NIDS or complementary anomaly detection algorithms.

In the following, we present how we address these aspects. Based on the properties of the features, we divide them into groups (as in [9]) and incorporate feature constraints in the adversarial crafting algorithm. We propose weighted optimisation for crafting adversarial examples in order to ensure feature constraints. As with previous work, we apply perturbation constraints to remain stealthy.

4.1 Feature Analysis and Grouping

Hashemi *et al.* [9] proposed the idea of grouping flow-based features by their *feasibility*, i.e. grouping flows based on whether they can be modified by an adversary and still yield correct flows. We follow a similar approach and group features, as presented in Table 1.

We exclude features that are related to backward flows, as it is reasonable to assume that an adversary generally does not have control over traffic that is generated by other hosts in the network (unless they are compromised). Features that are derived from other features are also not considered. These two groups are merged into a group (G0). Next, we consider features that are independent, e.g. the total number of forwarded packets or maximum length of the forwarded packets. These are further divided into features that are not used to derive other features (G1) and those which are (G2). Changes to features of the latter group requires recalculating dependent features; therefore, we consider them harder to change. The last group contains features that are difficult or impossible to change directly. For instance, to influence statistical summaries of the flows requires the modification of multiple packets. The last group (G3) also includes features with underlying physical constraints (e.g. Inter-Arrival-Time (IAT) features), whose modification could cause potential violations and break the communication.

Table 1. The proposed feature grouping, including those from Hashemi *et al.* [9]

Group	[9]	Description	Weight w
G0	(1)	Features extracted from backward flows	0
	(3)	Features whose values depend on the other features and can be calculated directly by a set of them	0
G1	(2)	Independent and not used to derive other features	1
G2	(2)	Independent and used to derive other features	2
G3	(4)	Features dependent on batches of packets (e.g., mean and frequency based features)	3
		Features with underlying physical constraints (e.g., IAT)	3

Based on the proposed grouping of features, we assign a weight w to each of the groups (as shown in Table 1). The weights give an intuition about how difficult it is for an adversary to perturb a feature, wherein $w = 0$ denotes that the feature cannot be changed and $w = 1, 2, 3$ indicates increasing difficulty. The crafting algorithm is intended to favour features with $w = 1$ over higher weights.

These weights are used in our crafting algorithm. They can be assigned to groups of features or individually to each feature. In this work, we have used constraints that are imposed by the implementation of adversarial perturbation through changes in network flows. Assuming a different threat model, these constraints can differ. For example, weights could also reflect the risk – to the adversary – associated with their change (e.g. due to complementary security measures). Moreover, weights can be assigned empirically using a feature sensitivity analysis [8].

4.2 Crafting Algorithm

For crafting adversarial examples, we extend the Carlini and Wagner (C&W) attack [3]. This method is among the most powerful crafting algorithms and a benchmark technique to evaluate the robustness of deep learning algorithms. Carlini and Wagner formulated an optimisation-based approach to craft adversarial examples. They derived an objective function that maximizes the desired target prediction, while minimising the size of the perturbation:

$$\min_{\delta}(||\delta||_p) \; + \; c \cdot g(x + \delta) \quad \text{s.t. } x + \delta = x^* \in [0, 1]^n, \tag{2}$$

where $\delta = x - x^*$ is the distance between the input x and the adversarial sample x^*, c is a coupling constant and $g(x)$ is a target function. This approach ensures minimal perturbation while minimizing the desired target function. For the L_2 (i.e. Euclidean) norm attack, p is set to 2. The constant c in this equation links the minimization of the distance with the minimization of the target function – smaller values of c result in a bias toward minimizing the distance. The optimisation is solved with the Adam algorithm [12].

As this crafting algorithm performs a distance minimization, it is possible to extend it with our proposed weighted features approach. Features are assigned weights w according to their grouping (0 to 3). Using these weights, along with a mask that specifies the set of features that are considered by the algorithm, we extend the C&W attack, as follows:

$$\min_{\delta}(||\delta \odot w||_2) \ + \ c \cdot g(x + \delta \odot mask) \quad \text{s.t. } x + \delta = x^* \in [0,1]^n, \tag{3}$$

where $\odot$ indicates an element-wise vector-vector multiplication. The weights added to the distance in Eq. 3 forces the algorithm to favour modifications on low-weighted features and avoid adding too much perturbation to high-weighted features. The *mask* represents our restriction on the feature space, e.g. it sets the perturbation of undesired features to 0 (in our case features from G0). As the function $g(x)$ in Eq. 3, we used the f_5 function, as presented in [3]:

$$g(x) = log(2 - 2 \cdot F(x)_t), \tag{4}$$

where $F(x)_t$ is the prediction of the classification model of target label t. This function becomes minimal when $F(x)_t \approx 1$.

4.3 Attack Budget (Parameters) and Metrics

The proposed crafting algorithm performs optimisation with respect to two types of constraints: feature space (feature budget) and the magnitude of feature change (perturbation budget). We define a feature budget f, based on the *mask* and w, and calculate it as follows:

$$f = \frac{mask \cdot w}{|w|_1} \tag{5}$$

where $mask \cdot w$ denotes a vector-vector product. If all features of groups G1-3 are used, the value of f is equal to 1, whereas with fewer features it decreases. This value should give an indication of the cost of an attack. Therefore, if an adversary can craft adversarial example with only a few, low-weight features, f is close to 0, hence the cost of the attack is low. Alongside the reduction on the feature space, we restrict our attacks with a maximum perturbation δ_{max}.

To assess the strength of the attack for a given budget f and δ_{max}, we compute the success rate as follows:

$$s_{j \to t} = \frac{1}{N} \sum_{x \in D_j} \mathbb{1}_{F(x+\delta_x)=t} \quad \text{s.t. } \forall \delta_x : \bar{\delta_x} \leq \delta_{max}, \tag{6}$$

where F is a given classifier with $F : D \rightarrow Y$ (Y being a set of labels), t is the desired label ($t \in Y$) and D_j is the data distribution of instances with true and predicted label j ($D_j \subset D$ with $F(x) = j$ for all $x \in D_j$ and $|D_j| = N$). $\mathbb{1}_{\text{condition}}$ is an indicator function, which is 1 if the condition is true, 0 otherwise. The perturbation δ_x, which aims to turn x into an adversarial example is restricted with the $mask$. The perturbation budget (δ_{max}) restricts the average perturbation per feature $\bar{\delta_x}$ of each instance x. As we only consider attacks that aim to be stealthy (target label t is benign), we are going to denote $s_{j \rightarrow t}$ as s_j. The overall success rate s would then be the average over all labels $j \in Y$. The success rate only makes sense for a sufficiently large number of test samples N.

Goodfellow *et al.* [7] interpreted adversarial examples as 'blind spots' due to incomplete training data. Using this metaphor the success rate can intuitively be seen as the relative number of detected 'blind-spots' within a sphere with radius δ_{max} in a hyperspace defined by $mask$. The success rate is dependent on the technique used for crafting adversarial examples and the set of input samples. Therefore, we restrict our evaluation to the *empirical success rate*, which is the overall success rate for a given crafting algorithm that is tested on particular set of samples.

To give an intuition about the vulnerability of the deep learning model against a given attack, we introduce a *vulnerability score*:

$$vs = \frac{2 \cdot (1/f) \cdot s}{(1/f) + s}, \tag{7}$$

which is the harmonic mean between the success rate s and the inverse feature budget f. The vs metric takes values in the range $[0, 2]$. The closer vs is to 0, the less vulnerable is the model under test. This metric is intended to reflect the trade-off between the empirical success rate s and the hyperspace defined by the attack budget.

5 Experimental Analysis

In this section, we introduce the experimental setup. We explain and justify the choice of datasets and how they are used for both anomaly detection (binary) and multi-label classification. Furthermore, we present our approach to preprocessing and feature grouping on the datasets. Subsequently, the models are evaluated (their accuracy) and then attacks on those models, to compare their vulnerability (robustness) against the adversarial examples, are performed.

5.1 Datasets and Preprocessing

In our experiments, we use two publicly available IDS datasets: *(i)* NSL-KDD [22], a relatively old but still widely-used benchmark dataset; and *(ii)* CICIDS2017 [19], which is a more recent network flow-based dataset.

Datasets. The NSL-KDD dataset is a refined version of the well-known KDD CUP 99 dataset that was developed by DARPA. The dataset includes information that has been extracted from network traffic (e.g. TCP connections), as well as high-level features (e.g. the number of failed logins). The data records are attributed with 41 features (intrinsic, content, time-based and host-based). The dataset contains 49 different labels that are grouped into five categories: Normal, Denial of Service (DoS), Probing, User to Root (U2R) and Remote to Local (R2L) attack. The NSL-KDD dataset is divided into training and testing sets. The distribution of the attacks in each of the subsets are presented in Fig. 1.

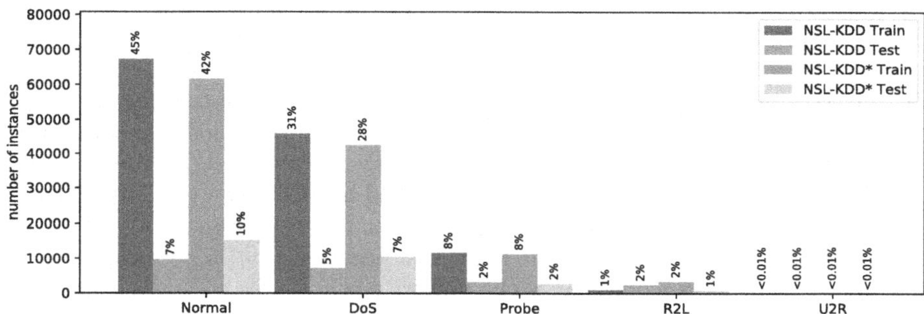

Fig. 1. The distribution of samples in the NSL-KDD dataset

A challenge when using the NSL-KDD dataset is the high diversity of testing samples – the testing set contains labels that are not included in the training set. In addition, for U2R and R2L attacks, the training set is smaller than the testing set, which can have a negative impact on the accuracy of trained classifiers. To address this issue, Rezvy *et al.* [18] defined their own training and testing subsets (further referred to as NSL-KDD*) to train their classifier with more samples of U2R and R2L attacks (see Fig. 1). In our experiments, we aim to reproduce the results of the Rezvy *et al.* DNN model; therefore, we use both variants of the NSL-KDD dataset.

The second dataset (CICIDS2017) [19] contains five days of network traffic that were recorded in an emulated environment with 25 hosts. The data is provided as network packets and bidirectional network flows. In total, this set contains about 2.8 million records, which are described with 80 features and grouped into 15 label categories (14 attacks plus benign). The dataset is quite imbalanced – some attacks are very sparse, e.g. the *Heartbleed* attack appears only eleven times in the whole dataset, whereas almost 84% of labels are normal samples. In our experiments, we used a subset of the CICIDS2017 dataset (due to computational constraints). We used an 80/20 random split to create training and testing sets. For multi-label classification, we utilized an oversampling technique for the training phase, by adding redundant data to low-frequency labels.

We also removed random samples from the benign label (undersampling). For the anomaly-based detection, we kept the original distribution of the CICIDS2017 dataset, as the benign and total attack samples are sufficiently balanced.

Data Preprocessing. Similar to Gao *et al.* [6], we have applied three pre-processing methods; these are necessary for the datasets to be used as input to machine learning models. First, we have performed *one-hot-encoding* to map categorical features to numerical values. For instance, the 'Protocol' feature can be of three distinct categories, namely 'TCP', 'UDP' or 'ICMP'. In one-hot-encoding, this feature is represented by a 3×1 vector, in which the value 'TCP' protocol translates to [1, 0, 0], 'UDP' to [0, 1, 0], etc. This procedure has been applied to the NSL-KDD dataset, encoding 41 categorical features as 122 numerical features. This step was not necessary for the CICIDS2017 dataset, as it does not include categorical features. Second, since the range of the features in the IDS datasets may vary significantly (e.g. some packet-size related features range from 0 to 10^8, others from 0 to 10^3), we apply the following log-transformation to all features: x_i: $x_i = log(1 + x_i)$. Consequently, a value $x_i \in [0, 10^8]$ is transformed to $x_i \in [0, 18]$. This approach was applied by Hawkins *et al.* [10]. Finally, we normalize the data using a *min-max transform*, such that the range of all the features is set to $[0, 1]$. Without the log-transformation that is performed in the previous step, outliers would cause the majority of features to be set to zero.

Feature Groups. The features in the datasets were arranged into groups, as discussed in Sect. 4.1. For the CICIDS2017 dataset, we assigned all the flows in a backward direction to G0, along with features that relate to both backward and forward directions (total flow bytes/s). Groups 1, 2 and 3 are features in the forward direction. The independent features are placed in G1, those that are used to derive other features are placed in G2, and derived features in G3. Additionally 'hard to access' features and those with physical limitations (IAT features) are placed into G3. Meanwhile, for the NSL-KDD dataset, we put all the categorical and binary features (flags) into G0. Content-based features that are based on flows in the forward direction are located in G1, alongside (independent) counters. Group 2 contains counters that are used to derive other features. Finally, frequency-based features (e.g. error rates) are placed into G3. We consider 30 out of 122 (25%) features for the NSL-KDD set and 32 out of 78 (41%) for the CICIDS2017 as accessible features, i.e. features that could be manipulated by an adversary. Therefore, the maximum number of $f = 1$ in Eq. 5 can only be achieved by using all 30 and 32 accessible features for NSL-KDD and CICIDS2017 datasets, respectively.

5.2 NIDS Model Evaluation

We start our experiments by establishing the baseline performance of the considered algorithms for network intrusion detection (described in Sect. 3.2). We evaluate both variants of NIDS models: attack detection (multi-label classification models) and anomaly detection (binary classification models).

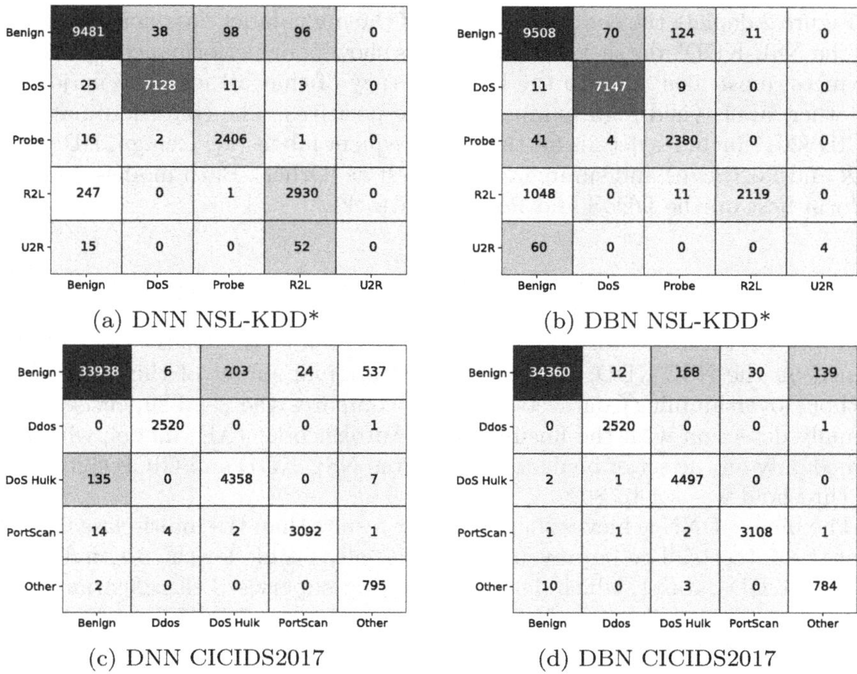

(a) DNN NSL-KDD* (b) DBN NSL-KDD*

(c) DNN CICIDS2017 (d) DBN CICIDS2017

Fig. 2. The confusion matrix for the multi-class models

Attack Detection (Multi-Class Models). Two classifiers have been trained and tested: a Deep Neural Network (DNN) [18] and a Deep Belief Network (DBN) [6]. The architecture and training parameters were chosen to be similar to the proposed models, with slight modifications to optimize the performance. Table 2 shows the performance of the models in terms of overall Accuracy, Recall, Precision and F1-score. The performance of both of the models are acceptable and aligned with the original papers [6,18]. It can also be noted that, as expected, both models achieve significantly better accuracy on the NSL-KDD* dataset than NSL-KDD.

Table 2. The results of the attack detection models

Model	Dataset	Accuracy	Precision	Recall	F1
DNN	CICIDS2017	0.979	0.933	0.983	0.957
	NSL-KDD	0.742	0.914	0.603	0.777
	NSL-KDD*	0.973	0.982	0.971	0.976
DBN	CICIDS2017	0.991	0.969	0.996	0.982
	NSL-KDD	0.762	0.929	0.630	0.751
	NSL-KDD*	0.938	0.983	0.908	0.944

Figure 2 depicts the confusion matrix of the multi-label classification models. For the NSL-KDD* dataset, both classifiers show poor performance for the U2R instances, most likely due to the low frequency of that attack. The majority of the other labels yield high numbers of true positives. The confusion matrix for CICIDS2017 includes details for the most frequent labels (i.e. Benign, DDos, DoS Hulk and PortScan) and summarizes the rest as 'Other'. Both models appear to perform best on the DDoS and PortScan attacks.

Anomaly Detection (Binary Models). For anomaly detection, the DNN model [18] was used again. However, in this case, it was trained for binary classification, i.e. there are only two output classes: benign or attack. The DNN was trained on the NSL-KDD, NSL-KDD* and original subset of the CICIDS2017 (without oversampling) datasets. Table 3 compares the semi-supervised DNN anomaly detection with the unsupervised AutoEncoder (AE) model, which was trained only on the set of benign samples from NSL-KDD and CICIDS2017. The AE threshold was set to 80%.

The binary DNN achieves slightly better results than the multi-class DNN for all of the datasets. The improvement is especially visible for the original split of the NSL-KDD dataset, which demonstrates that supervised classification is very sensitive to the distribution of labels in the training set. The AE model achieves surprisingly good results for the NSL-KDD data, with precision and recall above 0.88; however, its accuracy on the CICIDS2017 data is drastically lower. The recall of attack detection is just slightly above 50% and low precision indicates a high number of false positives. The reconstruction error of the anomalous instances seems to be insufficient to efficiently differentiate attacks from benign samples. In our evaluation of the adversarial example attacks, we focus only on sufficiently accurate models; hence, we will not consider the AutoEncoder (AE) trained on the CICIDS2017 dataset.

Table 3. The results of the anomaly detection models

Model	Dataset	Accuracy	Precision	Recall	F1
DNN	CICIDS2017	0.990	0.965	0.996	0.980
	NSL-KDD	0.794	0.921	0.698	0.798
	NSL-KDD*	0.975	0.984	0.971	0.978
AE	NSL-KDD	0.870	0.890	0.880	0.885
	CICIDS2017	0.628	0.273	0.548	0.365

Our goal with these models is to reproduce a representation of the established deep learning algorithms and test their robustness against adversarial samples. The accuracy and F1-score in Tables 2 and 3 demonstrate that the classifiers are reliable. In further experiments, we will use the strongest variants of the classifiers – for the DNN and DBN models, we choose those trained on the

CICIDS2017 and NSL-KDD* datasets (as they yield higher accuracy than the ones trained on the original NSL-KDD dataset).

5.3 Attack Evaluation

In this section, we evaluate the proposed algorithm for crafting adversarial examples. As mentioned in Sect. 3.1, our threat model assumes a white-box attack, i.e. the architecture and parameters of the NIDS model are known. The attacker's goal is to launch a stealthy attack through the use of adversarial examples. The idea is to modify the attack sample in such way that a NIDS classifies it as benign. For the multi-label classifiers, we chose the top two attacks (labels with the highest accuracy), as indicated in Fig. 2. The best accuracy of the DNN and DBN models was reported for DoS (99.6%/99.6%) and Probe (99.4%/99.1%) attacks from the NSL-KDD dataset, and Distributed Denial of Service (DDoS) (99.1%/99.6%) and PortScan (99.8%/99.0%) from the CICIDS2017 dataset. These four labels are considered for crafting adversarial examples. For anomaly detection, we selected a random subset of the NSL-KDD attack samples. Some assumptions were made in the evaluation of the proposed adversarial example attacks:

- Adversarial examples are only crafted for inputs that are correctly classified with at least 80% confidence.
- The parameter c in Eq. 3, which is the trade-off between minimizing the perturbation (distance) and maximizing the loss function, is set using a binary search (see [3]).
- We always list the worst-case attack, thus if not stated explicitly, the parameters are always set to maximise the success rate.
- The perturbation constraint δ_{max} should be understood as the average distance per feature; therefore, the actual perturbation δ must be smaller than $\delta_{max} \cdot |mask|_1$.
- The list of *considered features*, formally defined by $mask$, specifies which features can be modified by the adversarial crafting algorithm. The $mask$ is created by randomly adding features from groups in the order of their weights (starting with G1 up to G3), until the budget is reached.
- If all features of G1 to G3 are considered then $f = 1$, whereas $f \approx 0$ indicates that only a few features from G1 were selected. For all of the classifiers, we used the same $mask$ to get comparable results.

In the following, we experimentally evaluate the strength of the adversarial example attacks for the considered deep learning algorithms under a given budget, expressed in terms of feature space constraints (f) and perturbation magnitude (δ_{max}).

Attacks on Multi-class Models. We measure the success rate (see Eq. 6) of the adversarial examples that are crafted by the proposed algorithm, using different combinations of attack parameters. Figure 3 depicts the highest achieved

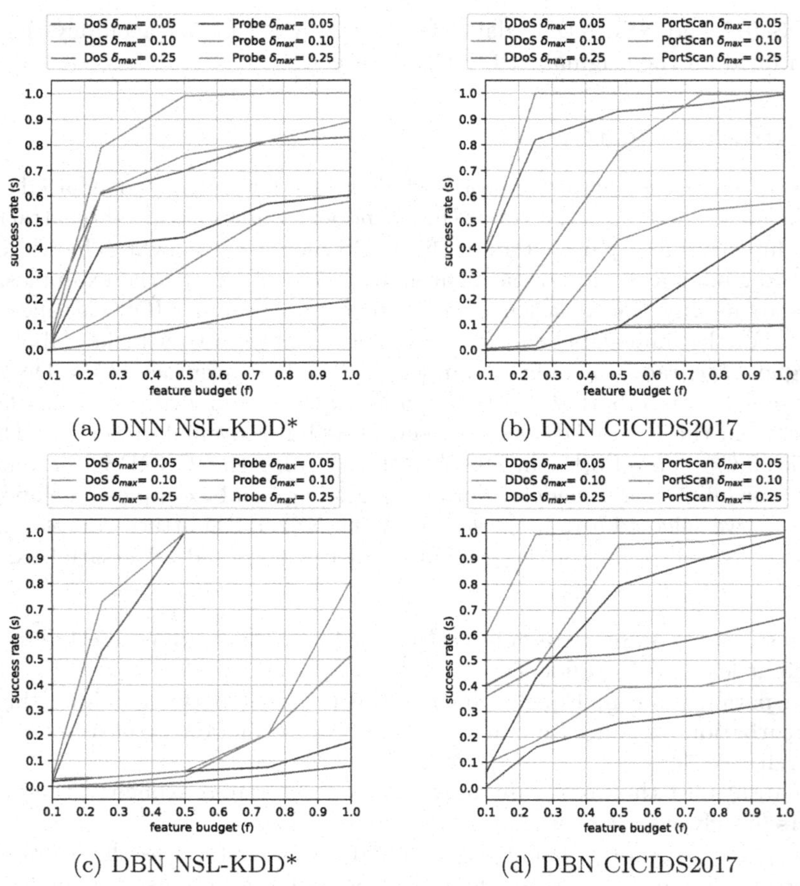

(a) DNN NSL-KDD* (b) DNN CICIDS2017

(c) DBN NSL-KDD* (d) DBN CICIDS2017

Fig. 3. Evaluation of the attack parameters for multi-class models

success rate for the DNN and DBN models for $\delta_{max} = \{0.05, 0.1, 0.25\}$ against varying $f = \{0.1, 0.25, 0.5, 0.75, 1\}$. The overall success rate is still quite high, given the fact that we consider only 41% of the features in the CICIDS2017 dataset as accessible and 25% of the NSL-KDD dataset (see Sect. 5.1). The results indicate that it is more difficult to craft adversarial examples for DoS attacks. Surprisingly, the DBN model seems to be less vulnerable for low budget attacks than the DNN model for the NSL-KDD* set, even though the DNN model outperforms the former in detection (see Table 2). As expected, the success rate increases with higher values of f – the attacks are more effective if an adversary is allowed to manipulate more features. The plots (Fig. 3) reveal some intuition about a trade-off between the attack parameters. We can analyse for which δ_{max} an attacker can reach the optimum success rate with a small feature budget. For instance, the most successful attacks can be noted for PortScan against both the DNN and DBN models with $\delta_{max} = 0.25$. Furthermore, we can observe that the success rate of the attack is more sensitive to changes of δ_{max} rather than f. Sometimes we can observe that with sufficient δ_{max} adding more features does not improve the success rate (e.g. for Probe and PortScan, the optimal feature budget can be found below 0.5). Analogically, for DoS and DDoS attacks, reasonable success rates can only be achieved for the highest δ_{max} value. For the majority of attacks, the optimal feature budget can be found below 0.5; afterwards there is only a gradual, small increase in success rate.

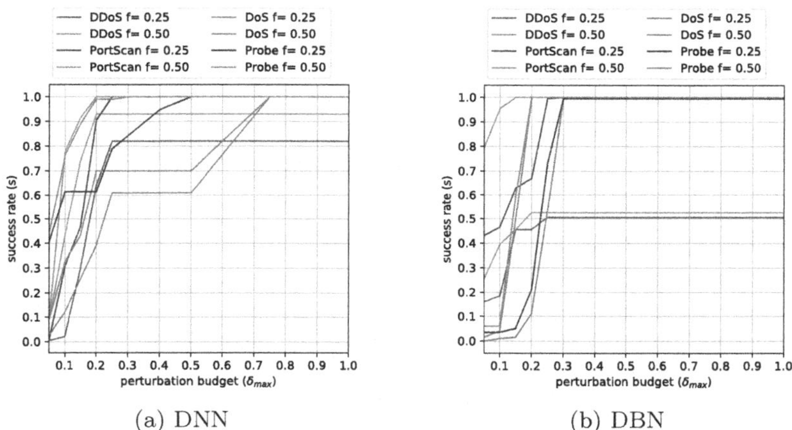

Fig. 4. The success rate of attacks against the DNN and DBN models for different values of δ_{max} parameter

We have investigated different values of perturbation budget δ_{max} for $f = 0.25$ and $f = 0.5$. Figure 4 visualizes the influence of δ_{max} on the success rate. We observe that for most graphs there exists a certain threshold after which the success rate stays constant. For the DBN model, the optimal value of perturbation budget is reached around $\delta_{max} = 0.3$, whereas for DNN it is on average slightly higher $\delta_{max} = 0.5$. Overall, this threshold appears to be slightly higher for the NSL-KDD dataset. This is due to the fact that the relative amount of features we consider is larger for the CICIDS2017 dataset. Therefore, a smaller perturbation-per-feature is necessary to reach the adversarial goal. An average perturbation above 0.3 seems rather extensive; however, we managed to achieve considerable success rates for δ_{max} below this value with $f = 0.5$. This budget for the NSL-KDD* dataset, for example, means that we only perturb around 10% of the features by ≈ 0.1 and still find adversarial examples for many instances.

Attacks on Anomaly-Based (Binary) Models. We performed a similar parameter analysis for adversarial example attacks against binary models. We

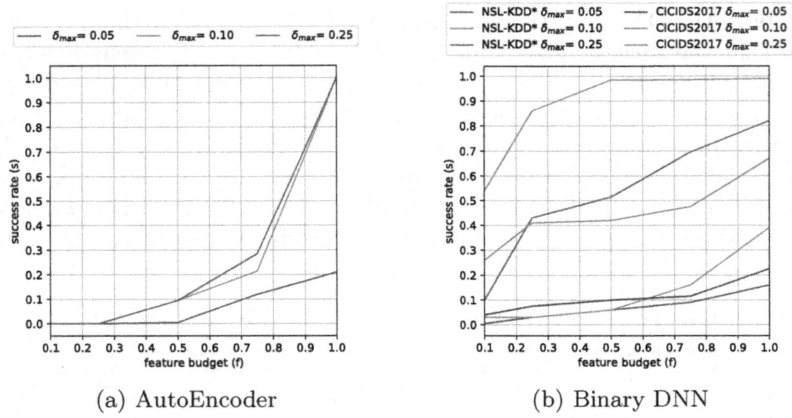

(a) AutoEncoder (b) Binary DNN

Fig. 5. Evaluation of the attack parameters for binary models

recorded the highest achieved success rate for given perturbation restrictions. The results are depicted in Fig. 5.

The AE model treats anomalies as outliers and detects them by measuring the reconstruction error (see Sect. 3.2). As Fig. 5a suggests, a rather high budget is necessary to achieve the adversarial goal. Surprisingly, the feature budget (f) seems to have more influence on the success rate than perturbation budget (δ_{max}). Even though the AE achieves lower accuracy than the other (supervised) models, it has a significant advantage of being more robust to adversarial examples. In Fig. 5b the success rates of adversarial example attacks against the binary DNN model are presented. We can clearly observe that attacks using NSL-KDD* dataset show better performance than CICIDS2017. Furthermore, for the CICIDS2017 dataset it is possible to craft strong attacks even with a small feature budget and relatively small δ_{max}. This might indicate that the distance between benign and anomalous samples is rather low for that dataset, making it challenging for outlier-based anomaly detection. This is why the AE model performed so poorly on the CICIDS2017 dataset (as shown in Table 3).

Vulnerability Analysis. In Fig. 6, we compare the algorithms in terms of their vulnerability to adversarial examples. The vulnerability score vs (see Eq. 7) is listed per attack against each model. The experiments were performed for three different values of δ_{max}.

We can observe that vs confirms our findings from the previous experiments. The classification models are relatively robust against the DoS attack of the NSL-KDD dataset, but rather vulnerable to the Probe and PortScan attacks. The low vs for the DoS attack may be explained by the fact that the most discriminative features for this type of attack are the IAT and frequency-based features. However, these features are assigned to G3 in the proposed grouping, thus considered hard to access and modify by an attacker. Considering features

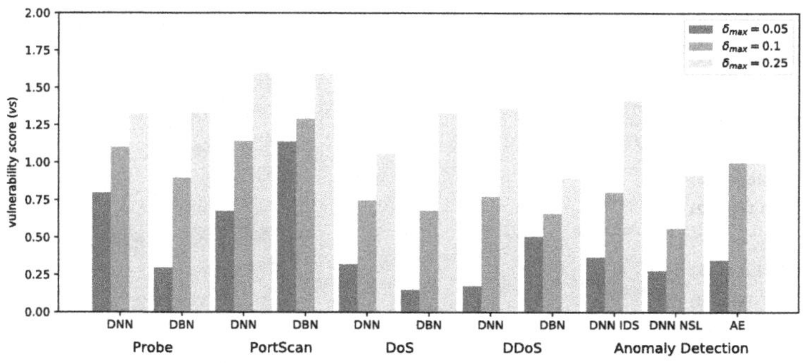

Fig. 6. The vulnerability score of all the models for both datasets

with high weights to craft successful adversarial examples targeted towards DoS attacks would increase the overall feature budget f and, therefore, decrease the vulnerability score. As previously shown, the AE model is robust against low-budget adversarial attacks. This is reflected by $vs \leq 1$ for all values of δ_{max}.

5.4 Feature Perturbation Analysis

To show the impact of the feature weights in the proposed algorithm (see Eq. 3), we performed a feature perturbation analysis. For this experiment, we used the DNN classifier trained on the CICIDS2017 dataset and crafted adversarial examples for the DDoS label. We compare the proposed crafting algorithm with the original C&W [4] and iterative Fast Gradient Sign Method (iFGSM) [13] attacks. The latter attack performs iterative FGSM [7], which maximises the loss using gradient sign. This algorithm terminates when either the desired label is reached or the limit of maximum iterations is exceeded; hence, it does not perform any distance (perturbation) minimisation. Therefore, we neglect the restriction on perturbation budget (maximum distance constraint) in the C&W and our method, since this restriction is not directly relevant for the analysis. As *considered features*, four features of each group have been chosen arbitrarily. The resulting feature budget sums up to $f = 0.31$. We measure the average perturbation per each feature for the successfully created adversarial examples. The results are depicted in Fig. 7.

As expected, the average perturbation for iFGSM and C&W does not depend on the feature group but feature importance with respect to the classifier. Furthermore, for C&W and our proposed extension, we compare the average perturbation per feature using two different values of the hyperparameter c, which controls the impact between distance and target function minimisation. A low value of $c = 0.1$, assigns less importance to target function minimisation and enforces a small distance over desired attack, hence the weights of the extended C&W algorithm strongly influence the results. As can be observed in Fig. 7 (left), our algorithm favours features from G1 over the other groups. This effect is less visible with higher $c = 10$, in which adversarial examples are optimised

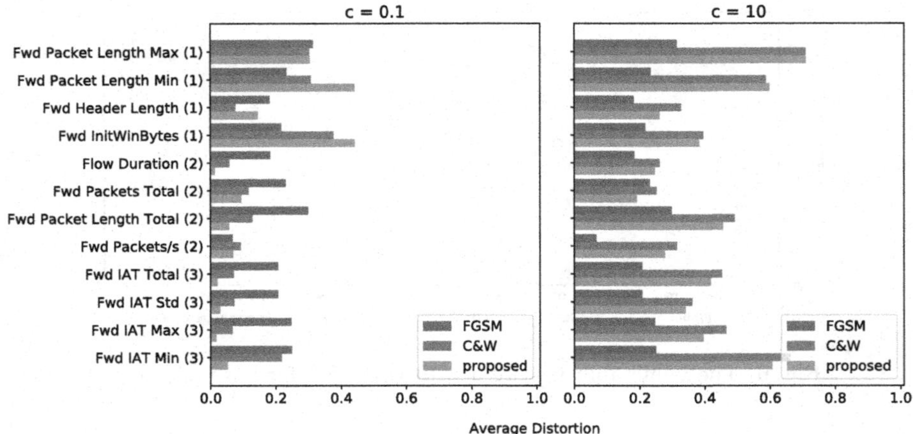

Fig. 7. The average distortion per feature for the DDoS attack label – feature group numbers are shown in parentheses

mostly with respect to target function. The success rate of the iFGSM in Fig. 7 was 73.3% (left and right). With emphasis on the distance minimization (left, $c = 0.1$) our proposed algorithm reached a success rate of 50.8 %, the original C&W 55.6%, even though the proposed algorithm applied only a perturbation close to 0 to the G3 features. By increasing c to 10, we achieved 87% for the proposed method and 87.7% for the C&W.

For an adversary that intends to attack a NIDS through adversarial examples it is vital to account for not only the feature space constraints (e.g. only a subset of features might be accessible) but also perturbation restrictions that are specific for some features. We demonstrate that using our weighted C&W approach, we are able to control the amount of perturbation per group of features. Our results show that the proposed method kept the perturbation of IAT features (G3) as low as possible, since these features are important for maintaining the goal of the DDoS attacks. In our experiments, we assigned weight values to $v = \{1, 2, 3\}$ for Group 1, 2 and 3, respectively. However, the impact of weighted perturbation could be amplified by using different weight ratios.

6 Conclusions

In this paper, we have proposed a novel approach to crafting adversarial examples that accounts for domain-specific constraints in the feature space. Features are assigned weights to reflect the difficulty of their modification. To achieve this, we have extended a well-established C&W attack [3] to perform optimisation with respect to feature weights and perturbation constraints. To express the difficulty of an attack, we consider two types of constraints: feature budget and perturbation budget. We have presented different methods to analyse the impact of attack budget on the strength of adversarial attacks against considered DL models. We demonstrate that by modifying only a few features by less than an average of 0.2, we can achieve considerable success rates for adversarial example attacks. Our weighted crafting algorithm is able to restrict the perturbation mostly to independent and easy to access features, which increases the chance of creating a valid adversarial flow instance. We introduced a vulnerability score to provide an empirical, yet realistic, measure of robustness of network intrusion detection models against attacks of a given perturbation budget. The measure gives an intuition about the difficulty of the attacks that are required to achieve considerable success rates. Our results indicate that DNN and DBN models are more robust to adversarial examples that are targeted to hide DoS attacks than Probe or PortScan attacks. Furthermore, an AutoEncoder (AE) model, even though it achieves slightly worse accuracy in anomaly detection than other methods, seem to be the least vulnerable to adversarial examples. In future work, we will explore different threat models, investigate the transferability of adversarial examples [17] and test the feasibility of black box attacks, given a more restrictive validity constraints in the NIDS domain.

Acknowledgments. The research leading to this publication was supported by the EU H2020 project SOCCRATES (833481) and the Austrian FFG project Malori (873511).

References

1. Azami, M.E., Lartizien, C., Canu, S.: Converting SVDD scores into probability estimates: application to outlier detection. Neurocomputing **268**, 64–75 (2017)
2. Carlini, N., et al.: On evaluating adversarial robustness. arXiv:1902.06705 [cs, stat] (2019)
3. Carlini, N., Wagner, D.: Towards evaluating the robustness of neural networks. arXiv:1608.04644 [cs] (2016)
4. Carlini, N., Wagner, D.: Adversarial examples are not easily detected: bypassing ten detection methods. arXiv:1705.07263 [cs] (2017)
5. Dong, B., Wang, X.: Comparison deep learning method to traditional methods using for network intrusion detection. In: 2016 8th IEEE International Conference on Communication Software and Networks (ICCSN), pp. 581–585. IEEE (2016)
6. Gao, N., Gao, L., Gao, Q., Wang, H.: An intrusion detection model based on deep belief networks. In: 2014 Second International Conference on Advanced Cloud and Big Data, pp. 247–252 (2014)
7. Goodfellow, I.J., Shlens, J., Szegedy, C.: Explaining and harnessing adversarial examples. arXiv:1412.6572 [cs, stat] (2014)
8. Hartl, A., Bachl, M., Fabini, J., Zseby, T.: Explainability and adversarial robustness for RNNs. arXiv:1912.09855 [cs, stat] (2020)
9. Hashemi, M.J., Cusack, G., Keller, E.: Towards evaluation of NIDSs in adversarial setting. In: Proceedings of the 3rd ACM CoNEXT Workshop on Big DAta, Machine Learning and Artificial Intelligence for Data Communication Networks - Big-DAMA 2019, pp. 14–21 (2019)
10. Hawkins, S., He, H., Williams, G., Baxter, R.: Outlier detection using replicator neural networks. In: Kambayashi, Y., Winiwarter, W., Arikawa, M. (eds.) DaWaK 2002. LNCS, vol. 2454, pp. 170–180. Springer, Heidelberg (2002). https://doi.org/10.1007/3-540-46145-0_17

11. Kim, J., Shin, N., Jo, S.Y., Kim, S.H.: Method of intrusion detection using deep neural network. In: 2017 IEEE International Conference on Big Data and Smart Computing (BigComp), pp. 313–316 (2017)
12. Kingma, D.P., Ba, J.: Adam: a method for stochastic optimization. arXiv:1412.6980 [cs] (2017)
13. Kurakin, A., Goodfellow, I., Bengio, S.: Adversarial machine learning at scale. arXiv:1611.01236 [cs, stat] (2017)
14. Mishra, P., Varadharajan, V., Tupakula, U., Pilli, E.S.: A detailed investigation and analysis of using machine learning techniques for intrusion detection. IEEE Commun. Surv. Tutorials **21**, 686–728 (2019)
15. Moosavi-Dezfooli, S.M., Fawzi, A., Frossard, P.: DeepFool: a simple and accurate method to fool deep neural networks. In: 2016 IEEE Conference on Computer Vision and Pattern Recognition (CVPR), pp. 2574–2582 (2016)
16. Papernot, N., McDaniel, P., Jha, S., Fredrikson, M., Celik, Z.B., Swami, A.: The limitations of deep learning in adversarial settings. In: arXiv:1511.07528 [cs, stat], pp. 372–387, March 2016
17. Papernot, N., McDaniel, P., Goodfellow, I.: Transferability in machine learning: from phenomena to black-box attacks using adversarial samples. arXiv:1605.07277 [cs] (2016)
18. Rezvy, S., Petridis, M., Lasebae, A., Zebin, T.: Intrusion detection and classification with autoencoded deep neural network. In: Lanet, J.-L., Toma, C. (eds.) SECITC 2018. LNCS, vol. 11359, pp. 142–156. Springer, Cham (2019). https://doi.org/10.1007/978-3-030-12942-2_12
19. Sharafaldin, I., Habibi Lashkari, A., Ghorbani, A.A.: Toward generating a new intrusion detection dataset and intrusion traffic characterization. In: Proceedings of the 4th International Conference on Information Systems Security and Privacy, pp. 108–116 (2018)
20. Shone, N., Ngoc, T.N., Phai, V.D., Shi, Q.: A deep learning approach to network intrusion detection. IEEE Trans. Emerg. Top. Comput. Intell. **2**, 41–50 (2018)
21. Szegedy, C., et al.: Intriguing properties of neural networks. arXiv:1312.6199 [cs] (2013)
22. Tavallaee, M., Bagheri, E., Lu, W., Ghorbani, A.A.: A detailed analysis of the KDD CUP 99 data set. In: Proceedings of the IEEE Symposium on Computational Intelligence for Security and Defense Applications, pp. 1–6 (2009)
23. Weng, T.W., et al.: Evaluating the robustness of neural networks: an extreme value theory approach. arXiv:1801.10578 [cs, stat] (2018)
24. Yang, K., Liu, J., Zhang, C., Fang, Y.: Adversarial examples against the deep learning based network intrusion detection systems. In: MILCOM 2018–2018 IEEE Military Communications Conference (MILCOM), pp. 559–564 (2018)
25. Zhang, X., Zhou, Y., Pei, S., Zhuge, J., Chen, J.: Adversarial examples detection for XSS attacks based on generative adversarial networks. IEEE Access **8**, 10989–10996 (2020)

Scenario-Based Requirements Elicitation for User-Centric Explainable AI

A Case in Fraud Detection

Douglas Cirqueira[1](✉), Dietmar Nedbal[2], Markus Helfert[3], and Marija Bezbradica[1]

[1] Dublin City University, Dublin, Ireland
douglas.darochacirqueira2@mail.dcu.ie
[2] University of Applied Sciences Upper Austria, Steyr, Austria
[3] Maynooth University, Maynooth, Ireland

Abstract. Explainable Artificial Intelligence (XAI) develops technical explanation methods and enable interpretability for human stakeholders on why Artificial Intelligence (AI) and machine learning (ML) models provide certain predictions. However, the trust of those stakeholders into AI models and explanations is still an issue, especially domain experts, who are knowledgeable about their domain but not AI inner workings. Social and user-centric XAI research states it is essential to understand the stakeholder's requirements to provide explanations tailored to their needs, and enhance their trust in working with AI models. Scenario-based design and requirements elicitation can help bridge the gap between social and operational aspects of a stakeholder early before the adoption of information systems and identify its real problem and practices generating user requirements. Nevertheless, it is still rarely explored the adoption of scenarios in XAI, especially in the domain of fraud detection to supporting experts who are about to work with AI models. We demonstrate the usage of scenario-based requirements elicitation for XAI in a fraud detection context, and develop scenarios derived with experts in banking fraud. We discuss how those scenarios can be adopted to identify user or expert requirements for appropriate explanations in his daily operations and to make decisions on reviewing fraudulent cases in banking. The generalizability of the scenarios for further adoption is validated through a systematic literature review in domains of XAI and visual analytics for fraud detection.

Keywords: Explainable artificial intelligence · Requirements elicitation · Domain expert · Fraud detection

1 Introduction

Digital platforms in retail and banking have enabled customers to experience convenience through personalization and tailored technologies for shopping and performing transactions [1–4]. However, the convenience is also accompanied by the danger of frauds

Published by Springer Nature Switzerland AG 2020
A. Holzinger et al. (Eds.): CD-MAKE 2020, LNCS 12279, pp. 321–341, 2020.
https://doi.org/10.1007/978-3-030-57321-8_18

[5, 6]. Transaction frauds are growing every year, and organizations such as retailers and banks realized the potential of AI models for automating the fraud detection task [7].

However, organizations leveraging AI technologies are considering the importance of automating their processes and understanding the predictions made by those models [8], as users are increasingly demanding transparency from their daily software assistants [9]. This understanding is enabled through explanations provided by Explainable AI (XAI) methods [10]. The field of XAI aims to implement and develop explanation methods, enabling transparency and traceability for statistical black-box ML models, such as deep learning approaches, which are increasingly used by industry due to their potential to reveal useful insights into the Big Data present in companies businesses [11].

While in some domains automation is relevant, it is essential for others to understand AI predictions and decisions for human stakeholders [10], as explanations can impact the work of stakeholders who adopt such tools for decision-making [12]. For instance, in healthcare, doctors can adopt explanation methods to understand the diagnosis provided by AI models predictions [10]. In finance, researchers seek to leverage explanations for better decision-making of fraud experts in reviewing fraudulent applications for credit and loans [13]. Therefore, a diversity of explanation methods for AI predictions has been developed in the XAI literature [6].

In addition, while it is essential to develop those methods, researchers from the social perspective highlight XAI research tended to adopt particular notions of what is a good explanation, not considering, for instance, the usability and causability requirements of stakeholders for understanding explanations [14–17]. Such requirements are essential as they enable an understanding of the quality of explanations associated with a human agent's properties and his cognitive and intelligence capabilities for working with AI models [18].

This lack of user-centric perspective in XAI is a context also observed in the domain of fraud detection. Nevertheless, fraud experts need to act on predictions provided by AI models which they do not understand or trust. However, XAI literature is rarely addressed from a user-centric perspective in fraud detection. User-centric XAI researchers highlight the importance of considering users' needs for a trustworthy relationship with AI models for decision-making [19, 20].

Aiming a user-centric view into decision-making for fraud detection, the domain of visual analytics has also been providing contributions through visualization tools and capabilities for fraud detection [21]. Indeed, some researchers have acknowledged the importance of the human-computer interaction or human-in-the-loop perspectives contributing to research in XAI, and the need to investigate new human-AI interfaces for Explainable AI [22–26]. Therefore, a user-centric perspective is essential for reviewing fraud cases, whether in XAI or visual analytics research, as every wrong decision made causes financial harm for customers and organizations.

In the meantime, Information Systems (IS) research has been studying, for years, the cognitive tasks of stakeholders, and how to designing information systems that can support in their decision-making processes [27, 28]. For support in decision-making, IS research states it is fundamental to identify user requirements in a problem space for developing artifacts as systems aligned with the needs of practitioners, causing a successful impact within an organization [29, 30]. This research follows an IS theoretical perspective in XAI for fraud detection, and aims to investigate the cognitive tasks of fraud experts for decision-making, and how those tasks can be adopted to identify their requirements for explanations of AI predictions aiding in their reviewing process of fraud cases.

To uncover the cognitive tasks of fraud experts, the main goal of this study is to demonstrate the usage of a scenario-based requirements elicitation method, and to develop scenarios illustrating the process for decision-making in fraud detection. Scenarios have the potential to bridge the gap between the social and operational focus with the organizational focus of information systems development [31]. Our stakeholder is regarded as a fraud expert, which is not knowledgeable about AI inner workings, and would benefit from explanations for reviewing fraudulent transaction cases daily in a bank. That is a context seldom addressed by the employment of scenarios within XAI.

We outline the following elements as contributions of this study:

- The demonstration of the suitability of scenario-based requirements elicitation method in the context of XAI for fraud detection.
- The development and validation of fraud scenarios for XAI literature, which can be adopted for identifying fraud experts' requirements for explanations, and designing explanation methods suitable for this domain.

The rest of this paper is organized as follows: Sect. 2 describes related work; Sect. 3 discusses the scenario-based method adopted in this study; Sect. 4 presents the results of the method as fraud scenarios; Sect. 5 describes the validation of the developed fraud scenarios given existing literature; Sect. 6 discusses how the developed scenarios can be adopted for requirements elicitation in XAI for fraud detection; Sect. 7 concludes the study with final remarks and future work.

2 Related Work

The concept of explaining has been studied for a long time by research disciplines other than information systems or computer science, such as social sciences [14, 32]. Following those lenses, Miller [33] defines explanations in XAI as an answer to a question an explainee would have to an explainer, which can be a why-question such as "Why is that transaction marked as a fraud?". Researchers in the discipline of computer science and machine learning have been developing XAI methods as explainers, which provide explanations or human-AI interfaces for different stakeholders, including domain experts, who adopt them for decision-making processes [23]. Research in XAI usually classifies explanations by their scope or dependency [33–37]. The scope can be global, when explanations provide an understanding of the whole logic of an AI model, or local when explanations provide an understanding of individual predictions. Dependency can be model-specific, which enables explanations of a particular AI model, or model-agnostic, which enables post-hoc explanations independently of the underlying AI model. Each of those methods has particular features, which enable understanding of particular aspects of AI predictions.

Within XAI literature, researchers have tried to assess the impact of explanations on the decision-making of fraud experts working with AI models in domains such as intrusion detection, fraudulent warranty claims, and banking transaction frauds. In [38], the authors provide a service architecture for security experts with explanations, aiming to introduce more context for the outlier score given to anomalous records of network flows. The work of [39] provides domain experts with shapely additive explanations (SHAP) [40] for why particular warranty claims are marked as anomalies by an ML model. In [41], the authors also work with SHAP explanations for fraud alerts, and observe through experiments that SHAP explanations impact decision-making for fraud cases. The same authors in [42] go further and provide a case-based SHAP explanation based on neighborhood, and enable experts to visualize similar instances to an observation for which a fraud alert was issued. Their goal is to increase the trust of domain experts in AI models analyzing transaction frauds in banking.

Some researchers consider the aid of visual analytics for understanding AI models, also in the fraud domain [43, 44]. In this context, [21] provides a visual analytics tool to support domain experts in their fraud detection workflow. The contribution was developed in close collaboration with fraud teams, through a user-centric iterative design process [45]. The authors make an essential contribution towards extending a fraud detection workflow with human analysis through visual analytics. However, they focus on interactive visualizations, but not on XAI methods. In [46], the authors focus on developing a visual analytics tool for supporting cyber analysts in making decisions when dealing with intrusion detection alerts. However, the authors also do not consider explanations in XAI. Their scenario is focused on network intrusion, which has different constraints than transaction fraud.

Regarding requirements elicitation in XAI, the literature is still at an early stage. Nevertheless, it was identified proposals for this elicitation in the literature. In [47], the authors provide a systematic methodology composed of five steps. Their goal is to understand requirements for XAI from multiple perspectives, assess explanation capabilities, and steer future research to industrial cases. In [48], also inspired by the requirements engineering literature, the authors propose a workflow to elucidate requirements for explanations, considering those requirements are non-functional. The methodology is assessed in a hypothetical hiring scenario. In [49], a Question-driven approach to assess explanation needs is proposed. The authors adopt a taxonomy of XAI methods mapped to user question types. They assume an explanation can be seen as an answer to a question, and represent user needs for XAI methods in terms of the questions a user might ask. In [50], the authors propose a stage-based participatory process for designing transparent interfaces incorporating perspectives of users, designers, and providers. They map requirements considering real-world needs influencing how to explain, such as company-specific style guidelines.

The work of [51] is one of the first proposals discussing the usage of scenarios in the context of XAI. Their goal is to anticipate scenarios of XAI usage to system development. They present a case study of aging-in-place monitoring, and argue that such a method can become a design resource to tackle the gaps between XAI, IS and Human-Computer Interaction communities for understanding how end users might interact with explanations capabilities and its workplace implications.

In summary, it is observed in [38, 39, 41, 42] proposals aiming for the integration of explanations in a fraud detection context. Within visual analytics literature, it is also observed studies aiming to support the decision-making of fraud experts through visualizations [21, 45, 46]. However, a social and user-centered perspective has been lacking in those works, by first understanding the needs of fraud experts for explanations which can enhance their trust in AI models and decision-making processes. Moreover, the adoption of scenario-based elicitation in XAI is introduced by Wolf [51]. Nevertheless, the author has not presented the process in the context of fraud detection, which is complex by itself, as fraud experts need to deal with critical decisions daily, relating to financial losses of customers [52]. Therefore, it is essential to understand the needs of those experts for explanations, given their context and cognitive tasks for reviewing fraud cases.

For the reasons illustrated, we chose and demonstrate the scenario-based method to uncover the cognitive tasks of fraud experts, creating scenarios that can be further employed to identify their requirements regarding socio-technical and operational constraints in their real context, to reflect appropriate explanations for their operations and trust in AI predictions.

3 Scenario-Based Requirements Elicitation

3.1 The Method

Scenario-based elicitation is considered a problem-centered method for identifying stakeholder needs early in the development of information systems [53]. The idea is not to discuss solutions beforehand with stakeholders, but to understand their socio and operational context. Therefore, stakeholders are not asked what they want a system to provide them with, but what they want to achieve [54].

Scenarios can bridge the cognitive or psychological focus of traditional HCI methods, with the organizational focus of information systems development, creating a hybrid lens into ways in which these concerns are co-constituted in practice [30, 55]. We add to this argument, with the fact that scenarios enable the possibility to uncover the needs of stakeholders from a qualitative perspective, which is valuable for research from interpretivist and subjective philosophical lenses targeting the cognitive tasks of human decision-makers.

Therefore, scenarios can be used to analyze software requirements, such as to guide the design of user interface layouts and controls [54]. They are narratives on the sequence of events and steps performed by a stakeholder in their daily operations [56]. Scenarios consist of particular elements, including scenes with one or more actors in their settings, their goals, knowledge, and tools, providing them with capabilities to manipulate and working on their particular tasks [54].

The method is also referred to as Scenario-based task analysis, especially within the HCI community [57, 58]. Indeed, it enables an overview of human-computer interactions and tasks through stories of past or future use of a system by a human agent. This perspective intersects well with the concept adopted in this research for scenarios, given we aim to uncover the cognitive tasks and requirements of fraud experts during the decision-making of fraud cases.

Finally, given this study adopts an IS theoretical lens for XAI research, it is crucial to consider the role of the domain experts in consuming explanations, which should be tailored to follow their user requirements. We aim to develop scenarios that can be adopted for a following requirements elicitation stage in XAI for fraud detection, considering the role of the fraud expert and his socio-technical context. Figure 1 depicts the scenario-based method, and research design adopted, inspired by [54] and [56]. In Sect. 6, we discuss how the scenarios obtained in this study can be used for requirements elicitation.

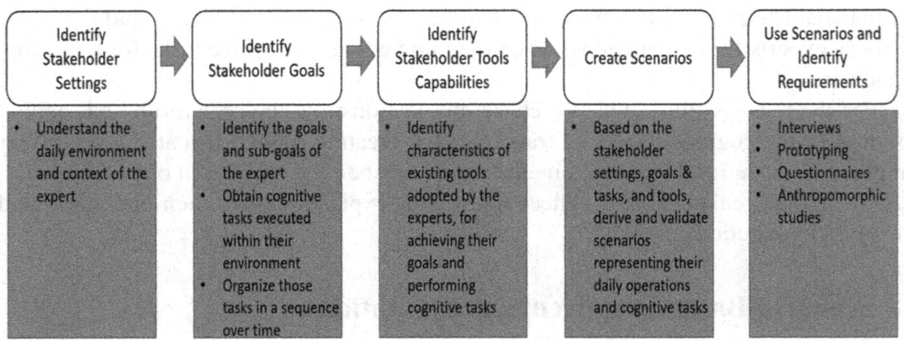

Fig. 1. Scenario-based requirements elicitation method

3.2 Fraud Detection Context

We focus on the type of fraud naming transaction fraud. In banking, transaction fraud happens when a customer card or online account balance is used to perform a transaction without the customer's consent or awareness [59]. The fraud can happen trough a shopping transaction in a retailer or money transfer between customers of an institution. Organizations have their workflows for transaction fraud detection, derived from research and fraud experts' knowledge. Those workflows, in general, contain events and processes reported as: 1) Transaction Attempt, 2) Transaction Blocking Rules, 3) Transaction Classification, and 4) Transaction Investigation [60]. In the end, there is the Transaction Investigation step, where fraud experts review fraud cases issued by a fraud detection system.

Therefore, domain experts investigate fraud cases and make the final decision if an alert represents a false or true positive for fraud. Nevertheless, it is usually tricky for fraud experts to understand how AI models work, and consequently trust the alerts issued by those models [42]. We illustrate how scenarios would work to identify fraud experts' requirements for providing them with tailored explanations to review fraud cases.

3.3 Using and Demonstrating the Method

We follow the steps depicted in Fig. 1, inspired by [54] and [56], to compose the aimed fraud detection scenarios by uncovering the settings with a fraud expert as an actor, their goals and sub-goals, cognitive tasks, and tools providing them with capabilities to review fraud transaction cases.

Those steps are implemented through a problem-centered expert interview [61]. This approach emphasizes the uncovering of problems within the operational context of interviewees. Three experts in banking fraud are interviewed within an Austrian bank, to guarantee multiple perspectives for the creation of the aimed scenarios. Following [61], the interview starts with a brief introduction into the project in which this study is being developed. Given the experts are already users of a fraud detection system, but not based on AI models, we asked them to think of their current settings and decision-making or cognitive tasks to perform their daily analyses.

In order to demonstrate the steps and the usage of the method depicted in Fig. 1, Table 1 brings the interview guide designed to create the aimed fraud detection scenarios. Following the guidelines of [61], we avoided a continuous interruption with questions for the fraud experts, aiming to uncover their context. When they considered the answer was complete, we used the questions in Table 1 to continue the discussion. The questions are inspired by [49], and we tailor them to our context to uncover the elements of scenarios [54].

Table 1. Expert interview guide for scenario-based requirements elicitation for XAI in fraud detection

Step	Example
1) Introduction into the Project	The introduction of the researcher and a brief overview into the project within this study is situated
2) Identify Stakeholder Settings	a) Can you describe a typical day of work within your department?
	b) What is the event that needs to be analyzed during your daily operations?
	c) Do you have preferences for colors and visualizations for performing your analysis?
	d) What type of data is adopted at your fraud detection system and on which you perform your analysis?
	e) How many experts do you have for analyzing outcomes of your system? Do you share tasks for the analyses?
	f) Do you conduct analysis before, during, or after receiving an output from your system?
3) Identify Stakeholder Goals	a) Can you describe what is your end goal when analyzing an output from your fraud detection system?
	b) What are the tasks you need to perform to achieve your end goal?
	c) Do you consider this analysis in a particular order?
4) Identify Stakeholder Tools Capabilities	a) What is the usual medium or channel for obtaining outputs from your fraud detection systems?
	b) Are you interacting with the interfaces for conducting your analysis?
	c) Are you aware of your fraud detection system's capabilities and limitations, and consider those when analyzing fraud cases?
	d) How long can you take to review a fraud case and make a decision during your daily operations?
	e) How many screens do you usually have for performing your analysis?
5) Short Questionnaire	a) Can you give me a summary of your professional experience? b) What is your role in this department?

4 Results: Fraud Detection Scenarios

From the interviews, it was possible to obtain detailed narratives on the daily operations of the experts. A second meeting was arranged with the experts to validate the narratives and qualitative data obtained. On this occasion, they confirmed the existence of two particular scenarios, which are described next using a fictitious name.

"Robert is a fraud expert with years of experience in reviewing fraudulent transaction cases. On a typical day in his work, he receives an alert for a case from his company's fraud detection system. Ideally, the system should deliver fraud cases based on their risk priority as a ranking, followed by the confidence level of a transaction being fraudulent. Robert has three computer screens with interfaces to analyze the fraud case. The interfaces illustrate tables, raw data, and graphical visualizations. He needs more information on the detected fraud in order to make a decision for it being a true positive, as the whole fraud case is composed of little pieces. Robert is interested in the most important pieces of information for analyzing the fraud case and no distractions. He needs to make a decision as soon as possible for the case, as there is no time to think in hours. It should be less to avoid more harm to that customer. Robert starts the analysis of the case by looking into similar cases for which fraud alerts were issued, and tries to understand that fraud by similarities. He realizes more information is needed, and then analyses the destination of that transaction, to observe if it is, for instance, a first time beneficiary. Given that it was detected as an anomalous beneficiary, he looks further into important attributes highlighted by the system to issue the alert and observes that the transaction's location is a high indicator for fraud. He finishes the analysis observing details on the customer data registered in the bank, such as his usual location for performing transactions. He observes a clear anomaly regarding the location indicator, and similar cases where this attribute was the determinant factor for considering the case as a fraud. He reports the case, and the transaction is not processed by the system".

The second scenario is described as follows.

"In similar settings, Robert receives a new alert from the fraud detection system. In this case, he finds it difficult to observe similar past cases for the current case reported. When analyzing the destination of the transaction, he finds it is a usual beneficiary. He then observes the important attributes highlighted by the system and realizes they match to the customer's data. In this scenario, Robert is unsure about the reported case, and performs more actions to investigate the incident. His next moves focus on analyzing further important attributes in the current transaction, and triggered rules by his fraud detection system. Then, he tries to observe the impact of attributes on the transaction and rules influencing the system's outcome. With those in mind, he observes past transactions of the customer to see if they have familiarity with this current behavior. Furthermore, he analyzes the transactions that happened after this alert was issued. Usually, Robert analyzes fraud cases by himself, but in such novel and more complex cases, he collaborates with colleagues to make decisions. They have to analyze it as soon

as possible to understand the case, as many customers can be victims of the same scheme. After discussing with his colleagues, Robert realizes the reasons for the transaction being considered fraudulent by the system, and reports it for avoiding harm to the customer."

Consulting with the experts, we name the first scenario as "Clear Transaction Fraud", when they are certain about the case being a fraud, but need to clarify the reasons for the diagnosis. In the second case, we label it as an "Uncertain Transaction Fraud", as the experts need to go for more cognitive tasks to clarify the case and protect the customer.

Therefore, we depict in Fig. 2 the cognitive tasks performed in both scenarios, which are executed by experts to review fraud cases in their environment and daily operations.

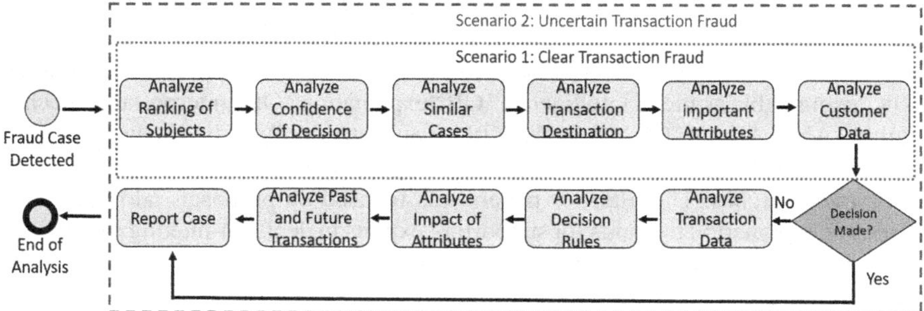

Fig. 2. Fraud detection cognitive tasks identified in scenarios developed with experts in banking fraud

5 Validation of Fraud Scenarios

The expert interviews lasted for approximately one hour each, and the researcher facilitated the discussion. It was noticed that the experts felt comfortable and confident in giving the answers. That is the aim of the problem-centered interview methodology [61], which empowers the interviewee for the provision of real information into their context and problems [62]. Therefore, we recommend the usage of the problem-centered interview methodology for creating scenarios with domain experts.

We omit some details regarding specific attributes of datasets, which were mentioned during the interviews. That is due to privacy concerns and national regulations limiting the banking industry's sharing of fraud detection policies for the safety of their customers. However, we also aim to achieve a level of abstraction for those scenarios, which can enable their adoption for researchers working in XAI for fraud detection.

Therefore, for validation, we conducted a systematic literature review following Webster and Watson [63]. The goal was to investigate studies focused on adopting explanation methods or visual analytics for supporting fraud experts in decision-making. Indeed, it is possible to validate the scenarios and cognitive tasks uncovered when analyzing the literature in visual analytics for fraud detection, as presented in Sect. 2, given researchers in this domain work on providing fraud experts with visualization tools for examining and reviewing fraud cases. Such tools can be related to explanations being adopted for our current scenarios.

We started the review by identifying comprehensive surveys and references in the field of XAI, to adopt search terms within this literature. The works of [13, 33, 64–66] were selected based on these criteria. Given the intersection with visual analytics literature for decision-making in fraud, we also adopt terminology from this domain for our systematic review based on [21, 43] and [67–72]. Next, core and most cited surveys in fraud detection were analyzed for extracting coherent keywords for our review [73–75]. Then, we defined the key terms for our review as: "("visual analytics" OR "explainable ai" OR "explainable artificial intelligence" OR "explanation" OR "interpretable machine learning") AND ("fraud" OR "anomaly" OR "fraud detection")". The databases selected were Scopus, ACM, IEEEXplore, and arXiv. Google Scholar was adopted for backward and forward searches. The filter for papers was focused on proposals adopting visual analytics or explanation methods for supporting experts in decision-making. It was identified 367 potentially relevant papers, from which 52 are deemed relevant for analysis. From those, 38 papers are added as new references in this study.

Table 2 illustrates the cognitive tasks mapped from the systematic literature review, and their association with the scenarios obtained through interviews with fraud experts. We managed to map 13 cognitive tasks. It is shown the supporting papers for each task identified, and whether they are observable from the expert interviews performed to develop fraud detection scenarios. The tasks can inform design principles for the integration of explanation methods and interfaces into fraud detection processes. Finally, a description is available for each task.

We hypothesize that the provided set of cognitive tasks and requirements can better inform the design of user-centric explanation methods and interfaces for fraud detection, promoting the trust of fraud experts for collaboration with AI models predictions. Researchers in XAI can refer to those cognitive tasks when designing explanation methods and interfaces for the domain of fraud detection.

It is noticeable that every cognitive task from fraud scenarios is identified in the XAI and visual analytics literature in fraud detection. When discussing with the experts regarding the non-presence in their scenarios of the tasks *Analyze Contrast Between*, *Analyze Cases in Clusters*, *Analyze Relationships Between Attributes*, they highlighted it is due to the available capabilities of the current fraud detection system in use. However, they highlighted that such tasks are also valuable and useful in their context.

Table 2. Cognitive tasks in fraud detection scenarios and their presence in the literature of XAI and visual analytics for fraud detection

Literature support	Total of literature supporting papers	Observable in experts fraud scenarios	Cognitive task for decision-making in fraud detection	Description
[22, 36, 43, 44, 55, 68, 71, 72, 80, 88, 89, 92, 93, 95–98, 101–107]	24	Yes	Analyze relationships between subjects	This task is associated with the analysis of a transaction destination. Experts observe the relationship between different subjects, which can be different customers within a network of transactions. The aim is to see, for instance, if a customer is usually performing transfers to another, or if it is a sign of an anomaly
[21, 22, 27, 43, 55, 67, 68, 71, 72, 76, 79, 82, 88, 89, 92, 93, 95, 106, 107, 110, 112]	21	Yes	Analyze attributes over temporal perspective	This task relates to the analysis of past and future transactions by experts. The aim is to analyze the values of attributes over time. For example, to analyze the number of transactions performed in a specific time frame, or the number of transfers to a destination in past and future dates
[21, 39, 41–44, 67, 72, 78, 80, 81, 83, 88–94]	19	Yes	Analyze the importance of attributes on decisions	Analyze the most important attributes as reasons for a transaction being considered as a fraud by the system
[22, 72, 76, 80, 83, 84, 86, 89, 90, 92, 99, 100, 108–111]	16		Analyze relationships between attributes	Observe how changes in the values of two attributes are influencing the predictions of a system for fraud
[38, 41, 43, 68, 72, 82, 91–97]	13	Yes	Analyze feature distribution	This task is associated with the analysis of current transaction data, or the common distribution of attributes, which represent the known pattern and behavior of users. That can be represented by averages, minimum and maximum thresholds for attributes

(continued)

Table 2. (*continued*)

Literature support	Total of literature supporting papers	Observable in experts fraud scenarios	Cognitive task for decision-making in fraud detection	Description
[16, 38, 42, 67, 76–83]	12	Yes	Analyze similar cases	Analyze fraud cases which are similar to the current case detected by the fraud detection system
[22, 27, 32, 72, 80, 88, 90, 101, 102, 110, 111, 113]	12	Yes	Analyze decision path rules	This task is associated with the analysis of decision rules by experts. Detailed observation on the decision path made by a fraud detection system, such as rules and attributes associated with the rules to provide predictions
[42, 79–81, 83, 87, 88, 94, 98–100]	11	Yes	Analyze impact of attributes	Analyze what is the influence of an attribute in the prediction of a system when changing the value of attributes
[71, 72, 79, 85–87]	6		Analyze cases in clusters	Observe cases in groups according to the characteristics of the transactions and their attributes
[31, 41, 83, 92, 94]	5	Yes	Analyze confidence of decision	Observe the confidence of the system in predicting and detecting frauds
[79, 83, 84]	3		Analyze contrast between cases	Detect differences between a legitimate and a fraudulent transaction
[21, 44]	2	Yes	Analyze the ranking of subjects	Visualize the most important transactions and attributes to be analyzed, given the time constraints fraud experts have in their scenarios
[71, 93]	2		Analyze decision in natural language	Analyze rationales on the reasons for predictions, such as textual descriptions of the reasons for a transaction being classified as fraudulent

6 Usage of Scenarios for Requirements Elicitation for Explanations

With the usage of the scenario-based method, we can establish scenarios as templates for further requirements elicitation steps. As illustrated by the scenario narratives and cognitive tasks in Sects. 4 and 5, it is possible to envision an actor's real context in a scenario, the fraud expert in this study. With these scenarios, it is possible to better plan experiments deploying explanations for the usage by the expert, according to his cognitive tasks.

The scenarios start by describing the settings of a fraud expert and the system he works with. Based on the narratives, it is clear that an AI model deployed in this environment should provide the riskiest transactions for a productive relationship with the expert. It is also described by the expert the common interface he is used to operating, which can guide on the deployment of explanations aligned with such design, including tables and graphical charts. It is possible to observe non-functional requirements in the scenarios already. For instance, the experts stated they need only the most important pieces of evidence for making a decision, which is aligned with the non-functional requirement stated by Miller [33] that explanations should be selective, and not overload their users with unnecessary reasons for an AI prediction. In the context of fraud in banking, the experts also point out a decision should be made promptly, which might indicate the need to support his decision-making with explanations that do not require heavy mental workload for understandability [42]. Those constraints are vital as they can dictate which XAI methods fit, for instance, into the time an expert has to review fraudulent transactions.

From the first scenario, with a clear transaction fraud, it is noticeable the specific tasks and sequence of cognitive tasks performed by the expert. The narrative helps in defining specific explanation which can be provided in experiments. Given the expert is usually focusing on reviewing individual fraud cases, a preliminary filter for explanation methods can be already established, such as to adopt local explanations provided by post-hoc XAI methods [13]. As the expert starts comparing cases and looking into destinations of transactions, an explanation interface might be presented with a case-based and network visualization explanation for reviewing cases. Furthermore, it could be deployed a feature importance explanation [98], as fraud experts need to investigate the most critical attributes impacting the prediction, such as the location of a transaction.

In the second scenario, it is also possible to think of explanations to be adopted in experiments. The expert goes further in his analysis by examining inference rules and the impact of attributes in the outcome of the system, which can be supported by explanations showing decision rules, such as Anchors [114], and counterfactuals and what-if scenarios [115]. Besides, he analyzes the past and further transactions of a customer, which can be aided by a temporal explanation component in the sequence of customer transactions.

Therefore, a scenario enables the establishment of assumptions regarding explanation interfaces that can be deployed in experiments as prototypes for uncovering experts' requirements [54]. Questions concerning the order of steps enable the potential design of workflows for fraud detection with the support of explanation methods, as the expert details the order of steps during his analysis of fraud cases. The assumptions for explanations to deploy on scenarios are based on XAI literature describing explanation interfaces and tools [116, 117]. Figure 3 depicts the usage of the cognitive tasks in scenario 1 in an experiment with prototypes of explanations interfaces.

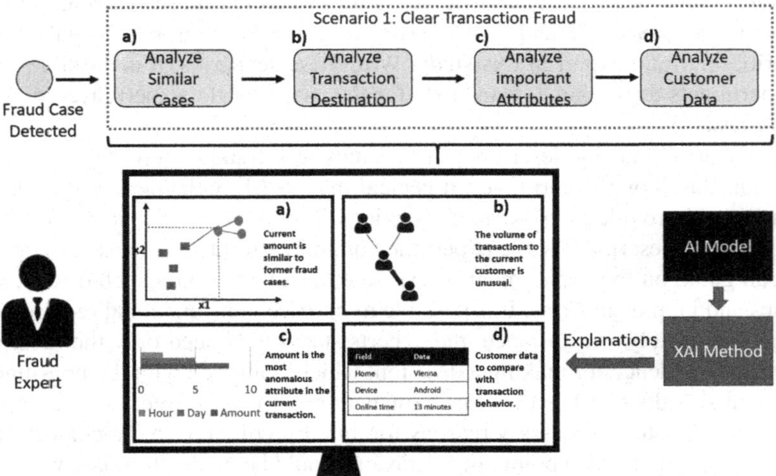

Fig. 3. Using scenarios within an experiment and prototyping to identify requirements of experts

7 Conclusions

This study calls for the potential of developing XAI research with an information systems theoretical lens. This research is aligned with user-centric XAI, which regards the vital role of stakeholders of explanations, their requirements, and their needs for understanding AI predictions. This study reinforces the need and benefits of understanding the socio-technical and operational environment of a stakeholder before deploying explanations to support their decision-making processes.

We demonstrate the usage of the scenario-based method for requirements elicitation, well regarded in IS and software engineering research. The method is adopted within a domain rarely addressed from a user perspective in XAI, which is fraud detection. We derived two fraud detection scenarios, discuss how they can be adopted for developing user-centric explanation methods in prototypes, and further elicit user requirements for explanations, such as having a selective set of explanations and enabling experts to perform local comparisons of fraud cases, respectively.

It is demonstrated the potential of the scenario-based method in uncovering directions and opportunities for developers of XAI methods and explanations in the early stage of their implementation. We aim to provide these scenarios for the XAI community interested in developing explanation methods tailored for the particularities of the fraud detection domain. Regarding limitations, the focus of this study was on domain experts, the users of AI predictions. Therefore, the scenarios are not focused on AI engineers who work in developing and improving AI models. Scenarios serve as a template for elicitation of requirements, so the direct relationships with specific explanations are inferred by the researcher based on previous literature defining explainability features.

As future work, the scenarios will be adopted through experiments with fraud experts and user-centric explanation prototypes. The aim is to follow the discovered tasks for decision-making to identify user requirements for appropriate explanation methods. The goal is to detect patterns and reveal potential design principles for integrating explanations into the domain of fraud detection, from a user-centric XAI perspective.

Acknowledgements. This research was supported by the European Union Horizon 2020 research and innovation programme under the Marie Sklodowska-Curie grant agreement No. 765395; and supported, in part, by Science Foundation Ireland grant 13/RC/2094.

References

1. Cirqueira, D., Hofer, M., Nedbal, D., Helfert, M., Bezbradica, M.: Customer purchase behavior prediction in e-commerce: a conceptual framework and research agenda. In: Ceci, M., Loglisci, C., Manco, G., Masciari, E., Ras, Z. (eds.) NFMCP 2019. LNCS (LNAI), vol. 11948, pp. 119–136. Springer, Cham (2020). https://doi.org/10.1007/978-3-030-48861-1_8
2. Bielozorov, A., Bezbradica, M., Helfert, M.: The role of user emotions for content personalization in e-commerce: literature review. In: Nah, F.F.-H., Siau, K. (eds.) HCII 2019. LNCS, vol. 11588, pp. 177–193. Springer, Cham (2019). https://doi.org/10.1007/978-3-030-22335-9_12
3. Cakir, G., Bezbradica, M., Helfert, M.: The Shift from financial to non-financial measures during transition into digital retail–a systematic literature review. In: International Conference on Business Information Systems, pp. 189–200. Springer, Cham, June 2019. https://doi.org/10.1007/978-3-030-20485-3_15
4. Iftikhar, R., Pourzolfaghar, Z., Helfert, M.: Omnichannel value chain: mapping digital technologies for channel integration activities. In: Siarheyeva, A., Barry, C., Lang, M., Linger, H., Schneider, C. (eds.) Information Systems Development: Information Systems Beyond 2020 (ISD2019 Proceedings). ISEN Yncréa Méditerranée, Toulon, France (2019)
5. Cirqueira, D., Helfert, M., Bezbradica, M.: Towards preprocessing guidelines for neural network embedding of customer behavior in digital retail. In: Proceedings of the 2019 3rd International Symposium on Computer Science and Intelligent Control, pp. 1–6, September 2019
6. Ryman-Tubb, N.F., Krause, P., Garn, W.: How artificial intelligence and machine learning research impacts payment card fraud detection: a survey and industry benchmark. Eng. Appl. Artif. Intell. **76**, 130–157 (2018)
7. Mohseni, S., Zarei, N., Ragan, E.D.: A Multidisciplinary survey and framework for design and evaluation of explainable AI systems. arXiv: Human-Computer Interaction (2019)
8. Miller, A.T.: "But why?" understanding explainable artificial intelligence. XRDS: Crossroads ACM Mag. Students **25**(3), 20–25 (2019)
9. Chazette, L., Schneider, K.: Explainability as a non-functional requirement: challenges and recommendations. Requirements Eng. **22**, 1–22 (2020). https://doi.org/10.1007/s00766-020-00333-1
10. Holzinger, A., Biemann, C., Pattichis, C.S., Kell, D.B.: What do we need to build explainable AI systems for the medical domain? (2017). arXiv preprint arXiv:1712.09923

11. Samek, W., Montavon, G., Vedaldi, A., Hansen, L.K., Müller, K.-R. (eds.): Explainable AI: Interpreting, Explaining and Visualizing Deep Learning. LNCS (LNAI), vol. 11700. Springer, Cham (2019). https://doi.org/10.1007/978-3-030-28954-6
12. Goebel, R., et al.: Explainable AI: the new 42? In: Holzinger, A., Kieseberg, P., Tjoa, A.M., Weippl, E. (eds.) CD-MAKE 2018. LNCS, vol. 11015, pp. 295–303. Springer, Cham (2018). https://doi.org/10.1007/978-3-319-99740-7_21
13. Adadi, A., Berrada, M.: Peeking inside the black-box: a survey on explainable artificial intelligence (XAI). IEEE Access **6**, 52138–52160 (2018)
14. Wang, D., Yang, Q., Abdul, A., Lim, B.Y.: Designing theory-driven user-centric explainable AI. In: Proceedings of the 2019 CHI Conference on Human Factors in Computing Systems, pp. 1–15, May 2019
15. Miller, T., Howe, P., Sonenberg, L.: Explainable AI: Beware of inmates running the asylum or: How I learnt to stop worrying and love the social and behavioural sciences (2017). arXiv preprint arXiv:1712.00547
16. Moalosi, M., Hlomani, H., Phefo, O.S.: Combating credit card fraud with online behavioural targeting and device fingerprinting. Int. J. Electron. Secur. Digital Forensics **11**(1), 46–69 (2019)
17. Holzinger, A., Langs, G., Denk, H., Zatloukal, K., Müller, H.: Causability and explainability of artificial intelligence in medicine. Wiley Interdisc. Rev. Data Min. Knowl. Disc. **9**(4), e1312 (2019)
18. Holzinger, A., Carrington, A., Müller, H.: Measuring the quality of explanations: the system causability scale (SCS). KI-Künstliche Intelligenz **20**, 1–6 (2020). https://doi.org/10.1007/s13218-020-00636-z
19. Akula, A.R., et al.: X-tom: explaining with theory-of-mind for gaining justified human trust (2019). arXiv preprint arXiv:1909.06907
20. Delaney, B.C., Fitzmaurice, D.A., Riaz, A., Hobbs, F.R.: Can computerised decision support systems deliver improved quality in primary care? Bmj **319**(7220), 1281 (1999)
21. Leite, R.A., et al.: Eva: visual analytics to identify fraudulent events. IEEE Trans. Vis. Comput. Graph. **24**(1), 330–339 (2017)
22. Holzinger, A.: Interactive machine learning for health informatics: when do we need the human-in-the-loop? Brain Inf. **3**(2), 119–131 (2016). https://doi.org/10.1007/s40708-016-0042-6
23. Abdul, A., et al.: Trends and trajectories for explainable, accountable and intelligible systems: an HCI research agenda. In: Proceedings of the 2018 CHI Conference on Human Factors In Computing Systems. ACM (2018)
24. Spinner, T., Schlegel, U., Schäfer, H., El-Assady, M.: explAIner: a visual analytics framework for interactive and explainable machine learning. IEEE Trans. Vis. Comput. Graph. **26**(1), 1064–1074 (2019)
25. Chatzimparmpas, A., Martins, R.M., Jusufi, I., Kerren, A.: A survey of surveys on the use of visualization for interpreting machine learning models. Inf. Vis. **19**, 1473871620904671 (2020)
26. Chatzimparmpas, A., Martins, R.M., Jusufi, I., Kucher, K., Rossi, F., Kerren, A.: The State of the art in enhancing trust in machine learning models with the use of visualizations. In: Computer Graphics Forum (Print)
27. Bell, S.: Learning with Information Systems: Learning Cycles in Information Systems Development. Routledge, United Kingdom (2013)
28. Ostrowski, L., Helfert, M.: Reference model in design science research to gather and model information. In: AMCIS 2012 Proceedings 3 (2012). https://aisel.aisnet.org/amcis2012/proceedings/SystemsAnalysis/3

29. Browne, G.J., Rogich, M.B.: An empirical investigation of user requirements elicitation: comparing the effectiveness of prompting techniques. J. Manage. Inf. Syst. **17**(4), 223–249 (2001)
30. Carroll, J.M.: Becoming social: expanding scenario-based approaches in HCI. Behav. Inf. Technol. **15**(4), 266–275 (1996)
31. Malle, B.F.: Time to give up the dogmas of attribution: an alternative theory of behavior explanation. Advances in Experimental Social Psychology, pp. 297–352. Academic Press, Massachusetts (2011)
32. Preece, A., Harborne, D., Braines, D., Tomsett, R., Chakraborty, S.: Stakeholders in explainable AI (2018). arXiv preprint arXiv:1810.00184
33. Miller, T.: Explanation in artificial intelligence: insights from the social sciences. Artif. Intell. **267**, 1–38 (2019)
34. Linsley, D., Shiebler, D., Eberhardt, S., Serre, T.: Global-and-local attention networks for visual recognition (2018). arXiv preprint arXiv:1805.08819
35. Seo, S., Huang, J., Yang, H., Liu, Y.: August. Interpretable convolutional neural networks with dual local and global attention for review rating prediction. In: Proceedings of the Eleventh ACM Conference on Recommender Systems, pp. 297–305, August 2017
36. Doshi-Velez, F., Been, K.: Towards a rigorous science of interpretable machine learning (2017). arXiv preprint arXiv:1702.08608
37. Došilović, F.K., Brčić, M., Hlupić, N.: Explainable artificial intelligence: a survey. In: 2018 41st International Convention on Information and Communication Technology, Electronics and Microelectronics (MIPRO). IEEE (2018)
38. Laughlin, B., Sankaranarayanan, K., El-Khatib, K.: A service architecture using machine learning to contextualize anomaly detection. J. Database Manage. (JDM) **31**(1), 64–84 (2020)
39. Antwarg, L., Shapira, B., Rokach, L.: Explaining anomalies detected by autoencoders using SHAP (2019). arXiv preprint arXiv:1903.02407
40. Lundberg, S.M., Lee, S.I.: A unified approach to interpreting model predictions. In: Advances in Neural Information Processing Systems (2017)
41. Weerts, H.J.P., van Ipenburg, W., Pechenizkiy, M.: A human-grounded evaluation of shap for alert processing (2019). arXiv preprintarXiv:1907.03324
42. Weerts, H.J.P., van Ipenburg, W., Pechenizkiy, M.: Case-based reasoning for assisting domain experts in processing fraud alerts of black-boxmachine learning models (2019). arXiv preprint arXiv:1907.03334
43. Dilla, W.N., Raschke, R.L.: "Data visualization for fraud detection: practice implications and a call for future research". Int. J. Account. Inf. Syst. **16**, 1–22 (2015)
44. Leite, R.A., Gschwandtner, T., Miksch, S., Gstrein, E., Kuntner, J.: Visual analytics for event detection: focusing on fraud. Vis. Inf. **2**(4), 198–212 (2018)
45. Munzner, T.: A nested model for visualization design and validation. IEEE Trans. Vis. Comput. Graph. **15**(6), 921–928 (2009)
46. Franklin, L., Pirrung, M., Blaha, L., Dowling, M., Feng, M.: Toward a visualization-supported workflow for cyber alert management using threat models and human-centered design. In: 2017 IEEE Symposium on Visualization for Cyber Security (VizSec), pp. 1–8. IEEE, October 2017
47. Hall, M., et al.: A systematic method to understand requirements for explainable AI (XAI) systems. In: Proceedings of the IJCAI Workshop on eXplainable Artificial Intelligence (XAI 2019), Macau, China (2019)
48. Köhl, M.A., Baum, K., Langer, M., Oster, D., Speith, T., Bohlender, D.: Explainability as a non-functional requirement. In: 2019 IEEE 27th International Requirements Engineering Conference (RE), pp. 363–368. IEEE, September 2019

49. Liao, Q.V., Gruen, D., Miller, S.: Questioning the AI: informing design practices for explainable AI user experiences (2020). arXiv preprint arXiv:2001.02478
50. Eiband, M., Schneider, H., Bilandzic, M., Fazekas-Con, J., Haug, M., Hussmann, H.: Bringing transparency design into practice. In: 23rd International Conference on Intelligent User Interfaces, pp. 211–223, March 2019
51. Wolf, C.T.: Explainability scenarios: towards scenario-based XAI design. In: Proceedings of the 24th International Conference on Intelligent User Interfaces, pp. 252–257, March 2019
52. West, J., Bhattacharya, M.: Intelligent financial fraud detection: a comprehensive review. Comput. Secur. **57**, 47–66 (2016)
53. Dick, J., Hull, E., Jackson, K.: Requirements Engineering. Springer, United Kingdom (2017)
54. Rosson, M.B., Carroll, J.M.: Human-computer interaction. Scenario-Based Design, pp. 161–180. CRC Press, New Jersey (2009)
55. Maguire, M., Bevan, N.: User requirements analysis. In: IFIP World Computer Congress, TC 13, Boston, MA, pp. 133–148. Springer, August 2002. https://doi.org/10.1007/978-0-387-35610-5_9
56. Hertzum, M.: Making use of scenarios: a field study of conceptual design. Int. J. Hum. Comput. Stud. **58**(2), 215–239 (2003)
57. Diaper, D., Stanton, N.: The Handbook of Task Analysis for Human-Computer Interaction. CRC Press, New Jersey (2003)
58. Go, K., Carroll, J.M.: The handbook of task analysis for human-computer interaction. Scenario-Based Task Analysis, p. 117. CRC Press, New Jersey (2003)
59. Raj, S.B.E., Portia, A.A.: Analysis on credit card fraud detection methods. In: 2011 International Conference on Computer, Communication and Electrical Technology (ICCCET). IEEE (2011)
60. Dal Pozzolo, A., Boracchi, G., Caelen, O., Alippi, C., Bontempi, G.: Credit card fraud detection: a realistic modeling and a novel learning strategy. IEEE Trans. Neural Networks Learn. Syst. **29**(8), 3784–3797 (2017)
61. Witzel, A., Reiter, H.: The Problem-Centred Interview. Sage, California (2012)
62. Forstner, A., Nedbal, D.: A problem-centered analysis of enterprise social software project. Procedia Comput. Sci. **121**, 389–397 (2017)
63. Webster, J., Watson, R.T.: Analyzing the past to prepare for the future: writing a literature review. MIS Q. **18**, xiii–xxiii (2002)
64. Arrieta, A.B., et al.: Explainable artificial intelligence (XAI): concepts, taxonomies, opportunities and challenges toward responsible AI. Inf. Fusion **58**, 82–115 (2020)
65. Gunning: explainable artificial intelligence (XAI), Defense Advanced Research Projects Agency (DARPA) (2018). http://www.darpa.mil/program/explainable-artificial-intelligence, Accessed 6 June 2018
66. Mueller, S.T., Hoffman, R.R., Clancey, W., Emrey, A., Klein, G.: Explanation in human-AI systems: A literature meta-review, synopsis of key ideas and publications, and bibliography for explainable AI (2019). arXiv preprint arXiv:1902.01876
67. Leite, R.A., Gschwandtner, T., Miksch, S., Gstrein, E., Kuntner, J.: Visual analytics for fraud detection and monitoring. In: 2015 IEEE Conference on Visual Analytics Science and Technology (VAST), pp. 201–202. IEEE, October 2015
68. Novikova, E., Kotenko, I., Fedotov, E.: Interactive multi-view visualization for fraud detection in mobile money transfer services. Int. J. Mobile Comput. Multimedia Commun. (IJMCMC) **6**(4), 73–97 (2014)
69. Argyriou, E.N., Symvonis, A., Vassiliou, V.: A fraud detection visualization system utilizing radial drawings and heat-maps. In: 2014 International Conference on Information Visualization Theory and Applications (IVAPP), pp. 153–160. IEEE, January 2014
70. Chang, R., et al.: Scalable and interactive visual analysis of financial wire transactions for fraud detection. Inf. Vis. **7**(1), 63–76 (2008)

71. Shi, Y., Liu, Y., Tong, H., He, J., Yan, G., Cao, N.: Visual analytics of anomalous user behaviors: a survey (2019). arXiv preprint arXiv:1905.06720
72. Sun, J., et al: FraudVis: understanding unsupervised fraud detection algorithms. In: 2018 IEEE Pacific Visualization Symposium (PacificVis), pp. 170–174. IEEE, April 2018
73. Ahmed, M., Mahmood, A.N., Islam, M.R.: A survey of anomaly detection techniques in financial domain. Future Gener. Comput. Syst. **55**, 278–288 (2016)
74. Phua, C., et al.: A comprehensive survey of data mining-based fraud detection research (2010). arXiv preprint arXiv:1009.6119
75. Bolton, R.J., Hand, D.J.: Statistical fraud detection: a review. Stat. Sci. **14**, 235–249 (2002)
76. Weerts, H.J.P.: Interpretable machine learning as decision support for processing fraud alerts, 24 Jun 2019
77. Shrikumar, A., Greenside, P., Kundaje, A.: Learning important features through propagating activation differences (2017). arXiv preprintarXiv:1704.02685
78. Böhmer, K., Rinderle-Ma, S.: Mining association rules for anomaly detection in dynamic process runtime behavior and explaining the root cause to users. Inf. Syst. **90**, 101438 (2019)
79. Guo, S., Jin, Z., Chen, Q., Gotz, D., Zha, H., Cao, N.: Visual anomaly detection in event sequence data (2019). arXiv preprint arXiv:1906.10896
80. Zhao, X., Wu, Y., Lee, D.L., Cui, W.: iforest: interpreting random forests via visual analytics. IEEE Trans. Vis. Comput. Graph. **25**(1), 407–416 (2018)
81. Mejia-Lavalle, M.: Outlier detection with innovative explanation facility over a very large financial database. In: 2010 IEEE Electronics, Robotics and Automotive Mechanics Conference, pp. 23–27. IEEE, September 2010
82. Novikova, E., Kotenko, I.: Visualization-driven approach to fraud detection in the mobile money transfer services. In: Algorithms, Methods, and Applications in Mobile Computing and Communications, pp. 205–236. IGI Global (2019)
83. Collaris, D., van Wijk, J.J.: ExplainExplore: visual exploration of machine learning explanations. In: 2020 IEEE Pacific Visualization Symposium (PacificVis), pp. 26–35. IEEE, June 2020
84. Zhu, J., Liapis, A., Risi, S., Bidarra, R., Youngblood, G.M.: Explainable AI for designers: a human-centered perspective on mixed-initiative co-creation. In: 2018 IEEE Conference on Computational Intelligence and Games (CIG), pp. 1–8. IEEE, August 2018
85. Didimo, W., Liotta, G., Montecchiani, F., Palladino, P.: An advanced network visualization system for financial crime detection. In: 2011 IEEE Pacific Visualization Symposium, pp. 203–210. IEEE, March 2011
86. Ko, S., et al.: A survey on visual analysis approaches for financial data. Comput. Graph. Forum **35**(3), 599–617 (2016)
87. Olszewski, D.: Fraud detection using self-organizing map visualizing the user profiles. Knowl. Based Syst. **70**, 324–334 (2014)
88. Perez, D.G., Lavalle, M.M.: Outlier detection applying an innovative user transaction modeling with automatic explanation. In: 2011 IEEE Electronics, Robotics and Automotive Mechanics Conference, pp. 41–46. IEEE, November 2011
89. Huang, M.L., Liang, J., Nguyen, Q.V.: A visualization approach for frauds detection in financial market. In: 2009 13th International Conference Information Visualisation, pp. 197–202. IEEE, July 2009
90. Collaris, D., Vink, L.M., van Wijk, J.J.: Instance-level explanations for fraud detection: a case study (2018). arXiv preprint arXiv:1806.07129
91. Lin, H., Gao, S., Gotz, D., Du, F., He, J., Cao, N.: Rclens: Interactive rare category exploration and identification. IEEE Trans. Vis. Comput. Graph. **24**(7), 2223–2237 (2017)
92. Leite, R.A., Gschwandtner, T., Miksch, S., Gstrein, E., Kuntner, J.: Visual analytics for fraud detection: focusing on profile analysis. In: EuroVis (Posters), pp. 45–47, June 2016

93. Xie, C., Chen, W., Huang, X., Hu, Y., Barlowe, S., Yang, J.: VAET: a visual analytics approach for e-transactions time-series. IEEE Trans. Vis. Comput. Graph. **20**(12), 1743–1752 (2014)
94. Gal, G., Singh, K., Best, P.: Interactive visual analysis of anomalous accounts payable transactions in SAP enterprise systems. Manag. Auditing J. **31**, 35–63 (2016)
95. Didimo, W., Liotta, G., Montecchiani, F.: Network visualization for financial crime detection. J. Vis. Lang. Comput. **25**(4), 433–451 (2014)
96. Rieke, R., Zhdanova, M., Repp, J., Giot, R., Gaber, C.: Fraud detection in mobile payments utilizing process behavior analysis. In: 2013 International Conference on Availability, Reliability and Security, pp. 662–669. IEEE, September 2013
97. Leite, R.A., Gschwandtner, T., Miksch, S., Gstrein, E., Kuntner, J.: Network analysis for financial fraud detection. In: EuroVis (Posters), pp. 21–23, June 2018
98. Ribeiro, M.T., Singh, S., Guestrin, C.: Why should I trust you? Explaining the predictions of any classifier. In: Proceedings of the 22nd ACM SIGKDD International Conference on Knowledge Discovery and Data Mining, pp. 1135–1144, August 2016
99. Gupta, N., Eswaran, D., Shah, N., Akoglu, L., Faloutsos, C.: Beyond outlier detection: LOOKOUT for pictorial explanation. In: Berlingerio, M., Bonchi, F., Gärtner, T., Hurley, N., Ifrim, G. (eds.) ECML PKDD 2018. LNCS (LNAI), vol. 11051, pp. 122–138. Springer, Cham (2019). https://doi.org/10.1007/978-3-030-10925-7_8
100. Vojíř, S., Zeman, V., Kuchař, J., Kliegr, T.: EasyMiner. eu: web framework for interpretable machine learning based on rules and frequent itemsets. Knowl. -Based Syst. **150**, 111–115 (2018)
101. Chmielewski, M., Stąpor, P.: Hidden information retrieval and evaluation method and tools utilising ontology reasoning applied for financial fraud analysis. In: MATEC Web of Conferences, vol. 210, pp. 02019. EDP Sciences (2018)
102. Vaculík, K., Popelínský, L.: DGRMiner: anomaly detection and explanation in dynamic graphs. In: Boström, H., Knobbe, A., Soares, C., Papapetrou, P. (eds.) IDA 2016. LNCS, vol. 9897, pp. 308–319. Springer, Cham (2016). https://doi.org/10.1007/978-3-319-46349-0_27
103. Kobayashi, M., Ito, T.: A transactional relationship visualization system in Internet auctions. In: 2007 IEEE/WIC/ACM International Conference on Intelligent Agent Technology (IAT'07), pp. 248–251. IEEE, November 2007
104. Chmielewski, M., Stąpor, P.: Money laundering analytics based on contextual analysis. Application of problem solving ontologies in financial fraud identification and recognition. In: Information Systems Architecture and Technology: Proceedings of 37th International Conference on Information Systems Architecture and Technology–ISAT 2016–Part I, pp. 29–39. Springer, Cham (2017). https://doi.org/10.1007/978-3-319-46583-8_3
105. Wang, D., et al.: A Semi-supervised graph attentive network for financial fraud detection. In: 2019 IEEE International Conference on Data Mining (ICDM), pp. 598–607. IEEE, November 2019
106. Chang, R., et al.: WireVis: visualization of categorical, time-varying data from financial transactions. In: 2007 IEEE Symposium on Visual Analytics Science and Technology, pp. 155–162. IEEE, October 2007
107. Didimo, W., et al.: Vis4AUI: visual analysis of banking activity networks. In: GRAPP/IVAPP, pp. 799–802 (2012)
108. Mokoena, T., Lebogo, O., Dlaba, A., Marivate, V.: Bringing sequential feature explanations to life. In: 2017 IEEE AFRICON, pp. 59–64. IEEE, September 2017
109. Hao, M.C., Dayal, U., Sharma, R.K., Keim, D.A., Janetzko, H.: Visual analytics of large multidimensional data using variable binned scatter plots. In: Visualization and Data Analysis, vol. 7530, p. 753006. International Society for Optics and Photonics, January 2010
110. Turner, R.: A model explanation system. In: 2016 IEEE 26th International Workshop on Machine Learning for Signal Processing (MLSP), pp. 1–6. IEEE, September 2016

111. Dumas, M., McGuffin, M.J., Lemieux, V.L.: FinanceVis. net-a visual survey of financial data visualizations. In: Poster Abstracts of IEEE Conference on Visualization, vol. 2, p. 8, November 2014
112. Carminati, M., Caron, R., Maggi, F., Epifani, I., Zanero, S.: BankSealer: an online banking fraud analysis and decision support system. In: IFIP International Information Security Conference, pp. 380–394. Springer, Berlin, Heidelberg, June 2014. https://doi.org/10.1007/978-3-642-55415-5_32
113. Das, S., Islam, M.R., Jayakodi, N.K., Doppa, J.R.: Active anomaly detection via ensembles: insights, algorithms, and interpretability (2019). arXiv preprint arXiv:1901.08930
114. Ribeiro, M.T., Singh, S., Guestrin, C.: Anchors: high-precision model-agnostic explanations. In: Thirty-Second AAAI Conference on Artificial Intelligence, April 2018
115. Byrne, R.M.: Counterfactuals in explainable artificial intelligence (XAI): evidence from human reasoning. In: IJCAI, pp. 6276–6282, August 2019
116. Du, M., Liu, N., Hu, X.: Techniques for interpretable machine learning. Commun. ACM **63**(1), 68–77 (2019)
117. Molnar, C.: Interpretable Machine Learning. Lulu. com, North Carolina (2019)

On-the-fly Black-Box Probably Approximately Correct Checking of Recurrent Neural Networks

Franz Mayr, Ramiro Visca, and Sergio Yovine(✉)

Universidad ORT Uruguay, Montevideo, Uruguay
{mayr,visca,yovine}@ort.edu.uy

Abstract. We propose a procedure for checking properties of recurrent neural networks used for language modeling and sequence classification. Our approach is a case of black-box checking based on learning a probably approximately correct, regular approximation of the intersection of the language of the black-box (the network) with the complement of the property to be checked, without explicitly building individual representations of them. When the algorithm returns an empty language, there is a proven upper bound on the probability of the network not verifying the requirement. When the returned language is nonempty, it is certain the network does not satisfy the property. In this case, an explicit and interpretable characterization of the error is output together with sequences of the network truly violating the property. Besides, our approach does not require resorting to an external decision procedure for verification nor fixing a specific property specification formalism.

1 Introduction

Today, deep recurrent neural networks (RNN) are used for sequence modeling and classification in order to accomplish a variety of safety- and security-critical tasks in a number of application areas, such as autonomous driving [18,34], intrusion detection [17,46], malware detection [29,32,41], and human activity recognition [36]. Therefore, there is increasing interest in verifying their behavior with respect to the requirements they must fulfill to correctly perform their task.

Whenever a property is not satisfied, it is important to be able to adequately characterize and interpret network's misbehaviors, so as to eventually correct them. Here, we consider the notion of *interpretability* provided in [7,26], which defines it as the degree to which an observer can understand the cause of a decision. Neural networks' nature undermines human capabilities of getting such understanding since their deep and complex architectures, with up to thousands of millions of parameters, makes it impossible for a human to comprehend the rationale of their outputs, even if the underlying mathematical principles are understood and their internal structure and weights are known [33]. Moreover, when it comes to interpreting RNN errors, it is useful to do it through an *operational* and *visual* characterization, as a means for gaining insight into the set of incorrect RNN outputs in reasonable time.

Published by Springer Nature Switzerland AG 2020
A. Holzinger et al. (Eds.): CD-MAKE 2020, LNCS 12279, pp. 343–363, 2020.
https://doi.org/10.1007/978-3-030-57321-8_19

For RNN devoted to sequence classification, one way of checking properties consists in somehow extracting a deterministic finite automaton (DFA) from the network. Since RNN are more expressive than DFA [24], the language of the automaton is, in general, an approximation of the sequences classified as positive by the RNN. Once the automaton is obtained, it can be model-checked against a desired property using an appropriate model-checker [8]. This approach can be implemented by resorting to white-box learning algorithms such as the ones proposed in [42,44,45]. However, these procedures do not provide quantitative assessments on how precisely the extracted automaton characterizes the language of the RNN. Actually, this issue is overcome by the black-box learning algorithm proposed in [20] which outputs DFA which are probably correct approximations [39] of the RNN.

In practice, this general approach has several drawbacks, notably but not exclusively that the automaton learned from the RNN may be too large to be explicitly constructed. Another important inconvenience is finding real counterexamples on the RNN when the model-checker fails to verify the property on the DFA. Indeed, since the latter is an approximation of the former, counterexamples found on the DFA could be false negatives. Moreover, it has been advocated in [27] that there is also a need for property checking techniques that interact directly with the actual software that implements the network.

To some extent, these issues can be dealt with learning-based black-box checking (BBC) [30]. BBC is a refinement procedure where finite automata are incrementally built and model-checked against a requirement. Counterexamples generated by the model-checker are validated on the black-box and false negatives are used to refine the automaton. However, BBC requires fixing a formalism for specifying the requirements, typically linear-time temporal logic, and an external model-checker. Besides, the black-box is assumed to be some kind of finite-state machine.

To handle the problem of checking properties over RNN on a black-box setting without the downsides of BBC, we propose a method which performs on-the-fly checking during learning without resorting to an external model-checker.[1] Our approach considers both the RNN and the property as black-boxes and it does not explicitly build nor assumes any kind of state-based representation of them. The key idea consists in learning a regular language which is a probably correct approximation of the intersection of the language of the RNN and the negation of the property.

We show that, when the returned language is empty, the proposed procedure ensures there is an upper bound on the probability of the RNN not satisfying the property. This bound is a function of the parameters of the algorithm. Moreover, if the returned language is nonempty, we prove the requirement is guaranteed to be false with probability 1, and truly bad sequences of the RNN are provided

[1] Our approach differs from on-the-fly BBC as defined in [30] which relies on a strategy for seeking paths in the automaton of the requirement. Also, [45] applies a refinement technique, but it is white-box.

together with an interpretable characterization of the error, in the form of a DFA which is probably correct approximation of the language of faulty behaviors.

The paper is organized as follows. Section 2 briefly reviews probably approximately correct learning and defines the notion of on-the-fly property checking through learning. Section 3 revisits the problem of regular language learning and develops the main theoretical results. Section 4 experimentally validates practical application of the approach in various case studies from different domains. The other sections are devoted to related work and conclusions.

2 PAC Learning and Black-Box Property Checking

We briefly revisit here *Probably Approximately Correct* (PAC) learning [39]. This summary is mostly based on [5]. We also prove a few useful results regarding the use of PAC learning as a means for checking properties of black boxes.

2.1 PAC Learning

Let $\mathcal{X}$ be the *universe* of examples. The *symmetric difference* of X, $X' \subset \mathcal{X}$, denoted $X \oplus X'$, is defined as $X \setminus X' \cup X' \setminus X$, where $X \setminus X'$ is $X \cap \overline{X'}$ and $\overline{X}$ is the complement of X. Examples are assumed to be identically and independently distributed according to an unknown probability distribution $\mathcal{D}$ over $\mathcal{X}$.

A *concept* C is a subset of $\mathcal{X}$. A concept class $\mathcal{C}$ is a set of concepts. Given an *unknown* concept $C \in \mathcal{C}$, the purpose of a *learning* algorithm is to output a hypothesis $H \in \mathcal{H}$ that *approximates* the target concept C, where $\mathcal{H}$, called *hypothesis space*, is a class of concepts possibly different from $\mathcal{C}$.

Approximation between concepts C and H is measured with respect to $\mathcal{D}$ as the probability of an example $x \in \mathcal{X}$ to be in their symmetric difference. This measure, also called *prediction error*, is formalized as $\mathbb{P}_{x \sim \mathcal{D}}\left[x \in C \oplus H\right]$.

An *oracle* **EX**, which depends on C and $\mathcal{D}$, takes no input and draws i.i.d examples from $\mathcal{X}$ following $\mathcal{D}$, and tags them as *positive* or *negative* according to whether they belong to C or not. Calls to **EX** are independent of each other.

A PAC-learning algorithm takes as input an *approximation* parameter $\epsilon \in (0,1)$, a *confidence* parameter $\delta \in (0,1)$, a *target* concept $C \in \mathcal{C}$, an oracle **EX**, and a hypothesis space $\mathcal{H}$, and if it terminates, it outputs an $H \in \mathcal{H}$ which satisfies $\mathbb{P}_{x \sim \mathcal{D}}\left[x \in C \oplus H\right] \leq \epsilon$ with confidence at least $1-\delta$, for any $\mathcal{D}$. The output hypothesis H is said to be an ϵ-approximation of C with confidence $1-\delta$. Hereinafter, we refer to H as an (ϵ, δ)-approximation.

The concept class $\mathcal{C}$ is said to be *learnable* in terms of $\mathcal{H}$ if there exists a function $m_{\mathcal{H}} : (0,1)^2 \to \mathbb{N}$ and a PAC learning algorithm that, when run on a set of examples S, generated by **EX**, of size m_S larger than $m_{\mathcal{H}}(\epsilon, \delta)$, it terminates in polynomial time, measured in terms of its relevant parameters ϵ, δ, m_S, and the size of the representations of examples and concepts.

PAC-learning algorithms may be equipped with other oracles. In this paper, we consider algorithms that make use of *membership* and *equivalence* query oracles, denoted **MQ** and **EQ**, respectively. **MQ** takes as input an example

$x \in \mathcal{X}$ and returns whether $x \in C$ or not. **EQ** takes as input a hypothesis H and answers whether H is an (ϵ, δ)-approximation of C by drawing a sample $S \subset \mathcal{X}$ using **EX**, and checking whether for all $x \in S$, $x \in C$ iff $x \in H$, or equivalently, $S \cap (C \oplus H) = \emptyset$. We will make use of the following results in Sect. 2.2.

Lemma 1. *Let H be an (ϵ, δ)-approximation of C. For any $X \subseteq C \oplus H$, we have that $\mathbb{P}_{x \sim \mathcal{D}}[x \in X] \leq \epsilon$ with confidence $1 - \delta$.*

Proof. For any $X \subseteq C \oplus H$, we have that $\mathbb{P}_{x \sim \mathcal{D}}[x \in X] \leq \mathbb{P}_{x \sim \mathcal{D}}[x \in C \oplus H]$. Then, $\mathbb{P}_{x \sim \mathcal{D}}[x \in C \oplus H] \leq \epsilon$ implies $\mathbb{P}_{x \sim \mathcal{D}}[x \in X] \leq \epsilon$. Now, for any $S \subset \mathcal{X}$ such that $S \cap (C \oplus H) = \emptyset$, it follows that $S \cap X = \emptyset$. Therefore, any sample drawn by **EQ** that ensures $\mathbb{P}_{x \sim \mathcal{D}}[x \in C \oplus H] \leq \epsilon$ with confidence $1 - \delta$ also guarantees $\mathbb{P}_{x \sim \mathcal{D}}[x \in X] \leq \epsilon$ with confidence $1 - \delta$. □

Proposition 1. *Let H be an (ϵ, δ)-approximation of C. For any $X \subseteq \mathcal{X}$:*

$$\mathbb{P}_{x \sim \mathcal{D}}\left[x \in C \cap \overline{H} \cap X\right] \leq \epsilon \tag{1}$$

$$\mathbb{P}_{x \sim \mathcal{D}}\left[x \in \overline{C} \cap H \cap X\right] \leq \epsilon \tag{2}$$

with confidence at least $1 - \delta$.

Proof. From Lemma 1 because $C \cap \overline{H} \cap X$ and $\overline{C} \cap H \cap X$ are subsets of $C \oplus H$. □

2.2 Using Learning for Property Checking

Property checking consists in verifying whether given any two concepts $C, P \in \mathcal{C}$, it holds that $C \subseteq P$, or equivalently $C \cap \overline{P} = \emptyset$. P is called the *property* to be checked on C. Here, we are interested in devising a PAC-learning based approach to property checking.

2.2.1 Property Checking on PAC-Learned Hypothesis

A first idea consists in resorting to a *model-checking* approach. That is, build a model of C and then check whether it satisfies property P. In a black-box setting, we can apply it as follows. Let us assume property $P \in \mathcal{H}$. Given a concept $C \in \mathcal{C}$, use a PAC-learning algorithm to learn a hypothesis $H \in \mathcal{H}$, and then check whether H satisfies P. In order to do this, there must be an effective model-checking procedure. Let us assume there is such a procedure for checking emptiness in $\mathcal{H}$ and $\overline{P} \in \mathcal{H}$. Clearly, in this case, we can pose the problem as checking whether $H \cap \overline{P} = \emptyset$, where H is a PAC-learned model of C.

The question is what could be said about the outcome of this procedure. The following proposition shows that whichever the verdict of the model-checking procedure for $H \cap \overline{P}$, the probability of it not holding for C is bounded by the approximation parameter ϵ, with confidence at least $1 - \delta$.

Proposition 2. *Let H be an (ϵ, δ)-approximation of C. For any $\overline{P} \in \mathcal{H}$:*

1. *if $H \cap \overline{P} = \emptyset$ then $\mathbb{P}_{x\sim\mathcal{D}}\left[x \in C \cap \overline{P}\right] \leq \epsilon$, and*
2. *if $H \cap \overline{P} \neq \emptyset$ then $\mathbb{P}_{x\sim\mathcal{D}}\left[x \in \overline{C} \cap H \cap \overline{P}\right] \leq \epsilon$,*

with confidence at least $1 - \delta$.

Proof.
1. If $H \cap \overline{P} = \emptyset$ then $\overline{P} = \overline{H} \cap \overline{P}$. Thus, $C \cap \overline{P} = C \cap \overline{H} \cap \overline{P}$ and from Proposition 1(1) it follows that $\mathbb{P}_{x\sim\mathcal{D}}\left[x \in C \cap \overline{H} \cap \overline{P}\right] \leq \epsilon$, with confidence at least $1 - \delta$.
2. If $H \cap \overline{P} \neq \emptyset$, from Proposition 1(2) we have that $\mathbb{P}_{x\sim\mathcal{D}}\left[x \in \overline{C} \cap H \cap \overline{P}\right] \leq \epsilon$, with confidence at least $1 - \delta$. □

In practice, this approach has a few drawbacks.

- When $H \cap \overline{P} \neq \emptyset$, even if with small probability, counterexamples found by the model-checking procedure may not be in C. Therefore, whenever that happens, we would need to make use of the oracle **EX** to draw examples from $H \cap \overline{P}$ and tag them as belonging to C or not in order to trying finding a concrete counterexample in C.
- This approach could only be applied for checking properties for which there exists a model-checking procedure in $\mathcal{H}$. Moreover, the computational time of learning a hypothesis adds up to the time of checking whether it satisfies the property.

2.2.2 On-the-fly Property Checking Through Learning

To overcome the aforementioned issues, rather than learning an (ϵ, δ)-approximation of C, an appealing alternative is to use the PAC-learning algorithm to learn an (ϵ, δ)-approximation of $C \cap \overline{P} \in \mathcal{C}$. In this context, we have the following result.

Proposition 3. *Let H be an (ϵ, δ)-approximation of $C \cap \overline{P} \in \mathcal{C}$. Then:*

1. *if $H = \emptyset$ then $\mathbb{P}_{x\sim\mathcal{D}}\left[x \in C \cap \overline{P}\right] \leq \epsilon$, and*
2. *if $H \neq \emptyset$ then $\mathbb{P}_{x\sim\mathcal{D}}\left[x \in H \setminus (C \cap \overline{P})\right] \leq \epsilon$,*

with confidence at least $1 - \delta$.

Proof. Straightforward from the fact that $\mathbb{P}_{x\sim\mathcal{D}}\left[x \in (C \cap \overline{P}) \oplus H\right] \leq \epsilon$, with confidence at least $1 - \delta$. □

The above proposition shows that on-the-fly property checking through learning yields the same theoretical probabilistic assurance as the first one. Nevertheless, from a practical point of view, it has several interesting advantages over the latter:

- A model of the *target* concept C is not explicitly built. This may result in a lower computational time. Besides, it could also be used in cases where it is computationally too expensive to build a hypothesis for C.

Algorithm 1: Bounded-L^*

```
Input  : MaxQueryLength, MaxStates, ε, δ
Output: DFA A
Initialize;
i ← 0;
repeat
    i ← i + 1;
    while OT is not closed or not consistent do
        if OT is not closed then
            OT, QueryLengthExceeded ← Close(OT);
        end
        if OT is not consistent then
            OT, QueryLengthExceeded ← Consistent(OT);
        end
    end
    A ← BuildAutomaton(OT);
    Answer ← EQ(A, i, ε, δ);
    MaxStatesExceeded ← STATES(A) > MaxStates;
    if Answer ≠ Yes and not MaxStatesExceeded then
        OT ← Update(OT, Answer);
    end
    BoundReached ← QueryLengthExceeded or MaxStatesExceeded;
until Answer = Yes or BoundReached;
return A, Answer;
```

- There is no need to resort to model-checking procedures. It may be applied even for checking properties for which no such algorithms exist.
- If the result of the PAC-learning algorithm turns up to be nonempty, it may be the case the oracle **EX** does actually generate an example $x \in C \cap \overline{P}$ during the run of the algorithm. Thus, in this case, x serves as a real witness of the violation of the property.

Hereinafter, we exploit this idea in the context of property checking and error characterization for RNN. Concretely, concepts inside the black-box are sequence classifiers implemented as RNN, and properties are formal languages.

3 Learning-Based Property Checking over Languages

In this section, we consider the case where the universe $\mathcal{X}$ is the set of words Σ^* over a set of symbols Σ, the target concept is a language $C \subseteq \Sigma^*$, and the hypothesis class $\mathcal{H}$ is the set of *regular languages*, or equivalently of *deterministic finite automata* (DFA).

For the sake of simplicity, we refer to a regular language or its DFA representation indistinctly. For instance, we write $A = \emptyset$ and $A \neq \emptyset$ to mean the language of DFA A is empty and nonempty, respectively.

3.1 Learning DFA with Bounded-L^*

DFA can be learned with L^* [4] which is an iterative learning algorithm that constructs a DFA by interacting with a teacher which makes use of oracles **MQ** and **EQ**. The PAC-based version of L^* satisfies the following property.

Property 1 (From [4]). *(1) If L^* terminates, it outputs an (ϵ, δ)-approximation of the target language. (2) L^* always terminates if the target language is regular.*

However, when applied to learning regular approximations of concepts belonging to a more expressive class of languages, L^* may not terminate. In particular, this arrives when using this approach for learning languages of recurrent neural networks (RNN), since in general, this class of networks is strictly more expressive than DFA [24,35,37]. To cope with this issue, Bounded-L^* (Algorithm 1) has been proposed in [20]. It bounds the number of iterations of L^* by constraining the maximum number of states of the automaton to be learned and the maximum length of the words used to calling **EX**, which are typically used as parameters to determine the complexity of a PAC-learning algorithm [14].

Bounded-L^* works as follows. The learner builds a table of observations OT by interacting with the teacher. This table is used to keep track of which words are and are not accepted by the target language. OT is built iteratively by asking the teacher membership queries through **MQ**.

OT is a finite matrix $\Sigma^* \times \Sigma^* \rightarrow \{0, 1\}$. Its rows are split in two. The 'upper' rows represent a prefix-closed set words and the 'lower' rows correspond to the concatenation of the words in the upper part with every $\sigma \in \Sigma$. Columns represent a suffix-closed set of words. Each cell represents the membership relationship, that is, $OT[u][v] = \mathbf{MQ}(uv)$.

We denote $\lambda \in \Sigma^*$ the empty word and OT_i the value of the observation table at iteration i. The algorithm starts by initializing OT_0 (line 1) with a single upper row $OT_0[\lambda]$, a lower row $OT_0[\sigma]$ for every $\sigma \in \Sigma$, and a single column for the empty word $\lambda \in \Sigma^*$, with values $OT_0[u][\lambda] = \mathbf{MQ}(u)$.

At each iteration $i > 0$, the algorithm makes OT_i *closed* (line 7) and *consistent* (line 10). OT_i is closed if, for every row in the bottom part of the table, there is an equal row in the top part. OT_i is consistent if for every pair of rows u, v in the top part, for every $\sigma \in \Sigma$, if $OT_i[u] = OT_i[v]$ then $OT_i[u\sigma] = OT_i[v\sigma]$.

Once the table is closed and consistent, the algorithm proceeds to build the conjectured DFA A_i (line 13) which accepting states correspond to the entries of OT_i such that $OT_i[u][\lambda] = 1$.

Then, Bounded-L^* calls **EQ** (line 14) to check whether A_i is PAC-equivalent to the target language. For doing this, **EQ** draws a sample S_i of size [4]:

$$m_{S_i}(i, \epsilon, \delta) = \left\lceil \frac{i}{\epsilon} \log \frac{2}{\delta} \right\rceil \tag{3}$$

If for every $s \in S_i$, s belongs to the target language if and only if it belongs to the hypothesis A_i, the equivalence test is passed. In this case, Bounded-L^* terminates and returns A_i.

Property 2 (From [20]). *If Bounded-L^* terminates with an automaton A which passes the* **EQ** *test, A is an (ϵ, δ)-approximation of the target language.*

If **EQ** does not pass, the learner receives a counterexample which violates the test. If the maximum number of states of the output hypothesis and/or the maximum length of a **MQ** are not achieved, the learner uses the counterexample to update OT (line 17). Then, it performs a new iteration. Otherwise, it terminates. Thus, upon termination Bounded-L^* may output an automaton A which fails to pass the **EQ** test, that is, A and the target language eventually disagree in $k > 0$ sequences of the sample S drawn by **EQ**. In such cases, the approximation bound guaranteed by the hypotheses produced by Bounded-L^* is given by the following property, which subsumes the previous one (case $k = 0$).

Property 3 (From [20]). *If Bounded-L^* terminates with an automaton A producing $k \in [0, m]$* **EQ***-divergences on a sample of size m, computed as in Eq. (3), then A is an $(\hat{\epsilon}, \delta)$-approximation of the target language, for every $\hat{\epsilon} > \epsilon^*$, where*

$$\epsilon^*(m, k, \delta) = \frac{1}{m - k} \log \frac{\binom{m}{k}}{\delta} \tag{4}$$

That is, $\epsilon^*(m, k, \delta)$ is the infimum of the approximation bounds assured by the output hypothesis, with confidence at least $1 - \delta$, provided $k \geq 0$ divergences with the target language are found on a sample S of size m drawn by **EQ**.

Notice that, for fixed k and $\delta \in (0, 1)$, ϵ^* tends to 0 as m_S tends to ∞. That is, it is possible to make ϵ^* smaller than any desired approximation parameter ϵ by letting **EQ** to draw a large enough sample.

Example 1. *Figure 1 shows an example of a run of Bounded-L^* that outputs the DFA of $(ab)^*$ after 2 iterations.*

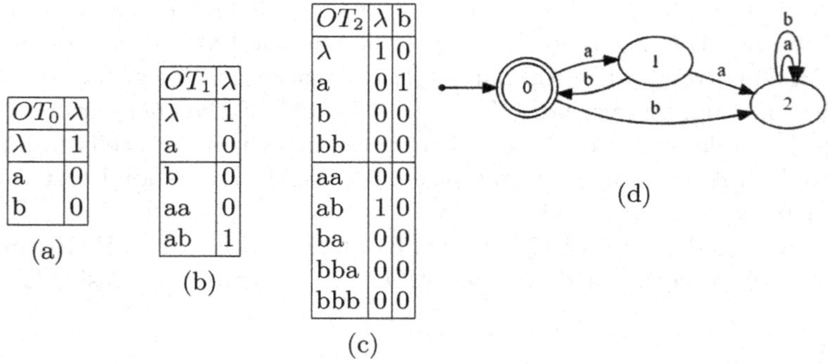

OT_0	λ
λ	1
a	0
b	0

(a)

OT_1	λ
λ	1
a	0
b	0
aa	0
ab	1

(b)

OT_2	λ	b
λ	1	0
a	0	1
b	0	0
bb	0	0
aa	0	0
ab	1	0
ba	0	0
bba	0	0
bbb	0	0

(c)

(d)

Fig. 1. Bounded-L^* example run.

3.2 Property Checking and Error Characterization

Given $C, P \subseteq \Sigma^*$, the property checking problem is posed as determining whether $C \cap \overline{P} = \emptyset$. The error characterization problem consists in learning a regular language which is an (ϵ, δ)-approximation of $C \cap \overline{P}$.

Remark 1. *It is important to notice that C, P, and $\overline{P}$ by no means need to or are assumed to be regular languages. DFA serve to characterize the error and Bounded-L^* is a tool to solve the problem. Hereinafter, no language is regular except otherwise stated.*

Let us start by showing that if the output of Bounded-L^* is nonempty, then the target language inside the black-box is also nonempty.

Lemma 2. *For every $i > 1$, if $A_i \neq \emptyset$ then the target language is nonempty.*

Proof. If $A_i \neq \emptyset$, there exists at least one accepting state, that is, there exists $u \in \Sigma^*$ such that $OT_i[u][\lambda] = 1$. Therefore, at some iteration $j \in [1, i]$, there is a positive membership query for u, i.e, $\mathbf{MQ}_j(u) = 1$. Hence, u belongs to the target language. □

This result is important because it entails that whenever the output for the target language $C \cap \overline{P}$ is nonempty, C does not satisfy P. Moreover, for every entry of the observation table such that $OT[u][v] = 1$, the sequence $uv \in \Sigma^*$ is a counterexample.

Corollary 1. *If Bounded-L^* returns a nonempty DFA for $C \cap \overline{P}$, then $C \cap \overline{P} \neq \emptyset$. Moreover, every $u, v \in \Sigma^*$ such that $OT[u][v] = 1$ is a counterexample.*

Proof. Immediate from Lemma 2. □

It is worth noticing that, by Lemma 2, the execution of Bounded-L^* for $C \cap \overline{P}$ could just be stopped as soon as the observation table has a non-zero entry. This would serve to prove C does not satisfy P. However, we seek providing a more detailed and explanatory characterization of the error, even if approximate, by running the algorithm upon normal termination.

Theorem 1 (Main result). *If Bounded-L^* terminates with an automaton A producing $k \in [0, m]$ $\mathbf{EQ}$-divergences on a sample of size m for $C \cap \overline{P}$, then:*

1. *A is an $(\hat{\epsilon}, \delta)$-approximation of $C \cap \overline{P}$, for every $\hat{\epsilon} > \epsilon^*(m, k, \delta)$.*
2. *If $A \neq \emptyset$ or $k > 0$, then $C \cap \overline{P} \neq \emptyset$.*

Proof
1. It follows directly from Property 3.
2. There are two cases. *a)* If $A \neq \emptyset$, then $C \cap \overline{P} \neq \emptyset$ by Corollary 1. *b)* If $A = \emptyset$ and $k > 0$, then $\emptyset \neq A \oplus (C \cap \overline{P}) = \emptyset \oplus (C \cap \overline{P}) = C \cap \overline{P}$. □

4 Experimental Results

We implemented a prototype of the proposed black-box on-the-fly property checking through learning based on Bounded-L^*. The approach consists in giving C and P as inputs to the teacher which serves as a proxy of $C \cap \overline{P}$. It is important to emphasize that this approach does not require modeling $\overline{P}$ in any particular way. Instead, to answer $\mathbf{MQ}(u)$ on a word u, the teacher evaluates $P(u)$, complements the output and evaluates the conjunction with the output of $C(u)$. To answer $\mathbf{EQ}(H)$, it draws a sample S of the appropriate size and evaluates $\mathbf{MQ}(u) \iff H(u)$ on every $u \in S$. Therefore, P may be any kind of property, even not regular, or another RNN. Here, we present the results obtained on case studies from different application domains.

1. In the first experiment, training and testing data is generated from a DFA specification of the behavior of a car's cruise-controller subsystem defined in [22]. This case study illustrates the situation where the model-checker found an error on the DFA extracted from the RNN but it was impossible to reproduce it back on the RNN under analysis.
2. The second experiment deals with the model of an e-commerce web service application described in [20,25]. In this case, we injected on purpose bad sequences in the training set in order to showcase they are actually found by our on-the-fly checking procedure which outputs a DFA depicting the error.
3. The third case study comes from the field of system security. Here, we analyze the behavior of an RNN trained with logs of a Hadoop Distributed File System (HDFS) from [10]. In this example, no a priori characterization of the language of normal logs was known. The experiment showed that on-the-fly checking exposed the fact that the RNN could actually incur in false positives, that is, predicting a sequence is normal when it is not, even if no such cases were found during training on a test dataset. The output DFA depicts the error and helps understanding the logs where such misleading classifications occur.
4. The last experiment analyzes a case study from bioinformatics, namely TATA-box subsequence recognition in promoter DNA sequences [28]. In this example, it was impossible to actually extract a DFA from the RNN. Nevertheless, on-the-fly checking managed to check the RNN was compliant with the specified requirement.

4.1 Cruise Controller

We trained an RNN with a dataset containing 200K positive and negative sequences upto a maximum length of 16 from a cruise controller model from [22] (Fig. 3). The measured error of the RNN on a test set of 16K sequences was 0,09%. The property P used in this example is shown in Fig. 2. It models the requirement that a *break* event can only happen if a *gas*|*acc* has already occurred before and no other *break* has happened inbetween.

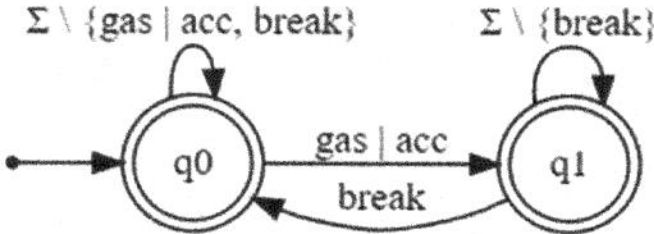

Fig. 2. Requirement of the cruise controller example

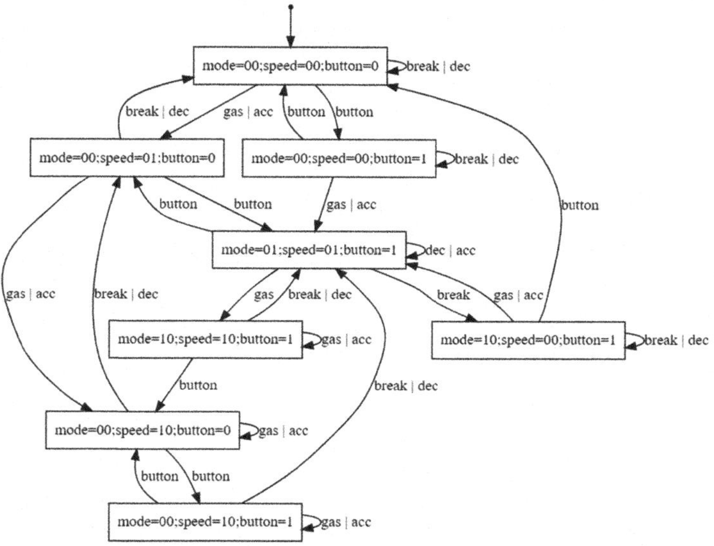

Fig. 3. Model of the cruise controller example

First, we used our on-the-fly technique and found out that every run ended up conjecturing $C \cap \overline{P} = \emptyset$ with perfect **EQ** tests. Running times, **EQ** test sizes and ϵ^* for different values of ϵ and δ of these experiments are shown in Table 1.

Table 1. Cruise controller: on-the-fly verification of RNN.

Configuration		Exec. time (s)			First counter-example	Average EQ test size	Average ϵ^*
ϵ	δ	Min	Max	Avg			
0.01	0.01	0.003	0.006	0.004	–	669	0.00688
0.001	0.01	0.061	0.096	0.075	–	6,685	0.00069
0.0001	0.01	0.341	0.626	0.497	–	66,847	0.00007

Second, we extracted PAC DFA from the network alone, with a timeout of 200 s (Table 2). For the first configuration, one run timed out and four completed. All extracted DFA exceeded the maximum number of states bound, and three of them did not verify the property. For the second one, there were two time outs, and three successful extractions. Every one of the extractions exceeded the maximum states bound and two of them did not verify the property. Finally, for the third one, every run timed out.

We then checked these DFA against the property with an external verification algorithm for computing intersection of DFA. It turned out that all the counterexamples found by the model-checking procedure where actually classified as negative by the RNN under analysis.

Table 2. Cruise controller: PAC DFA extraction from RNN.

Configuration		Exec. time (s)			Average EQ test size	Average ϵ^*
ϵ	δ	Min	Max	Avg		
0.01	0.01	11.633	200.000	67.662	808	0.05
0.001	0.01	52.362	200.000	135.446	8,071	0.03
0.0001	0.01	–	–	–	–	–

Then, we used **EX** to generate 2 million sequences for each of the DFA H not checking the property. It turned out that none was accepted by both $H \cap \overline{P}$ and the RNN. Thus, we cannot disprove the conjecture that the RNN is correct with respect to P obtained with the on-the-fly technique. Moreover, the second approach required considerable more effort because of its misleading verdict.

This experiment showcases a key aspect where on-the-fly property checking stands out: when it presents a witness it is real with probability 1, whereas this is not the case when verifying a property on a model of a target RNN.

4.2 E-commerce Web Application API

We analyzed an RNN trained with a dataset of 100K positive and negative sequences upto length 16 drawn from the model of the e-commerce system from [20,25], together with sequences that violate the properties to be checked. These *canary* sequences were added on purpose to check whether the RNN actually learned those faulty behaviors and whether our technique was able to figure that out. The RNN was trained until no error was measured on a test set of 16K.

We checked the RNN against the following regular properties. 1) It is not possible to buy products in the shopping cart (modelled by symbol $bPSC$) when the shopping cart is empty. Symbols $aPSC$ and eSC model adding products to and emptying the shopping cart, respectively (Fig. 4a). 2) It is not possible to execute the action $bPSC$ two or more times in a row (Fig. 4b).

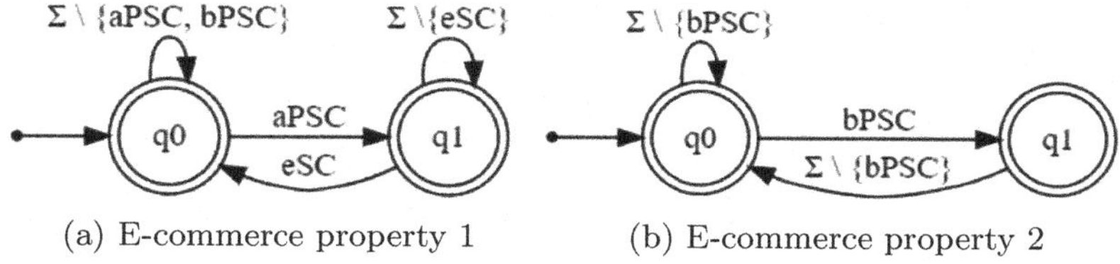

(a) E-commerce property 1 (b) E-commerce property 2

Fig. 4. E-commerce properties

In this experiment, we only checked properties with the on-the-fly approach. Nevertheless, we exctrated DFA for different values of ϵ and δ as a reference for comparing computational performance (Table 3).

Table 3. E-commerce: PAC DFA extraction from RNN.

Configuration		Exec. time (s)			Average EQ test size	Average ϵ^*
ϵ	δ	Min	Max	Avg		
0.01	0.01	16.863	62.125	36.071	863	0.00534
0.001	0.01	6.764	9.307	7.864	8,487	0.00054
0.0001	0.01	18.586	41.137	30.556	83,482	0.00006

On-the-fly property checking concluded both properties were not satisfied (Table 4). In average, it took more time to output a PAC DFA of the language of faulty behaviors than extracting a PAC DFA of the RNN alone. Nevertheless, counterexamples were found (in average) orders of magnitude faster than the latter for requirement 1), while it took comparable time for requirement 2), which revealed to be harder to check than the former.

Table 4. E-commerce: on-the-fly verification of RNN.

Prop	Configuration		Excecution time (s)			First counter-example	Average EQ test size	Average ϵ^*
	ϵ	δ	Min	Max	Avg			
1	0.01	0.01	87.196	312.080	174.612	3.878	891	0.00517
	0.001	0.01	0.774	203.103	102.742	0.744	9,181	0.00050
	0.0001	0.01	105.705	273.278	190.948	2.627	94,573	0.00005
2	0.01	0.01	0.002	487.709	148.027	80.738	752	0.00619
	0.001	0.01	62.457	600.000	428.400	36.606	8,765	0.00053
	0.0001	0.01	71.542	451.934	250.195	41.798	87,641	0.00005

Examples of outputs of the on-the-fly property checking algorithm for properties 1 and 2, with parameters $\epsilon = 0.0001$ and $\delta = 0.01$, are shown in Figs. 5 and 6, respectively. They contain valuable information about all possible consequences of the errors in terms of understanding and correcting them. At the

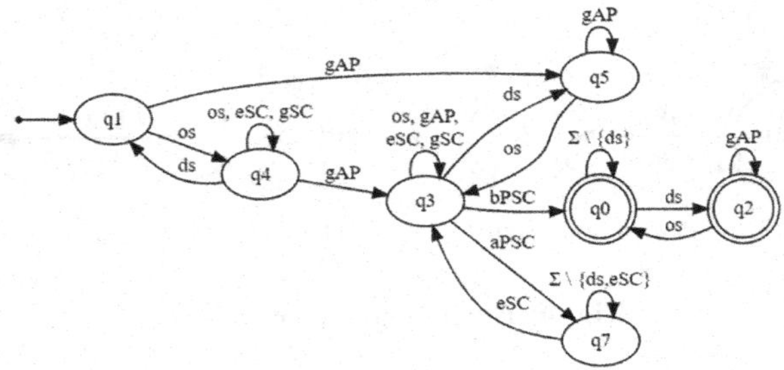

Fig. 5. Example of output for Property 1 on the e-commerce RNN.

same time, the technique is able to present real witnesses that belong to this language and to the network under analysis.

The DFA depicted in Fig. 5 shows that the RNN classifies as correct a sequence where event *gAP* (get available products) has occurred but either no product has been added to the shopping basket (i.e., no *aPSC* has occurred) or this has been emptied (i.e., *eSC* happened), within an active session (i.e, the last open session event *os* is not followed by a closed session event *cs*). This is illustrated, for instance, by the sub-DFA involving states q_1, q_4, q_3, and q_0. Actually, Fig. 6 shows that not only property 2 is not satisfied by the RNN but also property 1, as well, since it is possible to reach q_3 without executing *aPSC*.

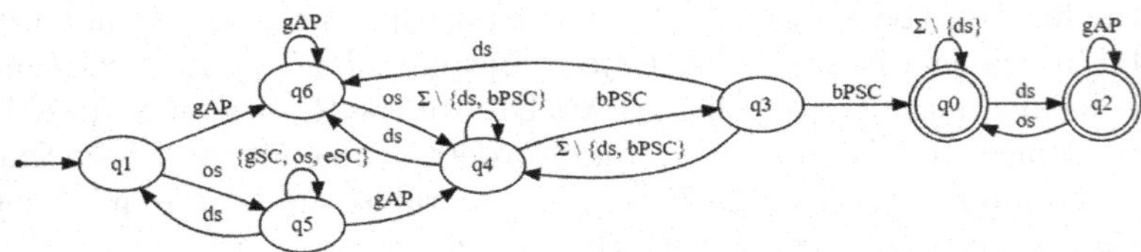

Fig. 6. Example of output for Property 2 on the e-commerce RNN.

4.3 Analysis of HDFS Logs

In this case study we deal with a dataset of logs of a Hadoop Distributed File System (HDFS) from [10]. The logs were labeled as normal or abnormal by Hadoop experts. It contains 4855 training normal variable-length logs. Each log is pre-processed into a sequence of numeric symbols from 0 to 28. These logs were used to train an RNN-based auto-regressive language model (LM). That is, the output of the RNN is the conditional probability of the next symbol given all the previous ones [6]. This RNN can be used to build a sequence classifier in several ways. In this case, we use the RNN to predict the probability of a sequence. Such prediction is then compared to a given threshold. If the probability is greater than the threshold, the sequence is considered to be normal (positive), otherwise is declared to be abnormal (negative).

Table 5. HDFS logs: on-the-fly verification of RNN.

Prop	Configuration		Excecution time (s)			First counter-example	Average EQ test size	Average ϵ^*
	ϵ	δ	Min	Max	Avg			
1)	0.01	0.01	209.409	1, 121.360	555.454	5.623	932	0.0050
	0.001	0.001	221.397	812.764	455.660	1.321	12,037	0.0006
2)	0.01	0.01	35.131	39.762	37.226	–	600	0.0077
	0.001	0.001	252.202	257.312	254.479	–	8,295	0.0008

For this experiment, the classifier was implemented as a Python function which queried the RNN and returned the prediction. We used a threshold of 2×10^{-7} and a perfectly balanced test set containing 33600 normal and abnormal logs. The classifier achieved an accuracy of 98.35% with no false positives. That is, no abnormal log in the test set is ever misclassified as normal by the classifier. We verified the following properties. 1) The classifier does not classify as normal a sequence that contains a symbol which only appears in abnormal logs. This set, identified as A, contains 12 symbols, namely $6, 7, 9, 11-14, 18, 19, 23, 26-28$. 2) The classifier always classifies as normal logs where the sum of occurrences of symbols "4" and "21", often seen at the beginning of normal logs, is at most 5. The purpose of checking these properties is to determine whether the RNN actually learned these patterns as characteristic of normal logs.

The results of on-the-fly checking are shown in Table 5. For each configuration, 5 runs were executed. For property 2), we found that it is satisfied by the classifier with PAC guarantees. However, in the case of property 1), all runs found counterexamples and output a PAC DFA of the sequences violating the property. This means the classifier can label as normal a log containing symbols in the set A of symbols that only appeared in logs tagged as abnormal by experts. Notice that this observation highlights a discrepancy with the results obtained on the test set where the classifier incurred in no false positives, therefore, it did not classify as normal any log containing symbols in A.

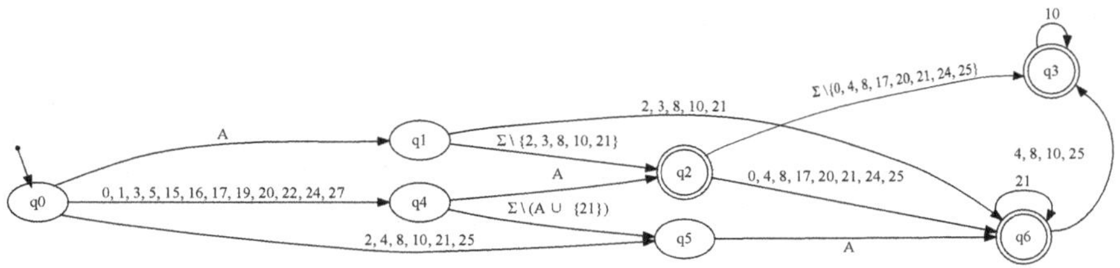

Fig. 7. Model of the error of the Deep Log network verified against property 1.

The output PAC DFA can be used to understand in more detail mistakes of the classifier in order to improve its performance. Figure 7 depicts the DFA obtained in a run of the algoritm with parameters $\epsilon = 0.01$ and $\delta = 0.01$. For instance, we can see that the RNN can recognize as normal logs of length two which start with a symbol in the set A. This is shown by paths q_0, q_1, q_2 and q_0, q_1, q_6 of the DFA. Figure 8 shows that the predicted probability of logs corresponding to these paths were always significantly above the threshold (by an order of magnitude of 4). The fact that the classifier could produce such classifications is not obvious, since the probability assigned by the RNN to an unseen symbol is expected to be low (because no such symbol has been seen during training).

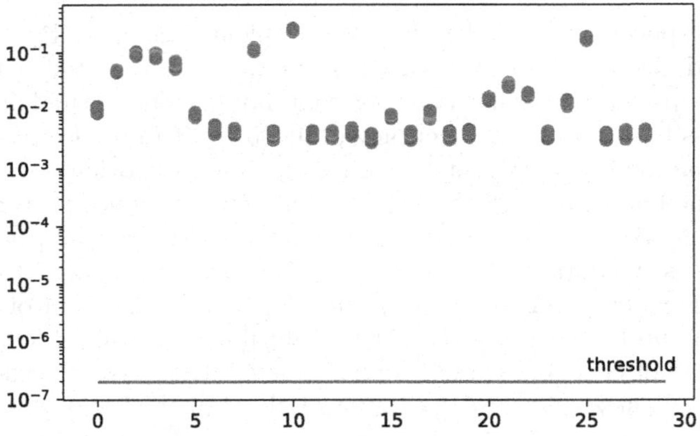

Fig. 8. Predicted probability for logs of length 2 starting with A (in log scale).

4.4 TATA-box Recognition in DNA Promoter Sequences

Promoter region recognition in DNA sequences is an active research area in bioinformatics. Recently, tools based on neural networks, such as CNN and LSTM, have been proposed for such matter [28]. Promoters are located upstream near the gene transcription start site (TSS) and control the activation or repression of the genes. The TATA-box is a particular promoter subsequence that indicates to other molecules where transcription begins. It is a T/A-rich (i.e., more T's and A's than C's and G') subsequence of 6 base pairs (bp) located between positions −30 bp to −25 bp, where +1 bp is the TSS. The goal of this experiment is not to develop a neural network for promoter classification, but to study whether an RNN trained with TATA and non-TATA promoter sequences is able to distinguish between them, that is, it is capable of determining whether a DNA sequence contains a TATA region. For such task, we trained an RNN composed of an LSTM and a dense layer for classification, with a dataset of the most representative TATA (2067 sequences) and non-TATA (14388 sequences) human promoters of length 50 bp from positions −48 bp to +1 bp. The dataset was downloaded from the website EPDnew[2]. The RNN was trained until achieving an accuracy of 100%.

[2] https://epd.epfl.ch//index.php.

Table 6. TATA-box: on-the-fly verification of RNN.

Configuration		Exec. time (s)			Average EQ test size	Average ϵ^*
ϵ	δ	Min	Max	Avg		
0.01	0.01	5.098	5.259	5.168	600	0.00768
0.001	0.001	65.366	66.479	65.812	8,295	0.00083
0.0001	0.0001	865.014	870.663	867.830	105,967	0.00008

We ran the on-the-fly algorithm to check whether the language of the RNN was included in the set of sequences containing a TATA-box. The property was coded as a Python program which counts the number of T's, A's, C's and G's in the subsequence from position −30 bp to −25 bp of the genomic sequence, and checks whether the sum of T's and A's is greater than the sum of C's and G's. In this case, the oracle **EX** was parameterized to generate sequences of length 50 over the alphabet $\{A, T, C, G\}$. We were not able to extract an automaton representing the target network because Bounded-L^* always hit a timeout before being able to construct a DFA. Therefore, extracting a model and then checking it was not achievable in practice due to state explosion. Nevertheless, we were able to perform the analysis with on-the-fly checking (Table 6). In this case, every run of the algorithm output an empty language of the error, thus conjecturing the RNN PAC-verifies the property. Notice that for parameters $\epsilon = \delta = 0.0001$, the PAC **EQ** sample is more than 6 times larger than the training set.

5 Related Work

Learning and automata-theoretic verification have been combined in several ways for checking temporal requirements of systems. For instance, [3,9,12] do compositional verification by learning assumptions. These methods are white-box and require an external decision procedure. Learning regular approximations of FIFO automata for verifying regular properties has been explored in [40]. A technique for verifying properties on learned automata is presented in [13]. It iteratively applies Trakhtenbrot-Barzdin algorithm [38] on several training sets until the inferred automaton is an invariant sufficient to prove the property.

Learning based testing (LBT) [23] is a BBC approach for generating test cases. It relies on incrementally building hypotheses of the system under test (SUT) and verifying whether they satisfy the requirement through an external model-checker. Counterexamples serve as test-cases for the SUT. To the best of our knowledge, it does not provide provable probabilistic guarantees. Recent work [21] proposes a sound extension but it requires relaxing the black-box setting by observing and recording the internal state of the SUT.

For checking safety properties on feed-forward neural networks (FFNN), a general white-box approach based on Linear Programming (LP) and Satisfiability Modulo Theories (SMT) has been first explored in [31]. Lately, this approach has been further explored, for instance, in [11,15,16]. For RNN, an approach for adversarial accuracy verification is presented in [43] based a white-box technique to extract DFA from RNN. Experimental evaluation is carried out work on Tomita grammars, which are small regular languages over the $\{0,1\}$-alphabet. That approach does not offer any guarantee on how well the DFA approximates the RNN. RNSVerify [2] implements white-box verification of safety properties by unrolling the RNN and resorting to LP to solve a system of constraints. The method strongly relies on the internal structure and weight matrices of the RNN. Overall, these techniques are white-box and are not able to handle non-regular properties. Besides, they do not address the problem of producing interpretable error characterizations.

Finally, statistical model checking (SMC) the system under analysis and/or the property is stochastic [1,19]. The objective of SMC is to check whether a stochastic system, such as a Markov decision process, satisfies a property with a probability greater or equal to a certain threshold θ. The problem we address in this work is different as neither the system nor the property is stochastic. Our approach provides statistical guarantees that the language of an RNN C is included in another language (the property P) or provides a PAC model of the language $C \cap \overline{P}$, along with actual counterexamples showing it is not.

6 Conclusions

The contribution of this paper is a black-box on-the-fly learning-based approach for checking properties on RNN. Our technique interacts with the software artifact implementing the RNN-based classifier through queries. It does not build a priori the state-space of the RNN but directly constructs an approximation of the intersection of the RNN with the negation of the requirement. Besides, in contrast to other approaches, the computational complexity of our technique does not depend on the size (hidden layers, weights) of the RNN and of external model-checkers or solvers, but rather on the size of its alphabet Σ, together with user-controlled inputs of the algorithm such as the approximation ϵ and confidence δ parameters, and the maximum number of states and length of membership queries. Moreover, it is not restricted to any particular class of RNN and can also be used to check non-regular properties. Our algorithm outputs an interpretable characterization of an approximation of the set of incorrect behaviors.

We implemented the approach and shown its practical applicability for checking properties on several case studies from different application domains. We compared, when possible, the results of on-the-fly checking through learning against model-checking the extracted PAC models of the RNN alone. The experiments were promising as they provided empirical evidence that the on-the-fly approach typically performs faster than extracting a DFA from the RNN under analysis whenever the property is probably approximately satisfied. Moreover, when a property is found not to be satisfied by the RNN, the experiments shown the output DFA contains valuable information about all possible consequences of the error in terms of understanding and correcting it.

Acknowledgments. This work has been partially funded by an ICT4V - Information and Communication Technologies for Verticals master thesis grant POS_ICT4V_2016_1_15, and ANII - Agencia Nacional de Investigación e Innovación research grants FSDA_1_2018_1_154419 and FMV_1_2019_1_155913.

References

1. Agha, G., Palmskog, K.: A survey of statistical model checking. ACM Trans. Model. Comput. Simul. **28**(1), 1–9 (2018)
2. Akintunde, M.E., Kevorchian, A., Lomuscio, A., Pirovano, E.: Verification of RNN-based neural agent-environment systems. In: AAAI, pp. 6006–6013 (2019)
3. Alur, R., Madhusudan, P., Nam, W.: Symbolic compositional verification by learning assumptions. In: Etessami, K., Rajamani, S.K. (eds.) CAV 2005. LNCS, vol. 3576, pp. 548–562. Springer, Heidelberg (2005). https://doi.org/10.1007/11513988_52
4. Angluin, D.: Learning regular sets from queries and counterexamples. Inf. Comput. **75**(2), 87–106 (1987)
5. Angluin, D.: Computational learning theory: survey and selected bibliography. In: STOC, pp. 351–369. ACM (1992)
6. Bengio, Y., Ducharme, R., Vincent, P., Janvin, C.: A neural probabilistic language model. J. Mach. Learn. Res. **3**, 1137–1155 (2003)
7. Biran, O., Cotton, C.V.: Explanation and justification in machine learning : a survey. In: IJCAI Workshop on Explainable Artificial Intelligence (XAI) (2017)
8. Clarke Jr., E.M., Grumberg, O., Peled, D.A.: Model Checking. MIT Press, Cambridge (1999)
9. Cobleigh, J.M., Giannakopoulou, D., Păsăreanu, C.S.: Learning assumptions for compositional verification. In: Garavel, H., Hatcliff, J. (eds.) TACAS 2003. LNCS, vol. 2619, pp. 331–346. Springer, Heidelberg (2003). https://doi.org/10.1007/3-540-36577-X_24
10. Du, M., Li, F., Zheng, G., Srikumar, V.: Deeplog: anomaly detection and diagnosis from system logs through deep learning. In: SIGSAC CCS, pp. 1285–1298. ACM (2017)
11. Ehlers, R.: Formal verification of piece-wise linear feed-forward neural networks. In: D'Souza, D., Narayan Kumar, K. (eds.) ATVA 2017. LNCS, vol. 10482, pp. 269–286. Springer, Cham (2017). https://doi.org/10.1007/978-3-319-68167-2_19
12. Feng, L., Han, T., Kwiatkowska, M., Parker, D.: Learning-based compositional verification for synchronous probabilistic systems. In: Bultan, T., Hsiung, P.-A. (eds.) ATVA 2011. LNCS, vol. 6996, pp. 511–521. Springer, Heidelberg (2011). https://doi.org/10.1007/978-3-642-24372-1_40
13. Habermehl, P., Vojnar, T.: Regular model checking using inference of regular languages. ENTCS **138**, 21–36 (2004)
14. Heinz, J., de la Higuera, C., van Zaanen, M.: Formal and empirical grammatical inference. In: ACL Annual Meeting, pp. 2:1–2:83. ACL (2011)
15. Huang, X., Kwiatkowska, M., Wang, S., Wu, M.: Safety verification of deep neural networks. In: Majumdar, R., Kunčak, V. (eds.) CAV 2017. LNCS, vol. 10426, pp. 3–29. Springer, Cham (2017). https://doi.org/10.1007/978-3-319-63387-9_1
16. Katz, G., Barrett, C., Dill, D.L., Julian, K., Kochenderfer, M.J.: Reluplex: an efficient SMT solver for verifying deep neural networks. In: Majumdar, R., Kunčak, V. (eds.) CAV 2017. LNCS, vol. 10426, pp. 97–117. Springer, Cham (2017). https://doi.org/10.1007/978-3-319-63387-9_5

17. Kim, J., Kim, J., Thu, H.L.T., Kim, H.: Long short term memory recurrent neural network classifier for intrusion detection. In: PlatCon, pp. 1–5. IEEE (2016)
18. Kocić, J., Jovičić, N., Drndarević, V.: An end-to-end deep neural network for autonomous driving designed for embedded automotive platforms. Sensors **19**(9), 2064 (2019)
19. Legay, A., Lukina, A., Traonouez, L.M., Yang, J., Smolka, S.A., Grosu, R.: Statistical model checking. In: Steffen, B., Woeginger, G. (eds.) Computing and Software Science. LNCS, vol. 10000, pp. 478–504. Springer, Cham (2019). https://doi.org/10.1007/978-3-319-91908-9_23
20. Mayr, F., Yovine, S.: Regular inference on artificial neural networks. In: Holzinger, A., Kieseberg, P., Tjoa, A.M., Weippl, E. (eds.) CD-MAKE 2018. LNCS, vol. 11015, pp. 350–369. Springer, Cham (2018). https://doi.org/10.1007/978-3-319-99740-7_25
21. Meijer, J., van de Pol, J.: Sound black-box checking in the learnlib. Innovations Syst. Softw. Eng. **15**(3–4), 267–287 (2019)
22. Meinke, K., Sindhu, M.A.: LBTest: a learning-based testing tool for reactive systems. In: STVV, pp. 447–454. IEEE, March 2013
23. Meinke, K.: Learning-based testing: recent progress and future prospects. In: Bennaceur, A., Hähnle, R., Meinke, K. (eds.) Machine Learning for Dynamic Software Analysis: Potentials and Limits. LNCS, vol. 11026, pp. 53–73. Springer, Cham (2018). https://doi.org/10.1007/978-3-319-96562-8_2
24. Merrill, W.: Sequential neural networks as automata. arXiv preprint arXiv:1906.01615 (2019)
25. Merten, M.: Active automata learning for real life applications. Ph.D. thesis, Technischen Universität Dortmund (2013)
26. Miller, T.: Explanation in artificial intelligence: insights from the social sciences. Artif. Intell. **267**, 1–38 (2019)
27. Odena, A., Olsson, C., Andersen, D., Goodfellow, I.J.: Tensorfuzz: debugging neural networks with coverage-guided fuzzing. In: ICML, vol. 97, pp. 4901–4911. PMLR (2019)
28. Oubounyt, M., Louadi, Z., Tayara, H., Chong, K.T.: Deepromoter: robust promoter predictor using deep learning. Front. Genet. **10**, 286 (2019)
29. Pascanu, R., Stokes, J.W., Sanossian, H., Marinescu, M., Thomas, A.: Malware classification with recurrent networks. In: ICASSP, pp. 1916–1920. IEEE (2015)
30. Peled, D., Vardi, M.Y., Yannakakis, M.: Black box checking. J. Automata Lang. Comb. **7**(2), 225–246 (2002)
31. Pulina, L., Tacchella, A.: Challenging SMT solvers to verify neural networks. AI Commun. **25**(2), 117–135 (2012)
32. Rhode, M., Burnap, P., Jones, K.: Early stage malware prediction using recurrent neural networks. Comput. Secur. **77**, 578–594 (2017)
33. Ribeiro, M.T., Singh, S., Guestrin, C.: "why should i trust you?": explaining the predictions of any classifier. In: SIGKDD Knowledge Discovery and Data Mining, pp. 1135–1144. ACM (2016)
34. Scheiner, N., Appenrodt, N., Dickmann, J., Sick, B.: Radar-based road user classification and novelty detection with recurrent neural network ensembles. In: Intelligent Vehicles Symposium, pp. 722–729. IEEE (2019)
35. Siegelmann, H.T., Sontag, E.D.: On the computational power of neural nets. In: COLT, pp. 440–449. ACM (1992)

36. Singh, D., et al.: Human activity recognition using recurrent neural networks. In: Holzinger, A., Kieseberg, P., Tjoa, A.M., Weippl, E. (eds.) CD-MAKE 2017. LNCS, vol. 10410, pp. 267–274. Springer, Cham (2017). https://doi.org/10.1007/978-3-319-66808-6_18
37. Suzgun, M., Belinkov, Y., Shieber, S.M.: On evaluating the generalization of LSTM models in formal languages. CoRR abs/1811.01001 (2018)
38. Trakhtenbrot, B.A., Barzdin, I.M.: Finite Automata : Behavior and Synthesis. North-Holland, Amsterdam (1973)
39. Valiant, L.G.: A theory of the learnable. Commun. ACM **27**(11), 1134–1142 (1984)
40. Vardhan, A., Sen, K., Viswanathan, M., Agha, G.: Actively learning to verify safety for FIFO automata. In: Lodaya, K., Mahajan, M. (eds.) FSTTCS 2004. LNCS, vol. 3328, pp. 494–505. Springer, Heidelberg (2004). https://doi.org/10.1007/978-3-540-30538-5_41
41. Vinayakumar, R., Alazab, M., Soman, K., Poornachandran, P., Venkatraman, S.: Robust intelligent malware detection using deep learning. IEEE Access **7**, 46717–46738 (2019)
42. Wang, Q., Zhang, K., Ororbia II, A.G., Xing, X., Liu, X., Giles, C.L.: A comparison of rule extraction for different recurrent neural network models and grammatical complexity. CoRR abs/1801.05420 (2018)
43. Wang, Q., Zhang, K., Liu, X., Giles, C.L.: Verification of recurrent neural networks through rule extraction. In: AAAI Spring Symposium on Verification of Neural Networks (VNN19) (2019)
44. Wang, Q., Zhang, K., Ororbia II, A.G., Xing, X., Liu, X., Giles, C.L.: An empirical evaluation of rule extraction from recurrent neural networks. Neural Comput. **30**(9), 2568–2591 (2018)
45. Weiss, G., Goldberg, Y., Yahav, E.: Extracting automata from recurrent neural networks using queries and counterexamples. In: ICML, vol. 80. PMLR (2018)
46. Yin, C., Zhu, Y., Fei, J., He, X.: A deep learning approach for intrusion detection using recurrent neural networks. IEEE Access **5**, 21954–21961 (2017)

Active Learning for Auditory Hierarchy

William Coleman[1,2(✉)], Charlie Cullen[1], Ming Yan[2], and Sarah Jane Delany[1]

[1] School of Computer Science, TU Dublin, Kevin Street, Dublin D08 X622, Ireland
d15126149@mytudublin.ie
[2] Xperi Corporation, Bangor BT19 7QT, UK

Abstract. Much audio content today is rendered as a static stereo mix: fundamentally a fixed single entity. Object-based audio envisages the delivery of sound content using a collection of individual sound 'objects' controlled by accompanying metadata. This offers potential for audio to be delivered in a dynamic manner providing enhanced audio for consumers. One example of such treatment is the concept of applying varying levels of data compression to sound objects thereby reducing the volume of data to be transmitted in limited bandwidth situations. This application motivates the ability to accurately classify objects in terms of their 'hierarchy'. That is, whether or not an object is a foreground sound, which should be reproduced at full quality if possible, or a background sound, which can be heavily compressed without causing a deterioration in the listening experience. Lack of suitably labelled data is an acknowledged problem in the domain. Active Learning is a method that can greatly reduce the manual effort required to label a large corpus by identifying the most effective instances to train a model to high accuracy levels. This paper compares a number of Active Learning methods to investigate which is most effective in the context of a hierarchical labelling task on an audio dataset. Results show that the number of manual labels required can be reduced to 1.7% of the total dataset while still retaining high prediction accuracy.

Keywords: Active Learning · Auditory hierarchy · Machine Learning · Support Vector Machine

1 Introduction

Recent technological advances have driven changes in how media is consumed in home, automotive and mobile contexts. Multi-channel audio home cinema systems have become more prevalent. The consumption of broadcast and gaming content on smart-phone and tablet technology via telecommunications networks is also more common. This has created new possibilities and consequently poses

This work was supported by the Irish Research Council and DTS Licensing Ltd. (now part of Xperi) under project code EBPPG/2016/339.

Published by Springer Nature Switzerland AG 2020
A. Holzinger et al. (Eds.): CD-MAKE 2020, LNCS 12279, pp. 365–384, 2020.
https://doi.org/10.1007/978-3-030-57321-8_20

new challenges for audio content delivery such as how media can be optimized for multiple contexts while minimizing file size.

Object-based audio [9] may offer a solution to this problem by providing audio content at an object level with meta-data which controls how the media is delivered dependant on mode of consumption. In this context, insight into the relative importance of different sounds in the auditory scene will be useful in forming content delivery strategies. In the following the concept of a hierarchy between audio objects in multimedia content which changes over time due to activity in the material, external factors and personal bias will be referred to as *audio object hierarchy*.

How sounds are noted as being of most interest, referred to as Foreground (FG) sounds in the following, is not explicitly understood. Section 2.1 outlines a number of factors hypothesised to have an influence, such as attention [63], prior training [5] and context [57]. It is reasonable to suggest that certain sounds (speech, or alert noises, such as alarms) would likely be consistently categorised as FG. However, detailed knowledge in this respect would be important in the design of any delivery solution for an object-based audio system as every potential influence can be thought of as requiring a weighting appropriate to the degree to which each influences the hierarchy. Accurately mapping such weightings requires a structured study in order to examine each influence in isolation, where possible. In order to do so a dataset of sounds is required, isolated from context in so far as this is possible, to examine the influence of external factors. To our knowledge no such dataset suited to the study of auditory hierarchy currently exists and the lack of labelled datasets of suitable scale is an acknowledged problem in the domain [46]. This paper outlines a method by which large numbers of audio objects can be labelled with minimal human input to high levels of accuracy into FG and Background (BG) categories.

Previous work has outlined evidence of an inherent FG, Neutral (N), BG hierarchy between isolated sounds [10]. Further studies have established that a supervised Machine Learning (ML) approach to auditory hierarchy prediction shows promise [11], in this instance by framing the problem as a binary 'FG'/'not FG' categorisation task, albeit using a small dataset. State-of-the-art audio ML requires large, labelled datasets [8] in order to achieve high accuracy levels. Datasets are difficult and expensive to compile and label manually, a problem which can be addressed using data augmentation techniques [49]. However, care must be taken that such augmentations do not alter the underlying semantic information of stimuli. It follows that other methods of minimising the manual effort required to compile large datasets are worthy of investigation.

Active Learning (AL) is a supervised ML technique that can be used to minimise the manual effort required to label large datasets [52]. AL strives to identify & label the most informative instances in a dataset, aiming to use a minimum of manual intervention to train a model capable of classifying unseen instances to a high level of accuracy. In this paper, AL is used to apply hierarchical labels to an audio corpus of environmental sounds. A number of selection strategies can be used in AL. Uncertainty Sampling AL (USAL) is a model-based approach which uses an uncertainty measure to identify instances that are most difficult to classify, assuming that these will be most informative for predicting other instances [52]. Exploration Guided AL (EGAL) [24] is a model-free approach which aims to identify dense clusters of instances that are most diverse from already labelled examples. This operates on the assumption that focusing on cluster centroids most distal from already labelled instances first will allow accurate predictions to be made early in the labelling process.

While popular, USAL is computationally expensive and time consuming, requiring models to be built repeatedly throughout the labelling process. EGAL addresses this problem by basing selection of informative instances solely on dataset features, avoiding the overhead of training models repeatedly. EGAL has been found to be more effective than model-based methods in some applications [41] and to our knowledge has not yet been applied to an audio problem. In addition, a random selection strategy is implemented as a baseline.

Results show that it is possible to dramatically reduce the number of labels required to hierarchically label the audio dataset used in this study. EGAL techniques outperform both USAL and random selection strategies, being able to label to high accuracy using only 1.7% of labelled dataset instances. The next best performing selection method requires 11.7% of labels to achieve the same accuracy level.

The following sections offer an overview of perceptual (Sect. 2.1) and ML (Sect. 2.2) research relevant to auditory hierarchy. Section 2.3 introduces AL and outlines the USAL and EGAL selection methods employed in this study. Section 3 offers an overview of methodology covering a subjective labelling exercise (Sect. 3.1), feature extraction methods (Sect. 3.2), classifier choice (Sect. 3.3), a cross validation experiment investigating audio data representation options (Sect. 3.4) and the structure of the AL experiment implemented in this instance (Sect. 3.5). Section 4 describes an experiment utilizing a number of AL selection methods and outlines the results observed from these efforts. Finally, Sect. 5 discusses these findings and suggests future areas for study.

2 Related Work

2.1 Auditory Scene Analysis

Research in object-based broadcasting [9] and auditory object categorization [62] has underlined a growing interest in how such concepts can be applied to modern media consumption. The concept of a variable compression codec is but one such possibility, addressed in this paper by outlining how a dataset can be formulated on which a model can be trained to predict auditory hierarchy. Auditory Scene Analysis (ASA) involves a constant activity of sound categorization which Bregman [7] outlines as both a conscious (schematic or *top-down*) and unconscious (primitive or *bottom-up*) process of soundscape perception. Guastavino [18] has noted converging evidence from both behavioral and neurophysiological domains that provides support for the notion that amalgamation of these processes is integrated, rather than serial. In the context of auditory hierarchy ASA can therefore be considered as a constant analysis of the surrounding sound scene, subject to varying levels of influence from a number of external factors. These have been noted to include physical properties of sounds [45], the level of attention granted by listeners [63], volume level [44], proximity [31], sound event context and listening mode [57], level of anticipation [26], prior training [5], experience [35] and even other senses (sight [17], smell [64] and touch [54]). This process involves continual identification of interesting sounds which may then be consciously analysed for semantic information or further meaning, or not, as deemed necessary.

This is therefore not a trivial problem to approach, as any fully-featured model predicting FG elements would be expected to incorporate input from many, continually changing, factors, each requiring careful examination both to evaluate the relative weight each carries with respect to auditory hierarchy and to assess how they interact over time. Furthermore, the process is subjective, each subject having a different perspective on which sounds are important and which are not, either explicitly or implicitly. Considering this, the most effective way to examine the effect of each factor is to first form a dataset with stimuli isolated from external influence in so far as this is possible. This paper therefore investigates audio object hierarchy prediction as it pertains to sounds isolated from context in so far as this is practical. Future work will involve investigation of other factors identified as having an influence on hierarchical categorization.

Predicting auditory hierarchy for modern media applications involves an investigation of individual subjective judgement of sound, specifically with regard to which sounds are most important when. As such, this should be seen as distinct from studies utilising ITU-R standards such as BS.1116-3 [28] and BS.1534-3 (MuSHRA) [29] which focus on the minutiae of variations in Basic Audio Quality (BAQ) [28] between experimental stimuli when evaluating output from different loudspeakers [53] or the qualities of ambisonic microphones [4], for instance. Our focus is on subjective perception of macro sound categorisation on a hierarchical level, rather than on micro differences between stimuli. This study focuses on stimuli suitable for use in game audio, visual streaming media and broadcasting content. This represents a broad palette of environmental sounds deemed most appropriate in terms of the envisaged end use of a hierarchical model. Framing the experimental and stimuli requirements in this manner allows us to prioritise accumulating volume of labels via an online environment over maintaining strict laboratory assessment conditions as required by the stricter standards.

2.2 Machine Learning for Auditory Hierarchy

There is a considerable extant audio ML literature [59] and a rich recent history in the application of such knowledge to the areas of acoustic scene classification [21], music information retrieval [60], various so-called 'hearable' technologies such as Google Home [16] and Amazon Echo [1] and many others [34, 36, 61]. In particular, Deep Learning (DL) algorithms such as Convolutional Neural Networks and Recurrent Neural Networks have gained a reputation as being good predictors for a wide variety of tasks and are considered state-of-the-art [8] in many audio domains such as speech recognition [23] and environmental sound categorization [48]. However, while these algorithms are capable of high accuracy they also require large amounts of data in order to achieve such scores [51]. Indeed, the lack of large, labelled datasets for experimental purposes is an acknowledged problem in the field [3,46].

It follows that securing a sufficient volume of suitable auditory stimuli is of primary importance in order to train a model that will accurately predict on unseen instances. This can be addressed by crowd sourcing labels for auditory stimuli and by using ML data augmentation techniques [46]. In the audio domain these include temporal and pitch variations, random cropping, dynamic range compression and the introduction of background noise [49]. However, it is still a difficult task to scale to large datasets using these methods and each are subject to limitations. Label quality is a concern with crowd sourced labels and care must be taken that data augmentation techniques do not change the underlying semantic content of the stimuli.

Auditory hierarchy has been investigated in a number of studies to date but there are methodological differences that preclude the use of these datasets for this study. For example, Lewis et al. [32] examine subject rating of approximately 256 sounds on an 'object like' versus 'scene like' axis for a selection of mechanical and environmental sounds. Thorogood et al. [55] use 200 soundscape recordings of 4 s in length derived from the World Soundscape Project Tape Library database [58] and categorize them in BG, FG and 'FG with BG' categories. These datasets are not of a suitable scale for our purposes, however. Salamon et al. [50] apply subjective labelling to 8,732 BG and FG urban sounds and validate label accuracy with experimental testing, but the sounds used are confined to urban settings and are not isolated from context. The authors are unaware of any large, publicly available database of sounds with hierarchical labels suitable for a study of multiple influences on auditory hierarchy.

A number of environmental sound databases are publicly accessible for research purposes (a useful summary is available [22]) and from these the Dataset for Environmental Sound Classification (ESC) [43] has been selected as it provides a large number of potential stimuli (>250,000 in total) which can be parsed for instances that contain isolated sounds suitable for hierarchical labelling. Further details on the stimuli selected for this experiment are given in Sect. 3.1.

2.3 Active Learning

AL is a supervised ML technique originally designed to build classifiers with minimal manual labelling effort which can be used to label large datasets [52]. As outlined in Fig. 1, when a prediction model cannot confidently predict class membership the informativeness of those instances can be assessed using a selection technique. Those deemed most informative are presented to a human oracle for labelling and used to improve the prediction model. The AL process is applied iteratively and more instances are presented for labelling until the performance of a model trained on labelled instances reaches a predetermined level or there

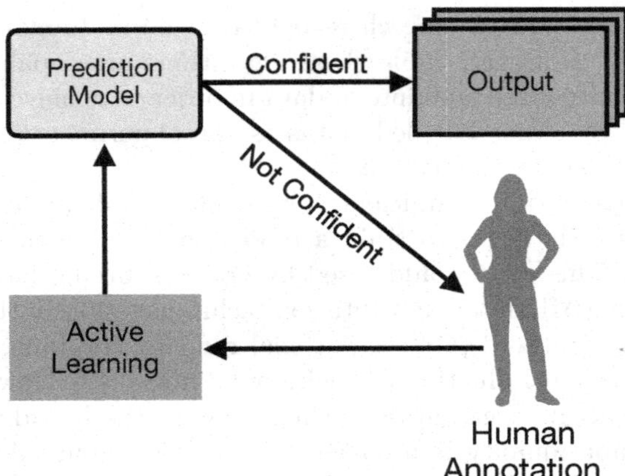

Fig. 1. An outline of the Active Learning process. The confidence of a prediction model (USAL) is one method of selecting instances for labelling. A feature space exploration technique (EGAL) will also be explored.

are no more instances to label. The objective is to use minimal manual effort to label the entire dataset to a high level of accuracy.

Two selection strategies are investigated in the following. The first of these is the most commonly used method, USAL, a model-based approach which uses uncertainty in model prediction as a metric to select instances for labelling. It has used in a variety of audio applications including environmental sound classification [20], bird sound categorization [47] and speech emotion recognition [65]. The hypothesis behind USAL holds that the instances about which the classifier is most confident will provide the least useful information and that the instances most difficult to categorize will be more informative, allowing greater accuracy from fewer manually applied labels. It therefore selects these instances for labelling first. Uncertainty can be identified in different ways. The least confident method ranks classification confidence based on the best prediction and takes the lowest ranking instance for labelling. An entropy measure can also be used to assess the average information content of an instance. The margin method is employed in this case, which ranks instances by their proximity to a classifier decision boundary, presenting those closest for labelling as they are the instances most difficult to categorize. This model-based approach is computationally expensive as it requires a model to be built at each iteration which can be time consuming and may not be practical for some applications.

The EGAL selection strategy addresses this shortcoming by eschewing use of a model and identifying useful instances for classification purposes in relation to their location in the feature space relative to neighbouring instances and proximity to already labelled instances. This can be expected to reduce the computational overhead and time required to label a corpus of instances compared to a model-based technique such as USAL as there is no need to retrain a model for each iteration. EGAL has been used in text classification applications [24] but to our knowledge this is the first application of this technique to an audio problem. The algorithm seeks to identify instances in clusters that are furthest from labelled instances on the assumption that dense clusters which are diverse from labelled instances will be most informative for classification purposes. This is implemented by first calculating a *density* value per instance, defined as the sum of similarities between the instance and all other instances within a certain radius. Here, the inverse of Euclidean distance is used for this measure. Secondly, a *diversity* value is calculated by measuring the distance between labelled and unlabelled instances.

3 Methodology

Audio stimuli and label collection methods used in a subjective labelling exercise are described in Sect. 3.1. Feature extraction and data preparation are covered in Sect. 3.2 and classifier choice is outlined in Sect. 3.3. A cross validation experiment investigating feature representations and classifiers is outlined in Sect. 3.4. The Python language was used for implementation using the associated Scikit-learn [42], SciPy [30] and Pandas [38] libraries.

3.1 Dataset

The ESC datasets [43] have been compiled from the Freesound website (*freesound.org*) for use in computational audio scene analysis contexts for training and testing automatic classification of sounds. They have been selected in this instance as they provide a large bank (>250,000) of potential stimuli with associated sound class metadata. Dataset recordings are of approximately 5 s duration and are provided in stereo at a sample rate of 44.1 kHz. In excess of 20,000 sounds were reviewed by the authors for suitability of use in this study with care taken to exclude sounds which evinced more than one sound event in order to provide a corpus of stimuli isolated from context in so far as this is possible. This resulted in the selection of 10,166 sounds as suitable for inclusion as they did not evince more than one audio 'object'.

A random selection of these sounds were used in a subjective labelling exercise carried out by participants from Xperi/DTS Inc. and from researchers in the School of Media, Technological University Dublin. The labelling environment was deployed using a website because this facilitates access for a physically distributed cohort of participants. As discussed in Sect. 2.1 auditory hierarchy categorisation concerns perception on a macro rather than a micro level so participants were asked to label sounds using headphones in a quiet environment accepting a variance in acoustic rendering in favor of maximising participant numbers. Presentation order was randomised using random orders were sourced from *random.org*, a source for true random sequences cited in a number of peer-reviewed publications [19] in order to ensure there was no imbalance in sound class representation for each labelling session. In all, 3,002 sounds were labelled a minimum of 3 times on a FG, Neutral, BG scale by 149 participants (73% male, 7% 18–24, 49% 25–44). An average of 83.42 sounds were rated per participant with each given the opportunity to rate 100 stimuli. The average time taken to complete the rating process excluding outliers >1 h in duration was 19 min 54 s. The numerical coding for each category (BG - 1, N - 2, FG - 3) was used to generate mean and standard deviation scores for each sound. For illustrative purposes the sounds are organized into 12 broad classes as outlined in Table 1 which reproduces the average rating score and standard deviation per class.

Table 1. A summary of instance count, average score and standard deviation (σ) per class for all 3,002 sounds rated. The highest occurrences are reproduced in **bold**, lowest are underlined.

Class	No.	Average score	σ
Nature	**523**	1.655	0.578
Ambience	507	1.477	0.504
Animal	408	2.121	0.569
Urban	370	1.382	0.437
Machine	285	1.941	0.585
Human	266	2.131	0.461
Other	226	2.325	0.564
Domestic	145	2.307	0.527
Travel	115	1.285	0.356
Actions	67	2.269	0.573
Alarms	55	**2.535**	0.41
Bells	35	2.41	**0.715**

This table shows that sounds such as 'Alarms' are likely to be labelled as FG. Sounds categorised as 'Travel' are most likely to be labelled BG reflecting the interior public transport hum ambience present in many of these sounds. Standard deviation per sound class varies between 0.41 and 0.715. The variance in average rating is outlined in the boxplots reproduced in Fig. 2 and this gives an indication of the variance in the data which in this instance shows the degree of subject consensus on BG - Neutral - FG sounds.

For illustrative purposes the sounds were organised into three average rating score bands. There are 1,156 instances with an average rating of 1.5 or under, designated BG sounds. There are 608 sounds with an average rating of >2.5 and these are designated FG sounds. The remaining 1,238 sounds have an average rating >1.5 & <2.5 and are referred to as neutral sounds. The width of each box plot is proportionate to the number of instances summarized in each rating band.

Similar to other research [10] a greater consensus is noted among subjects as regards sounds considered most FG or most BG; There is less variance in

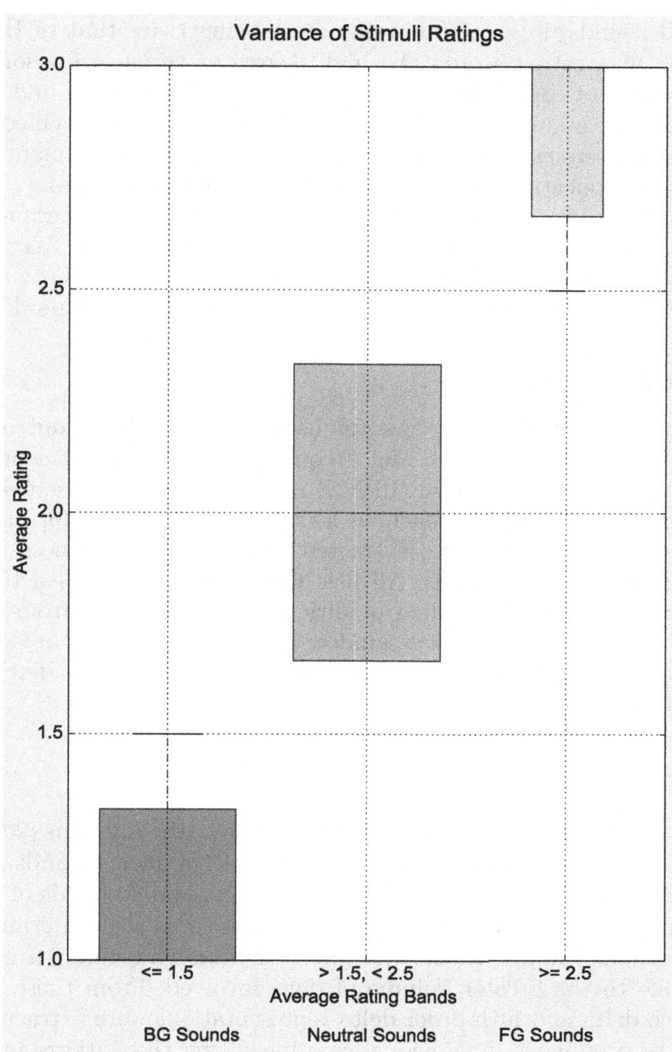

Fig. 2. Boxplots outlining the variance in average sound ratings grouped in broad bands. Note that the minimum average score for BG sounds is 1, hence there is no quartile or minimum whisker below this value. Similarly, the maximum average score for FG sounds is 3, hence this band has no quartile or maximum whisker above this value. Also, the width of each boxplot is proportional to the number of instances summarised in each band.

the ratings for these bands than those sounds considered Neutral. Interquartile range for both FG and BG bands is approximately 0.33 of a rating score. Neutral sounds on the other hand exhibit greater variance in rating scores compared to

BG and FG sounds, interquartile range here being twice that of BG and FG sounds, 0.67 of a rating score. The high degree of variance for some sounds, indicating a lack of consensus between subjects as to correct sound class, is to be expected with a subjective labelling task and the dataset evinces disagreement between raters as to the correct hierarchical category for many instances. The proposed application of a variable compression codec suggests a priority of identifying FG sounds so for the purposes of the following experiments it was decided to address the data as a binary classification problem. Accordingly, all sounds achieving an average score ≥2.5 (608 instances, 20.25%) are categorized as 'FG'. All others (2,394 instances, 79.7%) are categorized as 'nonFG' sounds.

3.2 Feature Extraction

The Python LibROSA [37] package was used to extract three different feature vectors for each audio stimulus. Mel Frequency Cepstral Coefficients (MFCC) and Log Power Mel Spectrogram (LPMS) representations were extracted based on their popularity in audio machine learning applications [46] and a Chromagram representation was also extracted based on its usefulness in previous experiments by the authors [11]. All files were first downsampled to 16kHz to account for the variable recording quality of sounds sourced from Freesound, such as the ESC datasets. A Hann window of the form outlined in Eq. 1, (where $n =$ sample number, $M =$ the number of points in the output window) is used to extract audio data.

$$w(n) = 0.5 - 0.5cos\left(\frac{2\pi n}{M-1}\right),\ 0 \leq n \leq M-1 \tag{1}$$

In line with similar experiments [14,49] a window size of 128 ms (2048 samples at 16 kHz) and stride of 32 ms was used to extract 12 frequency bands of Chromagram, 13 bands of zero-order MFCC feature vectors and 40 bands of LPMS features. A representation of 128 bands of LPMS data was also experimented with but no performance improvement was observed although training time increased markedly due to the greater volume of data involved. From these zero-order, delta, double delta and fifth-order delta representations were extracted as delta features were prominent in previous experiments by the authors investigating hierarchical categorization [11]. All data is scaled and bands from each data matrix are flattened and organized into 12 data subsets, 4 each for the MFCC, Chroma and LPMS data, a summary of which is presented in Table 2.

3.3 Classifier

A Support Vector Machine (SVM) classifier is used as it has been used extensively on audio ML applications [6,55,56]. SVMs aim to find the optimal hyperplane which separates instances by maximising the margin of distance from hyperplane to data point [12]. A number of different kernels can be used with a SVM. Here, three are investigated: the Radial Basis Function (RBF), Polynomial and Linear kernels.

Table 2. A summary of feature representation data vectors and their dimensions. For each representation (MFCC, Chroma & LPMS) zero-order and 1st, 2nd and 5th order delta vectors are computed, resulting in a total of 12 initial representations.

Type	Dimensions	Flattened dimensions
MFCC	$3002 \times 13 \times 156$	$3002 \times 2,028$
Chroma	$3002 \times 12 \times 156$	$3002 \times 1,872$
LPMS	$3002 \times 40 \times 156$	$3002 \times 6,240$

3.4 Cross Validation Experiment

In a preliminary experiment optimal feature representation for distinguishing between FG and nonFG sounds and which SVM kernel works best on this data is investigated. A SVM with three different kernels (RBF, polynomial and linear) is applied using default parameters outlined in Table 3. Class weights are adjusted to penalise mistakes inversely proportional to the number of instances in each class to adjust for the class imbalance in the dataset. Results showed that extracted delta representations give no improvement on zero-order representations and so these were discarded. Average Class Accuracy (ACA) and single class accuracy scores per kernel and representation are provided in Table 4.

Table 3. Default parameters used per kernel in the initial classification exercise. The 'scale' value for the gamma parameter uses $1/(no.features * variance)$ as value of gamma.

Kernel	Parameters
Radial Basis Function	C = 1, gamma = 'scale'
Linear	C = 1
Polynomial	C = 1, degree = 3, gamma = 'scale'

In addition to MFCC, Chroma and LPMS zero-order representations one further representation, a concatenation of these three, was investigated. This is labelled the 'All' representation in Table 4. Marginally better performance was observed using the 'All' representation at the cost of a significant increase in time taken to run the analysis due to its larger size. The MFCC and LPMS representations performed similarly to the 'All' representation, while the Chroma representation was notably poorer. It was decided to proceed with the LPMS representation as it performed slightly better than the MFCC and takes significantly less time to train than the 'All' representation, while achieving scores only slightly lower. With regard to kernel choice, RBF and polynomial kernels were observed to perform more strongly than the linear kernel. The overall difference between RBF and polynomial was marginal so the RBF kernel was selected as it is more commonly used [40].

Table 4. Average Class Accuracy (ACA), and Class Accuracy scores for FG and nonFG classes per kernel and feature representation. The 'All' representation is a concatenation of the other 3 representations.

Kernel	Measure	MFCC	Chroma	LPMS	All
RBF	ACA	72.2%	65.7%	73.9%	74.3%
	FG	67.3%	53.6%	67.1%	69.7%
	nonFG	77.2%	77.8%	80.7%	78.9%
Linear	ACA	63.9%	53.1%	63.1%	60.3%
	FG	45.9%	31.9%	38.5%	35.9%
	nonFG	81.9%	74.3%	87.8%	84.8%
Polynomial	ACA	72.4%	63.0%	73.4%	74.4%
	FG	66.6%	61.0%	69.1%	70.1%
	nonFG	78.3%	65.0%	77.7%	78.7%

Parameters were fitted for the RBF kernel to the LPMS representation using a grid search and a separate validation set of 20% of the dataset within a 5-fold cross validation. The ACA achieved was 76.9% which provides a point of comparison with ACA scores achieved using minimal labelled instances during AL labelling.

3.5 Active Learning Process

As 3,002 instances were pre-labelled as described in Sect. 3.1, a simulated labelling exercise was conducted to assess AL for auditory hierarchy, extracting a stratified, randomly selected hold-out test set of 501 instances to measure performance. The remaining 2,501 instances form the pool of 'unlabelled' examples. Due to the random nature of the hold-out test set and 'unlabelled' pool three random splits are formed in total to counteract the chance of a single iteration providing a misleading result. The results reported are therefore averages over 3 iterations.

To select the first set of instances agglomerative clustering was employed on the 'unlabelled' pool to form 5 distinct clusters and then select an initial batch of 10 instances as this has been shown to be an effective way to initiate AL [24, 25]. During labelling runs Average Class Accuracy (ACA) was used to measure performance due to the imbalanced class distribution. The initial instances are labelled, a model was trained on them and an ACA score calculated on the hold-out test set. The selection method was then used to pick the next batch of 10 instances from the 'unlabelled' pool, these were labelled, added to the other labelled instances and a new accuracy score calculated on the hold-out test set. This process continued until there were no more instances left to be 'labelled'. The ACA values were used to plot a learning curve which was then used to compare methods both visually and with an Area Under the Learning Curve

(AULC) value. As a baseline a random selection strategy was also implemented which does not seek to intelligently select instances for labelling.

4 Results

An overview of USAL and EGAL selection methods has previously been offered in Sect. 2.3. These methods are now applied to the selected representation to identify which is most effective in terms of identifying the minimal number of instances for manual labelling that allow a model to classify to high accuracy levels. In total five selection methods are investigated:

- USAL, which uses a SVM to identify the instances closest to the classification decision boundary.
- Diversity EGAL, which uses the diversity measure from EGAL to select instances that are most diverse from already labelled instances.
- Density EGAL, which uses the density measure from EGAL to select cluster centroids from the most densely populated areas of the feature space.
- Hybrid EGAL, which combines density and diversity EGAL measures to select cluster centroids that are most diverse from already labelled instances.
- Random selection, selects instances randomly. 3 random selection runs are executed to account for randomness.

Figure 3 shows results of labelling runs from 10 to eventually 2,501 'labelled' instances. It includes a shaded area that denotes the maximum and minimum values achieved by random selection for each batch which demonstrates large variance.

The EGAL runs are noticeably strongest early in the training runs, all quickly achieving scores in excess of 70% accuracy. USAL does not match this performance and indeed is surprisingly, given the effectiveness of the method in other domains [52], less effective than Random selection apart from the earliest section of the run under 70 labels. There is considerable variance between the maximum and minimum scores from the random selection method showing that this is not a reliable method for selection in this application. Figure 4 focuses on the early portion of the labelling run which tracks scores achieved between 0–500 labels.

This highlights the success of diversity EGAL, which achieves 74% ACA using only 50 labels. The other EGAL variants are fractionally behind this early result, but perform similarly up to approximately 120 labels with the performance of density EGAL being notably strong beyond this point. The random selection strategy does not improve on the accuracy level of diversity EGAL at 50 labels until it is provided 350 labels. USAL requires 1,410 labels to achieve the same. Table 5 offers a summary of ACA and AULC scores at different points from each labelling run.

Given the ACA achieved on the whole dataset is 76.9% across 5 stratified folds, the score of 74% from 50 labels is a strong result, meaning that AL in this instance can achieve 96.1% of total possible model accuracy using only 1.7% of

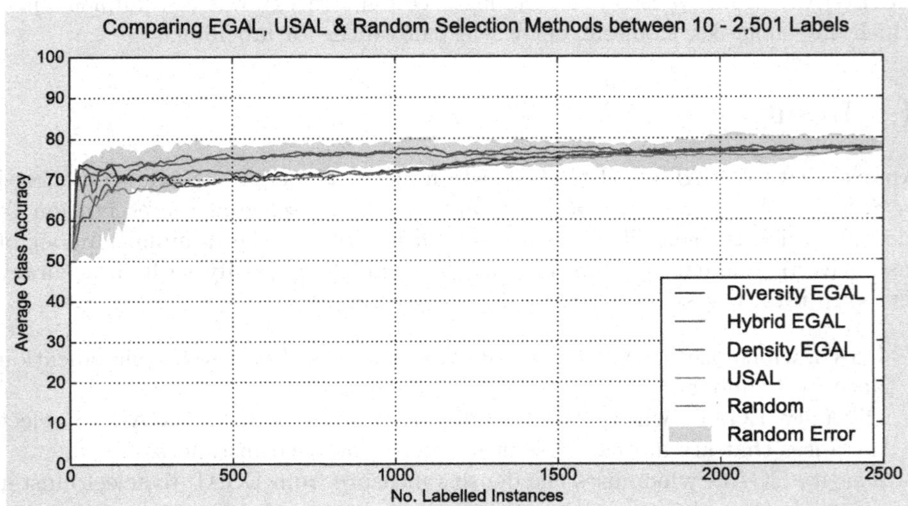

Fig. 3. Comparison of Active Learning selection methods displaying ACA scores (Balanced Accuracy) achieved from 10–2,501 labels. Each line denotes the overall average score for each method per batch. The shaded area denotes the variance observed from the random selection method.

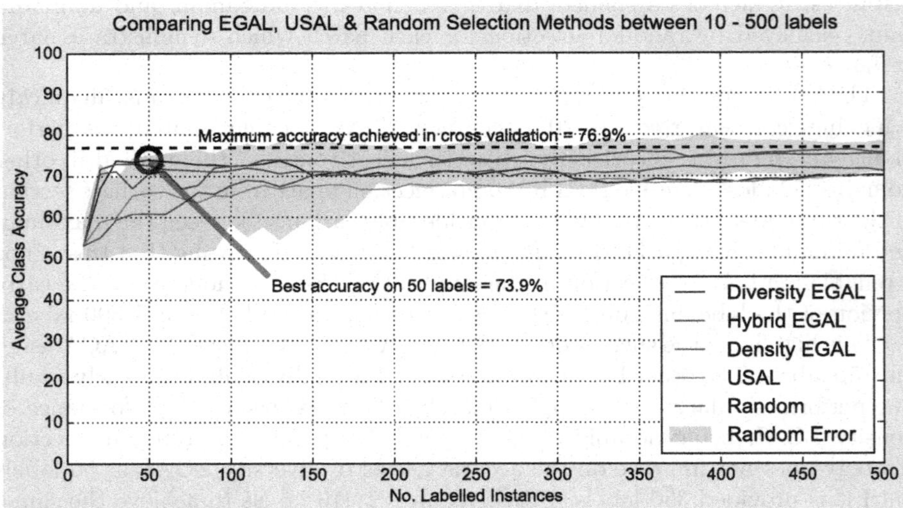

Fig. 4. Comparison of selection methods for early stage (between 0 and 500 labels) Active Learning runs. Each line denotes the overall average score for each method per batch. The shaded area denotes the variance observed from the random selection method.

Table 5. A summary of model accuracy and AULC scores for points in the labelling run per AL method. Using Diversity EGAL it is possible to achieve high classification accuracy (74%) relative to the model maximum using minimal manual labelling (50 labels) on this dataset.

Method	50	100	200	500	2501
	Average class accuracy scores				
Diversity EGAL	74.0%	72.5%	70.3%	70.2%	77.5%
Hybrid EGAL	72.7%	71.4%	70.5%	71.1%	77.5%
Density EGAL	70.7%	72.4%	73.8%	75.6%	77.5%
USAL	66.0%	65.2%	67.0%	70.1%	77.5%
Random	60.9%	67.8%	72.6%	75.4%	77.5%
	AULC scores				
Diversity EGAL	20.4	57.1	128.9	338.4	1838.2
Hybrid EGAL	20.8	56.7	127.7	341.6	1845.2
Density EGAL	20.2	54.9	128.2	353.3	1900.8
USAL	17.8	50.4	117.5	323.1	1808.6
Random	17.2	48.6	117.9	340.4	1877.5

labels. As noted, using random selection 350 labels, or 11.7% of the total, is required to improve on this accuracy level.

For statistical analysis the Friedman test was used to compare more than two samples with the Wilcoxon signed-rank test used as a post-hoc test between pairs of samples. In the case of the Wilcoxon test a Bonferroni correction was applied to the significance level in order to reduce the Type I error rate (identifying a significant effect where there is none) [15]. This resulted in a revised significance level of 0.005 for the post-hoc Wilcoxon tests as 10 comparisons were made. Additionally for the Wilcoxon test runs which have 20 measurements are compared as comparisons below this point are not recommended due to sample size [30]. The Friedman and Wilcoxon are non-parametric tests that look for differences between related samples and are noted to be a safer option than using parametric tests as they do not assume normal distributions or homogeneity of variance [13].

A Friedman test on the AL ACA values up to 200 labels provided is significant at the 95% level ($p = 8.03E\text{-}10$). The Wilcoxon tests reveal that the differences between EGAL variants are not significant to the revised significance level. However, the differences between EGAL and USAL, and between EGAL and Random selection methods are significant to the revised significance level. This indicates that EGAL is superior to both USAL and Random selection at selecting instances on which a classifier can be built to achieve high accuracy levels with minimal labelling. These results also suggest that there is little difference between the EGAL variants in this instance, as the results of the Wilcoxon comparisons between EGAL runs are not significant.

5 Discussion

This research has explored a series of Active Learning approaches to an auditory hierarchy labelling problem. It has been found that in this instance it is possible to classify to 96.1% of maximum model accuracy by labelling only 1.7% of dataset instances using the EGAL selection method. Using a random selection strategy it is necessary to select 350 instances (11.7% of the total) to surpass this accuracy level, however, as noted the large variance observed in scores from using the random selection strategy makes this an unreliable method in this instance. These results suggest EGAL is an effective method to minimise the manual effort required to label audio instances with hierarchical labels.

DL techniques are acknowledged as state-of-the-art in the audio classification domain [8] but are limited in terms of application to specific problems by the existence of suitable, large, appropriately labelled datasets. In a real-world scenario where potentially millions of labelled instances are required for DL applications the performance of EGAL in this instance suggests a potential for significant savings on manual labelling effort in both time and money terms for many different audio ML problems based on subjective human perception and evaluation of environmental sounds.

This is particularly interesting given the significance accorded to the emergence of datasets of this scale in other domains. For instance, the existence of ImageNet [27], consisting of over 14 million labelled images, is considered an important factor in the success of computer vision techniques and the influence of the DL methods applied to them [46]. While a number of large audio datasets are available [2,33,39] they are not universally appropriate for all audio ML problems, particularly those where subjective judgement is required. Therefore, the ability to quickly and efficiently take existing sound corpora and label them for a bespoke categorization tasks has the potential to facilitate the study of many more specific questions than would be the case if datasets were restricted to those consisting of manually labelled instances. Auditory hierarchy applied to the concept of a variable compression codec is one example of such a task.

6 Future Work

Our intention is to use these methods to label a large corpus and build a DL classifier to improve classification accuracy on hierarchically labelled audio data, ultimately validating machine labelled instances with human subjects. This extended corpus will also be suitable for use in deeper investigations on the functioning of auditory hierarchy which has been noted in Sect. 2.1 to be influenced by a series of factors such as sound context, the experience level of the subject and the physical characteristics of the sound itself. Having in-depth knowledge of the functioning of auditory hierarchy has application to media file delivery strategies, auto-mixing applications and object-based audio broadcasting scenarios.

Further combinations of AL methods with Self Learning elements, where labels are assigned to instances based on predictions from a model, or the concept of Co-Training, where labels are derived via a combination of prediction and selection methods on different feature representations may also lead to improvements.

References

1. Amazon Echo (2nd generation) – Alexa Speaker. https://www.amazon.com/all-new-amazon-echo-speaker-with-wifi-alexa-dark-charcoal/dp/B06XCM9LJ4. Accessed 27 Aug 2018
2. AudioSet. https://research.google.com/audioset/ontology/index.html. Accessed 27 Aug 2018
3. Aytar, Y., Vondrick, C., Torralba, A.: SoundNet: learning sound representations from unlabeled video. In: 30th Conference on Neural Information Processing Systems (NIPS 2016), Barcelona, Spain, 5–10 December 2016, pp. 892–900 (2016)
4. Bates, E., Gorzel, M., Ferguson, L., O'Dwyer, H., Boland, F.M.: Comparing ambisonic microphones: Part 1. In: 2016 AES International Conference on Sound Field Control, Guildford, UK, no. 6–3, pp. 1–10. AES (2016)
5. Bigand, E., Poulin-Charronnat, B.: Are we "experienced listeners"? A review of the musical capacities that do not depend on formal musical training. Cognition **100**(2006), 100–130 (2006). https://doi.org/10.1016/j.cognition.2005.11.007
6. Bountourakis, V., Vrysis, L., Papanikolaou, G.: Machine learning algorithms for environmental sound recognition. In: Proceedings of the Audio Mostly 2015 on Interaction With Sound - (AM15), Thessaloniki, Greece, 07–09 October 2015, pp. 1–7 (2015). https://doi.org/10.1145/2814895.2814905
7. Bregman, A.S.: Auditory Scene Analysis: The Perceptual Organisation of Sound. The MIT Press, Cambridge (1990)
8. Cakir, E., et al.: Convolutional recurrent neural networks for polyphonic sound event detection. IEEE/ACM Trans. Audio Speech Lang. Process. (TASLP) **25**(6), 1291–1303 (2017)
9. Churnside, T.: Object-Based Broadcasting (2013). http://www.bbc.co.uk/rd/blog/2013-05-object-based-approach-to-broadcasting. Accessed 27 Oct 2017
10. Coleman, W., Cullen, C., Yan, M.: Categorisation of isolated sounds on a background - neutral - foreground scale. In: Proceedings of the 144th Convention of the Audio Engineering Society, Milan, Italy, 23–26 May 2018, pp. 1–9 (2018)
11. Coleman, W., Cullen, C., Yan, M., Delany, S.J.: A machine learning approach to hierarchical categorisation of auditory objects. J. Audio Eng. Soc. **68**(1/2), 48–56 (2020)
12. Cunningham, P., Cord, M., Delany, S.J.: Supervised learning. In: Cord, M., Cunningham, P. (eds.) Machine Learning Techniques for Multimedia. Cognitive Technologies, pp. 21–49. Springer, Heidelberg (2008). https://doi.org/10.1007/978-3-540-75171-7_2
13. Demšar, J.: Statistical comparisons of classifiers over multiple data sets. J. Mach. Learn. Res. **7**, 1–30 (2006)
14. Espi, M., Fujimoto, M., Kinoshita, K., Nakatani, T.: Exploiting spectro-temporal locality in deep learning based acoustic event detection. EURASIP J. Audio Speech Music Process. **2015**(1), 1–12 (2015). https://doi.org/10.1186/s13636-015-0069-2

15. Field, A.: Discovering Statistics Using SPSS, vol. 58, 3rd edn. SAGE Publications, London (2009). https://doi.org/10.1234/12345678
16. Google Home - Smart Speaker & Home Assistant - Google Store. https://store.google.com/product/google_home. Accessed 27 Aug 2018
17. Gruters, K.G., Murphy, D.L.K., Smith, D.W., Shera, C.A., Groh, J.M.: The eardrum moves when the eyes move: a multisensory effect on the mechanics of hearing. bioRxiv 156570 (2017). https://doi.org/10.1101/156570
18. Guastavino, C.: Everyday sound categorization. In: Virtanen, T., Plumbley, M.D., Ellis, D. (eds.) Computational Analysis of Sound Scenes and Events, pp. 183–213. Springer, Cham (2018). https://doi.org/10.1007/978-3-319-63450-0_7
19. Haahr, M., Haahr, S.: Random.org (2018). https://www.random.org/media/. Accessed 04 Jan 2018
20. Han, W., et al.: Semi-supervised active learning for sound classification in hybrid learning environments. PloS One **11**(9), e0162075 (2016)
21. Han, Y., Park, J.: Convolutional neural networks with binaural representations and background subtraction for acoustic scene classification. Technical report, DCASE2017 Challenge, Munich, Germany, 16th November, September 2017
22. Heittola, T.: Datasets - Toni Heittola. https://www.cs.tut.fi/~heittolt/datasets. Accessed 28 Aug 2019
23. Hinton, G., et al.: Deep neural networks for acoustic modeling in speech recognition: the shared views of four research groups. IEEE Signal Process. Mag. **29**(6), 82–97 (2012). https://doi.org/10.1109/MSP.2012.2205597
24. Hu, R., Delany, S.J., Mac Namee, B.: EGAL: exploration guided active learning for TCBR. In: Proceedings of ICCBR, Alessandria, Italy, 19–22 July 2010, pp. 156–170 (2010). https://doi.org/10.1007/978-3-642-14274-1_13
25. Hu, R., Mac Namee, B., Delany, S.J.: Off to a good start: using clustering to select the initial training set in active learning. In: Twenty-Third International FLAIRS Conference, Florida, 19–21 May 2010 (2010). https://doi.org/10.21427/D7Q89W
26. Huron, D.: Sweet Anticipation: Music and the Psychology of Expectation. The MIT Press, Cambridge (2006)
27. ImageNet. http://www.image-net.org/. Accessed 23 Sep 2019
28. International Telecommunication Union: ITU-R BS.1116-3, Methods for the Subjective Assessment of Small Impairments in Audio Systems. ITU-R Recommendation 1116-3 (2015)
29. International Telecommunication Union: ITU-R BS.1534-3, Method for the Subjective Assessment of Intermediate Quality Level of Audio Systems. ITU-R Recommendation 1534-3 (2015)
30. Jones, E., Oliphant, T., Peterson, P., et al.: SciPy: Open source scientific tools for Python (2001). http://www.scipy.org/
31. Lavandier, C., Defréville, B.: The contribution of sound source characteristics in the assessment of urban soundscapes. Acta Acustica united Acustica **92**, 912–921 (2006)
32. Lewis, J.W., Talkington, W.J., Tallaksen, K.C., Frum, C.A.: Auditory object salience: human cortical processing of non-biological action sounds and their acoustic signal attributes. Front. Syst. Neurosci. **6**, 1–15 (2012). https://doi.org/10.3389/fnsys.2012.00027
33. Linguistic Data Consortium. https://catalog.ldc.upenn.edu/. Accessed 23 Sep 2019
34. Malfante, M., Mars, J.I., Dalla Mura, M., Gervaise, C.: Automatic fish classification. J. Acoust. Soc. Am. **143**(5), 2834–2846 (2018). https://doi.org/10.1121/1.5036628

35. McAdams, S.: Recognition of sound sources and events. In: McAdams, S., Bigand, E. (eds.) Thinking in Sound: The Cognitive Psychology of Human Audition, pp. 146–198. Clarendon Press, Oxford (1993). chap. 6
36. McFee, B.: Statistical methods for scene and event classification. In: Virtanen, T., Plumbley, M.D., Ellis, D.P.W. (eds.) Computational Analysis of Sound Scenes and Events, 1st edn., pp. 103–146. Springer, Cham (2018). https://doi.org/10.1007/978-3-319-63450-0_5
37. Mcfee, B., et al.: librosa: audio and music signal analysis in Python. In: Proceedings of the 14th Python in Science Conference (SciPy 2015), Austin, USA, 6–12 July 2015 (2015)
38. Mckinney, W.: Data structures for statistical computing in Python. In: Proceedings of the 9th Python in Science Conference (SCIPY 2010), Austin, USA, 28 June–3 July 2010, p. 51 (2010)
39. Million Song Dataset. http://millionsongdataset.com/. Accessed 23 Sep 2019
40. Nisbet, R., Miner, G., Yale, K., Nisbet, R., Miner, G., Yale, K.: Advanced algorithms for data mining. In: Handbook of Statistical Analysis and Data Mining Applications, pp. 149–167. Academic Press (2018). https://doi.org/10.1016/B978-0-12-416632-5.00008-6
41. O'Neill, J., Jane Delany, S., MacNamee, B.: Model-free and model-based active learning for regression. In: Angelov, P., Gegov, A., Jayne, C., Shen, Q. (eds.) Advances in Computational Intelligence Systems. AISC, vol. 513, pp. 375–386. Springer, Cham (2017). https://doi.org/10.1007/978-3-319-46562-3_24
42. Pedregosa, F., et al.: Scikit-learn: machine learning in Python. J. Mach. Learn. Res. **12**, 2825–2830 (2011)
43. Piczak, K.J.: ESC: Dataset for Environmental Sound Classification (2015). https://doi.org/10.1145/2733373.2806390
44. Pollack, I., Pickett, J.: Cocktail party effect. J. Acoust. Soc. Am. **29**(11), 1262 (1957)
45. Pressnitzer, D., Graves, J., Chambers, C., de Gardelle, V., Egré, P.: Auditory perception: Laurel and Yanny together at last. Curr. Biol. **28**(13), R739–R741 (2018). https://doi.org/10.1016/j.cub.2018.06.002
46. Purwins, H., Li, B., Virtanen, T., Schlüter, J., Chang, S.Y., Sainath, T.: Deep learning for audio signal processing. J. Sel. Top. Signal Process. **13**(2), 206–219 (2019). https://doi.org/10.1109/JSTSP.2019.2908700
47. Qian, K., Zhang, Z., Baird, A., Schuller, B.: Active learning for bird sound classification via a Kernel-based extreme learning machine. J. Acoust. Soc. Am. **142**(4), 1796–1804 (2017). https://doi.org/10.1121/1.5004570
48. Sailor, H.B., Agrawal, D.M., Patil, H.A.: Unsupervised filterbank learning using convolutional restricted Boltzmann machine for environmental sound classification. In: Proceedings of Interspeech 2017, pp. 3107–3111 (2017)
49. Salamon, J., Bello, J.P.: Deep convolutional neural networks and data augmentation for environmental sound classification. IEEE Signal Process. Lett. **24**(3), 279–283 (2017)
50. Salamon, J., Jacoby, C., Bello, J.P.: A dataset and taxonomy for urban sound research. In: Proceedings of the ACM International Conference on Multimedia - MM 2014, Orlando, Florida, USA, 3–7 November 2014, pp. 1041–1044 (2014). https://doi.org/10.1145/2647868.2655045
51. Schröder, J., Moritz, N., Anemüller, J., Goetze, S., Kollmeier, B.: Classifier architectures for acoustic scenes and events: implications for DNNs, TDNNs, and perceptual features from DCASE 2016. IEEE/ACM Trans. Audio Speech Lang. Process. (2017). https://doi.org/10.1109/TASLP.2017.2690569

52. Settles, B.: Active learning. Synth. Lect. Artif. Intell. Mach. Learn. **6**(1), 1–114 (2012)
53. Soren, B.: Listening tests on loudspeakers: a discussion of experimental procedures and evaluation of the response data. In: Proceedings of the 8th International Conference of the Audio Engineering Society, Washington D.C., USA, May 1990 (1990)
54. Steffens, J., Steele, D., Guastavino, C.: Situational and person-related factors influencing momentary and retrospective soundscape evaluations in day-to-day life. J. Acoust. Soc. Am. **141**(3), 1414–1425 (2017). https://doi.org/10.1121/1.4976627
55. Thorogood, M., Fan, J., Pasquier, P.: Soundscape audio signal classification and segmentation using listener's perception of background and foreground sound. J. Audio Eng. Soc. **64**(7/8), 484–492 (2016). https://doi.org/10.17743/jaes.2016.0021
56. Torija, A.J., Ruiz, D.P., Ramos-Ridao, Á.F.: A tool for urban soundscape evaluation applying support vector machines for developing a soundscape classification model. Sci. Total Environ. **482–483**(1), 440–451 (2014). https://doi.org/10.1016/j.scitotenv.2013.07.108
57. Truax, B.: Acoustic Communication, 1st edn. Ablex Publishing Corporation, Norwood (1984)
58. Truax, B.: World Soundscape Project Tape Library (2015). http://www.sfu.ca/sonic-studio/srs/index2.html. Accessed 07 Mar 2017
59. Virtanen, T., Plumbley, M.D., Ellis, D. (eds.): Computational Analysis of Sound Scenes and Events. Springer, Cham (2018). https://doi.org/10.1007/978-3-319-63450-0
60. Virtanen, T., Plumbley, M.D., Ellis, D.P.W.: Introduction to sound scene and event analysis. In: Virtanen, T., Plumbley, M.D., Ellis, D.P.W. (eds.) Computational Analysis of Sound Scenes and Events, pp. 3–12. Springer, Cham (2018). https://doi.org/10.1007/978-3-319-63450-0_1
61. Wang, D., Chen, J.: Supervised speech separation based on deep learning: an overview. Computing Research Repository (CoRR) abs/1708.0 (2017)
62. Woodcock, J., Davies, W.J., Cox, T.J.: A cognitive framework for the categorisation of auditory objects in urban soundscapes. Appl. Acoust. **121**(2017), 56–64 (2017). https://doi.org/10.1016/j.apacoust.2017.01.027
63. Woods, K.J.P., McDermott, J.H.: Attentive tracking of sound sources. Curr. Biol. **25**(17), 2238–2246 (2015)
64. Yong Jeon, J., Jik Lee, P., Young Hong, J., Cabrera, D.: Non-auditory factors affecting urban soundscape evaluation. J. Acoust. Soc. Am. **130**(6), 3761–3770 (2011). https://doi.org/10.1121/1.3652902
65. Zhang, Z., Schuller, B.: Active learning by sparse instance tracking and classifier confidence in acoustic emotion recognition. In: 13th Annual Conference of the International Speech Communication Association (INTERSPEECH 2012), Portland, OR, USA, 9–13 September 2012, pp. 362–365 (2012)

Improving Short Text Classification Through Global Augmentation Methods

Vukosi Marivate[1,2(✉)] and Tshephisho Sefara[2]

[1] University of Pretoria, Pretoria, South Africa
vukosi.marivate@cs.up.ac.za
[2] Council for Scientific and Industrial Research, Pretoria, South Africa
tsefara@csir.co.za

Abstract. We study the effect of different approaches to text augmentation. To do this we use three datasets that include social media and formal text in the form of news articles. Our goal is to provide insights for practitioners and researchers on making choices for augmentation for classification use cases. We observe that Word2Vec-based augmentation is a viable option when one does not have access to a formal synonym model (like WordNet-based augmentation). The use of *mixup* further improves performance of all text based augmentations and reduces the effects of overfitting on a tested deep learning model. Round-trip translation with a translation service proves to be harder to use due to cost and as such is less accessible for both normal and low resource use-cases.

Keywords: Natural Language Processing · Data augmentation · Deep Neural Networks · Text classification

1 Introduction

In this paper, we look at data augmentation for Natural Language Processing (NLP) applications. Encouraged by the ever-present use of data augmentation in computer vision applications [4], we want to be able to provide researchers and practitioners with a better understanding of augmentation for NLP tasks. Augmentation has benefited many image classification tasks [4], the structure of images are changed in order to increase the number of samples available to the machine learning algorithm while introducing resilience in the final model. Augmentation of text data to be able to create robust models has had different factors of success. Some approaches require more direct information about the language at hand than others [20], while others are more agnostic given a learned language model that can be used [17].

Over the last few years, the development of distributed word representations (word embeddings) [22] has improved the modelling of semantic relations between words in a text. This has created many new approaches to understanding text, in the case of this work, text classification tasks. To improve the classification accuracy, as well as make models more robust, one can look at data

Published by Springer Nature Switzerland AG 2020
A. Holzinger et al. (Eds.): CD-MAKE 2020, LNCS 12279, pp. 385–399, 2020.
https://doi.org/10.1007/978-3-030-57321-8_21

augmentation as a way to improve performance and create robustness. More recently, the development of unsupervised language models [13,26], makes it possible for us to use more data-driven language models that can be combined with data augmentation methods to improve performance and robustness of machine learning models for NLP.

We are motivated by several factors. We would like to be able to train classification models that do not necessarily have a large amount of labelled data. Labelling of data comes at a cost. Whether it is for identifying fake news [18], understanding political phenomena [29], feedback on government services [31], or better coordination during emergencies [14], getting labels is always challenging. As such, knowing that building machine learning models requires a large amount of data, we need to still be able to build models with smaller data. A large organisation might have access to large data sets as well as resources to label a large chunk of it. A smaller organisation tends to not have large data and fewer resources to label. To extend the use of the classifiers further than the distribution of information fed into it, we need to be able to change the input data in a way that makes the final learned model more robust to slight changes in the input distribution. This could be caused by the evolution of language or even geographical changes. Another use is in semi-supervised learning, where we use the few labels we have to create a classifier (that is likely noisy) to label more unlabelled data and then feed this back to train another classifier.

Our contributions, in this paper, is a short survey of several data augmentation methods, specifically looking at methods that augment data with more of a global view. That is, the schemes replace words that are used similarly from a global view instead of a contextually local view. So how are similar words used across texts, instead of what might be the best word to replace in this specific sentence in this specific document? We discuss methods that use linguistic features, a model that uses a translation service and then augmentation methods that act on embeddings/language models. To better understand the behaviour of the augmentation methods, we evaluate the approaches on several classification datasets under several conditions and provide insights into the different approaches. We also show the effect of the *mixup* [36] method on NLP tasks as an augmentation approach. This paper is organised as follows; We cover different text augmentation methods first. The approach in our comparative study is described in Sect. 3. Section 4 discusses the experimental results and then we conclude in Sect. 5.

2 Augmentation Methods for Text

For many machine learning tasks, data augmentation has been employed as a regularisation method while training supervised machine learning models. The more diverse examples fed to the model during training, the better the model generalises, and consequently, the better they predict when presented with new examples. Data augmentation is famously used in images, audio and more recently in text [4,16,21]. In this section, we describe prior approaches to text augmentation.

For our work, we categorise text augmentation techniques into two categories. Namely, *augmentation on text source* and *augmentation on text representation*. In the rest of this section, we discuss methods that fall in either of these categories. A summary of the methods we discuss in this section is shown in Table 1 and Fig. 1 illustrates how these methods augment data.

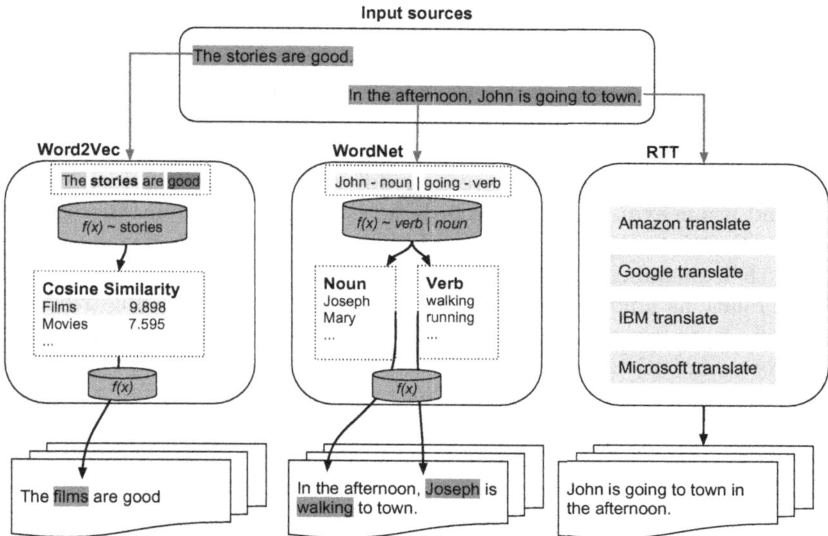

Fig. 1. Overview of augmentation structures

Table 1. Augmentation techniques

Method	Category: Augmentation on	Labels	Linguistics	Semantic
Synonyms from WordNet [37]	*text source*	No	Yes	Yes
Words from Word2Vec [17]	*text source*	No	Yes	Yes
Round-trip Translation [19,32]	*text source*	No	Yes	Yes
mixup [36]	*text representation*	Yes	No	No

2.1 Augmentation on Source Text

Augmenting textual data requires language modelling rules, written by linguistic experts, which are limited for low-resource languages. The alternative way is to use a dictionary/thesaurus or database of synonyms to make word replacements.

In a situation where there is no dictionary, the other way is to use distributed word representation where semantically similar words are identified together. In this subsection, we present how word replacements and sentence paraphrasing can be used as augmentation techniques.

Synonym Augmentation. We first begin with methods that use linguistic features. The best way to augment data is by using human rephrasing of sentences, but this is expensive. Therefore, the most natural option in data augmentation for most authors is to replace words or phrases with their synonyms. Verbs and nouns are the best name classes to have synonyms in various contexts. The popular open-source lexical database for the English language is WordNet [23]. It groups words like nouns, verbs, adjectives and adverbs into sets of cognitive synonyms called *synsets* each expressing different concept, provides short definitions and usage examples, and records several relations among these synonym sets. WordNet thus superficially resembles a thesaurus in that it groups words based on their meanings. However, with the distinction that WordNet labels the semantic relations among words and it interlinks word forms and strings of letters specific to senses of words resulting in words found close to one another in the network semantically disambiguated. A good illustration of synonym augmentation is shown in Fig. 1 as WordNet.

The thesaurus-based augmentation method has been applied to training a Siamese adaptation of the Long Short-Term Memory (LSTM) network to assess the semantic similarity between sentences [24]. Zhang *et al.* [37] used a WordNet-based augmentation method to augment their training data by using a Geometric function to help select words from a given dataset, using the selected words to find their synonyms to train a temporal convolutional network that learns text understanding from character level input up to abstract text concepts.

Semantic Similarity Augmentation. Using distributed word representation (word embeddings) [22], one can identify semantically similar words [17]. This approach requires either pre-trained word embedding models for the language at hand or enough data from the target application to be able to build the embedding model. This approach thus does not require access to a dictionary or thesaurus for a language to find synonyms. This can benefit languages where such resources might be harder to obtain but there might be enough unsupervised text data to be able to build the embedding models. With recent advances in building complete language models [7,10,26,27], further advances can be made to identify syntactic and semantic similarity for word augmentation.

For this paper, we are not exploring the use of language models. One can view language models as enabling a more localised replacement of words given the local context in the sentence. On the other hand, word embeddings give a global context. Language Models such as that by [7] allow the filling in of blanks in any part of a sentence. While other language models can be more used to fill in the *next* missing word in a sentence [27], reading a sentence left to right then filling in the missing word at the end. This exploration remains an area of future work.

Round-Trip Translation. Round-trip translation (RTT) is also known as recursive, back-and-forth, and bi-directional translation. It is the process of translating a word, phrase or text into another language (forward translation), then translating the results back into the original language (back translation) [1]. RTT can be used as an augmentation technique to increase the training data. An example is shown in Fig. 1. Fadaee *et al.* [9] used a method called translation data augmentation that uses rare word substitution to augment data for low-resourced neural machine translation (NMT). Their method augments both the source and target sentence to create a new pair preserving the meaning of the sentence. They proposed a weaker notion of label preservation that allows alteration of sentence pairs as long as the sentences remain translations of each other.

Sennrich *et al.* [32] used back translation as a data augmentation method to leverage the target monolingual data. In their method, both the NMT model and training algorithm are kept unaltered, and they employed back translation to construct training data. That is, target monolingual sentences are translated with an existing machine translation system into source language, that is used as additional parallel data to retrain the source-to-target NMT model. Aroyehun and Gelbukh [2] used English RTT on four intermediate languages (French, Spanish, German, and Hindi) that increased the size of their training set by a factor of 5. This method improved the performance of their model for identification of aggression in social media posts. Although back-translation has been proven to be effective and robust [2], one major problem for further improvement is the quality of automatically generated training data from monolingual sentences. Some of the incorrect translations are very likely to decrease the performance of a source-to-target model due to the deficiency of a machine translation system.

2.2 Augmentation on Representation

Augmentation on source text requires that we can have access to a method to replace words in the source text to create more examples while at the same time keeping the meaning of the full sentence the same. In this subsection, we present a method that was introduced as a regularisation technique on Deep Neural Networks but can be viewed as an augmentation that instead acts on the text representation. We discuss *mixup* which acts both on the input and the outputs.

***mixup* Augmentation.** *mixup*, introduced in [36] can be seen as an augmentation method that can be classified as *augmentation on representation*. *mixup* is data agnostic and is applied to images, speech and tabular data in the original paper [36]. *mixup* creates new training examples by drawing samples (sets of two or more) from the original data and combining them convexly. It combines the data both in terms of the input and output. The simplest implementation, which the authors suggest, creates a new augmented dataset by taking pairs of samples from the initial dataset and convexly summing both the input and output. That is, given two examples $(X_1, y_1), (X_2, y_2)$, where X is the input vector and y is the one-hot encoded labels, we construct a new example:

$$\hat{X} = \lambda X_1 + (1 - \lambda)X_2$$

$$\hat{y} = \lambda y_1 + (1 - \lambda)y_2$$

where $\lambda \in [\,0, 1]$ and is drawn from Beta distribution, $\lambda = \beta(\alpha, \alpha)$, α is set [36]. It is somewhat akin to soft-labelling but is best suited for learning algorithms that use the cross-entropy loss and also changes the input. The standard method is used for classification problems (it remains further work to explore the uses for regression). For text problems, augmentation by *mixup* can be done on the text representation. As such we can use *mixup* with bag-of-words models, TFIDF [28], word embeddings and language models.

3 Method and Approach

Our goal is to measure the impact of augmentation methods on the performance of classification algorithms. We compare methods across different datasets and on a level, as possible, playing field. It is important to do this so that insights can be used by other researchers as they build tools for different classification problems in text. We first describe the data we will use for classification, then the learning algorithms we will be using, and finally the last subsection details the experiments we will perform to test the augmentation approaches to better understand their strengths and limitations.

3.1 Data

The data we will use is from three different datasets that represent different challenges with text. For short text, we use the Sentiment 140 data set [11] as well as the Hate Speech data set [6]. For longer text, we use the AG News data set used in [37]. The Sentiment 140 uses noisy labelling [11] in the form of weak supervision to label the training data. The Hate Speech dataset uses human-annotated labels. Even though the Sentiment 140 has a separate test set that is made up of human-annotated labels, we will first focus on splitting the original data. The data is summarised in Table 2.

Table 2. Summary of data

Data source	Words	Approx. sentences	Avg number of words	Labels
Sentiment 140	18M	2M	13	Binary
AG News	3M	154K	31	Categorical
Hate Speech	243K	24K	14	Categorical

3.2 Augmentation Algorithms

We augment each data set using four types of augmentation methods: WordNet-based augmentation, Word2Vec-based augmentation, Round-trip translation as well as *mixup*. The first three methods augment data on text and can be combined with *mixup* which augments data on the fly. As part of this paper, we also release a library that allows the use of all text-based augmentation methods.[1]

WordNet-Based Synonym Augmentation. WordNet-based augmentation is a type of augmentation that randomly selects r words from a sentence (if they exist) using any distribution. To decide on which words to replace, we selected replaceable words like verbs, nouns, and the combination of them using a part-of-speech tagger implemented in the natural language toolkit (NLTK) [3] from a given text and randomly selects r of them. The probability of r is calculated by a Geometric distribution $P[r] \sim p^r$ where parameter p is the probability of success. The synonym s chosen given a word is also determined by another Geometric distribution in which $P[s] \sim p^s$ using the same probability of success $p = 0.5$ [37]. The new sentence is constructed by replacing the selected verb or noun with their synonyms. The algorithm has options to choose to augment using either verbs or nouns or even a combination. We report the results choosing the outcome of p on the first trial.

Word2Vec-Based (Learned Semantic Similarity) Augmentation. Word2Vec is another robust augmentation method that uses a word embedding model [22] trained on the public dataset to find the most similar words for a given input word. We use both a pretrained Wikipedia Word2Vec model for formal text. For social media data, we convert a GloVe model, pretrained on Twitter data, to Word2Vec format using Gensim [30]. We load the converted models in our algorithm to augment data by randomly selecting a word in a sentence to determine its similar words using cosine similarity. To select a similar word, we use the cosine similarity as a relative weight to select a similar word that replaces the input word. Our algorithm is illustrated in Algorithm 1, it receives a string and an integer where the string is an input data and the integer represents the number of repetitions to augment a given input data. The advantage of Word2Vec is that it tends to produce vectors that are more topically related, in other words, it allows words with similar meaning to have similar representation.

Round Trip Translation (RTT) Augmentation. We implement RTT augmentation using Google translation services[2] as well as Amazon translate[3]. We translate text in English to a target language then back to English. To measure

[1] https://github.com/dsfsi/textaugment.
[2] http://translate.google.com.
[3] https://aws.amazon.com/translate/.

Algorithm 1: Word2Vec-based augmentation algorithm [34].

Input: s: a sentence, run: a number
Output: $\hat{s}$ a sentence with words replaced

def Augment(s,run):
  Let $\vec{V}$ be a vocabulary;
  for i **in** range(run) :
    $w_i \leftarrow$ randomly select a word from s;
    $\vec{w} \leftarrow$ find similar words of w_i;
    $s_0 \leftarrow$ randomly select a word from $\vec{w}$ given weights as distance;
    $\hat{s} \leftarrow$replace w_i with similar word s_0;
  return($\hat{s}$);

the effect of RTT on a different number of augmentations, we translated text to French then back to English. We ensured that the paraphrased back-translated texts carry the same meaning as the source text. Due to the cost of doing the augmentation, we are unable to show results on our larger datasets. This is a challenge in using RTT.

***Mixup* Augmentation.** We implement this method with the α variable set to 0.2. We run *mixup* on its own as well as in combination with the other methods described.

Evaluation Metrics. For all of the experiments, we use error, and with some experiments loss, as metrics to give insight into the behaviour of the augmentation algorithms and their impact on model performance. We use the *error* for the rest of the paper defined as.

$$error = 1 - accuracy \tag{1}$$

We also present cross-entropy loss when investigating overfitting.

3.3 Learning Algorithms

We test two types of learning algorithms for the classification of text. Specifically, we use a deep learning approach as well as a logistic regression (LR). The inputs of the algorithms will be slightly different given the different types of augmentation. We would like to be able to show the impact of augmentation on the state of the art approaches as well as the impact on traditional algorithms and NLP representation.

We implement our models using Keras[4] (a deep learning toolkit). For logistic regression, the model contains a dense layer given a few arguments; the number of labels, and activation function as *softmax*. We compile the model using an adaptive learning rate method for gradient descent called ADADELTA [35] as

[4] http://keras.io.

our optimiser, and categorical cross entropy as our loss function. For the DNN, we use a Bidirectional LSTM network [12] coupled with 1 dimensional convolutional neural network and 3 fully connected layers activated by a *rectified linear unit* and *softmax* illustrated in Table 3.

Table 3. Table of a DNN architecture. Dropout layers use a probability of 0.4. Tanh represents a rectified linear unit. The number of filters for the last layer corresponds to the number of classes of the given dataset.

Layer	Type	Filters/Neurons	Kernel
1	Bidirectional LSTM+tanh	256	–
2	Dropout	–	–
3	Conv1D+sigmoid	512	3
4	GlobalMaxPool1D	512	–
5	Fully connected+tanh	512	–
6	Dropout	–	–
7	Fully connected+tanh	200	–
8	Dropout	–	–
9	Fully connected+softmax	4	–

4 Experiments and Results

This section explains detailed experiments on the effectiveness of augmentation in several settings. We conduct three types of experiments on the datasets. The first experiment tests the importance of augmentation on limited data. The second experiment tests the effectiveness of augmentation under overfitting settings. The last experiment tests how the number of augmentations affects performance.

4.1 Effect of Augmentation on Less Data

Limited data is a challenge both in getting well-labelled data for supervised learning problems [8] and also continues to be a bigger challenge for low-resource languages [5]. Here we present what the effect of the different augmentation schemes are when labelled data is reduced.

Here we show the effect of augmentation on learning for logistic regression and Deep Neural Network (DNN) models. For logistic regression, we use a TFIDF vector scheme [28]. For TFIDF, we fit the vector model using only the training data. For the DNN, we use pre-trained word vector representations from GloVe [25]. For GloVe we use the pre-trained Wikipedia model for the AG News dataset and pre-trained Twitter model for the social media datasets. For all of the datasets in this experiment, we augment the data 5 times. We also include the original dataset, resulting in an augmented dataset that is 6 times the size of the original. To make results comparable, when we use no augmentation we just repeat the same original dataset 6 times. Due to limitations of RTT we were only able to run experiments on logistic regression on AG News and the Hate Speech Dataset. As we cannot compare RTT across all experiments, we discuss it at the end.

First looking at the AG News results (Figs. 2a and 2b), we start noticing a few trends. We use 10000 articles for training and a further 10000 for validation. We repeat the experiment 5 times. When looking at the validation error for logistic regression on the AG News dataset, Fig. 2a, we note that augmented data leads to better results. For the logistic regression results (Fig. 2a), the WordNet-based Synonym and W2V augmentation lead to lower validation error. At the same time, across all augmentation schemes, *mixup* improved performance. With the DNN, WordNet-based Synonym augmentation with *mixup* leads to the lowest validation error. We believe this is because the AG News dataset is made up of news articles that have a longer length and are written formally, as such a synonym database is likely to make good substitutions.

Turning our attention to the two social media based datasets, we now have to deal with more informal language. In the Sentiment 140 dataset experiments (Figs. 3a and 3b), we use 100000 posts for training and 10000 for validation. Again augmentation outperforms no augmentation. We are not able to get results for *mixup* on Logistic regression with TFIDF due to computational constraints. *mixup* still provides better performance, when combined with another augmentation method for the DNN, and we expect that this is the same for LR. *mixup* also affects the performance of the learning even when it is starting to overfit. We discuss more details of this later.

Finally, for the Hate Speech dataset, we use the smallest amount of training data. We have a training set of size 2000 and a validation set of the same size. For the logistic regression (Fig. 4a), the *mixup* augmentation provides good performance. The same result is seen for the DNN (Fig. 4b).

RTT Augmentation proved to have differing effects. On the logistic regression, its performance on AG News was the best while on the Hate Speech dataset it was less successful. On the DNN, we observe similar results for both AG News and the Hate Speech data sets. We do think that this does likely indicate that on social media data, RTT will have a hard time doing translations and as such will increase error. At the same time, the more formal AG News dataset benefits from the augmentation. More still needs to be done to explore this area. In the results, we present for RTT, for AG News we used Amazon Translate with *English to French and back to English* as well as *English to German and back to English.* For the Hate Speech dataset, we used Google translate for *English to French and back to English.*

4.2 Effect of Different Number of Augmentations

Multiple augmentations may have an impact on the error. The next subsections discuss how multiple augmentations impact the error. We focus on using LR to

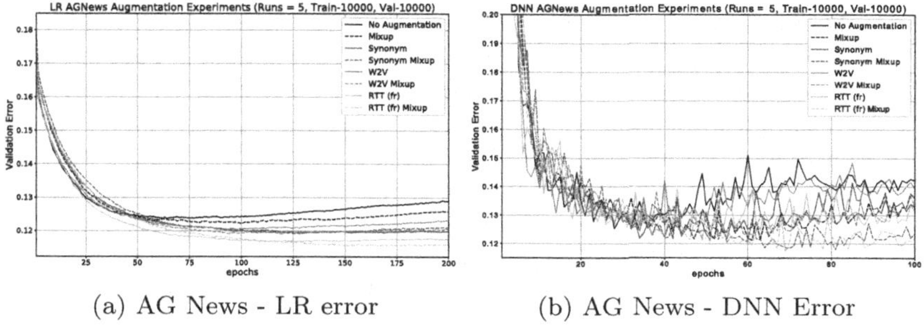

(a) AG News - LR error (b) AG News - DNN Error

Fig. 2. Effect of augmentation on different training set sizes for AG News

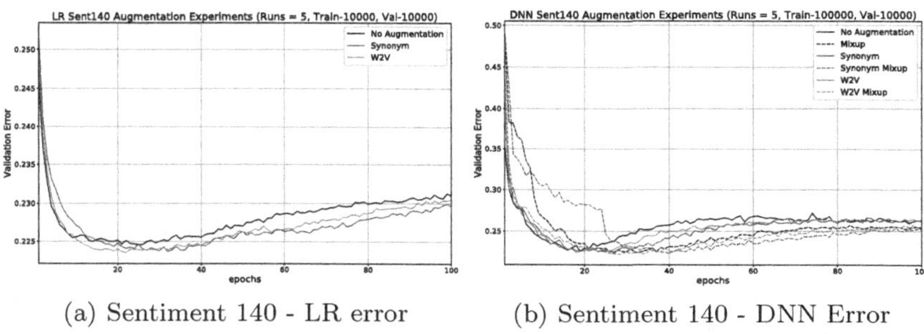

(a) Sentiment 140 - LR error (b) Sentiment 140 - DNN Error

Fig. 3. Effect of augmentation on different training set sizes for Sentiment 140

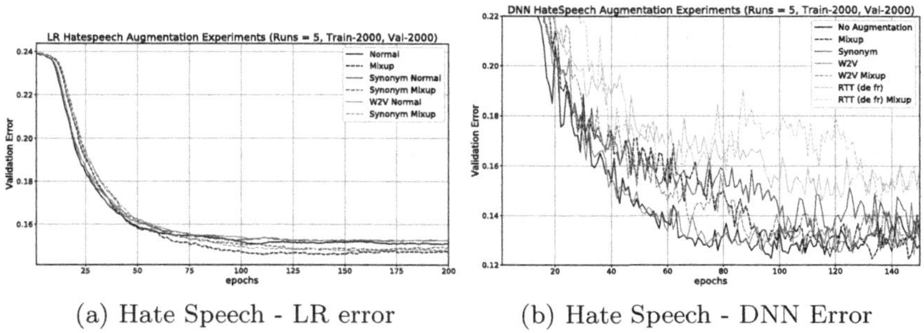

(a) Hate Speech - LR error (b) Hate Speech - DNN Error

Fig. 4. Effect of augmentation on different training set sizes for Hate Speech (Synonym Mixup omitted for readability)

conduct the experiments. We augment the data in portions of different sizes. For AG News, we augment 1000 and 10000 tokens for 5 and 10 times and report on the error using WordNet-based augmentation. We obtain the error of 0.1824 when augmenting 1000 tokens for 5 times. The error reduced to 0.1809 when we increase the number of augmentations to 10. This shows the effect of increasing number of augmentation on error is very low. As such, we increase the data size and augment 10k of the data. We observe an error of 0.12136 when augmenting

5 times. Then, we increase the number of augmentations to 10 and the error slightly reduce to 0.121. With these results for longer text, we observe that the number of augmentations has an impact on the error and when augmenting larger data the error is slightly reduced by a difference of 0.12136–0.1824.

For Sentiment 140, we augment 10000 tokens using the same settings. We observe an error of 0.25434 when augmenting for 5 times, we increased the number of augmentations to 10 then the error increased to 0.25764, this shows Word2Vec introduced more noise on the data.

What we observe is that moving from 5 to 10 augmentations had only slight effects on the lowest error for the cases we studied (Fig. 5).

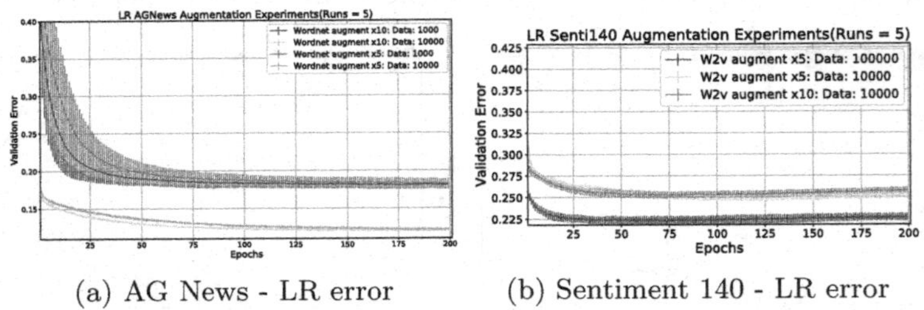

(a) AG News - LR error (b) Sentiment 140 - LR error

Fig. 5. Effects of different sizes of augmentation given different input data on error. (a) WordNet-based augmentation slightly reduces the error with more number of augmentations. (b) Word2Vec increase the error by introducing more noise.

4.3 Effect of Augmentation on Overfitting

Augmentation is viewed as a form of regularisation [33]. We can look at the effect of the different augmentation methods on how they reduce the effects of overfitting. Figure 6 shows the effect of the different methods we tested on overfitting. On both the AG News dataset (Fig. 6a) and the Sentiment 140 dataset (Fig. 6b) augmentation reduces the overfitting. *mixup* has the largest impact. On AG News, overfitting effect is reduced by Synonym, W2V and RTT augmentations, even without *mixup*.

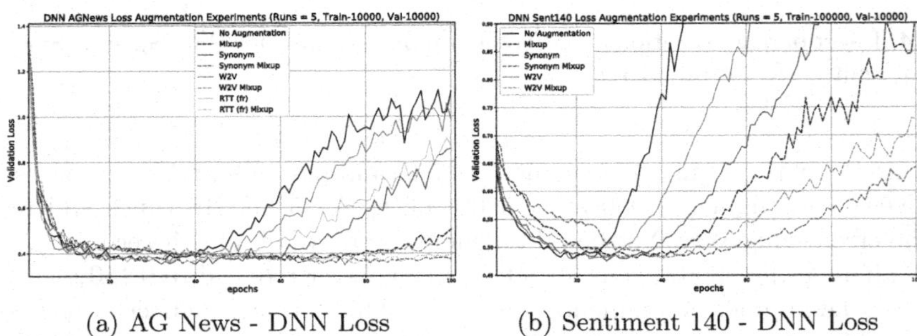

(a) AG News - DNN Loss (b) Sentiment 140 - DNN Loss

Fig. 6. Effect of overfitting on DNN model shown through cross-entropy loss for the AG News and Sentiment 140 datasets

5 Conclusion and Future Work

The use of WordNet-based Synonym augmentation on AG News or long text does result in most of the words found from the database. Hence, the probability of those words to be augmented is higher and the resulting augmented data does not change the meaning of the message. And this results in WordNet-based augmentation approach being a rich augmentation compared to RTT and Word2Vec-based approach. The WordNet-based augmentation approach highly depends on an existing database. Hence, the disadvantage is when such a database is not available for low-resourced languages, it first needs to be created at a great cost. The alternative way of augmenting low-resource language is to use unsupervised word embedding models that can be trained using GloVe, Word2Vec, and fastText [15] on pre-collected available corpora such as Wikipedia, Newspapers or literature. The vector representations in the models can be used to identify the nearest neighbours via the cosine similarity (such as used in the Word2Vec based augmentation). Such an approach becomes more feasible for augmenting data for lower resourced languages. As shown in the paper experiments Word2Vec-based augmentation resulted with good results compared to synonym-based approach on Sentiment 140, this shows that augmentation can be done with only Word2Vec. Even on AG News, Word2Vec-based augmentation is competitive.

RTT-based augmentation is expensive in many ways. If using an online service, the commercial services available require financial resources. The free tiers made available will only be able to translate a few thousand words for free. If one wants to reduce the cost, then one can train or use a pre-trained neural machine translation model. Commercial strength grade translation models though are hard to come by and will require a lot of data to train (which is another cost). As such they are even less feasible for lower resourced languages. We were only able to use RTT augmentation on the smaller datasets of AG News and Social Media Hate Speech. Even with this, we had to use two different services (Google and Amazon) to keep costs low. In our academic setting, it is not feasible to use RTT on very large datasets and remains future work.

There are some avenues of future work. We have provided experiments showing the efficacy of different augmentation schemes on a level playing field. More local context augmentation using language models is an avenue of extending this work. Another avenue is investigating how to improve semi-supervised learning of low resourced languages using augmentation. Given the success of *mixup*, one can explore other methods that augment the data as a way of regularisation.

References

1. Aiken, M., Park, M.: The efficacy of round-trip translation for MT evaluation. Transl. J. **14**(1), 1–10 (2010)
2. Aroyehun, S.T., Gelbukh, A.: Aggression detection in social media: using deep neural networks, data augmentation, and pseudo labeling. In: Proceedings of the First Workshop on Trolling, Aggression and Cyberbullying (TRAC 2018), pp. 90–97 (2018)

3. Bird, S., Klein, E., Loper, E.: Natural Language Processing with Python: Analyzing Text with the Natural Language Toolkit. O'Reilly Media, Inc., Sebastopol (2009)
4. Cubuk, E.D., Zoph, B., Mane, D., Vasudevan, V., Le, Q.V.: Autoaugment: learning augmentation policies from data. arXiv preprint arXiv:1805.09501 (2018)
5. Das, A., Ganguly, D., Garain, U.: Named entity recognition with word embeddings and Wikipedia categories for a low-resource language. ACM Trans. Asian Low-Resour. Lang. Inf. Process. (TALLIP) **16**(3), 18 (2017)
6. Davidson, T., Warmsley, D., Macy, M., Weber, I.: Automated hate speech detection and the problem of offensive language. In: Proceedings of the 11th International AAAI Conference on Web and Social Media, pp. 512–515 (2017)
7. Devlin, J., Chang, M.W., Lee, K., Toutanova, K.: Bert: pre-training of deep bidirectional transformers for language understanding. arXiv preprint arXiv:1810.04805 (2018)
8. Dundar, M., Kou, Q., Zhang, B., He, Y., Rajwa, B.: Simplicity of kmeans versus deepness of deep learning: a case of unsupervised feature learning with limited data. In: 2015 IEEE 14th International Conference on Machine Learning and Applications (ICMLA), pp. 883–888. IEEE (2015)
9. Fadaee, M., Bisazza, A., Monz, C.: Data augmentation for low-resource neural machine translation. arXiv preprint arXiv:1705.00440 (2017)
10. Fedus, W., Goodfellow, I., Dai, A.M.: MaskGAN: better text generation via filling in the _. arXiv preprint arXiv:1801.07736 (2018)
11. Go, A., Bhayani, R., Huang, L.: Twitter sentiment classification using distant supervision. CS224N Project Report, Stanford, vol. 1, no. 12 (2009)
12. Hochreiter, S., Schmidhuber, J.: Long short-term memory. Neural Comput. **9**(8), 1735–1780 (1997)
13. Howard, J., Ruder, S.: Universal language model fine-tuning for text classification. In: Proceedings of the 56th Annual Meeting of the Association for Computational Linguistics, pp. 328–339 (2018)
14. Imran, M., Castillo, C., Diaz, F., Vieweg, S.: Processing social media messages in mass emergency: a survey. ACM Comput. Surv. (CSUR) **47**(4), 67 (2015)
15. Joulin, A., Grave, E., Bojanowski, P., Mikolov, T.: Bag of tricks for efficient text classification. In: Proceedings of the 15th Conference of the European Chapter of the Association for Computational Linguistics, vol. 2, pp. 427–431 (2017)
16. Ko, T., Peddinti, V., Povey, D., Khudanpur, S.: Audio augmentation for speech recognition. In: Sixteenth Annual Conference of the International Speech Communication Association (2015)
17. Kobayashi, S.: Contextual augmentation: data augmentation by words with paradigmatic relations. In: Proceedings of the 2018 Conference of the North American Chapter of the Association for Computational Linguistics: Human Language Technologies, Volume 2 (Short Papers), vol. 2, pp. 452–457 (2018)
18. Krishnan, S., Chen, M.: Identifying tweets with fake news. In: 2018 IEEE International Conference on Information Reuse and Integration (IRI), pp. 460–464. IEEE (2018)
19. Lau, J.H., Clark, A., Lappin, S.: Unsupervised prediction of acceptability judgements. In: Proceedings of the 53rd Annual Meeting of the Association for Computational Linguistics and the 7th International Joint Conference on Natural Language Processing (Volume 1: Long Papers), Beijing, China, pp. 1618–1628. Association for Computational Linguistics, July 2015
20. Li, Y., Cohn, T., Baldwin, T.: Robust training under linguistic adversity. In: EACL 2017, p. 21 (2017)

21. Mikołajczyk, A., Grochowski, M.: Data augmentation for improving deep learning in image classification problem. In: 2018 International Interdisciplinary PhD Workshop (IIPhDW), pp. 117–122. IEEE (2018)
22. Mikolov, T., Sutskever, I., Chen, K., Corrado, G.S., Dean, J.: Distributed representations of words and phrases and their compositionality. In: Advances in Neural Information Processing Systems, pp. 3111–3119 (2013)
23. Miller, G.A.: WordNet: a lexical database for English. Commun. ACM **38**(11), 39–41 (1995)
24. Mueller, J., Thyagarajan, A.: Siamese recurrent architectures for learning sentence similarity. In: AAAI, vol. 16, pp. 2786–2792 (2016)
25. Pennington, J., Socher, R., Manning, C.: Glove: global vectors for word representation. In: Proceedings of the 2014 Conference on Empirical Methods in Natural Language Processing (EMNLP), pp. 1532–1543 (2014)
26. Peters, M.E., et al.: Deep contextualized word representations. arXiv preprint arXiv:1802.05365 (2018)
27. Radford, A., Narasimhan, K., Salimans, T., Sutskever, I.: Improving language understanding with unsupervised learning. Technical report, OpenAI (2018)
28. Ramos, J., et al.: Using TF-IDF to determine word relevance in document queries. In: Proceedings of the First Instructional Conference on Machine Learning, vol. 242, pp. 133–142 (2003)
29. Ratkiewicz, J., Conover, M., Meiss, M.R., Gonçalves, B., Flammini, A., Menczer, F.: Detecting and tracking political abuse in social media. In: ICWSM, vol. 11, pp. 297–304 (2011)
30. Řehůřek, R., Sojka, P.: Software framework for topic modelling with large corpora. In: Proceedings of the LREC 2010 Workshop on New Challenges for NLP Frameworks, Valletta, Malta, pp. 45–50. ELRA, May 2010
31. Sano, Y., Yamaguchi, K., Mine, T.: Automatic classification of complaint reports about city park. Inf. Eng. Express **1**(4), 119–130 (2015)
32. Sennrich, R., Haddow, B., Birch, A.: Improving neural machine translation models with monolingual data. In: Proceedings of the 54th Annual Meeting of the Association for Computational Linguistics (Volume 1: Long Papers), vol. 1, pp. 86–96 (2016)
33. Smirnov, E.A., Timoshenko, D.M., Andrianov, S.N.: Comparison of regularization methods for imagenet classification with deep convolutional neural networks. Aasri Procedia **6**, 89–94 (2014)
34. Wang, W.Y., Yang, D.: That's so annoying!!!: a lexical and frame-semantic embedding based data augmentation approach to automatic categorization of annoying behaviors using# petpeeve tweets. In: Proceedings of the 2015 Conference on Empirical Methods in Natural Language Processing, pp. 2557–2563 (2015)
35. Zeiler, M.D.: ADADELTA: an adaptive learning rate method. arXiv preprint arXiv:1212.5701 (2012)
36. Zhang, H., Cisse, M., Dauphin, Y.N., Lopez-Paz, D.: mixup: Beyond empirical risk minimization. arXiv preprint arXiv:1710.09412 (2017)
37. Zhang, X., Zhao, J., LeCun, Y.: Character-level convolutional networks for text classification. In: Advances in Neural Information Processing Systems, pp. 649–657 (2015)

Interpretable Topic Extraction and Word Embedding Learning Using Row-Stochastic DEDICOM

Lars Hillebrand[1,2(✉)], David Biesner[1,2], Christian Bauckhage[1,2], and Rafet Sifa[1]

[1] Fraunhofer IAIS, Sankt Augustin, Germany
lars.patrick.hillebrand@iais.fraunhofer.de
[2] University of Bonn, Bonn, Germany

Abstract. The DEDICOM algorithm provides a uniquely interpretable matrix factorization method for symmetric and asymmetric square matrices. We employ a new row-stochastic variation of DEDICOM on the pointwise mutual information matrices of text corpora to identify latent topic clusters within the vocabulary and simultaneously learn interpretable word embeddings. We introduce a method to efficiently train a constrained DEDICOM algorithm and a qualitative evaluation of its topic modeling and word embedding performance.

Keywords: Word embeddings · Topic analysis · Matrix factorization · Natural language processing

1 Introduction

Matrix factorization methods have always been a staple in many natural language processing (NLP) tasks. Factorizing a matrix of word co-occurrences can create both low-dimensional representations of the vocabulary, so-called word embeddings [11,15], that carry semantic and topical meaning within them, as well as representations of meaning that go beyond single words to latent topics.

DEcomposition into DIrectional COMponents (DEDICOM) is a matrix factorization technique that factorizes a square, possibly asymmetric, matrix of relationships between items into a loading matrix of low-dimensional representations of each item and an affinity matrix describing the relationships between the dimensions of the latent representation (see Fig. 1 for an illustration).

We introduce a modified row-stochastic variation of DEDICOM, which allows for interpretable loading vectors and apply it to different matrices of word co-occurrence statistics created from Wikipedia based semi-artificial text documents.

L. Hillebrand and D. Biesner—First author equal contribution.

Electronic supplementary material The online version of this chapter (https://doi.org/10.1007/978-3-030-57321-8_22) contains supplementary material, which is available to authorized users.

Published by Springer Nature Switzerland AG 2020
A. Holzinger et al. (Eds.): CD-MAKE 2020, LNCS 12279, pp. 401–422, 2020.
https://doi.org/10.1007/978-3-030-57321-8_22

Our algorithm produces low-dimensional word embeddings, where one can interpret each latent factor as a topic that clusters words into meaningful categories. Hence, we show that row-stochastic DEDICOM successfully combines the task of learning interpretable word embeddings and extracting representative topics.

Another interesting aspect of this type of factorization is the interpretability of the affinity matrix. An entry in the matrix directly describes the relationship between the topics of the respective row and column and one can therefore use this tool to extract topics that a certain text corpus deals with and analyse how these topics are connected in the given text.

In this work we first describe the aforementioned DEDICOM algorithm and provide details on the modified row-stochasticity constraint and on optimization. We then present results of various experiments on semi-artificial text documents (combinations of Wikipedia articles) that show how our approach is able to capture hidden latent topics within text corpora, cluster words in a meaningful way and find relationships between these topics within the documents.

2 Related Work

The DEDICOM algorithm has a long history of providing interpretable matrix factorization, mostly for rather low-dimensional tasks. First described in [6], it since has been applied to analysis of social networks [1], email correspondence [2] and video game player behaviour [16,17]. DEDICOM also has successfully been employed to NLP tasks such as part of speech tagging [4], however to the best of our knowledge we provide the first implementation of DEDICOM for simultaneous word embedding learning and topic modeling.

Many works deal with the task of putting constraints on the factor matrices of the DEDICOM algorithm. In [2,17], the authors constrain the affinity matrix $\boldsymbol{R}$ to be non-negative, which aids interpretability and improves convergence behaviour if the matrix to be factorized is non-negative. However, their approach relies on the Kronecker product between matrices in the update step, solving a linear system of $n^2 \times k^2$, where n denotes the number of items in the input matrix and k the number of latent factors. These dimensions make the application on text data, where n describes the number of words in the vocabulary, a computationally futile task. Constraints on the loading matrix, $\boldsymbol{A}$, include non-negativity as well (see [2]) or column-orthogonality as in [17].

In contrast, we propose a new modified row-stochasticity constraint on $\boldsymbol{A}$, which is tailored to generate interpretable word embeddings that carry semantic meaning and represent a probability distribution over latent topics.

Previous matrix factorization based methods in the NLP context mostly dealt with either word embedding learning or topic modeling, but not with both tasks combined.

For word embeddings, the GloVe [15] model factorizes an adjusted co-occurrence matrix into two matrices of the same dimension. The work is based on a large text corpus with a vocabulary of $n \approx 400,000$ and produces word embeddings of dimension $k = 300$. In order to maximize performance on the word analogy task, the authors adjusted the co-occurrence matrix to the logarithmized co-occurrence matrix and added bias terms to the optimization objective.

A model conceived around the same time, word2vec [13], calculates word embeddings not from a co-occurrence matrix but directly from the text corpus using the skip-gram or continuous-bag-of-words approach. More recent work [11] has shown that this construction is equivalent to matrix factorization on the pointwise mutual information (PMI) matrix of the text corpus, which makes it very similar to the glove model described above.

Both models achieve impressive results on word embedding related tasks like word analogy, however the large dimensionality of the word embeddings makes interpreting the latent factors of the embeddings impossible.

On the topic modeling side, matrix factorization methods are routinely applied as well. Popular algorithms like non-negative matrix factorization (NMF) [10], singular value decomposition (SVD) [5,18] and principal component analysis (PCA) [7] compete against the probabilistic latent dirichlet allocation (LDA) [3] to cluster the vocabulary of a word co-occurrence or document-term matrix into latent topics.[1] Yet, we empirically show that the implicitly learned word embeddings of these methods lack semantic meaning in terms of the cosine similarity measure.

We benchmark our approach qualitatively against these methods in Sect. 4.3 and the appendix.

3 The Row-Stochastic DEDICOM Model

In this section we provide a detailed theoretical view at the proposed row-stochastic DEDICOM algorithm for factorizing word co-occurrence based positive pointwise mutual information matrices.

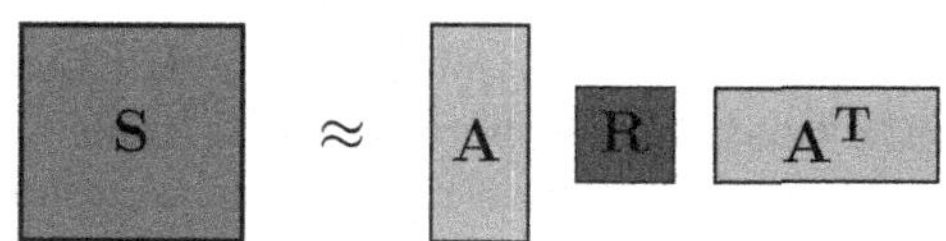

Fig. 1. The DEDICOM algorithm factorizes a square matrix $\boldsymbol{S}$ into a loading matrix $\boldsymbol{A}$ and an affinity matrix $\boldsymbol{R}$.

For a given language corpus consisting of n unique words $X = x_1, \ldots, x_n$ we calculate a co-occurrence matrix $\boldsymbol{W} \in \mathbb{R}^{n \times n}$ by iterating over the corpus on a word token level with a sliding context window of specified size. Then

$$\boldsymbol{W}_{ij} = \#\text{word } i \text{ appears in context of word } j. \tag{1}$$

Note that the word context window can be applied symmetrically or asymmetrically around each word. We choose a symmetric context window, which implies a symmetric co-occurrence matrix, $\boldsymbol{W}_{ij} = \boldsymbol{W}_{ji}$.

[1] More recent expansions of these methods can be found in [9,14].

We then transform the co-occurrence matrix into the pointwise mutual information matrix (PMI), which normalizes the counts in order to extract meaningful co-occurrences from the matrix. Co-occurrences of words that occur regularly in the corpus are decreased since their appearance together might be nothing more than a statistical phenomenon, the co-occurrence of words that appear less often in the corpus give us meaningful information about the relations between words and topics. We define the PMI matrix as

$$\mathbf{PMI}_{ij} := \log \boldsymbol{W}_{ij} + \log N - \log N_i - \log N_j \tag{2}$$

where $N := \sum_{ij=1}^{n} \boldsymbol{W}_{ij}$ is the sum of all co-occurrence counts of $\boldsymbol{W}$, $N_i := \sum_{j=1}^{n} \boldsymbol{W}_{ij}$ the row sum and $N_j := \sum_{i=1}^{n} \boldsymbol{W}_{ij}$ the column sum.

Since the co-occurrence matrix $\boldsymbol{W}$ is symmetrical, the transformed PMI matrix is symmetrical as well. Nevertheless, DEDICOM is able to factorize both symmetrical and non-symmetrical matrices. We expand details on symmetrical and non-symmetrical relationships in Sect. 3.2.

Additionally, we want all entries of the matrix to be non-negative, our final matrix to be factorized is therefore the positive PMI (PPMI)

$$\boldsymbol{S}_{ij} = \mathbf{PPMI}_{ij} = \max\{0, \mathbf{PMI}_{ij}\}. \tag{3}$$

Our aim is to decompose this matrix using row-stochastic DEDICOM as

$$\boldsymbol{S} \approx \boldsymbol{A}\boldsymbol{R}\boldsymbol{A}^T, \quad \text{with} \quad \boldsymbol{S}_{ij} \approx \sum_{b=1}^{k}\sum_{c=1}^{k} \boldsymbol{A}_{ib}\boldsymbol{R}_{bc}\boldsymbol{A}_{jc}, \tag{4}$$

where $\boldsymbol{A} \in \mathbb{R}^{n\times k}$, $\boldsymbol{R} \in \mathbb{R}^{k\times k}$, $\boldsymbol{A}^T$ denotes the transpose of $\boldsymbol{A}$ and $k \ll n$. Literature often refers to $\boldsymbol{A}$ as the loading matrix and $\boldsymbol{R}$ as the affinity matrix. $\boldsymbol{A}$ gives us for each word i in the vocabulary a vector of size k, the number of latent topics we wish to extract. The square matrix $\boldsymbol{R}$ then provides possibility for interpretation of the relationships between these topics.

Empirical evidence has shown that the algorithm tends to favor columns unevenly, such that a single column receives a lot more weight in its entries than the other columns. We try to balance this behaviour by applying a column-wise z-normalization on $\boldsymbol{A}$, such that all columns have zero mean and unit variance.

In order to aid interpretability we wish each word embedding to be a distribution over all latent topics, i.e. entry $\boldsymbol{A}_{ib}$ in the word-embedding matrix provides information on how much topic b describes word i.

To implement these constraints we therefore apply a row-wise softmax operation over the column-wise z-normalized $\boldsymbol{A}$ matrix by defining $\boldsymbol{A}' \in \mathbb{R}^{n\times k}$ as

$$\begin{aligned} \boldsymbol{A}'_{ib} &:= \frac{\exp(\bar{\boldsymbol{A}}_{ib})}{\sum_{b'=1}^{k} \exp(\bar{\boldsymbol{A}}_{ib'})}, \quad \bar{\boldsymbol{A}}_{ib} := \frac{\boldsymbol{A}_{ib} - \mu_b}{\sigma_b}, \\ \mu_b &:= \frac{1}{n}\sum_{i=1}^{n} \boldsymbol{A}_{ib}, \quad \sigma_b := \sqrt{\frac{1}{n}\sum_{i=1}^{n} (\boldsymbol{A}_{ib} - \mu_b)^2} \end{aligned} \tag{5}$$

and optimizing $\boldsymbol{A}$ for the objective

$$\boldsymbol{S} \approx \boldsymbol{A}'\boldsymbol{R}(\boldsymbol{A}')^T. \tag{6}$$

Note that after applying the row-wise softmax operation all entries of $\boldsymbol{A}'$ are non-negative.

To judge the quality of the approximation (6) we apply the Frobenius norm, which measures the difference between $\boldsymbol{S}$ and $\boldsymbol{A}'\boldsymbol{R}(\boldsymbol{A}')^T$. The final loss function we optimize our model for is therefore given by

$$\mathcal{L}(\boldsymbol{S}, \boldsymbol{A}, \boldsymbol{R}) = \left\| \boldsymbol{S} - \boldsymbol{A}'\boldsymbol{R}(\boldsymbol{A}')^T \right\|_F^2 \tag{7}$$

$$= \sum_{i=1}^{n} \sum_{j=1}^{n} \left(\boldsymbol{S}_{ij} - \left(\boldsymbol{A}'\boldsymbol{R}(\boldsymbol{A}')^T \right)_{ij} \right)^2 \tag{8}$$

with

$$\left(\boldsymbol{A}'\boldsymbol{R}(\boldsymbol{A}')^T \right)_{ij} = \sum_{b=1}^{k} \sum_{c=1}^{k} \boldsymbol{A}'_{ib} \boldsymbol{R}_{bc} \boldsymbol{A}'_{jc} \tag{9}$$

and $\boldsymbol{A}'$ defined in (5).

To optimize the loss function we train both matrices using alternating gradient descent similar to [17]. Within each optimization step we apply

$$\boldsymbol{A} \leftarrow \boldsymbol{A} - f_\theta(\nabla_{\boldsymbol{A}}, \eta_{\boldsymbol{A}}), \quad \text{where} \quad \nabla_{\boldsymbol{A}} = \frac{\partial \mathcal{L}(\boldsymbol{S}, \boldsymbol{A}, \boldsymbol{R})}{\partial \boldsymbol{A}} \tag{10}$$

$$\boldsymbol{R} \leftarrow \boldsymbol{R} - f_\theta(\nabla_{\boldsymbol{R}}, \eta_{\boldsymbol{R}}), \quad \text{where} \quad \nabla_{\boldsymbol{R}} = \frac{\partial \mathcal{L}(\boldsymbol{S}, \boldsymbol{A}, \boldsymbol{R})}{\partial \boldsymbol{R}} \tag{11}$$

with $\eta_{\boldsymbol{A}}, \eta_{\boldsymbol{R}} > 0$ being individual learning rates for both matrices and $f_\theta(\cdot)$ representing an arbitrary gradient based update rule with additional hyperparameters θ. For our experiments we employ automatic differentiation methods. For details on the implementation of the algorithm above refer to Sect. 4.2.

3.1 On Symmetry

The DEDICOM algorithm is able to factorize both symmetrical and asymmetrical matrices $\boldsymbol{S}$. For a given matrix $\boldsymbol{A}$, the symmetry of $\boldsymbol{R}$ dictates the symmetry of the product $\boldsymbol{A}\boldsymbol{R}\boldsymbol{A}^T$, since

$$(\boldsymbol{A}\boldsymbol{R}\boldsymbol{A}^T)_{ij} = \sum_{b=1}^{k} \sum_{c=1}^{k} \boldsymbol{A}_{ib} \boldsymbol{R}_{bc} \boldsymbol{A}_{jc} = \sum_{b=1}^{k} \sum_{c=1}^{k} \boldsymbol{A}_{ib} \boldsymbol{R}_{cb} \boldsymbol{A}_{jc} \tag{12}$$

$$= \sum_{c=1}^{k} \sum_{b=1}^{k} \boldsymbol{A}_{jc} \boldsymbol{R}_{cb} \boldsymbol{A}_{ib} = (\boldsymbol{A}\boldsymbol{R}\boldsymbol{A}^T)_{ji} \tag{13}$$

iff $\boldsymbol{R}_{cb} = \boldsymbol{R}_{bc}$ for all b, c. We therefore expect a symmetric matrix $\boldsymbol{S}$ to be decomposed into $\boldsymbol{A}\boldsymbol{R}\boldsymbol{A}^T$ with a symmetric $\boldsymbol{R}$, which is confirmed by our experiments. Factorizing a non-symmetric matrix leads to a non-symmetric $\boldsymbol{R}$, the asymmetric relation between items leads to asymmetric relations between the latent factors.

3.2 On Interpretability

We have

$$S_{ij} \approx \sum_{b=1}^{k} \sum_{c=1}^{k} A_{ib} R_{bc} A_{jc}, \tag{14}$$

i.e. we can estimate the probability of co-occurrence of two words w_i and w_j from the word embeddings A_i and A_j and the matrix R, where A_i denotes the i-th row of A.

If we want to predict the co-occurrence between words w_i and w_j we consider the latent topics that make up the word embeddings A_i and A_j, and sum up each component from A_i with each component A_j with respect to the relationship weights given in R.

Two words are likely to have a high co-occurrence if their word embeddings have larger weights in topics that are positively connected by the R matrix. Likewise a negative entry $R_{b,c}$ makes it less likely for words with high weight in the topics b and c to occur in the same context. See Fig. 2 for an illustrated example.

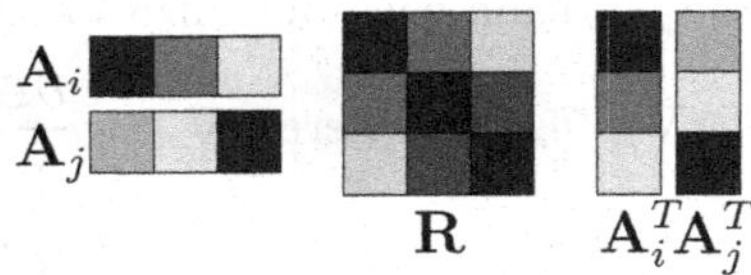

Fig. 2. The affinity matrix R describes the relationships between the latent factors. Illustrated here are two word embeddings, corresponding to the words w_i and w_j. Darker shades represent larger values. In this example we predict a large co-occurrence at S_{ii} and S_{jj} because of the large weight on the diagonal of the R matrix. We predict a low co-occurrence at S_{ij} and S_{ji} since the large weights on A_{i1} and A_{j3} interact with low weights on R_{13} and R_{31}.

Having an interpretable embedding model provides value beyond analysis of the affinity matrix of a single document. The worth of word embeddings is generally measured in their usefulness for downstream tasks. Given a prediction model based on word embeddings as one of the inputs, further analysis of the model behaviour is facilitated when latent input dimensions easily translate to semantic meaning.

In most word embedding models, the embedding vector of a single word is not particularly useful in itself. The information only lies in its relationship (i.e. closeness or cosine similarity) to other embedding vectors. For example, an analysis of the change of word embeddings and therefore the change of word meaning within a document corpus (for example a news article corpus) can only show how various words form different clusters or drift apart over time. Interpretabilty of latent dimensions would provide tools to also consider the development of single words within the given topics.

4 Experiments and Results

In the following section we describe our experimental setup in full detail[2] and present our results on the simultaneous topic (relation) extraction and word embedding learning task. We compare these results against competing matrix factorization methods for topic modeling, namely NMF, LDA and SVD.

4.1 Data

To conduct our experiments we leverage a synthetically created text corpus, whose documents consist of triplets of individual English Wikipedia articles. The articles are retrieved as raw text via the official Wikipedia API using the `wikipedia-api` library. Always three articles a time get concatenated to form a new artificially generated text document. We differentiate between thematically similar (e.g. "Dolphin" and "Whale") and thematically different articles (e.g. "Soccer" and "Donald Trump"). Each synthetic document is categorized into one of three classes: All underlying Wikipedia articles are thematically different, two articles are thematically similar and one is different, and all articles are thematically similar. Table 3 in the appendix shows this categorization and the overall setup of our generated documents.

On each document we apply the following textual preprocessing steps. First, the whole document gets lower-cased. Second, we tokenize the text making use of the word-tokenizer from the `nltk` library and remove common English stop words, including contractions such as "you're" and "we'll". Lastly we clear the text from all remaining punctuation and delete digits and single characters.

As described in Sect. 3 we utilize our preprocessed document text to calculate a symmetric word co-occurrence matrix, which, after being transformed to a positive PMI matrix, functions as input and target matrix for the row-stochastic DEDICOM algorithm. To avoid any bias or prior information from the structure and order of the Wikipedia articles, we randomly shuffle the vocabulary before creating the co-occurrence matrix. When generating the matrix we only consider context words within a symmetrical window of size 7 around the base word. Like in [15], each context word only contributes $1/d$ to the total word pair count, given it is d words apart from the base word.

The next section sheds light upon the training process of row-stochastic DEDICOM and the above mentioned competing matrix factorization methods, which will be benchmarked against our results in Sect. 4.3 and in the appendix.

4.2 Training

As theoretically described in Sect. 3 we train row-stochastic DEDICOM with the alternating gradient descent paradigm utilizing automatic differentiation from the `PyTorch` library.

[2] All results are completely reproducible based on the information in this section. Our `Python` implementation to reproduce the results is available on https://github.com/LarsHill/text-dedicom-paper.

First, we initialize the factor matrices $\boldsymbol{A} \in \mathbb{R}^{n \times k}$ and $\boldsymbol{R} \in \mathbb{R}^{k \times k}$, by randomly sampling all elements from a uniform distribution centered around 1, $\mathcal{U}(0,2)$. Note that after applying the softmax operation on $\boldsymbol{A}$ all rows of $\boldsymbol{A}$ are stochastic. Therefore, scaling $\boldsymbol{R}$ by

$$\bar{s} := \frac{1}{n^2} \sum_{ij}^{n} \boldsymbol{S}_{ij}, \tag{15}$$

will result in the initial decomposition $\boldsymbol{A}'\boldsymbol{R}(\boldsymbol{A}')^T$ yielding reconstructed elements in the range of $\bar{s}$, the element mean of the PPMI matrix $\boldsymbol{S}$, and thus, speeding up convergence.

Second, $\boldsymbol{A}$ and $\boldsymbol{R}$ get iteratively updated employing the Adam optimizer [8] with constant individual learning rates of $\eta_{\boldsymbol{A}} = 0.001$ and $\eta_{\boldsymbol{R}} = 0.01$ and hyperparameters $\beta_1 = 0.9$, $\beta_2 = 0.999$ and $\epsilon = 1 \times 10^{-8}$. Both learning rates were identified through an exhaustive grid search. We train for `num_epochs` $= 15,000$ until convergence, where each epoch consists of an alternating gradient update with respect to $\boldsymbol{A}$ and $\boldsymbol{R}$. Algorithm 1 illustrates the just described training procedure.

Algorithm 1. The row-stochastic DEDICOM algorithm

initialize $\boldsymbol{A}, \boldsymbol{R} \leftarrow U(0,2) \cdot \bar{s}$ ▷ See Equation (15) for the definition of $\bar{s}$
initialize β_1, β_2, ϵ ▷ Adam algorithm hyperparameters
initialize $\eta_{\boldsymbol{A}}$, $\eta_{\boldsymbol{R}}$ ▷ Individual learning rates

for i in $1, \ldots,$ `num_epochs` **do**
  Calculate loss $\mathcal{L} = \mathcal{L}(\boldsymbol{S}, \boldsymbol{A}, \boldsymbol{R})$ ▷ See Equation (8)
  $\boldsymbol{A} \leftarrow \boldsymbol{A} - \text{Adam}_{\beta_1,\beta_2,\epsilon}(\nabla_{\boldsymbol{A}}, \eta_{\boldsymbol{A}})$, where $\nabla_{\boldsymbol{A}} = \frac{\partial \mathcal{L}}{\partial \boldsymbol{A}}$
  $\boldsymbol{R} \leftarrow \boldsymbol{R} - \text{Adam}_{\beta_1,\beta_2,\epsilon}(\nabla_{\boldsymbol{R}}, \eta_{\boldsymbol{R}})$, where $\nabla_{\boldsymbol{R}} = \frac{\partial \mathcal{L}}{\partial \boldsymbol{R}}$
return $\boldsymbol{A}'$ and $\boldsymbol{R}$, where $\boldsymbol{A}' = \text{row\_softmax}(\text{col\_norm}(\boldsymbol{A}))$ ▷ See Equation (5)

We implement NMF, LDA and SVD using the `sklearn` library. In all cases the learnable factor matrices are initialized randomly and default hyperparameters are applied during training. For NMF the multiplicative update rule from [10] is utilized. Fig. 3 shows the convergence behaviour of the row-stochastic DEDICOM training process and the final loss of NMF and SVD. Note that LDA optimizes a different loss function, which is why the calculated loss is not comparable and therefore excluded. We see that the final loss of DEDICOM locates just above the other losses, which is reasonable when considering the row stochasticity contraint on $\boldsymbol{A}$ and the reduced parameter amount of $nk + k^2$ compared to NMF ($2nk$) and SVD ($2nk + k^2$).

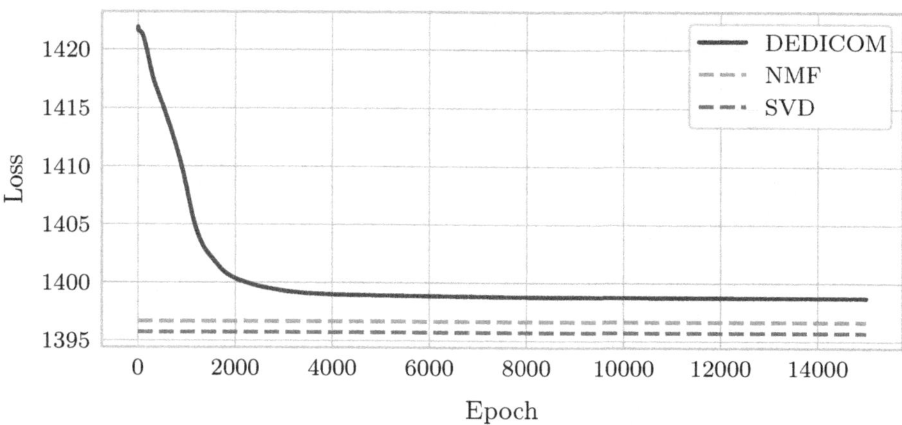

Fig. 3. Reconstruction loss development during training. The x-axis plots the number of epochs, the y-axis plots the corresponding reconstruction error for each matrix factorization method.

4.3 Results

In the following, we present our results of training row-stochastic DEDICOM to simultaneously learn interpretable word embeddings and meaningful topic clusters and their relations. For compactness reasons we focus our main analysis on document id 3 in Table 3, "Soccer, Bee and Johnny Depp", and set the number of latent topics to $k = 6$. We refer the interested reader to the appendix for results on other article combinations and comparison to other matrix factorization methods.[3]

In a first step, we evaluate the quality of the learned latent topics by assigning each word embedding $\boldsymbol{A}'_i \in \mathbb{R}^{1\times k}$ to the latent topic dimension that represents the maximum value in $\boldsymbol{A}'_i$, i.e.

$$\begin{aligned} \boldsymbol{A}'_i &= \begin{bmatrix} 0.05 \; 0.03 \; 0.02 \; 0.14 \; 0.70 \; 0.06 \end{bmatrix} \\ \operatorname{argmax}(\boldsymbol{A}'_i) &= 5, \end{aligned}$$

and thus, $\boldsymbol{A}'_i$ gets matched to Topic 5. Next, we decreasingly sort the words within each topic based on their matched topic probability. Table 1 shows the overall number of allocated words and the resulting top 10 words per topic together with each matched probability.

Indicated by the high assignment probabilities, one can see that columns 1, 2, 4, 5 and 6 represent distinct topics, which easily can be interpreted. Topic 1 and 4 are related to soccer, where 1 focuses on the game mechanics and 4 on the organisational and professional aspect of the game. Topic 2 and 6 clearly refer

[3] We provide a large scale evaluation of all article combinations listed in Table 3, including different choices for k, as supplementary material at https://bit.ly/3cBxsGI.

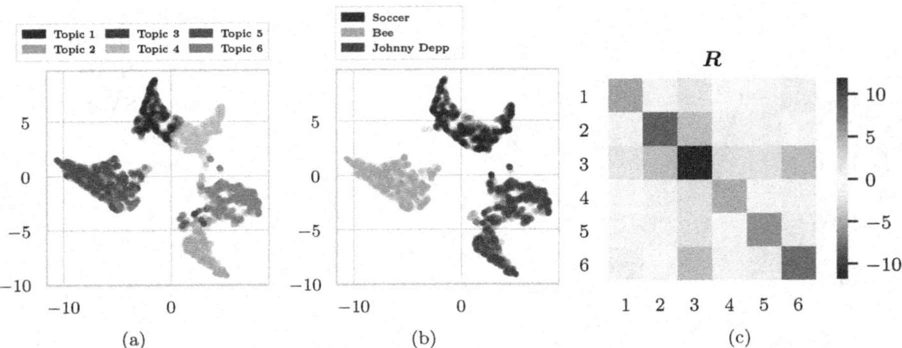

Fig. 4. (a) 2-dimensional representation of word embeddings $\boldsymbol{A}'$ colored by topic assignment. (b) 2-dimensional representation of word embeddings $\boldsymbol{A}'$ colored by original Wikipedia article assignment (words that occur in more than one article are excluded). (c) Colored heatmap of affinity matrix $\boldsymbol{R}$.

Table 1. Each column lists the top 10 representative words per dimension of the basis matrix $\boldsymbol{A}'$.

	Topic 1 #619	Topic 2 #1238	Topic 3 #628	Topic 4 #595	Topic 5 #612	Topic 6 #389
1	ball (0.77)	film (0.857)	salazar (0.201)	cup (0.792)	bees (0.851)	heard (0.738)
2	penalty (0.708)	starred (0.613)	geoffrey (0.2)	football (0.745)	species (0.771)	court (0.512)
3	may (0.703)	role (0.577)	rush (0.2)	fifa (0.731)	bee (0.753)	depp (0.505)
4	referee (0.667)	series (0.504)	brenton (0.199)	world (0.713)	pollen (0.658)	divorce (0.454)
5	goal (0.66)	burton (0.492)	hardwicke (0.198)	national (0.639)	honey (0.602)	alcohol (0.435)
6	team (0.651)	character (0.465)	thwaites (0.198)	uefa (0.623)	insects (0.576)	paradis (0.42)
7	players (0.643)	played (0.451)	catherine (0.198)	continental (0.582)	food (0.536)	relationship (0.419)
8	player (0.639)	director (0.45)	kaya (0.198)	teams (0.576)	nests (0.529)	abuse (0.41)
9	play (0.606)	success (0.438)	melfi (0.198)	european (0.57)	solitary (0.513)	stating (0.408)
10	game (0.591)	jack (0.434)	raimi (0.198)	association (0.563)	eusocial (0.505)	stated (0.402)

Table 2. For the most significant two words per topic, the four nearest neighbors based on cosine similarity are listed.

	Topic 1	Topic 2	Topic 3	Topic 4	Topic 5	Topic 6
0	ball (1.0)	film (1.0)	salazar (1.0)	cup (1.0)	bees (1.0)	heard (1.0)
1	penalty (0.994)	starred (0.978)	geoffrey (1.0)	fifa (0.995)	bee (0.996)	court (0.966)
2	referee (0.992)	role (0.964)	rush (1.0)	national (0.991)	species (0.995)	divorce (0.944)
3	may (0.989)	burton (0.937)	bardem (1.0)	world (0.988)	pollen (0.986)	alcohol (0.933)
4	goal (0.986)	series (0.935)	brenton (1.0)	uefa (0.987)	honey (0.971)	abuse (0.914)
0	penalty (1.0)	starred (1.0)	geoffrey (1.0)	football (1.0)	species (1.0)	court (1.0)
1	referee (0.999)	role (0.994)	rush (1.0)	fifa (0.994)	bees (0.995)	divorce (0.995)
2	goal (0.998)	series (0.985)	salazar (1.0)	national (0.983)	bee (0.99)	alcohol (0.987)
3	player (0.997)	burton (0.981)	brenton (1.0)	cup (0.983)	pollen (0.99)	abuse (0.982)
4	ball (0.994)	film (0.978)	thwaites (1.0)	world (0.982)	insects (0.977)	settlement (0.978)

to Johnny Depp, where 2 focuses on his acting career and 6 on his difficult relationship to Amber Heard. The fifth topic obviously relates to the insect "bee". In contrast, Topic 3 does not allow for any interpretation and all assignment probabilities are significantly lower than for the other topics.

Further, we analyze the relations between the topics by visualizing the trained $\boldsymbol{R}$ matrix as a heatmap (see Fig. 4c).

One thing to note is the symmetry of $\boldsymbol{R}$ which is a first indicator of a successful reconstruction, $\boldsymbol{A}'\boldsymbol{R}(\boldsymbol{A}')^T$, (see Sect. 3.1). Also, the main diagonal elements are consistently blue (positive), which suggests a high distinction between the topics. Although not very strong one can still see a connection between Topic 2 and 6 indicated by the light blue entry $\boldsymbol{R}_{26} = \boldsymbol{R}_{62}$. While the suggested relation between Topic 1 and 4 is not clearly visible, element $\boldsymbol{R}_{14} = \boldsymbol{R}_{41}$ is the least negative one for Topic 1. In order to visualize the topic cluster quality we utilize UMAP (Uniform Manifold Approximation ad Projection) [12] to map the k-dimensional word embeddings to a 2-dimensional space. Fig. 4a illustrates this low-dimensional representation of $\boldsymbol{A}'$, where each word is colored based on the above described word to topic assignment. In conjunction with Table 1 one can nicely see that Topic 2 and 6 (Johnny Depp) and Topic 1 and 4 (Soccer) are close to each other. Hence, Fig. 4a implicitly shows the learned topic relations as well and arguably better than $\boldsymbol{R}$.

As an additional benchmark, Fig. 4b plots the same 2-dimensional representation, but now each word is colored based on the original Wikipedia article it belonged to. Words that occur in more than one article are not considered in this plot.

Directly comparing Fig. 4b and 4a shows that row-stochastic DEDICOM does not only recover the original articles but also finds entirely new topics, which in this case represent subtopics of the articles. Let us emphasize that for all thematically similar article combinations, the found topics are usually not subtopics of a single article, but rather novel topics that might span across multiple Wikipedia articles (see for example Table 5 in the appendix). As mentioned at the top of this section, we are not only interested in learning meaningful topic clusters, but also in training interpretable word embeddings that capture semantic meaning.

Hence, we select within each topic the two most representative words and calculate the cosine similarity between their word embeddings and all other word embeddings stored in $\boldsymbol{A}'$. Table 2 shows the 4 nearest neighbors based on cosine similarity for the top 2 words in each topic. We observe a high thematical similarity between words with large cosine similarity, indicating the usefulness of the rows of $\boldsymbol{A}'$ as word embeddings.

In comparison to DEDICOM, other matrix factorization methods also provide a useful clustering of words into topics, with varying degree of granularity and clarity. However, the application of these methods as word embedding algorithms mostly fails on the word similarity task, with words close in cosine similarity seldom sharing the same thematical similarity we have seen in DEDICOM. This can be seen in Table 4, which shows for each method, NMF, LDA and SVD, the resulting word to topic clustering and the cosine nearest neighbors of the top two word embeddings per topic. While the individual topics extracted by NMF look very reasonable, its word embeddings do not seem to carry any semantic meaning based on cosine similarity; e.g. the four nearest neighbors of "ball" are "invoke", "replaced", "scores" and "subdivided". A similar nonsensical picture can be observed for the other main topic words. LDA and SVD perform slightly better on the similar word task, although not all similar words appear to be sensible, e.g. "children", "detective", "crime", "magazine" and "barber". Also, some topics cannot be clearly defined due to mixed word assignments, e.g. Topic 4 for LDA and Topic 1 for SVD.

For a comprehensive overview of our results for other article combinations, we refer to Tables 5, 6, 7, 8 and Figs. 5, 6 in the Appendix.

5 Conclusion and Outlook

We propose a row-stochasticity constrained version of the DEDICOM algorithm that is able to factorize the pointwise mutual information matrices of text documents into meaningful topic clusters all the while providing interpretable word embeddings for each vocabulary item. Our study on semi-artificial data from Wikipedia articles has shown that this method recovers the underlying structure of the text corpus and provides topics with thematic granularity, meaning the extracted latent topics are more specific than a simple clustering of articles. A comparison to related matrix factorization methods has shown that the combination of top modeling and interpretable word embedding learning given by our algorithm is unique in its class.

In future work we will expand on the idea of comparing topic relationships between multiple documents, possibly over time, with individual co-occurrence matrices resulting in stacked topic relationship matrices but shared word embeddings. Further extending this notion, we plan to utilize time series analysis to discover temporal relations between extracted topics and to potentially identify trends.

Acknowledgement. The authors of this work were supported by the Competence Center for Machine Learning Rhine Ruhr (ML2R) which is funded by the Federal Ministry of Education and Research of Germany (grant no. 01—S18038C). We gratefully acknowledge this support.

Appendix

Table 3. Overview of our semi-artifical dataset. Each synthetic sample consists of the corresponding Wikipedia articles 1–3. We differentiate between *different* articles, i.e. articles that have little thematical overlap (for example a person and a city, a fish and an insect or a ball game and a combat sport), and *similar* articles, i.e. articles with large thematical overlap (for example European countries, tech companies or aquatic animals). We group our dataset into different samples (3 articles that are pairwise different), similar samples (3 articles that are all similar) and mixed samples (2 similar articles, 1 different).

ID	Selection Type	Article 1	Article 2	Article 3
1	different	Donald Trump	New York City	Shark
2		Shark	Bee	Elephant
3		Soccer	Bee	Johnny Depp
4		Tennis	Dolphin	New York City
5	mixed	Donald Trump	New York City	Michael Bloomberg
6		Soccer	Tennis	Boxing
7		Brad Pitt	Leonardo Dicaprio	Rafael Nadal
8		Apple (company)	Google	Walmart
9	similar	Shark	Dolphin	Whale
10		Germany	Belgium	France
11		Soccer	Tennis	Rugby football
12		Apple (company)	Google	Amazon (company)

Table 4. For each evaluated matrix factorization method we display the top 10 words for each topic and the 5 most similar words based on cosine similarity for the 2 top words from each topic.

Articles: "Soccer", "Bee", "Johnny Depp"

		Topic 1	Topic 2	Topic 3	Topic 4	Topic 5	Topic 6
		#619	#1238	#628	#595	#612	#389
NMF	1	ball	bees	film	football	heard	album
	2	may	species	starred	cup	depp	band
	3	penalty	bee	role	world	court	guitar
	4	referee	pollen	series	fifa	alcohol	vampires
	5	players	honey	burton	national	relationship	rock
	6	team	insects	character	association	stated	hollywood
	7	goal	food	films	international	divorce	song
	8	game	nests	box	women	abuse	released
	9	player	solitary	office	teams	paradis	perry
	10	play	eusocial	jack	uefa	stating	debut
	0	ball	bees	film	football	heard	album
	1	invoke	odors	burtondirected	athenaeus	crew	jones
	2	replaced	tufts	tone	paralympic	alleging	marilyn
	3	scores	colour	landau	governing	oped	roots
	4	subdivided	affected	brother	varieties	asserted	drums
	0	may	species	starred	cup	depp	band
	1	yd	niko	shared	inaugurated	refer	heroes
	2	ineffectiveness	commercially	whitaker	confederation	york	bowie
	3	tactical	microbiota	eccentric	gold	leaders	debut
	4	slower	strategies	befriends	headquarters	nonindian	solo
		#577	#728	#692	#607	#663	#814
LDA	1	film	football	depp	penalty	bees	species
	2	series	women	children	heard	flowers	workers
	3	man	association	life	ball	bee	solitary
	4	played	fifa	role	direct	honey	players
	5	pirates	teams	starred	referee	pollen	colonies
	6	character	games	alongside	red	food	eusocial
	7	along	world	actor	time	increased	nest
	8	cast	cup	stated	goal	pollination	may
	9	also	game	burton	scored	times	size
	10	hollow	international	playing	player	larvae	egg
	0	film	football	depp	penalty	bees	species
	1	charlie	cup	critical	extra	bee	social
	2	near	canada	february	kicks	insects	chosen
	3	thinking	zealand	script	inner	authors	females
	4	shadows	activities	song	moving	hives	subspecies
	0	series	women	children	heard	flowers	workers
	1	crybaby	fifa	detective	allison	always	carcases
	2	waters	opera	crime	serious	eusociality	lived
	3	sang	exceeding	magazine	allergic	varroa	provisioned
	4	cast	cuju	barber	cost	wing	cuckoo

(*continued*)

Table 4. (*continued*)

Articles: "Soccer", "Bee", "Johnny Depp"							
		Topic 1	Topic 2	Topic 3	Topic 4	Topic 5	Topic 6
		#1228	#797	#628	#369	#622	#437
SVD	1	bees	depp	game	cup	heard	beekeeping
	2	also	film	ball	football	court	increased
	3	bee	starred	team	fifa	divorce	honey
	4	species	role	players	world	stating	described
	5	played	series	penalty	european	alcohol	use
	6	time	burton	play	uefa	paradis	wild
	7	one	character	may	national	documents	varroa
	8	first	actor	referee	europe	abuse	mites
	9	two	released	competitions	continental	settlement	colony
	10	pollen	release	laws	confederation	sued	flowers
	0	bees	depp	game	cup	heard	beekeeping
	1	bee	iii	correct	continental	alleging	varroa
	2	develops	racism	abandoned	contested	attempting	animals
	3	studied	appropriation	maximum	confederations	finalized	mites
	4	crops	march	clear	conmebol	submitted	plato
	0	also	film	ball	football	court	increased
	1	although	waters	finely	er	declaration	usage
	2	told	robinson	poised	suffix	issued	farmers
	3	chosen	scott	worn	word	restraining	mentioned
	4	stars	costars	manner	appended	verbally	aeneid

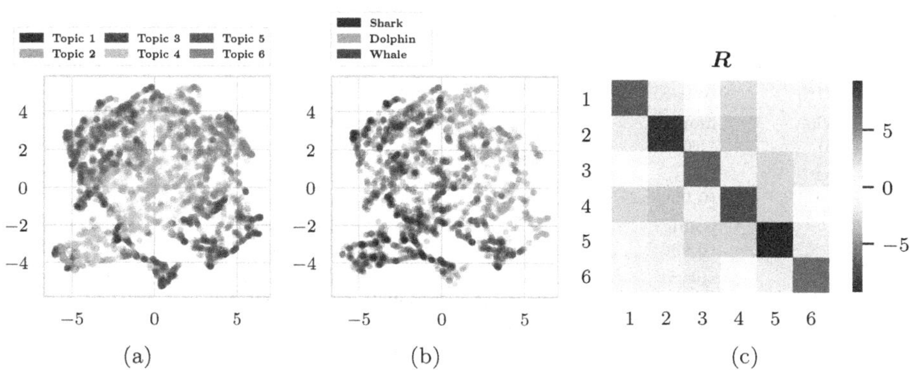

Fig. 5. (a) 2-dimensional representation of word embeddings $\boldsymbol{A}'$ colored by topic assignment. (b) 2-dimensional representation of word embeddings $\boldsymbol{A}'$ colored by original Wikipedia article assignment (words that occur in more than one article are excluded). (c) Colored heatmap of affinity matrix $\boldsymbol{R}$.

Table 5. Top half lists the top 10 representative words per dimension of the basis matrix A, bottom half lists the 5 most similar words based on cosine similarity for the 2 top words from each topic.

Articles: "Dolphin", "Shark", "Whale"

	Topic 1 #460	Topic 2 #665	Topic 3 #801	Topic 4 #753	Topic 5 #854	Topic 6 #721
1	shark (0.665)	calf (0.428)	ship (0.459)	conservation (0.334)	water (0.416)	dolphin (0.691)
2	sharks (0.645)	months (0.407)	became (0.448)	countries (0.312)	similar (0.374)	dolphins (0.655)
3	fins (0.487)	calves (0.407)	poseidon (0.44)	government (0.309)	tissue (0.373)	captivity (0.549)
4	killed (0.454)	females (0.399)	riding (0.426)	wales (0.304)	body (0.365)	wild (0.467)
5	million (0.451)	blubber (0.374)	dionysus (0.422)	bycatch (0.29)	swimming (0.357)	behavior (0.461)
6	fish (0.448)	young (0.37)	ancient (0.42)	cancelled (0.288)	blood (0.346)	bottlenose (0.453)
7	international (0.442)	sperm (0.356)	deity (0.412)	eastern (0.287)	surface (0.344)	sometimes (0.449)
8	fin (0.421)	born (0.355)	ago (0.398)	policy (0.286)	oxygen (0.34)	human (0.421)
9	fishing (0.405)	feed (0.349)	melicertes (0.395)	control (0.285)	system (0.336)	less (0.42)
10	teeth (0.398)	mysticetes (0.341)	greeks (0.394)	imminent (0.282)	swim (0.336)	various (0.418)
0	shark (1.0)	calf (1.0)	ship (1.0)	conservation (1.0)	water (1.0)	dolphin (1.0)
2	sharks (0.981)	calves (0.978)	dionysus (0.995)	south (0.981)	prey (0.964)	dolphins (0.925)
3	fins (0.958)	females (0.976)	riding (0.992)	states (0.981)	swimming (0.959)	sometimes (0.909)
4	killed (0.929)	months (0.955)	deity (0.992)	united (0.978)	allows (0.957)	another (0.904)
5	fishing (0.916)	young (0.948)	poseidon (0.987)	endangered (0.976)	swim (0.947)	bottlenose (0.903)
0	sharks (1.0)	months (1.0)	became (1.0)	countries (1.0)	similar (1.0)	dolphins (1.0)
2	shark (0.981)	born (0.992)	old (0.953)	eastern (0.991)	surface (0.992)	behavior (0.956)
3	fins (0.936)	young (0.992)	later (0.946)	united (0.989)	brain (0.97)	sometimes (0.945)
4	tiger (0.894)	sperm (0.985)	ago (0.939)	caught (0.987)	sound (0.968)	various (0.943)
5	killed (0.887)	calves (0.984)	modern (0.937)	south (0.979)	object (0.965)	less (0.937)

Table 6. For each evaluated matrix factorization method we display the top 10 words for each topic and the 5 most similar words based on cosine similarity for the 2 top words from each topic.

Articles: "Dolphin", "Shark", "Whale"

		Topic 1	Topic 2	Topic 3	Topic 4	Topic 5	Topic 6
		#492	#907	#452	#854	#911	#638
NMF	1	blood	international	evidence	sonar	ago	calf
	2	body	killed	selfawareness	may	teeth	young
	3	heart	states	ship	surface	million	females
	4	gills	conservation	dionysus	clicks	mysticetes	captivity
	5	bony	new	came	prey	whales	calves
	6	oxygen	united	another	use	years	months
	7	organs	shark	important	underwater	baleen	born
	8	tissue	world	poseidon	sounds	cetaceans	species
	9	water	endangered	mark	known	modern	male
	10	via	islands	riding	similar	extinct	female
	0	blood	international	evidence	sonar	ago	calf
	1	travels	proposal	flaws	poisoned	consist	uninformed
	2	enters	lipotidae	methodological	signals	specialize	primary
	3	vibration	banned	nictating	–	legs	born
	4	tolerant	iniidae	wake	emitted	closest	leaner
	0	body	killed	selfawareness	may	teeth	young
	1	crystal	law	legendary	individuals	fuel	brood
	2	blocks	consumers	humankind	helping	lamp	lacking
	3	modified	pontoporiidae	helpers	waste	filterfeeding	accurate
	4	slits	org	performing	depression	krill	consistency
		#650	#785	#695	#815	#635	#674
LDA	1	killed	teeth	head	species	meat	air
	2	system	baleen	fish	male	whale	using
	3	endangered	mysticetes	dolphin	females	ft	causing
	4	often	ago	fin	whales	fisheries	currents
	5	close	jaw	eyes	sometimes	also	sounds
	6	sharks	family	fat	captivity	ocean	groups
	7	countries	water	navy	young	threats	sound
	8	since	includes	popular	shark	children	research
	9	called	allow	tissue	female	population	clicks
	10	vessels	greater	tail	wild	bottom	burst
	0	killed	teeth	head	species	meat	air
	1	postures	dense	underside	along	porbeagle	australis
	2	dolphinariums	cetacea	grooves	another	source	submerged
	3	town	tourism	eyesight	long	activities	melbourne
	4	onethird	planktonfeeders	osmoregulation	sleep	comparable	spear
	0	system	baleen	fish	male	whale	using
	1	dominate	mysticetes	mostly	females	live	communication
	2	close	distinguishing	swim	aorta	human	become
	3	controversy	unique	due	female	cold	associated
	4	agree	remove	whole	position	parts	mirror

(*continued*)

Table 6. (*continued*)

Articles: "Dolphin", "Shark", "Whale"

		Topic 1	Topic 2	Topic 3	Topic 4	Topic 5	Topic 6
		#1486	#544	#605	#469	#539	#611
SVD	1	dolphins	water	shark	million	poseidon	dolphin
	2	species	body	sharks	years	became	meat
	3	whales	tail	fins	ago	ship	family
	4	fish	teeth	international	whale	riding	river
	5	also	flippers	killed	two	evidence	similar
	6	large	tissue	fishing	calf	melicertes	extinct
	7	may	allows	fin	mya	deity	called
	8	one	air	law	later	ino	used
	9	animals	feed	new	months	came	islands
	10	use	bony	conservation	mysticetes	made	genus
	0	dolphins	water	shark	million	poseidon	dolphin
	1	various	vertical	corpse	approximately	games	depicted
	2	finding	unlike	stocks	assigned	phalanthus	makara
	3	military	chew	galea	hybodonts	statue	capensis
	4	selfmade	lack	galeomorphii	appeared	isthmian	goddess
	0	species	body	sharks	years	became	meat
	1	herd	heart	mostly	acanthodians	pirates	contaminated
	2	reproduction	resisting	fda	spent	elder	harpoon
	3	afford	fit	lists	stretching	mistook	practitioner
	4	maturity	posterior	carcharias	informal	wealthy	pcbs

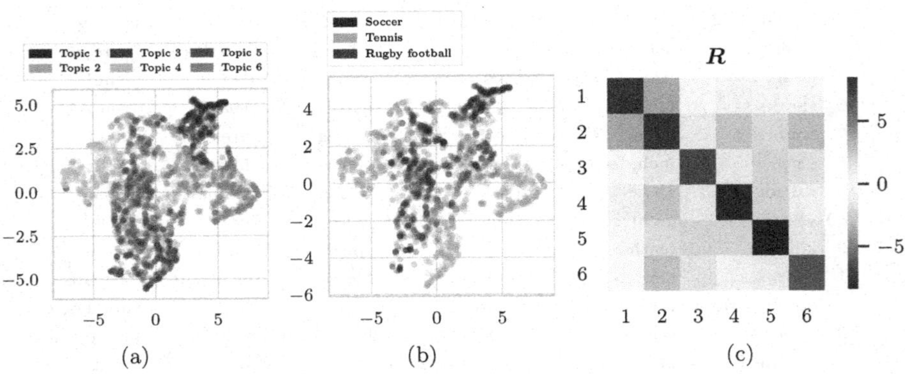

Fig. 6. (a) 2-dimensional representation of word embeddings $\boldsymbol{A}'$ colored by topic assignment. (b) 2-dimensional representation of word embeddings $\boldsymbol{A}'$ colored by original Wikipedia article assignment (words that occur in more than one article are excluded). (c) Colored heatmap of affinity matrix $\boldsymbol{R}$.

Table 7. Top half lists the top 10 representative words per dimension of the basis matrix A, bottom half lists the 5 most similar words based on cosine similarity for the 2 top words from each topic.

Articles: "Soccer", "Tennis", "Rugby"

	Topic 1 #539	Topic 2 #302	Topic 3 #563	Topic 4 #635	Topic 5 #650	Topic 6 #530
1	may (0.599)	leads (0.212)	tournaments (0.588)	greatest (0.572)	football (0.553)	net (0.644)
2	penalty (0.576)	sole (0.205)	tournament (0.517)	tennis (0.497)	rugby (0.542)	shot (0.629)
3	referee (0.564)	competes (0.205)	events (0.509)	female (0.44)	south (0.484)	stance (0.553)
4	team (0.517)	extending (0.204)	prize (0.501)	ever (0.433)	union (0.47)	stroke (0.543)
5	goal (0.502)	fixing (0.203)	tour (0.497)	navratilova (0.405)	wales (0.459)	serve (0.537)
6	kick (0.459)	triggered (0.203)	money (0.488)	modern (0.401)	national (0.446)	rotation (0.513)
7	play (0.455)	bleeding (0.202)	cup (0.486)	best (0.4)	england (0.438)	backhand (0.508)
8	ball (0.452)	fraud (0.202)	world (0.467)	wingfield (0.394)	new (0.416)	hit (0.507)
9	offence (0.444)	inflammation (0.202)	atp (0.464)	sports (0.39)	europe (0.406)	forehand (0.499)
10	foul (0.443)	conditions (0.201)	men (0.463)	williams (0.389)	states (0.404)	torso (0.487)
0	may (1.0)	leads (1.0)	tournaments (1.0)	greatest (1.0)	football (1.0)	net (1.0)
2	goal (0.98)	tiredness (1.0)	events (0.992)	female (0.98)	union (0.98)	shot (0.994)
3	play (0.959)	ineffectiveness (1.0)	tour (0.989)	ever (0.971)	rugby (0.979)	serve (0.987)
4	penalty (0.954)	recommences (1.0)	money (0.986)	navratilova (0.967)	association (0.96)	hit (0.984)
5	team (0.953)	mandated (1.0)	prize (0.985)	tennis (0.962)	england (0.958)	stance (0.955)
0	penalty (1.0)	sole (1.0)	tournament (1.0)	tennis (1.0)	rugby (1.0)	shot (1.0)
2	referee (0.985)	discretion (1.0)	events (0.98)	greatest (0.962)	football (0.979)	net (0.994)
3	kick (0.985)	synonym (1.0)	event (0.978)	female (0.953)	union (0.975)	serve (0.987)
4	offence (0.982)	violated (1.0)	atp (0.974)	year (0.951)	england (0.961)	hit (0.983)
5	foul (0.982)	layout (1.0)	money (0.966)	navratilova (0.949)	wales (0.949)	stance (0.98)

Table 8. For each evaluated matrix factorization method we display the top 10 words for each topic and the 5 most similar words based on cosine similarity for the 2 top words from each topic.

Articles: "Soccer", "Tennis", "Rugby"

		Topic 1	Topic 2	Topic 3	Topic 4	Topic 5	Topic 6
		#511	#453	#575	#657	#402	#621
NMF	1	net	referee	national	tournaments	rackets	rules
	2	shot	penalty	south	doubles	balls	wingfield
	3	serve	may	football	singles	made	december
	4	hit	kick	cup	events	size	game
	5	stance	card	europe	tour	must	sports
	6	stroke	listed	fifa	prize	strings	lawn
	7	backhand	foul	union	money	standard	modern
	8	ball	misconduct	wales	atp	synthetic	greek
	9	server	red	africa	men	leather	fa
	10	service	offence	new	grand	width	first
	0	net	referee	national	tournaments	rackets	rules
	1	defensive	retaken	serbia	bruno	pressurisation	collection
	2	closer	interference	gold	woodies	become	hourglass
	3	somewhere	dismissed	north	eliminated	equivalents	unhappy
	4	center	fully	headquarters	soares	size	originated
	0	shot	penalty	south	doubles	balls	wingfield
	1	rotated	prior	asian	combining	express	experimenting
	2	execute	yellow	argentina	becker	oz	llanelidan
	3	strive	duration	la	exclusively	bladder	attended
	4	curve	primary	kong	woodbridge	length	antiphanes
		#413	#518	#395	#776	#616	#501
LDA	1	used	net	wimbledon	world	penalty	clubs
	2	forehand	ball	episkyros	cup	score	rugby
	3	use	serve	occurs	tournaments	goal	schools
	4	large	shot	grass	football	team	navratilova
	5	notable	opponent	roman	fifa	end	forms
	6	also	hit	bc	national	players	playing
	7	western	lines	occur	international	match	sport
	8	twohanded	server	ad	europe	goals	greatest
	9	doubles	service	island	tournament	time	union
	10	injury	may	believed	states	scored	war
	0	used	net	wimbledon	world	penalty	clubs
	1	seconds	mistaken	result	british	measure	sees
	2	restrictions	diagonal	determined	cancelled	crossed	papua
	3	although	hollow	exists	combined	requiring	admittance
	4	use	perpendicular	win	wii	teammate	forces
	0	forehand	ball	episkyros	cup	score	rugby
	1	twohanded	long	roman	multiple	penalty	union
	2	grips	deuce	bc	inline	bar	public
	3	facetiously	position	island	fifa	fouled	took
	4	woodbridge	allows	believed	manufactured	hour	published

(*continued*)

Table 8. (*continued*)

Articles: "Soccer", "Tennis", "Rugby"							
		Topic 1	Topic 2	Topic 3	Topic 4	Topic 5	Topic 6
		#1310	#371	#423	#293	#451	#371
SVD	1	players	net	tournaments	stroke	greatest	balls
	2	player	ball	singles	forehand	ever	rackets
	3	tennis	shot	doubles	stance	female	size
	4	also	serve	tour	power	wingfield	square
	5	play	opponent	slam	backhand	williams	made
	6	football	may	prize	torso	navratilova	leather
	7	team	hit	money	grip	game	weight
	8	first	service	grand	rotation	said	standard
	9	one	hitting	events	twohanded	serena	width
	10	rugby	line	ranking	used	sports	past
	0	players	net	tournaments	stroke	greatest	balls
	1	breaking	pace	masters	rotates	lived	panels
	2	one	reach	lowest	achieve	female	sewn
	3	running	underhand	events	face	biggest	entire
	4	often	air	tour	adds	potential	leather
	0	player	ball	singles	forehand	ever	rackets
	1	utilize	keep	indian	twohanded	autobiography	meanwhile
	2	give	hands	doubles	begins	jack	laminated
	3	converted	pass	pro	backhand	consistent	wood
	4	touch	either	rankings	achieve	gonzales	strings

References

1. Andrzej, A.H., Cichocki, A., Dinh, T.V.: Nonnegative dedicom based on tensor decompositions for social networks exploration. Aust. J. Intell. Inf. Process. Syst. **12** (2010)
2. Bader, B.W., Harshman, R.A., Kolda, T.G.: Pattern analysis of directed graphs using dedicom: an application to enron email (2006)
3. Blei, D.M., Ng, A.Y., Jordan, M.I.: Latent Dirichlet allocation. J. Mach. Learn. Res. **3**, 993–1022 (2003)
4. Chew, P., Bader, B., Rozovskaya, A.: Using DEDICOM for completely unsupervised part-of-speech tagging. In: Proceedings of the Workshop on Unsupervised and Minimally Supervised Learning of Lexical Semantics, pp. 54–62. Association for Computational Linguistics, Boulder (2009)
5. Furnas, G.W., et al.: Information retrieval using a singular value decomposition model of latent semantic structure. In: Proceedings of ACM SIGIR (1988)
6. Harshman, R., Green, P., Wind, Y., Lundy, M.: A model for the analysis of asymmetric data in marketing research. Mark. Sci. **1**, 205–242 (1982)
7. Jolliffe, I.: Principal Component Analysis. Wiley, New York (2005)
8. Kingma, D.P., Ba, J.: Adam: A method for stochastic optimization. arXiv preprint arXiv:1412.6980 (2014)

9. Lebret, R., Collobert, R.: Word embeddings through hellinger PCA. In: Proceedings of the 14th Conference of the European Chapter of the Association for Computational Linguistics, pp. 482–490. Association for Computational Linguistics, Gothenburg (2014)
10. Lee, D.D., Seung, H.S.: Algorithms for non-negative matrix factorization. In: Proceedings of the 13th International Conference on Neural Information Processing Systems, NIPS 2000, pp. 535–541. MIT Press, Cambridge (2000)
11. Levy, O., Goldberg, Y.: Neural word embedding as implicit matrix factorization. In: Proceedings of the 27th International Conference on Neural Information Processing Systems - Volume 2, NIPS 2014, pp. 2177–2185. MIT Press, Cambridge (2014)
12. McInnes, L., Healy, J., Melville, J.: Umap: Uniform manifold approximation and projection for dimension reduction (2018)
13. Mikolov, T., Sutskever, I., Chen, K., Corrado, G., Dean, J.: Distributed representations of words and phrases and their compositionality (2013)
14. Nguyen, D.Q., Billingsley, R., Du, L., Johnson, M.: Improving topic models with latent feature word representations. Trans. Assoc. Comput. Linguist. **3**, 299–313 (2015)
15. Pennington, J., Socher, R., Manning, C.: Glove: global vectors for word representation. In: Proceedings of the 2014 Conference on Empirical Methods in Natural Language Processing (EMNLP), pp. 1532–1543. Association for Computational Linguistics, Doha (2014)
16. Sifa, R., Ojeda, C., Bauckhage, C.: User churn migration analysis with dedicom. In: Proceedings of the 9th ACM Conference on Recommender Systems, RecSys 2015, pp. 321–324. Association for Computing Machinery, New York (2015)
17. Sifa, R., Ojeda, C., Cvejoski, K., Bauckhage, C.: Interpretable matrix factorization with stochasticity constrained nonnegative dedicom (2018)
18. Wang, Y., Zhu, L.: Research and implementation of SVD in machine learning. In: 2017 IEEE/ACIS 16th International Conference on Computer and Information Science (ICIS), pp. 471–475 (2017)

A Clustering Backed Deep Learning Approach for Document Layout Analysis

Rhys Agombar(✉), Max Luebbering, and Rafet Sifa

Fraunhofer Institute for Intelligent Analysis and Information Systems, Schloss Birlinghoven, 53757 Sankt Augustin, Germany
rhys.agombar@iais.fraunhofer.de

Abstract. Large organizations generate documents and records on a daily basis, often to such an extent that processing them manually becomes unduly time consuming. Because of this, automated processing systems for documents are desirable, as they would reduce the time spent handling them. Unfortunately, documents are often not designed to be machine-readable, so parsing them is a difficult problem. Image segmentation techniques and deep-learning architectures have been proposed as a solution to this, but have difficulty retaining accuracy when page layouts are especially dense. This leads to the possibilities of data being duplicated, lost, or inaccurate during retrieval. We propose a way of refining these segmentations, using a clustering based approach that can be easily combined with existing rules based refinements. We show that on a financial document corpus of 2675 pages, when using DBSCAN, this method is capable of significantly increasing the accuracy of existing deep-learning methods for image segmentation. This improves the reliability of the results in the context of automatic document analysis.

Keywords: Document layout analysis · Faster R-CNN · DBSCAN · Post-processing · Bounding box refinement

1 Introduction

Any significant organization generates documents as part of its day-to-day running. Examples of these include invoices, accounting records, and structured plans. Unfortunately, as an organization grows in size, the volume of these documents increase, often to the point where organizing and searching them becomes time prohibitive. Automated document processing systems have been proposed as a solution to this, but encounter a serious problem: the majority of documents are human, not machine, readable. For digitized documents, the PDF format is one of the most commonly used, but it is difficult to parse automatically. PDFs are designed to visualize elements without storing ordering or semantic information, which makes data retrieval difficult. Even when data can be extracted from them, PDF layouts are notoriously non-standard, with many organizations having their own unique ones. This makes effectively labeling the data difficult without human supervision.

Published by Springer Nature Switzerland AG 2020
A. Holzinger et al. (Eds.): CD-MAKE 2020, LNCS 12279, pp. 423–430, 2020.
https://doi.org/10.1007/978-3-030-57321-8_23

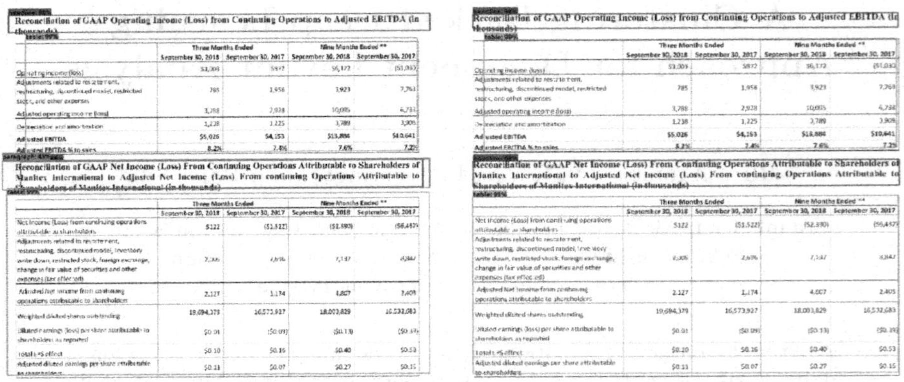

(a) The unmodified output of an FRCNN. Note the text cut off in the first table, the duplicate prediction, and the sloppy fitting of the bounding boxes.

(b) The output, once refined using only a rules based approach.

Fig. 1. The base and rule-refined bounding box predictions when classifying a document page. Here, a page excerpt containing two headers and two tables is segmented and labeled.

One proposed solution to this is to approach it as an image segmentation or object detection problem. Typically, this means we pass the PDF renderings through a neural network trained to output and label bounding boxes. In theory, the appearance of different elements in a PDF (images, headers, paragraphs, tables, etc.) should be distinct from each other, and allow a network to classify them. Previous work has shown that Faster R-CNN (FRCNN), [5,7], or models inspired by it, [6], are suitable for this task, but require refinement in order to be feasible. As shown in Fig. 1a, though a well-trained FRCNN model provides reasonably accurate bounding boxes, there are still errors that make it unusable as is. Overlaps, missing text, and sloppy box fitting all impact the accuracy of the system, especially when a document's layout is particularly dense. Indeed, [1] mentions a situation where FRCNN is known to struggle (dense tables) and claims a new approach is needed. Likewise, the problems described are present in the figures of [5], with their 'small table' example cutting off text, and 'page column alike' partially including the caption above it. To improve the usability of systems like this, accuracy must be increased, particularly when it comes to the precision of bounding box generation. Some of the mentioned problems can be fixed with rules based approaches, but alone, these can be unreliable. That is why, in this paper, we propose a clustering based approach that can improve bounding box generation in a more reliable and generalized manner, allowing automated systems to better handle diversities in layouts and improve precision when working with densely populated documents. This method is evaluated by computing a set of mAP scores for its predictions at multiple different IoU levels (0.75, 0.85, 0.95 and 0.99), and comparing them against the scores from predictions with only rule-based refinement, or without any refinement at all. For this, we used a custom dataset of assorted financial documents, consisting of 2675 individual pages that have been annotated with labeled bounding boxes for training and testing.

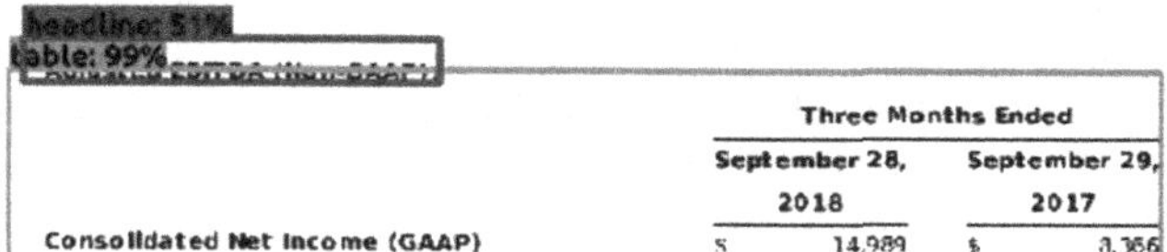

Fig. 2. Intersecting bounding boxes pose a problem for rule based refinement, especially when they contain parts of the same text.

2 Layout Analysis with Deep Learning

As mentioned in the introduction, an FRCNN is an architecture for identifying and classifying regions in an image, producing a series of labeled bounding boxes as its output. The architecture consists of two parts: a region proposal network (RPN), and a classification layer. The RPN works by generating a set of 'anchor points' spread evenly across the input image. At each of these points, pyramids of boxes (called 'anchors') are computed at multiple different scales and aspect-ratios. During training, sets of ground-truth bounding boxes are provided and used to train the network to regress its anchor boxes into usable bounding boxes. Here, the anchors overlapping the ground-truths by the greatest amount (determined by calculating the intersection over union (IoU) score) are used, and the anchors that only overlap slightly or not at all are discarded. The bounding boxes generated by this proposal network are then passed to the classification layer for labeling, and the boxes, their labels, and confidence scores are output. To improve performance, the network shares certain layers, but the details of this are not necessary to understand the basic principle. If desired, more detailed explanation can be found in the paper introducing this architecture [4].

As shown in Fig. 1a, this architecture is capable of reasonable bounding box generations, but merely reasonable accuracy is not sufficient for the use case of document analysis. In the first table prediction, the left-most column has been cut off, and any text extracted from this box would be missing letters. Additionally, the second header has two overlapping bounding boxes for it, which would lead to duplicated text being extracted. Though problematic, some of these issues can be fixed with rules based approaches. To deal with the overall sloppy fitting of the boxes, we take advantage of the fact that there is always a high contrast between the colour of the text and colour of the background, and apply a threshold to the image to retrieve the coordinates of the non-background pixels. The number of pixels yielded this way, however, can be substantial, especially if the page rendering contains a graphic or image. To reduce this to a more manageable size, we pass the threshold image through a Canny edge detector and use the edge points for refinement instead. The bounding boxes can then be contracted until they fit exactly around the minimum and maximum x and y values of their contained edge points. Once the boxes have been shrunk, we compute the IoU scores between each of them. If a set of boxes overlap by more than a given threshold value (IoU of 0.75 in the first iteration, 0.3 in subsequent ones), we merge them and match the new box's label to the label from the set with the highest confidence. The two exceptions to this are: if an unacceptably large number of boxes are set to be merged, and if the set includes a table.

In the first case, we assume that an erroneous 'super-box' has been predicted, covering far too large of an area, and delete the box responsible for it instead. Though this can lead to good bounding boxes being discarded, the chance of a single box being wrong is much less likely than multiple boxes having errors. Experimentally, we found that this caused a significant increase in overall accuracy, making this trade-off acceptable.

In the special case of a table being merged, due to the typically large size of tables, and the tendency of elements within a table to be classified as something else (usually a paragraph), we assign a higher weight to the table's confidence, increasing the likelihood that it will be chosen. Again, this runs the risk of altering correct box predictions, but empirically we have observed these instances are few and far between.

We repeat this shrink-merge process once more, to arrive at a much more accurate set of predictions. Occasionally some boxes will be predicted where there they contain either no elements, or insignificant ones (like specks of dust if the digital document was generated by scanning a physical one), so to finalize the refinement, we examine the threshold image again and delete any boxes containing only a sparse set of threshold points (less than 1% of the box area).

These rules lead to the output of Fig. 1b, which improves upon the classification and fitting of Fig. 1a, but still has the problem of boxes not fully capturing the desired text. At some point, these boxes need to be expanded to achieve this.

This problem is a difficult one because of the nature of the document layouts. Many layouts have sections that are densely populated with distinct elements. For example, a paragraph might have a header just above it, with very little white-space separating them, and relies on bold or underlined text to be easily distinguishable for humans. Additionally, sometimes bounding boxes intersect each other very slightly. In these cases, its usually not enough to justify a merge, but is enough for both of them to partially envelope the same line of text. An example of this is shown in Fig. 2. These situations mean that simple, imprecise approaches like iteratively expanding bounding boxes or matching points to the best fitting ones are unlikely work. To maximize the odds of success, we propose an approach using clustering to intelligently handle these overlaps (Fig. 3).

Fig. 3. By clustering edge points using DBSCAN, bounding boxes can be more accurately refined.

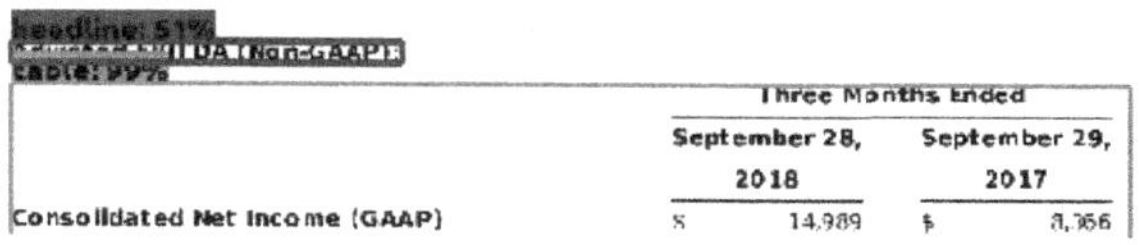

Fig. 4. Using DBSCAN, the problems of text being caught by multiple bounding boxes has been solved.

3 Improving Detection Performance by a Clustering Based Refinement

In order to effectively classify items in a document that are covered by two or more bounding boxes, we need to understand the spatial extent of the intersected element. Using Fig. 2 as an example, if a table's bounding box has been drawn slightly too large and it partially intersects a headline, we want to ensure that all of the text is assigned to the better fitting bounding box, rather than just parts of it. This will allow the other to contract to a more accurate shape. We solve this, and other inaccuracies, by using the clustering algorithm DBSCAN [2]. This process is our main contribution.

Since we do not know the number of 'clusters' that may be present in a given document page, DBSCAN's property of not requiring this number in advance is useful to us, and was the primary reason for the selection of this algorithm. The basic principle behind the algorithm is that it selects a data point, then counts to see if a certain number of points (including the selected one) are within a given radius ϵ of it. It then adds these points to a set of neighbours, labels the initial point as belonging to a specific cluster, and applies this process again to each of the neighbouring points, further expanding the set and classifying more and more points as belonging to the cluster at hand. Once it has exhausted its list of neighbours, it moves on to another unclassified point, increments the cluster label, and begins the process anew. In the end, the vast majority of points in the document should be labeled as belonging to different clusters. The method also classifies certain points as noise, but due to the clean images that most PDF renderings produced, these classifications were exceptionally rare. As such, we elected to ignore them, since they did not affect the system's accuracy. A more detailed description of the clustering algorithm can be found in [2].

Our use of DBSCAN clusters the given edge-points of the rendering such that each cluster will approximately cover an entire word in the text. In the cases of special formats like underlined or italicized text, they may span an entire line.

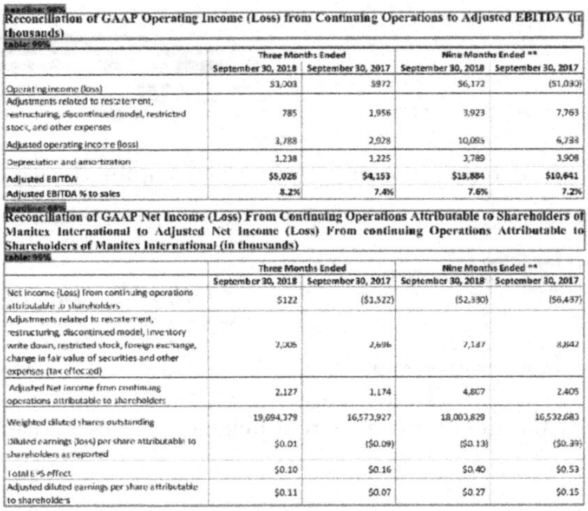

headline: 98%

Reconciliation of GAAP Operating Income (Loss) from Continuing Operations to Adjusted EBITDA (in thousands)

table: 99%

	Three Months Ended		Nine Months Ended **	
	September 30, 2018	September 30, 2017	September 30, 2018	September 30, 2017
Operating income (loss)	$3,003	$972	$6,172	($1,030)
Adjustments related to restatement, restructuring, discontinued model, restricted stock, and other expenses	785	1,956	3,923	7,763
Adjusted operating income (loss)	3,788	2,928	10,085	6,733
Depreciation and amortization	1,238	1,225	3,789	3,908
Adjusted EBITDA	**$5,026**	**$4,153**	**$13,884**	**$10,641**
Adjusted EBITDA % to sales	**8.2%**	**7.4%**	**7.6%**	**7.2%**

headline: 69%

Reconciliation of GAAP Net Income (Loss) From Continuing Operations Attributable to Shareholders of Manitex International to Adjusted Net Income (Loss) From continuing Operations Attributable to Shareholders of Manitex International (in thousands)

table: 99%

	Three Months Ended		Nine Months Ended **	
	September 30, 2018	September 30, 2017	September 30, 2018	September 30, 2017
Net income (Loss) from continuing operations attributable to shareholders	$122	($1,522)	($2,330)	($6,437)
Adjustments related to restatement, restructuring, discontinued model, inventory write down, restricted stock, foreign exchange, change in fair value of securities and other expenses (tax effected)	2,005	2,696	7,137	8,842
Adjusted Net income from continuing operations attributable to shareholders	2,127	1,174	4,807	2,405
Weighted diluted shares outstanding	19,694,379	16,573,927	18,003,829	16,532,683
Diluted earnings (loss) per share attributable to shareholders as reported	$0.01	($0.09)	($0.13)	($0.39)
Total EPS effect	$0.10	$0.16	$0.40	$0.53
Adjusted diluted earnings per share attributable to shareholders	$0.11	$0.07	$0.27	$0.15

Fig. 5. The boxes from Fig. 1a, now refined using both rules and clustering based techniques.

This behavior is intended, as said formatted text likely all belongs to the same element in the page. Once the clusters are computed, the following set of rules based on their points are applied:

1. If only a single bounding box contains points from the cluster, the box will be expanded to encompass all of them.
2. If multiple bounding boxes contain points from the cluster, the box that will expand the least is chosen.
3. If multiple bounding boxes contain points from the cluster, but require no expansion, a bounding box is computed from the cluster. The IoU scores between it and the other boxes are then calculated and the box with the highest score is the one that will be chosen.

In the end, this allows the box predictions from Fig. 2 to be refined to produce the image shown in Fig. 4.

4 Experiments

Though the system shows good results qualitatively (Fig. 5), a quantitative evaluation is needed to truly demonstrate the effectiveness of this extension. To do this, we ran a set of experiments and recorded the resulting mAP scores at multiple IoU levels.

The dataset we used for this consists of 2675 pages from assorted financial documents, with 2169 pages used for training the FRCNN and 506 used for the evaluation. To compensate for this relatively small amount of data, the network

Table 1. The mAP scores at different IoU levels for the base network predictions, predictions refined using rules, and predictions refined using a combination of rules and clustering techniques.

	Base	Rule	Cluster
mAP@0.75	0.7839	0.7537	**0.7948**
mAP@0.85	0.5036	0.7521	**0.7948**
mAP@0.95	0.2654	0.7115	**0.7268**
mAP@0.99	0.0000	0.0000	**0.3183**

was pretrained using the MS COCO dataset [3], before being refined by our training set. Regions of the dataset pages are classified using labeled bounding boxes corresponding to five different categories ('header/footer', 'headline', 'image', 'paragraph' and 'table'). Due to the level of precision needed when extracting text from documents with dense layouts, we restricted our evaluations to mAP scores using between 0.75 and 0.99 IoU. IoUs any lower than this would be wholly unusable in the context of text extraction.

The 'Base' mAP values are computed from the unmodified output of the trained FRCNN, and as shown in Table 1, do not perform well when high levels of precision are required. Our rule-refined method results in higher levels of accuracy, but due to the problems mentioned before, the lack of expansion rules limit its ability to perform optimally. For our clustering experiments, we keep the existing rule-refinements in place and add our clustering rules to allow for the expansion of too-small bounding boxes. This results in a higher level of accuracy overall, and even allows the system to function (albeit with a lower mAP score) when the required IoU ratio is raised to 0.99. The ability to work at such high levels of precision mean that the idea of backing rules based refinements with a clustering algorithm shows merit when attempting to analyse documents with dense layouts.

5 Conclusion and Future Work

In conclusion, automatic document analysis has the potential to be very useful for large organizations, but problems with non-standard layouts and densely populated documents mean approaches based on image segmentation need improvement in order to be viable. To solve this, we propose a clustering based approach using DBSCAN that can be combined with simple, rules based, refinements. As our experiments show, this successfully increases the performance of a deep-learning system when high levels of precision are required. For future work, we would like to improve the run-time of this method. Our clustering approach solves the problem it set out to, but does so at a significant computational cost. While it is usable as is, we would like to investigate other, less computationally expensive methods to refine our bounding boxes. This would improve run-time performance and increase our contribution's viability when dealing with mass amounts of documents.

References

1. Déjean, H., Meunier, J.L., et al.: Versatile layout understanding via conjugate graph. In: 2019 International Conference on Document Analysis and Recognition (ICDAR), pp. 287–294. IEEE (2019)
2. Ester, M., Kriegel, H.P., Sander, J., Xu, X.: A density-based algorithm for discovering clusters in large spatial databases with noise. In: Proceedings of the Second International Conference on Knowledge Discovery and Data Mining (KDD 1996), pp. 226–231. AAAI Press (1996)
3. Lin, T.-Y., et al.: Microsoft COCO: common objects in context. In: Fleet, D., Pajdla, T., Schiele, B., Tuytelaars, T. (eds.) ECCV 2014. LNCS, vol. 8693, pp. 740–755. Springer, Cham (2014). https://doi.org/10.1007/978-3-319-10602-1_48
4. Ren, S., He, K., Girshick, R., Sun, J.: Faster R-CNN: towards real-time object detection with region proposal networks. In: Advances in Neural Information Processing Systems, pp. 91–99 (2015)
5. Schreiber, S., Agne, S., Wolf, I., Dengel, A., Ahmed, S.: DeepDeSRT: deep learning for detection and structure recognition of tables in document images. In: 2017 14th IAPR International Conference on Document Analysis and Recognition (ICDAR), vol. 1, pp. 1162–1167. IEEE (2017)
6. Singh, P., Varadarajan, S., Singh, A.N., Srivastava, M.M.: Multidomain document layout understanding using few shot object detection. arXiv preprint arXiv:1808.07330 (2018)
7. Soto, C., Yoo, S.: Visual detection with context for document layout analysis. In: Proceedings of the 2019 Conference on Empirical Methods in Natural Language Processing and the 9th International Joint Conference on Natural Language Processing (EMNLP-IJCNLP), pp. 3464–3470. Association for Computational Linguistics, Hong Kong, China, November 2019

Calibrating Human-AI Collaboration: Impact of Risk, Ambiguity and Transparency on Algorithmic Bias

Philipp Schmidt[1(✉)] and Felix Biessmann[1,2]

[1] Amazon Research, Berlin, Germany
{phschmid,biessman}@amazon.com
[2] Einstein Center Digital Future, Berlin, Germany
felix.biessmann@beuth-hochschule.de

Abstract. Transparent Machine Learning (ML) is often argued to increase trust into predictions of algorithms however the growth of new interpretability approaches is not accompanied by a growth in studies investigating how interaction of humans and Artificial Intelligence (AI) systems benefits from transparency. The right level of transparency can increase trust in an AI system, while inappropriate levels of transparency can lead to algorithmic bias. In this study we demonstrate that depending on certain personality traits, humans exhibit different susceptibilities for algorithmic bias. Our main finding is that susceptibility to algorithmic bias significantly depends on annotators' affinity to risk. These findings help to shed light on the previously underrepresented role of human personality in human-AI interaction. We believe that taking these aspects into account when building transparent AI systems can help to ensure more responsible usage of AI systems.

Keywords: Transparent AI · Machine learning · HCI · Risk affinity

1 Introduction

Decision support by Machine Learning (ML) models has become ubiquitous in everyday life. Responsible usage of such assistive technology requires an appropriate level of trust into ML systems [7]. Trust into this technology is often argued to require interpretability of ML predictions. This is why transparent ML methods have become an active focus of research. A central research question in this field is how methodological advances translate into improvements in human-AI interaction and trust. Transparent ML research aims at better explaining ML predictions and systems to humans, but it is difficult to assess how much human-AI interaction profits from scientific advances in the field. Many studies proposing new interpretable ML methods do report results with human-in-the-loop experiments to test the impact of their proposed method on

P. Schmidt and F. Biessmann—Equal contribution.

Published by Springer Nature Switzerland AG 2020
A. Holzinger et al. (Eds.): CD-MAKE 2020, LNCS 12279, pp. 431–449, 2020.
https://doi.org/10.1007/978-3-030-57321-8_24

human-AI collaboration [26,37]; and there are approaches to compare the quality interpretability methods in psychophysical experiments with humans [43]. Yet there appears to be no consensus in the community on how the impact of interpretability methods on human-AI interaction should be evaluated [14].

So while there has been substantial growth in the research field of transparent AI, studies on the impact of transparency in AI systems on human cognition remain underrepresented. This development is at odds with the increased usage of ML systems as decision support systems. In many societies humans interact more often with computer systems than with other humans and the importance of a better understanding of machine behaviour and human machine interaction is widely recognized [36]. When humans interact with ML systems as often as with machines, studying the interdependence of machine behaviour and human behaviour becomes increasingly important. Everyday work in many professions with high responsibility employs assistive ML technology, including doctors, policemen and judges. To what extent these professions can profit from increased transparency or are negatively affected by algorithmic bias, here referring to humans trusting an AI too much, is an open research question. Algorithmic bias can have severe negative consequences, for instance when policemen trust biased ML predictions too much. Similarly, algorithm aversion can have devastating consequences, for example when experienced doctors ignore correct ML predictions. We argue that the danger of algorithmic bias or algorithm aversion should motivate not only calibrating the transparency level of AI systems. An equally important focus of research is the calibration of humans for responsible usage of transparent AI systems. The goal of this study is to highlight the potential of existing psychological research for a better calibration of human-AI interaction by taking into account personality traits. Our working hypothesis is that adding transparency does not have the same effect on users of an AI system, depending on their personality. We employ concepts from psychological research to investigate how different personality characteristics influence the impact of transparency in AI assisted decision making.

Human decision making in a collaborative context has been studied extensively in the psychological literature. One major focus of this research is on personality traits that are related to how tolerant subjects are with respect to risk and ambiguity. Risk affinity or aversion is studied in decisions in which subjects have access to the odds of a certain outcome. Tolerance to ambiguity is studied in decisions in which subjects to not have access to the probabilities associated with each outcome in a decision. Being optmistic in presence of ambiguity has recently been reported to be an important personality trait for trust. For instance the authors of [50] show that tolerance to ambiguity reliably predicts prosocial behaviour. We hypothesize that such behavioural traits are also involved in human-AI collaboration. We propose to leverage this research to better understand how humans interact with AI systems. Our results indicate that not only in human interaction but also in the context of assistive AI technology, these two factors, tolerance of risky and ambiguous uncertainty, play an important role. After all, most attempts to render AI systems more transparent can be motivated to reduce these very aspects: Transparency of an AI system is often increased by exposing the model likelihoods for an uncertain decision, or by showing explanations. Users with high or low affinity to risk and ambiguity could benefit differently from these transparency aspects.

Our study combines established methods from experimental psychology to determine personality traits indicative for risk and ambiguity tolerance with experiments that investigate the susceptibility to algorithmic bias of subjects. This combination allows to study the influence of these personality traits on the impact of transparency induced algorithmic bias. More importantly our findings can be directly applied to real world application scenarios of human-AI interaction in which responsible usage of AI systems is of paramount importance, such as policing, jurisdiction, medicine and many others. After illustrating cases of algorithmic bias and the differential susceptibility of humans, depending on their personality traits, we derive guidelines that help to reduce detrimental algorithmic bias and to maximise the benefits of transparent assistive AI.

2 Related Work

The work on interpretability of ML models has become a central topic of research in both theoretical aspects of statistical learning as well as applied ML. Many of the relevant publications at major ML conferences and dedicated workshops can be broadly categorized in more conceptual contributions or position papers and technical contributions to the field of interpretability.

In the category of position papers, an important aspect dealt with in [17] is the question of how we balance our concerns for transparency and ethics with our desire for interpretability. Herman points out the dilemma in interpretability research: there is a tradeoff between explaining a model's decision *faithfully* and *in a way that humans easily understand.* Interpreting ML decisions in an accessible manner for humans is also referred to as *simulatability* [28]. A reasonable working hypothesis is that the subjective value of transparency is an important factor for algorithmic bias. Studying these cases of bias is challenged by the fact that these biases can occur independently of the conscious perception of users. And even worse, these biases are likely to affect humans differently depending on their personality traits.

Intuitive comprehensibility and low cognitive friction of ML prediction explanations that is desired for explanations, and can be used as the basis of quantitative comparisons of interpretability approaches [8,29,32,43], is a two sided sword: Explanations should be comprehensible, but at the same time the negative aspects of algorithmic biases should be avoided. The need for unbiased and automated evaluation metrics for transparency in combination with human-in-the-loop experiments is widely recognized. For instance the authors of [8] highlight the necessity of *understandability* of explanations as well as the lack of consensus when it comes to evaluating interpretability of ML models. They propose an evaluation taxonomy that comprises both automated evaluations but also involves evaluations by human laymen. However, the negative and positive effects of algorithmic biases are not a central focus of that work.

Interpretability Approaches. On the AI side of human-AI interaction studies, there is a large body or work advancing the state of the art in transparent AI. The category of technical contributions can be broadly subdivided into two types of methods. First there are methods that aim at rendering specific models interpretable, such as interpretability methods for linear models [16,54] or interpretability for neural network models [33,44,53]. Second there are interpretability approaches that aim at rendering *any* model interpretable, a popular example are the *Local Interpretable Model-Agnostic Explanations* (LIME) [37]. As these latter interpretability methods work without considering the inner workings of an ML model, they are often referred to as *black box interpretability methods.* Due to the popularity of neural network models especially in the field of computer vision there have been a number of interpretability approaches specialized for that application scenario and the method of choice in this field, deep neural networks. Some prominent examples are *layerwise relevance propagation* (LRP), sensitivity analysis [44] and deconvolutions [53]. For comparing these different approaches the authors of [40] propose a greedy iterative perturbation procedure for comparing LRP, sensitivity analysis and deconvolutions. The idea is to remove features where the perturbation probability is proportional to the relevance score of each feature given by the respective interpretability method. An interesting finding in that study is that the results of interpretability comparisons can be very different depending on the metric: the authors of [13] performed an evaluation of sensitivity analysis and came to a different conclusion than [40].

The idea of using perturbations gave rise to many other interpretability approaches, such as the work on *influence functions* [5,15,24] and methods based on game theoretic insights [30,47]. In [47] evaluations are entirely qualitative; in [30] the authors compare interpretability methods by testing the overlap of explanations with human intuitions. While this approach can be considered quantitative, it is difficult to scale as it requires task specific user studies. Another metric used in that study for comparisons of evaluations is computational efficiency, which is simple to quantify, but is not directly related to interpretability. Other studies also employ user studies and comparisons with human judgements of feature importance. An interesting approach is taken in [38] in which the authors let students of an ML class guess what a model would have predicted for a given instance when provided with an explanation. Similarly the authors of [26] perform user studies in which they present rules generated by an interpretability method and measure how good and how fast students can replicate model predictions. This approach has been taken also in [18] in which the speed and accuracy are measured with which humans can replicate model decisions. Overall many studies investigate the impact of transparent AI on human-AI collaboration. Yet the details of when an explanation leads to detrimental algorithmic bias and the personality traits governing susceptibility to algorithmic bias remain underrepresented. We build our work on the ideas put forward in the above studies, but we place a special focus on the factors determining algorithmic bias in both ML models and human personality.

Decision Making Under Uncertainty. In almost every human-AI collaboration the final decision is made by humans. For this reason it is of utmost importance to understand how humans decide. Human decision making [3] is studied in a number of different fields such as mathematics [12,42], behavioural economics [20,48] and psychology [46]. The existing literature can be divided into work that focuses on normative theory, i.e., how decisions should be made with logical consistency, descriptive models, i.e., how people make decisions, and prescriptive approaches that try to help make people better decisions. Further, decision making problems can be divided by whether a decision maker has access to outcome probabilities, i.e., a decision task associated with risky uncertainty, or is lacking such information, i.e., a decision problem with ambiguous uncertainty. Depending on whether uncertainty is risky or ambiguous [23], humans tend to exhibit different behaviour, generally favoring risky options over ambiguous ones [4,6,45]

Expected utility theory [51] attempts to explain human choice behaviour using utility functions that take into account the objective value of a choice. Prior work has recognized the discrepancy between how people should choose under an expected value maximization principle and their actual choices [39]. It has been found that choices might deviate from the optimal one for a number of reasons, including risk aversion [1,19,34]. A widely known example of this is the St. Petersburg paradox, where players are reluctant to bet on a game with infinite expected value [39]. Further work in this field introduced subjective expected utility (SEU) [41] that allows for subjective variations in decision making behaviour under risk. However the explanatory power of SEU was questioned in [2] and it was later demonstrated by the Ellsberg paradox [10] that the rationality assumptions introduced by SEU did not hold in cases where outcome probabilities are not known, i.e., in cases of ambiguous uncertainty. Ambiguity aversion and its effects were studied thoroughly in [4] and hence it was found that ambiguity sensitive behaviour cannot be explained by SEU. Follow up work then explicitly developed models to explain decision behaviour under ambiguity [9,12,22,42].

In Psychology risk and ambiguity tolerance are considered two distinct personality traits [46]. Attitudes towards risky and ambiguous uncertainty can be estimated using choice models [12], as it was done in [50] to explain pro-social behaviour. In line with these findings, individuals that exihibt ambiguity tolerance were found to be generally optimistic when faced with uncertainty [35,52].

In this work, we employ an utility model that is used to specify subjective value of an option taking into account risky and ambiguous uncertainty [12]. This model has been used in prior work to determine a subjects attitude to risky and ambiguous uncertainty [11,27,50]. We believe that human-AI interaction is inherently associated with risky and ambiguous uncertainty, regardless of whether the interaction occurs during online shopping sessions or when judges draw on algorithmic decision support for bail decisions.

3 Experiment

In order to investigate the impact of levels of transparency and its relationship to risk and ambiguity affinity we ran an annotation task on the crowdworking platform Amazon Mechanical Turk[1]. The annotation task was based on a text classification task, a binary sentiment classification task of IMDb reviews. A ML model was trained on the task and its predictions and explanations thereof were exposed to the annotators. We varied the level of transparency and measured the effect on the agreement between annotators' responses and a) ground truth labels and b) model predictions. In order to examine how risk and ambiguity affinity relates to trust in an AI system with varying levels of transparency we first determined the affinity of annotators to risk and ambiguity in their decisions, using a well established psychological task that involves playing a lottery with known odds (risk) or with unknown odds (ambiguity) [11,27,49,50].

3.1 Risk and Ambiguity Affinity Experiment

The first part of the experiment was an incentivized gambling task for which the experiment participants had to choose between a safe payout and an uncertain monetary option. This type of task is known to yield reliable estimates for subjective risk and ambiguity attitudes. Across trials, participants were exposed to different levels of risk (25%, 50% and 75%) and ambiguity (24%, 50% and 74%). In half of the trials, participants were exposed to risky gambling options, where the winning odds were fully observable. The remaining trials had varying levels of ambiguity associated to them, where the winning probabilities could not be fully observed. See Fig. 1 for a depiction of a risky and ambiguous trial respectively. All of the ambiguous trials had an objective winning probability of 50%. The safe payout option had a monetary value of \$0.25 whereas the uncertain, risky and ambiguous, trials were allocated to equally represent monetary values of \$0.25, \$0.4, \$1.0, \$2.5 and \$6.25.

We have adopted a subjective utility function based on [12], as it has been defined in [50] as

$$\mathrm{SV}(p, A, v) = \left(p - \beta\frac{A}{2}\right) v^{\alpha} \tag{1}$$

where the subjective value (SV) is calculated as a function of three parameters, the objective winning probability (p), the level of ambiguity (A) and the monetary amount v in that trial. The two free parameters α and β indicate a subjects sensitivity to risk and ambiguity respectively. We modelled choice of the lottery, i.e., whether a subject chose the variable payout option on a given trial as

$$P\,(\text{play lottery}) = \frac{1}{1 + e^{\gamma(\mathrm{SV}_F - \mathrm{SV}_V)}}. \tag{2}$$

[1] https://www.mturk.com/.

The fixed monetary option is referred to as SV_F and the variable, risky or ambiguous, option is referred to as SV_V. For each subject we estimated three parameters; α, β and a slope of the logistic function γ using maximum likelihood given choice data that was collected as part of the experiment.

For subjects that are unaffected by ambiguity in their gambling choices, ambiguity sensitivity β will be 0. A positive β indicates ambiguity aversion, i.e., the winning probability is perceived as being less than 50% in ambiguous trials. On the other hand, a negative β indicates that a subject perceives the winning probability to be more than 50% in ambiguous trials. Risk neutral subjects will have an α of 1. A risk averse subject will have an α smaller than 1, and for a risk tolerant subject α is greater than 1.

Overall, the subjective value function explained participants choice behaviour extremely well, in 83.5% of trials across all subjects the model predicted choice correctly. According to the model fit, 41.5% of experiment participants were identified as being risk and ambiguity averse; the second largest group (31.8%) was tolerant to both risky and ambiguous uncertainty.

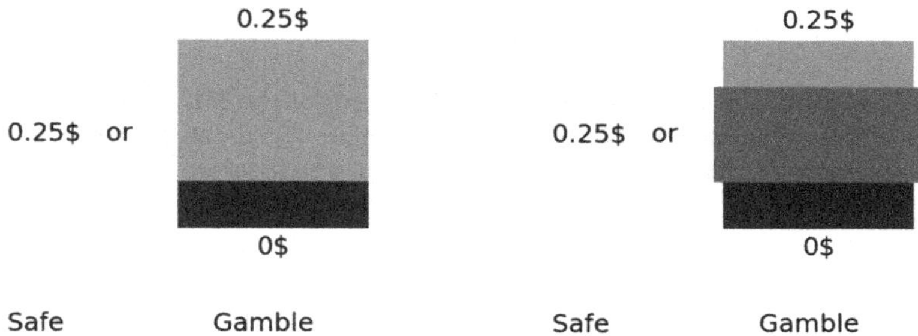

Fig. 1. User interface of the experiment to assess risk affinity and ambiguity tolerance. *Left:* Risk condition, users know the odds of winning the lottery. *Right:* Ambiguity tolerance condition, subjects do not know the odds, the winning probability in these trials was always 50%.

3.2 Annotation Task Experiment

In the second part of the experiment, we asked participants to annotate binary sentiments for 50 movie reviews from IMDb. Depending on the condition, participants were exposed to different levels of algorithmic transparency, see Fig. 2 for an exemplary depiction of the experimental conditions.

3.3 Data Set

The task uses the publicly available IMDb movie review sentiment dataset[2] which was introduced in [31]. The IMDb rating scale is defined from one to

[2] https://www.imdb.com/conditions.

ten stars where all reviews that have less than five stars are considered to have negative sentiment and all reviews that have more than six stars positive. For more controlled experimental conditions we further reduced the complexity of the dataset: We subsampled the full dataset to 50 movie reviews and controlled for various factors in that sample. Reviews were selected such that they were all between 400 and 1000 characters long to ensure comparable cognitive load for all reviews. Positive and negative reviews occurred equally often (25 times each) and had varying degrees of (relative) ease. This assessment of task ease is based on prior work in which subjects classified reviews without support; these values range between 0.5 and 1.0, indicating the fraction of subjects classifying the reviews correctly. In order to avoid learning and adoption effects, the true labels were never revealed throughout the experiment. We selected a set of reviews for which the ML model's classification accuracy was 80%. Moreover, this accuracy was symmetrical across positive and negative reviews. Given this design, all other conventional performance measures such as precision, recall, and specificity amount to 80% as well. Previous research on IMDb review classification found that typical human accuracy ranges between 75% and 80% on similar samples of the same data [43]. All participants were exposed to the same reviews.

Table 1. Held-out per label precision/recall/f1 scores of the ML model used for comparing ML interpretability methods on the full IMDb test dataset. In the annotation task a subsample of this full data set was used, in which several variables were controlled for to ensure comparable cognitive load across data points.

Sentiment	Precision	Recall	f1-score	Support
Negative	0.88	0.87	0.87	12500
Positive	0.87	0.88	0.87	12500
Avg/total	0.87	0.87	0.87	25000

3.4 Machine Learning Model

The ML model was trained on the complete training dataset which consists of 25000 movie reviews and achieved precision/recall/f1 metrics close to 90% on the test dataset, see Table 1. In all experiments we used unigram bag-of-words features that was term-frequency inverse document frequency normalized. English stopwords were removed prior to the feature extraction. Bag-of-words feature vectors $\boldsymbol{x} \in \mathbb{R}^d$, where d denotes the number of unigram features, were used to train an L_2 regularized multinomial logistic regression model. Let $y \in \{1, 2, \ldots, K\}$ be the true label, where K is the total number of labels and $\boldsymbol{W} = [\boldsymbol{w}_1, \ldots, \boldsymbol{w}_K] \in \mathbb{R}^{d \times K}$ is the concatenation of the weight vectors $\boldsymbol{w}_k \in \mathbb{R}^d$ associated with the kth class then

$$p(y = k|\boldsymbol{x}, \boldsymbol{W}) = \frac{e^{z_k}}{\sum_{j=1}^{K} e^{z_j}} \qquad \text{with } z_k = \boldsymbol{w}_k^\top \boldsymbol{x} \tag{3}$$

We estimated $\boldsymbol{W}$ using stochastic gradient descent (SGD) using the python library `sklearn` and used a regularization parameter of 0.0001, other values for the regularizer lead to similar model performance.

3.5 Interpretability Method

A simple and efficient approach for rendering linear models interpretable is provided in [16]. While this approach is limited to linear models, it is a special case of the feature importance ranking measure (FIRM) [54] that can be applied to arbitrary non-linear models and there are other non-linear extensions [21]. Following Eq. (6) in [16] we obtain the feature importances for each class k separately by

$$\boldsymbol{a}_k = \boldsymbol{X}^\top \hat{\boldsymbol{y}}_k \tag{4}$$

where the matrix $\boldsymbol{X} \in \mathbb{R}^{N \times d}$ denotes the N samples in the held out test data set and the and d denotes the number of unigram features extracted from the training data set. The predictions of the model for class k on the test data are denoted $\hat{\boldsymbol{y}}_k \in \mathbb{R}^{N \times 1}$. Each dimension of $\boldsymbol{a}_k \in \mathbb{R}^d$ is associated with a feature, in our case a word in the unigram dictionary. To compute the explanations, i.e. the highlighted words for sample $\boldsymbol{x}_i$, we selected the feature importances $\boldsymbol{a}_k$ associated with the most likely predicted class k under the model and ranked the words in a text according to the element-wise product of features $\boldsymbol{x}_i$ and feature/prediction covariances $\boldsymbol{a}_k$. The highlighted words were those that were present in the text and scored high in terms of their covariance between features and model predictions. The use of this interpretability method was motivated by its general applicability, by its simplicity and by its speed. Also this approach was found to be superior to other interpretability methods including LIME [37] for this particular combination of data set and ML model [43].

3.6 Experimental Setup

All user study experiments were run on Mechanical Turk where we asked annotators to provide the correct sentiment of 50 movie reviews. The annotation user interface (UI) is shown in Fig. 2. In total we collected annotations from 248 distinct workers. For each worker we selected one out of three levels of transparency:

- **control**: only the move review was shown
- **highlights**: movie reviews were shown along with the ML model prediction and the top 3 words according to interpretability score in Eq. 4 were highlighted
- **highlights with confidence**: same as *highlights* condition but with the likelihood for the predicted class as in Eq. 3.

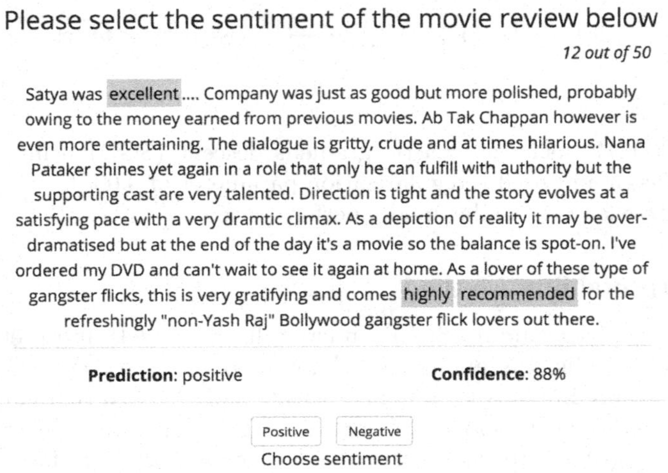

Please select the sentiment of the movie review below

12 out of 50

Satya was excellent.... Company was just as good but more polished, probably owing to the money earned from previous movies. Ab Tak Chappan however is even more entertaining. The dialogue is gritty, crude and at times hilarious. Nana Pataker shines yet again in a role that only he can fulfill with authority but the supporting cast are very talented. Direction is tight and the story evolves at a satisfying pace with a very dramtic climax. As a depiction of reality it may be over-dramatised but at the end of the day it's a movie so the balance is spot-on. I've ordered my DVD and can't wait to see it again at home. As a lover of these type of gangster flicks, this is very gratifying and comes highly recommended for the refreshingly "non-Yash Raj" Bollywood gangster flick lovers out there.

Prediction: positive **Confidence**: 88%

Positive Negative

Choose sentiment

Fig. 2. Annotation user interface for the AI-assisted IMDb movie review sentiment classification experiment. Three transparency levels were examined, shown is only the highest transparency level where the ML prediction with the model confidence was shown along with the explanation in form of highlighted words; the medium transparency level did not show the model confidence and the lowest level of transparency only showed the review text.

Each experimental subject was exposed to a transparency condition drawn uniformly at random. To control for effects related to the number of words highlighted we kept the number of words highlighted fixed to three words in each text, samples with more words highlighted (e.g. due to duplicate words) were discarded. For each annotation we recorded the annotation time, the experimental condition, the true label and the label provided by the annotator.

4 Results

We analysed the effects of increased transparency of ML predictions on human annotators performance. In particular, we investigated the agreement of human annotators with the ground truth labels and the ML predictions. Analysing the effects of transparency on annotators' agreement with the model predictions allows to investigate algorithmic bias of annotators, meaning the overlap of annotators' predictions and the predictions of the ML model. Studying the impact of transparency on human annotators' agreement with ground truth labels allows to differentiate cases of beneficial or detrimental algorithmic bias. These effects were then analysed with respect to the risk and ambiguity affinity of each annotator.

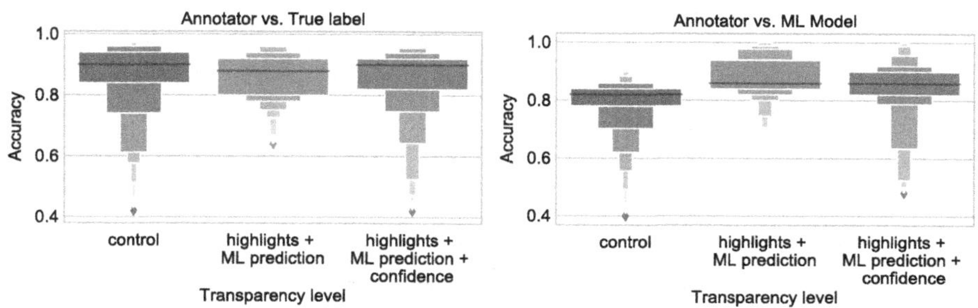

Fig. 3. Agreement between annotations by humans and ground truth (*left*) and ML model predictions (*right*) at increasing levels of transparency. Adding transparency significantly increased overlap between human annotations and ML predictions. But overlap with ground truth labels is not increased.

4.1 Transparency Increases Algorithmic Bias

When increasing transparency of ML predictions the annotators' agreement with the ground truth labels was not affected significantly. As shown in Fig. 3, there seems to be a slight decrease in human annotation accuracy when explanations and the model prediction were shown. In contrast, the annotators' agreement with the ML model predictions are increased significantly when adding model transparency. In particular, compared to the control group, algorithmic bias was increased in the first treatment group where word highlights and the model prediction were shown (Mann-Whitney, $p < 0.001$, bonferroni-adjusted). Similarly, algorithmic bias was also significantly increased in the second treatment group where in addition to the transparency from the first treatment group also model confidence scores were shown (Mann-Whitney, $p < 0.001$, bonferroni-adjusted). These results show that transparency mainly leads to algorithmic bias in our setting, but does not improve the performance of the annotators significantly.

Transparency Biases Annotators to Wrong ML Predictions. In order to better understand these effects we divided the data into cases when the ML prediction was correct and when the ML prediction was wrong. The results shown in Fig. 4 indicate that the effects observed in the overall aggregates in Fig. 3 can be mainly attributed to those cases when the AI was wrong. When the ML prediction was wrong, adding transparency led to a significant decrease in annotators agreement with the ground truth (Kruskal Wallis, $p < 0.001$). In contrast, there was a significant increase in the agreement of annotators with the ML model when the ML prediction was wrong (Kruskal Wallis, $p < 0.001$). When the ML prediction was correct, the effect of adding transparency was not significant.

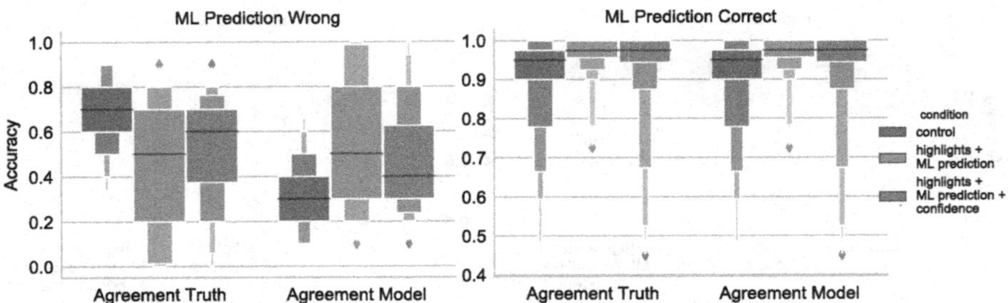

Fig. 4. Agreement between annotations by humans and ground truth or ML model predictions, respectively, when the ML prediction was *wrong* (*left*) and when the ML prediction was correct (*right*) at increasing levels of transparency. When the ML prediction was wrong, transparency decreases annotators' agreement with ground truth but increases their agreement with the ML prediction.

4.2 Algorithmic Bias and Model Uncertainty

While intuitive, these insights from conditioning on whether the model was right or wrong are difficult to translate in real world scenario advices: in most real world applications the true labels are not known. What often is known is the uncertainty of a ML prediction. We investigated how algorithmic bias due to transparency is influenced by model uncertainty. In some cases, when the model has high accuracy and its uncertainty estimates are well calibrated, this quantity is closely related to the accuracy of a model, but that is not necessarily the case. In order to condition on model uncertainty we first computed the entropy of the binary classifier for each data point

$$-p(\text{pos})\log(p(\text{pos})) - p(\text{neg})\log(p(\text{neg})) \tag{5}$$

where $p(\text{pos})$, $p(\text{neg})$ is the predicted likelihood of the ML model for a positive or negative review, respectively. We split the data at the median entropy of all data points into low entropy samples, for which the model was relatively certain about its prediction, and high entropy samples, for which the model was uncertain. Note that only in the condition with the highest transparency degree subjects had access to the probability score, which is in this case directly related to the entropy. In the two other conditions, the entropy of the model was not exposed.

Model Uncertainty Decreases Algorithmic Bias. The agreement of subjects with ground truth labels and model predictions split into low and high entropy samples is shown in Fig. 5. Similar to the overall effect of algorithmic bias in Fig. 3, also in this illustration we observe a pronounced algorithmic bias induced by adding transparency. The agreement between annotators and ML model increases when adding transparency, especially when only explanations and model prediction are shown. However, when conditioning on model entropy we see a strong effect of uncertainty on annotators' bias: their algorithmic bias is

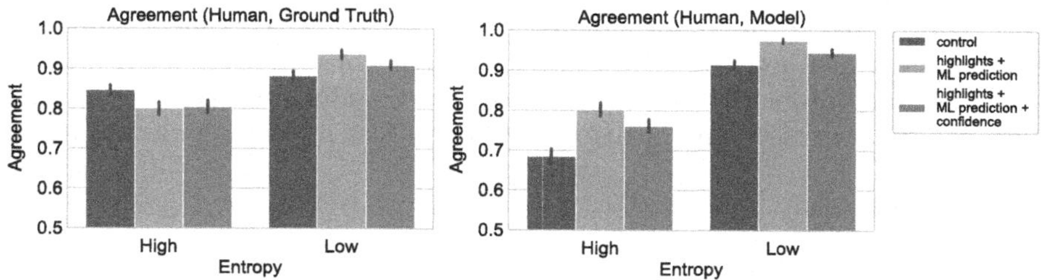

Fig. 5. Effect of model uncertainty on agreement between annotations by humans and ground truth (*left*) and ML model predictions (*right*) at increasing levels of transparency. *Left*: Algorithm transparency is associated with a decrease in annotators' agreement with true labels when predictions are uncertain, but with an increase when the ML model is certain. *Right*: Transparency induces algorithmic bias – especially when the model is certain.

reduced significantly in all transparency conditions when the model is uncertain (chi-square test of independence, $p < 0.001$).

Positive and Negative Effects of Algorithmic Bias. While the overall impact of transparency, shown in Fig. 3, is mainly algorithmic bias, there appears to be no effect on the annotators' agreement with the ground truth. Our results however suggest that when controlling for model uncertainty, transparency does have an effect on annotators' accuracy, but this effect is opposite for low and high entropy predictions of an ML model. In Fig. 5 (*left*) we observe that adding transparency *decreases* annotators' accuracy – but only for high entropy samples (chi-square test of independence, $p = 0.018$). In contrast when the model is certain, annotation accuracy is increased with transparency (chi-square test of independence, $p < 0.001$). These findings have direct implications for the calibration of human interaction with transparent AI systems. As annotators' accuracy becomes worse with added transparency when a model is uncertain, one should consider carefully exposing biasing information in such human-AI interaction when the model is uncertain. Interestingly, this is true also for conditions in which annotators had access to the model entropy. This finding is somewhat in line with the results in [25] in which the authors reported that exposing the probabilities of a prediction did not have a strong positive effect on human subjects.

4.3 Impact of Risk and Ambiguity Tolerance on Transparency Induced Algorithmic Bias

The above results confirm that transparency induces algorithmic bias, meaning annotators are more likely to replicate the ML prediction. In this section we investigate whether annotators exhibit different algorithmic bias susceptibility depending on the personality traits risk aversion and ambiguity tolerance. We partitioned the annotators into risk averse and risk affine as well as ambiguity averse and ambiguity tolerant subjects according to the coefficients in Eq. 1

which were fitted to the data obtained in the gambling experiment. Following [50] annotators with $\alpha > 1$ were classified as risk tolerant and and risk averse otherwise, annotators with $\beta < 0$ were classified as ambiguity tolerant and ambiguity averse otherwise. The histogram of annotators in each segment is shown in Table 2.

Table 2. Histogram of annotators classified as risk and ambiguity averse or tolerant

# annotators	Ambiguity averse	Ambiguity tolerant
Risk averse	103	45
Risk tolerant	21	79

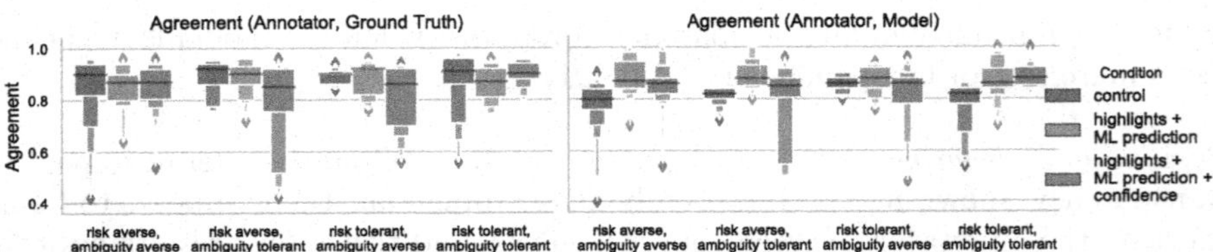

Fig. 6. Same data as in Fig. 3 but here the data is split by risk and ambiguity tolerant behaviour of annotators. When adding transparency, risk and ambiguity averse annotators exhibit higher agreement with the ML model and less agreement with ground truth. Risk tolerant and ambiguity averse annotators show the opposite effect. (Color figure online)

Risk Aversion Correlates with Algorithmic Bias Susceptibilty. The results in Fig. 6 show that annotators with different risk and ambiguity behaviour are impacted differently by adding transparency to the assistive ML system. The most prominent effect is the relationship between risk aversive behaviour and algorithmic bias. Annotators that tended to be risk averse showed the most pronounced algorithmic bias, as shown in Fig. 6, *right*, blue (control) vs. orange (highlights) and green (highlights and confidence) (Mann-Whitney, $p < 0.001$, bonferroni-adjusted). Interestingly, the strongest algorithmic bias was observed for the intermediate level of transparency, when the model prediction confidence was not shown (orange). This suggests that while risk averse subjects are most susceptible to algorithmic bias induced by transparency, this tendency is alleviated when the model confidence is shown. In contrast to risk averse annotators, risk tolerant annotators were not as susceptible to transparency induced algorithmic bias, the agreement of their annotations with the ML model predictions was less affected (Mann-Whitney, $p = 0.003$) by the level of transparency.

Ambiguity Tolerance and Transparency. We also investigated the relationship between ambiguity tolerance and the impact of transparency on algorithmic bias and annotation accuracy. Ambiguity tolerance is generally associated with prosocial behaviour in human interaction [50] and we hypothesized that it could be important for human AI interaction as well. While our results suggest that there is an effect of ambiguity tolerance in combination with risk aversion on the impact on transparency (Fig. 6), these differences are not statistically significant. This suggests, that while ambiguity tolerance is an important personality trait for interactions between humans it is less important for the trust relationship in human-AI interaction. We emphasize however that when conditioning on all combinations of risk aversion and ambiguity tolerance some groups of subjects were too small for detecting a significant effect of ambiguity and risk behaviour on transparency induced algorithmic bias, see also Table 2.

5 Conclusion

Human-Machine interaction has become a central part of everyday life. A large body of literature is dedicated to improving transparency of ML systems for more responsible usage of AI systems. We believe that transparency in itself does not necessarily have positive consequences on human-AI interaction. Both parts, AI systems and human users, should be calibrated well to avoid cases of unjustified algorithmic bias, or cases of ignorance of helpful assistive-AI predictions. Optimal calibration however requires an in-depth understanding of both parties and how they interact. To the best of our knowledge the role of human personality has been underrepresented in the literature on transparent machine learning. In this study we investigated the impact of transparency added to an ML system onto human-AI interaction with a special focus on personality traits that are associated with trust. We analyzed human-AI interaction by conditioning on various aspects of the underlying ML model, such as uncertainty or correctness of a prediction, but also by conditioning on personality traits.

Our results demonstrate that transparency leads to algorithmic bias in human-AI interaction. Extending previous work, we find that both model correctness and model uncertainty have an effect on algorithmic bias. In particular we find that transparency and the induced algorithmic bias can lead to worse annotation accuracy when the ML model prediction is uncertain or wrong – but we also find that algorithmic bias can lead to increased annotation accuracy when the model is certain or correct in its predictions. This finding has direct implications for practical applications: for uncertain model predictions, transparency should be used with care to avoid detrimental algorithmic biases. This is especially important as many cases, when unjustified algorithmic bias can have far reaching negative impact, are cases with high uncertainty, such as time critical decisions in hospitals or policing.

Most importantly however we find that not all subjects were equally susceptible to transparency induced algorithmic bias. Our results show that risk averse annotators were more susceptible to algorithmic bias than risk affine subjects.

When increasing transparency risk aversion was associated with an increase in agreement between annotators and the ML prediction and at the same time with a decrease in annotation accuracy – a sign of blind trust in ML predictions that can be attributed to increased transparency. These findings can also be directly transferred into practical applications. Determining the risk affinity of subjects can help to optimally calibrate the level of transparency for human-AI interaction. In contrast to the effects of risk aversion we did not find a significant effect of ambiguity tolerance on algorithmic bias. This result is different from studies on interaction between humans [50] and suggests that ambiguity tolerance could play a different role in interactions between humans and interactions between humans and an ML system.

Taken together our results highlight the potential of methods from psychology for improving the quality of human-AI interaction. A better understanding of how different personalities use AI can help to design systems that are both easier to use and less prone to algorithmic bias. We hope that this line of research will ultimately help to foster more responsible usage of AI systems.

References

1. Arrow, K.: Aspects of the theory of risk-bearing. Yrjö Jahnsson lectures, Yrjö Jahnssonin Säätiö (1965). https://books.google.de/books?id=hnNEAAAAIAAJ
2. Aumann, R.J.: Agreeing to disagree. Ann. Stat. **4**, 1236–1239 (1976)
3. Bell, D.E., Raiffa, H., Tversky, A.: Decision Making: Descriptive, Normative, and Prescriptive Interactions. Cambridge university Press, Cambridge (1988)
4. Camerer, C., Weber, M.: Recent developments in modeling preferences: uncertainty and ambiguity. J. Risk Uncertainty (1992). https://doi.org/10.1007/BF00122575
5. Cook, R.D.: Detection of influential observation in linear regression. Technometrics **19**(1), 15–18 (1977). http://www.jstor.org/stable/1268249
6. Curley, S.P., Yates, J.F., Abrams, R.A.: Psychological sources of ambiguity avoidance. Organ. Behav. Hum. Decis. Processes **38**(2), 230–256 (1986)
7. Dietvorst, B.J., Simmons, J.P., Massey, C.: Algorithm aversion: people erroneously avoid algorithms after seeing them err. J. Exp. Psychol. Gen. **144**(1), 114–126 (2015). https://doi.org/10.1037/xge0000033
8. Doshi-Velez, F., Kim, B.: Towards a rigorous science of interpretable machine learning. arXiv preprint arXiv:1702.08608 (2017)
9. Einhorn, H.J., Hogarth, R.M.: Decision making under ambiguity. J. Bus. **59**, S225–S250 (1986)
10. Ellsberg, D.: Risk, ambiguity, and the savage axioms. Q. J. Econ. **75**, 643–669 (1961)
11. FeldmanHall, O., Glimcher, P., Baker, A.L., Phelps, E.A.: Emotion and decision-making under uncertainty: physiological arousal predicts increased gambling during ambiguity but not risk. J. Exp. Psychol. Gen. **145**(10), 1255 (2016)
12. Gilboa, I., Schmeidler, D.: Maxmin expected utility with non-unique prior. In: Uncertainty in Economic Theory, pp. 141–151. Routledge (2004)
13. Goodfellow, I.J., Shlens, J., Szegedy, C.: Explaining and harnessing adversarial examples. CoRR abs/1412.6572 (2014). http://arxiv.org/abs/1412.6572

14. Guidotti, R., Monreale, A., Ruggieri, S., Turini, F., Giannotti, F., Pedreschi, D.: A survey of methods for explaining black box models. ACM Comput. Surv. **51**(5), 1–42 (2018). https://doi.org/10.1145/3236009. http://dl.acm.org/citation.cfm?doid=3271482.3236009
15. Hampel, F.R., Ronchetti, E.M., Rousseeuw, P.J., Stahel, W.A.: Robust Statistics: The Approach Based on Influence Functions, vol. 196. Wiley, Hoboken (2011)
16. Haufe, S., et al.: On the interpretation of weight vectors of linear models in multivariate neuroimaging. Neuroimage **87**, 96–110 (2014)
17. Herman, B.: The promise and peril of human evaluation for model interpretability. CoRR abs/1711.07414 (2017)
18. Huysmans, J., Dejaeger, K., Mues, C., Vanthienen, J., Baesens, B.: An empirical evaluation of the comprehensibility of decision table, tree and rule based predictive models. Decis. Support Syst. **51**(1), 141–154 (2011). https://doi.org/10.1016/j.dss.2010.12.003, http://www.sciencedirect.com/science/article/pii/S0167923610002368
19. Kahneman, D., Tversky, A.: Choices, values, and frames. In: Handbook of the Fundamentals of Financial Decision Making: Part I, pp. 269–278. World Scientific (2013)
20. Kahneman, D., Tversky, A.: Prospect theory: an analysis of decision under risk. In: Handbook of the Fundamentals of Financial Decision Making: Part I, pp. 99–127. World Scientific (2013)
21. Kindermans, P., Schütt, K.T., Alber, M., Müller, K., Dähne, S.: Patternnet and patternlrp - improving the interpretability of neural networks. CoRR abs/1705.05598 (2017). http://arxiv.org/abs/1705.05598
22. Klibanoff, P., Marinacci, M., Mukerji, S.: A smooth model of decision making under ambiguity. Econometrica **73**(6), 1849–1892 (2005)
23. Knight, F.H.: Risk, Uncertainty and Profit. Courier Corporation, North Chelmsford (2012)
24. Koh, P.W., Liang, P.: Understanding black-box predictions via influence functions. In: Precup, D., Teh, Y.W. (eds.) ICML. vol. 70, pp. 1885–1894 (2017). http://proceedings.mlr.press/v70/koh17a.html
25. Lai, V., Tan, C.: On human predictions with explanations and predictions of machine learning models: a case study on deception detection (2019). https://doi.org/10.1145/3287560.3287590
26. Lakkaraju, H., Bach, S.H., Leskovec, J.: Interpretable decision sets: a joint framework for description and prediction. In: Proceedings of the 22nd ACM SIGKDD International Conference on Knowledge Discovery and Data Mining, pp. 1675–1684. ACM (2016)
27. Levy, I., Snell, J., Nelson, A.J., Rustichini, A., Glimcher, P.W.: Neural representation of subjective value under risk and ambiguity. J. Neurophysiol. **103**(2), 1036–1047 (2009)
28. Lipton, Z.C.: The mythos of model interpretability. arXiv preprint arXiv:1606.03490 (2016)
29. Lipton, Z.C.: The doctor just won't accept that! arXiv preprint arXiv:1711.08037 (2017)
30. Lundberg, S.M., Lee, S.: A unified approach to interpreting model predictions. In: NIPS, pp. 4768–4777 (2017)
31. Maas, A.L., Daly, R.E., Pham, P.T., Huang, D., Ng, A.Y., Potts, C.: Learning word vectors for sentiment analysis. In: ACL, pp. 142–150 (2011). http://www.aclweb.org/anthology/P11-1015

32. Miller, T.: Explanation in artificial intelligence: insights from the social sciences. arXiv preprint arXiv:1706.07269 (2017)
33. Montavon, G., Lapuschkin, S., Binder, A., Samek, W., Müller, K.: Explaining nonlinear classification decisions with deep taylor decomposition. Pattern Recogn. **65**, 211–222 (2017). https://doi.org/10.1016/j.patcog.2016.11.008
34. Pratt, J.W.: Risk aversion in the small and in the large. In: Uncertainty in Economics, pp. 59–79. Elsevier (1978)
35. Pulford, B.D.: Short article: is luck on my side? optimism, pessimism, and ambiguity aversion. Q. J. Exp. Psychol. **62**(6), 1079–1087 (2009)
36. Rahwan, I., et al.: Machine behaviour. Nature **12**(11), 26. https://doi.org/10.1038/s41586-019-1138-y
37. Ribeiro, M.T., Singh, S., Guestrin, C.: "why should I trust you?": explaining the predictions of any classifier. In: SIGKDD, pp. 1135–1144 (2016)
38. Ribeiro, M.T., Singh, S., Guestrin, C.: Anchors: high-precision model-agnostic explanations. In: AAAI Conference on Artificial Intelligence (2018)
39. Rieger, M.O., Wang, M.: Cumulative prospect theory and the St. Petersburg paradox. Econ. Theory **28**(3), 665–679 (2006)
40. Samek, W., Binder, A., Montavon, G., Lapuschkin, S., Müller, K.: Evaluating the visualization of what a deep neural network has learned. IEEE Trans. Neural Netw. Learning Syst. **28**(11), 2660–2673 (2017). https://doi.org/10.1109/TNNLS.2016.2599820
41. Savage, L.J.: The Foundations of Statistics. Courier Corporation, North Chelmsford (1972)
42. Schmeidler, D.: Subjective probability and expected utility without additivity. Econometrica J. Econometric Soc. **57**, 571–587 (1989)
43. Schmidt, P., Bießmann, F.: Quantifying interpretability and trust in machine learning systems. vol. abs/1901.08558 (2019). http://arxiv.org/abs/1901.08558
44. Simonyan, K., Vedaldi, A., Zisserman, A.: Deep inside convolutional networks: Visualising image classification models and saliency maps. CoRR abs/1312.6034 (2013). http://arxiv.org/abs/1312.6034
45. Slovic, P., Tversky, A.: Who accepts savage's axiom? Behav. Sci. **19**(6), 368–373 (1974)
46. Stanley Budner, N.: Intolerance of ambiguity as a personality variable 1. J. Pers. **30**(1), 29–50 (1962)
47. Strumbelj, E., Kononenko, I.: An efficient explanation of individual classifications using game theory. J. Mach. Learn. Res. **11**, 1–18 (2010). https://doi.org/10.1145/1756006.1756007
48. Tversky, A., Kahneman, D.: Advances in prospect theory: cumulative representation of uncertainty. J. Risk Uncertainty **5**(4), 297–323 (1992)
49. Tymula, A., et al.: Adolescents' risk-taking behavior is driven by tolerance to ambiguity. Proc. National Acad. Sci. (2012). https://doi.org/10.1073/pnas.1207144109
50. Vives, M.L., Feldmanhall, O.: Tolerance to ambiguous uncertainty predicts prosocial behavior. Nat. Commun. (2018). https://doi.org/10.1038/s41467-018-04631-9
51. Von Neumann, J., Morgenstern, O., Kuhn, H.W.: Theory of Games and Economic Behavior (Commemorative Edition). Princeton University Press, Princeton (2007)
52. Wally, S., Baum, J.R.: Personal and structural determinants of the pace of strategic decision making. Acad. Manag. J. **37**(4), 932–956 (1994)

53. Zeiler, M.D., Fergus, R.: Visualizing and understanding convolutional networks. In: ECCV, pp. 818–833 (2014)
54. Zien, A., Krämer, N., Sonnenburg, S., Rätsch, G.: The feature importance ranking measure. In: Buntine, W., Grobelnik, M., Mladenić, D., Shawe-Taylor, J. (eds.) ECML PKDD 2009. LNCS (LNAI), vol. 5782, pp. 694–709. Springer, Heidelberg (2009). https://doi.org/10.1007/978-3-642-04174-7_45

Applying AI in Practice: Key Challenges and Lessons Learned

Lukas Fischer[1(✉)], Lisa Ehrlinger[1,2], Verena Geist[1], Rudolf Ramler[1], Florian Sobieczky[1], Werner Zellinger[1], and Bernhard Moser[1]

[1] Software Competence Center Hagenberg GmbH (SCCH), Hagenberg, Austria
{lukas.fischer,lisa.ehrlinger,verena.geist,rudolf.ramler, florian.sobieczky, werner.zellinger,bernhard.moser}@scch.at

[2] Johannes Kepler University, Linz, Austria
lisa.ehrlinger@jku.at

Abstract. The main challenges along with lessons learned from ongoing research in the application of machine learning systems in practice are discussed, taking into account aspects of theoretical foundations, systems engineering, and human-centered AI postulates. The analysis outlines a fundamental theory-practice gap which superimposes the challenges of AI system engineering at the level of data quality assurance, model building, software engineering and deployment.

Keywords: Machine learning systems · Data quality · Domain adaptation · Hybrid models · Software engineering · Embedded systems · Human centered AI

1 Introduction

Many real-world tasks are characterized by uncertainties and probabilistic data that is hard to understand and hard to process for humans. Machine learning and knowledge extraction [46] help turning this data into useful information for realizing a wide spectrum of applications such as image recognition, scene understanding, decision-support systems, etc. that enable new use cases across a broad range of domains.

The success of various machine learning methods, in particular Deep Neural Networks (DNNs), for challenging problems of computer vision and pattern recognition, has led to a "Cambrian explosion" in the field of Artificial Intelligence (AI). In many application areas, AI researchers have turned to deep learning as the solution of choice [54,97]. A characteristic of this development

---

Special thanks go to A Min Tjoa, former Scientific Director of SCCH, for his encouraging support in bringing together data and software science to tackle the research problems discussed in this paper. The research reported in this paper has been funded by BMK, BMDW, and the Province of Upper Austria in the frame of the COMET Programme managed by FFG.

Published by Springer Nature Switzerland AG 2020
A. Holzinger et al. (Eds.): CD-MAKE 2020, LNCS 12279, pp. 451–471, 2020.
https://doi.org/10.1007/978-3-030-57321-8_25

is the acceleration of progress in AI over the last decade, which has led to AI systems that are strong enough to raise serious ethical and societal acceptance questions. Another characteristic of this development is the way how such systems are engineered. Above all, there is an increasing interconnection of traditionally separate disciplines such as data analysis, model building and software engineering. In particular, data-driven AI methods such as DNNs allow data to shape models and software systems that operate them. System engineering of AI-driven software therefore faces novel challenges at all stages of the system lifecycle [51]:

- **Key Challenge 1:** *AI intrinsic challenges* due to peculiarities or shortcomings of today's AI methods; in particular, current data-driven AI is characterized by:
  - data challenge in terms of quality assurance and procurement;
  - challenge to integrate expert knowledge and models;
  - model integrity and reproducibility challenge due to unstable performance profiles triggered by small variations in the implementation or input data (adversarial noise);
- **Key Challenge 2:** Challenges in the process of *AI system engineering* ranging from requirements analysis and specification to deployment including
  - testing, debugging and documentation challenges;
  - challenge to consider the constraints of target platforms at design time;
  - certification and regulation challenges resulting from highly regulated target domains such as in a bio-medical laboratory setting;
- **Key Challenge 3:** *Interpretability and trust challenge* in the operational environment, in particular
  - trust challenge in terms of lack of interpretability and transparency by opaque models;
  - challenge posed by ethical guideline;
  - acceptance challenge in terms of societal barriers to AI adoption in society, healthcare or working environments;

2 Key Challenges on System Engineering Posed by Data-Driven AI

2.1 AI Intrinsic Challenges

There are peculiarities of deep learning methods that affect the correct interpretation of the system's output and the transparency of the system's configuration.

Lack of Uniqueness of Internal Configuration: First of all, in contrast to traditional engineering, there is a lack of uniqueness of internal configuration causing difficulties in model comparison. Systems based on machine learning, in particular deep learning models, are typically regarded as black boxes. However, it is not just simply the complex nested non-linear structure which matters as often pointed out in the literature, see [86]. There are mathematical or physical systems which are also complex, nested and non-linear, and yet interpretable (e.g., wavelets, statistical mechanics). It is an amazing, unexpected phenomenon that such deep networks become easier to be optimized (trained) with an increasing number of layers, hence complexity, see [100,110]. More precisely, to find a reasonable sub-optimum out of many equally good possibilities. As consequence, and in contrast to classical engineering, we lose uniqueness of the internal optimal state.

Lack of Confidence Measure: A further peculiarity of state of the art deep learning methods is the lack of confidence measure. In contrast to Bayesian based approaches to machine learning, most deep learning models do not offer a justified confidence measure of the model's uncertainties. E.g., in classification models, the probability vector obtained in the top layer (predominantly softmax output) is often interpreted as model confidence, see, e.g., [26] or [35]. However, functions like softmax can result in extrapolations with unjustified high confidence for points far from the training data, hence providing a false sense of safety [39]. Therefore, it seems natural to try to introduce the Bayesian approach also to DNN models. The resulting uncertainty measures (or, synonymously, confidence measures) rely on approximations of the posterior distribution regarding the weights given the data. As a promising approach in this context, variational techniques, e.g., based on Monte Carlo dropout [27], allow to turn these Bayesian concepts into computationally tractable algorithms. The variational approach relies on the Kullback-Leibler divergence for measuring the dissimilarity between distributions. As a consequence, the resultant approximating distribution becomes concentrated around a single mode, underestimating the uncertainty beyond this mode. Thus, the resulting measure of confidence for a given instance remains unsatisfactory and there might be still regions with misinterpreted high confidence.

Lack of Control of High-Dimensionality Effects: Further, there is the still unsolved problem of lack of control of high-dimensionality effects. There are high dimensional effects which are not yet fully understood in the context of deep learning, see [31] and [28]. Such high-dimensional effects can cause instabilities as illustrated, for example, by the emergence of so-called adversarial examples, see e.g. [3,96].

2.2 AI System Engineering Challenges

In a data-driven AI systems there are two equally consequential components: software code and data. However, some input data are inherently volatile and may change over time. Therefore, it is important that these changes can be identified and tracked to fully understand the models and the final system. To this end, the development of such data-driven systems has all the challenges of traditional software engineering combined with specific machine learning problems causing additional hidden technical debts [87].

Theory-Practice Gap in Machine Learning: The design and test principles of machine learning are underpinned by statistical learning theory and its fundamental theorems such as Vapnik's theorem [99]. The theoretical analysis relies on idealized assumptions such as that the data are drawn independent and identically distributed from the same probability distribution. As outlined in [81], however, this assumption may be violated in typical applications such as natural language processing [48] and computer vision [106,108].

This problem of data set shifting can result from the way input characteristics are used, from the way training and test sets are selected, from data sparsity, from shifts in data distribution due to non-stationary environments, and also from changes in activation patterns within layers of deep neural networks. Such a data set shift can cause misleading parameter tuning when performing test strategies such as cross-validation [58,104].

This is why engineering machine learning systems largely relies on the skill of the data scientist to examine and resolve such problems.

Data Quality Challenge: While much of the research in machine learning and its theoretical foundation has focused on improving the accuracy and efficiency of training and inference algorithms, less attention has been paid to the equally important practical problem of monitoring the quality of the data supplied to machine learning [6,19]. Especially heterogeneous data sources, the occurrence of unexpected patterns, and a large number of schema-free data pose additional problems for data management which directly impact data extraction from multiple sources, data preparation, and data cleansing [7,84].

For data quality issues, the situation is similar to the detection of software bugs. The earlier the problems are detected and resolved, the better for model quality and development productivity.

Configuration Maintenance Challenge: ML system developers usually start from ready-made, pre-trained networks and try to optimize their execution on the target processing platform as much as possible. This practice is prone to the entanglement problem [87]: If changes are made to an input feature, the meaning, weighting, or use of the other features may also change. This means that machine learning systems must be designed so that feature engineering and selection changes are easily tracked. Especially when models are constantly revised and subtly changed, the tracking of configuration updates while maintaining the clarity and flexibility of the configuration become an additional burden.

Deployment Challenge: The design and training of the learning algorithm and the inference of the resulting model are two different activities. The training is very computationally intensive and is usually conducted on a high performance platform [103]. It is an iterative process that leads to the selection of an optimal algorithm configuration, usually known as hyperparameter optimization, with accuracy as the only major goal of the design [105]. While the training process is usually conducted offline, inference very often has to deal with real-time constraints, tight power or energy budgets, and security threats. This dichotomy determines the need for multiple design re-spins (before a successful integration), potentially leading to long tuning phases, overloading the designers and producing results highly depending on their skills. Despite the variety of resources available, optimizing these heterogeneous computing architectures for performing low-latency and energy-efficient DL inference tasks without compromising performance is still a challenge [5].

2.3 Interpretability and Trust Challenge

In contrast to traditional computing, AI can now perform tasks that previously only humans were able to do. As such it contains the possibility to revolutionize every aspect of our society. The impact is far-reaching. First, with the increasing spread of AI systems, the interaction between humans and AI will increasingly become the dominant form of human-computer interaction [1]. Second, this development will shape the future workforce. PwC[1] predicts a relatively low displacement of jobs (around 3%) in the first wave of AI, but this could dramatically increase up to 30% by the mid-2030's. Therefore, human centered AI has started coming to the forefront of AI research based on postulated ethical principles for protecting human autonomy and preventing harm. Recent initiatives at national[2] and supra-national[3] level emphasize the need for research in trusted AI.

Interpretability Challenge: Essential aspects of trusted AI are explainability and interpretability. While interpretability is about being able to discern the mechanics without necessarily knowing why. Explainability is being able to quite literally explain what is happening, for example, by referring to mechanical laws. It is well known that the great successes of machine learning in recent decades in terms of applicability and acceptance are relativized by the fact that they can be explained less easily with increasing complexity of the learning model [44,60,90]. Explainability of the solution is thus increasingly perceived as an inherent quality of the respective methods [9,15,33,90]. Particularly in the case of deep learning methods attempts to interpret the predictions made using parameters fail [33]. The necessity to obtain not only increasing prediction accuracy but also the interpretation of the solutions determined by ML or Deep Learning arises at the latest with the ethical [10,76], legal [13], psychological [59], medical [25,45], and sociological [111] questions tied to their application. The common element of these questions is the demand to clearly interpret the decisions proposed by artificial intelligence (AI). The complex of problems that derives from this aspect of artificial intelligence for explainability, transparency, trustworthiness, etc. is generally described with the term Explainable Artificial Intelligence, synonymously

[1] https://www.pwc.com/gx/en/services/people-organisation/workforce-of-the-future/workforce-of-the-future-the-competing-forces-shaping-2030-pwc.pdf.

[2] https://www.whitehouse.gov/wp-content/uploads/2019/06/National-AI-Research-and-Development-Strategic-Plan-2019-Update-June-2019.pdf.

[3] https://ec.europa.eu/digital-single-market/en/news/ethics-guidelines-trustworthy-ai.

"Explainable AI" or "XAI". Its broad relevance can be seen in the interdisciplinary nature of the scientific discussion that is currently taking place on such terms as interpretation, explanation and refined versions such as causability and causality in connection with AI methods [30,33,42,43].

Trust Challenge: In contrast to Interpretability, trust is a much more comprehensive concept. Trust is linked to the uncertainty about a possible malfunctioning or failure of the AI system as well as to circumstances of delegating control to a machine as a "black box". Predictability and dependability of AI technology as well as the understanding of the technology's operations and the intentions of its creators are essential drivers of trust [12]. Particularly, in critical applications the user wants to understand the rationale behind a classification, and under which conditions the system is trustful and when not. Consequently, AI systems must make it possible to take these human needs of trust and social compatibility into account. On the other hand, we have to be aware of limitations and peculiarities of state of the art AI systems. Currently, the topic of trusted AI is discussed in different communities at different levels of abstraction:

- in terms of high level ethical guidelines (e.g. ethics boards such as algorithmwatch.org[4], EU's Draft Ethics Guidelines[5]);
- in terms of regulatory postulates for current AI systems regarding e.g. transparency (working groups on standardization, e.g. ISO/IEC JTC 1/SC 42 on artificial intelligence[6]);
- in terms of improved features of AI models (above all by explainable AI community [34,41]);
- in terms of trust modeling approaches (e.g. multi-agent systems community [12]).

In view of the model-intrinsic and system-technical challenges of AI that have been pointed out in the Sects. 2.1 and 2.2, the gap between the envisioned high-level ethical guidelines of human-centered AI and the state of the art of AI systems becomes evident.

3 Approaches, In-Progress Research and Lessons Learned

In this section we discuss ongoing research facing the outlined challenges in the previous section, comprising:

(1) Automated and Continuous Data Quality Assurance, see Sect. 3.1;
(2) Domain Adaptation Approach for Tackling Deviating Data Characteristics at Training and Test Time, see Sect. 3.2;
(3) Hybrid Model Design for Improving Model Accuracy, see Sect. 3.3;

[4] https://algorithmwatch.org/en/project/ai-ethics-guidelines-global-inventory/.

[5] https://ec.europa.eu/digital-single-market/en/news/ethics-guidelines-trustworthy-ai.

[6] https://www.iso.org/committee/6794475/x/catalogue/p/0/u/1/w/0/d/0.

(4) Interpretability by Correction Model Approach, see Sect. 3.4;
(5) Software Quality by Automated Code Analysis and Documentation Generation, see Sect. 3.5;
(6) The ALOHA Toolchain for Embedded Platforms, see Sect. 3.6;
(7) Human AI Teaming as Key to Human Centered AI, see Sect. 3.7.

3.1 Approach 1: Automated and Continuous Data Quality Assurance

In times of large and volatile amounts of data, which are often generated automatically by sensors (e.g., in smart home solutions of housing units or industrial settings), it is especially important to, (i), automatically, and, (ii), continuously monitor the quality of data [22,88]. A recent study [20] shows that the continuous monitoring of data quality is only supported by very few software tools. In the open-source area these are Apache Griffin[7], MobyDQ[8], and QuaIIe [21]. Apache Griffin and QuaIIe implement data quality metrics from the reference literature (see [21,40]), whereby most of them require a reference database (gold standard) for calculation. MobyDQ, on the other hand, is rule-based, with the focus on data quality checks along a pipeline, where data is compared between two different databases. Since existing open-source tools were insufficient for the permanent measurement of data quality within a database or a data stream used for data analysis and machine learning, we developed the Data Quality Library (DaQL). DaQL allows the extensive definition of data quality rules, based on the newly developed DaQL language. These rules do not require reference data and DaQL has already been used for a ML application in an industrial setting [19]. However, to ensure their validity, the rules for DaQL are created manually by domain experts.

Lesson Learned: In literature, data quality is typically defined with the "fitness for use" principle, which illustrates the high contextual dependency of the topic [11,102]. Thus, one important lesson learned is the need for more research into the automated generation of domain-specific data quality rules. In addition, the integration of contextual knowledge (e.g., the respective ML model using the data) needs to be considered. Here, knowledge graphs pose a promising solution, which indicates that knowledge about the quality of data is part of the bigger picture outlined in Approach (and lesson learned) 7: the usage of knowledge graphs to interpret the quality of AI systems. In addition to the measurement (i.e., detection) of data quality issues, we consider research into the automated correction (i.e., cleansing) of sensor data as additional challenge [18]. Especially since automated data cleansing poses the risk to insert new errors in the data (cf. [63]), which is specifically critical in enterprise settings.

[7] https://griffin.incubator.apache.org.
[8] https://github.com/mobydq/mobydq.

3.2 Approach 2: The Domain Adaptation Approach for Tackling Deviating Data Characteristics at Training and Test Time

In [106] and [108] we introduce a novel distance measure, the so-called Centralized Moment Discrepancy (CMD), for aligning probability distributions in the context of domain adaption. Domain adaptation algorithms are designed to minimize the misclassification risk of a discriminative model for a target domain with little training data by adapting a model from a source domain with a large amount of training data. Standard approaches measure the adaptation discrepancy based on distance measures between the empirical probability distributions in the source and target domain, i.e., in our setting this means training time and test time, respectively. In [109] we can show that our CMD approach, refined by practice-oriented information-theoretic assumptions of the involved distributions, yield a generalization of the conditions of Vapnik's theorem [99].

As a result we obtain quantitative generalization bounds for recently proposed moment-based algorithms for unsupervised domain adaptation which perform particularly well in many practical tasks [74, 95, 106–108].

Lesson Learned: It is interesting that moment-based probability distance measure are the most weakest among those utilized in the machine learning and, in particular, domain adaptation. Weak in this setting means that convergence by the stronger distance measures entails convergence of the weaker. Our lesson learned is that a weaker distance measure can be more robust than stronger distance measures. At the first glance, this observation might appear counterintuitive. However, at a second look, it becomes intuitive that the minimization of stronger distance measures are more prone to the effect of negative transfer [77], i.e. the adaptation of source-specific information not present in the target domain. Further evidence can be found in the area of generative adversarial networks where the alignment of distributions by strong probability metrics can cause problems of mode collapse which can be mitigated by choosing weaker similarity concepts [17]. Thus, it is better to abandon stronger concepts of similarity in favour of weaker ones and to use stronger concepts only if they can be justified.

3.3 Approach 3: Hybrid Model Design for Improving Model Accuracy by Integrating Expert Hints in Biomedical Diagnostics

For diagnostics based on biomedical image analysis, image segmentation serves as a prerequisite step to extract quantitative information [70]. If, however, segmentation results are not accurate, quantitative analysis can lead to results that misrepresent the underlying biological conditions [50]. To extract features from biomedical images at a single cell level, robust automated segmentation algorithms have to be applied. In the Austrian FFG project VISIOMICS[9], which

[9] Platform supporting an integrated analysis of image and multiOMICs data based on liquid biopsies for tumor diagnostics – https://www.visiomics.at/.

is devoted to cell analysis, we tackle this problem by following a cell segmentation ensemble approach, consisting of several state-of-the-art deep neural networks [38,85]. In addition to overcome the lack of training data, which is very time consuming to prepare and annotate, we utilize a Generative Adversarial Network approach (GANs) for artificial training data generation [53][10]. The underlying dataset was also published [52] and is available online[11]. Particularly for cancer diagnostics, clinical decision-making often relies on timely and cost-effective genome-wide testing. Similar to biomedical imaging, classical bioinformatic algorithms, often require manual data curation, which is error prone, extremely time-consuming, and thus has negative effects on time and cost efficiency. To overcome this problem, we developed the DeepSNP[12] network to learn from genome-wide single-nucleotide polymorphism array (SNPa) data and to classify the presence or absence of genomic breakpoints within large genomic windows with high precision and recall [16].

Lesson Learned: First, it is crucial to rely on expert knowledge when it comes to data augmentation strategies. This becomes more important the more complex the data is (high number of cores and overlapping cores). Less complex images do not necessarily benefit from data augmentation. Second, by introducing so-called localization units the network is able to gain the ability to exactly localize anomalies in terms of genomic breakpoints despite never experiencing their exact location during training. In this way we have learned that localization and attention units can be used to significantly ease the effort of annotating data.

3.4 Approach 4: Interpretability by Correction Model Approach

Last year, at a symposium on predictive analytics in Vienna [93], we introduced an approach to the problem of formulating interpretability of AI models for classification or regression problems [37] with a given basis model, e.g., in the context of model predictive control [32]. The basic idea is to root the problem of interpretability in the basic model by considering the contribution of the AI model as correction of this basis model and is referred to as "Before and After Correction Parameter Comparison (BAPC)". The idea of small correction is a common approach in mathematics in the field of perturbation theory, for example of linear operators. In [91,92] the idea of small-scale perturbation (in the sense of linear algebra) was used to give estimates of the probability of return of an odyssey on a percolation cluster. The notion of "small influence" appears here in a similar way via the measures of determination for the AI model compared to the basic model.

According to BAPC, an AI-based correction of a solution of these problems, which is previously provided by a basic model, is interpretable in the sense of

[10] Nuclear Segmentation Pipeline code available: https://github.com/SCCH-KVS/NuclearSegmentationPipeline.

[11] BioStudies: https://www.ebi.ac.uk/biostudies/studies/S-BSST265.

[12] DeepSNP code available: https://github.com/SCCH-KVS/deepsnp.

this basic model, if its effect can be described by its parameters. Since this effect refers to the estimated target variables of the data. In other words, an AI correction in the sense of a basic model is interpretable in the sense of this basic model exactly when the accompanying change of the target variable estimation can be characterized with the solution of the basic model under the corresponding parameter changes. The basic idea of the approach is thus to apply the explanatory power of the basic model to the correcting AI method in that their effect can be formulated with the help of the parameters of the basic model. BAPC's ability to use the basic model to predict the modified target variables makes it a so-called surrogate [9].

The proposed solution for the interpretation of the AI correction is of course limited from the outset by the interpretation horizon of the basic model. Furthermore, it must be assumed that the basic model is too weak to describe the phenomena underlying the correction in accordance with the actual facts. We therefore distinguish between explainability and interpretability and, with the definition of interpretability in terms of the basic model introduced above, we do not claim to always be able to explain, but rather to be able to describe (i.e. interpret) the correction as a change of the solution using the basic model. This is achieved by means of the features used in the basic model and their modified parameters. As with most XAI approaches (e.g., feature importance vector [33]), the goal is to find the most significant changes in these parameters.

Lesson Learned: This approach is work in progress and will be tackled in detail in the upcoming Austrian FFG research project "inAIco". As lesson learned we appreciate the BAPC approach as result of interdisciplinary research at the intersection of mathematics, machine learning and model predictive control. We expect that the approach generally only works for "small" AI corrections. It must be possible to formulate conditions about the size (i.e. "smallness") of the AI correction under which the approach will work in any case. However, it is an advantage of our approach that interpretability does not depend on human understanding (see the discussion in [33] and [9]). An important aspect is its mathematical rigidity, which avoids the accusation of "quasi-scientificity" (see [57]).

3.5 Approach 5: Software Quality by Code Analysis and Automated Documentation

Quality assurance measures in software engineering include, e.g., automated testing [2], static code analysis [73], system redocumentation [69], or symbolic execution [4]. These measures need to be risk-based [23,83], exploiting knowledge about system and design dependencies, business requirements, or characteristics of the applied development process.

AI-based methods can be applied to extract knowledge from source code or test specifications to support this analysis. In contrast to manual approaches, which require extensive human annotation work, machine learning methods have been applied for various extraction and classification tasks, such as comment classification of software systems with promising results in [78,89,94].

Software engineering approaches contribute to automate (i) AI-based system testing, e.g., by means of predicting fault-prone parts of the software system that need particular attention [68], and (ii) system documentation to improve software maintainability [14,69,98] and to support re-engineering and migration activities [14]. In particular, we developed a feed-back directed testing approach to derive tests from interacting with a running system [61], which we successfully applied in various industry projects [24,82]. In an ongoing redocumentation project [29], we automatically generate parts of the functional documentation, containing business rules and domain concepts, and all the technical documentation.

Lesson Learned: Keeping documentation up to date is essential for the maintainability of frequently updated software and to minimise the risk of technical debt due to the entanglement of data and sub-components of machine learning systems. The lesson learned is that for this problem also machine learning can be utilized when it comes to establishing rules for detecting and classifying comments (accuracy of >95%) and integrating them when generating readable documentation.

3.6 Approach 6: The ALOHA Toolchain for Embedded Platforms

In [66] and [65] we introduce ALOHA, an integrated tool flow that tries to make the design of deep learning (DL) applications and their porting on embedded heterogeneous architectures as simple and painless as possible. ALOHA is the result of interdisciplinary research funded by the EU[13]. The proposed tool flow aims at automating different design steps and reducing development costs by bridging the gap between DL algorithm training and inference phases. The tool considers hardware-related variables and security, power efficiency, and adaptivity aspects during the whole development process, from pre-training hyperparameter optimization and algorithm configuration to deployment. According to Fig. 1 the general architecture of the ALOHA software framework [67] consists of three major steps:

- (Step 1) algorithm selection,
- (Step 2) application partitioning and mapping, and
- (Step 3) deployment on target hardware.

Starting from a user-specified set of input definitions and data, including a description of the target architecture, the tool flow generates a partitioned and mapped neural network configuration, ready to the target processing architecture, which also optimizes predefined optimization criteria. The criteria for optimization include both application-level accuracy and the required security

[13] https://www.aloha-h2020.eu/.

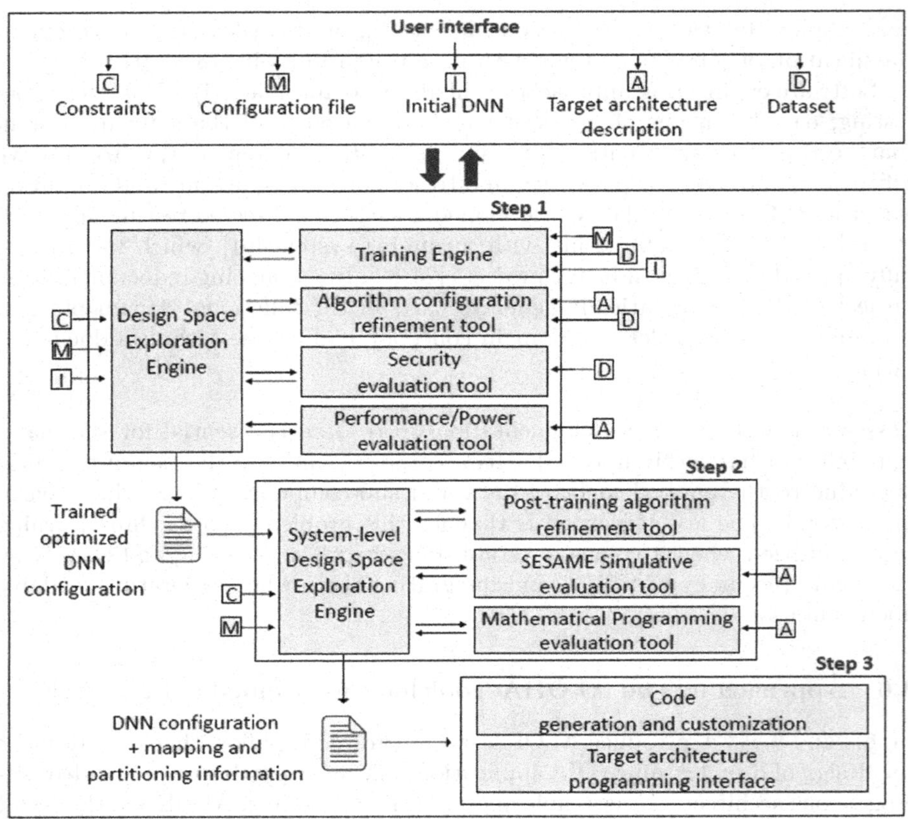

Fig. 1. General architecture of the ALOHA software framework. Nodes in the upper part of the figure represent the key inputs of the tool flow specified by the users, for details see [67].

level, Inference execution time and power consumption. A RESTful microservices approach allows each step of the development process to be broken down into smaller, completely independent components that interact and influence each other through the exchange of HTTP calls [71]. The implementations of the various components are managed using a container orchestration platform. The standard ONNX[14] (Open Neural Network Exchange) is used to exchange deep learning models between the different components of the tool flow.

In Step 1 a Design Space comprising admissible model architectures for hyperparamerter tuning is defined. This Design Space is configured via satellite tools that evaluate the fitness in terms of the predefined optimization criteria such as accuracy (by the Training Engine), robustness against adversarial attacks (by the Security evaluation tool) and power (by the Power evaluation tool). The

[14] https://onnx.ai/.

optimization is based on a) hyperparameter tuning based on a non-stochastic infinite-armed bandit approach [55], and b) a parsimonious inference strategy that aims to reduce the bit depth of the activation values from initially 8bit to 4bit by a iterative quantization and retraining steps [47]. The optimization in Step 2 exploits genetic algorithm for surfing the design space and requiring evaluation of the candidate partitioning and mapping scheme to the satellite tools Sesame [80] and Architecture Optimization Workbench (AOW) [62].

The gain in performance was evaluated in terms of inference time needed to execute the modified model on NEURAghe [64], a Zynq-based processing platform that contains both a dual ARM Cortex A9 processor (667 MHz) and a CNN accelerator implemented in the programmable logic. The statistical analysis on the switching activity of our reference models showed that, on average, only about 65% of the kernels are active in the layers of the network throughout the target validation data set. The resulting model loses only 2% accuracy (baseline 70%) while achieving an impressive 48.31% reduction in terms of FLOPs.

Lesson Learned: Following the standard training procedure deep models tend to be oversized. This research shows that some of the CNN layers are operating in a static or close-to-static mode, enabling the permanent pruning of the redundant kernels from the model. But, the second optimization strategy dedicated to parsimonious inference turns out to more effective on pure software execution, since it more directly deactivates operations in the convolution process. All in all, this study shows that there is a lot of potential for optimisation and improvement compared to standard deep learning engineering approaches.

3.7 Approach 7: Human AI Teaming Approach as Key to Human Centered AI

In [36], we introduce an approach for human-centered AI in working environments utilizing knowledge graphs and relational machine learning ([72,79]). This approach is currently being refined in the ongoing Austrian project Human-centred AI in digitised working environments (AI@Work). The discussion starts with a critical analysis of the limitations of current AI systems whose learning/training is restricted to predefined structured data, most vector-based with a pre-defined format. Therefore, we need an approach that overcomes this restriction by utilizing a relational structures by means of a knowledge graph (KG) that allows to represent relevant context data for linking ongoing AI-based and human-based actions on the one hand and process knowledge and policies on the other hand. Figure 2 outlines this general approach where the knowledge graph is used as an intermediate representation of linked data to be exploited for improvement of the machine learning system, respectively AI system. Methods applied in this context will include knowledge graph completion techniques that aim at filling missing facts within a knowledge graph [75]. The KG flexibly will allow tying together contextual knowledge about the team of involved human and AI based actors including interdependence relations, skills and tasks together with application and system process and organizational knowledge [49].

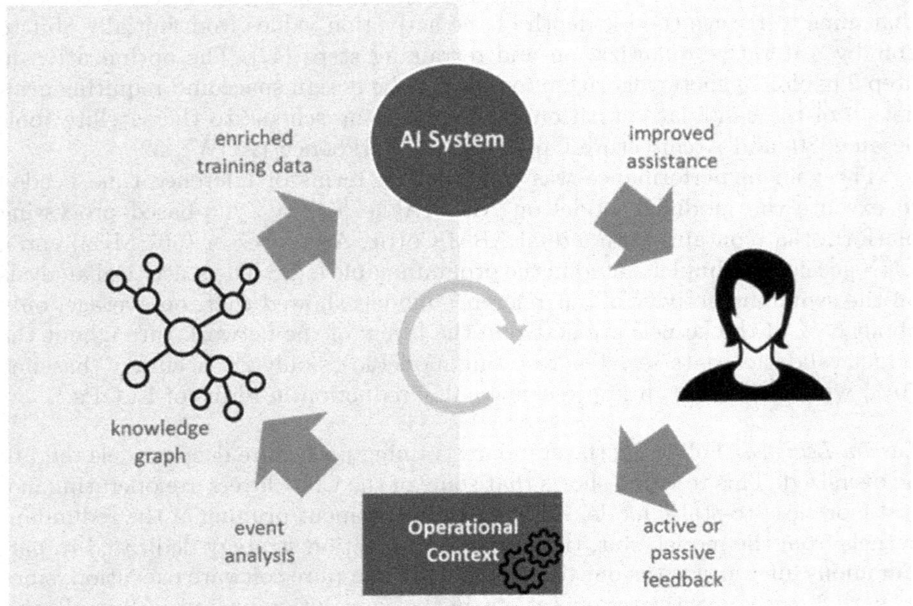

Fig. 2. A knowledge-graph approach to enhance vector-based machine learning in order to support human AI teaming by taking context and process knowledge into account.

Relational machine learning will be developed in combination with an updatable knowledge graph embedding [8,101]. This relational ML will be exploited for analysing and mining the knowledge graph for the purpose of detecting inconsistencies, curating, refinement, providing recommendations for improvements and detecting compliance conflicts with predefined behavioural policies (e.g. ethic or safety policies). The system will learn from the environment, user feedback, changes in the application or deviations from committed behavioral patterns in order to react by providing updated recommendations or triggering actions in case of compliance conflicts. But, the construction of the knowledge graph and keeping it up-to-date is a critical step as it usually includes laborious efforts for knowledge extraction, knowledge fusion, knowledge verification and knowledge updates. In order to address this challenge, our approach pursues bootstrapping strategies for knowledge extraction by recent advances in deep learning and embedding representations as promising methods for matching knowledge items represented in diverse formats.

Lesson Learned: As pointed out in Sect. 2.3 there is a substantial gap between current state-of-the-art research of AI systems and the requirements posed by ethical guidelines. Future research will rely much more on machine learning on graph structures. Fast updatable knowledge graphs and related knowledge graph embeddings might a key towards ethics by design enabling human centered AI.

4 Discussion and Conclusion

This paper can only give a small grasp of the broad field of AI research in connection with the application of AI in practice. The associated research is indeed inter- and even transdisciplinary [56]. Whatever, we come to the conclusion that a discussion on "Applying AI in Practice" needs to start with its theoretical foundations and a critical discussion about the limitations of current data-driven AI systems as outlined in Sect. 2.1. Approach 1, Sect. 3.1, and Approach 2, Sect. 3.2, help to stick to the theoretical prerequisites. Approach 1 contributes by reducing errors in the data and Approach 2 by extending the theory by relaxing its preconditions, bringing statistical learning theory closer to the needs of practice. However, building such systems and addressing the related challenges as outlined in Sect. 2.2 requires a bunch of skills from different fields, predominantly model building and software engineering know-how. Approach 3, Sect. 3.3, and Approach 4, Sect. 3.4, contribute to model building: Approach 3 by creatively adopting novel hybrid machine learning model architectures and Approach 4 by means of system theory that investigates AI as addendum to a basis model in order to be able to establish a notion of interpretability in a strict mathematical sense. Every model applied in practice must be coded in software. Approach 5, Sect. 3.5, outlines helpful state-of-the-art approaches in software engineering for maintaining the engineered software in good traceable and reusable quality which becomes more and more important with increasing complexity. Approach 6, Sect. 3.6, is an integrative approach that takes all the aspects discussed so far into account by proposing a software framework that supports the developer in all these steps when optimizing an AI system for an embedded platform. Finally, the challenge for human centered AI as outlined in Sect. 2.3 is somehow beyond of the state of the art. While the Key Challenges 1 and 2 require, above all, progress in the respective disciplines, Key Challenge 3 addressing "trust" in the end will require a mathematical theory of trust, that is a trust modeling approach at the level of system engineering that takes the psychological and cognitive aspects of human trust into account as well. Approach 7, Sect. 3.7, contributes to this endeavour by its conceptional approach for human AI teaming and its analysis of its prerequisites from relational machine learning.

References

1. Amershi, S., et al.: Guidelines for human-AI interaction. In: Proceedings of the 2019 CHI Conference on Human Factors in Computing Systems, CHI 2019 (2019)
2. Anand, S., et al.: An orchestrated survey of methodologies for automated software test case generation. J. Syst. Softw. **86**(8), 1978–2001 (2013)

3. Athalye, A., Engstrom, L., Ilyas, A., Kwok, K.: Synthesizing robust adversarial examples. arXiv e-prints (2017)
4. Baldoni, R., Coppa, E., D'elia, D.C., Demetrescu, C., Finocchi, I.: A survey of symbolic execution techniques. ACM Comput. Surv. (CSUR) **51**(3), 1–39 (2018)
5. Bensalem, M., Dizdarević, J., Jukan, A.: Modeling of deep neural network (DNN) placement and inference in edge computing. arXiv e-prints (2020)
6. Breck, E., Zinkevich, M., Polyzotis, N., Whang, S., Roy, S.: Data validation for machine learning. In: Proceedings of SysML (2019)
7. Cagala, T.: Improving data quality and closing data gaps with machine learning. In: Settlements, B.F.I. (ed.) Data Needs and Statistics Compilation for Macroprudential Analysis, vol. 46 (2017)
8. Cai, H., Zheng, V.W., Chang, K.C.C.: A comprehensive survey of graph embedding: problems, techniques and applications (2017)
9. Carvalho, D.V., Pereira, E.M., Cardoso, J.S.: Machine learning interpretability: a survey on methods and metrics. Electronics **8**(8), 832 (2019)
10. Char, D.S., Shah, N.H., Magnus, D.: Implementing machine learning in health care - addressing ethical challenges. N. Engl. J. Med. **378**(11), 981–983 (2018). https://doi.org/10.1056/NEJMp1714229. pMID: 29539284
11. Chrisman, N.: The role of quality information in the long-term functioning of a geographic information system. Cartographica Int. J. Geogr. Inf. Geovisualization **21**(2), 79–88 (1983)
12. Cohen, R., Schaekermann, M., Liu, S., Cormier, M.: Trusted AI and the contribution of trust modeling in multiagent systems. In: Proceedings of the 18th International Conference on Autonomous Agents and MultiAgent Systems, AAMAS 2019, pp. 1644–1648 (2019)
13. Deeks, A.: The judicial demand for explainable artificial intelligence. Columbia Law Rev. **119**(7), 1829–1850 (2019)
14. Dorninger, B., Moser, M., Pichler, J.: Multi-language re-documentation to support a COBOL to Java migration project. In: 2017 IEEE 24th International Conference on Software Analysis, Evolution and Reengineering (SANER), pp. 536–540. IEEE (2017)
15. Doshi-Velez, F., Kim, B.: Towards a rigorous science of interpretable machine learning. arXiv (2017)
16. Eghbal-Zadeh, H., et al.: DeepSNP: an end-to-end deep neural network with attention-based localization for breakpoint detection in single-nucleotide polymorphism array genomic data. J. Comput. Biol. **26**(6), 572–596 (2018)
17. Eghbal-zadeh, H., Zellinger, W., Widmer, G.: Mixture density generative adversarial networks. In: Proceedings of the IEEE Conference on Computer Vision and Pattern Recognition, pp. 5820–5829 (2019)
18. Ehrlinger, L., Grubinger, T., Varga, B., Pichler, M., Natschläger, T., Zeindl, J.: Treating missing data in industrial data analytics. In: 2018 Thirteenth International Conference on Digital Information Management (ICDIM), pp. 148–155. IEEE, September 2018
19. Ehrlinger, L., Haunschmid, V., Palazzini, D., Lettner, C.: A DaQL to monitor data quality in machine learning applications. In: Hartmann, S., Küng, J., Chakravarthy, S., Anderst-Kotsis, G., Tjoa, A.M., Khalil, I. (eds.) DEXA 2019. LNCS, vol. 11706, pp. 227–237. Springer, Cham (2019). https://doi.org/10.1007/978-3-030-27615-7_17

20. Ehrlinger, L., Rusz, E., Wöß, W.: A Survey of data quality measurement and monitoring tools. CoRR abs/1907.08138 (2019)
21. Ehrlinger, L., Werth, B., Wöß, W.: Automated continuous data quality measurement with quaiie. Int. J. Adv. Softw. **11**(3&4), 400–417 (2018)
22. Ehrlinger, L., Wöß, W.: Automated data quality monitoring. In: 22nd MIT International Conference on Information Quality (ICIQ 2017), pp. 15.1–15.9 (2017)
23. Felderer, M., Ramler, R.: Integrating risk-based testing in industrial test processes. Software Qual. J. **22**(3), 543–575 (2014)
24. Fischer, S., Ramler, R., Linsbauer, L., Egyed, A.: Automating test reuse for highly configurable software. In: Proceedings of the 23rd International Systems and Software Product Line Conference-Volume A, pp. 1–11 (2019)
25. Forcier, M.B., Gallois, H., Mullan, S., Joly, Y.: Integrating artificial intelligence into health care through data access: can the GDPR act as a beacon for policymakers? J. Law Biosci. **6**(1), 317–335 (2019)
26. Gal, Y.: Uncertainty in deep learning. Thesis (2016)
27. Gal, Y., Ghahramani, Z.: Dropout as a Bayesian approximation: representing model uncertainty in deep learning. In: Proceedings of the 33rd International Conference on International Conference on Machine Learning, ICML 2016, vol. 48. pp. 1050–1059. JMLR.org (2016)
28. Galloway, A., Taylor, G.W., Moussa, M.: Predicting adversarial examples with high confidence. arXiv e-prints (2018)
29. Geist, V., Moser, M., Pichler, J., Beyer, S., Pinzger, M.: Leveraging machine learning for software redocumentation. In: 2020 IEEE 27th International Conference on Software Analysis, Evolution and Reengineering (SANER), pp. 622–626. IEEE (2020)
30. Gilpin, L.H., Bau, D., Yuan, B.Z., Bajwa, A., Specter, M., Kagal, L.: Explaining explanations: an overview of interpretability of machine learning. In: 2018 IEEE 5th International Conference on Data Science and Advanced Analytics (DSAA), pp. 80–89 (2018)
31. Gorban, A.N., Tyukin, I.Y.: Blessing of dimensionality: mathematical foundations of the statistical physics of data. Philos. Trans. R. Soc. A Math. Phys. Eng. Sci. **376**(2118), 20170237 (2018)
32. Grancharova, A., Johansen, T.A.: Nonlinear model predictive control, In: Explicit Nonlinear Model Predictive Control, vol. 429, pp. 39–69. Springer, Heidelberg (2012). https://doi.org/10.1007/978-3-642-28780-0_2
33. Guidotti, R., Monreale, A., Ruggieri, S., Turini, F., Giannotti, F., Pedreschi, D.: A survey of methods for explaining black box models. ACM Comput. Surv. **51**(5), 1–42 (2018)
34. Gunning, D.: Darpa's explainable artificial intelligence (XAI) program. In: Proceedings of the 24th International Conference on Intelligent User Interfaces. p. ii. IUI 2019. Association for Computing Machinery, New York (2019)
35. Guo, C., Pleiss, G., Sun, Y., Weinberger, K.Q.: On calibration of modern neural networks. arXiv e-prints (2017)
36. Gusenleitner, N., et al.: Facing mental workload in AI-transformed working environments. In: h-WORKLOAD 2019: 3rd International Symposium on Human Mental Workload: Models and Applications (2019)
37. Hastie, T., Tibshirani, R., Friedman, J.: The Elements of Statistical Learning. SSS. Springer, New York (2009). https://doi.org/10.1007/978-0-387-84858-7
38. He, K., Gkioxari, G., Dollár, P., Girshick, R.: Mask R-CNN. In: IEEE International Conference on Computer Vision (ICCV) (2017). arXiv: 1703.06870

39. Hein, M., Andriushchenko, M., Bitterwolf, J.: Why ReLU networks yield high-confidence predictions far away from the training data and how to mitigate the problem. In: Proceedings of the IEEE Conference on Computer Vision and Pattern Recognition, pp. 41–50 (2019)
40. Heinrich, B., Hristova, D., Klier, M., Schiller, A., Szubartowicz, M.: Requirements for data quality metrics. J. Data Inform. Qual. **9**(2), 1–32 (2018)
41. Hoffman, R.R., Mueller, S.T., Klein, G., Litman, J.: Metrics for explainable AI: challenges and prospects. CoRR abs/1812.04608 (2018)
42. Holzinger, A.: Interactive machine learning for health informatics: when do we need the human-in-the-loop? Brain Inform. **3**(2), 119–131 (2016). https://doi.org/10.1007/s40708-016-0042-6
43. Holzinger, A., Carrington, A., Müller, H.: Measuring the quality of explanations: the system causability scale (SCS). Special Issue on Interactive Machine Learning. Künstliche Intelligenz (Ger. J. Artif. Intell. 34, 193–198 (2020)
44. Holzinger, A., Kieseberg, P., Weippl, E., Tjoa, A.M.: Current advances, trends and challenges of machine learning and knowledge extraction: from machine learning to explainable AI. In: Holzinger, A., Kieseberg, P., Tjoa, A.M., Weippl, E. (eds.) CD-MAKE 2018. LNCS, vol. 11015, pp. 1–8. Springer, Cham (2018). https://doi.org/10.1007/978-3-319-99740-7_1
45. Holzinger, A., Langs, G., Denk, H., Zatloukal, K., Müller, H.: Causability and explainability of artificial intelligence in medicine. WIREs Data Min. Knowl. Discov. **9**(4), e1312 (2019)
46. Holzinger, A.: Introduction to machine learning and knowledge extraction (make). Mach. Learn. Knowl. Extr **1**(1), 1–20 (2017)
47. Jacob, B., et al.: Quantization and training of neural networks for efficient integer-arithmetic-only inference. CoRR abs/1712.05877 (2017)
48. Jiang, J., Zhai, C.: Instance weighting for domain adaptation in NLP. In: Proceedings of the 45th Annual Meeting of the Association of Computational Linguistics, pp. 264–271 (2007)
49. Johnson, M., Vera, A.: No AI is an island: the case for teaming intelligence. AI Mag. **40**(1), 16–28 (2019)
50. Jung, C., Kim, C.: Impact of the accuracy of automatic segmentation of cell nuclei clusters on classification of thyroid follicular lesions. Cytometry. Part A J. Int. Soc. Anal. Cytol **85**(8), 709–718 (2014)
51. Kelly, C.J., Karthikesalingam, A., Suleyman, M., Corrado, G., King, D.: Key challenges for delivering clinical impact with artificial intelligence. BMC Med. **17**(1), 195 (2019)
52. Kromp, F., et al.: An annotated fluorescence image dataset for training nuclear segmentation methods. Nat. Sci. Data (2020, in press)
53. Kromp, F., et al.: Deep learning architectures for generalized immunofluorescence based nuclear image segmentation. arXiv e-prints (2019)
54. Lecun, Y., Bengio, Y., Hinton, G.: Deep learning. Nature **521**(FEB), 436–444 (2015)
55. Li, L., Jamieson, K., DeSalvo, G., Rostamizadeh, A., Talwalkar, A.: Hyperband: a novel bandit-based approach to hyperparameter optimization. J. Mach. Learn. Res. **18**(1), 6765–6816 (2017)
56. Li, S., Wang, Y.: Research on interdisciplinary characteristics: a case study in the field of artificial intelligence. IOP Conf. Ser. Mater. Sci. Eng. **677**, 052023 (2019)
57. Lipton, Z.C.: The mythos of model interpretability. Queue **16**(3), 31–57 (2018)
58. Little, M.A., et al.: Using and understanding cross-validation strategies. Perspectives on saeb et al. GigaScience **6**(5), gix020 (2017)

59. Lombrozo, T.: Explanatory preferences shape learning and inference. Trends Cogn. Sci. **20**(10), 748–759 (2016)
60. London, A.: Artificial intelligence and black-box medical decisions: accuracy versus explainability. Hastings Cent. Rep. **49**, 15–21 (2019)
61. Ma, L., Artho, C., Zhang, C., Sato, H., Gmeiner, J., Ramler, R.: GRT: program-analysis-guided random testing (t). In: 2015 30th IEEE/ACM International Conference on Automated Software Engineering (ASE), pp. 212–223. IEEE (2015)
62. Masin, M., et al.: Pluggable analysis viewpoints for design space exploration. Procedia Comput. Sci. **16**, 226–235 (2013)
63. Maydanchik, A.: Data Quality Assessment. Technics Publications, LLC, Bradley Beach (2007)
64. Meloni, P., et al.: NEURAghe: exploiting CPU-FPGA synergies for efficient and flexible CNN inference acceleration on Zynq SoCs. CoRR abs/1712.00994 (2017)
65. Meloni, P., et al.: ALOHA: an architectural-aware framework for deep learning at the edge. In: Proceedings of the Workshop on INTelligent Embedded Systems Architectures and Applications - INTESA, pp. 19–26. ACM Press (2018)
66. Meloni, P., et al.: Architecture-aware design and implementation of CNN algorithms for embedded inference: the ALOHA project. In: 2018 30th International Conference on Microelectronics (ICM), pp. 52–55 (2018)
67. Meloni, P., et al.: Optimization and deployment of CNNS at the edge: the ALOHA experience. In: Proceedings of the 16th ACM International Conference on Computing Frontiers, CF 2019, pp. 326–332 (2019)
68. Menzies, T., Milton, Z., Turhan, B., Cukic, B., Jiang, Y., Bener, A.: Defect prediction from static code features: current results, limitations, new approaches. Autom. Softw. Eng. **17**(4), 375–407 (2010)
69. Moser, M., Pichler, J., Fleck, G., Witlatschil, M.: RbGG: a documentation generator for scientific and engineering software. In: 2015 IEEE 22nd International Conference on Software Analysis, Evolution, and Reengineering (SANER), pp. 464–468. IEEE (2015)
70. Méhes, G., et al.: Detection of disseminated tumor cells in neuroblastoma: 3 log improvement in sensitivity by automatic immunofluorescence plus FISH (AIPF) analysis compared with classical bone marrow cytology. Am. J. Pathol. **163**(2), 393–399 (2003)
71. Newman, S.: Building Microservices, 1st edn. O'Reilly Media Inc. (2015)
72. Nickel, M., Murphy, K., Tresp, V., Gabrilovich, E.: A review of relational machine learning for knowledge graphs. Proc. IEEE **104**(1), 11–33 (2016)
73. Nielson, F., Nielson, H.R., Hankin, C.: Principles of Program Analysis. Springer, Heidelberg (2015). https://doi.org/10.1007/978-3-662-03811-6
74. Nikzad-Langerodi, R., Zellinger, W., Lughofer, E., Saminger-Platz, S.: Domain-invariant partial-least-squares regression. Anal. Chem. **90**(11), 6693–6701 (2018)
75. Noy, N., Gao, Y., Jain, A., Narayanan, A., Patterson, A., Taylor, J.: Industry-scale knowledge graphs: lessons and challenges. Commun. ACM **62**(8), 36–43 (2019)
76. Obermeyer, Z., Powers, B., Vogeli, C., Mullainathan, S.: Dissecting racial bias in an algorithm used to manage the health of populations. Science **366**(6464), 447–453 (2019)
77. Pan, S.J., Yang, Q.: A survey on transfer learning. IEEE Trans. Knowl. Data Eng. **22**(10), 1345–1359 (2009)
78. Pascarella, L., Bacchelli, A.: Classifying code comments in java open-source software systems. In: 2017 IEEE/ACM 14th International Conference on Mining Software Repositories (MSR), pp. 227–237. IEEE (2017)

79. Paulheim, H.: Knowledge graph refinement: a survey of approaches and evaluation methods. Semant. Web **8**(3), 489–508 (2017)
80. Pimentel, A.D., Erbas, C., Polstra, S.: A systematic approach to exploring embedded system architectures at multiple abstraction levels. IEEE Trans. Comput. **55**(2), 99–112 (2006)
81. Quionero-Candela, J., Sugiyama, M., Schwaighofer, A., Lawrence, N.D.: Dataset Shift in Machine Learning. The MIT Press, Cambridge (2009)
82. Ramler, R., Buchgeher, G., Klammer, C.: Adapting automated test generation to gui testing of industry applications. Inf. Softw. Technol. **93**, 248–263 (2018)
83. Ramler, R., Felderer, M.: A process for risk-based test strategy development and its industrial evaluation. In: Abrahamsson, P., Corral, L., Oivo, M., Russo, B. (eds.) PROFES 2015. LNCS, vol. 9459, pp. 355–371. Springer, Cham (2015). https://doi.org/10.1007/978-3-319-26844-6_26
84. Ramler, R., Wolfmaier, K.: Issues and effort in integrating data from heterogeneous software repositories and corporate databases. In: Proceedings of the Second ACM-IEEE International Symposium on Empirical Software Engineering and Measurement, pp. 330–332 (2008)
85. Ronneberger, O., Fischer, P., Brox, T.: U-Net: convolutional networks for biomedical image segmentation. In: Navab, N., Hornegger, J., Wells, W.M., Frangi, A.F. (eds.) MICCAI 2015. LNCS, vol. 9351, pp. 234–241. Springer, Cham (2015). https://doi.org/10.1007/978-3-319-24574-4_28
86. Samek, W., Wiegand, T., Müller, K.R.: Explainable artificial intelligence: understanding, visualizing and interpreting deep learning models. arXiv e-prints (2017)
87. Sculley, D., et al.: Hidden technical debt in machine learning systems. In: 28th International Conference on Neural Information Processing Systems (NIPS), pp. 2503–2511 (2015)
88. Sebastian-Coleman, L.: Measuring Data Quality for Ongoing Improvement. Elsevier, Amsterdam (2013)
89. Shinyama, Y., Arahori, Y., Gondow, K.: Analyzing code comments to boost program comprehension. In: 2018 25th Asia-Pacific Software Engineering Conference (APSEC), pp. 325–334. IEEE (2018)
90. Dosilovic, F.K., Brçiç, M., Hlupic, N.: Explainable artificial intelligence: a survey. In: Skala, K. (ed.) Croatian Society for Information and Communication Technology, Electronics and Microelectronics - MIPRO (2018)
91. Sobieczky, F.: An interlacing technique for spectra of random walks and its application to finite percolation clusters. J. Theor. Probab. **23**, 639–670 (2010)
92. Sobieczky, F.: Bounds for the annealed return probability on large finite percolation graphs. Electron. J. Probab. **17**, 17 (2012)
93. Sobieczky, F.: Explainability of models with an interpretable base model: explainability vs. accuracy. In: Symposium on Predictive Analytics 2019, Vienna (2019)
94. Steidl, D., Hummel, B., Juergens, E.: Quality analysis of source code comments. In: 2013 21st International Conference on Program Comprehension (ICPC), pp. 83–92. IEEE (2013)
95. Sun, B., Saenko, K.: Deep CORAL: correlation alignment for deep domain adaptation. In: Hua, G., Jégou, H. (eds.) ECCV 2016. LNCS, vol. 9915, pp. 443–450. Springer, Cham (2016). https://doi.org/10.1007/978-3-319-49409-8_35
96. Szegedy, C., et al.: Intriguing properties of neural networks. arXiv e-prints (2013)
97. Sünderhauf, N., et al.: The limits and potentials of deep learning for robotics. Int. J. Robot. Res. **37**(4–5), 405–420 (2018)

98. Van Geet, J., Ebraert, P., Demeyer, S.: Redocumentation of a legacy banking system: an experience report. In: Proceedings of the Joint ERCIM Workshop on Software Evolution (EVOL) and International Workshop on Principles of Software Evolution (IWPSE), pp. 33–41 (2010)
99. Vapnik, V.N.: Statistical Learning Theory. Wiley-Interscience, New York (1998)
100. Vidal, R., Bruna, J., Giryes, R., Soatto, S.: Mathematics of deep learning. arXiv e-prints (2017). arxiv:1712.04741
101. Wang, Q., Mao, Z., Wang, B., Guo, L.: Knowledge graph embedding: a survey of approaches and applications. IEEE Trans. Knowl. Data Eng. **29**(12), 2724–2743 (2017)
102. Wang, R.Y., Strong, D.M.: Beyond accuracy: what data quality means to data consumers. J. Manage. Inform. Syst. **12**(4), 5–33 (1996)
103. Wang, Y.E., Wei, G.Y., Brooks, D.: Benchmarking TPU, GPU, and CPU platforms for deep learning. arXiv e-prints (2019)
104. Xu, G., Huang, J.Z.: Asymptotic optimality and efficient computation of the leave-subject-out cross-validation. Ann. Stat. **40**(6), 3003–3030 (2012)
105. Yu, T., Zhu, H.: Hyper-parameter optimization: a review of algorithms and applications. arXiv e-prints (2020)
106. Zellinger, W., Grubinger, T., Lughofer, E., Natschläger, T., Saminger-Platz, S.: Central moment discrepancy (CMD) for domain-invariant representation learning. In: International Conference on Learning Representations (2017)
107. Zellinger, W., et al.: Multi-source transfer learning of time series in cyclical manufacturing. J. Intell. Manuf. **31**(3), 777–787 (2020)
108. Zellinger, W., Moser, B.A., Grubinger, T., Lughofer, E., Natschläger, T., Saminger-Platz, S.: Robust unsupervised domain adaptation for neural networks via moment alignment. Inf. Sci. **483**, 174–191 (2019)
109. Zellinger, W., Moser, B.A., Saminger-Platz, S.: Learning bounds for moment-based domain adaptation. arXiv preprint arXiv:2002.08260 (2020)
110. Zhang, C., Bengio, S., Hardt, M., Recht, B., Vinyals, O.: Understanding deep learning requires rethinking generalization. In: International Conference on Learning Representations (201z)
111. Zou, J., Schiebinger, L.: AI can be sexist and racist - it's time to make it fair. Nature **559**, 324–326 (2018)

Function Space Pooling for Graph Convolutional Networks

Padraig Corcoran(✉)

School of Computer Science and Informatics, Cardiff University, Cardiff, Wales, UK
corcoranp@cardiff.ac.uk

Abstract. Convolutional layers in graph neural networks are a fundamental type of layer which output a representation or embedding of each graph vertex. The representation typically encodes information about the vertex in question and its neighbourhood. If one wishes to perform a graph centric task, such as graph classification, this set of vertex representations must be integrated or pooled to form a graph representation. In this article we propose a novel pooling method which maps a set of vertex representations to a function space representation. This method is distinct from existing pooling methods which perform a mapping to either a vector or sequence space. Experimental graph classification results demonstrate that the proposed method generally outperforms most baseline pooling methods and in some cases achieves best performance.

Keywords: Graph neural network · Vertex pooling · Function space

1 Introduction

Many real world systems have a relational structure which can be modelled as a graph. These include physical systems where the bodies and joints correspond to the vertices and edges respectively [20]; robot swarms where robots and communication links correspond to the vertices and edges respectively [21]; and topological maps where locations and paths correspond to the vertices and edges respectively [4]. Given this, there exists great potential for the application of machine learning to graphs. With the great successes of neural networks and deep learning to the analysis of images and natural language, there has recently been much research considering the application or generalization of neural networks to graphs. In many cases this has resulted in state of the art performance for many tasks [25].

Graph convolution is a neural network architecture commonly applied to graphs which consists of a sequence of convolutional layers. The output of a sequence of such layers is a set of vertex representations where each element in this set encodes properties of a corresponding vertex and the vertices in its neighbourhood. In their seminal work, Gilmer et al. [9] showed that many different types of convolutional layers can be formulated in terms of a framework

A. Holzinger et al. (Eds.): CD-MAKE 2020, LNCS 12279, pp. 473–483, 2020.
https://doi.org/10.1007/978-3-030-57321-8_26

containing two steps. In the first step message passing is performed where each vertex receives messages from adjacent vertices regarding their current representation. In the second step, each vertex performs an update of its representation which is a function of its current representation and the messages it received in the previous step. Graph convolution is fundamentally different to the more commonly used image convolution. Unlike an image where each pixel will have an equal number of adjacent pixels (excluding boundary pixels), each vertex in a graph may have a different number of adjacent vertices. Furthermore, unlike an image where the set of pixels adjacent to a given pixel can be ordered, the set of vertices adjacent to a given vertex cannot be easily ordered. Given these facts, generalizing image convolution methods to graphs is non-trivial.

If one wishes to perform a vertex centric task such as vertex classification, then one may operate directly on the set of vertex representations output from a sequence of convolutional layers. However, if one wishes to perform a graph centric task such as graph classification, then the set of vertex representations must somehow be integrated to form a graph representation. We refer to this integration step as *pooling* and it represents the focus of this article. Note that, this step is sometimes referred to as global pooling. Performing pooling represents a challenging problem for a couple of reasons. Firstly, the size of the set of vertex representations will equal the number of vertices in the graph in question and this number will vary from graph to graph. Furthermore, the elements in this set will not be ordered. Therefore the set of vertex representations cannot be directly fed as input to feed-forward or recurrent architecture which require as input an element in a vector space of fixed dimension and an element in a sequence space respectively.

Commonly employed pooling methods include computing summary statistics of the set of vertex representations such as the mean or sum. However these simple pooling methods are not a *complete invariant* in the sense that many different sets of vertex representations may result in the same graph representation leading to weak discrimination power [26]. To overcome this issue and increase discrimination power a number of authors have proposed more sophisticated pooling methods. For example, Ying et al. [28] proposed a pooling method which performs a hierarchical clustering of the set of vertex representations to produce an element in a vector space of fixed dimension.

In this article we propose a novel pooling method which maps a set of vertex representations to a function space representation. This method is illustrated in Fig. 1 in the context of a complete graph classification architecture. The proposed pooling method is parameterized by a single learnable parameter which controls the discrimination power of the method. This makes the method applicable to both finer and coarser classification tasks which require greater and less discrimination power respectively. The proposed pooling method is inspired by related methods in the field of applied topology which map sets of points in $\mathbb{R}^2$ to function space representations [1].

The layout of this paper is as follows. Section 2 reviews related works on graph convolution architectures and pooling methods. Section 3 describes the proposed

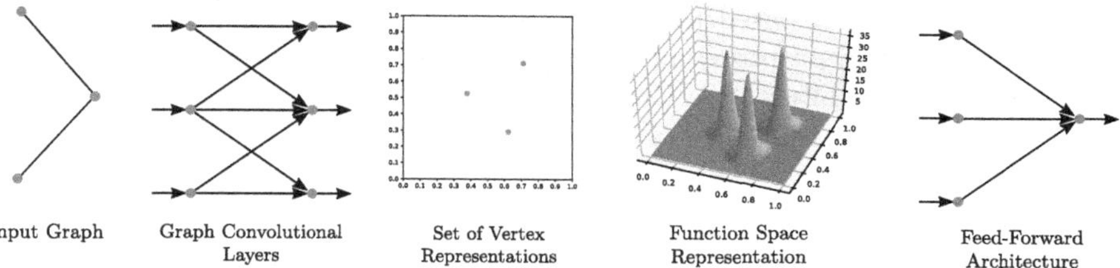

Fig. 1. The proposed pooling method is illustrated in the context of a complete graph classification architecture. The input graph is first fed to a sequence of graph convolutional layers which outputs a set of vertex representations. The number of elements in this set equals the number of vertices in the original graph. This set is next mapped to a function space representation. This function space representation is then fed to a feed-forward architecture which outputs a predicted graph class.

pooling method. Section 4 presents an evaluation of this method. Finally Sect. 5 draws some conclusions from this work.

2 Background and Related Works

In the following two subsections we review related works on graph convolution architectures and pooling methods.

2.1 Graph Convolution Architectures

There exist a wide array of graph convolution architectures. In this section we only review those architectures representing theoretical breakthroughs and state of the art. However the interested reader can consult the following review papers for greater details [25,30]. Hamilton et al. [10] proposed a graph convolution layer known as GraphSAGE which updates a vertex representation by first performing an aggregation of adjacent vertex representations. This aggregation is then concatenated with the current representation of the vertex in question before applying a linear transformation and non-linearity. The authors considered the aggregation functions of mean vertex representation and LSTM (Long Short-Term Memory) applied to a random ordering of vertex presentations. Xu et al. [26] proposed to apply a multi-layer perceptron, as opposed to a single layer which is most common, to the aggregation of adjacent vertex representations and demonstrated that this improve discrimination power. In a later work the same authors [27] proposed an architecture known as the jumping knowledge architecture which allows vertices to aggregate information from neighbouring vertices over different ranges. The authors showed that this architecture allows deeper convolutional architectures to be used and outperforms the use of residual connections commonly used in computer vision applications [12]. Given the successes of attention based architectures in natural language processing [22], Velickovic et al. [23] proposed an attention based architecture for graphs. For a given vertex this architecture allows different weights to be specified for different adjacent vertices.

2.2 Pooling Methods

There exist two main categories of pooling methods: those which map the set of vertex representations to a vector space of fixed dimension and those which map the set of vertex representations to a sequence space. The output of these mappings can then be fed as input to a feed-forward or recurrent architecture respectively. We now review pooling methods belonging to each of these categories.

The simplest pooling methods for mapping to a vector space of fixed dimension involve computing summary statistics such as mean and sum of vertex representations [7]. Despite the simple nature of these methods, a recent study by Luzhnica et al. [18] demonstrated that in some cases they can outperform more complex methods. To improve discrimination power more sophisticated pooling methods have been proposed. The SortPooling method proposed by Zhang et al. [29] first sorts the vertices with respect to structural roles in the graph. The vertex representations corresponding to the first k vertices in this order are then concatenated to give a fixed dimensional vector. The value k is a fixed hyper-parameter in the model. Set2Set is a general approach for producing a fixed dimensional vector space representation of a set which is invariant to the order in which the elements are processed [24]. Gilmer et al. [9] proposed to use this method to perform pooling. Ying et al. [28] proposed a pooling method known as DiffPool which performs a hierarchical clustering of vertex representations and returns an element in a fixed dimensional vector space. Kearnes et al. [13] proposed a pooling method based on fuzzy histograms. This method has similarities to that proposed in this article but is formulated in terms of fuzzy theory as opposed to function spaces. The method proposed in this article is in turn distinct. Tarlow et al. [17] proposed a pooling method which outputs an element in sequence space. Finally, all of the above pooling methods are supervised methods. Many unsupervised pooling methods have also been proposed but we do not review them here [2].

3 Function Space Pooling

In this section we present the proposed pooling method. Let graph $G = (V, E)$ denote a graph we wish to classify where V and E are the corresponding sets of vertices and edges respectively. Let $l : V \rightarrow \Sigma$ denote a vertex labelling function that assigns each vertex $v \in V$ a label $l(v)$ in the finite set Σ.

Let D be the set of vertex representations output from a sequence of convolutional layers applied to G. We assume that each element in this set is an element of $\mathbb{R}^n$ where n is a fixed hyper-parameter. The proposed pooling method takes

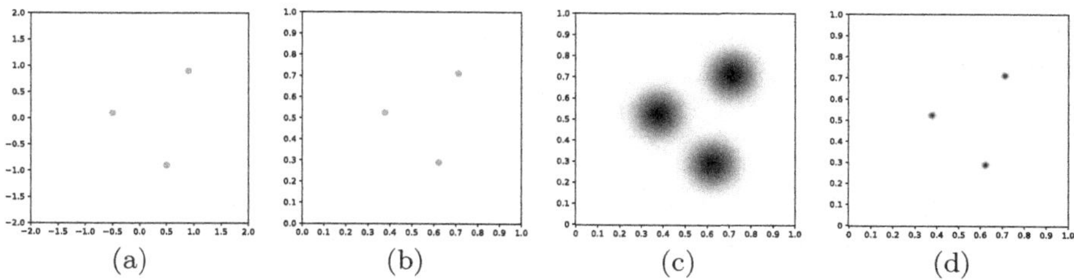

Fig. 2. A set D of vertex representations output from a sequence of convolutional layers is displayed in (a) where each element is represented by a red dot. The result of applying the map S to the set D is the set $s(D)$ displayed in (b). The result of applying the map F to $S(D)$ with the parameter $\sigma = 0.005$ is the function $\rho : I \rightarrow \mathbb{R}$ displayed in (c). The result of applying the map F to $S(D)$ with the parameter $\sigma = 0.0001$ is the function $\rho : I \rightarrow \mathbb{R}$ displayed in (d). (Color figure online)

as input D and returns an element in a function space. That is, the method is a map from the space of sets to the space of functions. It contains two steps which we now describe in turn.

The set of vertex representations D is an object in the space of sets which we denote Ω. Let Sigmoid : $\mathbb{R}^n \rightarrow I$ be the n-dimensional Sigmoid function defined in Eq. 1 where $I = \{(x_1, \ldots, x_n) \in [0,1]^n\}$ is the n-dimensional interval. In the first step of the proposed pooling method we apply the n-dimensional Sigmoid elementwise to D to give a map $S : \Omega \rightarrow \Omega$. To illustrate this map consider Fig. 2(a) which displays an example set D containing three elements in $\mathbb{R}^n$ where $n = 2$. The result of applying the map S to this set is illustrated in Fig. 2(b).

$$\text{Sigmoid}(x) = \frac{1}{1 + e^{-x}} \tag{1}$$

Let $g_u : \mathbb{R}^n \rightarrow \mathbb{R}$ be a probability distribution. For the purposes of this work we used the n-dimensional Gaussian distribution defined in Eq. 2 with mean u and variance σ^2.

$$g_u(x) = \frac{1}{2\pi\sigma^2} e^{-((x-u)^T(x-u))/2\sigma^2} \tag{2}$$

In the second step of the proposed pooling method we apply a map $F : \Omega \rightarrow L^p(I)$ to $S(D)$. Here $L^p(I)$ is the space of real valued functions on I equipped with the L^p-norm defined in Eq. 3 [5]. Note that, function addition and subtraction is performed pointwise in this space.

$$\|f\|_p = \left(\int_I |f(x)|^p dx \right)^{1/p} \tag{3}$$

The function resulting from the map F is defined in Definition 1. To illustrate this map consider again the example set $S(D)$ illustrated in Fig. 2(b). Figure 2(c) displays the function $\rho : I \rightarrow \mathbb{R}$ resulting from applying the map F to this set with a σ parameter value of 0.005.

Definition 1. *For $D \in \Omega$ the corresponding function representation $\rho : I \to \mathbb{R}$ is defined in Eq. 4*

$$\rho(z) = \sum_{u \in S(D)} g_u(z) \tag{4}$$

The elements of $L^p(I)$, and in turn the function representation $\rho : I \to \mathbb{R}$, are infinite dimensional vector spaces. That is, there are an infinite number of elements in the domain I of ρ. We approximate this function as a finite dimensional vector space by discretizing the function domain using a regular grid of elements. For example, the image in Fig. 2(c) corresponds to a discretizing of the function domain using a 250×250 grid.

The proposed pooling method is parameterized by σ in the probability distribution of Eq. 2 where this parameter takes a value in the range $[0, \infty]$. As the value of σ approaches 0 the probability distribution approaches an indicator function on the domain I. On the other hand, as the value of σ approaches ∞ the probability distribution approaches a uniform function on the domain I. For example, Fig. 2(c) and 2(d) display the functions $\rho : I \to \mathbb{R}$ resulting from applying the map F to the set $S(D)$ in Fig. 2(b) with σ parameter values of 0.005 and 0.0001 respectively.

The parameter σ may be interpreted as follows. As the value of σ approaches 0 the function representation $\rho : I \to \mathbb{R}$ becomes a sum of indicator functions on the set D of vertex representations. In this case distinct sets D map to distinct functions where the distance between these functions as defined by the norm in Eq. 3 is greater than zero. On the other hand, as σ approaches ∞, differences between the functions are gradually smoothed out and in turn the distance between the functions gradually reduces. Therefore, one can view the parameter σ as controlling the discrimination power of the method.

4 Results

To evaluate the proposed pooling method we considered the task of graph classification on a number of datasets. The layout of this section is as follows. Section 4.1 describes the neural network architecture used in all experiments. Section 4.3 describes the datasets considered. Section 4.2 describes the optimization method used to optimize the network parameters. Finally Sect. 4.4 presents the classification accuracy achieved by the proposed pooling method relative to a number of baseline methods.

4.1 Network Architecture

Recall from Sect. 3 that $G = (V, E)$ denotes a graph we wish to classify and $l : V \to \Sigma$ denotes a vertex labelling function where Σ is a finite set. In order to perform classification of G the following feed-forward neural network architecture was used which consists of six layers.

The first two layers are convolutional layers similarly to the GraphSAGE convolutional layers [10]. Only two convolutional layers were used because a number of studies have found that the use of two layers empirically gives best performance [16].

Let $\cdot$ denote matrix multiplication and CONCAT denote horizontal matrix concatenation. The kth convolutional layer is implemented using Eq. 5 where A is the adjacency matrix corresponding to G, W_k are the layer weights and b_k are the layer biases. The weights W_k is a matrix of dimension $2d_{k-1} \times d_k$ where d_k the dimension of the kth layer. The biases b_k is a vector of dimension d_k. The term h_0 denotes a matrix of size $|V| \times |\Sigma|$ where each matrix row equals the one-hot-encoding of an individual vertex label. The term h_k denotes a matrix of size $|V| \times d_k$ where each matrix row equals the representation of an individual vertex output from the kth convolutional layer and d_k is the dimension of this representation. Note that, since two convolutional layers are used, k takes values in the set $\{1, 2\}$. The dimension of the input layer d_0 is equal to the number of vertex types since one-hot encoding was used. The dimensions of the two convolutional layers d_1 and d_2 were both set to 20.

$$\begin{aligned} h_k &\leftarrow \text{CONCAT}(h_{k-1}, A \cdot h_{k-1}) \\ h_k &\leftarrow \text{ReLu}\left(W_k \cdot h_k + b_k\right) \end{aligned} \tag{5}$$

The third architecture layer is a fully connected linear layer of dimension 10. The fourth layer is the pooling method used. The fifth layer is another fully connected linear layer of dimension 20. The final layer is a softmax function and returns a probability distribution over the classes. The output of the first linear layer equals the input to the pooling method. Therefore the multi-dimensional interval corresponding to the domain of the function ρ in Definition 1 is of dimension 10. We approximate this function as a finite dimensional vector space by discretizing the function domain using a regular grid with 3 elements in each dimension. This gives a finite dimensional vector space of dimension $3^{10} = 59049$.

4.2 Optimization

The model parameters to be optimized in the architecture of Sect. 4.1 are the weights and biases of the convolutional layers, the weights and biases of the linear layers and the parameter σ of the pooling method. In all experiments the neural network parameters were initialized as follows. All weight matrices in the convolutional and linear layers were initialized using Kaiming initialization [11]. All biases in the convolutional and linear layers were initialized to zero. Finally, the parameter σ in Eq. 2 of the pooling layer was initialized to 0.125.

For loss function Cross Entropy plus an L^2 regularization term with weight of 0.2 was used. The Adam optimization algorithm was used to optimize all model parameters with a learning rate of 1×10^{-3} [15]. In all experiments optimization was performed for 350 data epochs and the model which achieved the minimum loss during this process was returned. In all cases the optimization procedure converged well before 350 data epochs.

Table 1. For each of the MUTAG, PROTEINS and ENZYMES datasets, the mean classification accuracy of 10-fold cross validation for each pooling method are displayed.

Pooling method	MUTAG	PROTEINS	ENZYMES
Sum	0.66 ± 0.60	0.60 ± 0.18	0.26 ± 0.07
Mean	0.78 ± 0.18	0.58 ± 0.16	0.30 ± 0.05
DiffPool	**0.85 ± 0.11**	**0.73 ± 0.04**	**0.32 ± 0.07**
SortPooling	0.74 ± 0.11	0.72 ± 0.05	0.23 ± 0.04
Set2Set	0.73 ± 0.08	0.72 ± 0.04	0.30 ± 0.07
Function space	0.83 ± 0.11	**0.73 ± 0.19**	**0.32 ± 0.06**

4.3 Datasets

To evaluate the proposed pooling method we used three graph classification datasets. The datasets in question are commonly used to evaluate graph classification methods and were obtained from the TU Dortmund University graph dataset repository [14].

The first dataset was the MUTAG dataset which consists of 188 graphs corresponding to chemical compounds where there are 7 distinct types of vertices. The classification problem is binary and concerns predicting if a chemical compound has mutagenicity or not [6].

The second dataset was the PROTEINS dataset which consists of 1113 graphs corresponding to protein molecules where there are 3 distinct types of vertices. The classification task is binary and concerns predicting if a protein is an enzyme or not [3].

The third dataset was the ENZYMES dataset which consists of 600 graphs corresponding to enzymes where there are 3 distinct types of vertices. The classification task is multi-class and concerns predicting enzyme class where there are 6 distinct classes.

4.4 Classification Accuracy

The proposed pooling method was benchmarked against the following five baseline pooling methods: mean vertex representation, sum of vertex representations, DiffPool by Ying et al. [28], SortPooling by Zhang et al. [29] and Set2Set by Vinyals et al. [24]. As described in the background and related works section of this paper, these are some of the most commonly used pooling methods.

For all baseline models we used a neural network architecture similar to that described in Sect. 4.1 with the exception that the pooling layer was replaced and the dimension of the linear layer before this layer was changed from 10 to 20. All experiments were implemented in Python3 using the PyTorch library [19] and run on an Nvidia GeForce RTX 2080 GPU. For the baseline pooling methods we used the corresponding implementations available in the *PyTorch Geometric* Python library [8].

For each dataset considered we computed the mean accuracy of 10-fold cross validation for each pooling method. The results of this analysis are displayed in Table 1. For each dataset, the proposed pooling method outperformed most baseline methods and achieved equal best performance on two of the three datasets. This demonstrates the utility of the proposed pooling method.

5 Conclusions

Pooling is a fundamental type of layer in graph neural networks which involves compute a representation of the set of vertex representations output from a sequence of convolutional layers. In this work we proposed a novel pooling method which computes a function space representation of the set of vertex representations. This method is distinct from existing pooling methods which compute either a vector or sequence space representation.

Experimental results on a number of graph classification benchmark datasets demonstrate that the proposed method generally outperforms most baseline pooling methods and in some cases achieves best performance. The benchmark datasets in question contain graphs corresponding to molecules and chemical compounds which are the most common types of dataset used to evaluate graph classification methods. Despite this fact, the proposed pooling method is general in nature and can be applied to any type of graph. Finally, the authors hope this work will serve as a platform for future work investigating the use of function space representations for pooling.

References

1. Adams, H., et al.: Persistence images: a stable vector representation of persistent homology. J. Mach. Learn. Res. **18**(1), 218–252 (2017)
2. Bai, Y., et al.: Unsupervised inductive whole-graph embedding by preserving graph proximity. In: Methods and Applications, First International Workshop on Deep Learning on Graphs (2019)
3. Borgwardt, K.M., et al.: Protein function prediction via graph kernels. Bioinformatics **21**(suppl_1), i47–i56 (2005)
4. Chen, K., et al.: A behavioral approach to visual navigation with graph localization networks. arXiv preprint arXiv:1903.00445 (2019)
5. Christensen, O.: Functions, Spaces, and Expansions: Mathematical Tools in Physics and Engineering. Springer, Boston (2010). https://doi.org/10.1007/978-0-8176-4980-7
6. Debnath, A.K., Lopez de Compadre, R.L., Debnath, G., Shusterman, A.J., Hansch, C.: Structure-activity relationship of mutagenic aromatic and heteroaromatic nitro compounds. correlation with molecular orbital energies and hydrophobicity. J. Med. Chem. **34**(2), 786–797 (1991)
7. Duvenaud, D., et al.: Convolutional networks on graphs for learning molecular fingerprints. In: Advances in Neural Information Processing Systems, pp. 2224–2232 (2015)
8. Fey, M., Lenssen, J.E.: Fast graph representation learning with PyTorch geometric. In: ICLR Workshop on Representation Learning on Graphs and Manifolds (2019)

9. Gilmer, J., Schoenholz, S.S., Riley, P.F., Vinyals, O., Dahl, G.E.: Neural message passing for quantum chemistry. In: Proceedings of the 34th International Conference on Machine Learning-Volume 70, pp. 1263–1272 (2017)
10. Hamilton, W., Ying, Z., Leskovec, J.: Inductive representation learning on large graphs. In: Advances in Neural Information Processing Systems, pp. 1024–1034 (2017)
11. He, K., Zhang, X., Ren, S., Sun, J.: Delving deep into rectifiers: surpassing human-level performance on imagenet classification. In: Proceedings of the IEEE International Conference on Computer Vision, pp. 1026–1034 (2015)
12. He, K., Zhang, X., Ren, S., Sun, J.: Deep residual learning for image recognition. In: Proceedings of the IEEE Conference on Computer Vision and Pattern Recognition, pp. 770–778 (2016)
13. Kearnes, S., McCloskey, K., Berndl, M., Pande, V., Riley, P.: Molecular graph convolutions: moving beyond fingerprints. J. Comput. Aided Mol. Des. **30**(8), 595–608 (2016). https://doi.org/10.1007/s10822-016-9938-8
14. Kersting, K., Kriege, N.M., Morris, C., Mutzel, P., Neumann, M.: Benchmark data sets for graph kernels (2016). http://graphkernels.cs.tu-dortmund.de
15. Kingma, D.P., Ba, J.: Adam: a method for stochastic optimization (2014)
16. Kipf, T.N., Welling, M.: Semi-supervised classification with graph convolutional networks. In: International Conference on Learning Representations (2017)
17. Li, Y., Tarlow, D., Brockschmidt, M., Zemel, R.: Gated graph sequence neural networks. In: Proceedings of International Conference on Learning Representations (2016)
18. Luzhnica, E., Day, B., Liò, P.: On graph classification networks, datasets and baselines. In: ICML Workshop on Learning and Reasoning with Graph-Structured Representations (2019)
19. Paszke, A., et al.: Automatic differentiation in PyTorch. In: NIPS Autodiff Workshop (2017)
20. Sanchez-Gonzalez, A., et al.: Graph networks as learnable physics engines for inference and control. In: International Conference on Machine Learning, pp. 4467–4476 (2018)
21. Tolstaya, E., Gama, F., Paulos, J., Pappas, G., Kumar, V., Ribeiro, A.: Learning decentralized controllers for robot swarms with graph neural networks. arXiv preprint arXiv:1903.10527 (2019)
22. Vaswani, A., et al.: Attention is all you need. In: Proceedings of the 31st International Conference on Neural Information Processing Systems, pp. 6000–6010. Curran Associates Inc. (2017)
23. Veličković, P., Cucurull, G., Casanova, A., Romero, A., Liò, P., Bengio, Y.: Graph attention networks. In: International Conference on Learning Representations (2018)
24. Vinyals, O., Bengio, S., Kudlur, M.: Order matters: sequence to sequence for sets. In: International Conference on Learning Representations (2016)
25. Wu, Z., Pan, S., Chen, F., Long, G., Zhang, C., Yu, P.S.: A comprehensive survey on graph neural networks. arXiv preprint arXiv:1901.00596 (2019)
26. Xu, K., Hu, W., Leskovec, J., Jegelka, S.: How powerful are graph neural networks? In: International Conference on Learning Representations (2019)
27. Xu, K., Li, C., Tian, Y., Sonobe, T., Kawarabayashi, K.I., Jegelka, S.: Representation learning on graphs with jumping knowledge networks. In: International Conference on Machine Learning, pp. 5449–5458 (2018)

28. Ying, Z., You, J., Morris, C., Ren, X., Hamilton, W., Leskovec, J.: Hierarchical graph representation learning with differentiable pooling. In: Advances in Neural Information Processing Systems, pp. 4800–4810 (2018)
29. Zhang, M., Cui, Z., Neumann, M., Chen, Y.: An end-to-end deep learning architecture for graph classification. In: Thirty-Second AAAI Conference on Artificial Intelligence (2018)
30. Zhang, Z., Cui, P., Zhu, W.: Deep learning on graphs: a survey. arXiv preprint arXiv:1812.04202 (2018)

Analysis of Optical Brain Signals Using Connectivity Graph Networks

Marco Antonio Pinto-Orellana[1(✉)] and Hugo L. Hammer[2,3]

[1] Department of Mechanical, Electronics and Chemical Engineering, Faculty of Technology, Art and Design, Oslo Metropolitan University, Oslo, Norway
marcop@oslomet.no

[2] Department of Information Technology, Faculty of Technology, Art and Design, Oslo Metropolitan University, Oslo, Norway
hugoh@oslomet.no

[3] Simula Metropolitan Center, Oslo Metropolitan University, Oslo, Norway

Abstract. Graph network analysis (GNA) showed a remarkable role for understanding brain functions, but its application is mainly narrowed to fMRI research. Connectivity analysis (CA) is introduced as a signal-to-graph mapping in a time-causality framework. In this paper, we investigate the application of GNA/CA in fNIRS. To solve the inherent challenges of using CA, we also propose a novel metric: a maximum cross-lag magnitude (MCLM) that efficiently extracts major causality information. We tested MCLM in four types of cognitive activities (mental arithmetic, motor imagery, word generation, and brain workload) from 55 participants. CA/MCLM showed a compelling modeling capacity and revealed unexpected cross-subject network patterns. We found that motion imagery and mental arithmetic share a background network structure, and that the right prefrontal cortex, in AFp8, is an invariable destination for information flows in every stimuli and participant. Therefore, CA/MCLM-fNIRS showed potential for its use along with fMRI in clinical studies.

Keywords: Brain signals · fNIRS · Graph network analysis · Connectivity analysis

1 Introduction

Time-frequency analysis of biomedical signals is a traditional and fundamental mechanism in the evaluation and interpretation of brain activity [20]. In the past decade, the advances in computing processing increased the interest of further types of analysis, in particular those that offered models of the connections between brain regions. Thus, outcomes from classical graph theory could be used in biomedical research. Graph, a.k.a network, analysis (GNA) represents the relationships between node entities (electrode channels, or brain regions in biomedical signals). However, the method to convert multivariate time series

A. Holzinger et al. (Eds.): CD-MAKE 2020, LNCS 12279, pp. 485–497, 2020.
https://doi.org/10.1007/978-3-030-57321-8_27

into a single network graph is an open problem, because compared with other types of data, interpretability is highly relevant and essential. GNA in brain research, mostly in functional magnetic resonance imaging (fMRI) studies, relies on connectivity analysis (CA) for this mapping. CA is a robust technique that can map any time series (under mild conditions) through cross-time dependencies between a set of signals. In this mapping, a link (edge) between a node A and B describes an amount of signal causal information that circulates from A to B [23]. This relationship with causality in the time series domain is based on the Granger's definition of causality: a measure of the influence of a time series on the future values of another signal that cannot be explained the latter itself [9]. This joint use of GNA/CA has shown an impressive role in understanding and describing brain functions and dynamics [1].

We can distinguish three levels of connectivity: a) structural connectivity (SC) that is associated to the anatomical or physical linkages among brain regions; b) functional connectivity (FC) as the undirected, or symmetric, interaction map generated by the linear correlations between unexplained stochastic oscillations in the observed time series; and c) effective connectivity (EC) as the directed graph network constructed by measures of the time-causality (Granger-causality) that each signal has over the other observed channels [1,23]. These three degrees of connectivity yield practical knowledge about the underlying brain interactions from different viewpoints. EC and FC show the information-level dynamics inside the brain (FC highlights the correlation between channels, while EC focuses on their non-symmetric time-causality). Both are highly time-varying because of their dependency on external (stimuli) and internal factors. However, SC is the sole type of connectome that is almost constant over time, and it can only be reliably estimated through structural magnetic resonance imaging (sMRI) [8]. Nevertheless, we can infer EC and FC through (mid- or high-frequency sampled) electrical, magnetic, or optical signals [1].

Functional near-infrared spectroscopy (fNIRS) is a noninvasive method to quantify the hemodynamic changes in the brain using the absorption properties of the near-infrared (NIR) light waves (the spectral region in the range of 700 nm and 900 nm) [14]. Even though that fNIRS and fMRI shared the same goal of estimating hemodynamic changes, connectivity analysis has been widely used in fMRI, but only in a few studies with fNIRS signals: Liu et al. compared the statistical difference between the functional connectivity maps in a driving context against a resting state [13]; Behboodi et al. analyzed functional connectivity over fNIRS filtered through neural networks [3]. However, some recognized software packages, as the NIRS AnalyzIR toolbox, have also integrated some functions for inferring FC [18].

In this paper, we explore the use of connectivity analysis and GNA in fNIRS in order to reveal underlying brain dynamics. This application is not straightforward because of the processing challenges that are inherent to fNIRS with respect to fMRI: ten times higher sampling rate and high dimensionality. Even though that fMRI data is highly dimensional, the extracted time courses are restricted and summarized using specific regions of interest, typically defined through parcellation maps [6]. This anatomical clustering reduces the signal dimensionality substantially. However, in fNIRS, there is no standard anatomical map that can be used for the same dimension-reduction purpose. Therefore, CA models incorporate a larger set of parameters when applied in fNIRS, and consequently, introduce interpretability issues. To solve this issue, we also propose a novel metric denoted as maximum cross-lag magnitude (MCLM) that summarizes CA parameters extracting the most significant causality information.

The rest of this paper is organized as follows: in Sect. 2, we describe the formulation of CA and MCLM in a graph network framework. Later, in Sect. 2.2, we describe the fNIRS data (4 cognitive activities, 9 events in 55 participants) where we tested our connectivity analysis proposal. In Sect. 3, we describe the outcomes of our model and its implications. Finally, in Sect. 4, we summarized the conclusions of our study.

2 Method

2.1 Model

Compared with machine learning methods, traditional time series models offer a slightly lower performance in prediction [10], but the latter keeps a robust and understandable model of the signals. This robustness property is advantageous in the analysis of biomedical signals because of the presence of several sources of artifacts, i.e., biological interference, device's mechanical noise, or other types of external noise [1]. In CA, the kernel technique is the vector (or multivariate) autoregressive model (VAR) [9] that models a set of M channels $\{X_1(t), X_2(t), \ldots, X_M(t)\}$ sampled every T_S seconds. Under this method, the observed value for a channel i at a time t is considered to be generated as a linear combination of the previous p points, of all M channels, and a stochastic increment $\varepsilon_i(t)$:

$$X_i(t) = \sum_{\ell=1}^{p} \sum_{j=1}^{M} \phi_{j\to i}^{(\ell)} X_j(t - \ell T_s) + \varepsilon_i(t) \quad i = 1, \ldots, M \tag{1}$$

In this notation, $\phi_{j\to i}^{(\ell)}$ measures the effect of the channel j at the time ℓT_s on channel i. The stochastic component $\varepsilon(t) = (\varepsilon_1(t), \varepsilon_2(t), \ldots, \varepsilon_M(t))^T$ is a multivariate white noise $\varepsilon(t) \sim \mathcal{N}(0, \Sigma_\varepsilon)$ with Σ_ε as the variance-covariance noise matrix, and $X\varepsilon(t)$ is uncorrelated with any previous point, $\mathbb{E}\left[\varepsilon(t)\varepsilon^T(t - \ell T_s)\right] = 0\,\forall \ell > 0$.

For a vectorial notation, let us define the multivariate recording at t as $X(t) = (X_1(t), X_2(t), \ldots, X_M(t))^T$, and the dependency matrix at lag ℓ:

$$\Phi_\ell = \begin{pmatrix} \phi_{1\to 1}^{(\ell)} & \phi_{1\to 2}^{(\ell)} & \cdots & \phi_{1\to M}^{(\ell)} \\ \phi_{2\to 1}^{(\ell)} & \phi_{2\to 2}^{(\ell)} & \cdots & \phi_{2\to M}^{(\ell)} \\ \vdots & \vdots & \ddots & \vdots \\ \phi_{M\to 1}^{(\ell)} & \phi_{M\to 2}^{(\ell)} & \cdots & \phi_{M\to M}^{(\ell)} \end{pmatrix} = \left(\phi_{2\to 1}^{(\ell)}\right)_{i,j=1\ldots M} \tag{2}$$

Then, the VAR model of Eq. 1 can be expressed as a linear matrix combination,

$$X(t) = \sum_{\ell=1}^{p} \Phi_\ell X(t - \ell T_s) + \varepsilon(t) \quad i = 1, \ldots, M \tag{3}$$

We should remark that Σ_ε measures the linear covariance between the stochastic variations in the channels that are not explained by this model, i.e., it serves as a quantification of the functional connectivity among the measured channels [1].

The set of matrices $\Phi = \{\Phi_1, \Phi_2, \ldots, \Phi_M\}$ describes the magnitude of non-symmetrical temporal dependencies among the channels in the dataset. Therefore, these pieces of information can be employed to quantify the effective connectivity in the set of signals: a) in the time domain, these coefficients can estimate the time information flow between channels; b) in the frequency domain, these matrix set can estimate the cross-spectrum and determine the magnitude of information that circulates through frequency bands [1,23]. These possibilities allow us to use different metrics: partial directed coherence [2], directed transfer function [12], as well, other improved formulations [17].

Due to our current interest in time-domain characteristics, we introduce a simple metric derived from the VAR model: the maximum cross-lag magnitude (MCLM). MCLM is an operator $\mathbb{R}^{p\times p\times M} \rightarrow \mathbb{N}^{p\times p} \times \mathbb{R}^{p\times p}$ that maps the set Φ into a tuple (L, Θ) where L is the max-lag matrix, and Θ is the max-dependency matrix. L is defined as a $p \times p$ matrix where each item $l_{i,j}$ is the time lag with the strongest absolute coefficient ϕ:

$$l_{i,j} = \arg \max_{\ell=1,\ldots,p} \left| \phi_{i\rightarrow j}^{(\ell)} \right| \tag{4}$$

Θ is defined as a $p\times p$ matrix where each item is the cross-lag maximum coefficient between channel i and j:

$$\theta_{i,j} = \phi_{i\rightarrow j}^{(l_{i,j})} \tag{5}$$

Sample estimators of both parameters, $\hat{l}_{i,j}$ and $\hat{\theta}_{i,j}$ can be estimated from the data and their confidence interval obtained through subsampling Monte Carlo simulations given that the distributions of $\hat{\phi}_{i\rightarrow j}^{(\ell)}$ are known [4,15,16].

The MCLM max-lag matrix, Θ, can be interpreted as an adjacency matrix of a weighted graph network. Therefore, a graph $G_\Theta = (V, E, \omega)$ can be constructed where $V = 1, \ldots, M$ is the set of channels in the observations as vertices; E is the ordered set of edges or links $E \in V \times V$, and the weight function $\omega : E \rightarrow \mathbb{R}$ that assigns the maximum dependency magnitude $\theta_{i,j}$ as weight for the link $i \rightarrow j$. Furthermore, Σ_ε can also be reinterpreted as an undirected graph $G_\Sigma = (V, E, \omega)$ under a similar formulation (Table 1).

Considering that a specific event for each subject τ will be associated with a matrix $\Theta^{(\tau)}$, we introduce two terms for further cross-subject analysis: a representative max-dependency matrix $\Theta^{(*)}$ as the average of all $\Theta^{(\tau)}$; and a coverage metric of each magnitude $\theta_{i,j}^{(*)}$ defined as the proportion of connections that are non-null:

Table 1. Experiments and events recorded in the two datasets. The number of participants and channels employed in the dataset are also indicated. Each fNIRS channel corresponds to the midpoint between the optical source and detector with the equivalent label according to the extended 10–20 EEG standard layout.

Experiment	Events	Dataset	Partici-pants	fNIRS Channels
N-back (NB)	0-back 2-back 3-back	NBWG	26	*Pre-frontal* (16): AF1, AF2, AF5h, AF6h, AF7, AF8, AFF3h, AFF4h, AFF5, AFF6, AFFz, AFp3, AFp4, AFp7, AFp8, AFpz *Central region* (8): C3h, C4h, C5h, C6h, FCC3, FCC4, CCP3, CCP4 *Centro-parietal* (6): CPP3, CPP4, P3h, P4h, P5h, P6h *Parieto-occipital* (6): PO1, PO2, POOz, PPO3, PPO4, PPOz
Word Generation (WG)	WG WG baseline			
Motor Imagery (MI)	Right MI Left MI	MIMA	29	*Pre-frontal* (7): AF1, AF2, AFp5h, AFp6h, AFp7, AFp8, AFpz *Central region* (26): C3h, C4h, C5h, C6h, CCP1, CCP2, CCP3, CCP4, CCP5, CCP6, CP3h, CP4h, CP5h, CP6h, FC3h, FC4h, FC5h, FC6h, FCC1, FCC2, FCC3, FCC4, FCC5, FCC6, Fp1h, Fp2h *Occipital* (3): O1h, O2h, POOz
Mental Arithmetic (MA)	MA MA baseline			

$$\text{coverage}\left\{\theta_{i,j}^{(*)}\right\} = \frac{\left|\left\{\theta_{i,j}^{(\tau)} \neq 0 | \forall\tau\right\}\right|}{\left|\left\{\theta_{i,j}^{(\tau)} | \forall\tau\right\}\right|} \tag{6}$$

2.2 Data Description

In order to show the expressiveness and capabilities of the model in fNIRS signals, we used two recorded datasets by Shin et al. [11,19]. These sources of data are publicly available and contribute to the reproducibility of the results with the presented model. Even though that both datasets contain other non-optical biomedical signals, we restricted to the analysis of their fNIRS time series.

In the first dataset (NBWG), twenty-six participants were requested to perform three cognitive activities (n-back, word generation, and discrimination/selection response task) from which we selected two relevant activities for our goals [11]:

- *N-back tasks (NB).* In this exercise, every participant performed a 0-, 2-, or 3-back task during 60 s (40 s for the activity, and 20 s for the resting period). The experiment is organized in three sessions, wherein each session, nine n-back tasks were performed (3 times per n-back type) in a counter-balanced order per session.
- *Word generation activity (WG).* In three sessions, consisting of twenty trials each one, the subjects were presented a single letter for WG or a fixation-cross in a screen for baseline. The task included 10 s for the task and 13–15 s for a resting interval.

In the second data source (MIMA), twenty-nine subjects performed two types of activities that represent typical mental tasks commonly used in brain-computer studies [19]:

- *Motor imagery (MI).* MI is a classical test for brain-computer interfaces for different purposes: computer-assisted rehabilitation, games, and virtual reality systems. In MIMA, all participants performed a mental process consisting of imaging the scene of opening and closing their hands while grabbing a ball. They were also requested to imagine this movement with a speed of one cycle per second. The experiment was organized in three sessions, with ten trials for left hand MI, and ten trials for right hand MI.
- *Mental arithmetic (MA).* In this activity, the subjects were requested to subtract a one-digit number from a three-digit number in the lapse of twelve seconds (two seconds for displaying the instruction, and ten for solving it) with a resting time of 15–17 s. This session was repeated 20 times per subject.

Further details about the datasets, and experimental designs, we refer to [11] and [19].

2.3 Data Analysis

The biomedical signals from MIMA and NBWG datasets were processed according to the steps as follows:

1. Signals are subsampled in MIMA from 12.5 Hz to 10 Hz in order to ensure the same sampling frequency across datasets.
2. Time series are frequency filtered in the range 0.01–0.1 Hz using a finite impulse filter of 100th order. The extracted spectral range is typically associated with cerebral autoregulation, cognition, and neural activity [14].
3. Signals are partitioned into sections according to their recorded time events.
4. A VAR(20) model is fit for each segment allowing to model dependencies up to 2 s in the past, removing the estimated parameters with p-values greater than 0.0001. The remaining estimated components have strong evidence to be non-null, and therefore, are appropriate for our analysis.
5. Matrix Θ and L, and the link coverages are calculated according to Eqs. 4, 5 and 6.

6. The approximate distribution for each coefficient θ_{ij} was estimated using a Monte Carlo simulation and a subsampling as described in [15] and [16].
7. The mean magnitude for each link is estimated across all subjects as well as their approximated distribution.
8. For our exploratory analysis, we calculate two primary metrics: centrality and information flow. We refer to [8] for a more comprehensive review of alternative network graph metrics.

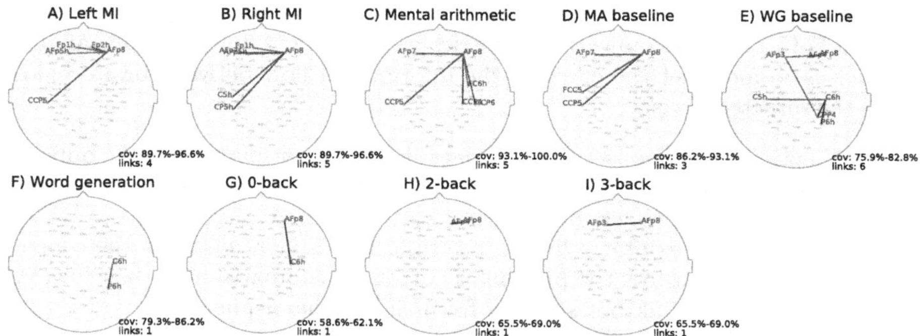

Fig. 1. General connections in the functional connectivity.

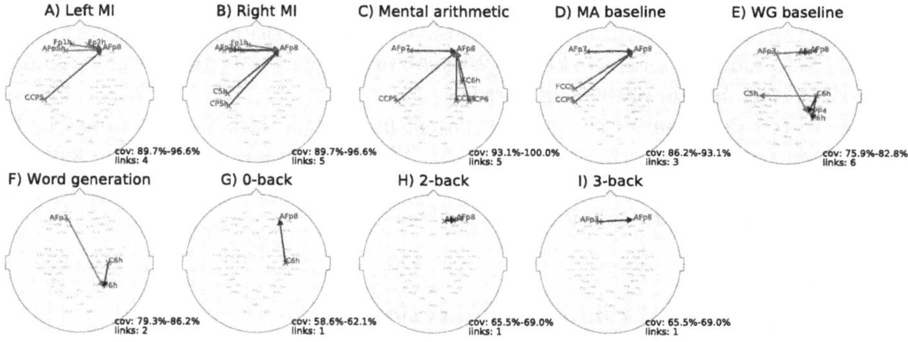

Fig. 2. General connections in the effective connectivity using MCML. Note that MCLM as a connectivity metric is able to capture the same links than raw effective connectivity, as it is shown in Fig. 1.

3 Results and Discussion

Based on the described procedure, a network map was estimated for each event and person (246 networks in total). This large amount of data motivated us to reduce the parameters to analyze and describe in a concise but informative manner.

3.1 Cross-Subject General Connections

A link was considered general if their coverage is above the 95% percentile in the network graph related to a specific stimulus/event. No general coverage threshold was used because the maximum coverage in the data can be lower than 100% (as a direct consequence of the p-value filtering of step 5 in Sect. 2.3). Although the uncertainty-based filtering increased the confidence of the link magnitudes estimated, it also removed relevant connections that present high levels of uncertainty.

The most significant directed and undirected connections (effective and functional connectivity) are displayed in Fig. 2 and Fig. 1, respectively. Most connections in both types of connectivity metrics were similar. Moreover, this analysis allowed us to interpret the effect of the information flow between brain regions using the directed links:

- In MI activities, it is observed that data flows were originated in the opposite hemisphere of the imagined motion hand, i.e., the left MI had a dependency link from the right to left hemisphere, and vice-versa.
- MA tasks always exhibit a link in the right hemisphere between the central-parietal region towards the prefrontal cortex. In comparison, its baseline MA denoted a similar link but starting from the left hemisphere.
- WG experiment shows relevant flows in the right central, parietal, and left prefrontal cortex, but with an additional link from the left prefrontal cortex. We should emphasize that the activity on the central-parietal region was confirmed as activated areas in WG tasks through an fMRI study by Brannet el al. [5],
- Attention tasks (0-back) appeared to have similar information flows compared with MA, while mental workload (2-back and 3-back) data flows were strongly evident only in the prefrontal cortex.
- It is worth mentioning that, in all cases, numerous data flows seemed to be oriented towards the right hemisphere. This phenomenon can be associated with the fact that the participants were mostly right-handed. However, further research is needed to ratify this hypothesis.

3.2 Cross-Subject Common Connections

We define a link as common if their coverage in the dataset is above the median of the signal amplitude on the event's coverage. The common links in effective connectivity are shown in Fig. 3. Compared with the network maps in Fig. 2, these maps can be slightly different, because of the presence of frequent, but not general, links.

Maps of common links allowed us to observe more details about the reconfiguration of the connectivity in the brain under different experimental tasks.

Connectivity maps showed a natural organization intro three large groups, or clusters, of tasks: mental activity (mental imagery and arithmetic), verbal fluency (word generation and its baseline), and mental workload (0-, 2-, and 3-tasks).

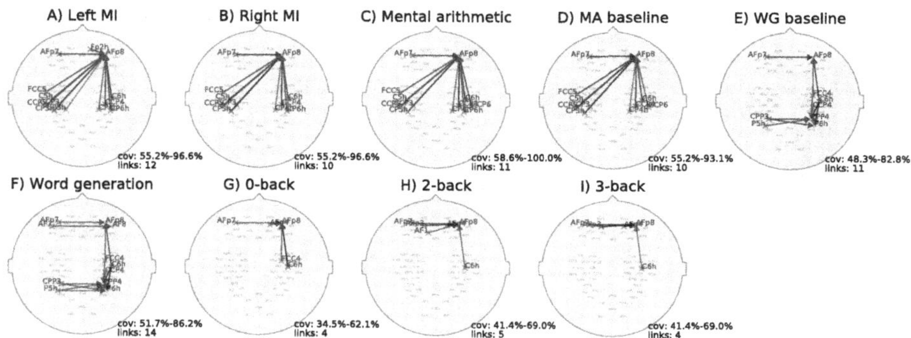

Fig. 3. Common connections in the effective connectivity

All connectivity maps showed a "gravity effect" of the electrode AFp8 (right prefrontal cortex): it is the preferred destination point for all the data flows in every event of each subject in the datasets. The influence of the right prefrontal cortex was denoted in MA tasks by Tanida et al. [21], in MA in a study by Ehrlichman et al. [7], and in n-back tasks according to Vermeij et al. [22].

3.3 Net Information Flow

For a node (channel) i, net information flow (NIF) is defined as the total flow that enters into the node (out-flow) subtracted from the total flow originated in the node (in-flow):

$$\mathrm{NIF}_i = \sum_{v \in V} \theta_{i \to v} - \sum_{v \in V} \theta_{v \to i} \tag{7}$$

This property estimates the final impact that the electrode had in the connectivity network. The electrode channel shows a higher dependency on the other channels when the net flow is negative; otherwise, it exhibits a particular impact on the network. The most relevant channels' NIF is shown in Fig. 4. As it was discussed before, AFp8 was the electrode that is more influential on the network. However, its dependency magnitude varies according to the type of activity, demanding mental tasks, and effortless lexical tasks. It is also remarkable that the net information flow can provide insights to identify the type of task: lexical activities have a notable dependent effect in the right hemisphere (channel CPP4 and P6h), while mental tasks have a more role as sources' flow in the left hemisphere (channel CCP5).

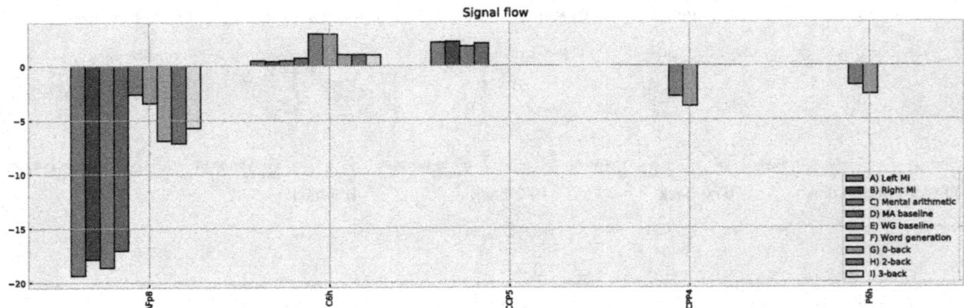

Fig. 4. Net information flow. The most significant NIF values (NIF > 2) are displayed (channel AFp8, C6h, CCP5, CPP4, P6h) and classified according to the datasets' events: A) Left MI, B) Right MI, C) Mental arithmetic, D) MA baseline, E) WG baseline, F) Word generation, G) 0-back, H) 2-back, and I) 3-back.

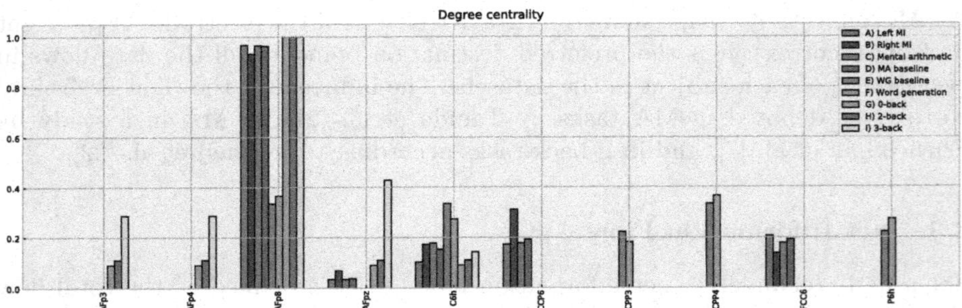

Fig. 5. Network degree centrality. The most significant NDC values (NDC > 0.2) are shown (channels AFp3, AFp4, AFp8, AFpz, C6h, CCP6, CPP3, CPP4, FCC6, and P6h). Each bar corresponds to the NDC of datasets' event: A) Left MI, B) Right MI, C) Mental arithmetic, D) MA baseline, E) WG baseline, F) Word generation, G) 0-back, H) 2-back, and I) 3-back.

3.4 Network Degree Centrality

For each node i, degree centrality (NDC) is defined as the proportion of information flows that have i as a source or destination with respect to the total links in the network:

$$\mathrm{NDC}_i = \frac{\sum_{v \in V} \mathbb{I}\left[\theta_{i \to v} \neq 0\right] - \sum_{v \in V} \mathbb{I}\left[\theta_{v \to i} \neq 0\right]}{\sum_{i \in V} \sum_{j \in V} \mathbb{I}\left[\theta_{i \to j} \neq 0\right]} \tag{8}$$

where $\mathbb{I}[\cdot]$ is the indicator function: $\mathbb{I}[x] = \begin{cases} 1 & x \text{ is true} \\ 0 & \text{otherwise} \end{cases}$.

The results are shown in Fig. 5. In concordance with the previous assessments, the centrality role of the channel AFp8 is general across all experimental tasks. However, a partial relevance is displayed for channel AFpz, CPP4, and CCP6, in mental workload, lexical, and MI/MA tasks, respectively.

4 Conclusions

Biomedical time series are often analyzed through their time changes or their spectral responses. Other types of analysis, such as network analysis, are usually only performed in fMRI data, where cross-dependency patterns are used to create and study brain graph networks. This signal-to-graph transformation is based on connectivity analysis (CA) and allows us to create complex network structures that associate sets of time series in a time-causality framework. Despite its proven effectiveness in fMRI, this methodology was not completely explored in optical biomedical signals.

In this paper, we investigated the possibilities of using CA with a new connectivity metric based on the classical, but robust, multivariate autoregressive model. This metric, a maximum cross-lag magnitude, relates each pair of signal channels with a quantified inter-channel time-dependency measure. We applied this formulation into fNIRS signals (from two different datasets) that contained four types of cognitive activities (mental arithmetic, motor imagery, word generation, and brain workload) organized into nine different categories of events. Each event was repeated at least four times in 55 participants (distributed in 26 participants in the first dataset and 29 in the second one).

Combining CA with our connectivity metric showed a compelling modeling potential and allowed us to reveal unexpected cross-subject dynamic causality patterns. Our results showed that motion imagery shares a similar background structure with mental arithmetic tasks; while channel AFp8 is always a destination for information flows regardless of the stimuli or participant. Simultaneously, the method provided event-related individual patterns that let to identify each event individually using some simple network properties. These results offer exciting possibilities for further extensions as complementary input in machine learning algorithms as well as possible clinical applications due to the availability of uncertainty measures of each dependency magnitude and the selection of potential regions of interest for more comprehensive MRI analysis.

Acknowledgments. This work is financially supported by the Research Council of Norway to the Project No. 273599, "Patient-Centric Engineering in Rehabilitation (PACER)".

References

1. Anwar, A.R., et al.: Effective connectivity of cortical sensorimotor networks during finger movement tasks: a simultaneous fNIRS, fMRI, EEG study. Brain Topogr. **29**(5), 645–660 (2016)
2. Baccalá, L.A., Sameshima, K.: Partial directed coherence: a new concept in neural structure determination. Biol. Cybern. **84**(6), 463–474 (2001)
3. Behboodi, B., Ji-Woong, C., Hyeon-Ae, J.: Deep neural networks for assessing functional connectivity: an fNIRS study. PhD thesis, Daegu Gyeongbuk Institute of Science and Technology (2018)

4. Botev, Z., L'Ecuyer, P.: Simulation from the tail of the univariate and multivariate normal distribution. In: Puliafito, A., Trivedi, K.S. (eds.) Systems Modeling: Methodologies and Tools. EICC, pp. 115–132. Springer, Cham (2019). https://doi.org/10.1007/978-3-319-92378-9_8
5. Brannen, J.H., Badie, B., Moritz, C.H., Quigley, M., Elizabeth Meyerand, M., Haughton, V.M.: Reliability of functional MR imaging with word-generation tasks for mapping broca's area. Am. J. Neuroradiol. **22**(9), 1711–1718 (2001)
6. Chen, J.E., Glover, G.H.: Functional magnetic resonance imaging methods. Neuropsychol. Rev. **25**(3), 289–313 (2015)
7. Ehrlichman, H., Barrett, J.: Right hemispheric specialization for mental imagery: a review of the evidence. Brain Cogn. **2**(1), 55–76 (1983)
8. Farahani, F.V., Karwowski, W., Lighthall, N.R.: Application of graph theory for identifying connectivity patterns in human brain networks: a systematic review. Front. Neurosci. **13**, 585 (2019)
9. Goebel, R., Roebroeck, A., Kim, D.-S., Formisano, E.: Investigating directed cortical interactions in time-resolved fMRI data using vector autoregressive modeling and granger causality mapping. Magn. Reson. Imaging **21**(10), 1251–1261 (2003)
10. Guo, J.: Oil price forecast using deep learning and ARIMA. In: 2019 International Conference on Machine Learning, Big Data and Business Intelligence (MLBDBI). IEEE, November 2019
11. Shin, J., et al.: Simultaneous acquisition of EEG and NIRS during cognitive tasks for an open access dataset. Sci. Data **5**(1), 180003 (2018)
12. Kaminski, M.J., Blinowska, K.J.: A new method of the description of the information flow in the brain structures. Biol. Cybern. **65**(3), 203–210 (1991)
13. Liu, Z., et al.: Effective connectivity analysis of the brain network in drivers during actual driving using near-infrared spectroscopy. Front. Behav. Neurosci. **11**, 211 (2017)
14. Pinti, P., Scholkmann, F., Hamilton, A., Burgess, P., Tachtsidis, I.: Current status and issues regarding pre-processing of fNIRS neuroimaging data: an investigation of diverse signal filtering methods within a general linear model framework. Front. Hum. Neurosci. **12**, 505 (2019)
15. Politis, D.N., Romano, J.P., Wolf, M.: Subsampling. Springer, New York (1999). https://doi.org/10.1007/978-1-4612-1554-7
16. Romano, J.P., Wolf, M.: Subsampling inference for the mean in the heavy-tailed case. Metrika **50**(1), 55–69 (1999)
17. Sandhya, C., Srinidhi, G., Vaishali, R., Visali, M., Kavitha, A.: Analysis of speech imagery using brain connectivity estimators. In: 2015 IEEE 14th International Conference on Cognitive Informatics & Cognitive Computing. IEEE (2015)
18. Santosa, H., Zhai, X., Fishburn, F., Huppert, T.: The NIRS brain AnalyzIR toolbox. Algorithms **11**(5), 73 (2018)
19. Shin, J., et al.: Open access dataset for EEG+NIRS single-trial classification. IEEE Trans. Neural Syst. Rehabil. Eng. **25**(10), 1735–1745 (2017)
20. Subasi, A.: Biomedical signal analysis and its usage in healthcare. In: Paul, S. (ed.) Biomedical Engineering and its Applications in Healthcare, pp. 423–452. Springer, Singapore (2019). https://doi.org/10.1007/978-981-13-3705-5_18
21. Tanida, M., Sakatani, K., Takano, R., Tagai, K.: Relation between asymmetry of prefrontal cortex activities and the autonomic nervous system during a mental arithmetic task: near infrared spectroscopy study. Neurosci. Lett. **369**(1), 69–74 (2004)

22. Vermeij, A., et al.: Prefrontal activation may predict working-memory training gain in normal aging and mild cognitive impairment. Brain Imaging Behav. **11**(1), 141–154 (2016)
23. Zeidman, P., et al.: A guide to group effective connectivity analysis, part 1: first level analysis with DCM for fMRI. NeuroImage **200**, 174–190 (2019)

Property-Based Testing for Parameter Learning of Probabilistic Graphical Models

Anna Saranti[1(✉)], Behnam Taraghi[3], Martin Ebner[3], and Andreas Holzinger[1,2]

[1] Medical University Graz, Auenbruggerplatz 2, 8036 Graz, Austria
{anna.saranti,andreas.holzinger}@medunigraz.at
[2] xAI Lab, Alberta Machine Intelligence Institute, Edmonton T6G 2H1, Canada
[3] Department Educational Technology, Graz University of Technology, Münzgrabenstrasse 36/I, 8010 Graz, Austria
{b.taraghi,martin.ebner}@tugraz.at

Abstract. Code quality is a requirement for successful and sustainable software development. The emergence of Artificial Intelligence and data driven Machine Learning in current applications makes customized solutions for both data as well as code quality a requirement. The diversity and the stochastic nature of Machine Learning algorithms require different test methods, each of which is suitable for a particular method. Conventional unit tests in test-automation environments provide the common, well-studied approach to tackle code quality issues, but Machine Learning applications pose new challenges and have different requirements, mostly as far the numerical computations are concerned. In this research work, a concrete use of property-based testing for quality assurance in the parameter learning algorithm of a probabilistic graphical model is described. The necessity and effectiveness of this method in comparison to unit tests is analyzed with concrete code examples for enhanced retraceability and interpretability, thus highly relevant for what is called explainable AI.

Keywords: Machine learning · Probabilistic graphical models · Property-based testing

1 Introduction

Most Machine Learning (ML) approaches are stochastic. Consequently, most existing testing techniques are inadequate for ML code implementations. Consequently, the ML community uses numerical testing, metamorphic testing, mutation testing, coverage-guided fuzzing testing, proof-based testing, and especially property-based testing to detect problems in ML code implementations as early as possible [1]. Because these ML models are increasingly used for decision support, e.g. in the medical domain, there is an urgent need for quality assurance - particularly with a focus on domain-dependent properties. On such is monotonicity and specifies a software as learned by an ML model to provide a prediction.

A. Holzinger et al. (Eds.): CD-MAKE 2020, LNCS 12279, pp. 499–515, 2020.
https://doi.org/10.1007/978-3-030-57321-8_28

Interestingly, approaches for checking monotonicity of the generated model, in particular of black-box models, are lacking [13].

The concept of property-based testing (PBT) relies on randomly generated test cases and it is a very relevant extension for unit tests. Defining concrete test cases is a central task when developing unit tests. However, it is very time-consuming and still often incomplete. Therefore methods for automatic generation of a variety of test-cases with only one specification, are more effective and profitable. Test developers don't have to define all possible edge cases anymore; those are automatically discovered by the corresponding frameworks [9]. The task of the developer shifts from listing and programming a lot of use-cases, to analyzing the constraints and the properties of the software under test and let the framework randomly generate values that fulfil the constraints and explore the relevant edge-cases automatically.

Since Artificial Intelligence applications have become prevalent, the need of corresponding quality management tools is rising. Frameworks like ProbFuzz [4], tailored for the needs of probabilistic programming systems and generate lots of different probability distributions. Several examples of machine learning programs involving neural networks are described in [3] and one of the most popular and useful ones, the Markov Chain Monte Carlo (MCMC) is indeed exercised with property-based techniques [5]. An extensive study is provided by [15]. This research work focuses on a particular probabilistic graphical model with a defined structure, where the parameters need to be learned with the expectation-maximization algorithm. The testing of the implementation follows the paradigm of property-based testing.

2 Previous Work

Previous research work was based on data of the learning analytics application "1x1 trainer"[1], developed by the department Educational Technology of Graz University of Technology, Austria. Users answer 1-digit multiplication questions that are posed to them sequentially. Detailed information about the gathered data, student modelling and analysis can be found in [12,14]. The student model that was designed and provided valuable insights, is used in the forthcoming sections and its structure is depicted in Fig. 1. Each question has its own probabilistic graphical model; the structure of all models is basically the same.

In Bayesian parameter estimation the computation of the posterior distribution with regard to the prior is computed with the Bayes rule 1:

$$\overbrace{P(\Theta|\mathcal{D})}^{posterior} = \frac{\overbrace{P(\mathcal{D}|\Theta)}^{likelihood}\overbrace{P(\Theta)}^{prior}}{\underbrace{P(\mathcal{D})}_{marginal\ likelihood}} \tag{1}$$

[1] https://schule.learninglab.tugraz.at/einmaleins/, Last accessed 26 April 2020.

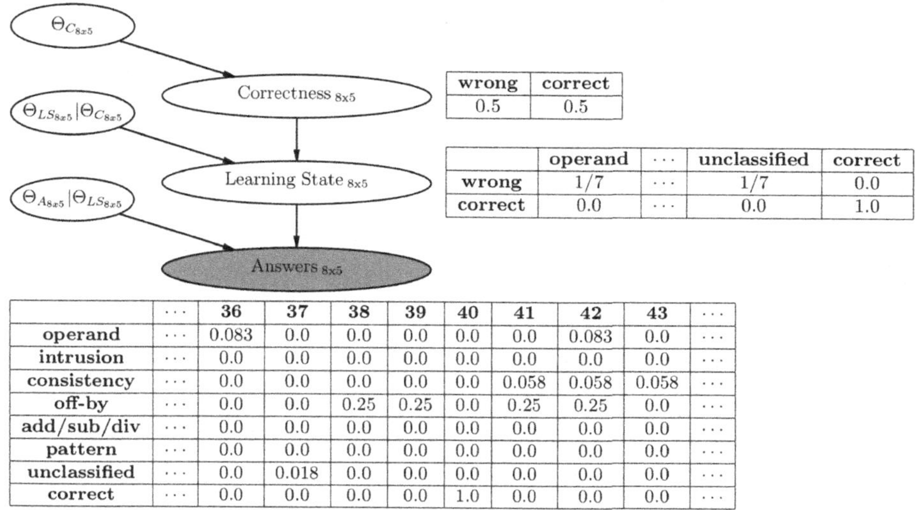

wrong	correct
0.5	0.5

	operand	...	unclassified	correct
wrong	1/7	...	1/7	0.0
correct	0.0	...	0.0	1.0

	...	36	37	38	39	40	41	42	43	...
operand	...	0.083	0.0	0.0	0.0	0.0	0.0	0.083	0.0	...
intrusion	...	0.0	0.0	0.0	0.0	0.0	0.0	0.0	0.0	...
consistency	...	0.0	0.0	0.0	0.0	0.0	0.058	0.058	0.058	...
off-by	...	0.0	0.0	0.25	0.25	0.0	0.25	0.25	0.0	...
add/sub/div	...	0.0	0.0	0.0	0.0	0.0	0.0	0.0	0.0	...
pattern	...	0.0	0.0	0.0	0.0	0.0	0.0	0.0	0.0	...
unclassified	...	0.0	0.018	0.0	0.0	0.0	0.0	0.0	0.0	...
correct	...	0.0	0.0	0.0	0.0	1.0	0.0	0.0	0.0	...

Fig. 1. Parameters of the learning competence probabilistic graphical model

The parameters of the student model in Fig. 1 are the ones corresponding to the uniform (uninformative) prior. The data that were collected from the students by their interaction with the learning application, are used to update the parameters, as it will be described in the following sections. The equation of the joint distribution 2 will be very valuable in the following sections for the update of the parameters.

$$\begin{aligned} P(\mathbf{Correctness_q}, \mathbf{Learning\ State_q}, \mathbf{Answers_q}) = \\ P(\mathbf{Correctness_q})\ P(\mathbf{Learning\ State_q}|\mathbf{Correctness_q}) \\ P(\mathbf{Answers_q}|\mathbf{Learning\ State_q}) \end{aligned} \tag{2}$$

3 Learning the Model's Parameters with Batch Expectation-Maximization (EM)

Bayesian parameter learning is applicable when all variables are visible [7]; in that case all components of the Eq. 1 are computable. The model of the learning competence contains hidden variables, therefore the computation of the posterior of each random variable cannot be made directly. In this case the method that is used is expectation-maximization (abbreviated by EM). The concepts of prior, likelihood and posterior that were described in the previous Sect. 2 are used in the description of this method.

3.1 Notation

The entities that are necessary for the analytical solution for the computation of the posterior distributions of all model's variables are the following:

N : Number of all samples in dataset

n : One sample of N

M : Number of $\mathbf{Correctness_q}$ possible outcomes ($M = 2$)

μ : Index of $\mathbf{Correctness_q}$ outcome

w_μ : Parameters of $\mathbf{Correctness_q}$

K : Number of $\mathbf{Learning\ State_q}$ possible error types and correct outcome ($K = 8$)

k : Index of $\mathbf{Learning\ State_q}$ outcome (one error type out of $K - 1$ or correct)

$\pi_{k|\mu}$: Parameters of the $\mathbf{Learning\ State_q}$ variable

Q : Number of $\mathbf{Answers_q}$ random variables (90 in total)

q : Index of $\mathbf{Answers_q}$ (one question of Q)

X : Number of all possible answers of each question (columns of conditional probability tables of $\mathbf{Answers_{1x1}}$ to $\mathbf{Answers_{10x9}}$)

x : one answer out of X

x_n : the answer of the n-th sample

$\theta_{x|k}$: The parameters of the $\mathbf{Correctness_q}$ random variable

Θ : All current parameters of the model : (set of all w_μ, $\pi_{k|\mu}$, $\theta_{x|k}$).

Θ_{old} : All parameters of the previous EM iteration.

$\mathbf{X}$: The set of all visible variables. In this model, they are all $\mathbf{Answers_q}$ variables.

$\mathbf{Z}$: The set of all latent variables or hidden causes. In this model, they are all $\mathbf{Correctness_q}$ and $\mathbf{Learning\ State_q}$ variable.

3.2 Expectation-Maximization (EM) Algorithm

The goal of the EM-Algorithm is to find appropriate values for all parameters Θ. In general a better model will fit the data better, although it must not overfit. The latent variables $\mathbf{Correctness_q}$ and $\mathbf{Learning\ State_q}$ are not observed, so the direct maximization of the likelihood $P(\mathbf{X}; \Theta)$ of the data according to this model is not possible; the observed data $\mathbf{X}$ (not to be confused with the number of possible answers of each question X) is incomplete. Each iteration of the EM-algorithm computes a different instantiation of the table CPDs.

By using marginalization:

$$P(\boldsymbol{X}; \Theta) = \sum_{\boldsymbol{Z}} P(\boldsymbol{X}, \boldsymbol{Z}; \Theta) \tag{3}$$

$$\ln P(\boldsymbol{X};\Theta) = \ln\left\{\sum_{\boldsymbol{Z}} P(\boldsymbol{X},\boldsymbol{Z};\Theta)\right\} \tag{4}$$

If the complete data set $\{\boldsymbol{X},\boldsymbol{Z}\}$ were known, then it would be straightforward to try to maximize the complete data log-likelihood. To avoid multiplication of very small floating point numbers that can lead to zero, one can equivalently maximize the log-likelihood function $\ln P(\boldsymbol{X};\Theta)$.

The EM-Algorithm works iteratively and consists of four steps:

1. Initialization of all parameters to Θ_0 of the complete dataset $\{\boldsymbol{X},\boldsymbol{Z}\}$ and set $\Theta_0 = \Theta_{old}$.
2. E-Step: Computation of the posterior distribution $P(\boldsymbol{Z}|\boldsymbol{X};\Theta_{old})$ of $\mathbf{Z}$ given the visible variables and the previous parameters.
3. M-Step: Compute new Θ parameters by trying to maximize 6 the expected value of the posterior distribution 5 over the latent variables $\boldsymbol{Z}$:

$$\mathcal{Q}(\Theta,\Theta_{old}) = \sum_{\boldsymbol{Z}} P(\boldsymbol{Z}|\boldsymbol{X};\Theta_{old}) \ln P(\boldsymbol{X},\boldsymbol{Z};\Theta) \tag{5}$$

$$\Theta = \underset{\Theta}{\operatorname{argmax}}\ \mathcal{Q}(\Theta,\Theta_{old}) \tag{6}$$

4. Compute the incomplete data likelihood $P(\boldsymbol{X};\Theta)$ or equivalently the log-likelihood $\ln P(\boldsymbol{X};\Theta)$ 4. If the log-likelihood's increase or the Θ parameters' change is not significant compared to the previous iteration, then stop. Else, set current Θ with the values computed in M-Step and return to E-Step. The EM-algorithm is a "meta-algorithm" since it contains an inference in the E-Step [11]. The iterative process is depicted in Fig. 2.

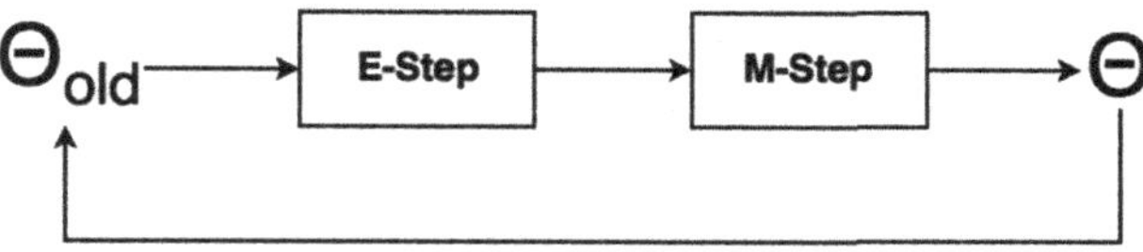

Fig. 2. The iteration loop of the EM-algorithm

3.3 Analytical Solution of Expectation-Maximization (EM) for the Model of Learning Competence

The steps of the EM-algorithm are applied to the model of the Learning Competence for the derivation of the analytical solution for the update of the parameters. We apply those steps to the model of Learning Competence of each question q separately. The equations in this subsection omit the subscript q; they apply to the model of each question independently.

The Eq. 7 expresses the joint probability distribution Eq. 8 is derived from:

$$P(\boldsymbol{X}, \boldsymbol{Z}; \Theta) = \prod_{n} \prod_{\mu} \prod_{k} w_{\mu} \pi_{k|\mu} \theta_{x_n|k} \tag{7}$$

$$\ln P(\boldsymbol{X}, \boldsymbol{Z}; \Theta) = \sum_{n=1}^{N} \ln \left(\sum_{\mu=1}^{M} \sum_{k=1}^{K} w_{\mu} \pi_{k|\mu} \theta_{x_n|k} \right) \tag{8}$$

The expected value of the complete log-likelihood $\mathcal{Q}(\Theta, \Theta_{old})$ is:

$$\begin{aligned} \mathcal{Q}(\Theta, \Theta_{old}) = \mathbb{E}_{P(\boldsymbol{Z}|\boldsymbol{X};\Theta_{old})} \left[\ln P(\boldsymbol{X}, \boldsymbol{Z}; \Theta) \right] = \\ \sum_{\boldsymbol{Z}} P(\boldsymbol{Z}|\boldsymbol{X}; \Theta_{old}) \ln P(\boldsymbol{X}, \boldsymbol{Z}; \Theta) = \\ \sum_{n} \sum_{\mu} \sum_{k} \gamma(z_{\mu k}^{(n)}) \Big(\ln w_{\mu} + \ln \pi_{k|\mu} + \ln \theta_{x_n|k} \Big) \end{aligned} \tag{9}$$

The responsibility $\gamma(z_{\mu k}^{(n)})$ of the hidden error cause or correct k for $n-$th sample coupled with the probability of the answer being answered correctly, can be computed by using the Bayes rule and the factorization of the joint probability distribution from Eq. 2:

$$\gamma(z_{\mu k}^{(n)}) = P(z_{\mu k}^{(n)} | x^{(n)}; \Theta_{old}) \propto P(x^{(n)} | z_{\mu k}^{(n)}; \Theta_{old}) P(z_{\mu k}^{(n)}; \Theta_{old}) \tag{10}$$

The values of all $\gamma(z_{\mu k}^{(n)})$ values in Eq. 10 are provided up to a normalization factor. Since $\gamma(z_{\mu k}^{(n)})$ depends only on Θ_{old}, it can be considered a constant in the process of maximization of $\mathcal{Q}$. At the same time following constraints that reflect the conditional probability rules must be fulfilled:

$$\sum_{\mu=1}^{M} w_{\mu} = 1 \tag{11}$$

$$\sum_{k=1}^{K} \pi_{k|\mu} = 1 \tag{12}$$

$$\sum_{x=1}^{X} \theta_{x|k} = 1 \tag{13}$$

The maximization of the complete log-likelihood $\mathcal{Q}(\Theta, \Theta_{old})$ leads to the parameters of the model. The maximization process must also fulfil the constraints in Eqs. 11, 12, 13, which can be made with the use of Lagrange Multipliers. The maximum of the following expression must be found:

$$\mathcal{Q}(\Theta, \Theta_{old}) + \lambda \Big(\sum_{\mu} w_{\mu} - 1 \Big) + \sum_{\mu} \lambda_{\mu} \Big(\sum_{k} \pi_{k|\mu} - 1 \Big) + \sum_{k} \lambda_{k} \Big(\sum_{x} \theta_{x|k} - 1 \Big) \tag{14}$$

First, the update of the parameters of a particular $\mathbf{Correctness_q}$ value $w_{m|q}$, is made from the data samples n' that have as question $q = q_{n'} \in [q_1 \cdots q_Q]$, and answer m being either correct or wrong:

$$\sum_{n'=1}^{N'} \gamma(z_{\mu k}^{(n')}) \frac{1}{w_{m|q}} + \lambda \stackrel{!}{=} 0 \quad \| \cdot w_{m|q} \tag{15}$$

$$\sum_{n'=1}^{N'} \gamma(z_{\mu k}^{(n')}) + \lambda w_{m|q} \stackrel{!}{=} 0 \quad \| \sum_{m=1}^{M} \tag{16}$$

$$\sum_{m=1}^{M} \sum_{n'=1}^{N'} \gamma(z_{\mu k}^{(n')}) + \lambda \sum_{m=1}^{M} w_{m|q} \stackrel{!}{=} 0 \tag{17}$$

$$\lambda = - \sum_{m=1}^{M} \sum_{n'=1}^{N'} \gamma(z_{\mu k}^{(n')}) = -N' \tag{18}$$

because :

$$\sum_{m=1}^{M} \gamma(z_{\mu k}^{(n')}) = 1 \tag{19}$$

$$w_{m|q} = \frac{\sum_{n'=1}^{N'} \gamma(z_{\mu k}^{(n')})}{N} \tag{20}$$

Secondly, the maximization with respect to a particular $\pi_l \in [\pi_1 \cdots \pi_K]$ is computed. The derivative must be set to 0 and all parameters of the expression 14 not related to π_l can be eliminated as constants. If the number of samples that are answered wrongly is N', the following steps provide the analytical solution for the update rule for any π_k:

$$\sum_{n'=1}^{N'} \gamma(z_{\mu k}^{(n')}) \frac{1}{\pi_l} + \lambda_\mu \stackrel{!}{=} 0 \quad \| \cdot \pi_l \tag{21}$$

$$\sum_{n'=1}^{N'} \gamma(z_{\mu k}^{(n')}) + \lambda_\mu \pi_l \stackrel{!}{=} 0 \quad \| \sum_{k=1}^{K} \tag{22}$$

$$\sum_{n'=1}^{N'} \gamma(z_{\mu k}^{(n')}) + \lambda_\mu \sum_{k=1}^{K} \pi_l \stackrel{!}{=} 0 \tag{23}$$

$$\lambda_\mu = - \sum_{k=1}^{K} \sum_{n'=1}^{N'} \gamma(z_{\mu k}^{(n')}) \tag{24}$$

$$\pi_k = \frac{\sum_{n'=1}^{N'} \gamma(z_{\mu k}^{(n')})}{\sum_{k=1}^{K} \sum_{n'=1}^{N'} \gamma(z_{\mu k}^{(n')})} \tag{25}$$

Thirdly, the maximization with respect to $\theta_{x|q,k}$, is performed in a similar manner. The update of the parameters of a particular **Answers$_\mathbf{q}$** value $\theta_{x|q,k}$, is made from the data samples n' that have as question $q = q_{n'} \in [q_1 \cdots q_Q]$, and answer $x = x_{n'} \in [x_1 \cdots x_X]$:

$$\sum_{n'=1}^{N'} \frac{\gamma(z_{\mu k}^{(n')})}{\theta_{x|k}} + \lambda_k \stackrel{!}{=} 0 \quad \| \cdot \theta_{x|k} \tag{26}$$

$$\sum_{n'=1}^{N'} \gamma(z_{\mu k}^{(n')}) + \lambda_k \theta_{x|k} \stackrel{!}{=} 0 \quad \| \sum_{x=1}^{X} \tag{27}$$

$$\sum_{x=1}^{X} \sum_{n'=1}^{N'} \gamma(z_{\mu k}^{(n')}) + \lambda_k \sum_{x=1}^{X} \theta_{x|k} \stackrel{!}{=} 0 \tag{28}$$

$$\lambda_k = - \sum_{x=1}^{X} \sum_{n'=1}^{N'} \gamma(z_{\mu k}^{(n')}) \tag{29}$$

$$\theta_{x|k} = \frac{\sum_{n'=1}^{N'} \gamma(z_{\mu k}^{(n')})}{\sum_{x=1}^{X} \sum_{n'=1}^{N'} \gamma(z_{\mu k}^{(n')})} \tag{30}$$

The steps of the EM-Algorithm for updating the parameters of this Bayesian Model are as follows:

1. Initialization of all parameters Θ_0. In this case that is the uniform prior.
2. E-Step: Computation of $\gamma(z_{\mu k}^{(n)})$ using Eq. 10
3. M-Step: Compute new Θ parameters $w_{\mu|q}$, π_k and $\theta_{x|k}$ using Eqs. 20, 25 and 30
4. Compute the likelihood $P(\boldsymbol{X};\Theta)$ or log-likelihood $\ln P(\boldsymbol{X};\Theta)$:

$$\begin{aligned} P(\mathbf{Correctness_q}, \mathbf{Answers_q}; \Theta) = \\ \frac{P(\mathbf{Correctness_q}, \mathbf{LearningState_q}, \mathbf{Answers_q}; \Theta)}{P(\mathbf{LearningState_q} | \mathbf{Correctness_q}, \mathbf{Answers_q}; \Theta)} \\ P(\mathbf{Correctness_q}; \Theta) P(\mathbf{Correctness_q} | \mathbf{LearningState_q}; \Theta) \end{aligned} \tag{31}$$

If the likelihood or the parameters values do not converge, then set current Θ with the values computed in M-Step and goto E-Step.

Figure 3 depicts the steps of the EM-algorithm updating procedure. The dataset used for training is called training set.

It is proven that the EM-algorithm increases the log-likelihood of the observed data X at each iteration [2]:

$$\ln P(\boldsymbol{X};\Theta) \geq \ln P(\boldsymbol{X};\Theta_{old}) \tag{32}$$

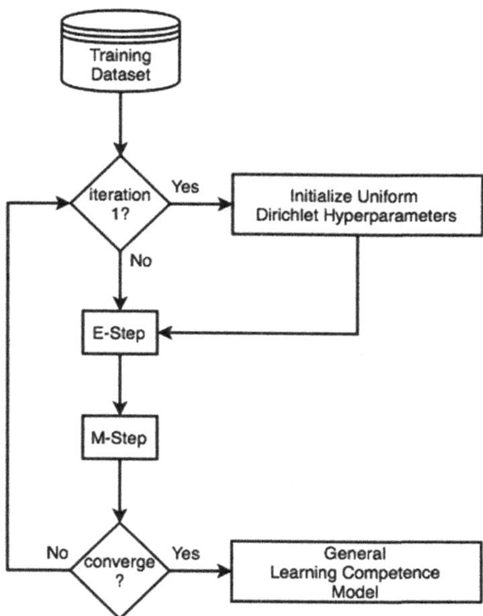

Fig. 3. Expectation-maximization training algorithm applied on the training set. In the first step the uniform Dirichlet hyperparameters are used. Then alternating E- and M-steps bring the parameters/log-likelihood convergence.

The procedure of updating the log-likelihood in this manner is shown to guarantee convergence to a stationary point, which can be a local minimum, local maximum or saddle point. Fortunately, by initializing the iterations from different starting Θ_0 and injecting small changes to the parameters, the local minima and saddle points can be avoided [7].

4 Fractional Updating

Since the learning application proposes questions continuously, it is important to update the beliefs about the learning competence of the student as soon as an answer is present. As new evidence is observed - in the form of answered questions - the model shifts the value of the parameters to reflect the fact that the belief about the learning competence of the user is changed.

With fractional updating [6], the initialization and updating of the parameters is made by means of the Dirichlet pseudocounts. The starting pseudocount number is set to 1.0 to express a weak belief about the learning competence of the student. In this application, for each question-answer pair, only one probabilistical graphical model needs to be updated. The data sample only contains the value of the corresponding observed variable $\mathbf{Answers_q}$. The update of the pseudocounts α is provided by equation:

$$\alpha_{ijk}^{l+1} = \alpha_{ijk}^{l} + P(\boldsymbol{X}_i = k, Parents_G(\boldsymbol{X}_i) = j|\mathcal{D}) \tag{33}$$

where the current joint probability of the updated variable and the value of its parents are used to update the value of the pseudocounts, which may no longer be an integer. $\mathcal{D}$ denotes the dataset of samples.

The fractional updating procedure can be explained by an example where a student provides the wrong answer 42 to the question 8×5. The probabilities start with the following values (Table 1 and 2):

Table 1. Probabilistic graphical model of the question 8×5 where all conditional probabilities (all rows of the conditional probability tables) are set uniformly.

wrong	**correct**
$\frac{1}{2}$	$\frac{1}{2}$

operand	**intrusion**	**consistency**	**off-by**	**add/sub/div**	**pattern**	**unclassified**
$\frac{1}{7}$	$\frac{1}{7}$	$\frac{1}{7}$	$\frac{1}{7}$	$\frac{1}{7}$	$\frac{1}{7}$	$\frac{1}{7}$

	...	**42**	...
operand	...	$\frac{1}{12}$	...
intrusion	...	0	...
consistency	...	$\frac{1}{17}$	...
off-by	...	$\frac{1}{4}$	...
add/sub/div	...	0	...
pattern	...	0	...
unclassified	...	0	...

The corresponding pseudocounts start with the following values:

There are three error types that can cause the answer 42. The weights for each case, corresponding to the entity $P(\boldsymbol{X}_i = k, Parents_G(\boldsymbol{X}_i) = j|\mathcal{D})$ of the Eq. 33, are computed as follows:

$\frac{1}{2}\frac{1}{7}\frac{1}{12}/(\frac{1}{2}\frac{1}{7}\frac{1}{12} + \frac{1}{2}\frac{1}{7}\frac{1}{17} + \frac{1}{2}\frac{1}{7}\frac{1}{4}) = 0.21259$
$\frac{1}{2}\frac{1}{7}\frac{1}{17}/(\frac{1}{2}\frac{1}{7}\frac{1}{12} + \frac{1}{2}\frac{1}{7}\frac{1}{17} + \frac{1}{2}\frac{1}{7}\frac{1}{4}) = 0.15006$
$\frac{1}{2}\frac{1}{7}\frac{1}{4}//(\frac{1}{2}\frac{1}{7}\frac{1}{12} + \frac{1}{2}\frac{1}{7}\frac{1}{17} + \frac{1}{2}\frac{1}{7}\frac{1}{4}) = 0.63776$

The value of the updated pseudocounts of the **operand**, **intrusion**, and **consistency** error types, are presented in the following table:

	$\mathbf{CQ_{8\times5}}$	$\mathbf{LS_{8\times5}}$	$\mathbf{AS_{8\times5}}$	pseudocounts	probability
$D_{8\times5,\ 42,\ operand}$	wrong	operand	42	$1 + 0.21259$	0.151
$D_{8\times5,\ 42,\ consistency}$	wrong	consistency	42	$1 + 0.15006$	0.144
$D_{8\times5,\ 42,\ off-by}$	wrong	off-by	42	$1 + 0.63776$	0.205

The pseudocounts of the rest of the error types will remain to the value 1, so the total sum of pseudocounts that will be used as normalization value is:

Table 2. Probabilistic graphical model of the question 8×5 where all pseudocounts are set to value 1.

wrong	**correct**
1	1

operand	**intrusion**	**consistency**	**off-by**	**add/sub/div**	**pattern**	**unclassified**
1	1	1	1	1	1	1

	...	**26**	...
operand	...	1	...
intrusion	...	0	...
consistency	...	1	...
off-by	...	1	...
add/sub/div	...	0	...
pattern	...	0	...
unclassified	...	0	...

$4 \times 1 + 1.21259 + 1.15006 + 1.63776 = 8.0004$. The actual probabilities of the involved error types are listed in the table above; the rest have the value 0.12499. The pseudocounts of "wrong" are increased by +1, setting the probability of "wrong" to $\frac{2}{3}$ and "correct" to $\frac{1}{3}$. The values of the $\mathbf{Answers_{8x5}}$ random variable are computed accordingly.

This comprises a full iteration of the online EM-algorithm. In the next iteration, the newly computed pseudocounts will play the role of the prior that needs updating. Drawbacks and extensions of the fractional updating algorithm can be explained in the work of [6].

5 Evaluation of Parameter Learning

The evaluation of the parameter learning EM-algorithm is firstly made by computing the likelihood of a training set at each iteration. It is expected that the likelihood is increasing monotonically and converging with increasing number of iterations. As seen in Fig. 4, this also applies for the likelihood of the models as a whole.

If the EM-algorithm is repeated for many iterations, the values of the parameters will be adjusted too much to the training set, without being able to generalize to the properties of the test set; an unseen user's learning competence must be also modelled sufficiently by the model. Figure 5 depicts the evolution of the likelihood of the test set, with respect to the number of EM-iterations of the training set. The likelihood of the test set decreases after 4 iterations; this is an indication of overfitting [2].

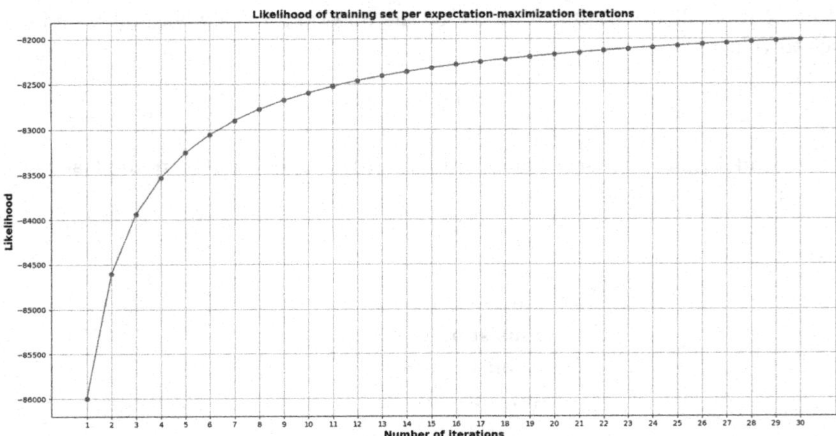

Fig. 4. Evolution of the likelihood of the training set with respect to the number of EM-iterations in the training set.

The expectation-maximization algorithm bases on the fact that all possible outcomes of all questions present at least one sample of the dataset. This was not the case in this application; the sufficient statistics condition was not fulfilled [7,8]. Nevertheless, it has been shown that the models performance is sufficient for practical purposes and that as new data are gathered, this problem might be solved.

6 Testing

Software testing in python is made with the use of the pytest framework[2] [10]. The expectation-maximization update rules were tested with some examples and compared to numerically computed results. But since the number of possible cases that must be tried out is very large, property-based testing was used [9]. The hypothesis framework[3] gives the ability to write tests in an abstract manner, where the concrete numerical values are generated automatically.

An extended description of property-based testing is out of scope of this work, but the main idea is describing the properties of the function that is tested. By that means, generating several numerical examples was proven to be very effective. The fractional expectation-maximization update rule 4 has the following properties:

[2] https://docs.pytest.org/, Last accessed 10 March 2020.
[3] https://hypothesis.readthedocs.io/en/latest/, Last accessed 10 March 2020.

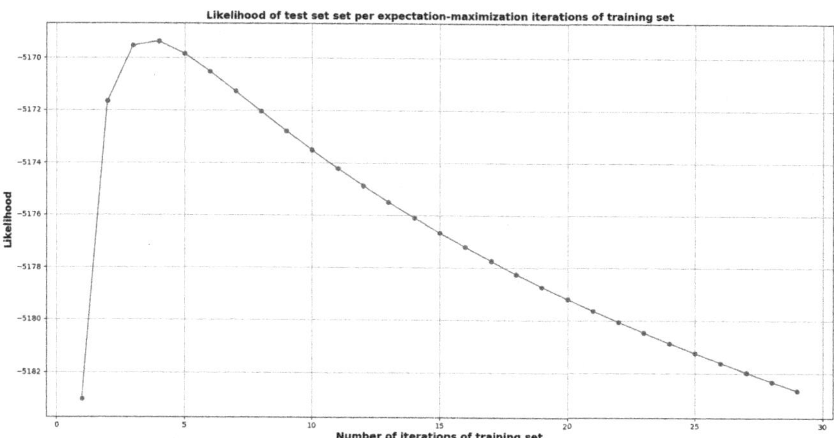

Fig. 5. Evolution of the likelihood of the test set with respect to the number of EM-iterations in the training set. The test set contains 1000 samples.

- The sum of each row of the conditional probability tables must equal to 1.0 after the update.
- Only one of the $\mathbf{Answers_q}$ (namely the one that corresponds to the posed question), as well as the corresponding $\mathbf{Learning\ State_q}$ and $\mathbf{Correctness_q}$ will change.
- A sampled answer can belong to one or more error types. The conditional probability of this answer will be increased in the $\mathbf{Answers_q}$ conditional probability table. Because the sum must remain 1.0, the conditional probabilities of the other answers will be decreased after the update. Similarly, the error types that could be responsible for this answer will have an increased conditional probability in the $\mathbf{Learning\ State_q}$, whereas the rest conditional probabilities will decrease. If the answer is wrong, then the belief that the student's ability to answer a question correctly will fall, and the $\mathbf{Correctness_q}$ will change by the same means.

The following code in Listing 1.1, is the definition of one pytest test-case which covers several valid scenarios at once. The test-case exercises the fractional expectation-maximization learner and updater algorithm. During each scenario, one of the questions is randomly sampled, as well a valid corresponding answer between a minimum and a maximum value. The number of iterations of expectation-maximization also varies. Up to 10 tests are run at each execution (controlled by the parameter `max_examples`) and the execution can have unlimited time. The test's fixture that defines all those values, is passed as a parameter.

Listing 1.1. Property-based test-case definition

```
@given(question=sampled_from(
    elements=['1x1', '1x2', '1x3', '1x4', '1x5',
              '1x6', '1x7', '1x8', '1x9',
              '2x1', '2x2', '2x3', '2x4', '2x5',
              '2x6', '2x7', '2x8', '2x9',
              '3x1', '3x2', '3x3', '3x4', '3x5',
              '3x6', '3x7', '3x8', '3x9',
              '4x1', '4x2', '4x3', '4x4', '4x5',
              '4x6', '4x7', '4x8', '4x9',
              '5x1', '5x2', '5x3', '5x4', '5x5',
              '5x6', '5x7', '5x8', '5x9',
              '6x1', '6x2', '6x3', '6x4', '6x5',
              '6x6', '6x7', '6x8', '6x9',
              '7x1', '7x2', '7x3', '7x4', '7x5',
              '7x6', '7x7', '7x8', '7x9',
              '8x1', '8x2', '8x3', '8x4', '8x5',
              '8x6', '8x7', '8x8', '8x9',
              '9x1', '9x2', '9x3', '9x4', '9x5',
              '9x6', '9x7', '9x8', '9x9',
              '10x1', '10x2', '10x3', '10x4', '10x5',
              '10x6', '10x7', '10x8', '10x9']),
    answer=integers(min_value=0, max_value=99),
    number_of_em_iterations=integers(min_value=1,
                                     max_value=5))
@settings(max_examples=10, timeout=unlimited)
def test_fractional_em(
    question: str,
    answer: int,
    number_of_em_iterations: int,
    init_fractional_em_fixture: typing.Tuple):
```

Part of the implementation properties in the test-case are listed in 1.2. After the fractional updater is applied, the properties are checked one by one. The probability distributions at each row of the Conditional Probability Tables must sum up to one all the time. Depending on the answer the "Correct" or "InCorrect" proportion must increase, as well as the corresponding error types that could generate it. The probabilities of the other error types that could not have generated this answer must decrease correspondingly, while the sum remains equal to 1. The likelihood of the training set data must increase, as described by the Eq. 32.

Listing 1.2. Properties of the test-case

```
for index in range(0, number_of_em_iterations):

    em_fractional_updater.update_alpha(users_questions,
                                       users_answers)

    # Returned parameters after update
    w_prob_dist = em_fractional_updater.get_w_prob()
    pi_prob_dist = em_fractional_updater.get_pi_prob()
    theta_prob_dist = em_fractional_updater.get_theta_prob()

    # Constraint: Probability distributions must sum up to 1
    learning_state_types = init_fractional_em_fixture [2]
    constraint_prob_dist_sum_one(w_prob_dist,
                                 pi_prob_dist,
                                 theta_prob_dist,
                                 question,
                                 learning_state_types)

    # Probabilities that must increase or decrease
    is_correct_answer = em_utils.is_correct_answer(question,
                                                   answer)

    if index >= 1:
        if is_correct_answer:
            assert w_prob_dist[question]["Correct"] >
                   w_prob_dist_prev[question]["Correct"], \
                   "The proportion of correct must increase"
            assert w_prob_dist[question]["InCorrect"] <
                   w_prob_dist_prev[question]["InCorrect"], \
                   "The proportion of incorrect must decrease"
        else:
            assert w_prob_dist[question]["Correct"] <
                   w_prob_dist_prev[question]["Correct"], \
                   "The proportion of correct must decrease"
            assert w_prob_dist[question]["InCorrect"] >
                   w_prob_dist_prev[question]["InCorrect"], \
                   "The proportion of incorrect must increase"

        learning_state_types = init_fractional_em_fixture [2]
        for learning_state_type in learning_state_types:
            if answer in \
            theta_prob_dist[question][learning_state_type].keys():

                # pi_prob_dist
                assert pi_prob_dist[question][learning_state_type] > \
                    pi_prob_dist_prev[question][learning_state_type], \
                    "The proportion of error type " +
                    learning_state_type + " must increase"

                assert theta_prob_dist[question]
                                      [learning_state_type]
                                      [answer] > \
                    theta_prob_dist_prev[question]
                                        [learning_state_type]
                                        [answer], \
                    "The probability of the given answer must increase"

                # theta_prob_dist
```

```
            for other_answer in \
                theta_prob_dist[question][learning_state_type].keys():
                if other_answer != answer:
                    assert theta_prob_dist[question]
                                          [learning_state_type]
                                          [other_answer] < \
                        theta_prob_dist_prev[question]
                                            [learning_state_type]
                                            [other_answer], \
                        "The probability other answers must decrease"
        else:
            assert pi_prob_dist[question][learning_state_type] < \
                pi_prob_dist_prev[question][learning_state_type], \
                "The proportion of error type " +
                learning_state_type + " must decrease"

    # Copy
    likelihood = em_fractional_updater.
                 compute_log_likelihood(users_questions,
                                        users_answers)
    likelihood_training_set_array.append(likelihood)

    w_prob_dist_prev = copy.deepcopy(w_prob_dist)
    pi_prob_dist_prev = copy.deepcopy(pi_prob_dist)
    theta_prob_dist_prev = copy.deepcopy(theta_prob_dist)

# Likelihood must increase because it is the training set
likelihood_decreasing = em_utils.\
    check_decreasing_likelihood(likelihood_training_set_array)
assert not likelihood_decreasing, \
"The likelihood must not decrease : " +
str(likelihood_training_set_array)
```

7 Conclusion

Property-based testing is an effective method to ensure the code quality of probabilistic graphical models parameter learning. The necessity and effectiveness of this method has justified its use and was beneficial for the quality management of a learning-aware application. This work provides a concrete paradigm, that can be used by other similar applications that use probabilistic programming and analytical solutions of their learned parameter updating rules.

References

1. On testing machine learning programs. J. Syst. Softw. **164**, 110542 (2020). https://doi.org/10.1016/j.jss.2020.110542
2. Bishop, C.: Pattern Recognition and Machine Learning. Springer, New York (2006)
3. Braiek, H.B., Khomh, F.: On testing machine learning programs. J. Syst. Softw. **164**, 110542 (2020)
4. Dutta, S., Legunsen, O., Huang, Z., Misailovic, S.: Testing probabilistic programming systems. In: Proceedings of the 2018 26th ACM Joint Meeting on European Software Engineering Conference and Symposium on the Foundations of Software Engineering, pp. 574–586 (2018)

5. Grosse, R.B., Duvenaud, D.K.: Testing MCMC code. arXiv preprint. arXiv:1412.5218 (2014)
6. Jensen, F.V., Nielsen, T.D.: Bayesian Networks and Decision Graphs, 2nd edn. Springer, New York (2007)
7. Koller, D., Friedman, N.: Probabilistic Graphical Models: Principles and Techniques. MIT Press, Cambridge (2009)
8. Murphy, K.P.: Machine Learning: A Probabilistic Perspective. MIT press, Cambridge (2012)
9. Nilsson, R.: ScalaCheck: the definitive guide. Artima (2014)
10. Okken, B.: Python Testing with Pytest: Simple, Rapid, Effective, and Scalable. Pragmatic Bookshelf (2017)
11. Pfeffer, A.: Practical Probabilistic Programming. Manning Publications, Greenwich (2016)
12. Saranti, A., Taraghi, B., Ebner, M., Holzinger, A.: Insights into learning competence through probabilistic graphical models. In: Holzinger, A., Kieseberg, P., Tjoa, A.M., Weippl, E. (eds.) CD-MAKE 2019. LNCS, vol. 11713, pp. 250–271. Springer, Cham (2019). https://doi.org/10.1007/978-3-030-29726-8_16
13. Sharma, A., Wehrheim, H.: Testing monotonicity of machine learning models. arXiv:2002.12278 (2020)
14. Taraghi, B., Saranti, A., Legenstein, R., Ebner, M.: Bayesian modelling of student misconceptions in the one-digit multiplication with probabilistic programming. In: Proceedings of the Sixth International Conference on Learning Analytics & Knowledge, pp. 449–453 (2016)
15. Zhang, J.M., Harman, M., Ma, L., Liu, Y.: Machine learning testing: survey, landscapes and horizons. arXiv preprint arXiv:1906.10742 (2019)

An Ensemble Interpretable Machine Learning Scheme for Securing Data Quality at the Edge

Anna Karanika[1], Panagiotis Oikonomou[1], Kostas Kolomvatsos[1(✉)], and Christos Anagnostopoulos[2]

[1] Department of Informatics and Telecommunications, University of Thessaly, Volos, Greece
{ankaranika,paikonom,kostasks}@uth.gr
[2] School of Computing Science, University of Glasgow, Glasgow, Scotland
christos.anagnostopoulos@gla.ac.uk

Abstract. Data quality is a significant research subject for any application that requests for analytics to support decision making. It becomes very important when we focus on Internet of Things (IoT) where numerous devices can interact to exchange and process data. IoT devices are connected to Edge Computing (EC) nodes to report the collected data, thus, we have to secure data quality not only at the IoT infrastructure but also at the edge of the network. In this paper, we focus on the specific problem and propose the use of interpretable machine learning to deliver the features that are important to be based on for any data processing activity. Our aim is to secure data quality for those features, at least, that are detected as significant in the collected datasets. We have to notice that the selected features depict the highest correlation with the remaining ones in every dataset, thus, they can be adopted for dimensionality reduction. We focus on multiple methodologies for having interpretability in our learning models and adopt an ensemble scheme for the final decision. Our scheme is capable of timely retrieving the final result and efficiently selecting the appropriate features. We evaluate our model through extensive simulations and present numerical results. Our aim is to reveal its performance under various experimental scenarios that we create varying a set of parameters adopted in our mechanism.

Keywords: Machine learning · Interpretable machine learning · Ensemble scheme · Features selection

1 Introduction

Nowadays we are witnessing the advent of Internet of Things (IoT) where numerous devices can interact with their environment and perform simple processing activities. Multiple services and applications are executed over humongous volumes of data collected by the IoT devices. These data are transferred to the

A. Holzinger et al. (Eds.): CD-MAKE 2020, LNCS 12279, pp. 517–534, 2020.
https://doi.org/10.1007/978-3-030-57321-8_29

Cloud infrastructure to be the subject of further processing. Due to the bandwidth of the network, latency and data privacy concerns, the research community has focused on the processing performed at the edge of the network. Edge Computing (EC) involves heterogeneous nodes close to IoT devices and end users capable of performing various activities and delivering analytics over the collected data. EC nodes act as mediators between the IoT infrastructure and Cloud. They can be sensors, home gateways, micro servers, and small cells while being equipped with storage and computation capabilities.

Every EC node is 'connected' to a number of IoT devices and become the host of the collected data. We focus on a multivariate data scenario where multiple variables/dimensions/features consist of vectors reported by IoT devices. Locally, at EC nodes, an ecosystem of distributed datasets is formulated depicting the geo-located aspect of the problem. Data, before being the subject of processing, should be validated concerning their quality to support efficient analytics. A metric, among others, that secures data quality is accuracy [25]. Accuracy refers to the closeness of estimates to the (unknown) exact or true values [26]. In other words, accuracy depicts the error between the observation/estimation and the real data. We consider that maintaining accuracy in a dataset will lead to 'solid' data repositories, i.e., datasets exhibiting a limited error/deviation (around the mean). Actually, 'solid' datasets is the target of data separation algorithms proposed in the relevant literature; these algorithms aim to deliver small non-overlapping datasets and distributed on the available nodes [42]. In this paper, we propose a model for securing accuracy in datasets present in EC nodes acting proactively and rejecting any data that could jeopardize their 'solidity'. We consider a Machine Learning (ML) algorithm that decides if the incoming data should be stored locally or offloaded in peer nodes/Cloud. Actually, we propose the use of Naive Bayesian Classifier (NBC) for getting the final decision. However, this decision is made over only features that are judged as significant for each dataset. We consider that the remaining features should not be part of the decision making as they do not exhibit the appropriate and necessary characteristics that will lead to efficient analytics.

Motivating Example. Feature selection models are widely adopted to filter irrelevant or redundant features in our datasets. It is a significant technique that is, usually, incorporated in dimensionality reduction models to deal with the so-called curse of dimensionality. In general, it always helps analyzing the data up front and, then, we are ready to support any decision making process. Instead of collecting the data and performing any pre-processing/analysis action afterwards, it would be better to make the analysis during their collection. Hence, data quality and preparation can be secured before the dataset be the subject of any processing activity. This process can become the groundwork for the subsequent engineering steps providing a solid foundation for building good ML schemes for decision making. When solid datasets are the final outcome, we can easily deliver analytics based on the specific features detected during the reception of data. Hence, no need for post-processing is present while the accuracy of data is at a high level. A representative real example could be the distributed data management in a Smart City infrastructure. In this scenario, we want the data to be ready to be used by additional applications that citizens may adopt during their movement in the city.

Our intention is to provide a decision making model for securing data quality based on an ML scheme that will produce the relevant knowledge about the domain relationships during the reception of data. A set of research efforts focus on the data quality management and have identified its necessity in any application domain. However, they seldom discuss how to effectively validate data to ensure data quality [13]. The poor quality of data could increase costs and reduce the efficiency of decision making [31]. In IoT, it is often necessary to detect correlations between the collected data and external factors. We propose to secure data quality by allocating them to the appropriate datasets and select beforehand a (sub-)set of features that can be adopted in interpretable/explainable ML schemes. Explainable models can be easily 'absorbed' by humans depicting the hidden correlations between data and giving the necessary insights to understand the reasons behind the adoption of the specific ML model. The decision of the data allocation is performed over the selected features to have the delivered datasets ready to be processed by the desired ML models. Instead of performing the feature selection process after the collection of data, we go a step forward and propose the execution of the activity during the reception of data. Evidently, feature selection and data allocation are utilized at the same time to secure quality over a streaming environment. With this approach, we can save time and resources compared to a scheme where a batch processing activity is realized.

We build on an ensemble scheme, i.e., we adopt three (3) different model-agnostic approaches: the Permutation Feature Importance (PFI) [6], Shapley Values [4] and the Feature Interaction Technique (FIT) [12]. It is our strategic decision to adopt an ensemble approach to seek for a better 'predictive' performance that could be obtained from any of the individual model alone. Additionally, we could also avoid individual models' drawbacks. For instance, most permutation based techniques ignore features dependence, thus, we can combine them with techniques that deal with the correlations between features to have the optimal outcome. In addition, for delivering the final significance value for each feature through an aggregation of the three aforementioned outcomes, we adopt an Artificial Neural Network (ANN) [1]. In our case, the adopted inputs of the ANN are the outputs of the aforementioned interpretable models to efficiently combine them in a final value. The ANN undertakes the responsibility of 'aggregating' the opinion of 'experts' (i.e., our interpretable models) and deliver the final outcome. Based on these technologies, we are able to detect the most significant features in the collected data and build a powerful scheme for securing the data quality at the edge of the network. We depart from legacy solutions and instead of collecting huge volumes of data and post-process them trying to derive knowledge, we propose their real time management and allocation keeping similar data to the same partitions. We have to notice that our approach is not 'bounded' by any application domain and can be incorporated to any service that deals with the preprocessing of data before they will be the subject of further processing activities. The difference from our previous work presented in [20] is that the current work proposes an interpretable ML approach to give meaning to the stored data and the results as delivered by the processing that end users desire. The following list reports on the advantages of the proposed model: (i) we proactively 'prepare' the data before the actual processing is applied; (ii) we offer an interpretable ML scheme for satisfying the meaningful knowledge extraction; (iii) we provide an ensemble scheme for aggregating multiple interpretable ML models; (iv) we offer an ANN for delivering the most significant features fully aligned with the collected data; (v) the proposed model proactively secures the quality of data as it excludes data that may lead to an increased error; (vi) our scheme leads to the minimum overlapping of the available datasets that is the target of the legacy data separation algorithms.

The rest of the paper is organized as follows. Section 2 reports on the related work while Sect. 3 presents the problme under consideration. In Sect. 4, we present the adopted interpretable ML models and our ensemble scheme for combining the provided outcomes. In Sect. 5, we perform an extensive evaluation assessment and Sect. 6 concludes our paper by giving insights in our future research plans.

2 Related Work

The interested reader can find a survey of data quality dimensions in [45]. Data mining and statistical techniques can be combined to extract the correlation of data quality dimensions, thus, assisting in the definition of a holistic framework. The advent of large-scale datasets as exposed by IoT define additional requirements on data quality assessment. Given the range of big data applications, potential consequences of bad data quality can be more disastrous and widespread [38]. In [27], the authors propose the '3As Data Quality-in-Use model' composed of three data quality characteristics i.e., contextual, operational and temporal adequacy. The proposed model could be incorporated in any large scale data framework as it is not dependent on any technology. A view on the data quality issues in big data is presented in [38]. A survey on data quality assessment methods is discussed in [7]. Apart from that, the authors present an analysis of the data characteristics in large scale data environments and describe the quality challenges. The evolution of the data quality issues in large scale systems is the subject of [3]. The authors discuss various relations between data quality and multiple research requirements. Some examples are: the variety of data types, data sources and application domains, sensor networks and official statistics.

ML interpretability [29,32] is significant to deliver models that can explainable to humans, thus, to support efficient decision making. There are varying definitions of it [10,23] without having a common ground, e.g., no formal ontology of interpretability types. However, in [23] is argued that these types can generally be categorised in (i) transparency (direct evidence of how the internals of a model work); or (ii) post hoc explanation (adoption of mapping methods to visualize input features that affect outputs) [28,39]. A common post hoc technique incorporates explanations by example, e.g., case-based reasoning approach to select an appropriately-similar example from training set [8] or natural language explanations [16]. The emergence of these methods shows there is no consensus on how to assess the explanation quality [9]. For instance, we have to decide the most appropriate metrics to assess the quality of an explanation. Especially, for edge computing such issues are critical; the interested reader can find a relevant survey of major research efforts where ML has been deployed at the edge of computer networks in [30].

In [51], the authors discuss the feasibility of running ML algorithms, both training and inference, on a Raspberry Pi, an embedded version of the Android operating system designed for IoT device development. The focus is to reveal the performance of various algorithms (e.g., Random Forests, Support Vector Machines, Multi-Layer Perceptron) in constrained devices. It is known that the highly regarded programming libraries consume to much resources to be ported to the embedded processors [47]. In [35], a service-provisioning framework for coalition operations is extended to address specific requirements for robustness and interpretability, allowing automatic selection of service bundles for intelligence, surveillance and reconnaissance tasks. The authors of [40] review explainable machine learning in view of applications in the natural sciences and discuss three core elements i.e., transparency, interpretability, and explainability. An analysis of the convergence rate of an ML model is presented in [50]. The authors focus on a distributed gradient descent scheme from a theoretical point of view and propose a control algorithm that determines the best trade-off between local update and global parameter aggregation.

The 'combination' between EC and deep learning is discussed in [15]. Application scenarios for both are presented together with practical implementation methods and enabling technologies. Deep learning models have been proven to be an efficient solution to the most complex engineering challenges while at the same time, human centered computing in fog and mobile edge networks is one of the serious concerns now-a-days [14]. In [36], the authors present a model that learns a set of rules to globally explain the behavior of black box ML models. Significant conditions are firstly extracted being evolved based on a genetic algorithm. In [24], an approach for image recognition having the process split into two layers is presented. In [21], the authors present a software accelerator that enhances deep learning execution on heterogeneous hardware. In [44] the authors propose the utilization of a Support Vector Machine (SVM) running on networked mobile devices to detect malware. A generic survey on employing networked mobile devices for edge computing is presented in [48]. A combination of ML with Semantic Web technologies in the context of model explainability is discussed in [43]. The aim is to semantically annotate parts of the ML models and offer the room for performing advanced reasoning delivering knowledge. All the above efforts aim at supporting the Explainable Artificial Intelligence (XAI) [22]. XAI will facilitate industry to apply AI in products at scale, particularly for industries operating with critical systems. Hence, end users will, finally, be able to enjoy high quality services and applications.

Explainable ML models are adopted in data management applications to provide outcomes that could be easily digested by end users. For this, researchers focus, among other, on causality. Explainable models might facilitate the task of finding data relationships that, should they occur, could be tested further for a stronger causal link between the involved features [37,49]. This way, we can build strong inference of causal relationships from data [33]. An example application is data fusion, i.e., a technique adopted to aggregate data and deliver analytics over the fused results. Future data fusion approaches may consider endowing deep learning models with explainability by externalizing domain data sources. Deep Kalman filters (DKFs) [19], Deep Variational Bayes Filters (DVBFs) [18], Structural Variational Autoencoders (SVAE) [17] or conditional random fields as Recurrent Neural Networks (RNNs) [52] are some representatives. These approaches provide deep models with the interpretability inherent to probabilistic graphical models [2].

3 Problem Definition

Consider a set of N edge nodes connected with a number of IoT devices. IoT devices interact with their environment and collect data while being capable of performing simple processing activities. Data are transferred in an upwards direction towards the Cloud infrastructure where they are stored for further processing. As exposed by the research community [34], processing at the Cloud faces increased latency compared to the processing at the edge of the network. Therefore, edge nodes can maintain local datasets that can be the subject of the desired processing activities close to end users. In each local dataset $D_l, l = 1, 2, \dots, N$, an amount of data (tuples/vectors) are stored. We focus on a multivariate scenario, i.e., D_l contains vectors in the form $\mathbf{x} = \langle x_1, x_2, \dots, x_M \rangle$ where M is the number of dimensions/features. Without loss of generality, we consider the same number of features in every local dataset.

The upcoming intelligent edge mesh [41] incorporates the necessary intelligence to have edge nodes acting autonomously when serving end users or applications. This way, we can deliver the desired services in real time fully aligned with the needs of end users/applications and the available data. Arguably, the intelligent edge mesh provides analytics capabilities over the collected contextual data, thus, edge nodes should conclude ML models that have meaning for end users/applications. For instance, edge nodes may perform ML models for novelty or anomaly detection. When delivering ML models, a challenging problem is to extract higher-valued features that 'represent' the local dataset, thus, we can get our strategic decisions only over them and deal with the so-called curse of dimensionality. Formally, we want to detect the most significant features $x_{ij}, j = 1, 2, \dots, M$ based on the available data vectors $\mathbf{x}_i, i = 1, 2, \dots, |D_l|$. Hence, we will be able to 'explain' the local ML model making end users/ applications to have faith in it. This is the main motivation behind the adoption of

ML model interpretability. We have to notice that the selected features are those: (i) being the most significant for each dataset, thus, they have to be part of any upcoming processing; (ii) being adopted to secure data quality by incorporating them in the decision for the allocation of the incoming data to the appropriate datasets; (iii) being the most appropriate to support the explainability of the subsequent ML schemes.

Local datasets are characterized by specific statistical information, e.g., mean and variation/standard deviation. The aim of each node is to keep the accuracy of the local dataset at high levels. The accuracy is affected by the error between D and $\mathbf{x}$. Edge nodes should decide if $\mathbf{x}$ 'matches' D, however, based on features that are detected as significant for the local dataset (and not all of them). Through this approach, we do not take into consideration features that are not important for the local ML model as exposed by the incoming data vectors. We perform a dimensionality reduction beforehand during the collection of data. This means that our scheme is fully aligned with the needs of the environment (where edge nodes and IoT devices act) and end users/applications. If $\mathbf{x}$ deviates from D, it can 'rejected' and transferred either in a peer node (where it exhibits a high similarity) or in Cloud (as proposed in [20]); its incorporation in D will affect the local statistics 'imposing' severe fluctuations in basic statistical measures (e.g., mean, deviation). A Naive Bayesian Classifier (NBC) is adopted to deliver the decision of locally storing $\mathbf{x}$ or offloading it in peers/Cloud. The NBC reports over the probability of having $\mathbf{x}$ 'generated' by the local dataset D. However, the decision is made over the most significant features as delivered by the proposed ensemble interpretable ML model aiming at having an ML model that can be explained in end users/applications. Our ensemble scheme involves three interpretable, model agnostic techniques, i.e., the PFI, Shapley Values and the FIT.

For handling the 'natural' evolution of data in the error identification (between D and $\mathbf{x}$), we consider a novelty detection model before the incoming data being subject of the envisioned NBC (for deciding the storage locally or the offloading to peers/Cloud). The novelty detection is applied over a copy of the latest W vectors and delivers if there is a significant update in the statistics of the incoming data. When the novelty detection module identifies the discussed update, the W data vectors are incorporated in the local dataset D and the proposed interpretable ML model is fired. In this paper, due to space limitations, we do not focus on a specific novelty detection scheme and consider a indicator function $I([\mathbf{x}]^W) \rightarrow \{0, 1, \}$ to depict the change in the incoming data statistics. For achieving the 'final' interpretability, we propose the use of an ANN over multiple model-agnostic interpretable models. The goal is to decouple the model from the interpretation paying more attention on the significance of each feature and the amount of its contribution in the 'black box' ML model (i.e., the NBC). The ANN receives as inputs the outcomes of each interpretable technique and deliver the final value to decide over the features that are significant for the local dataset. In any case, even if ANNs are not interpretable models, the interpretability in our approach is secured by the three aforementioned explainable schemes. The ANN is adopted to 'aggregate' the 'opinion' of three different interpretable models and get the final outcome based on which we, consequently, get the significance of a feature. The ANN is there to handle possible 'disagreements' for the significance of each feature. In Fig. 1, we can see the envisioned setup. In the first place of our future research plans is the aggregation of interpretable models originated in different edge nodes to deliver and interpretable model for a group of nodes covering a specific area.

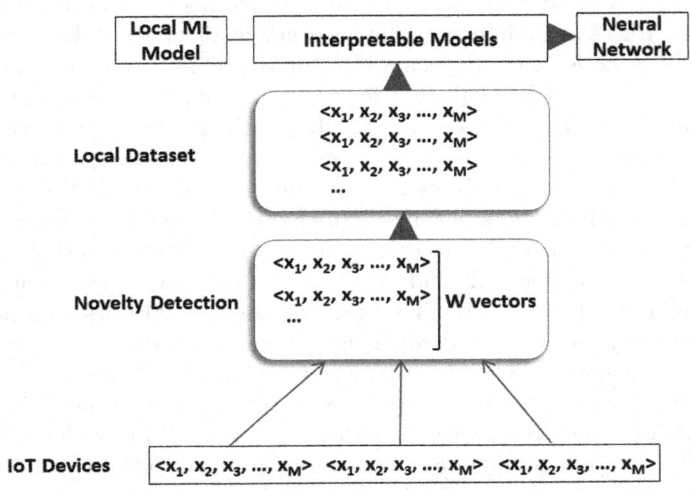

Fig. 1. The architecture of an edge node.

4 The Ensemble Scheme

4.1 Feature Effects and Selection

An NBC adopts the Bayes theorem of conditional probabilities to estimate the probability for a class given the value of the feature. This is realized for each feature independently; a similar approach as having an assumption of the independence of features. Given a dataset X and its values $[x_i]$, the probability of a class C_k is given by:

$$P\left(C_k|X\right) = \frac{1}{Q}P(C_k)\prod_{i=1}^{n}P(x_i|C_k) \tag{1}$$

where Q is a scaling parameter adopted to secure that probabilities for all the classes sum up to unity. The independence assumption leads to an interpretable model, i.e., for each classification, its contribution to the predicted class is easily perceived.

Let the dataset be $\mathbf{Z}$ $[y, X]$ where y is the output c-length vector and a cXp covariate matrix. In addition, we get the trained model f over our dataset and the $L(y, f)$ is a function delivering the error measure for our model based on the outcome y. The PFI scheme [11] adopts a number of steps for calculating each feature's importance to finally decide the final (sub-)set of the adopted features. The training dataset is split in half and values of the jth feature are swapped between the two halfs instead of producing permutation for the feature. Initially, the model estimates the f's error notated as $e^o = L(y, f(X))$ based on any technique (e.g., we can adopt the mean squared error). Afterwards, for each feature, we generate feature permutations in data breaking the correlation between the feature and the outcome y. For this permutation, we calculate the error $e^p = L(y, f(X^p))$ where X^p is the dataset delivered after the permutation. The PFI for the feature is calculated as follows: $F_j^{PFI} = \frac{e^p}{e^o}$.

Shapley values are originated in the coalition game theory. The interpretation of a Shapley value ξ_{ij} for the feature j and the instance i of the dataset is the feature value x_{ij} contributed ξ_{ij} towards the estimation for i compared to the average prediction for the dataset. A Shapley value aims at detecting the effect of the jth feature on the prediction of a data point. For instance, in a linear model, i.e., $\hat{f}(x_i) = \beta_0 + \beta_1 x_{i1} + \beta_2 x_{i2} + \ldots + \beta_p x_{ip}$, it is easy through the weight β_j to expose the effect of the jth feature. For retrieving the final Shapley value, we should examine all possible 'coalitions' of features which is a computational intensive task when we focus on a high number of features. In these coalitions, we have to incorporate or leave the feature in combination with other features to see its effect in the estimation of the target parameter. Hence, we rely on an approximation model proposed in [46]. The method is based on a Monte-Carlo simulation that delivers the final value, i.e., $F_j^{SV} = \frac{1}{M}\sum_{m=1]}^{M}\left(\hat{f}(x^{+j}) - \hat{f}(x^{-j})\right)$. In this equation, M is the number of iterations (we get the mean of the differences), $\hat{f}$ is the estimated value for the ith sample based on the black box ML model, x^{+j} is the selected instance with a random number of features replaced by values retrieved by a random data point x and x^{-j} is identical to x^{+j} but we exclude the jth feature. This means that we create two new instances x^{+j} & x^{-j} from the same dataset, however, performing a sampling for realizing permutations for our features. The steps of the approach are as follows: (i) select an instance of interest i and a feature j; (ii) select the number of samples M; (iii) for each sample, select a random instance and mix the order of features; (iv) create two new instances (as described above) for the ith sample; (v) get the difference of the estimated value; (vi) get the mean of the results as the final Shapley value.

We can estimate the FIT value for each feature based on the so-called Partial Dependence (PD) between features. The interaction of a feature with all the remaining ones in our model will depict the significance of the specific feature. Let two features x_j and x_k. For measuring if the jth feature interacts with the remaining features in the model, we get: $F_j^{FIT} = \frac{\sum_{i=1}^{n}\left[\hat{f}(x^{(i)}) - PD_j(x_j^{(i)}) - PD_{-j}(x_{-j}^{(i)})\right]}{\sum_{i=1}^{n}}$ ($-j$ represents the exclusion of the j feature from the instance). The partial function for a feature can be easily retrieved by a Monte Carlo simulation, i.e., $PD(x_j) = \frac{1}{n}\sum_{i=1}^{n} \hat{f}(x_j, \dot{x})$ where $\dot{x}$ are values from the dataset for features we are not interested in.

4.2 Combination of Multiple Models

The combination of the interpretable models is performed for each feature through the use of our ANN. ANNs are computational models inspired by natural neurons. The proposed ANN is a series of functional transformations involving C combinations of input values i.e., $o_f^1, o_f^2, \ldots, o_f^{|\mathcal{O}|}$ ($o_f^k, k = 1, 2, \ldots, |\mathcal{O}|$ (o_f^k is the final fused value for each metric) [5]. The linear combination of inputs has the following form: $\alpha_j = \sum_{k=1}^{|\mathcal{O}|} w_{jk} o_f^k + w_{j0}$, where $j = 1, 2, \ldots, C$. In the above equation, w_{jk} are weights and w_{j0} are the biases. Activation parameters α_j are, then, transformed by adopting a nonlinear activation function to give $z_j = g(\alpha_j)$. In our model, $g(.)$ is the sigmoid function. The overall ANN function is given by:

$$y(\mathbf{o_f}) = s\left(\sum_{j=1}^{C} w_j g\left(\sum_{k=1}^{|\mathcal{O}|} w_{jk} o_f^k + w_{j0}\right) + w_0\right), \tag{2}$$

where $s(.)$ is the sigmoid function defined as follows: $s(\alpha) = \frac{1}{1+exp(-\alpha)}$. In addition, C is the combinations of input values and $\mathcal{M}$ is the number of inputs.

The proposed ANN tries to aggregate heterogeneous metrics and pays attention on their importance. We adopt a three layered ANN. The first layer is the *input layer*, the second is the *hidden layer* and the third is the *output layer*. We adopt a feed forward ANN where data flow from the input layer to the output layer. In our ANN, there are $|\mathcal{O}|$ inputs i.e., the final estimated values for each performance metric depicted by the vector $\mathbf{o_f}$. The output $y(\mathbf{o_f})$ is the aggregated value that will be the basis for deciding the significance of each feature. Actually, we fire the ANN and get the significance value of each feature creating, at the end, a sorted list. We adopt a threshold d above which a feature is considered as significant for our model. The most important part of our decision scheme is the training of the proposed ANN. In the training phase, we adopt a training dataset depicting various strategies/scenarios concerning the interpretable ML models. This training dataset contains various combinations of outcomes of the adopted interpretable models. For a number of iterations, we produce values that correspond to multiple combinations of metrics depicting various states of the network and the node. The dataset is defined by experts.

5 Performance Assessment

5.1 Indicators and Simulation Setup

We present the experimental evaluation of the proposed model through a set of simulations. It is worth noticing that our simulator was developed in R and our experiments were performed relying on WS-DREAM datasets provided in [53][1] and more specifically the Dataset 1. This dataset describes real-world QoS measurements, including both response time and throughput values, obtained from 339 users on 5,825 Web services. From this dataset, we adopt all the available features and apply our model.

Our evaluation process focuses on the improvement of the decision-making process when deciding whether to keep data locally based on the most important features of the incoming data as opposed to all of them, i.e., no interpretability (feature selection) process is applied. Furthermore, we are concerned with keeping locally the instances of data that preserve the solidity of the current dataset maintained by an EC node. Solidity is very important as it can be used to enhance the confidence interval of the statistical information of datasets. In our experimental evaluation, we pay attention on the specific features that are selected in every evaluation scenario. The ultimate goal is to detect if the final outcome corresponds to something valid and interesting from the application point of view (i.e., secure quality by allocating data to the appropriate datasets). Lastly, we focus on the time required for a node to make a decision.

We define the metric Δ as the percentage of correct decisions. The following equation holds true: $\Delta = |CD|/|DS| * 100\%$. In the aforementioned equation, CD represents the set of correct decisions related to the storage of the appropriate data locally and DS represents the set of decisions taken in our experimental evaluation. When $\Delta \to 100\%$, it means that the model has a high accuracy, whereas as $\Delta \to 0\%$, the model's predictions are not reliable at all. Moreover, we establish the metric σ, which is depicted by the standard deviation of data and describes the 'solidity' of the local dataset. The lower the σ becomes, the more 'solid' a node's dataset is and the opposite is true when σ's value becomes high; specifically, when a dataset is quite 'solid', it means that its values are concentrated around the mean value, hence, giving us a concrete idea of the concentration of data. Having a 'solid' dataset can be highly useful in the efficient allocation of queries to datasets that can serve them in the most effective manner. In addition, we report on τ, representing the average time that is required for a decision to be made on whether a single data instance should be kept locally, or offloaded to another EC node into which it fits better or the Fog/Cloud.

We perform a set of experiments for a variety of M and w values. We adopt $M \in \{20, 50, 100\}$, i.e. different numbers of dimensions for the dataset, as well as $w \in \{10\%, 20\%, 50\%\}$, i.e. different percentages of features to be used for the final decision about a data instance's storage node.

5.2 Experimental Outcomes

We start by evaluating our model in terms of Δ (see Fig. 2). In this set of experiments, we compare the performance of two models, i.e., CD and wCD. The former depicts the percentage of correct decisions made by the NBC based on all the features of the adopted dataset. This is a baseline solution where equal

[1] https://github.com/wsdream/wsdream-dataset.

significance is paid for all the available features. The latter model illustrates the percentage of correct decisions made by the NBC based only on the w^*M most significant features of the dataset. It consists of the model where our 'reasoning' is adopted to detect the most important features of the dataset. We observe that in the majority of the experimental scenarios (except one case), the performance of wCD is decidedly improved when compared against the CD. This is quite rational as in wCD the NBC is able to focus solely on the most important features of an instance to make a decision about whether to keep it locally or not and does not take into account features that can result in a false prediction. This provides an evidence that our mechanism is capable of efficiently detecting significant features, thus, we can adopt them to support decision making. As M increases, Δ becomes low, since an increment in the number of features used by the classifier brings about the aforementioned false predictions. Features that are not significant steer the prediction away from the actual class, and even if only w^*M of the features are used, the features are still too many to make the decision-making process as clear as it needs to be. In general, the performance of the proposed system is affected by M and w, i.e., increased M & w lead to lower Δ values.

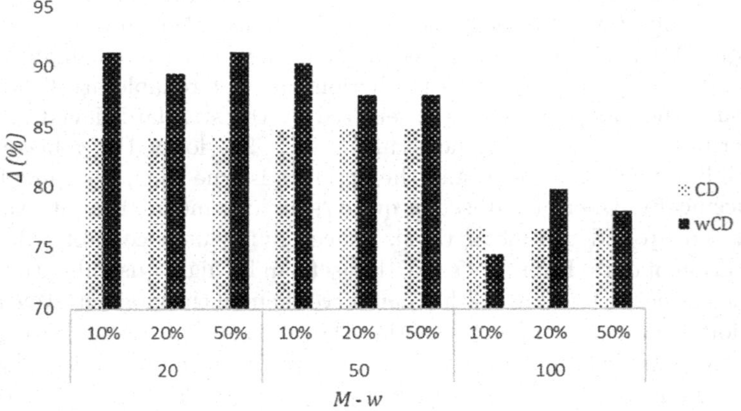

Fig. 2. Performance evaluation for the correct decisions derived by our model compared with the baseline solution, i.e., the Naïve Bayes Classifier.

In Fig. 3, we present our results for the solidity of the retrieved datasets after the selection of the most significant features. In this set of experiments, we compare three models, i.e., the OS, the BNS and the NNS. OS represents the model where we deliver the σ realization based on the entire set of data available in a node. The BNS depicts the solidity of the dataset when adopting the NBC and the entire set of the available features. Finally, the NNS represents the solidity of the dataset when adopting the features selected by the proposed interpretable approach. In all the experimental scenarios, our feature selection approach (i.e., the NNS) manages to achieve the best performance. This means that the final, delivered dataset is solid and the deviation from the mean is limited. Hence, we can increase the accuracy of data as they do not deviate from the mean limiting the possibilities of the presence of extreme values that can negatively affect the statistical characteristics of the dataset. Apart from that, in a latter step, we can create data synopses to be distributed in the upper layer of a Cloud-Edge-IoT architecture that could be characterized by an increased confidence interval. In Fig. 3, we also observe that the OS exhibits the worst performance among the compared models. Finally, a low M combined with a low w leads to the best possible performance.

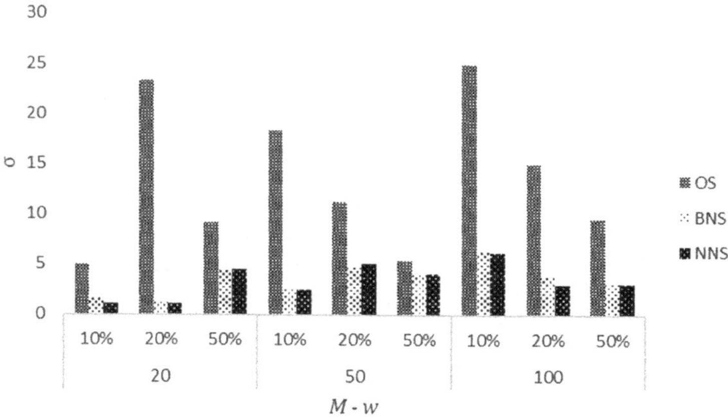

Fig. 3. Data solidity as delivered by the proposed model in comparison with other models found in the respective literature (i.e., the OS and the BNS models).

Another set of experiments deals with the time required to conclude the final sub-set of features. In Fig. 4, we plot τ for various combinations of M and w. We have to notice that τ is retrieved as the mean for a number of iterations. As it can be observed, w's increment does not reflect any change to τ. This is reasonable since the model has to do calculations for each of the M features to determine the most important ones. This procedure is repeated for each instance and its total duration is higher than the decision itself. Figure 4 also depicts that τ is (approx.) linear to the total number of features M. This observation becomes the evidence of the efficiency of the proposed approach as it is 'transparent' to the total number of features taken into consideration.

We compare our wCD scheme with a model that adopts the Principal Component Analysis (PCA) for dimensionality reduction. Table 1 reports on the comparative outcomes related to the accuracy of the decision making, i.e., the Δ metric. We observe that the wCD outperforms the PCA in the vast majority of the adopted experimental scenarios showing the ability of the proposed

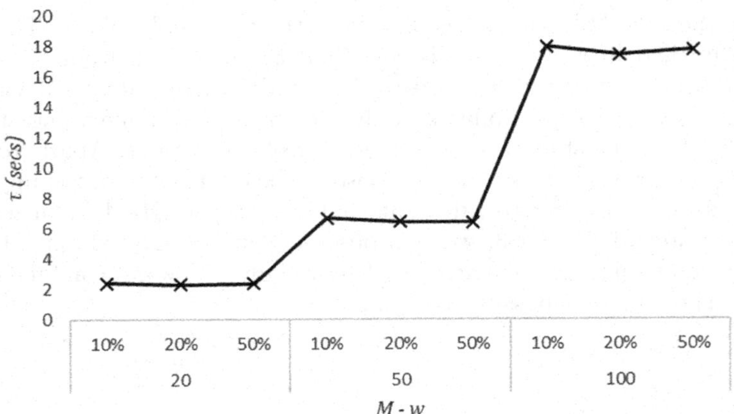

Fig. 4. Performance evaluation related to τ, i.e., the time requirements for concluding the final sun-set of features.

approach to secure the quality of data in the available datasets under the rationale explained above. This is another evidence that our mechanism is capable of efficiently detecting significant features, focusing on them and support the appropriate decision making for solving the problem under consideration.

Table 1. Comparative results for the Δ metric.

M	w	wCD	PCA
20	10%	91	71
	20%	89	89
	50%	91	84
50	10%	90	81
	20%	87	83
	50%	87	84
100	10%	83	78
	20%	79	78
	50%	77	74

6 Conclusions and Future Work

Data quality is significant because without it, we are not able to support efficient decision making. Securing data quality will give a competitive advantage especially to companies that are based on various analytics processing activities.

In this paper, we focus on the management of data quality and propose that any decision related to the acceptance of incoming data should be based on specific features and not all of them. Such features will exhibit the appropriate statistical characteristics that will make, afterwards, the desired analytics explainable to end users. We assume an edge computing environment and propose and ensemble scheme for features selection. We present the adopted algorithms and provide the aggregation process. In addition, we propose the use of a Neural Network that delivers the importance of each individual feature before we conclude the final sub-set. Based on the above, we are able to detect the most significant features for data present at edge nodes. Our experimental evaluation exhibits the performance of the system and its capability to select the proper features. Our numerical results denote the significance of our model and its capability to be adopted in real time applications. In the first place of our future research plans, we will provide a mechanism for covering the uncertainty around the significance of each feature. Additionally, we plan to incorporate into our model a scheme that delivers the selection decision based on a modelling of the available features adopting a sliding window approach.

Acknowledgment. This research received funding from the European's Union Horizon 2020 research and innovation programme under the grant agreement No. 745829.

References

1. Alpaydin, E.: Introduction to Machine Learning. MIT Press, Cambridge (2009)
2. Arrieta, A.B., et al.: Explainable artificial intelligence (XAI): concepts, taxonomies, opportunities and challenges toward responsible AI. Inf. Fus. **58**, 82–115 (2020)
3. Batini, C., Rula, A., Scannapieco, M., Viscusi, G.: From data quality to big data quality. J. Database Manag. **26**(1), 60–82 (2015)
4. Bertini, C.: Shapley value. In: Encyclopedia of Power (2011)
5. Bishop, C.: Pattern Recognition and Machine Learning. Springer, Heidelberg (2006)
6. Breiman, L.: Random forests. Mach. Learn. **45**(1), 5–32 (2011). https://doi.org/10.1023/A:1010933404324
7. Cai, L., Zhu, Y.: The challenges of data quality and data quality assessment in the big data era. Data Sci. J. **14**(2), 1–10 (2015)
8. Caruana, R., Kangarloo, H., Dionisio, J., Sinha, U., Johnson, D.: Case based explanation of non-case-based learning methods. In: Proceedings of the AMIA Symposium, pp. 212–215 (1999)
9. Carvalho, D., Pereira, E., Cardoso, J.: Machine learning interpretability: a survey on methods and metrics. Electronics **8**(8), 832 (2019)
10. Doshi-Velez, F., Kim, B.: Towards a rigorous science of interpretable machine learning (2017). arXiv preprint arXiv:1702.08608
11. Fisher, A., Rudin, C., Dominici, F.: All Models are Wrong, but Many are Useful: Learning a Variable's Importance by Studying an Entire Class of Prediction Models Simultaneously (2019). https://arxiv.org/pdf/1801.01489.pdf
12. Friedman, J., Popescu, B.: Predictive learning via rule ensembles. JSTOR Ann. Appl. Stat. **2**(3), 916–954 (2008)

13. Gao, J., Xie, C., Tao, C.: Big data validation and quality assurance - issues, challenges and needs. In: IEEE Symposium on Service-Oriented System Engineering (SOSE) (2016). https://doi.org/10.1109/SOSE.2016.63
14. Gupta, B., Agrawal, D., Yamagushi, S.: Deep learning models for human centered computing in fog and mobile edge networks. J. Ambient Intell. Humanized Comput. **10**, 2907–2911 (2019)
15. Han, Y., Wang, X., Leung, V., Niyato, D., Yan, X., Chen, X.: Convergence of Edge Computing and Deep Learning: A Comprehensive Survey (2019). arXiv:1907.08349
16. Hendricks, L.A., Akata, Z., Rohrbach, M., Donahue, J., Schiele, B., Darrell, T.: Generating visual explanations. In: Leibe, B., Matas, J., Sebe, N., Welling, M. (eds.) ECCV 2016. LNCS, vol. 9908, pp. 3–19. Springer, Cham (2016). https://doi.org/10.1007/978-3-319-46493-0_1
17. Johnson, M.J., Duvenaud, D.K., Wiltschko, A., Adams, R.P., Datta, S.R.: Composing graphical models with neural networks for structured representations and fast inference. In: Advances in Neural Information Processing Systems, vol. 29, pp. 2946–2954 (2016)
18. Karl, M., Soelch, M., Bayer, J., van der Smagt, V.: Deep Variational Bayes Filters: Unsupervised Learning of State Space Models from Raw Data (2016)
19. Krishnan, K.R., Shalit, U., Sontag, D.: Deep Kalman Filters (2015)
20. Kolomvatsos, K.: A distributed, proactive intelligent scheme for securing quality in large scale data processing. Computing **101**, 1–24 (2019). https://doi.org/10.1007/s00607-018-0683-9
21. Lane, N.D., Bhattacharya, S., Georgiev, P., Forlivesi, C., Kawsar, F.: Accelerated deep learning inference for embedded and wearable devices using DeepX. In: Proceedings of the 14th Annual International Conference on Mobile Systems, Applications, and Services Companion, p. 109 (2016)
22. Lecue, F.: On the role of knowledge graphs in explainable AI. In: Proceedings of the 18th International Semantic Web Conference (2019)
23. Lipton, Z.: The mythos of model interpretability. In: ICML Workshop on Human Interpretability in Machine Learning, vol. 2017, pp. 96–100 (2016)
24. Liu, C., et al.: A new deep learning-based food recognition system for dietary assessment on an edge computing service infrastructure. IEEE Trans. Serv. Comput. **11**(2), 249–261 (2017)
25. Loshin, D.: Monitoring Data Quality Performance Using Data Quality Metrics. Informatica, The Data Integration Company, White Paper (2011)
26. Management Group on Statistical Cooperation. Report of the Sixteenth meeting. European Commission, Eurostat, Doc. MGSC/2014/14 (2014)
27. Merino, J., Caballero, I., Rivas, B., Serrano, M., Piattini, M.: A data quality in use model for big data. Fut. Gen. Comput. Syst. **63**, 123–130 (2016)
28. Montavon, G., Lapuschkin, S., Binder, A., Samek, W., Muller, K.: Explaining nonlinear classification decisions with deep taylor decomposition. Pattern Recogn. **65**, 211–222 (2016)
29. Murdoch, W., Singh, C., Kumbier, K., Abbasi-Asl, R., Yu, B.: Interpretable machine learning: definitions, methods and applications. PNAS **116**(44), 22071–22080 (2019)
30. Murshed, M., Murphy, C., Hou, D., Khan, N., Ananthanarayanan, G., Hussain, D.: Machine Learning at the Network Edge: A Survey (2019). arXiv:1908.00080
31. Nelson, R.R., Todd, P.A., Wixom, B.H.: Antecedents of information and system quality: an empirical examination within the context of data warehousing. J. Manag. Inf. Syst. **21**(4), 199–235 (2005)

32. Olah, C., et al.: The building blocks of interpretability. Distill **3**(3), e10 (2018). https://doi.org/10.23915/distill.00010
33. Pearl, J.: Causality. Cambridge University Press, Cambridge (2009)
34. Pham, Q., et al.: A Survey of Multi-Access Edge Computing in 5G and Beyond: Fundamentals, Technology Integration, and State-of-the-Art (2019). https://arxiv.org/pdf/1906.08452.pdf
35. Preece, A., Harborne, D., Raghavendra, R., Tomsett, R., Braines, D.: Provisioning robust and interpretable AI/ML-based service bundles. In: MILCOM (2018)
36. Puri, N., Gupta, P., Agarwal, P., Verma, S.: MAGIX: Model Agnostic Globally Interpretable Explanations (2017). arXiv:1706.07160
37. Rani, P., Liu, C., Sarkar, N., Vanman, E.: An empirical study of machine learning techniques for affect recognition in human' robot interaction. Pattern Anal. Appl. **9**(1), 58–69 (2006)
38. Rao, D., Gudivada, V.N., Raghavan, V.V.: Data quality issues in big data. In: Proceedings of the IEEE International Conference on Big Data, Santa Clara, CA, USA (2015)
39. Ribeiro, M., Singh, S., Guestrin, C.: Why should i trust you? explaining the predictions of any classifier. In: Proceedings of the 22nd ACM SIGKDD International Conference on Knowledge Discovery and Data Mining (KDD'16), pp. 1135–1144. ACM (2016)
40. Roscher, R., Bihn, B., Duarte, M., Garcke, J.: Explainable Machine Learning for Scientific Insights and Discoveries (2019). arXiv:1905.08883
41. Sahni, Y., Cao, J., Zhang, S., Yang, L.: Edge mesh: a new paradigm to enable distributed intelligence in internet of things. IEEE Access **5**, 16441–16458 (2017)
42. Salloum, S., He, Y., Huang, J. Z., Zhang, X., Emara, T.: A Random Sample Partition Data Model for Big Data Analysis (2018). https://arxiv.org/abs/1712.04146
43. Seeliger, A., Pfaff, M., Krcmar, H.: Semantic web technologies for explainable machine learning models: a literature review. In: 1st Workshop on Semantic Explainability (2019)
44. Shamili, A.S., Bauckhage, C., Alpcan, T.: Malware detection on mobile devices using distributed machine learning. In: 20th IEEE International Conference on Pattern Recognition (ICPR), pp. 4348–4351 (2010)
45. Sidi, F., Panahy, P.H.S., Affendey, L.S., Jabar, M.A., Ibrahim, H., Mustapha, A.: Data quality: a survey of data quality dimensions. In: International Conference on Information Retrieval & Knowledge Management (CAMP), pp. 300–304 (2012)
46. Strumbelj, E., Komonenko, I.: Explaining prediction models and individual predictions with feature contributions. Knowl. Inf. Syst. **41**(3), 647–65 (2014)
47. Szydlo, T., Sendorek, J., Brzoza-Wosh, R.: Enabling machine learning on resource constrained devices by source code generation of the learned models. In: Proceedings of the 18th International Conference on Computational Science (2018)
48. Tran, T., Hosseini, M., Pompili, D.: Mobile edge computing: recent efforts and five key research directions. MMTC Commun.-Front. **12**(4), 29–34 (2017)
49. Wang, H.-X., Fratiglioni, L., Frisoni, G., Viitanen, M., Winblad, B.: Smoking and the occurence of alzheimer's disease: cross-sectional and longitudinal data in a population-based study. Ame. J. Epidemiol. **149**(7), 640–644 (1999)
50. Wang, S., et al.: When edge meets learning: adaptive control for resource-constrained distributed machine learning. In: IEEE Infocom (2018)
51. Yazizi, M., Basurra, S., Gaber, M.M.: Edge machine learning: enabling smart internet of things applications. In: Big Data and Cognitive Computing, vol. 2, no. 26 (2018)

52. Zheng, S., et al.: Conditional random fields as recurrent neural networks. In: Proceedings of the IEEE International Conference on Computer Vision, pp. 1529–1537 (2015)
53. Zheng, Z., Zhang, Y., Lyu, M.R.: Investigating QoS of real- world web services. IEEE Trans. Serv. Comput. **7**(1), 32–39 (2014)

Inter-space Machine Learning in Smart Environments

Amin Anjomshoaa(✉) and Edward Curry

Lero – the Irish Software Research Centre, National University of Ireland, Galway, Ireland
{amin.anjomshoaa,edward.curry}@nuigalway.ie

Abstract. Today, our built environment is not only producing large amounts of data, but –driven by the Internet of Things (IoT) paradigm– it is also starting to talk back and communicate with its inhabitants and the surrounding systems and processes. In order to unleash the power of IoT enabled environments, they need to be trained and configured for space-specific properties and semantics. This paper investigates the potential of communication and transfer learning between smart environments for a seamless and automatic transfer of personalized services and machine learning models. To this end, we explore different knowledge types in context of smart built environments and propose a collaborative framework based on Knowledge Graph principles and IoT paradigm for supporting transfer learning between spaces.

Keywords: Smart environment · Knowledge graph · Transfer learning

1 Introduction

Humans spend a significant portion of their lifetime indoors and are actively pursuing the vision of an ideal built environment which encompass the emergence of utopian concepts such as smart city, smart building, and smart home. In order to maintain our comfort, we have equipped our buildings and spaces with diverse information systems and services powered by the Internet of Things (IoT), which are generating a huge amount of data. Recently, the front-runners of ICT industry are exploiting the power of artificial intelligence and machine learning techniques to advance virtual assistants that facilitate the interaction with IoT devices and space services such as thermal comfort and ambient assisted living [19] in private environments. Examples of such virtual assistants are Google Home, Amazon Alexa, Microsoft Cortana, and Apple Siri. In order to integrate any of these virtual assistants, the services of virtual assistants need to be calibrated and configured based on space-specific properties and semantics and are captured in various ways such as dedicated information resources, service compositions, sense-actuate cycles, and well-trained machine-learning models. This task usually involves intensive human interventions to understand the implicit

Published by Springer Nature Switzerland AG 2020
A. Holzinger et al. (Eds.): CD-MAKE 2020, LNCS 12279, pp. 535–549, 2020.
https://doi.org/10.1007/978-3-030-57321-8_30

semantics of space, devices, as well relevant information resources and services. For instance, an Amazon Echo user may use Amazon's voice service, Alexa, to control smart devices such as cameras, door locks, entertainment systems, lighting, and thermostats. Furthermore, end-users are able to compose new services and sense-actuate cycles based on one or more IoT devices to accomplish more complicated tasks.

IoT-based systems are typically built following a three-layer model (cf. 1) that consists of: (i) a sensing layer, which acquires the observation of interest from the environment; (ii) a context layer, which is concerned with context acquisition, modeling, and reasoning; and (iii) an actuate layer that triggers an action or invokes a service according to some predefined logic. The main effort required for automatic change management in a private IoT space is hidden in the context layer. Unlike the sense and actuate layers which typically undertake straightforward tasks, the creation and configuration of the context layer is a complicated task which is not necessarily based on a syntactic or deterministic model. Instead, it needs a deep understanding of incoming events as well as the context of those events. Currently, human cognition is necessary to interpret the incoming data from the sensor layer and add the missing semantics about the events and their context.

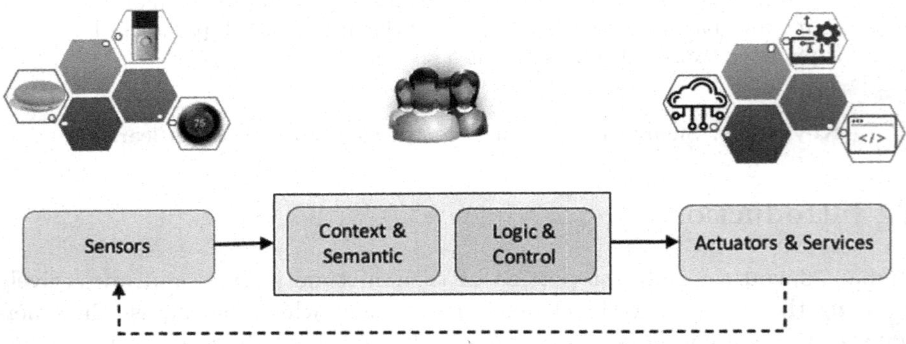

Fig. 1. Three-layer model of an IoT-based system including sensing, context, and actuation layers.

Additionally, in order to transfer the personalized services beyond the boundaries of private spaces, the technical details of sensing and actuation components needs to be adapted based on the smart nodes and IoT standards of the target space. For instance, in the thermal comfort scenario we might have different types of temperature sensors and control mechanisms to adjust the room temperature. While in one space we actuate the heater, in a second space the temperature might be controlled by opening and closing a vent. As such, we would need to adapt and customize the sensing and actuating layers in order to make personalized services transferable.

In summary, although human interventions for personalizing the smart environments work well, such methods may soon be infeasible due to the following challenges:

1. **Versatile IoT configurations:** Human contribution cannot cope with the ever-increasing number of IoT devices. By introducing new devices or applying changes to the smart environment, the configurations and rules needs to be revisited and checked. As such, we need a configuration management approach that supports flexibility, dynamicity, and incremental change in smart environments.
2. **IoT service transfer:** While users can manage, train, and configure the services in their private environment, it is not easy to transfer such configuration to semi-private spaces such as hotel rooms, cars, hospital rooms, open city spaces, and offices. For instance, suppose an individual has defined some rules to maintain his/her thermal comfort at home based on services such as motion detector, air conditioning system, and the body temperature from a wearable device. In order to achieve the same thermal comfort in a semi-private environment such as hotel room or office, the rules need to be adjusted based on the semantics and standards of the target spaces.
3. **Transfer learning:** The smart space services, embodied in machine learning models, are commonly associated with time-consuming and costly processes such as large-scale data collection, data labeling, network training, and fine-tuning models. Sharing and reuse of these elaborated models in a different space would facilitate the adoption of services for the inhabitants and accelerates the uptake of machine learning in smart building applications. The model adoption process, which is referred to as Transfer Learning, is commonly undertaken by a human who is able to understand the implicit semantics of spaces, devices, as well as the relevant information resources and services. Therefore, self-explaining and machine-understandable models are the key requirements to accelerate the transfer learning between smart spaces.

In this paper we introduce the concept of Inter-space learning which exploits efficient and economic realization of knowledge exchange and transfer learning between spaces. To this end, we will first introduce the different knowledge types in built environments and then explore the sharing and reuse of machine learning models within transfer learning scenarios.

2 Knowledge Types in Built Environment

Before discussing the Inter-space learning methods and concepts, we need to identify the different types of knowledge that are embodied in a physical space. Our built environment is made of various complex and interrelated systems and services that draws upon interdisciplinary areas such as economics, law, public policy, public health, management, geography, design, technology, and environmental sustainability. As such, the embodied knowledge in built environment comes in various types that cover different aspects of space information. The embodied knowledge ranges from simple facts and concepts such as basic space information to more complex knowledge types such as rules, procedures, and models. In order to use this knowledge effectively, part of this knowledge which is known as explicit knowledge is communicated through various mediums [10] and can be readily articulated, codified, stored, and accessed by human and machines [11].

Knowledge is a broad concept and has been extensively debated in philosophy for many centuries and still there is no universal agreement about its definition and different categories. However, due to the increasing interest in organizational knowledge and knowledge management systems, we need to take a pragmatic approach and define the knowledge types that are needed in the domains of interest to solve our day to day problems. Based on the existing works in knowledge management and knowledge management systems [1], we have identified five knowledge types, namely, Basic (Priori) knowledge, Inferred (Posteriori) knowledge, Procedural knowledge, Cognitive knowledge, and Descriptive Knowledge. These categories establish the basis of our inter-space learning framework and will be described in the following subsections.

As shown in Fig. 2, knowledge types are interrelated and may create new facts about the domain of interest. To this end, the inferred knowledge can be completed by applying rules to the basic knowledge, executing a procedure, or using cognitive models (e.g. machine learning models) to recognize new facts.

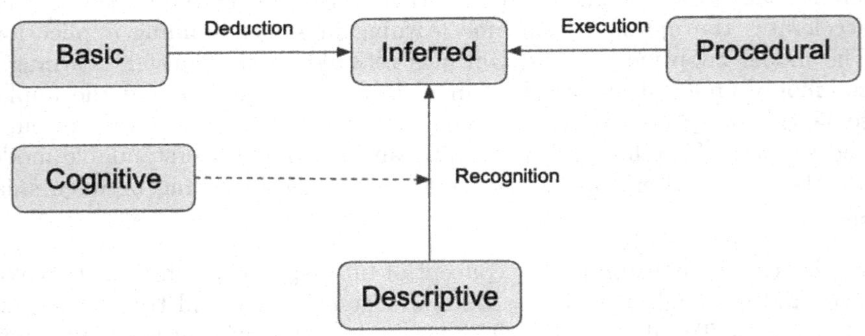

Fig. 2. Knowledge types and their inter-relations.

In the rest of this section we discuss these knowledge types and their corresponding learning objects in context of smart built environments.

2.1 Basic (Priori) Knowledge

In the context of the built environment, the basic knowledge is the explicit knowledge that covers various building artefacts and their relationships. Such knowledge can be readily assessed and acquired from the existing resources of a smart space and comprises various static space characteristics such as building elements, information models, and their physical and logical relationships. This information includes complex, multi-resolution, interrelated entities that are tightly connected to their surrounding environment. Identifying these components and their cross-links with surrounding entities such as people and devices will establish a preliminary base for enhancing various building processes.

Part of the basic knowledge of the built environment is currently captured via a wide array of Building Information Modeling (BIM) approaches of the Architecture, Engineering, and Construction (AEC) domain. Due to the complex nature of the built environment, there is no universal model that can capture all physical and functional requirements of buildings. As a result, there are several BIM standards and formats – each designed for specific building processes and use cases. Furthermore, the environments also include a growing number of IoT devices which form the virtual network of connected physical objects.

The basic knowledge of a smart built environment can be captured and documented in a number of ways. One such method is the use of ontologies and Linked Data where domain concepts and their relationships are represented by means of knowledge graphs. The knowledge graph provides a standardized descriptions of the physical (e.g. doors and windows, IoT devices), logical (e.g. neighbor-room and floor-room relationships), data streams, and virtual assets and their relationships. In order to establish these knowledge graphs, existing and well-known ontologies can be adopted and extended to fulfill the requirements of smart applications. For instance, in a smart building environment, we may reuse the Brick schema [5] that consists of an extensible dictionary of building terms and concepts, a set of relationships for linking and composing concepts together, and a flexible data model permitting seamless integration of Brick with other tools and databases.

2.2 Inferred (Posteriori) Knowledge

The basic knowledge can be extended by means of deductive reasoning, applying rules to existing facts, and use of cognitive models to process implicit knowledge. Furthermore, inference-based techniques can be used in discovering possible inconsistencies during the data integration processes. In semantic based and knowledge graph systems, the inference is commonly specified by means of semantic rules expressed by a description logic language. For instance, in a smart building environment semantic rules can be applied to real-time data streams of CO2 sensors to infer the space occupancy status.

2.3 Procedural Knowledge

This category of knowledge includes procedures or steps that are required to accomplish a task. For instance, the sense-actuate cycles in IoT-based solutions are simple procedures that connect sensors data to a specific task. Commonly, the creation and configuration of such procedures is a complicated task which is not necessarily based on a syntactic or deterministic model and is usually undertaken by human who has a profound understanding of incoming events as well as the context of those events.

Although the idea of connected things has opened up many possibilities for machine-to-machine communication, however these environments require an elaborated service layer around connected things in order to create smart environments. These services receive requests from hardware or software agents and process and analyze the input data according to their embedded logic to generate the appropriate output. In context of smart environments, the merge between data and services has led to the notion of data mashups. Using this analogy, the large amount of data produced by people, devices, buildings, and infrastructure streams between the processing nodes and services and the results are recycled back to the system. Efficient and intelligent programming of these data streams and services may turn spaces into even more productive entities.

2.4 Cognitive Knowledge

This type of knowledge includes information or sources of knowledge that cannot be explicitly defined and are acquired by observation and experimentation. An example of this type of knowledge is machine learning models that are taught to undertake complex tasks such as face recognition or energy optimizations using supervised, unsupervised, or reinforcement learning approaches. In context of smart built environments, these methods benefit from the huge amount of data in IoT-enabled spaces in their training processes which could yield significant profit over the lifetime of a building.

The cognitive models (machine learning models) can be refined and extended by technique such as transfer learning where a model trained on one task is re-purposed on a second related task. There are two main reasons why transfer learning is considered a key enabling technology in smart environments:

- In supervised machine learning approaches, we would need large training and test datasets in order to create reliable models. However, in many cases sufficient training and testing data does not exist.
- The real world is messy and contains various unpredicted scenarios that we have not encountered/considered during the training process. Including all exceptional cases and scenarios requires significant training which increases the model creation costs.

The high costs of creating machine learning models which also requires large amount of training and testing data sets, gives smart environments an incentive to reuse and re-purpose the existing models. For instance, in a smart environment the speech recognition model can be adopted and retrained in a new space to cope with the surrounding noise of the target space.

2.5 Descriptive Knowledge

This type of knowledge is declared in sentences, text documents, images and other formats that are not readily available to digital processes. Examples of this type of knowledge are safety guidelines of buildings, space history, images, and videos. In order to acquire explicit knowledge from such information, we would need advanced methods such as deep learning and machine learning to process and extract relevant information [24]. For instance, a video stream can be processed for inhabitant identification purposes or a text recognition system may be used to analyze the content of documents and semantically connect them to relevant resources.

3 Learning in Smart Spaces

This research aims to investigate the potential of communication and learning between smart environments for a seamless and automatic transfer of personalized services and applications. This process may range from simple sharing of data and information to more complex knowledge transfer method such as transfer learning where the knowledge gained in a specific space can be applied to a different space configuration. In this section, we will first explore the potential ways for communication between spaces for knowledge sharing and knowledge reuse purposes.

3.1 Space Knowledge Communication

Based on the introduced knowledge types in the previous section, we will now focus on the different methods for sharing and reuse of embodied knowledge in building spaces or zones. These communication methods are depicted in Fig. 3 and are classified as follows:

- The first and simplest method of communication between spaces is running queries on the explicit knowledge. Since the explicit knowledge can be articulated and codified, the spaces with a common understanding of domain concepts can formulate relevant queries based on common shared concepts (ontologies) and interpret the returning results in order to complete their inferred knowledge. For instance, two spaces that belong to the same thermal zone of a building can share the information about the corresponding Air Handling Unit (AHU) and its power meter.
- Procedures can be shared as a whole (black-box service on cloud) or get adopted and customized for use in context of the target space. As an example, consider a procedure that requires interaction with specific types of sensors/actuators or need to communicate with external services to accomplish a task. In order to adopt such procedures, we might need to replace the sensors and adjust its communications based on the resources available at the target space. For instance, in a temperature control scenario that includes a simple sense-actuate cycle, we need to adjust the procedure based on the available IoT services in the target space.
- Part of domain knowledge can be captured by elaborated models. These models are able to transform parts of the human's tacit knowledge into explicit

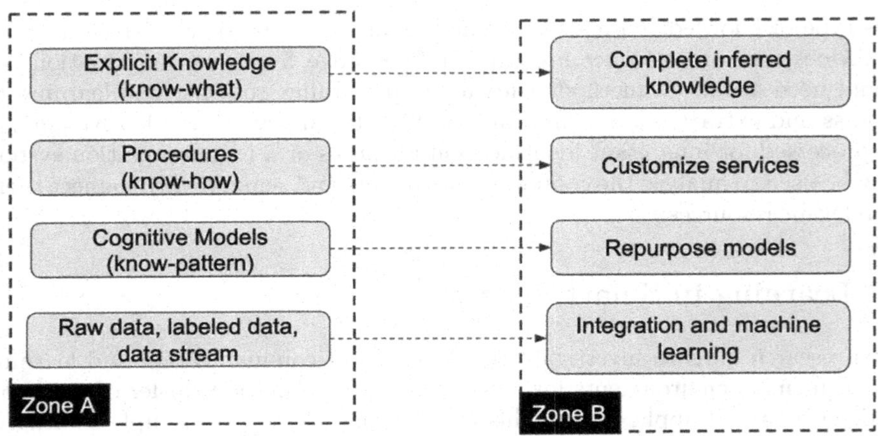

Fig. 3. Zone communication methods.

knowledge which can be used by machines. Machine learning models are examples of such knowledge acquisition method that facilitate sharing of cognitive-based approaches. Such models can be repurposed and retrained in the target zone in order to satisfy the contextual requirements. For instance, a speech recognition model can be adopted and repurposed to cope with the noise in the target space.

- A common type of communication between spaces is sharing data in different formats, frequencies, and structures. Such data could be in the form of raw data that is shared for data integration purposes or labeled data (e.g. images with labeled objects) for machine learning purposes.

There is already a handful of research work that exploits the power of semantic web, linked data, and knowledge graphs for capturing and conceptualization of information and procedures in smart environments. In the rest of this paper, we focus on the inter-space communication methods for cognitive knowledge and through a case study investigate the potential of transfer learning between spaces and zones.

4 Case-Study: Occupancy Prediction

In order to demonstrate the feasibility and effectiveness of transfer learning in smart built environments, we use an occupancy prediction use-case which plays an important role in energy efficiency applications of smart buildings. Counting space occupants can be implemented using various sensing technologies such as PIR sensors, visual cameras, Wi-Fi and Bluetooth enabled devices, and door sensors. Recently, there is an increasing interest to measure the occupant count based on environment sensors such as temperature, humidity, and CO2 level of target spaces. Due to the long response time and calibration errors, the environmental-based methods are not as accurate as other sensing methods such as visual cameras; however because of the privacy and cost concerns as well as the recent advances in machine learning approaches, these methods are gaining momentum. To this end, there are various research work for occupancy prediction based on environmental sensor data [4,17,21] that provide sophisticated methods based on a combination of sensor types to offer high accuracy prediction results. In our paper rather than creating high accuracy prediction results, we aim to demonstrate the sharing and reuse of knowledge between spaces. So, we use a simple occupancy prediction model based on the CO2 level of a source spaces and then will measure the efficiency of reusing these model reuse in a different space.

4.1 Dataset

We use an open dataset [18] that is collected via sensors on room-level occupant counts together with related data on indoor environmental indicators including airflow, CO2, relative humidity, illuminance, and temperature. The dataset comprises 44 full days, collated in the period of March 2018 to April 2019 for a lecture room and two study-zones in a public building in the University of Southern Denmark, Odense campus. Table 1 lists the spaces of this dataset and their attributes.

Table 1. Summary of target spaces.

Room ID	Room type	Size (m2)	Seating-capacity	Volume (m3)
Room-1	Lecture	139	84	461.48
Room-2	Study-zone	125	32	418.75
Room-3	Study-zone	125	32	418.75

Before using this data and in order to mitigate the long response time of CO2 sensor data, we have limited the study time to the building's peak hours (6:00 am to 14:00 pm) and aggregated the data to 30 min intervals. Then a collection of statistical metadata was calculated and added to the description of the dataset. We may use this metadata for finding top candidate models when a specific service such as occupancy prediction is offered by more than one space. For describing the statistical metadata, we use and extend the terms and relations defined by ML-Schema [16], an interchangeable format for description of machine learning experiments. ML-Schema will also provide us with a set of classes, properties, and restrictions for representing and interchanging information on machine learning algorithms, datasets, and experiments. Figure 4 depicts part of the knowledge graph that describes the dataset as well as statistical metadata.

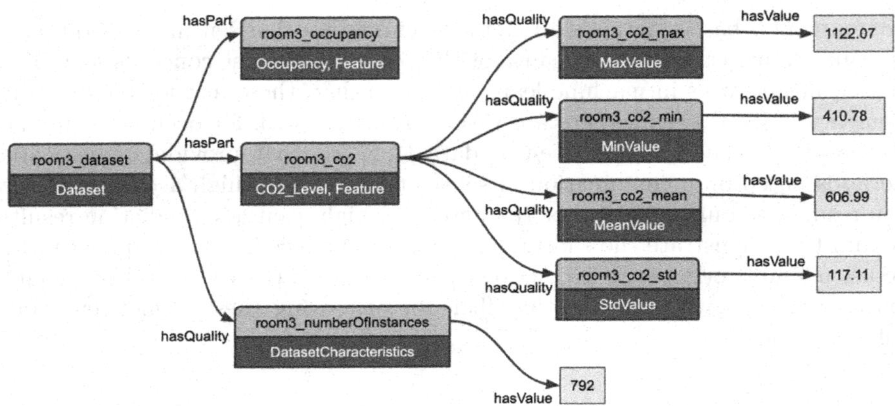

Fig. 4. Part of the knowledge graph describing dataset features such as occupancy, CO2, and their corresponding metadata.

4.2 Knowledge Graph

As described previously, the knowledge graph should include both the space information and the dataset description. So, in addition to the ML-Schema, we would also need a schema to describe metadata of smart spaces including sensors, subsystems and the relationships among them. To this end, we use the Brick schema [5] that is a uniform schema for representing metadata in IoT-enabled environments.

In the knowledge graph proposed in this research, we create a bridge between ML-Schema and Brick to describe dataset, building information, and machine learning processes. As depicted in Fig. 4, machine learning processes can be characterized based on their input data, output model, and model evaluation measures such as Mean Absolute Error (MAE) or Mean Squared Error (MSE) of learning processes. Furthermore, each model is dedicated to a specific task defined by ML-Schema which helps spaces to find the relevant models shared by other spaces. As such, the models are presented in a self-explainable and interpretable way to both human users as well as space agents (machines).

In the case of multiple competing models for transfer learning purposes, the system needs to assess the fitness of offered models based on the metadata of source and target spaces. This can be achieved by one or a combination of the following approaches:

- A number of spaces may have similar properties and use. As such, the models of a space that depend on those properties can be shared and reused by other similar spaces. The space similarity, depending on use case, can be characterized by features such as room's function, size, or capacity. In the case of our occupancy prediction model, rooms of the same size and capacity are expected to behave similarly.

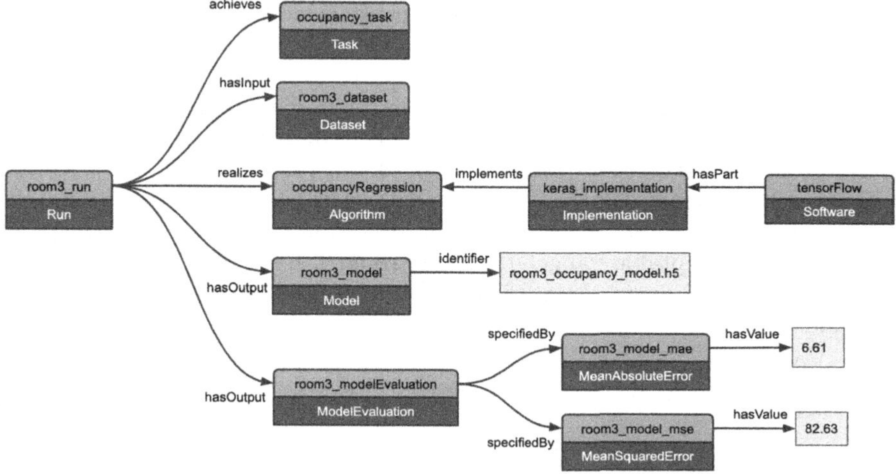

Fig. 5. Part of the Knowledge graph describing ML-Schema.

- Training dataset plays also an important role in the accuracy of model predictions. If the machine learning model is created based on a small or low variance feature, its behavior in a new space will be unpredictable. Since all such statistical metadata are included in the proposed knowledge graph, the space agent can compare the range of its input features to those of the training dataset of adopted model and make sure the model is adequately good for transfer learning purposes.
- The machine learning models are also characterized by their performance indicators. For instance, the loss indicator which is widely used in machine learning processes can be used for comparison and ranking of the available models for a specific task.

4.3 Transfer Learning

During the operation phase, buildings are now producing more data than ever before, such as energy usage statistics, utility information, occupancy patterns, scheduling information, and financial data. However, this information cannot be used directly for machine learning purposes and requires time-consuming processes for preparing and fine-tuning training datasets that are vital for creating high quality machine learning models. In the machine learning domain, transfer learning aims to eliminate the high cost of data preparation processes by sharing and reuse of pre-trained models.

In the proposed use case, we have used the CO2 time series of each room as input and created a simple logistic regression model [15] to predict the room occupancy count. Next, we use these models in other rooms and investigate their fitness and performance compared to the model trained by target room's data. Figure 6 depicts the performance matrix of these models on test dataset of each room. The rows in this matrix show the regression models and columns specify the applied test data.

As expected, the model performance should be best when it is applied to the test data of the room itself. Furthermore, the room with similar characteristics (e.g. size and volume) shows similar performances and as a result can adopt the models from each other. For instance, room-2 and room-3 in our use case have similar properties and also their training dataset is consistent (similar statistical indicators) and as shown in Fig. 6 the performances of transferred models are within an acceptable range. However, room-1 has different function and properties and as a result the performance of adopted models compared to its own model is not acceptable.

5 Related Work

Knowledge graph is a powerful tool for capturing digital representations of both physical and functional characteristics of buildings. They can play an important role in narrowing the physical-digital gap via applying a network of digital elements around our physical built environment for integration of brick-based (i.e. physical space and IoT devices) and bit-based (i.e. cyberspace and IT services) elements [14].

In order to build and populate the knowledge graph of smart environments, a number of methods and standards are introduced. For instance, the Industry Foundation Classes (IFC) developed by the BuildingSMART alliance [22] is one of the most mature Building Information Modeling (BIM) standards and defines an object-based hierarchy of building entities and concepts for data exchange and data sharing. In this context, several researches have proposed domain specific ontology schemas based on BIM and Linked Data principles for supporting the interoperability and data integration in smart built environments [3,8,20].

Although, the BIM standards provide a comprehensive description of buildings' physical elements and address a number of interoperability challenges between systems and services, but they fail to capture the relationship between static building information and real-time dynamic of IoT ecosystems in smart buildings [2]. To this end, the Brick schema [5] provides a broader coverage of concepts for smart buildings by standardizing semantic descriptions of the physical, logical and virtual assets in buildings and the relationships between them.

Recent advances in Knowledge graph [12] and machine learning domains has revealed their complementary nature and advantages of combining knowledge graphs and machine learning techniques [6]. More specifically, knowledge graphs and ontologies are introduced as key technologies for creating explainable and comprehensible machine learning models for both human and machines [13]. Furthermore, existing works [9,23] have shown the potential of transfer learning for IoT and edge devices but these approaches are not geared towards capturing the semantics of space, IoT devices, or the machine learning models.

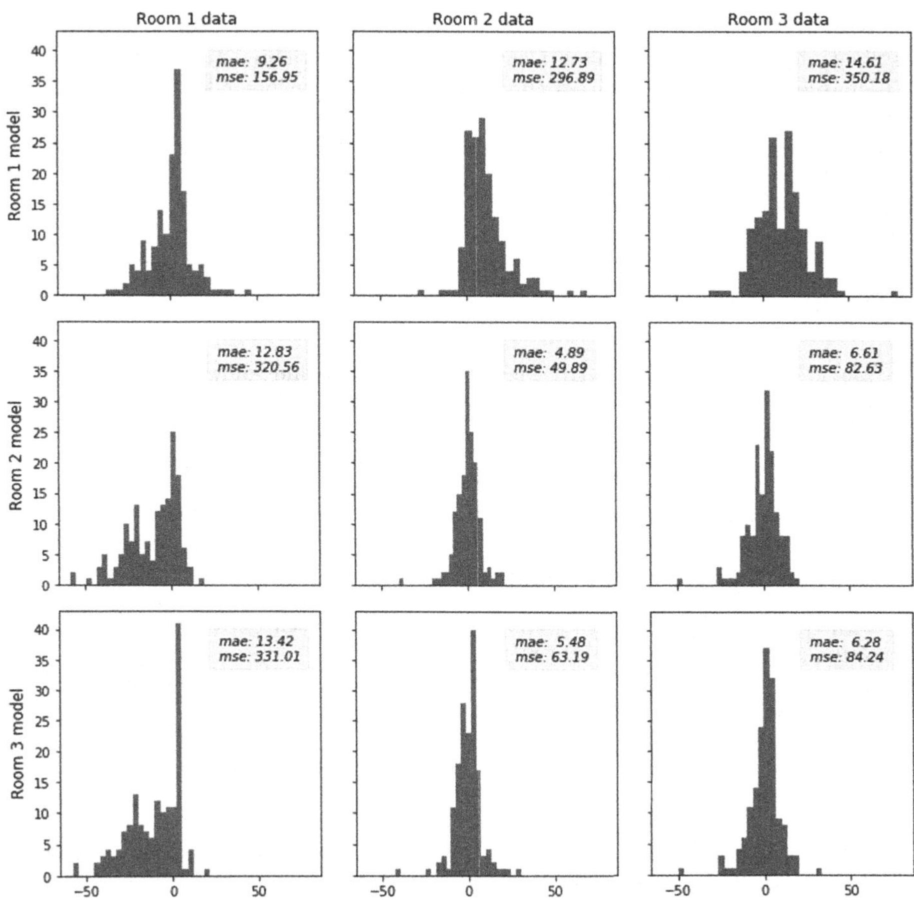

Fig. 6. Predicting space occupancy by self-trained model vs. transferred models. The histogram plot in each cell shows the distribution of errors for the occupancy counting task.

6 Conclusions and Future Work

Buildings as an integral part of urban settlements are being equipped with more IoT devices than even before. In this context, IoT industries and service providers strive to find more efficient ways to benefit from the growing IoT ecosystem and combine it with other available information resources in order to create smarter environments. In this research we discussed various knowledge types in built environments and described the relationship between them. Furthermore, we demonstrated that transfer learning based on building knowledge graphs can be effectively used in smart spaces. The presented showcase for occupancy prediction, shows the feasibility of this approach, however there are a number of challenges such as the fitness of adopted models and the efficacy of training datasets needs to be further investigated. As future work, we aim to explore the application of Real-time Linked Dataspaces [7] for enriching the context layer of IoT-enabled spaces and address the requirements of transfer learning use cases.

Acknowledgement. This work was supported with the financial support of the Science Foundation Ireland grant 13/RC/2094 and co-funded under the European Regional Development Fund through the Southern & Eastern Regional Operational Programme to Lero - the Irish Software Research Centre (www.lero.ie).

References

1. Alavi, M., Leidner, D.E.: Knowledge management and knowledge management systems: conceptual foundations and research issues. MIS Q. **25**, 107–136 (2001)
2. Anjomshoaa, A.: Blending building information with smart city data. In: S4SC@ ISWC, pp. 1–2. Citeseer (2014)
3. Anjomshoaa, A., Shayeganfar, F., Mahdavi, A., Tjoa, A.: Toward constructive evidence of linked open data in AEC domain. In: Proceedings of the 10th European Conference on Product and Process Modelling (ECPPM2014), Vienna, Austria, 17–19 September 2014, pp. 535–542 (2014)
4. Arief-Ang, I.B., Hamilton, M., Salim, F.D.: A scalable room occupancy prediction with transferable time series decomposition of co2 sensor data. ACM Trans. Sens. Netw. (TOSN) **14**(3–4), 1–28 (2018)
5. Balaji, B., et al.: Brick: towards a unified metadata schema for buildings. In: Proceedings of the 3rd ACM International Conference on Systems for Energy-Efficient Built Environments, pp. 41–50. ACM (2016)
6. Bonatti, P.A., Decker, S., Polleres, A., Presutti, V.: Knowledge graphs: new directions for knowledge representation on the semantic web (dagstuhl seminar 18371) (2019)
7. Curry, E.: Real-Time Linked Dataspaces: Enabling Data Ecosystems for Intelligent Systems. Springer, Cham (2020). https://doi.org/10.1007/978-3-030-29665-0
8. Curry, E., O'Donnell, J., Corry, E., Hasan, S., Keane, M., O'Riain, S.: Linking building data in the cloud: integrating cross-domain building data using linked data. Adv. Eng. Inform. **27**(2), 206–219 (2013)
9. Deng, L., Li, D., Yao, X., Cox, D., Wang, H.: Mobile network intrusion detection for IoT system based on transfer learning algorithm. Cluster Comput. **22**(4), 9889–9904 (2019)
10. Handzic, M.: Knowledge management: a research framework. In: Proceedings of the European Conference on Knowledge Management, pp. 219–229 (2001)
11. Hélie, S., Sun, R.: Incubation, insight, and creative problem solving: a unified theory and a connectionist model. Psychol. Rev. **117**(3), 994 (2010)
12. Hogan, A., et al.: Knowledge graphs (2020)
13. Holzinger, A.: From machine learning to explainable AI. In: 2018 World Symposium on Digital Intelligence for Systems and Machines (DISA), pp. 55–66. IEEE (2018)
14. Ishii, H., Ullmer, B.: Tangible bits: towards seamless interfaces between people, bits and atoms. In: Proceedings of the ACM SIGCHI Conference on Human factors in computing systems, pp. 234–241 (1997)
15. Kleinbaum, D.G., Dietz, K., Gail, M., Klein, M., Klein, M.: Logistic Regression. A Self-Learning Text. Springer, New York (2002). https://doi.org/10.1007/b97379

16. Publio, G.C., et al.: Ml-schema: exposing the semantics of machine learning with schemas and ontologies (2018)
17. Sangogboye, F.C., Arendt, K., Singh, A., Veje, C.T., Kjærgaard, M.B., Jørgensen, B.N.: Performance comparison of occupancy count estimation and prediction with common versus dedicated sensors for building model predictive control. Build. Simul. **10**, 829–843 (2017)
18. Schwee, J.H., et al.: Room-level occupant counts and environmental quality from heterogeneous sensing modalities in a smart building. Sci. Data **6**(1), 1–11 (2019)
19. Singh, D., et al.: Human activity recognition using recurrent neural networks. In: Holzinger, A., Kieseberg, P., Tjoa, A.M., Weippl, E. (eds.) CD-MAKE 2017. LNCS, vol. 10410, pp. 267–274. Springer, Cham (2017). https://doi.org/10.1007/978-3-319-66808-6_18
20. Törmä, S.: Semantic linking of building information models. In: 2013 IEEE Seventh International Conference on Semantic Computing, pp. 412–419. IEEE (2013)
21. Wang, W., Chen, J., Hong, T.: Occupancy prediction through machine learning and data fusion of environmental sensing and wi-fi sensing in buildings. Autom. Constr. **94**, 233–243 (2018)
22. Wikipedia: Buildingsmart, industry foundation classes (IFC). https://en.wikipedia.org/wiki/Industry_Foundation_Classes. Accessed 14 Apr 2020
23. Xing, T., Sandha, S.S., Balaji, B., Chakraborty, S., Srivastava, M.: Enabling edge devices that learn from each other: cross modal training for activity recognition. In: Proceedings of the 1st International Workshop on Edge Systems, Analytics and Networking, pp. 37–42 (2018)
24. Yadav, P., Curry, E.: VidCEP: complex event processing framework to detect spatiotemporal patterns in video streams. In: 2019 IEEE International Conference on Big Data (Big Data), pp. 2513–2522. IEEE (2019)

Author Index

Printed in the United States
By Bookmasters